Third World Colonialism and Strategies of Liberation
Eritrea and East Timor Compared

By analyzing Ethiopia's rule over Eritrea and Indonesia's rule over East Timor, *Third World Colonialism and Strategies of Liberation* compares the colonialism of powerful Third World countries on their small, less-powerful neighbors. Through a comparative study of Eritrean and East Timorese grand strategies of liberation, this book documents the inner workings of the nationalist movements and traces the sources of government types in these countries. In doing so, Awet Tewelde Weldemichael challenges existing notions of grand strategy as a unique prerogative of the West and opposes established understanding of colonialism as an exclusively Western project on the non-Western world. In addition to showing how Eritrea and East Timor developed sophisticated military and nonmilitary strategies, Weldemichael emphasizes that the insurgents avoided terrorist methods when their colonizers indiscriminately bombed their countries, tortured and executed civilians, held them hostage, starved them deliberately, and continuously threatened them with harsher measures.

Awet Tewelde Weldemichael is an assistant professor in the history department at the University of Kentucky. He is also Fernand Braudel Fellow at the French Humanities Foundation, University of Paris Diderot. He taught at the University of Asmara in Eritrea and has worked as a political affairs officer for the UN peacekeeping mission in East Timor.

Third World Colonialism and Strategies of Liberation

Eritrea and East Timor Compared

AWET TEWELDE WELDEMICHAEL

University of Kentucky

CAMBRIDGE
UNIVERSITY PRESS

32 Avenue of the Americas, New York NY 10013-2473, USA

Cambridge University Press is part of the University of Cambridge.

It furthers the University's mission by disseminating knowledge in the pursuit of
education, learning and research at the highest international levels of excellence.

www.cambridge.org
Information on this title: www.cambridge.org/9781107576520

First published 2013
First paperback edition 2015

A catalogue record for this publication is available from the British Library

Library of Congress Cataloguing in Publication data

Weldemichael, Awet Tewelde. Third world colonialism and strategies of liberation : Eritrea
and East Timor compared / Awet Tewelde Weldemichael.
p.   cm.
Includes bibliographical references and index.
ISBN 978-1-107-03123-4 (hardback)
1. Eritrea – History – Autonomy and independence movements.   2. National liberation
movements – Eritrea.   3. Eritrea – History – Revolution, 1962–1993.
4. Timor-Leste – History – Autonomy and independence movements.   5. National liberation
movements – Timor-Leste.   I. Title.
DT397.W45   2013
959.87–dc23   2012025692

ISBN 978-1-107-03123-4 Hardback
ISBN 978-1-107-57652-0 Paperback

I bow in front of you, I kiss your hands, kiss your knees, your feet, too; exemplars of moral rectitude; most humorous providers of unequaled teachings in life, my parents. You cannot directly read this because you spent the better part of your lives making sure that my siblings and I can read and write books. This is my first, I promise.

ገጸ-በረከት

ዝኸበርኩም ወለደይ፡ ብቐኑዕ ጠባይኩም ኣርኣያ ብምዃን፡ ዋዛ ምስ ቁም ነገር ዝመልኦ ምኽርን ተግሳጽን ብምሃብ ናቢኹም ከተዕብዩኒ ብምኽኣልኩም ምስጋናይ ይብጽሐኩም፡፡ እዚ ብቛንቋ እንግሊዝ ሳላ'ቲ ሓልዮትኩም ጾርኩምን ጽሒፈዮ ዘሎኹ ከተንብብዎ ኣይትኽእሉን ኢኹም፡ ምኽንያቱ ንዓና ንደቅኹም ከተምህሩ ዕድመኹም ብስራሕን ኣብ ስደትን ከርተት ኢልኩም ስለ ዘሕለፍክሞዎ፡፡ ስለዚ ኣብ ቅድሜኹም ድፍእ ኢለ ብትሕትና ኣእዳውኩምን ኣብራኽኩምን ብምስላም ንዝኽሪ ፍረ ጻማኹም ከኹውን እዚ ቦኹሪ ጽሑፈይ ብስምኩም ይውፍዮ፡፡ ቀጻሊ ድማ ኢዩ፡፡

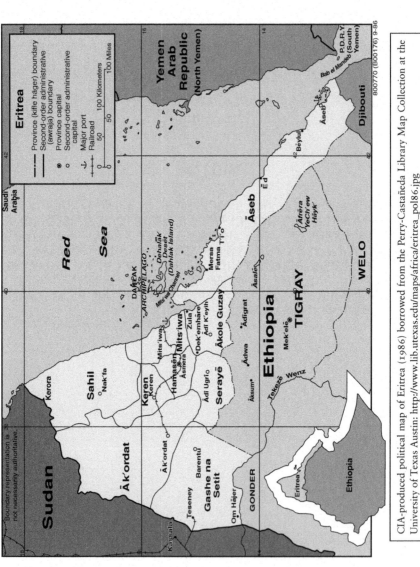

Eritrea

- - - Province (kifle hāger) boundary
——— Second-order administrative
(awraja) boundary
⊙ Province capital
○ Second-order administrative
capital
⚓ Major port
�┼╼ Railroad

0   50   100 Kilometers
0   50   100 Miles

Saudi Arabia

Red Sea

DAHLAK ARCHIPELAGO

Dehalāk Deset (Dahlak Island)

Mits'iwa Channel

Yemen Arab Republic (North Yemen)

Sudan

Kerora

Sahil

Nak'fa

Keren
Keren

Hamasēn
Asmera

Mits'iwa
Mits'iwa

Zula
Dek'emhāre
Ādi K'eyih
Ākole Guzay

Mersa Fatma
Ti'o

 Āseb

Ēd

Ādi Ugrio

Serayē

'Ādigrat

Āsaēta

Beylul

Āseb

Djibouti

Bab el Mandeb

P.D.R.Y. (South Yemen)

Āk'ordat

Āk'ordat

Teseney

Barentū

Gashe na Setit

Om Hājer

Kassala

GONDER

Ethiopia

Āksum

Ādwa

Mek'elē

TIGRAY

Tekezē Wenz

Ārā'ra YeCh'ew Hāyk'

WELO

Eritrea

Ethiopia

Boundary representation is not necessarily authoritative.

800770 (B00176) 9-86

CIA-produced political map of Eritrea (1986) borrowed from the Perry-Castañeda Library Map Collection at the University of Texas Austin: http://www.lib.utexas.edu/maps/africa/eritrea_pol86.jpg

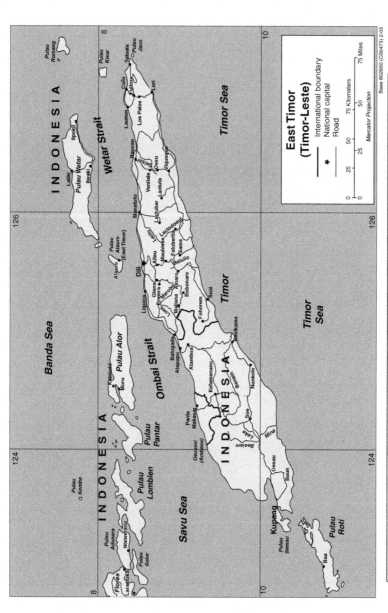

CIA-produced political map of East Timor (2003) borrowed from the Perry-Castañeda Library Map Collection at the University of Texas Austin: http://www.lib.utexas.edu/maps/middle_east_and_asia/east_timor_pol_03.jpg

Contents

Foreword

During our long struggle for independence, we sought and found examples in other independence movements that had been fighting similar wars against European and regional colonialism. We particularly took some lessons from African wars and drew inspiration from the Eritrean independence movement. Not surprisingly, Eritrean leaders kept well-informed about the dire predicament of the East Timorese people. Our knowledge about one another's struggle offered the basis for our mutual empathy, solidarity and collaboration.

At the height of our diplomatic campaigns, I worked closely with the Eritrean representative at the United Nations General Assembly, Bereket Habte Selassie, and I particularly remember the numerous occasions that him and I had been barred from or thrown out of international fora because Ethiopian and Indonesian representatives lodged complaints against us as terrorist.

The attendant hardship of occupation and domination that Timor-Leste and Eritrea endured in the hands of Indonesia and Ethiopia, respectively, are neither unique nor have East Timorese and Eritrean successes brought an end to that phenomenon aptly described in this book as secondary colonialism. Powerful countries have forcefully subjugated their weaker neighbors to brutal domination and are likely to continue doing so in pursuit of their geostrategic and resource needs. Through an analysis of our experiences parallel to that of Eritreans, Dr. Awet Weldemichael has done an excellent job in exposing the nature of such domination and the dynamics of resistance against it.

I first met Professor Weldemichael at the height of the brief conflict that afflicted independent Timor-Leste in 2006 – he was one of the very few foreigners who chose to stick it out when most of the expatriate community evacuated. As a young researcher then, and, later, as a political affairs offi-cer for the United Nations peacekeeping mission, Awet developed intimate knowledge of Timor-Leste's historical and contemporary political nuances all of which he richly represents throughout the pages of this book in comparison and contrast to Eritrea's, his native country.

Through a close examination of unprecedented detail and rigor, he captures the personal and collective drive of the East Timorese and Eritrean fighters, reconstructs the unique and complex processes of the two independence movements, and explains the current political realities in postwar Timor-Leste and Eritrea. In the process he offers important theoretical and practical insights with unique intellectual courage and boldness. He demonstrates how Third World countries – some of them former colonies themselves – have become colonial powers, hence secondary colonialism. He irrefutably projects colonial subjects as crafters of complex and successful grand strategies. And he proves how state terrorism was perpetrated against us when we – out of moral principle – avoided the temptation of expediently resorting to terrorism.

Rarely has any one succeeded to bring out so much detail and nuance of a single independence movement much less of two previously underestimated and subsequently neglected struggles in Timor-Leste and Eritrea. Awet has presented a lucid, brilliant and accessible comparative analysis that is indispensable for scholars, policy makers and aid organizations. This is a book that every politician, diplomat, development worker, academic and student should read not only on Timor-Leste and Eritrea but also on local resistance to regional domination, modern state formation and nation building at the age of globalization.

José Ramos-Horta
Dili, 25 September 2012

The former president of East Timor (between 2007 and 2012); and the co-Laureate of the 1996 Nobel Peace Prize.

Acknowledgments

The seed of this book was sown in 2001, a year that witnessed major political turmoil within the ranks of Eritrea's liberation leaders. In September, the President ordered the arrest of a dozen ministers, generals, and other highly placed civil servants in one fell swoop. The government simultaneously suspended the mushrooming private press. A sudden shadow and polarization descended across the Eritrean political landscape. As I started to grapple with the dizzying speed of Eritrean politics, I stumbled across the story of the equally arduous and inspiring East Timorese quest for liberation whose outcome seemed to defy the trite adage that "revolutions devour their children." I set out to comparatively examine the two.

I hypothesized that the contrasting outcomes of the seemingly similar struggles were attributable to the grand strategies that the nationalist movements adopted. My hypothesis nearly faltered during my fieldwork in East Timor in 2006 when the country descended into chaos. At the expiration of a deadline to reverse an earlier summary dismissal of a third of East Timor's army, young supporters of the sacked soldiers ran amok across the capital. In a constitutionally questionable move, the president demanded the resignation of the ministers of interior and defense, and ultimately of the prime minister as well. As East Timor teetered on the edge of the precipice, the Eritrean clean sweep seemed to be a better alternative.

Timely international intervention averted the brief conflict in independent East Timor from degenerating into irreversible tragedy, and the revolution from devouring its own children. This action stands in stark contrast to Eritrea's parallel experience with members of the international community, where the most powerful members of the United Nations Security Council are actively hostile toward the Eritrean government. In more ways than not, that situation is an attribute of the legacy of the two independence movements' grand strategies with which this book is concerned.

During the first phase of the project as a doctoral thesis, I had the unmatched mentoring of Drs. Edmond Keller, William Worger, Christopher

Ehret, Anthony Reid, Geoffrey Robinson, and Edward "Ned" Alpers, to whom I owe a heavy debt of gratitude. I am particularly indebted to Geoff and Ned, who believed in the feasibility of an idea that many wrote off out of hand and unfailingly supported me from start to finish. I thank the University of California Pacific Rim Research Program, UCLA's International Institute, and the Globalization Research Center–Africa for their generous research grants that made my fieldwork possible.

Contemporary history is incomplete by its very nature and this incomplete account of Eritrean and East Timorese contemporary histories took an exceptionally long time to complete because the allure of gaining new historical knowledge directly from its makers proved unrelenting, often to the detriment of writing it. I was humbled and privileged to sit at the bedside of the ailing Mohammed Omar Abdellah "Abu Tyara" and across the table from Dr. Taha Mohammed-Nur, Romedan Mohammed-Nur, and many others in Eritrea. It was an equal privilege for Bishop Carlos Filipe Ximenes Belo, President José Ramos-Horta, President Mário Soares, President Jorge Sampaio, Governor Mário Carrascalão, as well as many diplomats, politicians, and academics to make themselves available to me. Perhaps the most transformative moments of the entire exercise were my interviews with the Eritrean and East Timorese men and women who, at a young age, stood up to defend their people and rectify the wrongs they had suffered. Their respective peoples must be indebted to all of them – and to their fallen compatriots – for their exceptional sacrifices. I cannot thank them enough for opening their hearts and homes to me and sharing their experiences.

I have been extremely fortunate to have the support of numerous officials and private citizens who have generously granted me access to their personal and institutional resources. I am forever indebted to Zemhret Yohannes, Alemseged Tesfai, and Azeb Tewelde for their tireless mentoring, confidence, and unfailing support for me. I thank the young archivists at Eritrea's Research and Documentation Center (RDC) in Asmara, who were valuable in extending hands-on assistance during my research. My thanks also goes to the directors of and archivists at the Arquivo e Museo Resistência in Dili, the Fundacão Mário Soares and Arquivo Mário Soares in Lisbon, the Centro de Informação e Documentação Amílcar Cabral also in Lisbon, and Fentahun Tiruneh at the Library of Congress.

In East Timor, my research would not have gone far enough without the constant support of my friend Laurentina "Mica" Barreto Soares. She was generous with her direct knowledge (as a former active member of the clandestine student movement in Indonesia – RENETIL) of many of the important turning points of the resistance movement and of the Timorese personalities. She also helped me in interpreting all of the interviews conducted in Tetum. I am grateful to Mindo Rajagukguk, Lurdes Bessa, Jaquiline Siapono, Fernando de Araújo "Lasama," Cris Carrascalão, Zacarias Albano da Costa, David Diaz Ximenes, Gregorio Saldanha, and Joaquim Fonseca "Ruso" for their friendship and invaluable support. My thanks are also due to all of my Indonesian and Timorese friends who made me feel at home in Yogyakarta and across East Timor.

A number of well-connected and influential individuals supported my research in Portugal in ways that are too long to recount. Here I would like to particularly acknowledge Nuno Morais Sarmento, João Fialho, Gregory Arvoy, Antonio Barbedo Magalhães, and Moisés Fernandes.

The support of my friends and siblings across the world was instrumental for me to survive both the anticipated challenges and the unexpected shocks of being a globetrotting student and researcher – including getting caught up in the East Timorese conflict, narrowly avoiding the Indonesian earthquake that hit Yoga, surviving the targeted burglarizing of my apartment in Washington, DC, and the stealing of my data and research equipment. With encyclopedic knowledge of people, events, and processes, my eldest sister Almaz has always been the restraining voice of reason and sustaining encouragement during my entire research career. My sisters Natsinet and Belainesh supported me without reserve; I would not have made it this far without them. During my long nomadic existence they readily assumed my personal, family, and social responsibilities. They regularly followed my whereabouts, often calling in the middle of the night half the world away to pass family updates or to ask what kind of camera was better or what color to paint which room. My friends in Southern California were equally supportive, for which I am very thankful.

After UCLA, I spent three years in Europe as a research Fellow at the Institute of Advanced Studies of the University of Bologna, then as a Hiob Ludolf Guest Professor at Hamburg University, and finally as a Fernand Braudel Fellow of the Fondation Maison des sciences de l'homme at the University of Paris 7, which enabled me to work on this book. I thank them and their directors and scholars for their generous hospitality. I am especially grateful to Professor Irma Taddia (at Bologna); Professors Siegbert Uhlig and Alessandro Bausi (at Hamburg); and Professors Dominique Vidal, Mahamet Timera, and Jocelyne Streiff-Fenart (at Unité de recherches "Migrations et société" in Paris and Nice).

From its inception to its conclusion, many individuals offered critical feedback to many of the things that I brought, or did not bring, to the table and variously encouraged and supported me. They are too many to list, but I cannot pass without mentioning Uoldelul Chelati Dirar, Yemane Mesghina, Vijay Prashad, Lahra Smith, Tricia Reddeker Hepner, Elena Vezzadini, Daniel Gebremichael, Judith Byfield, Patrice and Margaret Higonnet, Peter Davies and Linda DeNoyer, Giulia Bonacci, Andrea Guazzi, Giridhar Babu, Ghislaine Lydon, Dawit Yohannes "Wedi John," and Manna Bahre. Nor can I pass on thanking Caroline Lees for meticulously copyediting the manuscript and Alex Meckelburg for excellent work on the index. I also thank Eric Crahan, Abigail Zorbaugh, Ken Karpinski, and Cambridge's editors. The constructive criticism and feedback of the anonymous review-ers proved extremely useful for which I remain grateful.

Clifford Geertz astutely noted that over time and after many consulta-tions of different materials and with different people, one is hard pressed to recognize where one's ideas come from, and which are one's own and which are others'. It is my hope that the views, ideas, and data of all of my oral and written sources are accurately represented and duly acknowledged. I take sole responsibility for any misrepresentations and/or errors.

Awet Tewelde Weldemichael

Introduction

[W]henever there are colonizer and colonized face to face, I see force, brutality, cruelty, sadism, conflict, and, in a parody of education, the hasty manufacture of a few thousand subordinate functionaries ... necessary for the smooth operation of business.

– Aimé Césaire[1]

Caught between disintegrating European colonialism and local expansionism, the former Italian colony of Eritrea and Portuguese Timor experienced secondary colonialism in the hands of their powerful neighbors. Ethiopia annexed Eritrea in 1962; Indonesia invaded and occupied East Timor in 1975. Nationalists in the two territories waged protracted struggles for independence. Their success in the 1990s established their respective countries as the last former colonies to gain independence – and the only ones to do so from non-European secondary colonial rule.

Despite their similar histories, Eritrea and East Timor had very different liberation strategies. Geography and demography enabled the Eritrean liberation movement to implement a robust military stratagem. Eritrean nationalists decisively defeated the Ethiopian military on the battleground. Eritrea achieved its independence with a secondary reliance on diplomacy.

By contrast, fully surrounded by geographically and demographically dominant Indonesia, the half island of East Timor was structurally handicapped and unable to wage an Eritrean-style resistance. Initial military attempts to halt the Indonesian invasion failed. But, convinced that "to resist is to win," Timorese nationalists did not lay down their weapons. Instead, they challenged Indonesia in the arena of international diplomacy, while maintaining a secondary reliance on guerilla tactics.

---

[1] Aimé Césaire, *Discourse on Colonialism*, trans. Joan Pinkham (Marlborough, England: Adam Matthew Digital, 2007), 42. Reproduced with permission of Monthly Review Press.

I

In a study of these two classic cases of secondary colonialism and anti-colonial grand strategies[2] this book challenges accepted master-narratives of history by examining how the Third World is perceived in several important respects.

First, colonialism is almost universally understood as the West's rule over the Rest. However, as this study shows, non-Western African and Asian powers (other than Japan) have colonized their neighbors. In pursuit of their own national interest, or those of a small ruling elite, important African and Asian powers implemented policies toward weaker entities that were no less colonial and sought no less imperially grandiose than Europe's. This book reveals two important Third-World countries – Ethiopia, well known as a symbol of freedom from Western oppression, and Indonesia, the fastest to have destroyed vestiges of colonialism – as perpetrators of oppressive colonialist projects against their less-powerful neighbors.

Second, grand strategies are conventionally considered a vocation for the militarily dominant West, with the Rest occasionally featuring on the receiving end. However, this Western-centered perspective is due for a reappraisal following the proliferation of sophisticated armed insurgencies, and the rise of the Global South[3] as an internationally important economic and military powerhouse. Colonial subjects have devised effective grand strategies that have enabled them to win independence against regional and global powers. The authors of these successful grand strategies have been catapulted into the canon until recently reserved for Western thinkers and military men. As this book shows, Eritrean and East Timorese nationalists drew on their respective strengths, resources, and allies to devise strategies that suited their particular circumstances against their different opponents.

Third, terrorism has been widely considered as a preserve of insurgencies in the Third World when the method has been widely used, and sometimes openly defended and endorsed by both states and nonstates around the globe. The turn of the twentieth century witnessed an accelerated paradigmatic shift that saw all movements against internationally recognized national governments lumped together as terrorist organizations, even retroactively.[4] This state-centric understanding of terrorism focuses on the actor(s), in other words the same two or more acts are regarded

---

[2] In this context, grand strategy is the term used to describe the sum total of military, diplomatic, propaganda and other strategies that belligerents devise in pursuit of their war and peacetime interests.

[3] The Global South refers to the countries, most of which are located in the Southern Hemisphere that, according to the 2005 United Nations Development Program Report, have a medium (eighty-eight countries) to low (thirty-two countries) human development of less than .8.

[4] After the September 11, 2001 terrorist attacks on the United State, the US PATRIOT ACT greatly expanded the definition of terrorism and those who support(ed) it that the newly established Department of Homeland Security withdrew the asylum status of some former

differently depending on the identity of the actor(s). In R. Woddis's oft-repeated parody,

Throwing a bomb is bad,

Dropping a bomb is good;

Terror, no need to add,

Depends on who is wearing the hood.

This book argues that Ethiopia and Indonesia took over Eritrea and East Timor through terrorist methods and that their subsequent counterinsurgencies constituted state terrorism. By contrast, the respective independence movements displayed remarkable restraint and discipline in rejecting terrorism as a method in spite of the odds stacked against them.

The book concludes with an analysis of how the divergent routes taken by Eritrean and East Timorese nationalists led to different political systems on independence. It aims to add to the growing body of knowledge of both the Eritrean and the East Timorese political systems. Because regime types are intrinsically linked to domestic and regional peace and/or conflict, this analysis will help our understanding of the prospects of peace in the Horn of Africa and Southeast Asia.

Just as their grand strategies were divergent, so, too, were the postindependence political systems in Eritrea and East Timor. For Eritrea, surviving domestic, regional, and global hostility while overcoming the mighty Ethiopian military necessitated secrecy, iron-fisted military discipline, and fierce autonomy from outside powers. These characteristics became deeply ingrained among Eritrean cadres during their struggle. After independence, the newly formed Eritrean government succumbed to these habits, instituting a monistic order.

The challenges of waging simultaneous diplomatic resistance and guerrilla warfare with leaders physically separated and autonomous, forced the East Timorese resistance to become a loose, amorphous body. Unable to indoctrinate and discipline all disparate elements of the resistance, the East Timorese independence movement settled for polyphony – even cacophony – among its specialized guerrilla, clandestine, and diplomatic fronts. They succeeded in making occupation unsustainable until Jakarta granted the East Timorese the right to decide their future in a United Nations–supervised referendum. In spite of the international community's pressure and the donor-based economy binding East Timorese leaders to their stated democratic ideals, however, collaboration rapidly gave way to fierce and often violent political contestation after independence. The lack of a power center and cohesion

Eritrean independence fighters because the nationalist movement that they once belonged to have now been determined to have been terrorist.

led to a precarious start for the East Timorese state, which continues to suffer from loose control, shaky institutions, and arrested reconstruction.

Imperialism by Adjacency and Colonialism

Empires are political arrangements under which various groups are bound together with a single individual leader (or a small group around the leader) assuming supreme military and legislative power over a territory embracing more than one political community.[5] Taking it as classic among the empires that rose and fell across time and space, Anthony Pagden contends that imperial Rome's fundamental qualities "as limited and independent or 'perfect' rule, as a territory embracing more than one political community, and as the absolute sovereignty of a single individual" lasted until recently.[6] Such formal or informal relationships, whereby "one state controls the effective political sovereignty of another political society . . . can be achieved by force, by political collaboration, by economic, social or cultural dependence."[7] Where they come into existence through nonviolent means, empires inaugurate and live off their attendant structural violence that is inevitably sustained by military might. This generally associates empires with military rule, and, more particularly, colonial or conquest empires with physical violence.

Extant theorizing on imperialism offers little help in explaining secondary colonialism much less Ethiopian and Indonesian colonial expansionism, which followed from their deep-seated expansionism. Committed to preparing the ground for socialism, classical Marxism offers structural explanations of imperialism as a materially driven phenomenon, and colonialism as its "highest stage."

In Marxism, according to Tom Kemp, the explanation for colonialism as an aspect of imperialism "has to be sought in material conditions rather than in ideology and politics."[8] Subsequent and differing discourses on imperialism placed the industrially advanced West at the center of diverse peripheries (that were also diverse within themselves).[9] That is why Patrick Wolfe critiqued the debate for being structured around misleading oppositions, one of which is "between the internal and the external, variously

---

[5] Anthony Pagden, *Lords of All the World. Ideologies of Empire in Spain, Britain and France c. 1500–c. 1800* (New Haven, CT: Yale University Press, 1995), 14–17; and Michael Doyle, *Empires* (Ithaca, NY: Cornell University Press, 1986), 45.

[6] Pagden, *Lords of All the World*, 14–17.

[7] Doyle, *Empires*, 45.

[8] Tom Kemp, "The Marxist Theory of Imperialism" in *Studies in the Theory of Imperialism*, ed. Roger Owen and Rob Sutcliffe (London: Longman, 1972), 17.

[9] For a succinct analysis of the various theories of imperialism until the end of the past century, see Patrick Wolfe, "History and Imperialism: A Century of Theory, from Marx to Postcolonialism," *American Historical Review* 102, no. 2 (April 1997):388–420.

manifesting as European versus colonial, core versus periphery, developed versus developing, etc.... this opposition is false because its two terms co-produce each other."[10] These oppositions are, however, accurate in cases of secondary colonialism because, at least in Wolfe's own terms, the center and the periphery did not produce each other for the simple fact that they all constituted peripheries of other rival centers.[11]

Nevertheless, whereas some non-Western, noncapitalist powers are recognized as empires, the colonialism of their imperialism is overlooked – and even celebrated in some circles – on grounds of causation, race and supposed distance that ought to be between the colonizer and colonized.[12] Imperialism, wrote the renowned Edward Said, for example, "means the practice, the theory, and the attitudes of a dominating metropolitan center ruling a distant territory; 'colonialism', which is almost always a *consequence* of imperialism, is the implanting of settlements on *distant* territories" (emphasis added).[13]

How "distant" is distant enough for imperial acquisition and domination to be deemed colonial? Although existing literature on empire does not sufficiently address this question, and Japanese imperial/colonial domination in Asia seems to have little bearing on this discourse, Said continues that Russia "acquired its imperial territories almost exclusively by adjacence." Said, of course, stopped short of suggesting that Russia's swallowing of "whatever land or people stood next to its borders ..."[14] was different from Western European colonial acquisition in Asia and Africa. For the repertoire of power, and the discourses and narratives of imperial domination transcend causative and geographical discrepancies. Moreover, if imperialism is "simply the process or policy of establishing or maintaining an empire," as Michael Doyle puts it,[15] its colonial essence does not change, regardless of whether it was driven by faraway capitalism or expanded overland to adjacent territories for strategic interests of nearby powers.

Secondary colonialism is not always the outcome of imperialism powered by capitalism in the Marxist sense. With their imperial thrusts made possible and sustained by geopolitically driven alliances with, and dependence on, bigger imperial systems of global reach, secondary colonial powers were in many respects different from their European predecessors. It, thus, requires discursive reinterpretation of the value of geopolitics to secondary colonialism that was as much homegrown as in the service of more powerful, faraway empires. So, too, does the political wherewithal that turn such an

[10] Wolfe, "History and Imperialism," 398.
[11] Ethiopia is an exception in a sense that as an independent empire state, it was on the periphery in contrast to the other three, which were formal colonies.
[12] Japanese colonial adventures in Asia seem to have little bearing on this discourse.
[13] Edward W. Said, *Culture and Imperialism* (London: Vintage Books, 1994), 8.
[14] Ibid., 9.
[15] Doyle, *Empires*, 45.

asset into tangible and consequential alliances. For that, the post–World War II international system offers many useful tools.

Margery Perham concluded as early as 1961 that the United Nations "provided a world platform from which to anathematise colonialism and it also established new principles and agencies with the help of which the attack could be pressed home."[16] Secondary colonialism is perhaps better understood within the context of a post–World War II international order that enunciated a paradigmatic shift as to what constituted colonialism. The Atlantic (and the United Nations) Charter resurrected Wilsonian ideals of self-government and liberty. Articles 1, 55, 56, and 73 of the UN Charter, and the Universal Declaration for Human Rights gave fuller expression to Wilson's objection to colonialism on grounds of human rights and rights of non–self-governing peoples to decide their political future. International legal prohibitions against lateral expansion are of the same stock as against European colonialism. And that is discernible beyond the political correctness of United Nations references to territories under secondary colonialism as "dependencies" and "non–self-governing."

In 1960, the UN General Assembly Declaration on the Granting of Independence to Colonial Countries and Peoples equated depriving non–self-governing territories of the right to decide their future to the denial of their people's fundamental human rights.[17] Then, Resolution 1541 spelled out how non–self-governing territories could end their dependent status through an inclusive, transparent process and their free and informed decision.[18] Short of a "freely expressed desire on the part of non-self-governing peoples and through an informed democratic procedure verifiable by the world body,"[19] the acquisition of former European colonies by other states is secondary colonialism. With none of the conditions of Resolution 1541 met, Ethiopian and Indonesian rule over Eritrea and East Timor, respectively, becomes no less colonial than Great Britain's over Kenya or France's over Vietnam. For colonialism is the imposition of an alien political entity's rule over another polity or territory – race and geography may be contributory factors, but are not its defining features.

Whereas the UN General Assembly decision to federate Eritrea with Ethiopia in 1950 took place without plebiscites involving the informed

[16] Margery Perham, *The Colonial Reckoning: The End of Imperial Rule in Africa in the Light of British Experience* (London: Collins, 1961), 52.
[17] UN General Assembly Resolution I514 (XV), December 1960.
[18] UN General Assembly Resolution 1541 (XV): "Principles which Should Guide Members in Determining whether or not an Obligation Exists to Transmit the Information Called for Under Article 73 e of the Charter," December 1960.
[19] UN General Assembly resolution 1541 (XV): "Principles which Should Guide Members in Determining whether or not an Obligation Exists to Transmit the Information Called for Under Article 73 e of the Charter," 15 December 1960.

participation of Eritreans,[20] Indonesian invasion of East Timor in 1975 "constituted an act of aggression forbidden by the United Nation Charter and customary law" and deprived the former Portuguese colony "of its right to self-determination [through] military intervention."[21]

Horn of African and Southeast Asian twentieth century imperialism by adjacency, therefore, did not lead to what Albert Memmi tellingly characterized as "profitable purgatory" in which European colonizers enjoyed "exorbitant rights."[22] Similarities of the physical environment, ethnographic overlap or proximity, and possible shared historical experiences between the adjacent colonizer and colonized lessened the secondary colonizers' "suffering" that their European counterparts had to endure in pursuit of their distant colonial projects. And the overall lack of rights and privileges in the secondary metropolitan center precluded the regime of exorbitant rights that European colonialism instituted in the colonies.

Nor did Ethiopian and Indonesian secondary colonialism inaugurate the "bifurcated state" of "citizens" and "subjects" of late European colonial despotism. Mahmood Mamdani shows such a state as comprising a vast majority of rightless rural subjects and urban middle- and working-class natives who are neither subject nor citizen.[23] Unlike European colonizers who were preoccupied with the native question, secondary colonizers sought to impose their preferred or elite identities (as opposed to that of their own marginalized periphery) on the colonized by erasing the identities (languages, cultures, histories and aspirations) of the latter. Because of the two factors – the aforementioned regime of rightlessness in the metropoles and ethnic and/or ethnographic similarities with the secondary colonial subjects – Ethiopia and Indonesia insisted that Eritreans were "Ethiopian" and East Timorese "Indonesian," respectively.

---

[20] On February 15, 1950, the UN Commission for Eritrea issued its first communiqué inviting "any individual or any group of individuals from among the inhabitants of Eritrea who so desire to send, as soon as possible and no later than 28 February 1950, to the Commission at its headquarters in Asmara any written statement relating to the future status of Eritrea" (emphasis added). "Communiqué by the Commission to the Inhabitants of Eritrea Inviting Written Statement by Individuals or Groups," 15 February 1950 (available at UCLA Research Library Special Collections, Ralph Bunche Papers, Box 92, "Eritrea Mission Cables"). According to the Fifth Confidential Report of the Principal Secretary of the Commission, Petrus J. Schmidt, to UN Secretary General Trygve Lie, the Mission ended its fact-finding in Eritrea on March 25, 1950. In less than two months, a disharmonious group of five quarreling envoys who also represented conflicting interests of their respective countries (or that of their allies) decided the fate of a people in less than two months.

[21] Roger S. Clark, "The 'Decolonization' of East Timor and the United Nations Norms on Self-determination and Aggression," *International Law and the Question of East Timor* (1995):73.

[22] Albert Memmi, *The Colonizer and the Colonized* (Boston: Beacon Press, 1965), 5, 8.

[23] Mahmood Mamdani, *Citizen and Subject. Contemporary Africa and the Legacy of Late Colonialism* (Princeton, NJ: Princeton University Press, 1996).

Lacking longevity and stability, Ethiopian and Indonesian secondary colonial systems are best characterization as *imposed provincialism* plagued by *counterinsurgency*. Yet, secondary colonialism in Eritrea and East Timor bore a strong resemblance to European colonialism. First, the colonial and secondary colonial centers imposed their administrative structures, languages, and rituals on the subjects who were not only expected to accept losing their own rights but also to sing their colonizers' praise songs. During the Dutch centennial independence celebrations in the Dutch East Indies (future Indonesia), Soewardi Soerjaningrat, an astute product of colonial education, wrote in the Dutch language, "If I were a Dutchman, then I would hold no independence celebrations in a land where we deny the people their independence."[24] In the same way that Soewardi's thinking and writing offered a conceptual basis to challenge Dutch colonialism, so, too, did Indonesian- and Ethiopian-educated East Timorese and Eritrean nationalists challenge their subjugation on the very principles that their colonial masters expected them to celebrate their lot.

As a result, and this is the second resemblance between European and secondary non-European colonial experiences, a native's imitation of the secondary colonizer was as much needed as rejected by the latter. Homi Bhahba has shown how the mimicry of Europe's colonial subjects was desired by the colonizer as it provided "a reformed, recognizable Other" at the same time that it was disavowed for its disruptive effect.[25] Out of conviction, or pure opportunistic expedience, Eritreans and East Timorese spoke Amharic and Indonesian, sang to their actual or mythical glories, and did their bidding, not only in their home territories but also in secondary metropoles of Addis Ababa and Jakarta.

The ambivalent secondary colonial masters celebrated such Eritreans and East Timorese as much as they reminded them of their otherness. Whereas the subordination of loyal East Timorese to Indonesian officials of inferior talent and experience is visible throughout the administration of and counterinsurgency across that territory, the legal advisor to Ethiopia's Emperor Haile Selassie was candid in disclosing how hailing from Eritrea was "a chink in the armor" of Eritreans in the employ of the Emperor in Addis Ababa.[26]

And finally, beyond the figurative penetration, opening up and fertilization of the colonized lands, colonial masters found luscious appeal in

---

[24] Quoted in R. E. Elson, "Constructing the Nation: Ethnicity, Race, Modernity and Citizenship in Early Indonesian Thought," *Asian Ethnicity* 6, no. 3 (2005):145–160.

[25] Homi K. Bhabha, *The Location of Culture* (London and New York: Routledge, 1998), 86–88.

[26] John H. Spencer, *Ethiopia at Bay. A Personal Account of the Haile Selassie Years*, 2nd ed. (Hollywood, CA: Tsehai Publishers 2006), 138. See also Amare Tekle, "A Response to Professor Bahru Zewde" of January 22, 1999, at http://www.dehai.org/conflict/articles/bahru.html.

their female colonial subjects.[27] "Wherever they have gone," writes Wolfe, "male colonizers have impregnated native women."[28] Ethiopia's project of "Amharizing" (the ethnicity of Ethiopian rulers) Eritrea by fighting the war in the wombs of Eritrean women and harvesting Eritrean children to Amhara fathers[29] is analyzed in Chapter Six.

There is circumstantial evidence that Indonesia had similar policies toward East Timor when the latter became a destination for Indonesian transmigration and, at the same time, was a garrison province, with soldiers made to live as civilians among the East Timorese people. Although this deliberate intermixing had immediate security objectives,[30] its long-term Indonesianizing influences were as important as the transmigrants.[31] Ironically and ominously perhaps, male colonial subjects and women of the colonizing societies fell for each other.[32] Defeating secondary colonialism, however, required as intricate grand strategies of liberation as those of imperial domination.

Grand Strategy and the Global South

When the nineteenth-century Prussian military thinker Karl von Clausewitz wrote of war as "the continuation of policy by other means,"[33] he argued that waging war required more than just military strategy aimed at winning

[27] Frantz Fanon, *The Wretched of the Earth*, trans. Constance Farrington (New York: Grove Press, 1968).

[28] Wolfe, "History and Imperialism," 416.

[29] "Eti Kale-ay Kwinat" reproduced in Alemseged Tesfai, *Two Weeks in the Trenches: Reminiscences of Childhood and War in Eritrea* (Trenton, NJ: The Red Sea Press, 2002), 167ff. Alemsged also offers the true story context to that play in *The Other War: An After Word*, 211ff.

[30] Samuel Moore, "The Indonesian Military's Last Years in East Timor: An Analysis of its Secret Documents," *Indonesia* 72 (October 2001):20–23.

[31] Bhabha articulates such a dual purpose of European colonial discourse – equally relevant to secondary colonial situations – when he minimally identified it "as an apparatus that turns on the recognition and disavowal of racial/cultural/historical differences. Its predominant strategic function is the creation of a space for the 'subject peoples' through the production of knowledges in terms of which surveillance is exercised and a complex form of pleasure/unpleasure is incited." Bhabha, *The Location of Culture*, 70.

[32] In *The Colonial Reckoning*, Perham alludes to male colonial subjects, who find their way to the colonial metropoles, finding luscious appeal for white women and eager to prove their prowess to them as if to prove a point to the colonizing male. Along the same lines, Tayeb Salih's *Season of Migration to the North*, trans. Denys Johnson-Davies (Oxford: Heinemann, 1969) offers sexualized metaphor of the dynamics of colonizer-colonized relationship with his inscrutable character Mustafa Sa'eed bragging to liberate Africa with his penis. This work was first published in Arabic in 1967 as *Mawsim al-Hijrah ila ash-Shamal*.

[33] Karl Von Clausewitz, *On War*, eds. and trans. Michael Howard and Peter Paret (Princeton, NJ: Princeton University Press, 1976), 99.

battles.[34] In 1943, leading grand strategy scholar Edward Mead Earle further advanced that view, arguing that given increasing complexity of war and society, effective strategy required the consideration of economic, psychological, moral, political, and technological factors as well as traditional military ones.[35] This came to be called grand strategy, "an art in the Clausewitzian sense," according to Paul Kennedy, that relies upon the regular review of one's goals and both military and nonmilitary capacities to best serve one's interests in war and in peace.[36]

Such conventional discussion of grand strategy presupposes the agency of state actors, often major Western powers. More recent Western scholarship and policy even speak of statecraft as the centerpiece of grand strategy. In the footsteps of Henry Kissinger, Charles Hill takes this point even further by assigning grand strategic significance to Western literary classics from Homer to Jane Austen and more.[37] Nevertheless, one does not have to imbibe Western literary classics, or wear a suit and tie, be housed in imposing buildings, or conduct oneself in a certain conventional way, to be able to plan and oversee the implementation of an elaborate and farsighted plan of action. Nor does one have to go through West Point, Sandhurst, or Saint-Cyr to command an army in one battle after another without losing sight of the war. Liberation movements in the colonies developed masterly grand strategies whose effectiveness can be measured by their success in gaining independence against many odds. Indeed, experience shows that these liberation movements can defeat even regional and global powers with legions of military theorists steeped in conventional lore. They have also won against statesmen conversant in Western literary classics.

In some important respects, the Eritrean and East Timorese liberation movements acted like sovereign states contesting Ethiopian and Indonesian power. Although Eritrea and East Timor did not have the official international recognition enjoyed by Ethiopia and Indonesia, their liberation movements displayed incremental statelike sophistication that contributed to their ultimate success. This is a condition that Trotsky famously called a state of "dual authority," in which a "state" within a state issued orders and offered its followers statelike services, or the hope thereof, and gradually eroded the internal legitimacy of the latter. However, unlike Trotsky's characterization of that period as a condition of "Dual Impotence,"[38] dual

---

[34] Liddell Hart, *Strategy*, rev. 2nd ed. (London: Meridian, 1991), 353.

[35] Edward Mead Earle (ed.), *Makers of Modern Strategy. Military Thought from Machiavelli to Hitler* (Princeton, NJ: Princeton University Press, 1943), viii.

[36] Paul Kennedy (ed.), *Grand Strategies in War and Peace* (New Haven, CT, and London: Yale University Press, 1991), 5–6.

[37] Charles Hill, *Grand Strategies: Literature, Statecraft, and World Order* (New Haven, CT, and London: Yale University Press, 2010).

[38] This best captures the state of affairs in Russia after the 1917 revolution when both the bourgeois government and the Soviets claimed to control the state and issued understandably

authority empowered the liberation movements in Eritrea and East Timor and was a stepping-stone to even greater authority. Indeed, this book concludes by relating how the ebb and flow of Eritrean and East Timorese grand strategies are intricately linked to their statehood-in-waiting. It can, therefore, be argued that the independence wars in Eritrea and East Timor were one long process of state formation, and the grand strategies of the liberation movements were statecraft-in-the-making.

Broadly speaking, the roots of Eritrean and East Timorese resistance were grounded in similar contexts of secondary colonialism and their liberation movements devised different dynamic strategies at various stages. A deeper analysis shows that during the height of their struggles the two adopted divergent grand strategies that best fit their respective circumstances: one centering on military victory and another on diplomatic and civil society endeavors.

Oppressive rule and Addis Ababa's diplomatic mastery and monopoly of the state-level international forums, inattention by the United Nations and fixed hostility of the superpowers, left Eritreans with no choice but to fight. The liberation movement formulated and implemented a robust militaristic grand strategy because structural factors like geography and demography offered cross-border sanctuaries, ensured reliable avenues of materiel and logistical supply, and replenished their ranks. In addition to defeating Ethiopian forces on the battlefield in Eritrea, Eritrean nationalists fostered rebel movements within Ethiopia as "democratic alternatives" to the government[39] and propped them up to take the helm of power in Addis Ababa.

Fully surrounded by Indonesia and with a population of less than one million throughout the occupation, East Timor lacked Eritrea's relative advantages. Structurally handicapped to wage an Eritrean-style resistance, the initial military attempts of the East Timorese to halt the Indonesian invasion failed. But convinced that "to resist is to win"[40] and without laying down their weapons, the East Timorese nationalists pragmatically devised alternative means of challenging Indonesia. Their initial military-centered strategy gave way to diplomatic efforts in the international arena, along with simultaneous ideological and political reorientation on the ground. While

---

conflicting orders. Leon Trotsky, "The Farce of Dual Power" in *The Proletarian Revolution in Russia*, by N. Lenin and Leon Trotsky, ed. Louis C. Fraina (New York: The Communist Press, 1918), 185ff.

[39] Voice of the Broad Masses, "The EPLF and its Relationship with the Democratic Movements in Ethiopia," 31 January–2 February 1985, reproduced in *Adulis* 1, no. 11 (May 1985).

[40] This is a famous slogan of the East Timorese resistance against Indonesian invasion, later popularized by the East Timorese nationalist leader, Xanana Gusmão. It is also the title of his autobiography and compilation of his writings and speeches edited by Sarah Niner, *To Resist Is to Win. The Autobiography of Xanana Gusmão* (Richmond, Australia: Aurora Books, 2000).

ideological moderation earned the movement the backing of the territory's influential Catholic Church, political pragmatism enabled the resistance to embrace politically diverse proponents of independence. By simultaneously shifting its focus to the Indonesian military's ceaseless violation of Timorese human rights, the resistance won the moral support of Indonesia's Western allies, isolating Jakarta and breaking its resolve to continue with its occupation.

State Terrorism and the Restraint of Nonstate Opponents

Terrorism has never been more menacing than its definition is polarizing and its discussion riddled with contradictions. The unprecedented increase in the incidence and scale of terrorism in the twentieth century continued into the twenty-first century and has become the single most salient policy preoccupation of our times. Nonetheless, negotiations on a Comprehensive Convention on International Terrorism faltered because of the trite cliché that one man's terrorist is a liberator to another.[41] No member state wants either to be branded terrorist or to face accusations of abetting terrorism according to the very terms that it participated in framing. In 2005, Thalif Deen captured the key descriptive and normative issues stalling the negotiations: "[W]hat distinguishes a 'terrorist organisation' from a 'liberation movement'? And do you exclude activities of national armed forces, even if they are perceived to commit acts of terrorism? If not, how much of this constitutes 'state terrorism'?"[42] Six years later and in spite of near consensual repugnance at the act itself, negotiations have not moved much, if at all.

Terrorism is understood in this study to mean a violent act – or the threat thereof – against innocent civilians and/or their property in order to achieve political or other end(s) directly or indirectly by intimidating and instilling fear among an audience other than those enduring the violence or the threat.[43] The moral question involved in the act and discussion of it aside, terrorism, as deployed by weak opponents of the state, is unique because it

---

[41] The draft Comprehensive Convention on International Terrorism defines terrorism as "unlawful and intentional act causing or threatening to cause violence by means of firearms, weapons, explosives, any lethal devices or dangerous substances, which results, or is likely to result, in death or serious bodily injury to a person, a group of persons or serious damage to property – whether for public use, a State or Government facility, a public transportation system or an infrastructure facility." The failure on this convention is in spite of numerous United Nations General Assembly and Security Council resolutions at different times condemning various acts of terrorism or devising mechanisms to mitigate the phenomenon.

[42] "U.N. Member States Struggle to Define Terrorism," IPS News, July 25, 2005: http://ipsnews.net/news.asp?idnews=29633.

[43] Igor Primoratz (ed.), *Terrorism. The Philosophical Issues* (New York: Palgrave Macmillan, 2004); see the first two chapters by C. A. J (Tony) Coady and Primoratz, pp. 3–29.

targets the few in a way that claims the attention of the many. Thus a lack of proportion between resources deployed and effects created, between the material power of actors and the fear their actions generate, is typical... terrorism is distinguished by its high symbolic and expressive value. The discrepancy between the secrecy of planning and the visibility of results gives it even more shock value.[44]

Terrorism is an act committed – and a method resorted to – by states as well. "Before 1914," reflected Eric Hobsbawm, "the view that war was against combatants and not non-combatants was shared by rebels and revolutionaries... Today this limitation is no more recognized by revolutionaries and terrorists than by governments waging war."[45] Condemning nonstate terrorism, terrorism scholar Walter Laqueur explains state terrorism as something that serves a different function and manifests itself differently.[46]

A number of scholars disagree and argue that terrorism is self-evident in its unfolding, regardless of who the actor may be. They range from Hanna Arndt's characterization of the Third Reich and Stalin's Soviet Union, to Igor Primoratz's philosophical classification of Allied bombing of German cities, among others, and Ruth Blakeley's analysis of the Global North's historical role in the South.[47] According to Primoratz, state terrorism is in fact far more damaging and repugnant for a number of reasons: capacity of states (even the weak ones) outweighs its nonstate opponents, state terrorism happens in secrecy and with deception that makes it hard to establish its full extent and that can be denied even if a limited aspect of it is known, terrorism is prohibited by international statutes to which states are signatories, and states have no acceptable grounds to resort to terrorism like nonstate actors who do so as a last resort.[48]

However, not all nonstate actors turn to terrorism. During the last two of four phases that constituted humanity's slide to what Hobsbawm characterized as barbarism – that is, "the four decades of the Cold War era, and ... the general breakdown of civilization as we know it over large parts

---

[44] Martha Crenshaw, "Thoughts on Relating Terrorism to Historical Contexts" in Martha Crenshaw (ed.) *Terrorism in Context* (University Park: The Pennsylvania State University Press, 2007), 4.

[45] Eric Hobsbawm, "Barbarism: A User's Guide," *New Left Review* 206 (July–August 1994):44–54.

[46] Walter Laqueur, *The Age of Terrorism* (Boston: Little, Brown, 1987), 146. Laqueur's pre-September 11 predications of what he called was "new terrorism" were not fully borne out by subsequent developments. But September 11 proved him right that terrorists had started to use tactics that had previously been considered science fiction.

[47] Hannah Arendt, "Ideology and Terror: A Novel Form of Government," *The Review of Politics* 15, no. 3 (July 1953):303–327; Primoratz (ed.), *Terrorism*; and Ruth Blakeley, *State Terrorism and Neoliberalism: The North in the South* (New York: Routledge, 2009). Also see Naom Chomsky et al., "What Anthropologists Should Know about the Concept of Terrorism..." in *Anthropology Today* 18, no. 2 (April 2002):22–23.

[48] Primoratz, "State Terrorism and Counter-terrorism" in *Terrorism*, ed. Primoratz, 117–119.

of the world in and since the 1980s"[49] – the Eritrean and East Timorese liberation movements set remarkable examples of overcoming seemingly insurmountable challenges in pursuit of a legitimate cause, without resorting to terrorism. Whereas the liberation movements were careful not to antagonize the civilians who sheltered and supported them and replenished their ranks, the Eritrean and East Timorese nationalists cautiously avoided using terroristic methods inside Ethiopia and Indonesia as well.[50] But their restraint was not matched by the states that they opposed.

The histories of the Eritrean and East Timorese independence struggles are full of stories of nationalists isolating legitimate targets and carefully timing their attacks and of Indonesian and Ethiopian governments retaliating for their losses on civilians. In the aftermath of every successful insurgent attack on Ethiopian or Indonesian positions (military or political), government forces carried out widespread arrests and tortured and killed civilians. From the July 1962 indiscriminate killing of civilians in the town of Agordat,[51] to the December 1970 obliteration of the villages of Ona and Besik-Dira,[52] and the May 1988 massacre at Shieb and Ghedghed[53] and more, no change of government made a difference to Ethiopian state terrorism against noncombatant Eritreans and their property. Ethiopian gains did not stop its military from terrorizing the civilian population of Eritrea. Captured fighters were publicly hanged and their bodies left to rot, while mutilated corpses of fighters were displayed in public squares to instill fear in the population under the Ethiopian military's control.

Similarly, in East Timor, whether in the aftermath of the independence fighters blowing up military and radio installations in June 1980,[54] or East

---

[49] Hobsbawm, "Barbarism: A User's Guide," 44–54.

[50] The young East Timorese activists in Indonesian universities, for example, stayed clear of growing militancy of the Indonesian youth and student body all the while identifying and collaborating with (and sometime leading) peaceful demonstrations in support of reform, respect of human rights and the right to self-determination of East Timorese (discussed in Chapter 6).

[51] This was in retaliation to the July 12, 1962 attack by the fledgling ELF units on the city hall where Ethiopia's most senior officials were gathered.

[52] In late November 1970, ELF units assassinated the highest Ethiopian commander in Eritrea General Teshome Ergetu in a daring broad daylight ambush. A week later, Ethiopian reinforcements that congregated at the scene descended on the nearby villages of Ona and Besik-Dira, killing more than one thousand innocent men, women, and children and setting every standing hut on fire.

[53] In March, EPLF forces had made their most strategic and irreversible gain against Ethiopian forces when they crushed the latter's Nadew Command at the gates of Nakfa and liberated the strategic town of Afabet.

[54] Conversations with David Diaz Ximenes (summer 2006, Dili, East Timor) and Francisco Carvalho "Chico" (interview, May 13, 2006, Dili, East Timor) were arrested, among many others who were innocent of collaborating with the attack but were jailed in Atauro islet, and tortured, and some even killed.

Timorese nonviolent defiance of November 1991,[55] or their victory to decide their future during the second half of 1999,[56] Indonesian atrocities were so widespread that its actions have been described as genocide (discussed in Chapter 3). Indonesian forces put the U.S.-supplied OV-10 Broncos to effective, gruesome use when they blanket-bombed vast tracts of rural East Timor, directly targeting the civilian population, defoliating their forested habitat, and burning their crops. Throughout, Eritrean and East Timorese nationalists resisted the temptation of retaliating in kind, retaining the moral high ground.

Building on her classic study of Algeria's National Liberation Front (FLN), Martha Crenshaw offers important insights into why nonstate actors (in this case, liberation movements) resort to terrorism. According to her, the imbalance between insurgents and centralized bureaucratic states leave the former no choice but to reach a "collective rational strategic choice" of terrorism as a calculated response in order to compensate for their numerical inferiority. This is compounded by the insurgents' organizational incapacity or laziness to work hard toward mass mobilization, a combination of untested optimism and urgency, and by innovation in identifying targets considered taboo or inviolable and so least expected and in using technology to spread and replicate their actions.[57]

In spite of their numerical and material inferiority, numerous Ethiopian and Indonesian weak targets, and a technological capacity to execute, replicate and spread their acts,[58] this book shows Eritrean and East Timorese nationalists making a rational, strategic choice not to resort to terrorism. Instead, they worked hard to mobilize their own people; garner regional and global material, diplomatic and military support; and exploit Addis Ababa's and Jakarta's weaknesses by, among other things, winning over Ethiopian and Indonesian allies who helped to take the fight to their respective governments' doorsteps.

---

[55] This is the funeral procession that turned into a peaceful political rally and culminated in the Santa Cruz massacre of November 12, 1991.

[56] The terror that descended on East Timor in the run up to the May 5, 1999, Accords and afterward took place because the Indonesian military in East Timor trained, armed and financed preexisting and new pro-autonomy militias with the express goal of cowing their pro-independence brethren into choosing continued association with Indonesia.

[57] Martha Crenshaw, "The Logic of Terrorism: Terrorist Behavior as a Product of Strategic Choice," in *Origins of Terrorism: Psychologies, Ideologies, Theologies, States of Mind*, ed. Walter Reich (Washington, DC: the Woodrow Wilson Center Press, 1998), pp. 7–23. Although later she made some concession to Jerrold M. Post's argument that terrorism has to do with state of mind of the terrorist, "psycho-logic" as he put it, she generally maintains her argument with regard to organized movements.

[58] For an analysis of how organized groups fine tuned their terrorist methods and generally evolve in response to technological and normative changes of our time, see Peter R. Neumann, *Old and New Terrorism: Late Modernity, Globalization and the Transformation of Political Violence* (Cambridge: Polity Press, 2009).

Colonial Nationalism Reified

As Ethiopia intensified its iron-fisted hold on Eritrea and Indonesia launched a full-scale invasion of East Timor, the two peoples' rejection of their subordinate status took the form of organized, violent resistance. The increasingly crude Ethiopian and Indonesian counterinsurgencies only increased the resolve to resist. Far from weakening nascent Eritrean and East Timorese sentiments, Ethiopian and Indonesian expansion of educational and other opportunities helped bolster and articulate Eritrean and East Timorese rejection of their imposed Ethiopian-ness and Indonesian-ness. If the toxic mix of education, economic, industrial, and infrastructural growth (or hopes thereof), and repression within the administrative frameworks of a defined territory saw the birth of territorial nationalisms and the undoing of colonialism in the former colonies,[59] Eritreans' and East Timorese's distinct identities evolved within, and in response to, the physical and structural violence that attended Ethiopian and Indonesian secondary colonialisms. Irrepressible desire for freedom outlasted the long and arduous process and the exorbitant sacrifices.

Ernest Renan wrote that the existence of a nation depended on the outcome of *"a daily plebiscite"* in which its people affirm their willingness to stay in that given nation,[60] but the exorbitant price tag of making that happen has left many to ponder its source. For the colossal sacrifices to be made in the name of a nation, one school of thought holds, the nation – or at least the seeds thereof – must have existed as a primordial basis for collective identity.[61] Nationalists in the former European colonies in Africa and Asia partially subscribed to this view and labored to establish the historicity of their nations-in-the-waiting. In a bid to legitimize and garner support for their independence, they glorified little traces of common history – and, where they did not exist, in mythmaking. Nevertheless, the fact that even such glorification or mythmaking is spatially and ethnographically constrained and limited through time lends itself to the conclusion that nationness is a historically contingent phenomenon, nonprimordialist scholars

---

[59] George McTurnan Kahin, *Nationalism and Revolution in Indonesia* (Ithaca: Cornell University Press, 1952); and Benedict Anderson, *Imagined Communities. Reflections on the Origin and Spread of Nationalism* (London: Verso, 1991 Revised Edition). Although this general frame of analysis emerges out of Kahin's earlier examination of Indonesian nationalism, Anderson broadened its application to other cases of colonial nationalism. Perham (*The Colonial Reckoning*, 35ff.) offer similar – albeit cursory – analysis in African context.

[60] Ernest Renan, "What Is a Nation?" in *Modern Political Doctrines*, ed. A. Zimmern (Oxford: Oxford University Press, 1939), 187–205.

[61] Anthony D. Smith, *The Ethnic Origins of Nations* (Oxford and New York: B Blackwell, 1986). But Smith goes on to make the debatable claim that colonial nationalisms do not have "a common myth of origin nor shared history." See his "Introduction" in *Nationalist Movements* (London: Macmillan, 1976), 5.

contend without dismissing outright the commonsensical primordial starting point into the roots of modern nationalism.[62]

The contradictory processes and events driven by nationalism complicate the discussion into its roots. Although the term and concept of nationalism are used to describe contradictory processes and events,[63] existing nation-states and nationalism in Africa and Asia followed on the heels of capitalism and relative industrial growth that colonialism ushered in. As much as the latter randomly split communities, its exploitative capitalist economy, legal system(s), administrative structures, and education systems had an integrative impact on the colonized. It also necessitated the education (however limited) of natives who, as nationalist vanguards of their newly reconstituted communities, appropriated the colonial paraphernalia to end colonialism.[64]

This is why Eric Hobsbawm characterized territorial or colonial nationalisms as "typically unificatory as well as emancipatory"[65]: *unificatory* because they bonded together peoples of diverse backgrounds who were cavalierly brought together during the colonial era and *emancipatory* because they took an unflinching stand in pursuit of independence and against colonialism.[66] Maturing through the violence of Ethiopian and Indonesian secondary colonialism, Eritrean and East Timorese territorial nationalisms could hardly afford to be less violent than the environment that gave birth to them and against which they struggled. If the colossal sacrifices nationalism demanded were offered out of love for the colonized, it persisted because of its enmity toward and, oftentimes, violence against the colonizer.[67] In the process, the nationalists lost many battles – from the smallest skirmishes to large-scale confrontations – but throughout the spiraling cycle of conflict, clandestine operations and diplomatic wrangling, they devised

---

[62] Anderson, *Imagined Communities*, 5–8, 22–26.

[63] "It has been the ideology of the weaker, less developed countries struggling to free themselves from alien oppression. But on the other hand … the term applies no less characteristically, to the history of Italian fascism and the Japanese military state of the 1930s," summarizes Tom Nairn, "The Modern Janus" in *New Left Review*, No. 94 (November–December 1975):5. Also in Nairn, *The Break-up of Britain. Crisis and Neo-Nationalism* (1981), chapter 9: "The Modern Janus," 329–364.

[64] Kahin, *Nationalism*; and Anderson, *Imagined Communities*.

[65] Eric Hobsbawm, *Nations and Nationalism since 1780: Program, Myth, Reality*, 2nd ed. (Cambridge: Cambridge University Press, 1992), 169–171.

[66] Throughout this period, Eritrea and East Timor were not peripheries to centers in Addis Ababa and Jakarta but to Rome and Lisbon.

[67] Revolutionary thinkers and early scholars of the former colonies accordingly identify colonial nationalism with visible anti-colonial action that "binds [the colonized people] together as a whole [and] each individual forms a violent link in the great chain" of resistance to the initial violence imposed by the colonizers, according to Fanon, *The Wretched of the Earth*, 50; James S. Coleman, "Nationalism in Tropical Africa," *American Political Science Review* V; Crawford Young, "Nationalism, Ethnicity and Class in Africa: A Retrospective," *Cahiers d'Etudes africaines* 103, no. 26-3 (1989).

intricate stratagem that outlasted Ethiopian and Indonesian superior numbers, and diplomatic and military prowess. Once Ethiopia and Indonesia
had unleashed systematic and blatant violence, Eritrean and East Timorese
nationalisms burst into action, and Addis Ababa and Jakarta resorted to even
heavier-handed counterinsurgencies. Superior grand strategy determined the
outcome of the David-versus-Goliath struggles.

Imperial Roots and Colonial Origins of the Recolonizers and the Recolonized

The government newspaper *The Ethiopian Herald* quoted His Imperial
Majesty Haile Selassie I condemning imperialism without apparent irony.
Similarly, the founding Indonesian President Sukarno repeatedly condemned
Dutch imperialism, only to glorify the imperial past of precolonial commercial empires of Majapahit and Srivijaya as essential cornerstones of an
independent Indonesia. While the Indonesian Republic's modern origins lay
in the history of Dutch imperialism, the modern Ethiopian Empire came to
being in competition against, and in negotiations with, its European imperial
counterparts in the Horn of Africa. Directly or indirectly, therefore, all the
political entities that are the subject of this book share a common legacy of
European colonialism's territorial imprint. Nevertheless, Ethiopia regained
its independence in 1941 and Indonesia won it in 1949–1950 before turning
on their small, weak neighbors.

The Ethiopian Empire
Ethiopian rulers prided themselves on being kings of kings and imperial
majesties, although contemporary scholars have debated the genesis and
transformations of the imperial polity.[68] Out of the so-called Era of Princes
that plagued the Northeast African Christian polity of Abyssinia since the
1760s,[69] Tewodros's accession to the throne in 1855 ushered in his dominion over a multinational and politically heterogeneous empire. During most
of his reign, Tewodros exercised as absolute authority as his military power
permitted. His relatively short reign left behind a legacy of wanting to build
a strong centralized polity that his effective successor Yohannes IV readily
took on. Although, as self-declared primus inter pares, Yohannes gave his

---

[68] The consensus among scholars is that Emperor Menelik (reign 1889–1913) presided over
the crystallization of a fluid process handed down to him from his immediate predecessors, Tewodros II (r, 1855–1868) and Yohannes IV (r. 1872–1889). The 1974 coup either
marked the transformation of the empire or heralded an era whereby the transformation
was effected.

[69] This was a period of warlordism characterized by regional royal families and aspiring
brigands fighting each other to become kingmakers. For a comprehensive examination of
this period, see Mordechai Abir, *Ethiopia: The Era of the Princes. The Challenge of Islam
and the Re-unification of the Christian Empire, 1769–1855* (New York: Praeger, 1968).

provinces extensive autonomy, he expected no less loyalty from his "equals" (regional princes governing the provinces) than Tewodros had. Meanwhile, Menelik II, the hereditary ruler of the then southernmost province of Shoa – while pledging allegiance to the north and bowing on the feet of Yohannes in submission – forcibly conquered new territories beyond his southern and western limits, creating a mini empire within a broader empire.[70] When Yohannes died at the hands of the Sudanese Mahdist forces in 1889, Menelik's power, partly emanating from his recent conquests, propelled him to the throne of an even more powerful, enlarged empire.

Onetime imperial peripheries become integral parts of the center that require the acquisition of more territory as a buffer, the latter acquisitions become periphery at a later stage, and so goes the cycle. When European imperial schemes carved up Italian, French, and British colonies in Northeast Africa, Menelik launched another all-out invasion of his neighbors to secure a buffer zone for his empire's peripheries, around the northern and central highlands of present-day Ethiopia.[71] His successful thwarting of Italian attempts to encroach upon his empire at the Battle of Adwa in 1896 crowned his territorial acquisitions and earned him European empire builders' recognition – in return for his leaving Italy's Eritrean colony unmolested.[72] As the Italians exited the scene after their humiliating defeat in World War II, however, Ethiopian recognition of Eritrea as a territory beyond its own domain lapsed. After the British restored Emperor Haile Selassie (r. 1930–1974) to his throne, subsequent to Ethiopia's liberation from Italian rule in 1941, he made access to the sea one of his top foreign policy priorities. Consistent with his predecessors' imperial practices, he sought to extend his domain over the former Italian colony of Eritrea.

Throughout this period, the Ethiopian empire state gradually modernized its governing apparatus (administrative, monetary, defense, and security). At the same time, successive Ethiopian rulers simultaneously held on to the traditional political, economic, and feudal means of legitimizing and consolidating their power. The cumulative outcome of these was a bureaucratic empire in which traditional political roles and modern administrative functions coexisted.[73] With corruption rampant, the benefits of limited reforms

---

[70] Bahru Zewde, *A History of Modern Ethiopia, 1855–1974* (Addis Ababa: Addis Ababa University Press, 1992), 60–61.

[71] Bahru, (*A History of Modern Ethiopia*, 61–66) gives a concise, vivid account of Menilek II's conquests of what today are Ethiopia's borderlands.

[72] For an account of the causes and outcome of the Battle of Adwa, see Bahru, *A History of Modern Ethiopia*, 72–84. Yosef Neguse's letter to Alfred Ilg and Leon Chefneux of March 31, 1896, gives a firsthand account of the battle, of which the translated version appears in Bairu Tafla's *Ethiopian Records of the Menilek Era: Selected Amharic Documents from the Nachlass of Alfred Ilg, 1884–1900* (Wiesbaden: Harrassowitz Verlag, 2000), 458 ff.

[73] Edmond J. Keller, *Revolutionary Ethiopia from Empire to Revolutionary Republic* (Bloomington: Indiana University Press, 1988), 15n1, 273.

were restricted to the already privileged elements of Ethiopian society.[74] Haile Selassie, indeed, gave precedence to strengthening his personal rule over all other concerns; every restructuring was either intended or manipulated to serve that purpose. By and large, Ethiopia remained a traditional polity under the growing domination of ethnic Amhara elite until a group of little known junior army officers called the Derg staged a successful coup d'état in 1974.

The Derg aborted Haile Selassie's desire to transform Ethiopia into a constitutional monarchy, "an empire built on refined principles of royal absolutism,"[75] but did little to transform the empire itself. In fact, the post–Haile Selassie regime in Addis Ababa determined to maintain the imperially acquired territories by whatever means necessary. Moreover, it pursued in earnest the Amharization process of cultural imperialism long after the supposed revolutionary order replaced the imperial system.[76] Founded through violence and held together through coercion, the Ethiopian state lived on as an imperial entity.

Recolonizing the "Firstborn" Italian Colony of Eritrea

For centuries before the nineteen-century European scramble for Africa, the territory of Eritrea had been a fighting ground for marauding Tigrayan warlords from present-day northern Ethiopia and successive Funj incursions, Turco-Egyptian expansion, and later Mahdyya invasions from Nilotic Sudan. Some inhabitants came to cultivate a sense of shared ancestry through waves of migrations while others lived collectively under the mercy of one or another of the invading regional powers and bonded with each other through seeking and offering refuge during times of war. Having grown war weary during the nineteenth century, a number of Eritrean communities welcomed the advent of Italians to the scene, while some individual warriors actively collaborated with setting up Italian colonial rule.[77]

Once Italy finished carving up its colony of Eritrea around 1890, Eritreans shared the curses and the blessings of colonial rule. On one hand, the brunt of Italian racist policies and exploitative practices were felt across the country.[78] On the other hand, the prolonged years of peace along with

---

[74] John Markakis, *Ethiopia: Anatomy of a Traditional Polity* (Oxford: Clarendon Press, 1974).

[75] Keller, *Revolutionary Ethiopia*, 1.

[76] This is addressed in greater detail in relation to Eritrea in subsequent sections.

[77] Asmerom Habtemariam, "100 years of Resistance and Endurance," *Hadas Eritra* (Eritrean daily newspaper), 30 December 1999 (No. 52)-25 January 2000 (No. 63); Alemseged Tesfai, "Diversity, Identity and Unity in Eritrea. A View from Inside" (an unpublished paper presented at the "Identity and Conflict in Africa" conference, African Studies Unit, University of Leeds, September 1997); and Michael Gabir, *The History of the Bilen* (Baghdad:, 1992).

[78] Okbazghi Yohannes argues that despite it quick suppression, Bahta Hagos's December 1894 rebellion against Italian confiscation of peasants' land was "crucial insofar as it marked the

the newly introduced capitalist economy afforded many of the colony's inhabitants employment opportunities, which required venturing out of their villages and hamlets and living among other groups that had come under the same jurisdiction. Prominently, a large number of able-bodied Eritreans were recruited into and constituted a major bloc of the Italian colonial army in which they assumed a collective identity as Askaris.[79] Italy's entry into World War II in 1940, however, was as fateful for its African colonies – and more so for Eritrea – as it was for Italy itself.

Perhaps the best indicator of the birth of distinct Eritrean identity became manifest at this time when British forces offered Eritreans the opportunity to do away with Italian rule. In line with the Allied objective of neutralizing Italy's dispersed forces in its colonies, British Commonwealth forces attacked them in Eritrea. As part of their war strategy, the British promised the Eritrean people the realization of their "national aspirations" if they would help the Allied cause of defeating the Italians.[80] Eritrean Askaris deserted their Italian commanders in response; a swift British victory and their takeover of Eritrea ensued to Eritreans' celebrations.

The British failed to deliver on wartime promises to Eritreans and the victors of World War II were unable to decide the fate of the territory. As a British Military Administration (BMA) held onto Eritrea for more than ten years while the fate of the territory debated – now at the newly established United Nations – Ethiopia found a perfect opportunity to seek to expand its dominion to Eritrea. As with the Portuguese toward Indonesia in East Timor, Ethiopia's acquisition of Eritrea involved the British and the United Nations granting Addis Ababa a right it did not have before.

Emperor Haile Selassie first laid claim to Eritrea in June 1942 on grounds of historic ties and ethnolinguistic affinities among the Ethiopians and Eritreans as well as Ethiopia's security concerns.[81] Ethiopia's fundamental interest in Eritrea, however, was its quest for what some Ethiopians still claim is "Ethiopia's natural right over the Red Sea,"[82] something the Emperor

beginning of Eritrean nationalism, which had to be reckoned with." Okbazgi Yohannes, *Eritrea, a Pawn in World Politics* (Gainesville: University of Florida Press, 1991), 9.

[79] Tekeste Negash, *Italian Colonialism in Eritrea, 1882–1941: Policies, Praxis and Impact* (Uppsala: Universitatis Upsaliensis, 1987). The forerunners of the pro-independence political parties in the 1940s, later hailed as the fathers of Eritrean nationalism by the nationalist movement, received their first exposure to modern education in Italian colonial education system.

[80] Alemseged Tesfai, *Aynefelale. Eritrea, 1941–1950* (Asmara: Hidri Publishers, 2001), 5. One of the leaflets dropped by the British said, "[Y]ou deserve your own flag! You have the right to become officers! You have the right to fight with better weapons than what the Italians are giving you! If you abandon the Italians, we promise to fulfill for you all of these . . . "

[81] Alemseged Tesfai, *Aynfelale*, 42–43; and Bahru, *A History of Modern Ethiopia*, 181.

[82] Negussay Ayele, *In Search of the DNA of the Ethiopia-Eritrea Problem: Recent Articles on the Nature and Evolution of the Conflict in Northeast Africa* (San Diego, CA: Media Ethiopia, 2003).

affirmed to Eritrean elders in Asmara in 1962. While Emperor Haile Selassie worked vigorously to secure Eritrea, the UN General Assembly took over the disposal of the former Italian colonies and dispatched its own Inquiry Commission.

The BMA allowed the formation of political parties in anticipation of the UN commission and, between 1946 and 1947, political parties espousing different political options emerged. Collective disillusionment with European rule compelled most of these political parties to demand an immediate break with European rule; some even believed that "union [with Ethiopia] was the only way to escape a repressive [European] colonial regime."[83] Such an opening-up of political space in Eritrea gave the Ethiopian Emperor enough room to exploit Eritrean political naïveté and curb the pro-independence tendencies in the territory through deceit, corruption, and intimidation.[84] This was particularly the case after Addis Ababa opened a liaison office in Asmara in March 1946 to direct Ethiopia's covert and overt work to secure Eritrea. The Ethiopian emperor dispatched a fellow Shoan member of the ruling Amhara nobility to serve as his liaison officer. Known for his arrogance and his ruthless, crude methods, Colonel Negga Haile Selassie's tenure was attended by organized violence against personalities and groups opposed to union with Ethiopia.[85] Fully financed and armed by Ethiopia, the Unionist Party became well-oiled machinery that easily outshone its pro-independence rivals.

Moreover, Ethiopia manipulated sociocultural cleavages of Eritrean society to weaken proponents of independence. There are nine widely recognized ethnic/linguistic groups in Eritrea almost evenly divided as Christian and Muslim. Of them, the Tigrigna-speaking, predominantly Christian (Coptic Orthodox) highlanders and the Tigre-speaking, predominantly Muslim

---

[83] A representative sentiment among many former Unionists quoted in Michela Wrong, *I Didn't Do it for You. How the World Betrayed a Small African Nation* (New York: HarperCollins, 2005), 184. For a more extensive analysis of this, see also Alemseged Tesfai, *Aynefelale* 22–36, 127–128; and Lloyd Schettle Ellingson, "Eritrea: Separatism and Irredentism, 1941–1985" (PhD Dissertation, Michigan State University, 1986), 15, 24–25.

[84] Alemseged, *Aynefelale*, 278ff; and G. K. N. Trevaskis, *Eritrea: A Colony in Transition* (Westport, CT: Greenwood Press, 1975), 96.

[85] Alemseged, *Aynefelale*, 278ff. details how after the arrival in March 1946 of Colonel Negga Haile Selassie as Ethiopia's Liaison Officer in Eritrea, organized political violence against personalities and groups opposed to union with Ethiopia intensified in Eritrean towns as well as Italian-owned business centers around the country. With its peak in 1948, prompting Alemseged to call it as "the year of banditry," this ranges from the 1947 unsuccessful assassination attempt against Weldeab Weldemariam in which Col. Negga was directly implicated in court (p. 280), to isolated attacks by Ethiopian-flag-carrying bandits against pro-independence youth in various Eritrean towns in 1948 (pp. 284–285), to the assassination of pro-independence leader Kahsai Malu on February 12, 1949 (p. 305) and that of Abdel-Kadir Kebire on March 27, 1949 (p. 307). Alemseged (pp. 358ff.) also details the initially spontaneous coming together of the pro-independence political parties and their becoming targets to intensified political terrorism. Trevaskis, *Eritrea*, p. 96.

lowlanders were (and still are) numerically dominant and influential in the country's politics. With this in mind, Ethiopia adopted a three-pronged strategy of dividing and conquering.

First, through the Eritrean Orthodox Churches, which were administered under the Ethiopian Coptic Church, Ethiopia threatened the excommunication of Christians who opposed union. Second, when Ethiopia-sanctioned actions pushed the independentist parties – the Muslim League and the Liberal Progressive Party – into a loose pro-independence coalition and cultivated a cozy relationship with the Italians, Italian promises to assist Eritrea were readily presented as selling out to the old European master. Party leaders, who formerly had justified their link with the Italians as a tactical arrangement, failed to adequately address the rampant Italophobic reaction of their constituencies. And third, Muslim advocates of independence (or at least the founding leaders) hailed from the less-privileged serf class among the Tigre-speaking Eritreans. Emancipation of serfs from Beni Amer lords was, thus, inextricable from their program for national political independence. Ethiopia's Haile Selassie and the British counterbalanced Tigre independence advocates by promising the privileged Beni Amer lords to maintain the status quo if they agreed to unite with Ethiopia. On the instigation and encouragement of Ethiopia and the British, therefore, a bulk of Muslim and Christian Eritreans walked on the proponents of independence; those who stayed on were subjected to systematic and blatant violence. [86]

On December 2, 1950, United Nations General Assembly resolved that "Eritrea shall constitute an *autonomous* unit federated with Ethiopia under *the sovereignty of the Ethiopian Crown*" (emphasis added).[87] With that, Ethiopia "acquired a great responsibility," concluded British Military Administration political officer GKN Trevaskis; how Addis Ababa would act with regard to the Federation, that is, Eritrean autonomy, would shape the Northeast African region. "The temptation to subject Eritrea firmly under her own control will always be great. Should she try to do so, she will risk Eritrean discontent and eventually revolt, which . . . might well disrupt both Eritrea and Ethiopia herself. . . . It is for Ethiopia to make her choice."[88] Ethiopia made a disastrous one.

Whereas Eritreans from across the political spectrum took a conciliatory stand and committed to respecting the terms of the federal arrangement, the Ethiopian government ruled from the start, in 1952, that Eritrea was no

[86] Trevaskis, *Eritrea*, 97–98; and Alemseged, *Aynefelale*, 422–435.

[87] UN General Assembly – Fifth Session, Resolution 390 (V). "Eritrea: Report of the United Nations Commission for Eritrea; Report of the Interim Committee of the General Assembly on the Report of the United Nations Commission to Eritrea," December 2, 1950.

[88] Trevaskis, *Eritrea*, 131. This book was first published in 1960, and if these conclusions were drawn between 1958 and 1960, Trevaskis was only prophesizing what had been unfolding openly in front of him.

different from any of the Ethiopian provinces. Accordingly, Ethiopia proceeded unilaterally to dismantle what it believed was a foreign aberration –
and an unholy one at that. An Ethiopia that included Eritrea was presented
as a heavenly ordained entity with territorial limits drawn by the mighty
Christian God himself. When opening the 1957 session of the Ethiopian
Parliament on his twenty-seventh coronation anniversary, Emperor Haile
Selassie put it thus:

> There is nothing new and startling in the reintegration of Eritrea with its motherland.
> With the passage of time, *a territorial boundary artificially erected by the hand of
> man has been broken down by the Almighty hand of God....* We [read: I] would
> also admonish you [parliamentarians] to be ever conscious of the fact that the unity
> of *Our Empire is not merely the work of man, but of God Almighty Himself...* [89]
> (emphasis added)

Disempowerment of Eritrea's Supreme Court, closure of its free press,
change of Eritrea's official languages from Tigrigna and Arabic to Amharic
(hence, Amharization), discarding of the Eritrean flag and symbols, renam-
ing of the government as "administration," and eventually disbanding of
the Eritrean Assembly followed in quick succession. A reign of terror and
intimidation designed to muffle Eritrean opposition attended these moves.[90]
An Eritrean columnist of the time captured the travesty of the "powerless,
dead word" *federation* in a rhetorical question: "What was the purpose
of debating the powers of the Imperial Representative [if] the major task
accomplished by the representative of the United Nations and delegates
of the Eritrean people becomes meaningless simply because the Ethiopian
Government does not like it... "[91]

Gullible and inexperienced, pro-independence Eritrean politicians were
not a match for Ethiopian savoir faire, but the more successful Ethiopia
was, the further Eritrean nationalist aspiration was dashed, swelling the
number and the intensity of discontents. The urge for independence grew

---

[89] Ethiopian Ministry of Information, *Speeches Delivered by His Imperial Majesty Haile
Selassie 1st, Emperor of Ethiopia, on Various Occasions, May 1957–December 1959*, 20–
21.

[90] Alemseged Tesfai, *Federation Ertra ms Ityopiya: Kab Matienzo kesab Tedla, 1951–1955*
(Asmara: Hidri Publishers, 2005), 274–179. While Alemseged's book is the first comprehensive coverage to have been written in Tigrigna entirely based on the perspectives and
experiences of the Eritrean participants in the early years of the troubled and troublesome
federation, Bereket Habte Selassie, *Conflict and Intervention in the Horn of Africa* (New
York and London: Monthly Review Press, 1980), 5960; Ruth Iyob, *The Eritrean Struggle
for Independence: Domination, Resistance, Nationalism, 1941–1993* (Cambridge: Cambridge University Press, 1995), 88; and Osman Saleh Denden, *Ma'erakat Iritriyah. Al-Juzu
Al-Awal* (City: NP, 1996), 11–17, offer succinct accounts of Ethiopian violations of the
Eritrean autonomy.

[91] A column in independent newspaper *Dehai Ertra*, 1st year, no. 10, November 22, 1952;
quoted in Alemseged, *Federation Ertra ms Ityopiya*, 278–279.

further in response to Ethiopia's tyrannical meddling in the internal Eritrean political landscape. While veteran Eritrean politicians (both pro-independence and unionists) became intensely frustrated with the corroding federal arrangement, and their electorate became increasingly mistrustful of them, a new breed of Eritrean nationalists living in exile turned combative.

When Eritreans finally resorted to violence, sparking the thirty-year independence war, Ethiopia dismissed their cause as one instigated by foreign enemies. Ethiopia accused Arabs, imperialists, narrow nationalists, or others of conspiring to carve out Eritrea from its "mother" Ethiopia. In the words of the Emperor, they were "hypocrites who are serving as instruments for marrying past history and betraying it to aliens."[92] Throughout the war years, successive Ethiopian governments insisted on the existence of an organic bond between Eritrea and Ethiopia and flaunted a mythical three thousand years of history when Eritrea allegedly constituted the core component – the irony of a centrifugal core and a centripetal periphery is shrouded in oblivion here.

Modern Indonesia: Srivijaya's Successor?

Much less evident than that of Ethiopia, the historical memory of Indonesia's imperial past shaped Jakarta's colonial project in East Timor. Modern Indonesia sits on a long history of precolonial Sirivijaya and Majapahit, whose commercial empires extended over much of archipelagic Southeast Asia.[93] Any intent of these polities to fuse the multitudes of islands that make up contemporary Indonesia into a potent empire crumbled in the face of European imperialism.[94] Dutch colonialism disrupted and displaced what local expansionism may have existed, and replaced it with a far more effective imperial lunge. Having first set foot in the Southeast Asian islands during early oceanic commercial voyages of the sixteenth century, the Dutch consolidated their new possessions into Indonesia in the 1820s.[95] With the

---

[92] The Ethiopian Government, *Selected Speeches of His Imperial Majesty Haile Selassie First, 1918 to 1967* (Addis Ababa: The Imperial Ethiopian Ministry of Information, 1967), 462.

[93] Clifford Geertz suggests that the expansionist tendencies of these pre-Dutch polities constituted the root of Indonesian imperialist impulses. Geertz, *Islam Observed: Religious Development in Morocco and Indonesia* (New Haven, CT, and London: Yale University Press, 1968), 11, 26.

[94] O. W. Wolters, *History, Culture, and Region in Southeast Asian perspectives*, rev. ed. (Ithaca, NY: Cornell University Southeast Asia Program Publications, 1999). After the decline of Sriwijaya, the ascendancy of Majapahit did not last long as its constituent polities broke away and started an independent existence in rivalry with each other. With the exception of Aceh in Sumatra, which retained its independence until the early twentieth century, these kingdoms fell to Dutch imperialism one after the other.

[95] Nicholas Tarling, "The Establishment of the Colonial Regime" in *The Cambridge History of Southeast Asia. Volume Three. From c. 1800 to the 1930s* (Cambridge: Cambridge University Press, 1999), 9.

earliest anticolonial resistance brutally crushed, successive colonial governments resorted to incarcerating and deporting prominent leaders when faced with rising agitation of a new breed of young and educated Indonesian nationalists.

Since their emergence in the 1920s as an organized group to be reckoned with, Indonesian nationalists were – or sought to be – active within this colonially delineated sphere, claiming to represent the entire population of the old commercial empires. Arrested for his nationalist agitation, one of the fathers of Indonesian nationalism – and founding president of independent Indonesia – pleaded his case in court in 1930. Condemning Dutch imperialism, Sukarno romanticized the glorious past of precolonial empires of Majapahit and Sriwijaya as progenitors of independent Indonesia in the waiting.[96] Moreover, a self-righteous nationalism that was also rooted in grandiose, universalist precepts helped nurture and consolidate the collective memory of glorious imperial inheritance.

In its early phase, Indonesian nationalism manifested itself in the form of a cultural movement of Western-educated elites, which led to the birth of the Taman Siswa school system in the 1920s.[97] Taman Siswa sought modern identity formation of its individual members and the collective forging of national identity, among other things, in freedom and humaneness.[98] Islam provided another inclusive and solid institution for Muslims in the Dutch school system. The Islamic reformist movement called Muhammadiyah, which was soon imitated by similar movements across rural Indonesia, emerged in 1912 as an alternative to Western education. These religious movements eventually merged into the Great Islamic Council of Indonesia (MIAI), providing a solid ally to secular nationalism in the struggle for independence and a formidable rival of secularism in the postindependence political scene.[99] Finally, and despite its early suppression by the Dutch, the widespread popularity of the Indonesian Communist Party (PKI) left long-lasting marks of inclusivity through progressive grassroots mobilization. Hence, a legacy of Marxist opposition to capitalism and an Islamic "us" against the infidel "them" became identifying features of Indonesian nationalism.[100]

Internally, the independent Unitary State of Indonesia – dominated by old and new Javanese elites – established uncontested dominion throughout

---

[96] Roger K. Paget (ed. and trans.), *Indonesian Accuses: Soekarno's Defence Oration in the Political Trial of 1930* (Kuala Lumpur: Oxford University Press, 1975), 80.

[97] Anthony Reid, "Indonesia: Revolution without Socialism," in *Asia – the Winning of Independence. The Philippines, India, Indonesia, Vietnam, Malaya*, ed. Robin Jeffrey (London: Macmillan, 1981), 125.

[98] Reid, "Indonesia: Revolution without Socialism," 126–127.

[99] Ibid., 127–128.

[100] Ibid., 130–131.

the ethnically and politically diverse country.[101] Externally, universalist features of Indonesian nationalism outlived the hardships of colonial rule and proved vital in shaping independent Indonesia's foreign policy toward its immediate neighbors. This first appeared during the opening session of the Committee for the Investigation of Independence (BPKI) around mid-1945. BPKI discussed and reached a consensus on the Pancasila (five principles: nationalism, humanity, popular sovereignty, social justice, and faith in God) as the official ideology of an independent Indonesian state. The transnationalism of Indonesian nationalism was sealed with Sukarno quoting Gandhi: "I am a nationalist, but my nationalism is humanity."[102] Besides its inherent breadth, the Indonesian sense of humanity drew inspiration from Marxism and Islam, transcending ethnic or linguistic boundaries.

Resuming deliberations, the BPKI set out to determine the territorial extent of Indonesia. Mohammed Yamin argued that Indonesian territory extended up to, and included, the whole of New Guinea, East Timor, Borneo, and Malaya. Accordingly, these territories formed "the nucleus of the People's State of Indonesia" and "ever since the beginning of history, they have been inhabited by the people of Indonesia forming part of our mother land."[103] Claiming that he was focusing on Papua, Timor, Borneo and the Malay Peninsula because they could not send their representatives to the DPKI deliberations, Yamin exhorted his colleagues to take it upon themselves to represent them. For "*[t]hey may be likened to an orphan who*

---

[101] Although secessionist and autonomist tendencies threatened to undermine Indonesia's unity and Jakarta's centralizing grip immediately after independence, the state brutally asserted its control. By the end of the 1950s, all regional rebellions had been quelled and the internecine war in Aceh subsided significantly. For a succinct analysis of the early independence years of Indonesia, see Audrey R. and George McT. Kahin, *Subversion as Foreign Policy: The Secret Eisenhower and Dulles Debacle in Indonesia* (New York: New Press 1995).

[102] Sukarno's speech during the BPKI meeting (June 1, 1945) in Herbert Feith and Lance Castles (eds.), *Indonesian Political Thinking: 1945–1965* (Ithaca, NY, and London: Cornell University Press, 1970), 40–49; and Bernhard Dahm, *History of Indonesia in the Twentieth Century*, trans. P. S. Falla (London: Praeger, ND), 102. The entire speech – "Lahirnja Pantja Sila" – is also available in *Pantja Sila: the Basis of the State of Republic Indonesia* (National Committee for the Commemoration of the Birth of Pantja Sila, 1964).

[103] Excerpts from Professor Mohammed Yamin's *Naskah Persiapkan Undang-Undang Dasar 1945, Vol. 1* (Jakarta: Jajasan Prapantja) in Tahanan Politik (TAPOL), *The Territory of the Indonesian State; Discussions in the Meeting of Badan Penjelidek Usaha Persiapkan Kemerdekaan Indonesia. Background to Indonesia's Policy Toward Malaysia* (no date), 1–3. Yamin's claim that the Japanese occupiers of Southeast Asia during World War II had agreed to transfer the territories under their occupation to Indonesia remains unsubstantiated. Imperial Japan consistently failed to uphold its promise of granting independence to the former Dutch colony until it became abundantly clear that the war was lost. Bernhard Dahm best captures this ill fortune when he writes that under Japanese occupation, "Indonesians had jumped from the frying-pan into the fire" for Japan had secretly decided to permanently incorporate the strategic and rich Indonesian Archipelago into its empire. Dahm, *History of Indonesia*, pp. 83 and 89.

deserves to be looked after with all the care and sincerity . . . lest there should be adduced any research material with the object of separating those territories or any one of them from the Indonesian motherland"[104] (emphasis added).

A lawyer by training, Yamin became a leading Indonesian ideologue through his prolific poems, his advocacy to make Bahasa Indonesia the national language and his hold on Sukarno's ear. His proposal captured the sentiment shared by many of his contemporaries that, as part of the pre-colonial empires of Majapahit and Sriwijaya, the islands beyond the archipelagic Dutch colony constituted the progenitor of postcolonial Indonesia.[105] Revealing his agreement with this Greater Indonesia view and perhaps the scope of his ambition, Sukarno added that had it not been already independent, he would have included the Philippines as well.[106]

Such seedlings of lateral expansionism did not go unchallenged by level-headed and farsighted Indonesians. Arguing against Yamin's proposal, Dr. Mohammed Hatta, another prominent nationalist leader, sternly warned the BPKI that such a principle would sound imperialistic and would instill in Indonesian youth an insatiable urge for imperialist expansion instead of governing and developing Indonesia proper. Unencumbered, the BPKI resolved – with applause – that "the territory of Free Indonesia will include the former Dutch East Indies with the addition of Malaka (Malaya), North Borneo, Papua, Timor and the adjacent islands."[107]

Preoccupied by its bid to "restore" West New Guinea and *Konfrontasi*, newly independent Indonesia did not pursue its leaders' pronouncements

---

[104] Dahm, *History of Indonesia*, 102–104.

[105] This was the gist of Sukarno's defense against the Dutch as early as 1930. Paget, *Indonesian Accuses*, 80.

[106] Ibid., 104; J.D. Legge, *Sukarno: A Political Biography*, 2nd ed. (Sydney: Allen and Unwin, 1984), 190–191.

[107] BPKI Chairman Radjiman Wedijodiningrat during the BPKI meeting of May 31, 1945, quoted in TAPOL, *The Territory of the Indonesian State; Discussions in the Meeting of Badan Penjelidek Usaha Persiapkan Kemerdekaan Indonesia. Background to Indonesia's Policy Toward Malaysia* (no date), 31. The importance of this expansionist claim to the potentially disastrous 1960s confrontation between Indonesia and the newly independent Malaysian Federation is debatable. Legge, *Sukarno*, 191, for example, points to the inaccuracy of linking Indo-Malaysian confrontation to the deliberations of the BPKI on Indonesian territorial limits. Instead, he elaborates the context within which the confrontation took place and offers a valid analysis of Indonesia's decisions that, however, fails to rule out the existence of an underlying expansionist tendency (pp. 361–365). Moreover, Legge understates the significance of these declarations as expansionist thus: "in the closing months of the war [i.e., World War II] there seemed a possibility of reshaping boundaries along 'natural' lines . . . The situation seemed fluid and to look to a 'greater Indonesia' in mid 1945 was not necessarily to look beyond the bounds of practical politics." This belated defense of Indonesian expansionist tendencies, however, fades in light of Dr. Hatta's concerns and warnings to the BPKI in 1945 and in light of Indonesian actions afterwards.

regarding Portuguese Timor.[108] Subsequently, the new pro-U.S. government of Suharto (in power since the second half of the 1960s) found common anticommunist ground with the Portuguese in one-half of the Timor island. Whereas Jakarta was too reliant on the United States to dislodge a NATO member, Lisbon was effective in using U.S. bases in its Azores islands as an indirect check on Suharto's New Order. Portuguese fears of Indonesian expansionism were temporarily contained. Nevertheless, there continued Indonesian interest in Portuguese Timor. In September 1963, for example, Indonesian Minister of Information Ruslan Abdulgani was reported as saying, "we can not allow people of common ancestry to be prosecuted and thrown in prison merely because they wanted to unite with the fatherland of their ancestors."[109] Later on, despite Suharto's self-control, influential and vocal Indonesians kept calling for the return of East Timor to Indonesia. In the early 1970s, the Vice-Chairman of the Indonesian House of Representatives (MPR), Johnny Naro, was the outspoken mouthpiece of this view.

Postoccupation official Indonesian publications resumed claims of East Timor's Indonesian-ness, such as "From the earliest times, Timor has been an integral part of the history of the Indonesian archipelago."[110] This integrality was portrayed as abruptly ruptured when European colonizers set foot in the archipelago, disintegrating Sriwijaya's and Majapahit's territorial legacies, "one result of which was the isolation of East Timor from Indonesia."[111] This isolation had to be exorcised through the initial bloody takeover and the blood-spattered decades that followed.

[108] Donald E. Weatherbee, "Portuguese Timor: An Indonesian Dilemma," *Asian Survey* 6, no. 12 (December 1966):695. By restoration of West New Guinea is meant the efforts to decolonize the half island from the Dutch and merge it with Indonesia; Konfrontasi refers to the confrontation between the newly emerging Malaysian Federation and Indonesia. Weatherbee predicted that once "Indonesian ideology and interest converge" on East Timor, Portugal would have no choice but to concede to Indonesia.

[109] Quoted in James Dunn, *Timor: A People Betrayed* (Auckland: Jacaranda Press, 1983), 103.

[110] Republic of Indonesia, *East Timor: Building for the Future* (Ministry of Foreign Affairs, 1992), 2.

[111] Republic of Indonesia, *The Province of East Timor: Development in Progress* (Department of Information, ND), 7. Such assertions permeated Indonesia's justification for its incorporation of its half island neighbor notwithstanding their stark contradiction with the Indonesian government's statements during and after the Irian Jaya affair. For instance, Indonesia's 1957 official statement to the 12th Session of the UN General Assembly reads: "the attempt to link West Irian with East New Guinea simply because the two territories happened to form one island would create a very dangerous precedent, for example, in the case of the islands of Borneo and Timor. Indonesia had no claims on any territories which had not been part of the former Netherlands East Indies." Excerpts of Indonesian statement at the 12th UN General Assembly session, November 26, 1957, in Heike Krieger (ed.), *East Timor and the International Community. Basic Documents*, Cambridge International Documents Series, Vol. 10 (Cambridge: Cambridge University Press, 1997), 27.

East Timor: From Portugal's Colony to Indonesia's "Orphan"

In the aftermath of the Crusades and the Ottoman takeover of Constantinople in 1453, the Portuguese set out in search of, among other things, an alternative route to Asian spices. They were also looking for a Christian ally, the mythical Prester John of the Indies, to the south of their archenemy, the Muslim Turks. This search led the Portuguese to establish fortresses all around the coast of the Indian Ocean, including Southeast Asia, as part of their strategy to establish the *Estado da Índia*. In the seventeenth century, their predominance was challenged by several emerging European rivals, notably by the Dutch and the British, who drove the Portuguese out of their Southeast Asian strongholds, except for half of the island of Timor. A series of boundary agreements between 1895 and 1913 defined East (Portuguese) Timor from West (Dutch) Timor.[112]

At the outset, Portuguese presence hardly altered the preexisting Timorese political landscape. The local kingdoms continued to rule through their traditional hierarchy of rulers – liurais (kings) at the top and Chefe de Povoação at the bottom of the hierarchy. In their effort to co-opt these rulers, the Portuguese bestowed the rank of colonel to the liurais and lieutenant to the Chefe de Povoação. But this neither enabled the Portuguese administration to penetrate deeply into the local social fabric nor pacified the indigenous population. Between their arrival in the sixteenth century and the anticolonial rebellion in 1959, João Saldanha identifies scores of anti-Portuguese revolts and uprisings of different intensity.[113] Nevertheless, under an archaic and isolationist colonial system,[114] East Timor subsequently remained insulated from the anti-colonialist fervor permeating Southeast Asia since the first half of the twentieth century.

With the decline of the sandalwood trade and of Portugal's status as a world power, East Timor had become a backwater of the Third Portuguese Empire,[115] but Lisbon held on to the territory into the second half of the twentieth century in defiance of repeated UN requests to decolonize.[116]

---

[112] Malyn Newitt (ed.), *The First Portuguese Colonial Empire* (University of Exeter, 1986).

[113] João Mariano de Sousa Saldanha, *The Political Economy of East Timor Development* (Jakarta: Pustakan Sinar Harapan, 1994), pp. 34 ff. Timorese nationalist historiography refers to these rebellions as nationalist inspired. Particular emphasis is placed on the most protracted and most recent of them – the late-nineteenth-century rebellion led by the Liurai of Manufahi, Don Boventura and the 1959 rebellion instigated by Indonesian army officers who sought refuge in Portuguese Timor when their secessionism was crushed by Jakarta's unitary army.

[114] Jim Dunn alternatively characterized it as not "particularly oppressive . . . akin to a benign paternalism." Dunn, *Timor*, 22, 31–32; and personal conversations (March 2007, Dili, East Timor).

[115] Gervase Clarence-Smith, *The Third Portuguese Empire, 1825–1975. A Study in Economic Imperialism* (Manchester: Manchester University Press, 1985), 61–66.

[116] While John G. Taylor, *Indonesia's Forgotten War. The Hidden History of East Timor* (London and City, NJ: Zed Books, 1991), 18, quotes a Portuguese official saying in 1964:

On April 25, 1974, the Salazar-Caetano regime was overthrown in the Carnation Revolution, and steered by the Portuguese Communist Party, the Movement of the Armed Forces (MFA) that staged the coup hauled Portugal onto the doorsteps of communist dictatorship.[117] The MFA's urge to cut losses and their ideological orientation suddenly drew the prospects of decolonization of East Timor nearer. One of the oldest and farthest "provinces" that had long fallen on Portugal's imperial backburner suddenly and transiently came to the fore, unnerving Indonesia and touching off turbulent political waves in East Timor itself.

Only around that time did questions of nationalism and independence resonate among East Timorese, who were kept largely unaware about the rest of the world.[118] Not until the 1970s were there a handful of high school graduates, fewer than a dozen of whom earned university degrees overseas. Whereas their limited numbers hamstrung their impact at home and access to resources abroad, the Timorese intelligentsia emerged too late into the anticolonial upsurge to tap into global ideological solidarity of the earlier decades. Moreover, the lack of objective conditions for nationalist agitation – outside fostering, education and the leadership of the intelligentsia, and blatant and rampant oppression – precluded a violent outburst of Timorese nationalism until the mid-1970s.

Despite the absence of visible anticolonial action, the formation of a distinct East Timorese national identity had started to take hold before the 1974 Portuguese Revolution. As the few educated East Timorese started

"'Portugal would no more give up Timor than America would give up Hawaii,'" Dunn, *Timor*, 37, claims that in the same year, "a senior Portuguese official confided that his country would be happy to turn East Timor over to the United Nations, if it were not for the implication such a move would carry for the other overseas provinces." Also see Roger S. Clark, "The 'Decolonization' of East Timor and the United Nations Norms on Self-determination and Aggression" in *International Law and the Question of East Timor* (1995), 67–68.

[117] Interview with Dr. Mário Soares (August 2006, Lisbon, Portugal). During the "Hot Summer" of 1975, Portugal was on the verge of an all out civil war. Henry Kissinger believed that this might be the start of a wave of communist dictatorships that would sweep through west European capitals and called the pro-pluralistic democracy advocate, the Socialist leader Mário Soares, the "Alexander Kerensky of Portugal." Effectively mobilizing the prodemocracy Portuguese citizens from across party lines and with strong backing from his Western allies, Mário Soares made a forceful comeback to avert the possible communist consolidation. Nonetheless, not only was that too late for East Timor, but also, at this point, the Portuguese state was too preoccupied with consolidating the precarious peace in the country to bother about East Timor.

[118] Portuguese scholar Moises Silva Fernandes argues that the first modern pan-Timorese nationalism made its presence felt when a group of Muslim Timorese formed a government in exile in Indonesia in the 1960s. "A Uniao da Republica de Timor: o atrofico movimento nacionalista islamico-malaio timorense, 1960–1975," Armando Marques Guedes e Nuno Canas Mendes (ed.), *Ensaios sobre nacionalismos em Timor-Leste* (Ministry of Foreign Affairs of Portugal, December 2005), 355–431.

taking posts in the colonial administration, the hollow rigidity of colonial hierarchy they encountered, along with the uncertainty that Lisbon would grant them independence, nurtured growing cynicism toward the colonial order. This small group of elites was encouraged by the post–World War II economic recovery to contemplate the prospects of independence. And once a nationalist vanguard emerged, some of the nationalist leaders' roots in the leading Timorese economic and political stakeholding families lent legitimacy to the creeping pan-Timorese and anticolonial sentiment.[119]

In the early 1970s, young Timorese clandestinely met in small groups to discuss how to challenge the status quo and started publishing in the only locally produced newspaper.[120] Others, studying in Portugal or banished to the African colonies because of their protests against the colonial system, were being influenced by the global radicalism of the 1970s and were equipping themselves with the intellectual, ideological, and organizational tools of popular mobilization, resistance, and alternative development.[121]

So too did rejection of association with Indonesia start to take hold among most East Timorese at the same pace as, and perhaps even faster than, the anticolonial sentiment.[122] Initially, Portuguese fear of Indonesian expansionism and anti-imperialist pretensions was imparted to the East Timorese. Later, the Timorese saw for themselves what they considered were the dangers of joining Indonesia – economic hardship as witnessed in West Timor, political instability reflected in the 1960s purges, and Javanese domination.

---

[119] John G. Taylor, *East Timor: The Price of Freedom* (London and New York: Zed Books, 1999), 18; Niner, *To Resist Is to Win*; interview with Dr. Abilio de Araújo (August 5, 2006, Vila Franca de Xida, Portugal, 5 August 2006). The founders of APODETI (José Osorio Soares), UDT (Mário Carrascalão) and ASDT/FRETLIN (Nicolao Lobato) were highly placed civil servants in the Portuguese colonial administration.

[120] Under the editorship of the late Father Martinho da Costa Lopes (later apostolic administrator of Dili diocese between 1977 and 1983), Seara hosted the writing of people like Francisco Xavier do Amaral and José Ramos-Horta. The latter was a journalist who, because of his writings, was banished to Mozambique for several years.

[121] José Ramos-Horta, *Funu. The Unfinished Saga of East Timor* (Lawrenceville, NJ, and Asmara: Red Sea Press, 1987); interview with Abilio de Araújo (Villa Franca de Xida, Portugal, 5 August 2006). Despite Abilio's insistence that he did not belong to the Portuguese Maoist Party (MRPP), a number of Portuguese former MRPP activists associate him with that party along with numerous other Timorese students who moved back to East Timor during the brief but crucial days of party politics in the former colony.

[122] Interview with Professor António Barbedo de Magalhães (August 29, 2006, Porto, Portugal). Serving on the Portuguese committee to decolonize the education system in East Timor between 1974 and 1975, Professor Barbedo "knew that the Timorese would never like to be Indonesians." This deep conviction sustained his vigorous and effective advocacy for the Timorese right to self-determination. He played a crucial role in awakening Portuguese public opinion to the fate their government had left their Timorese colonial subjects, in pushing the Portuguese governments into persistent diplomatic campaign and in promoting the understanding among early prodemocracy Indonesians that the right to self-determination of the Timorese people was an inseparable part of their struggle.

"There would be no point in our joining with Indonesia after decolonization," remarked an East Timorese returning from a visit to Indonesian Timor in mid-1974; "their side is poorer than ours, and instead of the Portuguese over us we would have the Javanese. This would be *recolonization*, not *decolonization*"[123] (emphasis added).

The overthrow of the dictatorship in Lisbon enabled open political discussions on the fate of East Timor in 1974–1975. Political parties, espousing different political platforms, were hastily organized. While the União Democrática Timorense (UDT, Timorese Democratic Union) called, initially, for a loose association with Portugal before eventual independence, the Associação Social-Democrata Timorense (ASDT, Timorese Social Democratic Association), later renamed the Frente Revolucionária do Timor Leste Independente (FRETILIN, Revolutionary Front for Independent East Timor), advocated for immediate independence. Although the overwhelming majority of East Timorese, thus, opted for independence from Portugal, there suddenly emerged a powerful minority choosing to be "independent" by joining Indonesia.

As the chain of events in Portugal and in East Timor helped break Indonesian restraint, developments within Indonesia itself revived Jakarta's perennial desire to absorb the Portuguese colony. Indonesia inaugurated a multipronged strategy. First, through its consulate in the East Timorese capital, Dili, it sponsored the launching of the small Associação Popular Democrática de Timor (APODETI, Timorese Popular Democratic Association) in May 1974 with the express goal of seeking the integration of East Timor with Indonesia.[124] In the same way that the British tolerated Ethiopian fostering and militarization of the Unionist Party in Eritrea, the Portuguese allowed the Indonesian Consulate in Dili to continue its political activities and ensure the logistical upkeep of APODETI, in order to avoid Indonesian wrath.[125]

East Timorese integrationists traveled to Jakarta to meet with Indonesian officials at the highest levels. After one such meeting, Indonesian General Ali Murtopo, the commander of the Operasi Khusus (OPSUS, Special Operations), called on Army Colonel Sugianto to start gathering intelligence on East Timor, all of its political parties and their leaders. Assisted by a small staff of intelligence and elite paracommando (KOPASSANDHA) officers, General Murtopo started Operasi Komodo in October in order to secure East Timor through subversion of the decolonization processes and the

---

[123] Dunn, *Timor*, 41.

[124] Ramos-Horta, *Funu*, chapter. 4, 29–39; Dunn, *Timor*, 52; Jill Jolliffe, *East Timor: Nationalism and Colonialism* (Queensland: University of Queensland Press, 1978), 62ff.

[125] Dunn, *Timor*, 52. Dunn observed quite correctly that by offering the option of integration to avoid angering Indonesia rather than as a response to popular demand, the Portuguese tacitly offered Indonesia a right it did not have before. The same analogy applies with regard to the British Military Administration's granting to Ethiopia rights it did not have over Eritrea.

manipulation of its politicians.[126] To that effect, Operasi Komodo armed
and trained East Timorese integrationists on the Indonesian side of their
shared border,[127] in order to terrorize and intimidate their pro-independence
counterparts. These were punctuated by a vigorous propaganda campaign
against pro-independence parties on Indonesian media outlets.[128] Whereas
the Indonesian military-affiliated paper *Berita Yudha* fanned fabricated stories of the arrival of Chinese and Vietnamese communists in East Timor,
Radio Kupang started to denigrate both UDT and FRETILIN as neofas-
cists and Marxists, respectively, and warned of the dire consequences of
independence.[129] Out of anxiety, UDT and FRETILIN formed a loose, and
even tense, coalition on a minimum pro-independence platform.[130] Only
then did Operasi Komodo strategists awake to APODETI's lack of sufficient
mass of popular support to influence developments on the ground. Indonesia
scrambled, and succeeded, to drive a wedge between the pro-independence
UDT and FRETILIN.[131]

[126] Ken Conboy, *KOPASSUS. Inside Indonesia's Special Forces* (Jakarta: Equinox Publishing, 2003), 196–197; Julius Pour, *Benny Moerdani: Profil Prajurit Negarawan* (Jakarta:
Kejuangan Panglima Besar Sudirman, 1993), 381. In this official biography of Murdani, it is
indicated that Operasi Komodo started in January 1975, which fails to explain Indonesian
activities before that date and contradicts the account of all other scholars and observers.
For his part, Taylor, *East Timor*, 31, traces the birth of Operasi Komodo even further back
to mid-1974, when he claims that Indonesian intelligence agency BAKIN had finalized its
scheme to integrate East Timor.
[127] CAVR, *Chega!*, Part Three: "The History of the Conflict," 25. The first person to receive
military training in Indonesia, Tomas Gonçalves told the Comissão de Acolhimento, Verdade e Reconciliacão de Timor-Leste (CAVR, Commission for Reception, Truth and Reconciliation) that he went to West Timor in August 1974 with the facilitation of the Indonesian
Consulate in Dili after APODETI requested Indonesian assistance for paramilitary training
of its members.
[128] Interview: João Carrascalão (June 28, 2006, Dili); Helen Hill, *The Timor Story* (Melbourne:
Timor Information Service, 1975), p. 5. This is against the backdrop of FRETILIN's
suspicion of and hostility toward UDT and Portugal, seeing, as it did then, the latter as a
bigger threat than Indonesia. See CAVR, *Chega!*, Part 3: "History of the Conflict", p. 26.
[129] Interview with João Carrascalão (June 28, 2006, Dili, East Timor); and Helen Hill, *The
Timor Story* (Melbourne: Timor Information Service, 1975), 5.
[130] Taylor, *East Timor*, 38–39, highlights the role of the Portuguese Governor Pires and his
advisor Major Jonatas in the formation of this coalition. Whatever the causes, personal
views of prominent Timorese leaders from the two parties show that the coalition was
stillborn. Surprised to hear about the coalition while FRETILIN's anti-UDT rhetoric was
ongoing, UDT President and João's older brother, Mário Carrascalão cut short his trip to
Portugal and returned to East Timor, and found the coalition in a squeaking motion. For his
part, prominent FRETILIN ideologue, Abilio de Araújo, had thought of APODETI leaders
as more nationalist than UDT and had proposed an alliance with APODETI before that
with UDT. Less than a month after Dr. de Araújo left East Timor for Portugal, FRETILIN
leaders on the ground forged a coalition with UDT and he disagreed with FRETILIN's
branding of APODETI as an enemy.
[131] Interview with Joao Carrascalao (June 28, 2006, Dili, East Timor); Ramos-Horta, *Funu*,
chapters 9 and 10; Dunn, *Timor*, 111ff.; Jolliffe, *East Timor*, 63–64; and Taylor, *Indonesia's Forgotten War*, 52.

General Murtopo invited separate UDT and FRETILIN delegates to Jakarta in April 1975. While FRETILIN delegates were entertained, UDT leader João Carrascalão claims that he was deceived and pinned down because of the collective fear of communism among UDT leaders.[132] Indonesia supposedly promised UDT that it would recognize Timorese independence only if the "communist" FRETILIN was excluded from the country's politics.[133] In May 1975, UDT withdrew from the coalition. In August, it staged a coup and seized power from Portugal.[134] FRETILIN escaped to the countryside, from where it launched a countercoup. Already eager to leave, the Portuguese evacuated to a neighboring islet off the main half island of East Timor and left the Timorese to fight it out. With the pro-Indonesian and integrationist leaders and their soldiers crossing into Indonesia, FRETILIN won the brief civil war – which nonetheless, was of enormous immediate and long-term consequence – only to grapple with governing the territory because the Portuguese were reluctant to return and finish the decolonization process.[135] The Indonesian military was only too happy to fill the vacuum left behind by the Portuguese, compelling FRETILIN to declare unilateral independence on November 28, 1975, in a bid to avert the imminent invasion. The Timorese UDI may have foiled Operasi Komodo's covert and overt efforts, but it gave Indonesia a convenient pretext for a full-blown invasion. FRETILIN did not comprehend the scale of the invasion and was incapable of repulsing it.

Conclusion

Addis Ababa's and Jakarta's lateral expansion into Eritrea and East Timor are classic cases of secondary colonialism, despite the disparity between the

---

[132] Ramos-Horta, *Funu*, chapters 9 and 10; Dunn, *East Timor*, 111ff.; and Taylor, *Indonesia's Forgotten War*, 52.

[133] Interview with João Carrascalão (June 28, 2006, Dili); Carmel Budiardjo and Liem Soei Liong, *The War against East Timor* (London: Zed Books, 1984), 5–7; and Taylor, *Indonesia's Forgotten War*, 51.

[134] João Carrascalão insists that what UDT calls the "August 11 Movement" was an expression of genuine homegrown anticommunism. Given Indonesia's expertise in what has come to be called a uniquely Javanese skill of softening the ground by separating groups and exploiting the weaknesses of the individual members, I am inclined to believe what other scholars and observers (Budiardjo and Liong, Taylor, and Dunn, to mention a few) believed; that is, Indonesia instigated UDT to withdraw from the coalition and stage the coup. It is interesting to note that while the UDT coup took Mário Carrascalão by surprise amid his tour of the countryside inspecting agricultural projects and was later herded back to Dili by UDT militants, Francisco Xavier Lopes da Cruz says that he was specifically told by João Carrascalão to not say or do anything because, as president of the party, all he needed to do was sit back for his lieutenants to do the work.

[135] According to Talyor, *East Timor*, 63, the last Portuguese governor of Timor, Colonel Limos Pires, to his credit, recommended the resumption of the derailed decolonization process through possible UN trusteeship. There is no evidence that Lisbon even considered that as an option.

geneses of their traditions of empire building, the temporal incongruity of their dynamics, and their geographical remoteness. Highly coercive, hierarchical, and multinational Ethiopia and Indonesia sought to camouflage their brute force by grandiose self-images – at least of the rulers. They also flaunted their legitimizations among international audiences. These included presumed a historical identity between the secondary colonizers and the colonized, the latter's supposed wish to join their powerful neighbors because of their inability to administer themselves, and the security advantages for both the rulers and their subjects.

Fundamentally, this book examines the making of armed revolutionaries in Eritrea and East Timor and the forging of their dynamic grand strategies out of the crucible of oppressed nationalism. In spite of geographical and cultural remoteness, or proximity, between the colonizer and the colonized, this book illustrates that Third-World countries – some former colonies themselves – took an active part in secondary colonialism. It shows how grand strategies were appropriated and perfected by two liberation movements in the Global South that actively eschewed terrorism as a method.

In examining the differences between the process of their struggles and their post-liberation governments, as well as the global, regional and domestic factors that led to such differences, this volume raises, and seeks to answer, the following questions: What were the quintessential features that differentiated Eritrean and East Timorese grand strategies of liberation through time? The preliminary answer raises another question: Why were the two grand strategies of liberation so divergent, despite their apparently similar circumstances? In other words, what compelled the East Timorese liberation movement to resort to a diplomacy-centered grand strategy when a similarly positioned liberation movement in Eritrea chose a military strategy? Finally, does an inquiry into their respective independence struggles help us understand Eritrea and East Timor today?

Local, regional, and global factors, against which the two movements were launched, offered limited policy choices. The leaderships' strategic decision making and their implementation by their members and the populations were equally critical. These grand strategies necessarily emerged out of the *interaction between* the local, regional, and global structural and nonstructural factors surrounding them. An in-depth comparative investigation of the interplay of these factors shows the genesis and the evolution of the grand strategies of the two independence movements. Moreover, Eritrean and Timorese strategies evolved in response to changing Ethiopian and Indonesian capabilities and their determination to pursue their counterinsurgency strategies (militarily or otherwise, locally and internationally). Understanding these is essential for a proper examination of the liberation movements themselves.

After capable horse-mounted Mongol raiders invaded China in the twelfth century, a wise Chinese Confucian mused: "You can conquer China on a horseback, but you cannot rule it from the horseback." The Eritrean and East Timorese governance toolkits overflowed with skills cultivated during their respective long and arduous years of resistance. Although not all of these skills could be transplanted into the new phase of complex administrative, political, and security challenges of independence, institutional memory and political culture do not crop up overnight. So it is only logical – in hindsight – that the different routes that the Eritrean and East Timorese movements took led them to different political systems upon independence.

I

Swaggering Empires and Defiant "New Provinces"

We did not want the process and the results of decolonization [in Portuguese Timor] to destabilize the area, which, in turn, could endanger our own stability and that of Southeast Asia in general.

Indonesian President Suharto after the 1975 takeover of East Timor

Jakarta is now sending guerilla units into the Portuguese half of the island in order to engage Fretilin forces, encourage pro-Indonesian elements, and provoke incidents that would provide the Indonesians with an excuse to invade should they decide to do so.

(United States Central Intelligence Agency (CIA), September 1975)

Ethiopia and Indonesia did not make their moves toward their neighbors until the bipolar world order of the Cold War presented them with favorable conditions. The British Military Administration and Portuguese colonial order granted Ethiopia and Indonesia rights they did not previously have in Eritrea and East Timor. Addis Ababa and Jakarta were offered the option of integration to accommodate their interests, rather than as a response to popular demand. Extreme distrust of, and disillusionment with, European powers compelled a sufficient mass of Eritreans and East Timorese to jockey for Ethiopian and Indonesian backing, unaware of the schemes these states had for them. While Eritrean and East Timorese political ineptitude were thus staggering, Ethiopia and Indonesia succeeded in dividing and weakening local independence groups.

The primacy of order became manifest long before Samuel Huntington's *Order in Changing Societies* laid bare the logic behind U.S. paradoxical dealings with oppressive client states in regions of strategic interest. Staking out their fortunes in step with superpower interests, Ethiopia and Indonesia also exploited U.S. (and later Soviet, in the case of Ethiopia) interests and rhetoric. They meticulously laid the groundwork for the U.S. backing by sufficiently destabilizing Eritrea and East Timor (or at least making them appear unstable) to arouse concern about their future. In the name of order and collective security, Ethiopia and Indonesia got away with improbable justifications of their actions.

Ironically, the more successful Addis Ababa and Jakarta were, the more proponents of independence in Eritrea and East Timor took to extreme measures of resorting to violence. They found sufficient domestic, regional, and global inspiration and support to defy powerful governments.

Locked in seemingly unbreakable cycles of violence, the positions of all four belligerents hardened. Ethiopian and Indonesian efforts to crush any resistance and pacify their newly acquired provinces dragged on. As the Eritrean resistance gathered momentum and its East Timorese counterpart persisted, heavy-handed Ethiopian and Indonesian administration and brutal counterinsurgency measures became apparent. This isolated pro-union Eritreans and East Timorese and bolstered the positions of their pro-independence compatriots.

This chapter examines the outbreak of the Eritrean independence war and the transformation of East Timor's defense against Indonesian incursions into a war of liberation. These two struggles are looked at within the context of the Cold War, by examining how the superpower rivalry gave Ethiopia and Indonesia strategic and diplomatic advantages. Of paramount importance to the survival and growth of the two liberation movements were the insurgents' clandestine grassroots political work and their eventual success in cultivating civilian support while preventing their opponents from doing the same.

The Cold War Curse

No sooner had the British restored Haile Selassie to the Ethiopian throne in 1941 than he sought to regain Ogaden (the Somali-inhabited eastern part of what is today Ethiopia). Ethiopia's claim to Ogaden was based on the fact that it was one of the territories that Menelik had acquired through conquest and that his empire held on to until the 1935 Italian invasion. Similarly, immediately after winning independence, Indonesia claimed West New Guinea (West Irian) on the grounds that the former Dutch colonies belonged with the independent Indonesian state that displaced the colonial order.

Ethiopia's arrogation of Ogaden (from the British in 1948) and Indonesian victory in West New Guinea (from the Dutch in 1962) foreshadowed the two states' schemes for Eritrea and East Timor. In fact, the Eritrean and East Timorese cases for independence rested on similar historical-legal foundations as Ethiopia's claim to Ogaden and Indonesia's to West New Guinea. But Cold War imperatives, and Eritrean and East Timorese failures within the bipolar world order, rendered these contradictions moot. In fact, the collective security panacea of the Cold War presented Addis Ababa and Jakarta with favorable conditions.

At the heart of the global power equation lay the U.S.-Soviet Cold War rivalry. The U.S. urge to build an "empire of overseas military bases"[1] and a revival of perennial Russian expansionism triggered each other.[2] With containment the catchphrase of U.S. foreign policy for decades to come, U.S. policy makers focused on placing the Soviet Union within overlapping tiers of alliances and military bases to check its physical expansion and to filter out its ideological influence beyond its borders. The Soviet Union was preoccupied with breaking out of this envelopment by winning allies far afield. Third-World countries, such as Ethiopia and Indonesia, looked on and tried to work the situation to their advantage as the two superpowers embarked on a dangerous course of interstate relations inflamed by their thermonuclear arms race. The geostrategic locations of Eritrea and East Timor and their inability to perform in the state system conveniently played into the hands of Addis Ababa and Jakarta.

Cold War Eritrea: Bullets for Rejecting a Merger with Ethiopia

In the context of this superpower rivalry, Eritrea assumed an unparalleled geopolitical significance in its region. Located on the African side of the Red Sea, Eritrea controlled a long swath of coastline along the shortest route between the Mediterranean Sea and the Indian Ocean. It also faced the oil-rich Middle East from which, in June 1948, the U.S. Joint Chiefs of Staff (JCS) had decided to bar all rival forces.[3] With the added advantage of an active spy station in its capital Asmara, Eritrea was ideally situated for bases and facilities from which U.S. forces could be quickly deployed to regions of strategic interest across Red Sea as the JCS recommended.

Asmara's unique location (in terms of latitude and altitude) is able, for yet unknown reasons, to receive and transmit radio signals to and from most parts of the globe. Aware of this, Americans turned the basic Radio Marina communication base that the Italians had left behind into a state-of-the-art intelligence-gathering facility, intercepting radio signals from around the world and eavesdropping on rivals and allies alike.[4] Acknowledging "the benefits now resulting from operation of our telecommunication center in

---

[1] Chalmers Johnson, *The Sorrows of Empire: Militarism, Secrecy, and the End of the Republic* (New York: Metropolitan Books, 2004).

[2] The Soviets sought to justify their expansionism by their need to avoid another invasion from the West; in the first half of the twentieth century alone, Russia had to endure two devastating invasions from across its western frontiers.

[3] Alemseged Tesfai, *Aynefelale. Eritrea, 1941–1950* (Asmara: Hidri Publishers, 2001), 323.

[4] During the war years, radio traffic between the Axis powers was monitored regularly with instant, valuable payback. The best example of this occurred in October 1943, when the Japanese ambassador to Germany radioed Tokyo with German military positions and capabilities. Intercepted and decoded in Asmara, the military secrets enabled General Eisenhower to plan the Allied landing at Normandy. Michela Wrong, *I Didn't Do It for You* (New York: Harper Collins, 2005), 198–200. Also see Harold G. Marcus, *The Politics of Empire: Ethiopia, Great Britain, and the United States, 1941–1974* (Berkeley: University of California Press, 1983]).

Asmara ... can be obtained from no other location in the entire Middle East-Mediterranean area," U.S. strategists resolved that "United States' rights in Eritrea should not be compromised."[5] The radio communication facility alone was a decisive factor for U.S. wartime and Cold War strategic thinking. Successive foreign policy architects were convinced that Ethiopia was crucial to their long-term interests.

Disgruntled by London's own scheme for Ethiopia, Emperor Haile Selassie saw an opportunity in the almost compulsive U.S. preoccupation with Eritrea. He went over the heads of the British to seek a quid pro quo deal with the United States. In January 1945, Emperor Haile Selassie met President Roosevelt in Egypt. According to John Spencer, who attended the meeting as Haile Selassie's advisor, "[h]ighest priority was given to the necessity of access to the sea and a request for US support for the return of Eritrea [to Ethiopia] to provide a solution to this need."[6] Roosevelt was noncommittal. Later that year, during a session of the Council of Foreign Ministers of the victors of World War II, the United States turned down Ethiopia's overtures and rejected its claims on the grounds that the UN Charter provides for the former Italian colonies' right to self-determination and independence, including Eritrea.[7] U.S. Secretary of State James F. Byrnes defended the U.S. position and added that the inhabitants of the former Italian colonies needed assistance to "develop the capacity for self-government so that the people might be granted independence" and "not be developed ... for the military advantage of anyone."[8]

From that point, Ethiopia aimed to destabilize Eritrea to make it unfavorable to U.S. strategic concerns. A political officer of the British Military Administration observed that the failure of World War II victors to decide Eritrea's fate four years after their victory "had already caused Eritrea serious injury."[9] Their indecision granted Ethiopia an opportunity to deprive Eritrean politicians of the space to cultivate unity of purpose that could sustain independence. Eritrean socioreligious and regional cleavages were politicized and deepened, and Ethiopia did not fail to bring exaggerated implications of those divisions to the attention of the superpower with vested interest in Eritrea.[10] Moreover, pro-independence Eritrean politicians either

---

[5] Admiral William Leahy to Secretary of Defense (1948) quoted in Marcus, *The Politics of Empire*, 84.

[6] John H. Spencer, *Ethiopia at Bay. A Personal Account of the Haile Selassie Years*, 2nd ed. (Hollywood, CA: Tsehai Publishers, 2006), 159.

[7] Okbazghi Yohannes, *Eritrea a Pawn in World Politics* (Gainesville: University of Florida Press, 1991), 80.

[8] Quoted in ibid., 79.

[9] G. K. N. Trevaskis, *Eritrea. A Colony in Transition: 1941–1952* (Westport: CT: Greenwood Press, 1975), 92.

[10] Trevaskis, *Eritrea*, 97–98, and Alemseged, *Aynefelale*, 422–435, illustrate British collusion in weakening Eritrea's case for independence by dividing the pro-independence politicians. The British by this time had succumbed to U.S. interests in the region.

failed to understand the Cold War political alignments or were unwilling to engage pragmatically with Cold War protagonists in pursuit of their right to self-determination. The fragmentation of the Eritrean political landscape climaxed as the Cold War escalated into a far-reaching missile and thermonuclear arms race and unsettling developments emerged in the Middle East.

Ethiopian strategic thinking was deeply rooted in its sense of being a Christian island in a turbulent Muslim-Arab sea, even though about half of Ethiopia's population was Muslim.[11] Supposedly fearing that Eritrean Muslims would align themselves with other Muslims of the region to suffocate it in an Islamic encirclement, the Ethiopian Christian state made incessant overtures to guarantee that the Red Sea was not an exclusive sphere of hostile Arab-Muslim countries. At the same time the Middle East plunged into yet unresolved conflict with the birth of the State of Israel. Finally, in November 1948, the Ethiopian Foreign Minister, Aklilu Habtewold reassured his American counterpart, George C. Marshall, that Addis Ababa would grant Washington the right to continue using the radio intelligence station in Asmara and more, if the United States supported Ethiopia's claim to Eritrea.[12] Ethiopia brilliantly used leading American diplomat John Foster Dulles's concept of the Northern Tier, one of the United States' containment cordons around the Soviet Union, to fortify its position by proposing a Southern Tier as a backup in the Horn of Africa and the Middle East.[13] The United States' acceptance of that idea meant that if Eritrea were not secured, it would risk becoming a hole in the U.S. chain of defense.

Ethiopia's ceaseless and creative overtures were simply irresistible to the decisive generalship of the U.S. foreign policy chief. By contrast, Eritrean leaders of the time did not sufficiently understand the dynamics of the Cold War alignments either to assuage the United States' concern that Eritrea would not be used "for the military advantage of anyone," as Secretary Byrnes cautioned, or to capitalize on his Soviet counterpart Andrey Gromyko's rejection as "inadmissible that Eritreans be taken away from one state and subjected to the control of another."[14] In a swift dismissal

---

[11] Perhaps the first time that present-day Ethiopia had been characterized as such in international diplomatic correspondences is when nineteenth-century English diplomat Gerald Portal famously wrote of it as a "Christian island set in the midst of a stormy Moslem sea." Gerald H. Portal, *My Mission to Abyssinia* (London: Edward Arnold, 1892; reprinted New York: Negro Universities Press, 1969), iv.

[12] Alemseged, *Aynefelale*, 322–323. Testifying before the 1974 Ethiopian commission that was set up to investigate the government of Emperor Haile Selassie, former Ethiopian foreign minister Aklilu Habtewold "boastfully claimed that Haile Selassie's diplomacy exploited the Cold War by openly staking the future and fortune of Ethiopia on the side of the Western powers... in return for a 'deal' on Eritrea." Bereket Habte Selassie, *Eritrea and the United Nations and other Essays* (Trenton, NJ: Red Sea Press, 1989), 35.

[13] Spencer, *Ethiopia at Bay*, 267.

[14] Quoted in Okbazghi, *Eritrea*, 106.

of the United States' stated position in favor of a people's right to self-determination, Secretary Marshal promised unreserved U.S. support for Ethiopia and a cooperation agreement that was to be formalized after Eritrea's fate was decided at the UN.[15]

In 1953, the United States and Ethiopia concluded an agreement granting the United States the right to use and expand the Radio Marina Station – newly renamed Kagnew Station after one of the Imperial Bodyguard Battalions dispatched by Emperor Haile Selassie to Korea – and other facilities in the Eritrean port of Massawa. A concurrent agreement granted Ethiopia economic and military assistance, which the United States saw as payment for Kagnew.[16] For the two decades following, Kagnew Station remained Haile Selassie's key bargaining chip. In the words of a U.S. defense official, the emperor would get his way even if he asked for Kagnew rent money in "solid gold Cadillacs."[17] When technological advancements made Kagnew redundant and political pressures too costly for the United States, Ethiopia jumped off Washington's bandwagon and into the Soviet Union's embrace, until the end of the Eritrean war.

The superpowers competed to add Ethiopia to their portfolio of African client states while Eritrean independence fighters were ignored. Ethiopia's mythical millennial history and its military victory against the Italians in 1896 made the country a symbol of African freedom. For many Pan-Africanists, Ethiopia represented the driving spirit behind the ideals that later crystallized as the key pillars of the Organization of African Unity (OAU) – the present-day African Union.[18] Haile Selassie capitalized on this reputation, and U.S. backing, to bring the headquarters of the OAU, and the UN Economic Commission for Africa, to Addis Ababa. Both organizations gave, and continue to give, Ethiopia enormous diplomatic and moral leverage over other African countries. Eritrean nationalists could not challenge Ethiopia's place in the master-narrative of a proud, free Africa, nor could any Eritrean rival Emperor Haile Selassie's status as a preeminent African statesman. Moreover, at no point did Eritrean insurgents match Ethiopia's masterful state-level diplomatic manipulation.

Militarily, the Ethiopian government's Second Division in northern Ethiopia hastily put together the Twelfth Brigade to takeover from the British Military Administration. This brigade, with initial force of about 2,500 men and later rising in numbers and units, took charge of Ethiopian military operations in Eritrea into the early 1970s. As the incremental erosion of Eritrea's autonomy heightened political tensions in the late 1950s,

---

[15] Alemseged, *Aynefelale*, 322–323.

[16] Spencer, *Ethiopia at Bay*, 261ff.

[17] Quoted in Wrong, *I Didn't Do It for You*, 201.

[18] Ruth Iyob, *The Eritrean Struggle for Independence: Domination, Resistance, Nationalism, 1941–1993* (Cambridge: Cambridge University Press, 1995), 50ff.

Ethiopia deployed the Twelfth Brigade in the streets of Eritrean towns.[19] They went on routine marches through Asmara's thoroughfares chanting, "Embi yale sew tiyit augrusow!" (literally, "Feed [a] bullet to whoever says 'no' [to merger]!") – a show of force that foretold a grim reality in Eritrea for decades to come.

On September 8, 1962, one week before the formal dissolution of the Eritrean-Ethiopian federation, the London-based *Observer* reported the prevailing tension in Eritrea and the security that Ethiopia had put in place: "the presence... of a crack Army division and of General Abeyi [Abebe], an Amhara (Ethiopian) Governor of proven professional integrity, seems to indicate that law and order will be efficiently maintained in the next fortnight."[20] The general and his forces did indeed maintain order while presiding over the breaking of the law, the dissolution of an international instrument: in mid-September 1962, Ethiopian soldiers held Eritrean parliamentarians at gunpoint to disband the Eritrean legislature and abolish the Federal Act.[21]

The UN resorted to legal obscurantism to avoid remaining involved in Eritrea, despite its 1950 promise. According to the American legal advisor to Haile Selassie, the Federal Act involved Ethiopia and the Eritrean Assembly in an agreement that they could consensually amend and/or terminate. UN legal experts had accordingly "divested the United Nations of all further jurisdiction in the federation."[22] In 1954, UN Assistant Secretary General Andrew Cordier ruled: "There now exists no basis on which the United Nations can show any interest in the political situation within the Federation."[23] By the time African countries had started to gain independence – and an African legal system based on the preceding colonial territorial designation was being born – Eritrea had long been an integral part of Ethiopia. This situation was fortified by the continental provision that African countries do not interfere in the internal affairs of others.

Cold War East Timor
After the division of Berlin and the Korean War, Southeast Asia became an important checkpoint, where the United States hoped to contain Sino-Soviet influences. To that effect and in the spirit of the North Atlantic Treaty

[19] Dawit Wolde Giorgis, *Red Tears. War, Famine and Revolution in Ethiopia* (Trenton, NJ: Red Sea Press, 1989), 80–81. *Ye 12gna Egregna Brigade-ena Bewestu Yemistedaderut Leyu-Leyu Kefloch Ye-Kefil Tarik* ("The History of the 12th Brigade and Its Special Units"), Ca. 1977/1978 (a classified document of the Ethiopian ministry of defense accessed in Eritrea's Research and Documentation Center).

[20] *Observer* (London), September 9, 1962.

[21] See Wrong, *I Didn't Do It for You*, 177ff, for an analysis of the groundwork that preceded the final act of dissolving the Eritrean-Ethiopian Federation.

[22] Spencer, *Ethiopia at Bay*, 236.

[23] Quoted in Wrong, *I Didn't Do it for You*, 190.

Organization (NATO), the United States and its regional allies (Australia, New Zealand, and Japan) fostered blocs of alliances with, and of, countries of Southeast Asia and the Pacific littoral: the Southeast Asia Treaty Organization (SEATO) and the Association of Southeast Asian Nations (ASEAN). Although these regional alliances did not engage in direct combat against communism,[24] their collective anticommunist firmness (and regional system of noninterference in one another's internal affairs) offered the United States a normative comfort zone to directly confront communism in Southeast Asia.

While thus shoring up the violent confrontation against communism in mainland Southeast Asia,[25] Washington precluded communist expansion in island Southeast Asia by lavishly propping up friendly governments and unleashing them against their respective peripheries and neighbors. The United States enabled Portugal to continue with its colonial project in East Timor (and its African colonies) against repeated UN resolutions to decolonize. U.S. intolerance of the slightest hint of leftist radicalism encouraged the overthrow, in a military coup, of left-leaning Indonesian President Sukarno in 1965–1966. Furthermore, U.S. intelligence and the State Department's "rotten apple" analogy supported Suharto, the new president, and his ruthless massacre of hundreds of thousands of communists and their sympathizers. Beside cleaning the home front of ideological pariahs (a strategy Jakarta called *linkungan bersih*, "clean environment"), Washington let the Orde Baru regime off the leash in East Timor, when its interests there seemed threatened.

The deep Wetar Strait off the north coast of East Timor gave U.S. nuclear submarines an undetected passage, allowing them to close in on the Soviet Union and China. Control of the Wetar Strait also ensured the safety and security of the maritime route between the Indian Ocean and the Pacific.[26] So long as Portugal and Indonesia belonged to the same camp, Indonesia left the Portuguese grip on East Timor unmolested and U.S. Cold War interests secure. But the 1974 coup in Lisbon threatened Portugal's position in, and loyalty to, the Western bloc. Consequent prospects for decolonization of East Timor emerged in the immediate aftermath of the U.S. defeat in Vietnam

---

[24] This is not to disregard the training and materiel support that member countries of either of these organizations offered to U.S. war effort in mainland Southeast Asia. For a brief synopsis of Indonesia's role, for example, see Ken Conboy, *KOPASSUS. Inside Indonesia's Special Forces* (Jakarta: Equinox Publishing, 2003), 190–191.

[25] Hence, the United States stepped into the footsteps of the French in Vietnam, escalating the Vietnam War (which the Vietnamese correctly call "the American War") that engulfed Laos and Cambodia.

[26] Nevertheless, American Admiral Gene R. La Rocque dismissed these claims on grounds of new technological advances and alternative strategic bases in the Indian and Pacific oceans, concluding in 1980 that "East Timor is of no military concern to the United States or other countries." CIDAC-CDPM, TL6531, "Statement delivered to the Fourth Committee of the United Nations General Assembly," October 20, 1980.

and rising tides of communism in Southeast Asia. Having purged itself of its domestic communist menace, Indonesia was shaken by Vietnamese communists' alleged intentions of spreading their ideology throughout the region. In July 1975, President Suharto assured President Ford at Camp David that Indonesia was devising a "National Resilience" plan to strengthen its political, economic, and military apparatus to contain possible communist expansion.[27] Fanatically opposed to communism and delicately located next to the vibrant communist world, New Order Indonesia was sensitive to, and intolerant of, any signs of leftist tendencies within its borders and without.[28]

Genuine or not, Indonesia's concerns that independent East Timor could become a hub of communist activities at its back door were heightened by homegrown progressive tendencies in East Timor and radical ideological influences brought from abroad. Since the 1940s, the Catholic Church in East Timor assumed a major role in providing the limited education that was available at the time.[29] Not only did the church's substantive teaching offer Timorese better education than government-run schools, but frustrated with racist, conservative colonial rule, church-educated emergent leaders also embraced Christian teachings of social progress and justice in pursuit of self-empowerment.[30] Moreover, East Timorese students affiliated with the Portuguese Maoist party (variously referred to as the Portuguese Workers or Reorganized Movement of the Party of the Proletariat, but commonly remembered as MRPP) gave the homegrown progressive tendencies

[27] U.S. National Security Archives, "For Newsom from Habib: Ford/Suharto Discussions, July 5," 1975.

[28] A conversation in April 1975 between Indonesian defense minister General Panggabean and Chairman of the American Joint Chiefs of Staff General Brown illustrates this perfectly. Panggabean discussed Indonesia's real concern about the prospect of communist victory in Vietnam and Indonesia's need to bolster its security "both within itself and within ASEAN context" as part of its "National Resilience." See U.S. National Security Archives, "General Brown Meeting with General Panggabean," April 7, 1975.

[29] Arnold S. Kohen, *From the Place of the Dead. The Epic Struggle of Bishop Belo of East Timor* (New York: St. Martin's Press, 1999), 39. The Concordat of 1940 between the Salazar dictatorship in Lisbon and the Vatican made East Timor a separate diocese and set the terms under which the Holy See regulated the activities of missionaries and the appointment of bishops.

[30] Interviews with Bishop Carlos Filipe Ximenes Belo (August 25, 2006, Mogofores, Portugal); Francisco Xavier do Amaral (July 8, 2006, Dili, East Timor); Father Domingos "Maubere" Soares (May 22, 2006, Dili); and Avelino Coelho da Silva (May 5, 2006, Dili). See also Kohen, *From the Place of the Dead*, 59. The Timorese adoption of church teachings to challenge repressive social order does not seem to have had an organic link with Liberation Theology, the ecclesiastical advocacy of exercising preferential treatment of the poor in order to liberate and empower them and improve their sociocultural well-being. Articulated by Gustavo Gutiérrez after the Second Vatican Council of the first half of the 1960s and adopted by the Medellín conference of Latin American bishops in 1968, Liberation Theology proved to be a potent force in Latin Americans' fight against inequality of all forms. Thomas E. Skidmore and Peter H. Smith, *Modern Latin America*, 6th ed. (New York: Oxford University Press, 2005), 207.

a further push when they returned from Portugal in September 1974 to join FRETILIN.[31]

Although many debate whether these students were the driving force behind ASDT's transformation into FRETILIN, their role in implementing its grassroots programs and spreading FRETILIN's reach is undisputed.[32] Literacy programs, agricultural cooperatives, and other communal projects that these students pioneered confirmed FRETILIN's shift.[33] Rival parties also blamed the straining of their relationships with FRETILIN on the sudden change in the latter's rhetoric after the students' return.[34] From the range of responsibilities they assumed, it is easy to surmise the influence that these radical elements wielded within the fledgling independence party.[35] The students remained strong until the late 1970s, when, apart from Abilio de Araujo, who had returned to Portugal before the invasion, all were killed during the resistance. Their influence within the leadership of guerrilla resistance, however, lasted into the 1980s.[36]

Two additional factors may have contributed to make integration attractive to Indonesia. First, the multibillion-dollar bankruptcy that engulfed state-owned oil company, Pertamina, when world oil prices skyrocketed,

---

[31] The students, who returned to participate in their country's political life, included FRETILIN's leading ideologue Abilio de Araújo, Vicente dos Reis (also known as Sahe, who helped set up UNETIM, FRETILIN's student organization and ran agricultural cooperatives), Antonio Duarte Carvarino (also known as Mau Lear, who was responsible for setting up the literacy campaign), Venâncio Gomes da Silva, and Guilhermina Araújo.

[32] Abilio Araújo even disclaims any ties with the Portuguese left and downplays the role of Timorese students who flocked back from Portugal to East Timor in 1974. Interview with Abilio de Araújo (August 5, 2006, Vila Franka de Xida, Portugal). Similarly, Dr. Roque Rodriguez insists that the transformation of ASDT into FRETILIN was decided weeks before the students arrived in East Timor mainly because "the cadres and activists of ASDT came into touch with our own people and decided to become more thorough in going to the roots of the question" and adapting an all-encompassing front – a goal that FRETILIN hardly achieved. For him, the notion of "radicalism coming from outside is nonsense." Interview wtih Dr. Roque Rodriguez (July 8, 2006, Dili, East Timor).

[33] Helen Hill, *The Timor Story* (Melbourne: Timor Information Service, 1975; Jill Jolliffe, *Report from East Timor. AUS Representative on Australian Delegation to East Rimor, March 12–20,1975* (Canberra: Australian National University Students' Association, 1975).

[34] Interviews with Mário Carrascalão (July 3 and 7, 2006, Dili, East Timor); João Carrascalão (June 28, 2006, Dili, East Timor); and Francisco Xavier Lopes da Cruz (August 21, 2006, Lisbon, Portugal).

[35] CAVR, *Chega!*, Part 3: "History of the Conflict", 26.

[36] In 1987, the second-generation leader of the resistance, Xanana Gusmão, declared that the resistance followed leftist ideologies out of loyalty to the fallen leaders who taught them these ideologies. Sahe, to whom Gusmão attributes his knowledge of progressive ideologies, for instance, influenced him so much so that when the latter, as a leader of the remaining independence fighters, started to reorient the resistance ideologically toward the center-left, he felt he was betraying his mentor. Sarah Niner, *To Resist Is to Win: The Autobiography of Xanana Gusmão with Selected Letters and Speeches* (Richmond, Australia: Urora Books, 2000), 129ff.

left important Indonesian policy makers spellbound by East Timor's integration. The Indonesian generals who ran Pertamina were looking for ways
out of the precarious situation when the sudden prospect of Portugal's departure made the oil deposits in the Timor Gap seem up for grabs, resurrecting
the long-stalled Indonesian scheme for the half-island.[37] This may have been
encouraged by politically powerful Australian oil interests disappointed by
the recent concessions Portugal had granted to U.S. companies in East Timorese waters.[38]

Second, a small but influential group of Indonesian Catholics may have
sought to incorporate the non-Muslim half-island of Timor in order to beef
up their Catholic constituency within Indonesia. Prominent members of this
group included General Benny Murdani from the Indonesian military's internal intelligence and Liem Bian-Kie (also known as Yusuf Wanandi), who
was director of the Center for Strategic and International Studies (CSIS)
and assistant to Intelligence Chief General Ali Murtopo. Such players were
strategically placed to shape the course of Indonesia's actions in their sectarian and personal interests.[39] Moreover, the shake-up of Indonesian Armed
Forces (ABRI) command in 1974[40] demoted some, put others in uncertain positions (Minister of Defense General Panggabean and General Ali
Murtopo), and promoted a few officers (General Benny Murdani). The latter
two groups wanted to prove their loyalty and worth to President Suharto.
Other officers may also have seen the prospect of attaining their delayed
promotions through some action in East Timor.[41]

[37] Benedict Anderson, "East Timor and Indonesia: Some Implications," in *East Timor at the
Cross Roads: The Forging of a Nation*, ed. Peter Carey and G. Carter Bentley (Honolulu:
University of Hawaii Press, 1995), 138–141; Anderson, "Statement delivered to the Fourth
Committee of the United Nations General Assembly on East Timor, October 20, 1980" in
*East Timor, Five Years After the Indonesian Invasion: Testimony Presented at the Decol-
onization Committee of the United Nations' General Assembly, October 1980*, ed. Jason
Clay, (Cambridge, MA: Cultural Survival, Occasional Paper No. 2, 1981), 29–34; also
quoted in José Ramos-Horta, *Funu. The Unfinished Saga of East Timor* (Lawrenceville, NJ,
and Asmara: Red Sea Press, 1987), 61.

[38] John G. Taylor, *East Timor: The Price of Freedom* (London and New York: Zed Books,
1999), 37–38.

[39] This concept came out of several discussions with Dr. Moises Silva Fernandes, scholar of
Portugal's former empire in Asia and professor of international relations at Universidade de
Lisboa.

[40] This was in the wake of "Malari Affair," the January 1974 riots (by students and the poor) in
Jakarta during the visit of Japanese prime minister Tanaka Kakuei. It was staged as a protest
against the increasingly corporatist state policies along with alleged corruption of Chinese-
Indonesian businesses, which grew closer to Suharto's regime, and Japan's exploitation of
Indonesian economy and the overall resentment of the poor over their worsening conditions.
Some of the highest-ranking army officers commandeering the state security and intelligence
agencies were implicated for steering it and allowing it to take the turn that it did.

[41] Anderson, "East Timor and Indonesia: Some Implications," 138–141.

Indonesia's case for intervention rested on East Timorese leftist tendencies and Portugal's failure to ensure an orderly decolonization (in addition to claims about Indonesian security concerns and historic oneness of the Timorese people with their Indonesian counterparts). Jakarta claimed that these factors threatened regional stability. Indonesia also claimed that Portugal had secretly turned over its weapons and soldiers to FRETILIN and evacuated the territory in face of the civil war it instigated.[42] Because of the "criminal absence of the Portuguese government itself in organizing decolonization process,"[43] East Timor "started to become turbulent and full of suffering,"[44] threatening "stability in Indonesia in particular and in Southeast Asia in general."[45] This is an accurate characterization at face value, but it hides the fact that Jakarta was the principal culprit behind it all. Military takeover was a quick-fix solution that its generals proposed for a problem that had been created by unscrupulously meddling in East Timor's internal affairs long before the Portuguese exited.

Indonesian interference aimed to deny East Timorese the space to cultivate the necessary unity of purpose that would sustain their nascent nationhood and expose those weaknesses for the world to see. The plan succeeded marvelously.[46]

Parallel to the coordinated scheme of making the half-island – or simply making it appear to be – too disorderly and uncertain to leave alone, Indonesia carefully softened the international community's response to its takeover. Following its withdrawal from Vietnam in the wake of communist victory, the United States did not want another "leftist" government in Southeast

---

[42] Republic of Indonesia, *East Timor: Building for the Future. Issues and Perspectives* (Ministry of Foreign Affairs, July 1992), ii–iii. The truth is, however, that FRETILIN won over the East Timorese soldiers of the Portuguese colonial army after UDT staged its ill-fated coup on the behest of Jakarta in August 1975.

[43] "Statement of the Government of the Republic of Indonesia on Portuguese Timor" December, 10, 1975, in *Government Statements on the East Timor Question*, by Department of Information (no publication information; a compilation of five statements issued in succession by the Indonesian government between December 4 and December 22–23, 1975), 15.

[44] Ibid., December 4, 1975, 6.

[45] Ibid., December 8, 1975, 9.

[46] A precedent was set with Operasi Tjendrawasih in West Irian when an efficient balance of infiltration and agitation among the local population, propaganda, diplomacy, and military action delivered the desired outcome: merger with Indonesia. That result was later legitimized through pro forma deliberations among selected representatives of the local population. J. D. Legge, *Sukarno: A Political Biography* (Sydney: Allen and Unwin, 1984), 360ff; James Dunn, *Timor: A People Betrayed* (Auckland: the Jacaranda Press, 1983), 112–113. Under General Suharto, who in the 1960s commanded KOSTRAD (Strategic Reserve), senior officers Ali Murtopo, Benny Murdani, Dading Kalbuadi and others served in Operasi Tjendrawasih. Under his Presidency in the 1970s, the same officers masterminded Operasi Komodo and other schemes to secure East Timor.

Asia. High-ranking U.S. policy makers favorably received Suharto's analysis of East Timor as a communist-FRETILIN-instigated source of regional instability, and Suharto's impeccable anticommunist credentials assured them that an Indonesian-controlled East Timor would not fall to the rival camp. How Jakarta went about ensuring that was inconsequential, so long as it happened "effectively, quickly and not [with] use [of] our weapons," to use U.S. Ambassador David D. Newsom's words.[47]

Parallel to orchestrating subversive operations and political deceit in East Timor, Deputy Chief of Badan Koordinasi Intelijen Negara (BAKIN, State Intelligence Coordinating Agency) General Ali Murtopo stage-managed Jakarta's successful diplomatic campaign, signing up Western backing for the integration project. In September 1974, Australian Prime Minister Gough Whitlam told President Suharto that he believed that "Portuguese Timor should become part of Indonesia" because it was "too small to be independent." President Suharto for his part explained how independent East Timor was likely to become "a thorn in the eye of Indonesia and a thorn in Indonesia's back." Whitlam endorsed Suharto's "Archipelagic Concept" whereby Indonesia would exercise sovereignty over the entire maritime limits of the archipelago.[48]

Indonesia then proceeded to conveniently take Portugal's ambivalence as a green light for merger. After his October 1974 meeting with high-ranking Portuguese officials in Lisbon, Murtopo brushed off his hosts' precondition that integration should be achieved through a democratic process. He instead came out with the "impression... that the Portuguese Government had practically committed itself to the eventual integration of Portuguese Timor with the Republic of Indonesia."[49] Former Indonesian foreign minister, Ali Alatas, dismissed this fundamental – and

---

[47] Quoted in "Secret Correspondence of Australian Ambassador in Jakarta to Canberra," August 23, 1975. CIDAC-CDPM, TL/6720, CPDM (Council for the Defense of the Maubere People) Collection at the Amilcar Cabral Information and Documentation Center (CIDAC), Lisbon.
[48] "Record of Meeting between Whitlam and Soeharto," Yogyakarta, September 6, 1974, Document No. 26, in *Australia and the Indonesian Incorporation of Portuguese Timor, 1974–1976*, ed. Wendy Way, (Melbourne: Melbourne University Press, 2000), 95–98.
[49] Ali Alatas, *The Pebble in the Shoe: The Diplomatic Struggle for East Timor* (Jakarta: Aksara Karunia, 2006), 3. After listening to Murtopo's insistence that Portugal had agreed to cede its half-island colony to Indonesia, Australian Ambassador to Lisbon, who had prior knowledge of Portugal's precondition, noted that there was no "meeting of minds... between Lisbon and Djakarta" on the question of East Timor. Australian Ambassador Cooper, Lisbon, to Canberra, October 14, 1974, "Timor" report on his meeting with General Murtopo, Document No. 45, in *Australia*, ed. Way, 119. Australian Ambassador Woolcott in Jakarta observed that "Ali Murtopo's report... does not suggest the degree of misunderstanding between the Portuguese and the Indonesians ..." Woolcott to Canberra, October 21, 1974, "Portuguese Timor" Document No. 50, in *Australia*, ed. Way, 124–125.

possibly deliberate – miscommunication as insignificant detail: Murtopo and his team simply "did not pay too much attention."[50]

Meanwhile, in early 1975, the hawkish Chief of Intelligence in Indonesia's Department of Defense and Security, General Benny Murdani, ordered Colonel Dading Kalbuadi to assemble an elite unit to "start a Timor operation for me."[51] Murdani envisaged a "tactical combat intelligence [operation] in the event of Indonesian military intervention,"[52] codenamed Operasi Flamboyan. Thinly disguised as pro-integration Timorese partisans, Kopassandha units (Indonesian special forces) thus began making incursions into East Timor.[53] When FRETILIN chased UDT out and took Dili in August 1975, Indonesia stepped up its direct involvement; in September alone, the CIA reported that close to 1,000 armed Indonesian special forces and "Timorese irregular troops" had crossed into East Timor.[54]

Portuguese disorderly evacuation was a favorable development for the Indonesians who now wanted to deny FRETILIN an opportunity to stabilize itself into a credible administration. Komodo and Flamboyan merged into one multifaceted operation staged from border outposts in East Timorese territory. In late August, the Komando Tugas Gabungan (KOGASGAB, Joint Task Force Command) was inaugurated to assume control over all of Indonesia's operations toward East Timor including the army's new plan, Operasi Seroja, of taking over and pacifying the half-island. The change from the intelligence-based Operasi Komodo and Flamboyan to a KOGASGAB-led military command marked the transition from "small-scale destabilization to larger-scale military operation."[55] The objective was to normalize the situation for a civilian administration to be set up after "smashing and clearing of the residual force of the Security Spoiler Groups (GPK)."[56] However, stiff resistance by FRETILIN along the Atsabe-Bobonaro line, the start of the rainy season, and the lack of naval support limited Indonesian success.

Having once overestimated the capability of its deployed troops, Indonesian intelligence now set the stage for a full-scale involvement of the armed forces. Indonesia successfully stirred nationalist sentiments by alleging that

---

[50] Alatas, *The Pebble in the Shoe*, 3.

[51] Colonel Dading Kalbuadi quoted in Conboy, *KOPASSUS*, 199. See also Julius Pour, *Benny Moerdani: Profil Prajurit Negarawn* (Jakarta: Kejuangan Panglima Besar Sudirman, 1993), 392ff.

[52] Conboy, *KOPASSUS*, 199.

[53] Pour, *Benny Moerdani*, 392–394. Carmel Budiardjo and Liem Soei Liong, *The War against East Timor* (London: Zed Books, 1984), 18, argue that these incursions began long before FRETILIN chased the integrationists toward the Indonesian border.

[54] Quoted in Taylor, *East Timor*, 58.

[55] CAVR, *Chega!*, Part 3: "History of the Conflict," 45, 62.

[56] Departmen Pertahanan Keamanan, "Keputusan Menteri Pertahanan-Keamanan/Panglima Angkatan Bersenjata nomor Kep/23/X/1978 tentang Normalisasi Penyelenggaraan Pertahanan-Keamanan di Daerah Timor-Timur dan Pembubaran KODHANKAM Tim-Tim," October 1978.

FRETILIN had carried out cross border attacks, killing Indonesian civilians as well as East Timorese who had chosen to become Indonesian. In October 1975, reinforced and reorganized Kopassandha units resumed incursions into East Timor. By midmonth, they had pushed FRETILIN out of Batugade and then Balibo.[57] In November, assisted from the sea and air, Indonesian attacks gained a new intensity and took positions deeper inside East Timor.[58]

After Batugade, Balibo, and Fatularan fell to Indonesian forces in late November, it was only a matter of time before the entire Atabae area followed suit.[59] Declaring that "the situation has reached a crisis point,"[60] FRETILIN adapted a two-pronged strategy against the growing Indonesian incursions, just before the full-blown invasion. First, in order to beef up its resistance and better secure the territory, the recruitment of a militia auxiliary force, the Popular Militia of National Liberation (MIPLIN, in its Portuguese acronym), started in earnest in November.[61] Second, it resolved to unilaterally declare independence because it feared that "the political vacuum would give Indonesia a pretext to launch a full-scale invasion of Timor-Leste."[62]

Despite warnings to the contrary from some CCF members, most FRETILIN leaders hoped that declaring independence would fill the void left behind by the Portuguese and improve their chances of gaining international attention and domestic support as an independent country. In fact, CCF members Mari Alkatiri and Cesar Mau Laka had just returned from Mozambique (newly independent from Portugal) with the news that twenty-five countries had reportedly promised to recognize independent East Timor.[63] This news, although never independently confirmed, gave the liberation movement renewed confidence. So after Indonesia occupied Atabae, FRETILIN Secretary General Nicolau Lobato shouted in an impromptu CCF meeting: "The Indonesian army have already . . . occupied Atabae! If we wait until 1 December we might not have time to declare independence in Dili. So we'd better proclaim independence today."[64] The next day, November 28, 1975, in a tense and hastily prepared ceremony, FRETILIN declared

---

[57] Balibo, where the invading Indonesian forces killed five journalists from Australia and New Zealand, is also the title of highly acclaimed Australian feature film based on the story. Only recently did highly placed Indonesian Colonel Gatot Purwanto, who has direct, firsthand knowledge of what happened, spoke out to confirm the veracity of the killings. See *Tempo online* (December 12, 2009)

[58] For a succinct analysis of this period, see Taylor, *East Timor*, 59–62.

[59] It is important to note that some UDT elements who did not cross into Indonesia joined FRETILIN.

[60] FRETILIN message to Australia and Papua New Guinea quoted in Jolliffe, *East Timor*, 207.

[61] CAVR, *Chega!*, Part 3: "History of the Conflict", 54.

[62] Quoted in CAVR, *Chega!*, Part 3: "History of the Conflict," 53.

[63] Jolliffe, *East Timor*, 215–216.

[64] Quoted in Ibid., 55.

independence.[65] Commanding a force close to 10,000 (about 2,500 regulars and about 7,000 militias), the first government of the Democratic Republic of East Timor (RDTL) was inaugurated on December 1 to do Amaral's defiant declaration: "If we must fight and die for our freedom, we will now do so as free men and women."[66] After the declaration, however, fewer than half a dozen lukewarm recognitions came forth, none from countries that could affect international public opinion.

This course of action became the proverbial straw that broke the camel's back, providing a convenient pretext for Indonesia to invade. First, East Timorese integrationists immediately rejected FRETILIN's declaration with what came to be called as the Balibo Declaration. Signed by leaders of the four political parties (UDT, APODETI, KOTA, and Trabalhista) on November 30, the controversial declaration announced East Timorese 'independence' through integration with Indonesia and urged the latter to "take steps immediately to protect the lives of the people who now regard themselves as Indonesians."[67] Portugal recognized neither of these declarations, insisting instead that it remained the administering power. But FRETILIN's actions and the unionists reaction had already provided Indonesian President Suharto with the final impetus to give his generals the green light for an all out invasion of East Timor.[68]

By the end of August 1975, the Indonesians had drawn a plan (to which they remained faithful to the word) to launch a three-pronged offensive on East Timor. Accordingly an airborne contingent from the Eighteenth Brigade of Komando Strategis Angkatan Darat (KOSTRAD – Strategic Reserve Command) parachuted into the heart of Dili first. Then Indonesian marines mounted a seaborne and amphibious invasion on the capital while units from KOSTRAD's Seventeenth Brigade took East Timor's second biggest town of Baucau.[69] The incursions from West Timor scaled up to a sweeping overland invasion assisted by naval barrage.[70] Once these

---

[65] A single foreign citizen from Australia, Roger East, attended – in his private capacity – this declaration.

[66] Hill, *The Timor Story*, 16.

[67] "Balibo Declaration" in *East Timor and the International Community: Basic Documents*, Cambridge International Documents Series, Vol. 10, ed. Heiki Krieger (Cambridge: Cambridge University Press, 1997), 40–41. The best analysis of the Balibo declaration to date is Akihisa Matsuno, "The Balibo Declaration: Between Text and Fact," *The East Timor Problem and the Role of Europe*, ed. Pedro Pinto Leite (Dublin: International Platform of Jurists for East Timor-IPJET, 1996), 159–194.

[68] CAVR, *Chega!*, Part 3: "History of the Conflict," p. 57. Indonesian Major Yusman Yutam, who had been spearheading KOGASGAB's incursions into East Timor for months before Suharto's "go ahead" similarly asserts that FRETILIN's unilateral declaration of independence "was the red line that was not supposed to be crossed. This forced our hand." Quoted in Conboy, *KOPASSUS*, 233.

[69] Pour, *Benny Moerdani*, 397; and Budiardjo and Liong, *The War against East Timor*, 22.

[70] Budiardjo and Liong, *The War against East Timor*, 22.

are accomplished, "special forces units would [then] push inland. Victory, it was calculated, with [*sic*] be easy and swift."[71]

One day after the visit of the U.S. president and his secretary of state (perhaps ironically on December 7, Pearl Harbor Day), Indonesian forces launched an all-out invasion of East Timor from air, sea and land.[72] However, the moment military operations began any hopes of replicating India's swift takeover of Portuguese Goa over a decade earlier faded.[73] Airborne units of KOSTRAD's Eighteenth Brigade were dropped over FALINTIL positions while the latter was withdrawing from Dili into the rugged hills above. After sustaining heavy casualties, the paratroopers came under friendly fire from their seaborne counterparts as they swept from the coast through the town. In the process, both the paratroopers and the seaborne brigades rampaged, looted, and killed indiscriminately.[74] Whereas as many as a dozen ships were allegedly moored to Dili harbor to transport the loot, corpses floated on some beaches and were strewn across the capital, and the only hospital was filled with the dead and wounded.[75]

Thus, bogged down by gross planning miscalculations, tactical errors of execution, and FALINTIL resistance, what was expected to be a quick operation lasted decades. In the ensuing war, Indonesia's campaign was continually thwarted by East Timor's challenging geographical terrain. The East Timorese interior, says a World War II Allied briefing, is "one lunatic contorted tangle of mountains. There is no main system of ranges, for the mountains run in all directions and fold upon one another in crazy

---

[71] Conboy, *KOPASSUS*, 239.
[72] Suharto and the Indonesian government insisted that the invasion was a counterattack by pro-integration Timorese assisted by Indonesian volunteers: "[o]ur volunteers supported those who regarded us as brothers." Moreover, as "Indonesia could not possibly remain a passive onlooker in the middle of the turmoil in the area, which had disrupted and could pose a threat to our territorial integrity...we opened the doors to the people of Portuguese Timor to integrate with...Indonesia, if this was according to their wish ..." Soeharto, *Pikiran, Ucapan dan Tindakan Saya* (Jakarta: PT Citra Lamtoro Gung Persada, 1988), 271.
[73] While there was little to no resistance from the Goans, the Indian action was not attended by the level of violence that Indonesia's intervention in East Timor caused. Moreover, whatever resistance may have existed to Indian takeover died peacefully as New Delhi managed to quickly integrate Goans into the Indian political fabric with equal rights as the rest of its population. The renowned Keynesian economist John Kenneth Galbraith served as the U.S. ambassador to India during this time and for his perspective, see Richard Parker's *John Kenneth Galbraith: His Life, His Politics, His Economics* (New York: Farrar, Straus and Giroux, 2005).
[74] Hamish McDonald, *Suharto's Indonesia* (Blackburn, Victoria, Australia: Fontana Books, 1980), 212.
[75] The former Australian consul in Dili James Dunn offered the earliest and best reconstruction of those ghastly days based on eyewitness accounts when East Timorese started to arrive in Portugal. *The East Timor Situation. Report on Talks with Timorese Refugees in Portugal* (Canberra: Legislative Research Services, Australian Parliament, 1977).

fashion."[76] From both sides of the coast, gigantic mountains sharply rise over the horizon as high as 2,900 meters (more than 9,000 feet) above sea level, unpredictably intersected by deep scenic gorges, always covered with thick vegetation. As early as 1975, Indonesian forces resorted to what Taylor called "saturation bombings," blanket aerial and artillery bombardments of "forested areas ... in an attempt to defoliate ground cover" in order to make military operations possible.[77]

FALINTIL "Special Forces" commander Paulino Gama claims that, relying on laboratory-generated maps, Indonesian generals were oblivious to challenges posed by the hostile landscape, and their forces did not have adequate counterguerrilla combat experience in such fierce terrain. This was why it took an Indonesian battalion four months to march a mere three kilometers into the interior and take the southern coastal town of Suai.[78] Similarly, after their landings, the advancing Indonesian troops took at least two weeks to reach Remexio, less than twenty kilometers outside of Dili, and when they did, they immediately withdrew because FRETILIN fighters were a stone's throw away, biding their time.[79]

Even before the territory had come under full control of Indonesian forces, a sham Provisional Government and a Popular Representative Assembly were hastily set up in late 1975. Within six months, their handpicked members "urge[d] the Government of the Republic of Indonesia to accept, in the shortest possible time, and to undertake constitutional measures for the full integration of the people and territory of East Timor into the unitary state of the Republic of Indonesia without any referendum."[80] Flaunting this call as a testament of East Timorese popular choice, Indonesia shrugged off calls for an act of self-determination.[81] Suharto did away with the fallacy of such justifications, however, by disclosing one of the main reasons for Indonesian intervention: "We did not want the process and the results of decolonization to destabilize the area, which, in turn, could endanger our own stability and that of Southeast Asia in general."[82] East Timor, thus, became twenty-seventh province of the Unitary State of Indonesia, and Western capitals recognized the merger.

Unlike the case of Eritrea, the United Nations and many of its individual members – prominently the Lusophone countries and their allies – rejected Indonesian claims and persisted in calling for a legitimate act of

---

[76] Quoted in Jolliffe, *East Timor*, 46.
[77] Taylor, *East Timor*, 85.
[78] Ibid., 71.
[79] Constâncio Pinto and Matthew Jardine, *East Timor's Unfinished Struggle: Inside the Timorese Resistance* (Boston: South End Press, 1997), 44.
[80] *East Timor and the International Community*, ed. Krieger, 45.
[81] Ibid., 10.
[82] Soeharto, *Pikiran, Ucapan dan Tindakan Saya*, 271.

self-determination. This had an impact on the independence movement's grand strategy. Like Eritrea, however, the violence that Ethiopia and Indonesia unleashed in the last phase of their incorporation schemes shaped the nationalist responses in the two territories, and presaged counterinsurgency strategies that Addis Ababa and Jakarta pursued.

Domestic Conditions Surrounding the Outbreak of Open Resistance

Whereas conventional forces, such as those of Ethiopia and Indonesia, are doctrinally compelled to seek a quick victory through the physical occupation and retention of territory, their weaker opponents lack the means to do so.[83] Hence, Eritreans and East Timorese who sought to break free of secondary colonialism resorted to what Clausewitz called "people's war." In so doing, they built on a millennial history of guerrilla warfare. In its crudest form, this purely military technique made its first recorded appearance during the Punic Wars of the third century BCE when Hannibal of Carthage besieged Rome. Having lost a considerable number of its forces to the enemy, the Roman Empire decided to avoid engaging the Carthaginians and, under Fabius Maximus, Roman troops resorted to what came to be called "Fabian [delaying] tactics," that is, "hanging about the Carthaginian camps ... nibbling at Hannibal's limited manpower but refusing at all times to come to grips."[84]

The first modern military thinker to theorize about it as viable method of the weak, Clausewitz similarly counseled leaders of guerrilla fighters to avoid engaging the enemy in major confrontations.[85] "Militant bands and

---

[83] Gebru Tareke, *The Ethiopian Revolution: War in the Horn of Africa* (New Haven and London: Yale University Press, 2009), 49.

[84] A. Richard Preston et. al., *Men in Arms. A History of Warfare and its Interrelationships with the Western Society*, 5th ed. (Fort Worth: Harcourt Brace Jovanovich College Publishers, 1991), 3233. The military usage of the term *guerrilla warfare* is traced to the Spanish popular resistance against Napoleon. The white Cossacks of Russia had to fight a guerrilla war to kick out the invading Napoleonic army and restore the monarchy. Similarly, at the peak of World War II, the Soviets and the Southeast Asian countries had to organize guerrilla units from among the peasants to harass German and Japanese forces, respectively, from directions inaccessible to the regular armies. In western and south-central Europe, the regular armies resorted to guerrilla activities and some guerrilla armies of radical orientation emerged, particularly in Yugoslavia under Tito. Carl Von Clausewitz, *On War*, ed. and trans. Michael Howard and Peter Paret (Princeton, NJ: Princeton University Press, 1976), 480–481; and B. H. Liddell Hart, *Strategy*, 2nd rev. ed. (London: Meridian, 1991), 361–363.

[85] In pure military terms, all guerrillas have the same characteristics: "the use of irregular troops, reliance on elusiveness, knowledge of the terrain, and sympathy from a large section(s) of the civilian population; sabotage and ambush; capture of arms and supplies from the enemy." Vladimir Dedijer, "The Poor Man's Power" in Nigel Calder (ed.), *Unless Peace Comes; a Scientific Forecast of New Weapons* (New York: Viking Press, 1968), 20.

armed civilians . . . are not supposed to pulverize the core but to nibble at the shell and around the edges," he coached.[86] A people's war such as outlined in the preceding becomes unpopular and is doomed to fail if it does not rely on the people or its goals do not match their aspirations. Since the mid-twentieth century, Mao Tse-tung and the Chinese revolutionary war, Vietnam's independence struggle, and the Cuban revolution followed each other in quick succession, giving guerrilla warfare a new resonance and making it almost synonymous with revolution and liberation.

According to these revolutionaries, guerrilla war is a double-edged military-political tool. Mao asserts that a guerrilla war's spirit is of a revolutionary nature and a "revolutionary war is never confined within the bounds of military action." Since they aim to destroy the pre-existing oppressive societal structures that necessitated the revolution in the first place and to replace them with new and just ones,[87] revolutionary guerrilla armies, unlike conventional armies, need to be thoroughly politicized to understand what precisely they have at stake. They must also be prepared to give their lives for its cause. Beyond their ability to exploit the difficulties – terrain, climate, society, and so on – that the superior adversary encounters while piercing their territory, the survival and success of these politically conscious fighters hinge on their relationship with the people in and around the war zone.[88] Hence, "arousing and organizing the people" is the first of the "fundamental steps" for success "because guerrilla warfare basically derives from the masses and is supported by them, [it] can neither exist nor flourish if it separates itself from their sympathies and cooperation."[89] In other words, it is imperative that "the water . . . [is] warm enough to accommodate the fish."[90]

Reinforcing Mao's point that a guerrilla war must have a political agenda that coincides with the aspirations of the people, Basil Davidson argues that "however difficult its circumstances, a resistance movement wins by developing an ideology of liberation, or dies by failing to do

---

[86] Clausewitz, *On War*, 480–481. Although leftist revolutionaries attach politico-ideological significance to guerrilla warfare, Mao Tse-tung and Ernesto "Che" Guevara are in total harmony with Clausewitz on the military essence of guerrilla warfare. Mao Tse-tung, *On Guerrilla Warfare*, trans. Brigadier General Samuel B. Griffith, (New York: Frederick A. Praeger, 1961), 67, 42–44; Che Guevara, *Guerrilla Warfare* (Lincoln: University of Nebraska Press, 1961), 10–12.

[87] As colonialism came into and prolonged its existence by imposing a new socio-political order and/or co-opting preexisting ones, anticolonial wars of liberation were necessarily waged to overthrow those structures (of local or external origin) that sustained colonial order. When it is successful, therefore, anticolonial war is revolutionary as it leads to a break with the past in a sense that it alters the old sociopolitical order in substance and appearance.

[88] Mao Tse-tung, *On Guerrilla Warfare*, 42.

[89] Ibid., 43–44.

[90] Ibid., 8.

that."[91] This ideology of liberation is achieved first through the harmonization of the "liberating objectives, policies, or methods, and the level or conditions of a people's consciousness [and then] . . . the use of that harmony as a basis for further development of that consciousness."[92] So how "warm" were the "waters" and how conducive was the environment for the violent opposition to which Eritrean and East Timorese nationalists resorted?

Inspired as they were by the rise of armed revolutionaries around the world, the Eritrean and East Timorese nationalists sought to replicate other successful liberation movements in taking calculated risks against their formidable foes. In its early stages the Eritrean movement learned from the clandestinity of the Sudanese Communist Party and, later, the Algerian war of independence. The East Timorese had the independence wars of the African Portuguese colonies to look up to, as well as the Vietnam War. Due to their diverse role models and differing individual circumstances, the Eritrean and East Timorese movements cultivated public political consciousness in different ways.

Fluctuating Eritrean Waters
In 1958, Eritreans staged labor strikes in Asmara, protesting against Haile Selassie's economic policies of uprooting factories from Eritrea and sending them to mainland Ethiopia. These strikes, although peaceful, were brutally suppressed by the Ethiopians, which made many Eritreans conclude that they needed an organized new movement with an altogether new approach. In early November, Mohammed Said Nauwd, leading a group of young Eritreans in Sudan, formed the Eritrean Liberation Movement (ELM) to achieve independence.[93] Founded on the principle that "Muslims and Christians are brothers, and their unity makes [secular] Eritrea one,"[94] in 1959, the ELM initiated a clandestine political mobilization based on the experience of the Sudanese Communist Party. Each founding member recruited six others, forming a cell of seven, and each member of the new cell was entrusted with enlisting another six members into a separate cell led by the recruiter, and so spread the chain.[95]

Several factors helped the ELM's mobilization reverberate across Eritrea. According to Gaim Kibreab, the ELM was assisted in its emergence

---

[91] Basil Davidson, *The People's Cause. A History of Guerrillas in Africa* (London: Longman, 1981), 115.

[92] Ibid.

[93] Mohammed Said Nawud, *Harakat al-Tahrir Al-Irytriyah* (Khartoum: No Publication Information); Tahir Ibrahim Feddab, *Harakat al-Tahrir Al-Irytriyah wa Masiretaha al-Tarikhiyah fi al-Fetrah ma bayna 1958 ila 1967. Kitab Watha'iqi* (Cairo: Metabi' al-Shurq, 1994); and Ruth, *The Eritrean Struggle for Independence*.

[94] Preamble of the ELM Constitution of 1962 quoted in John Markakis, *National and Class Conflict in the Horn of Africa* (Cambridge: Cambridge University Press, 1987), 106.

[95] Interview with Mohammed-Berhan Hassan (September 13, 2005, Asmara, Eritrea).

and expansion by Ethiopia's outright banning, or systematic smothering, of Eritrean associational life and the activities of nationwide civil society groups.[96] While Ethiopian cultural domination and political heavy-handedness pervaded the Eritrean sociopolitical landscape, dissent was not allowed. Clandestine activism became the only way to express popular disapproval of Ethiopian domination and Eritrean ineptitude. Its inclusive vision appealed to Eritreans disaffected with the schism-ridden political landscape presided over by older politicians. As a result, ELM secret cells quickly multiplied, and its grassroots base swelled.

Nevertheless, this pioneer combative movement was not without weakness; in fact, crucial failings that contributed to its ultimate demise in 1965. Most importantly, its ambivalence about the expediency of armed struggle sealed its fate. Whereas Eritrea-based activists believed that they were preparing the ground for an Algerian style insurrection,[97] ELM leadership in Port Sudan adhered to what they dubbed "al-thewra al-inqilabiyah" (literally "revolutionary coup d'état").[98] The unwieldy chain of communication between the leaders inside Eritrea and their superiors in Sudan exacerbated such critical misunderstandings, and made the work of clandestine organization even more cumbersome than it inherently is.

Meanwhile, ELM recruiter in chief Tahir Ibrahim Feddab met with apprehensive Eritrean students in Cairo in mid-1960 who declined his invitation to join on the grounds that ELM wavered on the expediency of armed struggle whereas they wanted to start one.[99] This coincided with the return to Cairo from Riyadh of two older pro-independence politicians – Ibrahim Sultan Ali (founding leader of the Muslim League and later the Independence Bloc) and Idris Mohammed Adem (former president of the Eritrean Parliament) – whom the students in Cairo approached with the idea of forming an armed movement.[100] In July 1960, led by Idris Mohammed Adem, these students launched the Eritrean Liberation Front (ELF). Declaring that "the only way out of this black colonialism [under Ethiopia] was to start a revolution,"[101] ELF thus faced off the Ethiopian Empire.

Idris Mohammed Adem sneaked back into western Eritrea to solicit the backing of the Sheikhs – elders – around his hometown of Aqordat. Under

---

[96] Gaim Kibreab, *Critical Reflections on the Eritrean War of Independence. Social Capital, Associational Life, Religion, Ethnicity and Sowing Seeds of Dictatorship* (Trenton, NJ, and Asmara: Red Sea Press, 2008), chap. 4, 97ff.

[97] Interview with Mohammed-Berhan Hassan (September 13, 2005, Asmara, Eritrea)

[98] Mohammed Said Nawud, *Harakat al-Tahrir Al-Irytriyah* (Khartoum: NP, 1995); and Tahir Ibrahim Feddab, *Harakat al-Tahrir Al-Irytriyah wa Masiretaha al- Tarikhiyah fi al-Fetrah ma bayna 1958 ila 1967. Kitab Watha'iqi* (Cairo: Metabi' al-Shurq, 1994).

[99] Interview with Dr. Taha Mohammed-Nur (September 17, 2005, Asmara Eritrea).

[100] Denden, *Ma'erakat Iritriyah*, 45–46.

[101] ELF, "Destur Jebhat al-Tahrir al-Iritriyah" (1960). A document in private possession of Dr. Taha Mohammed-Nur.

the auspices of these Sheikhs, about 160 important Eritrean personalities gathered secretly and pledged to support the ELF, among them Hamid Idris Awate, who was to become well known in the independence movement.[102] One of the elders, the revered Mohammed Sheikh Daud, had so resented Christian Ethiopia's abolition of Arabic as an official language in Eritrea that he called on Hamid Idris Awate to wage a jihad against Addis Ababa. Unconvinced of the efficacy of the ELM's revolutionary coup strategy, but sympathetic to the ELF's armed struggle and obedient to Mohammed Sheikh Daud, Awate led an armed insurrection.[103] Already known to Ethiopia for his past as an armed popular militia against local banditry, Awate drew the attention of the federation's Eritrean Police because of his travels between and meetings in Asmara and Aqordat and his hometown of Gherset between 1960 and 1961.[104] In August 1961, he was tipped off about their suspicions and possible plans to apprehend him. He quickly took to the bush with five rifles and ten of his closest associates. In the ensuing pursuit, the eleven men engaged the police in battle at Mount Adal on September 1, 1961. This battle marked the beginning of the thirty-year war for independence.

Meanwhile, ELM leaders in Sudan got embroiled in war of words with ELF's Middle East–based leaders.[105] The verbal diatribe betrayed the ELM to the Ethiopian security, which mounted multiple, simultaneous security operations in Eritrea (and some in Sudan), and by 1962 had arrested many Eritrea- and Ethiopia-based ELM leaders.[106] The ELM belatedly embraced

[102] Alamin Mohammed Said, *Al-Defe' wa al-Teredi: Al-Thewra al-Iritriyah. Qisat al-Inshiqaq al-Dakhiliyah Lil-Thewra al-Iritriyah* (Asmara: Dogoli Printing Press, 1992), 17; Denden, *Ma'erakat Iritriyah*, 49–50.

[103] Interview with Adem Mohammed Hamid "Gendifel" (January 7, 1988, Kassala, Sudan) in ELF/UO, 02847, Günter Schröder, "Interviews on E.L.F History."

[104] RDC/Biography/03, 006807: "Minutes of Meeting," April 9, 1962, held by the police with traditional administrators and the public in the Eritrean town of Haicota regarding Hamid Idris Awate; RDC/Biography/3, 006806: Haile Selassie Weldu, "Hatsir Tarikh Hamid Idris Awate kesab 1961," November 30, 1983.

[105] Markakis, *National and Class Conflict*, 107–108 notes that, strategy-wise, "the older and conservative nationalist leaders" of the ELF were "wary of the ELM's efforts to bridge the sectarian divide by recruiting Christians... Idris Mohammed Adam was deeply distrustful of Christians... and thought it folly to recruit officials of the unionist administration into an organization dedicated to its overthrow." Moreover, the founders of the nascent ELF were "wary of the unknown quality of the ELM leadership, and doubly so when they discovered the communist affiliation" of its two most prominent leaders. Indeed, according to Mohammed Said Nawud, *Harakat al-Tahrir*, the ELF started calling them communists and children of goatherds. While being a Marxist (read atheist) is, at best, inflammatory among the highly traditional and religious members of the Eritrean society, the children of shepherds reference was probably meant to humiliate ELM's young leaders as an unknown lot with low-status backgrounds.

[106] Denden, *Ma'erakat Iritriyah*, 44. One of those who were extradited to Ethiopia was a Sudanese national serving in the Sudanese Armed Forces. He was handed back to Sudan

armed struggle as a method, but, once alerted, Ethiopian security tightened its grip even further and its intelligence-gathering network penetrated Eritrean society so that no insurrection from within Eritrea could
be mounted.[107] The rise of the ELF, which jealously protected the remote
Eritrean region suitable to challenge Ethiopia, precluded the ELM's insurrection inside the country.[108]

At a time when ELM-affiliated nationalists had started to wonder who
their leaders were and what their strategy for action was,[109] familiar
and established personalities of the Federation dissociated themselves from
Ethiopia, took on a new face as ELF, and called on the people to rise up.
Eritrean response to their calls was swift. In April 1961, for example, on
Idris Mohammed Adem's behest a dozen Eritrean soldiers of the Sudanese
army, who had previously pledged allegiance to the ELM, signed up with the
ELF and went even further. They started going back into Eritrea in groups of
two or three, in order to win over ELM activists to ELF's line.[110] ELM bases
silently switched allegiance or actively supported the ELF, with some even
joining its ranks in the battlefield. Two years after the ELM was founded
and amid growing frustration with its inaction among the movement's
fiery activists inside Eritrea, the ELF made a bold entrance into nationalist politics. It was to thrive in the fertile political ground that the ELM had
prepared.

The ELF Constitution of 1960 promised to "Conscientize/awaken . . . and
organize the Eritrean people and unite their leadership."[111] Nevertheless, the
ELF's early activities inside Eritrea spoke to its limited and limiting vision
and its pursuit of a narrow support base for the armed struggle. Former
ELF Chief of Staff Tesfai Tekle attributes the movement's failures partially

upon the exposure of the cooperation of General Ibrahim Aboud's conservative govern-
ment. Those arrested in Eritrea included Saleh Ahmed Iyay, Mohammed-Berhan Hassan,
Kahsai Bahlebi and Ahmed-din Abdelqader. Those arrested in Addis Ababa included Gir-
mai Gebremesqel and Werede Yohannes. Mohammed-Berhan Hassan, *Menqisiqas Harenet
Ertra (Haraka): Me'arfo kab Me'arfotat Gu'ezo Hagherawi Qalsna*. *Welqawi Mezekir*
(Asmara, 2001), 68.

[107] Mohammed-Berhan, *Menqisiqas Harenet Ertra*, p. 65.

[108] Bent on defending its operational base in western Eritrea both against the Ethiopian forces
and from rival Eritrean organizations, ELF leader Osman Saleh Sabbe warned ELM's
Mohammed Said Nawud that the Eritrean field could only accommodate one organization
and that was the ELF. When the ELM defied this warning and dispatched an armed band
of fifty men into northern Eritrea in 1965, ELF liquidated them, marking ELM's effective
end. History Project Interview with Saleh Mohammed Idris "Abu-Ajaj" (June 26, 1996,
Eritrea). According to Abu-Ajaj, the ELM sent its forces into Eritrea around the same time
that ELF's military and political leaders were deliberating on the zonal division. It was
decided then to dispatch a force to confront the ELM while the deliberations continued.

[109] Interview with Adem Mohammed Hamid "Gendifel" (January 7, 1988, Kassala Sudan) in
ELF/UO, 02847, Günter Schröder, "Interviews on E.L.F History."

[110] Ibid.

[111] ELF, "Destur Jebhat al-Tahrir al-Iritriyah," Article 4.

to the early fighters' limited understanding of Eritrea. Tesfai believed that this was due to their lack of education and limited exposure to Eritrean diversity.[112] But the experienced and educated founders of the ELF in Cairo did not lay an inclusive foundation to guide field commanders. To begin with, either for reasons of political expediency or because they truly believed this to be the case, the leaders of the Eritrean student movement in Cairo presented the Eritrean case as an Arab, Muslim question.[113] In fact, ELF founders hailed from all geographical regions of Eritrea, including at least one Jeberti and a Saho, from Eritrean Muslim communities in the Christian-dominated southern highlands. But not only was the ELF superstructure exclusively Muslim but founded "in the name of Allah,"[114] the ELF disregarded the Christian God, disowning those Eritreans who worshipped Him. The ELF, thus, became the conceptual antithesis to the ELM's secular orientation.

Moreover, Idris Mohammed Adem blamed his Christian counterparts in the former Eritrean parliament for the dissolution of the Federation and became wary of recruiting Christians to ELF ranks.[115] As discussed in the next section, this problem was exacerbated by Muslim-Christian divisions among Eritreans that had been an enduring tool in the hands of the Machiavellian monarch in Addis Ababa and the credulous Orthodox/Coptic Church. Besides the church's support of union, however, Haile Selassie's unionist project had the crucial backing of important Muslim clerics and Muslim communities across Eritrea, including Idris Mohammed Adem himself. The ELF was unable or unwilling to come to terms with the fact that senior Muslims supported the union.

Unlike East Timor, where the resistance simultaneously drew on traditional loyalties and national allegiance at a relatively low cost,[116] the two proved mutually exclusive in the Eritrean nationalist movement and the leadership's heavier tilt toward subnational identities culminated in its splintering. ELF's most influential leaders had long lost the political innocence that had enabled the young ELM leaders to be imaginative, see beyond the distrust and division that had enveloped them, and rally Eritreans across

---

[112] Correspondence wtih Tesfai Tekle (Keren, January 1999).

[113] Interview with Mohammed-Berhan Hassan (September 13, 2005, Asmara, Eritrea); Denden, *Ma'erakat Iritriyah*, 44–45. At that time, Anwar al-Sadat was a member of the Egyptian Revolutionary Leadership, very close to President Jamal Abdal-Nasser, and Secretary of the Islamic Conference, which at that time included Egypt, Saudi Arabia, and Pakistan. The implications of Sadat's pledge (and several other similar meetings, promises of support and actual assistance) to the Eritrean independence movement were apparent.

[114] ELF, "Destur Jebhat al-Tahrir al-Iritriyah" (1960). This dilapidated document was made available to me by Dr. Taha Mohammed-Nur who was a student leader in Cairo and one of the founding members of the ELF.

[115] Markakis, *National and Class Conflict*, 107–108.

[116] Taylor, *East Timor*, 95, 115ff.

the board. Consequently, warming the water in Eritrea lagged far behind the armed struggle.[117] In an honest admission of failure to make the ELF more inviting and accommodating of diversity, and the failure to adequately lay an inclusive political foundation, Taha Mohammed-Nur says that the founders' primary preoccupation was to put something concrete in motion. They believed that once they managed to get something started, then whoever succeeded them would modify the movement depending on circumstances.[118]

In mobilizing the grassroots beyond regional and religious affinities between the recruiter and the potential recruit, ELF's methods remained rudimentary. After Mohammed Sheikh Daud's 1962 tour across western Eritrea to prepare the people to anticipate and assist Hamid and his followers, ELF fighters explained to the people, "We are not shifta [bandits]; we are a revolution; we are out for your liberation and we will die for you; we want to be free like Sudan, we live under colonialism, Ethiopia usurped our land."[119]

ELF's political-ideological orientation was also uncertain at the outset. Jordan Gebre-Medhin best summarized its shortcomings thus: "The question of defining 'enemies and friends' at the national and international levels was not posed, let alone answered.... [and] the leadership was not prepared to guide the rural population into a revolution which would have social implications."[120]

The one chance the ELF had to overcome some of its fundamental weaknesses was lost when the founding commander of the armed insurgents, Hamid Idris Awate, died. As a former Askari in the Italian colonial army and, later, leader of one of the "popular militia" bands of self-defense against widespread banditry of the 1940s and 1950s, Awate had gained considerable experience, respect and fame. Moreover, he embodied qualities that brought together several ethnic groups of western Eritrea. He belonged to the Nara ethnic group; had cultivated close ties with the Kunama neighbors through his long relations with Fayotingun Longhi and his popular anti-banditry militia.[121] He was also staunchly loyal to the spiritual guidance of a Beni Amer sheikh, belonging to, and wielding significant influence among, the Tigre of western Eritrea. Such "cosmopolitanism," if one may, is likely to have nurtured the nonregionalist and antisectarian beliefs that Awate was known for. It is widely told, for example, that Awate fiercely protected the

---

[117] Gaim, *Critical Reflections*, pp. 150–151, attributes that to the fact that ELM was founded on and carried on by people who had been active in the nascent Eritrean political and civil society associations.

[118] Interview with Dr. Taha Mohammed-Nur (September 17, 2005, Asmara, Eritrea).

[119] History Project Interview with Mahmoud Dinai (June 26, 1995).

[120] Jordan Gebre-Medhin, *Peasants and Nationalism in Eritrea. A Critique of Ethiopian Studies* (Trenton, NJ: Red Sea Press, 1989), 172.

[121] Ibid., 156–157.

only Christian highlander among his followers, instructing the latter to do the same and advising them that the participation of all Eritreans was necessary for the struggle to succeed. Unfortunately for the Eritrean independence movement, he did not live long enough to institutionalize his beliefs within the ranks of the nascent insurgency.

Awate's successors inside Eritrea had neither the experience to adopt an inclusive course of action nor the stature to stand up to the divisive regional politicking of competing power centers within the ELF's exiled political leadership. Coming as they did from long years of active service in the Sudanese military, the new leaders of the Eritrean Liberation Army (ELF's armed wing) lacked an understanding of Eritrean socio-political characteristics necessary to lead an all-embracing struggle.[122] Moreover, their patriotism and commitment to Eritrean independence notwithstanding, they either did not share Hamid's convictions or lacked his strength of personality to remain above the rivalry-ridden ELF Supreme Council's political leadership.

The Supreme Council trio – Idris Mohammed Adem (Beni Amer from Aqordat), Osman Idris Geladewos (Tigre-speaking Betjuk from the environs of Keren), and Osman Saleh Sabbe (Tigre-speaking eastern lowlander from the environs of Massawa) – became patrons to their co-regionists in the field whom they supplied generously with necessities and disproportionately promoted to positions of authority.[123] Individual leaders of the movement also took on the Islamic orientation of its founders and became susceptible to the jihadist pronouncement of the spiritual leaders who invoked Hamid to mount the insurrection. This was particularly so after Ethiopian-recruited Eritrean Christians formed specialized counterinsurgency commandos and ravaged through Muslim areas (discussed later). Yet, so many Eritreans (Muslim and Christian, urbane and rural) flocked to the ELF, or started mobilizing in its support, that it was forced to reorganize and expand its military structures. However, the preparation of the political ground trailed behind by over a decade.

ELM nonviolent activism laid the initial groundwork that empowered a growing number of disenfranchised Eritreans and channeled their resentment into coherent expressions of disapproval. However, rivalry between the two independence organizations – ELM and ELF – eroded the political foundation necessary for a successful people's war. Unlike the ELM, the ELF lacked the vision to break free from narrow primordial loyalties and mobilize people on its own terms, beyond the division and brutalities wrought by Ethiopian counterinsurgency. Consequently, the

---

[122] Interview with Alamin Mohammed Said (September 28, 2005, Asmara, Eritrea).
[123] This practice of promoting one's favorites continued throughout the existence of the ELF. In the winter of 2002 in Barentu, Eritrea, a former ELF fighter (then in his late forties) frankly admitted to me that he had been promoted through the ELF military hierarchy and had become a superior to his more-experienced longer-serving comrades.

Eritrean armed struggle for independence started with little political ground-work among Eritreans living in the country. Not until midway through the resistance did nationalist leaders make a concerted effort to organize and communicate with the grassroots inside, as well as outside Eritrea. By that time, the resistance movement had matured, evolving from a guer-rilla movement to a conventional army, while tending to the domestic political environment by capitalizing on popular disenfranchisement and disillusionment.

Just as the birth of the ELM lent some coherence to Eritrean discon-tent and empowered the disenfranchised, the advent of the ELF marked an important milestone toward the crystallization of Eritrean nationalism and the march toward independence. Despite the unifying appeal its boldness had on Eritreans, ELF leadership lacked the vision and capacity to trans-late this appeal into a united political vision that would propel the armed struggle even further. As the following chapter shows, the ELF's early strat-egy and activities on the ground had in fact worsened the already fractured sociopolitical Eritrean landscape. Despite the major strides the ELF made toward realizing nationalist political goals, its violent infighting undermined these achievements.

East Timor's Strong Political Base

Politically, East Timor was better prepared than Eritrea for a guerilla war because its armed resistance followed from the peaceful days of Portuguese-era party politics. Of the two pro-independence parties, the stronger, better-established party transformed itself into an independence movement, with a nascent institutional framework and infrastructure. The East Timorese resistance survived the death, capture, or surrender of its first-generation leaders because it based itself in revolutionary ideals as well as in traditional identity formations.[124] Its broad, grassroots base enabled it to make difficult readjustments upon the ascent to power of a new generation of leaders.

As the Frente Revolucionária do Timor Leste Independente (FRETILIN, Revolutionary Front for the Independence of East Timor) and the União Democrática Timorense (UDT, Timorese Democratic Union) competed to win the support of the people for their respective paths toward indepen-dence, they propelled Timorese political awareness to unprecedented levels. Relatively well-placed in Timorese colonial society, UDT leaders used their positions, as well as their personal wealth, to win the support of tradi-tional rulers and co-opt their respective retinues. FRETILIN's leadership was largely drawn from the educated urban elite and actively sought the support of local political leaders (from lurais to Chefe de Suco), but the bulk of their followers came from the urban and rural poor. Out of a desire to reconnect to their roots and counterbalance UDT's dominance in higher

---

[124] Taylor, *East Timor*, 95, 115ff.

echelons of society, FRETILIN made a concerted effort at the grassroots level with immediate results. So much so that the FRETILIN leadership was "a self-conscious, and to that extent self-dissolving elite . . . seek[ing] a return to and the redemption of its own people," concluded a close observer of the pre-invasion days.[125]

In the footsteps of Brazilian educationist Paulo Freire, FRETILIN leaders believed that the substance and method of teaching emanate from, and reflect, power relations within society.[126] With due cognizance to traditional values of their societies, they charted out several programs, prominently focusing on literacy and self-help projects, in a bid to empower their people and reverse prevailing power relations. Local decision making was devolved to regional bodies answerable to the FRETILIN Central Committee (CCF) and started dealing with areas of pressing necessity, like education, health, and economic development. Under the supervision of CCF member Antonio Duarte Carvarino, the party launched its literacy campaign in early 1975 along Freire's model, using the local lingua franca, Tetum.

FRETILIN Secretary General and future Prime Minister of the unilateral Democratic Republic of East Timor (RDTL) Nicolau Lobato initiated an agricultural cooperative in his home region of Liquiça. Another leader, Vicente (dos Reis) Sahe, set up a consumer cooperative while at the same time helping establish the FRETILIN student organization, UNETIM.[127] Similar organizations of women and workers sprang up in an unprecedented manifestation of self-empowerment. Foreign observers noted the potential of the small-scale experimentations in agricultural collectivization and consumer cooperatives that CCF members were undertaking.[128]

FRETILIN's work at the grassroots level was mutually beneficial to the party and many East Timorese – in the short and long term. Although its agricultural and other programs were meant to better physical conditions of the downtrodden, FRETILIN's popularization of long-denigrated folk culture endeavored to lay psychological foundations for a self-reliant society. A powerful example is the conscious embracing of the word and meaning of *Maubere*. Literally meaning "my brother" among the Mambai people of

---

[125] Jolliffe, *East Timor*, 79.

[126] Paulo Freire, *Pedagogy of the Oppressed*, trans. Myra Bergman Ramos (New York: Herder and Herder, 1970), chap. 1.

[127] Taylor, *East Timor*, 34–35; Jolliffe, *East Timor*, 101ff. Once these grassroots initiatives got underway, CCF members were quick to leave for the countryside to manage party activities and supervise what they named Revolutionary Brigades, the volunteers who were implementing FRETILIN projects in all sectors. At any given time, many of FRETILIN leaders were in the countryside, with the result that Portuguese officials often became exasperated because of the absence of enough number of CCF members to decide on important matters.

[128] Hill, *The Timor Story*; Jolliffe, *Report from East Timor*.

central East Timor, the Portuguese had used the word as a denigrating reference to a poor, despised underclass. FRETILIN restored the word's original meaning and attached nationalist connotations to it; activists, and later most Timorese, used it to refer to one another as proud children of Timor.[129] For many ordinary people, the ability to organize, acquire literacy, and recognize their folk culture proved empowering. For FRETILIN leaders, going to work with their grassroots constituents constituted valuable political canvassing, offering practical lessons that helped FRETILIN better articulate its policies as a political party and later as a resistance movement.

UDT's August 1975 coup offered FRETILIN an opportunity to test and fortify its gains with the addition of an armed force, composed of professional soldiers and militias. Having escaped to the countryside to avoid UDT's full force, FRETILIN infiltrated the three Portuguese army garrisons and won over most of Timorese soldiers in the colonial army. It renamed the more than two thousand professional soldiers as Forças Armadas da Libertação Nacional de Timor-Leste (FALINTIL, Armed Forces for the National Liberation of East Timor), and declared a general insurrection on August 20. Assisted by civilian militia of the pro-independence party, FALINTIL reversed the coup, chased its opponents – UDT and other integrationists – westward to the Indonesian border, and took their stronghold town of Batugade in mid-September. FRETILIN then quick declared itself sole "interpreter of the profound ideals of all East Timor and...the only representative of the people."[130]

FALINTIL's birth, its brief combat experience, and its quick military victory against UDT nurtured an early sense of camaraderie among its ranks and gave credence to the notion of national liberation that had taken hold within FRETILIN. Influenced by liberation movements in former Portuguese colonies in Africa – like PAIGC in Guinea Bissau, MPLA in Angola, and particularly the Mozambican FRELIMO – and by surging popular opinion articulated powerfully in Freire's dictum that freedom is not handed out but rather acquired by force, FRETILIN came to believe in the inevitability of a fight for independence.

---

[129] Taylor, *East Timor*, 42. As a self-proclaimed coiner of the politicized meaning of the word and inspired by Swedish success story and the need to reflect Timorese sociocultural and historical realities, Ramos-Horta writes, "I began therefore to concoct our own version of social democracy by coining the word Mauberism – from Maubere, a common name among the Mambai people...Though vaguely defined without any serious theoretical basis, Maubere and Mauberism proved to be the single most successful political symbol of our campaign. Within weeks, Maubere became the symbol of a cultural identity, of pride, of belonging." Ramos-Horta, *Funu*, 37. After independence, Mauberism became an issue of national discussion involving the highest political leaders of the country who initially gave the word an invigorated nationalist meaning.
[130] FRETILIN statement quoted in Jolliffe, *East Timor*, 74.

Nonetheless, the political haze of the day obscured against whom exactly the fight was to be: Portugal had initiated decolonization of its own volition, while Indonesia had not yet launched its invasion. In fact, Indonesian Foreign Minister Adam Malik had assured FRETILIN's chief diplomat, Ramos-Horta, in June 1974 that the Indonesian government believed independence was the right of every people, including the people of East Timor.[131]

However, Indonesia went back on its promises and invaded East Timor in December 1975. Although neither of East Timor's fledgling political establishments was sufficiently equipped to handle the scale of Indonesia's onslaught, FALINTIL and FRETILIN quickly transformed themselves into a resilient liberation movement. Indonesia's atrocities, combined with FRETILIN's modest political work, helped strengthen growing political consciousness across East Timor. Moreover, FALINTIL's defiant stand helped raise FRETILIN above the early divisions among East Timorese.[132] The moral and material support offered by the East Timorese people kept the military resistance alive through its most difficult times. While this "warm" demographic "sea," thus, helped nourish the resistance, the "lunatic contortion" of the terrain offered safe havens for guerrilla fighters throughout their resistance.[133]

Early Phases of Eritrean and East Timorese Resistance

Initial domestic political inexperience, Ethiopian and Indonesian abuses and international neglect left Eritrean and East Timorese nationalists with little

---

[131] Ramos-Horta, *Funu*, 43.

[132] Although they did not automatically pledge allegiance to FRETILIN, several of the former Timorese advocates of integration with Indonesia or those who had been manipulated into that position renounced their positions, condemned Indonesian atrocities and subsequent occupation, and identified with their resisting brethren. Immediately after the invasion, UDT leader and mastermind of the August 1975 coup João Carrascalão was sent by Jakarta on a tour to the Middle East to explain Indonesian actions and intentions. The tour was interrupted after his first landing in Egypt where he told his hosts that Indonesian actions were nothing short of invasion and Indonesian intentions were occupation of his homeland. Interview with João Carrascalão (June 28, 2006, Dili, East Timor). In an April 1976 letter to the UN Secretary General, KOTA leader José Martins similarly renounced his December 1975 statement before the UN Security Council. José Martins to Secretary General of the UN, April 29, 1976 in *East Timor, Indonesia and the Western Democracies. A Collection of Documents*, ed. Torben Retbøll (Copenhagen: IWGIA, 1980), 45–48.

[133] It is important to note at this juncture that from their attire, the weapons they carry and the equipment they need as well as overall mode of operation, conventional forces are inherently at a disadvantage in moving around difficult terrain. Moreover, the smaller the theatre of operation, as they were in East Timor immediately after the start of the invasion, the less useful the heavy weapons of a conventional army become, to the further detriment of their effectiveness.

choice but to rise up in arms.[134] Encouraged by support, or promises of support, from international underdogs, such as Egypt towards Eritrea, and Vietnam and the former Portuguese colonies in Africa towards East Timor, nationalists endeavored to halt and reverse initial Ethiopian and Indonesian gains.

It is important to acknowledge the context of these developments. At the time, key political and ideological rivalries were playing out. Globally, the ideological left seemed to be winning against the West in the Cold War, and anticolonial movements in the African Portuguese colonies had aligned themselves with the East and had won, or were on the verge of victory, through violent means. It was only natural to assume that at least some Eritrean and East Timorese sought to imitate these victories, although at a considerable cost to themselves. Ideological jockeying by Eritrean and East Timorese nationalists, and the network of alliances they sought, proved detrimental to their respective causes. This is because their search for leftist allies in the Eastern Bloc reinforced (or seemed to reinforce) Ethiopian and Indonesian justifications in the international arena.

Escalating Resistance and Attendant Challenges in Eritrea
Beyond stating its aim to use violent means against the Ethiopian Empire, the ELF did not offer a clear long-term strategy. The thirty-year war of independence started, and its initial strategy was formulated in 1961, in response to a police manhunt for Hamid Idris Awate and his band of followers.[135] In early 1962, Mohammed Omar Abdellah (also known as Abu Tyara) entered Eritrea with several other former members of the Sudanese army who wanted to join the armed struggle. Awate was elated: "Al-thewra sabatat al-yom!" ("The revolution solidified today!").[136] The band of about thirty men, however, carried only nine long rifles and a pistol, as well as several traditional weapons such as swords and daggers.

After an early battle, which killed two independence fighters, the founding commander of the insurgents lamented that their lack of weapons could be considered a moral defeat. Awate urged the insurgents to "become an undying flame of the revolution and if that flame dies it would not be easy to reignite it in a short period of time."[137] He quickly instructed Abu Tyara

---

[134] Besides their long history with warfare and soldiery, the logic of violence that Ethiopian and Indonesia followed and an international system that allows violence for self-defense are important factors to consider as a background.

[135] RDC/Biography/03, 006807: "Minutes of Meeting," April 9, 1962, held by the police with traditional administrators and the public in the Eritrean town of Haicota regarding Hamid Idris Awate; RDC/Biography/3, 006806: Haile Selassie Weldu, "Hatsir Tarikh Hamid Idris Awate kesab 1961," November 30, 1983.

[136] Interview with Mohammed Omar Abdellah "Abu Tyara" (September 2, 2005, Tessenei, Eritrea).

[137] Quoted in Denden, *Ma'erakat Iritriyah*, 57.

to go back to Sudan to "communicate with the politicians to secure enough weapons."[138] Awate was a soldier entrusted with accomplishing a political goal charted out by the politicians and activists, who had no knowledge or experience of military matters. His interactions with his subordinates and his communications with the ELF leadership abroad clearly show how little he wanted to intervene in what he believed were the politicians' prerogatives.

Awate devised hit-and-run tactics. He avoided marching into villages with all of his forces, choosing instead to send a small group to nearby villages to solicit provisions in his name without disclosing any information about him and his force.[139] Although known for his quietness and seclusion, Awate lived the same life as his followers, conveying information and instructions on a need-to-know basis. He is applauded in later publications of the ELF for grooming his followers (including the former soldiers in Sudan's conventional army) in his tactics of unconventional war so well that for several years after his death, they led the armed struggle in his footsteps.[140]

Hamid died in May 1962, leaving fewer than fifty fighters (only seventeen of whom carried firearms) in the care of the former soldiers in the Sudanese army. However, they could neither establish a firm authority or command structure nor cultivate consensus. One of these commanders was Mohammed Omar Abdellah "Abu Tyara," who had served for twelve years in the Sudanese army before joining the ELF. Along with Mohammed Idris Haj, he stepped up to fill the vacuum left by Awate's death until the December 1962 Bergheshish conference when his position was confirmed after a secret ballot of the fighters.[141] In the presence of one of their political leaders, Osman Saleh Sabbe, the fledgling liberation army (Eritrean Liberation Army – ELA) began to spread its activities across Eritrea. To do this the fighters reorganized themselves first in to two platoons and later into three, plus a separate fedayeen unit (semiclandestine hit squad).[142] Although the

[138] Interview with Mohammed Omar Abdellah "Abu Tyara" in *Irytriyah al-Haditha*, March 7, 1992.

[139] The early independence fighters capitalized on Sheikh Dawud's initial canvassing to secure the people's favorable attitude as well as material support, safe havens and the provision of information on police movements.

[140] ELF, *Erytriyah: Burkan Al-Qern Al-Afriqi (Eritrea: Volcano of the Horn of Africa*, 1986), 87–88. This is an Arabic publication by a faction of the ELF led by Abdellah Idris subsequent to the splintering of the early 1980s.

[141] ELF, *Erytriyah*, 87; and interview with Mohammed Omar Abdellah "Abu Tyara" (September 2, 2005, Tessenei, Eritrea). According to Abu-Tyara, the commander of the Ethiopian forces in Eritrea, Brigadier General Merid Gizaw, offered the independence fighter general amnesty in return for surrender. Abu-Tyara asked for the cessation of their manhunt until he consulted with the rest of the fighters. The Ethiopian commander agreed. Taking advantage of the brief lull, the fighters received Osman Saleh Sabbe of ELF's Supreme Council to reorganize their structure and forces during December 1962 conference.

[142] Denden, *Ma'erakat Iritriyah*, 59. Although his contemporaries do not corroborate his information, Mohammed Omar Abdellah "Abu Tyara" claims that he co-led the ELF after Bergheshish with Mohammed Idris Haj. Interview with Mohammed Omar Abdellah "Abu

ELF, thus, entered a new phase of planned tactical operation with better-organized forces, its leaders – the equally experienced military men – plunged into personal rivalry that quickly took a sectarian and regionalist turn.

In 1964, the first group of about two dozen Egyptian-educated fighters arrived in Eritrea from their Syrian training. They found rebellious rank and file openly calling for the removal from command of all the former soldiers from the Sudanese army. They alleged that their leaders had embezzled money for use in Sudan, as well as for their personal and sectarian rivalries. The new arrivals demanded that the Supreme Council address all the issues raised.[143] The pressure from the Eritrean field coincided with the October 1964 Sudanese coup that removed General Aboud's anti-Eritrean regime. Taking advantage of the favorable environment, the absentee political leadership took on the task of reorganizing the resistance structures.[144]

Crumbling of Conventional Defense Strategy in East Timor

East Timorese resistance against Indonesia proceeded from FRETILIN's challenge to UDT following the latter's coup in August 1975. The birth of FALINTIL and its quick knockout operations against UDT and other integrationists, boosted the confidence of FRETILIN leaders. Pursuit of the integrationists also gave FALINTIL practical combat experience and encouraged the development of camaraderie among its ranks. Nevertheless, Portuguese reluctance to return and resume administering the territory during the decolonization process left FRETILIN as a de facto "government," setting the scene for Indonesia's overt intervention in December. FALINTIL's victory during the brief Timorese civil war brought it face-to-face with Indonesian forces that were almost ten times in number.

In addition to its numerical and material disadvantages, the East Timorese resistance also suffered from structural weaknesses. The Portuguese colonial system trained its soldiers to uphold its military code of *apartidarismo* under which politicians controlled the military, and the latter remained above and out of political groupings. Although the alignment of Timorese soldiers with FRETILIN against UDT undermined this basic principle, the soldiers' transfer of allegiance was more to the political cause of independence than to the party itself.[145] Yet, their conventional doctrine proved hard to break

---

Tyara" in *Irytriyah al-Haditha*, March 7, 1992. This difference of opinion reflects the early rivalry among the former soldiers in the Sudanese Army who came to lead the liberation fighters after the death of its founder. While this rivalry played favorably into the hands of the divisive politicking of the leadership abroad, it came to a head around the same time that the ELF imploded in 1969.

[143] Interview with Romedan Mohammed-Nur (September 25, 2005).

[144] Interviews with Romedan Mohammed-Nur (September 25, 2005) and Ibrahim Idris Totil (September 22 and 27, 2005, Asmara, Eritrea).

[145] This is despite isolated incidents of police and military insubordination at the early stages. For pre-invasion police insubordination, see Jolliffe, *East Timor*, 185–186. CAVR, *Chega!*,

from. Individual and institutional inability and/or reluctance to transition into an army of national liberation led to a two-tiered resistance against Indonesian incursions and invasion.

Subordinate to political leaders with little or no military background, one tier of resistance was made up of well-trained soldiers and another of auxiliary militias.[146] This cost the independence movement a great deal during its early stages because, under instructions from their political superiors and ill positioned for alternative approach, FALINTIL waged positional warfare. Although it proved itself a force to be reckoned with, the superior Indonesian forces tore it asunder fairly quickly. Whereas FALINTIL commanders were unable to consider alternative viable options when conventional resistance became impracticable, political leaders were incapable of charting a political way out of the impending military catastrophe.

Atabae was the last place that FALINTIL managed to hold defensive position in and effectively resist Indonesian infantry advances from West Timor. After Atabae fell to Indonesia in late November 1975, FALINTIL's organized, positional resistance gave way to less-organized and small-scale mobile engagements. As Indonesian forces overwhelmed FALINTIL units, and Dili was reached from air and sea, the enfeebled Atsabe-Bobonaro defense line became redundant for the defense of the capital, and it crumbled as rank-and-file fighters as well as their commanders dispersed. Most FALINTIL regular soldiers retired to their home districts either to find safety with their families or to locate them and lead them to safety.

By contrast, armed civilians proved more adaptable to the challenges of confronting the massive force and materiel of Indonesia. A small special forces unit exclusively made up of FRETILIN's civilian militants was born upon the inauguration of FALINTIL in August 1975. Led by Paulino Gama (also known as "Mauk Muruk") and answerable only to the FRETILIN Secretary General and future Prime Minister Nicolau Lobato, this was a highly mobile unit specifically designed to be on the offensive at all times without engaging in prolonged confrontations. From a bodyguard-type unit of seven soldiers, FALINTIL "Special Forces" grew to perhaps several dozen just before Indonesian landings.[147] When positional defense failed to hold back

Part 5: Resistance: Structure and Strategy, pp. 17ff., also offers an incisive account of the internal conflict between most of the politicians, on the one hand, and the soldiers, on the other, in the period after the May-June 1976 Soibada Conference. As the report confirms, however, the conflicts were not caused by the total rejection of apartidarismo on the part of the soldiers. Rather, it was caused by the politicians' doctrinaire approach to the war in complete disregard to those who actually did the fighting. It is also possible that some personal, ethnic and/or class differences, or even grudges, may have added to the overall disaffection of the soldiers during this difficult period.

[146] It was not until reorientation that the political and military hierarchies of the resistance became more fully integrated around mid-1980s.

[147] According to Paulino Gama (interview, October 9, 2007, Rijswijk, the Netherlands) this unit had grown to 250 strong at the time of the Indonesian invasion. But given his generally

Indonesian overland advance, surviving FALINTIL units and its 'Special Forces' rushed back to Dili with the news. They immediately took charge of the capital's security during the FRETILIN's unilateral declaration of the Democratic Republic of East Timor (DRET) until the Indonesian assault on Dili on December 7, 1975.[148]

Discovering during the early morning hours of December 7 that the Indonesian navy had put the capital within its artillery's firing range, FALINTIL Special Forces Commander Gama claims that he took the field. Although Gama's assertion of sole command is questionable, especially given that FALINTIL's highest commanders like Guido Soares and Sebastiao Sarmento were in or around Dili, the damage that the Indonesians sustained speaks for itself. FALINTIL command declared Dili a war zone and when Indonesian paratroops started to land, FALINTIL soldiers received orders to shoot them before they touched down.[149]

The East Timorese resistance benefited from tactical inaccuracy of Indonesian planning and execution. Indonesian paratroopers from the Eighteenth Brigade of KOSTRAD (Komando Strategis Angkatan Darat, Army's Strategic Reserve Command) were dropped into Dili above the withdrawing FALINTIL units. After sustaining heavy casualties in the hands of the latter,

---

inflated estimates of FALINTIL's personnel, I assume 250 is a little exaggerated as well. As a trusted commander of this fledgling unit, however small or big, Paulino was instructed by Nicolau Lobato to accompany and give protection to the five foreign journalists who filmed Indonesian forces' incursions into East Timor and FALINTIL's resistance. Indonesian forces later killed the journalists at Balibo, but Gama managed to deliver some of their footage to Lobato. As FRETILIN was overtaken by the speed and gravity of the developments that followed the fall of Balibo, the recording did not make it to the international audience as Lobato had planned. For an account surrounding the disappearance of the journalists, see Jolliffe, *East Timor*, 166ff. Note the document on p. 173 carrying the name "Paul Gama" at the top; Gama still prefers to be called Paul "because it is easier for Westerners to know it," as he told me. Jolliffe also wrote the only comprehensive expose on the five foreign journalists killed in Balibo during the early phase of Indonesian invasion: *Cover-Up: The Inside Story of the Balibo Five* (Melbourne: Scribe Publications, 2001).

[148] The early phase of Timorese resistance is replete with stories of FALINTIL commanders and ranks retiring from battle in the thick of the resistance to rescue their families. Nonetheless, it is likely that, before proceeding to their home districts and families, many FALINTIL soldiers from the eastern part of the country and especially their high-ranking commanders, reported to Dili and were there when the invasion took place. For example, Aquiles Freitas, the commander of FALINTIL Cavalry Company on the Atabae front line in Bobonaro, could not have retired to his home district of Baucau and later be confirmed as sector commander there without having come to Dili between the fall of Atabae in late November and Dili in early December 1975.

[149] Interview with Paulino Gama (Mauk Muruk) (October 9, 2007, Rijswijk, the Netherlands). Paulino admits that he ordered his soldiers to shoot the Indonesian paratroopers in the air and that those orders and the subsequent acts were against international law. But he said that when ten aircrafts were simultaneously dropping paratroopers, the navy was bombarding from the sea, and the infantry was marching from the west, he had no choice but to do any and everything he could to defend his country and people.

the paratroopers came under friendly fire from Indonesian marines sweeping from the coast through the town. According to McDonald, "[t]he remnants of the paratroopers then rampaged through the town, killing and looting at random."[150] In the ensuing confusion, FALINTIL ensured the safe exit of FRETILIN leadership out of Dili toward Aileu through the hilly outskirts of the capital.

Diplomatically, FRETILIN did not completely shun the capitalist world in its rhetoric and pursuit of potential allies although, at the early stage, it sought the support of some progressive countries of the Eastern bloc.[151] About two weeks after the transformation of ASDT to FRETILIN, for example, FRETILIN's José Ramos-Horta wrote to the Chinese ambassador in Canberra asking for help: FRETILIN "as the only legitimate representative of people of East Timor... can count on the People's Republic of China, under President Mao, to give us... moral, political, diplomatic, economic, and military support." Expressing suspicion that "Indonesia is preparing a take-over of our country" and readiness to "fight if necessary," Ramos-Horta related East Timor's imminent struggle to that of North Vietnam, Cambodia and Mozambique and solicited Chinese assistance for their anti-colonial struggle.[152] Likewise, on December 3, 1975, when covert Indonesian incursions into the country had long started and their takeover of Dili was imminent, FRETILIN President Francisco Xavier do Amaral sent a letter to President Ton Duc Thang of North Vietnam, seeking support.[153]

Gusmão reflected in 1987, "when Fretilin assumed [a] leftist ideology it 'turned' unmistakably into a potential threat to the strategic interests of the

[150] McDonald, *Suharto's Indonesia*, 212.
[151] From early on, FRETILIN was embroiled in a highest-level debate about who to seek and receive help from: the United States was out of the question, while the Soviet Union was equally imperialist for some but social imperialist for others, whatever the two terms may have meant to the leaders at the time. In one such meeting in April 1976, FRETILIN President Francisco Xavier do Amaral blurted angrily, "I don't want to know if it is imperialism or social imperialism. I don't care if the help comes from America, the Soviet Union, China, or wherever. All I need is help. Isn't that what we need?" in Niner, *To Resist Is to Win*, 41. Interview with Abilio de Araújo (August 5, 2006, Vila Franka de Xida, Portugal). According to Abilio Araújo, who led FRETILIN's first delegation overseas, FRETILIN sought support from Yugoslavia and leftist political parties across Europe and Asia. It was not until the late 1970s that China started to support the resistance. It gave FRETILIN an undisclosed amount of cash in four installments with no strings attached.
[152] Arquivo e Museo Resistencia, 05000.274/Resistência, José Ramos-Horta's letter to the Ambassador of the People's Republic, Canberra, September 28, 1974. In the first few years after Indonesia's invasion of East Timor, China helped the Timorese resistance by giving financial assistance to the foreign delegation of FRETILIN. Without any strings attached, the undisclosed sum came in installments to shore up the diplomatic aspect of the struggle. Interview with Abilio de Araújo (August 5, 2006, Vila Franka de Xida, Portugal).
[153] Arquivo e Museo Resistencia, 05000.056/Resistência, President of the Democratic Republic of Vietnam Ton Duc Thang to President Francisco Xavier do Amaral, Ha Noi, January 27,

powerful."[154] Although that is not particularly inaccurate, it is important to note that Western and Indonesian policy-makers had already excluded the probability of East Timor's independence on the grounds that it would become a pawn for external interests as it was purportedly too small to sustain independence. FRETILIN's radical turn in late 1974 only legitimized such thinking and perhaps convinced the skeptics.

Conclusion

Beyond justificatory claims, Cold War imperatives played conveniently into the hands of Ethiopian and Indonesian contemporaneous interests. Like most Third-World countries, Eritrea and East Timor found themselves ensnared within the Cold War between U.S. containment endeavors and Soviet efforts to break out of that encirclement. Calculations in the best interests of superpowers and their allies – in the name of collective security – determined their fate. An American diplomat, for example, famously explained Washington's calculations to back Ethiopia's claim to Eritrea thus: "the strategic interests of the United States in the Red Sea basin and considerations of security and world peace make it necessary that the country has to be linked with our ally, Ethiopia."[155] This mind-set was to shape U.S. policy and that of their Western allies toward the Eritrean and East Timorese[156] liberation movements until the end of the Cold War. It was in this vein also that President Ford and his secretary of state Henry Kissinger granted Indonesia the green light to invade East Timor in order to reverse FRETILIN's takeover after "the Portuguese simply marched out and left a vacuum behind."[157] Rejecting the logic of imperial grandiosity

---

1976. "Being a nation which has waged protracted resistance wars against French colonialists and US imperialists," the North Vietnamese president assured his Timorese counterpart, "the Vietnamese people and the Government of the Democratic Republic of Viet Nam completely sympathize with and resolutely support the struggle for independence and freedom carried on by the people of East Timor..." Needless to say, the Timorese resistance did not receive Vietnam's assistance in any form, however.

[154] Niner, *To Resist Is to Win*, 129.

[155] John Foster Dulles quoted in Bereket, *Conflict and Intervention*, 58.

[156] As early as August 1975, U.S. Secretary of State Kissinger is on record saying, "[i]t is clear that the Indonesians are going to take over the island sooner or later," and questioning, "Why should [Australian Prime Minister] Whitlam care about the disappearance of a vestige of colonialism?" National Security Archives, "East Timor Revisited," proceeding of the meeting of "the Secretary's Principal and Regional Staff," August 12, 1975, http://www.gwu.edu/~nsarchiv/NSAEBB/NSAEBB62/doc2.pdf.⟨6:indentry o: id="1.584"⟩⟨/6:indentry⟩

[157] Testimony of U.S. Assistant Secretary of State for East Asian and Pacific Affairs, John Holdridge in "Recent Developments in East Timor," *Hearing before the Subcommittee*

in favor of nationalist particularism, the Eritrean and East Timorese peoples, for their part, waged protracted struggles to assert their territorial independence.

Ethiopian and Indonesian acquisition of Eritrea and East Timor could not have been more different from their rule over the newly acquired territories were similar. Eritrea was already linked to Ethiopia through a federation put in place by the UN General Assembly in 1950. Security services answerable to Addis Ababa thus existed within the territory in all possible forms to annex the autonomous region at the right time, which happened gradually until late 1962. East Timor was an altogether new acquisition made possible through violent aggression. Those differences aside, both cases represent grave violations of international law – Ethiopia's annexation violated an international instrument, Indonesian invasion was a blatant and unprovoked aggression. Once imposed, however, the two powers sought to maintain their rule over their newly acquired territories through similar means – continued violation of international law and the subjugation of the peoples to brute force that left indelible marks on Eritrean and East Timorese sociopolitical landscapes.

Eritrean and East Timorese resistance assumed different military and political dispositions at the beginning and evolved in opposite directions. Eritreans resorted to gradually escalating hit-and-run guerrilla warfare whereas East Timorese resistance started as conventional war and "regressed" to scattered guerrilla movement. Politically, likewise, the Eritrean Liberation Movement (ELM) lacked the capacity to act on its galvanizing vision, and the founders of the ELF-led armed struggle did not adequately understand the sociocultural complexity of Eritrea. Their first attempt to work out an inclusive strategy proved ill thought out and poorly managed. It exacerbated the cleavages within the Eritrean society and introduced practices that were of disservice to the struggle in the long-term. But Eritrean guerrilla insurgency escalated as its East Timorese counterpart rolled from conventional resistance back to guerrilla warfare, and a precarious one at that.

In East Timor, nationalists realized quite late in the game that their independence would have to be seized in the face of Portuguese inaction and Indonesian invasion. As the invasion became a reality and Portuguese authority dissipated, however, FRETILIN's political moves proved naïve, and FALINTIL was ill prepared to cope with the military challenge from Indonesia. Although the sheer enormity of Indonesian onslaught decimated East Timorese capabilities to effectively resist militarily, it did not weaken East Timorese political awareness gained during the period of party politics

on Asian and Pacific Affairs of the Committee on Foreign Affairs, House of Representatives, Ninety-Seven Congress (Second Session), September 14, 1982 (Washington: U.S. Government Printing Office, 1982), 48 and 70, respectively.

under the Portuguese. By contrast, the start of armed struggle in Eritrea exposed the clandestine work of the preceding secular nationalists and ironically eroded the fertile political ground that had led to the outbreak of guerrilla war. Outsmarted and taken by surprise at important junctures, therefore, Eritrean and East Timorese bold resistance initiatives nearly faltered in the face of excessive Ethiopian and Indonesian belligerence and for lack of realistic, sustainable, homegrown approaches.

2

Bittersweet Replicas of Foreign Experiences and Reform

> Become the undying flame of the revolution, because if that flame dies it would not be easy to reignite it.
>
> Hamid Idris Awate

Without realistic long-term contingency plans, Eritrean and East Timorese nationalists reacted against the shocking brutality of Ethiopian and Indonesian measures with a spontaneity that bordered on haphazardness. They endeavored to halt and reverse initial Ethiopian and Indonesian gains. But nationalists in Eritrea were ill prepared, and their counterparts in East Timor ill equipped and strategically handicapped, to overcome the challenges that Ethiopia and Indonesia threw their way.

In a bid to seize the initiative from the Ethiopian and Indonesian militaries, Eritrean and East Timorese nationalists improvised their organizational structures and strategies by absorbing lessons from successful armed independence struggles elsewhere. While Eritrean nationalists sought to replicate the Algerian nationalists' strategy, the East Timorese looked to the African Portuguese colonies for inspiration and organizational models. But neither of these experiences could prepare them for the heavy-handed Ethiopian and Indonesian counterinsurgencies. Both countries had enormous resources, and they never shied away from launching unrestrained counterinsurgencies against the nascent resistance movements.

Moreover, the nationalists had not anticipated the local challenges of adopting external strategies that were detached from their own domestic realities. This, coupled with internal rivalries within the nationalist movements, further limited the Eritreans and East Timorese, and only exposed them to harsher reactions from their antagonists. This chapter shows how heavy borrowing from foreign experiences did not help either group, and it reconstructs their respective elusive routes toward reforming their structures and methods.

Root Causes for Eritrean Reform and East Timorese Reorientation

Although the Eritrean independence movement was growing in size and diversity, it was not yet inclusive of all segments of Eritrean society. The flow of young, educated, and urban nationalists to the ELF awoke the movement to its internal difficulties and injected it with a new vision of Eritrea. While embodying the spread of the nationalist cause across ethno-regional, religious, and class lines, the new generation of fighters envisioned a unified leadership of an inclusive and cohesive movement, leading to *Islah* (literally meaning "Reform"). Reforming the ELF from within, however, remained at best incomplete, and early attempts at genuine reorganization culminated in the splintering of the ELF.

By contrast, in East Timor, it took the near annihilation of FRETILIN and FALINTIL for the nationalists to appreciate the urgency of reorientation. Successive military setbacks, the demolition of the *Bases de Apoio* (support bases), and their grave consequences to the civilians; the deaths, surrender, and/or capture of commanders and fighters of the resistance; and the elimination of the first generation of the leaders left the survivors scrambling for ways to survive physically and revive the resistance.

From Haphazard to Strategic: Faulty Eritrean Initiative

To contain rising sectarian divisions among commanders of its fighting force, while expanding the independence movement's horizons of operation, the ELF's Supreme Council opted to model itself on Algeria's nationalists. In 1965, the ELF invited its senior commanders to a meeting in Khartoum. They deliberated on, and adopted, the Algerian model: to divide the country into semiautonomous military zones with regional structures mostly composed of, and led by, local fighters. Some field commanders objected, notably Taher Salim, who saw it as emboldening extant sectarian tendencies. Instead, Salim wanted to overcome sectarianism through an Eritrea-based centralized command.[1] However, the ELF held that assigning military commanders their respective operational zones in their home regions would end their rivalry. Moreover, it was hoped that such reorganization would attract the commanders' fellow coethnics and/or regionists into the zones and persuade them to join the national struggle, undercutting Ethiopia's scheme (of setting Eritreans against each other). However lethargic this plan may have been, it constituted the ELF's first initiative to design a grand strategy of liberation, ending earlier ELA tactical measures against overall Ethiopian strategic initiatives.

---

[1] Interviews with Mohammed Omer Abdellah (September 2, 2005, Tessenei, Eritrea); and Mohammed Osman Ezaz (September 3, 2005, Tessenei, Eritrea).

With considerable success, the Supreme Council introduced four zones –
and, in late 1966, a fifth zone. It restructured its Kassala-based Revolutionary Command and introduced a centralized training center. Under ELF
Supreme Council member Osman Idris Geladewos, the Revolutionary Command was intended to serve as the intermediary between the zonal commanders in the field and the Middle East–based Supreme Council. It was also
expected to oversee the day-to-day activities and logistical provisions of the
zones. Taher Salim was dispatched to establish and lead the newly introduced training center, from where all new recruits were to be dispatched to
their assigned divisions, after a period of military and political training.

Zone One operated in the western Eritrean province of Barka. Although
its membership consisted of the Nara (formerly called Baria) and Tigre, this
was an exclusive sphere of the Tigre-speaking Beni Amer, who dominated
its ranks and leadership, with ELF cofounder and member of its Supreme
Council Idris Mohammed Adem as their patron.

Zone Two was active in Senhit, between the western lowlands and the
central highlands, inhabited by the Bilin ethnolinguistic group and also home
to the Tigre-speaking Betjuk. Several prominent fighters belonged to the
Betjuk, including the chief of the Kassala-based Revolutionary Command,
Osman Idris Geladewos.

Zone Three operated in the southern highland provinces of Akeleguzai
and Seraye. The Muslim Saho and Jeberti communities co-inhabit this area
with the predominating Tigrigna-speaking Christian groups. The zonal commander was Abdel-Kerim Ahmed, a Muslim Saho, although the political
commissar was a Tigrigna-speaking Christian, as were most members of
this zone.

And finally, Zone Four was assigned to the coastal province of Semhar.
Its members were the fighters of the western lowlands of Eritrea, from where
Osman Saleh Sabbe originally hailed.

Later, in October 1966, a fifth zone in the central highland province
of Hamasien[2] was introduced to accommodate the growing number of
Tigrigna-speaking Christians and to consolidate ELF's activities in the
region. Although its commander was a Tigrigna-speaking Christian, his
regional affiliation was with Senhit. Furthermore, his deputy was a Muslim
Bilin from the environs of Senhit's provincial capital, Keren.

The preceding thumbnail sketch shows that, objectively speaking, the
1965 reorganization expanded the independence movement's reach and

---

[2] Osman Saleh Denden, *Ma'erakat Iritriyah. Al-Juzu Al-Awal* (n.p., 1996), 64ff. Although
the history of the Eritrean independence war during the years of zonal division has been
touched upon by several scholars and Eritrean independence organizations, by far the most
authoritative account is offered by Denden, whose account is fully supported by previously
inaccessible documents including correspondences and proceedings of meetings. In particular,
he glaringly presents the religious, ethnic, logistical, territorial (among the zones), personality,
and other problems that were the hallmarks of the era of zonal division.

brought it physically closer to a broad cross section of Eritreans. The mush-rooming of ELF zones across Eritrea and the spreading of its activities attracted a growing numbers of new recruits, as shown by the quadrupling of its fighting force between 1965 and 1969. It also stretched Ethiopian forces and made their presence in Eritrea more vulnerable. This was demonstrated by the two dozen important operations that caused the deaths of hundreds of Ethiopian soldiers (but also that of important ELA commanders such as Taher Salim at Adobha, Jinger in Aqordat, and Omar Ezaz at Halhal, among others).

These gains were not without their deleterious effects, however. To begin with, when ELF leaders divided the Eritrean field into military zones, they ignored the fact that Algeria's National Liberation Front (FNL) had militar-ily been defeated in 1961 – leaving aside the longer-lasting negative political implications that its zonal division had on Algeria, which the ELF could not have known at that time.[3] Basil Davidson's observation of the Algerian zonal division resonates acutely with the Eritrean reality. Writing on the experience of the FNL, Davidson best captures the obstructions caused by the zonal division:

So long as the top leadership ... was "outside," each [zonal] command tended more and more to do as it thought best without reference to the centre of command or even to neighbouring wilayet. This vision of authority and control was then found to have played into the still more divisive hands of an old habit and attitude of provincial "regionalism" or "clan-ism" well known in Algerian history ... It bade fair to destroy the FNL and its army. The unifying politics of armed struggle began to decay into the military "commandism" of this or that local chieftain. The damage was considerable, and French action now increased it.[4]

Similarly, the zonal division in Eritrea failed to take note of the division-ridden Eritrean sociopolitical fabric, and intensified the latent rivalries among Eritreans along politicized ethnic, religious, and regional cleavages that had already started to plague the ELF, to the detriment of the indepen-dence struggle. Decentralizing the resistance in such a way that each of the rivals would reign supreme in his designated zone (also his home region) institutionalized the sectarian and regional rivalries. Each division had a significant mass of fighters, not native to its zone of operations, claiming

---

[3] Consistent with the Algerian experience such zonal division also exposed the Eritrean liber-ation movement to Ethiopia's attempts to improvise on France's Challe Plan (after General Maurice Challe who led the final phase of French counterinsurgency campaign), which effec-tively sealed off the whole of Algeria from its neighbors and took on FNL's zones one at a time, pounding them with highly mobile counterinsurgency units until their devastating defeat in battle.

[4] Basil Davidson, *The People's Cause. A History of Guerillas in Africa* (London: Longman, 1981), 81.

to have been dominated by one or the other ethnic/religious group.[5] On this account alone, the ELF's strategic thinking and planning was naïve and reflected an inadequate understanding of the fractured Eritrean social and political landscapes.

This weakness was compounded by the fact that the zonal division was neither coherently envisioned nor strictly applied. During inception, it was not clear what factors were taken into account (geographic, demographic, ethnolinguistic, or other features of Eritrea) in establishing the zonal division. This problem was not clarified even during implementation of zones. Assignment of leaders and staffing failed to follow a predictable formula. Left to the whims and interests of the leaders in Kassala and the Middle East, therefore, the zonal division plan lent itself to manipulation by rival Supreme Council members. While Zone One was supposed to be Idris Mohamed Adem's zone, Geladewos was the patron of Zone Two and Sabbe of Zone Four. The very leaders who introduced the scheme, at their own peril and to the detriment of the independence struggle, undermined it only to revive the latent rivalries among Eritreans along politicized ethnic, religious, and regional divisions.

As an extension of this fundamental structural failure, the Kassala-based Revolutionary Command failed to carry out its duties. The Supreme Council triumvirate circumvented the Revolutionary Command as an intermediary structure and directly supported the zones of their co-regionists, and the latter directly communicated with their respective patrons. All available sources are consistent in their allegations of rampant regional and ethnic favoritism when it came to supplying zones with necessities.

More particularly, without an overseas patron, remote from third-party countries and surrounded by Ethiopia's strongest presence in Eritrea, Zone Three and later Zone Five in the highlands were left impoverished. Despite having a powerful patron in Osman Saleh Sabbe, Zone Four in the coastal lowlands was not much better either. It is important to consider the relative ease of supplying Zones One and Two because of their proximity to Sudan, while Zones Three (in the southern highlands), Four (in the western/coastal lowlands) and later Five (in the central highlands) were farther from the Revolutionary Command's reach and under stronger control of the Ethiopian security apparatus.

In light of the leadership's lack of political will and the sectarian polarization of the base, this practical difficulty, if at all taken into consideration, did

---

[5] The non–Beni Amer in Zone One, for example, came to be called Kesser Movement. In Zone Two, the Betjuk and Maria were pitted against each other. The Saho and Tigre elements in Semhar's Zone Four also had a falling out. Christians across the ELF, and mainly in Zone Three, felt underrepresented and generally persecuted. Interview with Romedan Mohammed-Nur (September 25, 2005).

not dispel the distrust between the bulk of the fighters and their leaders, as well as among the fighters themselves. Lack of cooperation among the zones also added to the supply problems. The attendant endemic discrimination, inefficiency, and the lack of a long-term strategic vision compelled newer, younger, more-educated fighters to seek to rectify the situation.

And finally, as fiery high school and university students from the Eritrean highlands and mainland Ethiopia flocked to the battlefield, the ELF leadership's suspicion of the educated and Christian fighters increased. In several instances, newly arrived fighters were summarily executed for any sign of equivocation or for reasons only their executioners knew. The rocky start and eventual fiasco in the Christian Zone Five (see the following discussion) best epitomized the failure of the ELF's zonal division strategy and underlined the urgent need for reform. According to Haile "Deru'e" Weldetensae, the birth of the Christian division was, in the first place, an outcome of the rivalry between Supreme Council members Geladewos (who also doubled as chief of the Revolutionary Command) and Sabbe. This rivalry played out in many avenues available to these two adversaries – the provision of supplies and information, and the staffing offices in each zone.[6] Fearing that adjacent Zones One and Two were coming closer together, which could risk overshadowing his influence and the significance of his loyal Zone Four, Sabbe allegedly forged an alliance of sorts between the latter and its neighboring Zone Three, which did not have a patron among the top leaders. To maintain an upper hand, Geladewos then advocated for and succeeded in forming a fifth zone for the growing number of Christians/Tigrigna-speakers of Hamasien province, adjacent to Zone Two. To ensure the new zone's loyalty, which would function as a loose trizonal alliance against Sabbe's Zones One and Two, Geladewos appointed as commander Weldai Kahsai, a Tigrigna from the Anseba area of his home province of Senhit, deputized by a loyal lieutenant, Hishel Osman, from Bilini neighbors of Geladewos's Betjuks of Senhit.[7]

Internally, seven major challenges or flaws troubled Zone Five. First, to prove himself, the zonal commander had boasted that when all Christians joined him, his zone would be the strongest as an end in and of itself. Second, organized former university students wanted to strengthen the zone as

[6] It is important to note that their modus operandi compounded the rivalry among the field commanders of the liberation army that had been coming to a head. This is mainly the rivalry between Mohammed Omar Abdellah ("Abu-Tyara") and, to some extent, Omer Damer, on one hand, and Omer Ezaz and Mahmoud Dinai, on the other.

[7] Haile "Deru'e" Weldetensae in Dan Connell, *Conversations with Eritrean Political Prisoners* (Trenton, NJ: Red Sea Press, 2005), 33ff. Having lived in the Kassala office of the ELF between late 1966 and 1967, Haile gives by far the most vivid depiction of the unfolding of these rivalries.

a means of bargaining with the ELF leadership to reform the entire organization. They warned the zonal commander from falling into the trap of
the divisive leaders. Third, Deputy Commander Hishel and his men were
there to ensure that Zone Five was in line with its purpose as a satellite of
Zone Two.[8] Fourth, the zone was poorly supplied because it was far from
the supply lines to and from friendly third-party countries and it lacked
a powerful patron among the political leaders. Fifth, this zone was in a
vast, poor, and densely populated territory where Ethiopia's control was
significantly stronger than in the rest of the country. Sixth, forces from the
neighboring zones are believed to have made incursions into the highlands
to support themselves, exposing Zone Five to the people's wrath but failing
to come to its rescue when cornered by Ethiopian counterinsurgency operations. Last, to make matters worse, the Revolutionary Command stripped
the zone of its main potential source of income. Zone Five included the
Eritrean capital Asmara, which was expected to generate great resources to
sustain the activities of the guerrillas. However, the Revolutionary Command took over Asmara as a national capital, and *fedayin* units, answerable
to the Revolutionary Command, ran activities and collected donations.[9]

The turning point for Zone Five took place in the summer of 1967, in the
aftermath of Ethiopia's sweeping counterinsurgency operation. The expansion of the ELF zones had intensified nationalist activities across the country
and had nudged Ethiopia out of its complacency. Just as Eritrean nationalists replicated the Algerian experience, the Ethiopian government resorted
to France's Challe Plan against the FLN, targeting one ELF division at a
time, starting with the highlands. After a shattering government operation
against Zone Five in mid-1967, the deputy commander of Zone Five, Hishel
Osman, accused his Christian fighters of failing to put up an effective resistance and executed dozens of them, in the absence of the Christian zone
commander Weldai Kahsai.[10] The latter then defected to Ethiopia, as did
dozens of other Christian fighters.[11] This may have reinforced the rampant
fear among ELA commanders that the influx of Christians into the struggle
was being orchestrated by Ethiopia in order to destroy the ELF from within.

---

[8] Haile in Connell, *Conversations*, 34–38.

[9] Haile in Connell, *Conversations*, 37.

[10] John Markakis, *National and Class Conflict in the Horn of Africa* (Cambridge: Cambridge
University Press, 1987), 122. This brutal and senseless act does not seem to have been
committed out of religious zeal as is widely believed. Hishel was known for being ruthlessly
nationalist and for taking harsh measures even against Muslims under his command whom
he suspected of not being nationalist enough. He came from a mixed Christian-Muslim
background from near Keren, and some of his closest cousins were Christians. Similarly,
Haile "Deru'e" emphasized the importance of the ethno-regionally centered loyalties over
religious ones. Hishel's assignment to the second highest position in Zone Five was necessitated by Geladewos's desire to have his kind control the zone and tip the balance in his
favor against Sabbe. Haile in Connell, *Conversations*, 34–38, 31–32.

[11] Markakis, *National and Class Conflicts*, 122.

But the distrust and fratricide along regional and religious lines boded ill to the Eritrean nationalist movement.

Elusive Reform of ELF Zonal Command and Bifurcation of the Eritrean Movement

As the spiraling Eritrean insurgency attracted – and the indiscriminate Ethiopian reprisals pushed – many Eritreans into the independence movement, ELF ranks grew increasingly diverse as its organizational weakness became manifest. Younger and more-educated volunteers found appalling the ELF's lack of a long-term strategic vision against Ethiopia, its ideological inconsistencies, and divisive mismanagement of the increasingly diverse fighters. No sooner did they seek to reform the organization into an all-embracing and effective revolutionary movement than the ELF started to target urbanites and the intelligentsia – Christian and Muslim alike – culminating in its implosion.

Three easily identifiable groups championed reform of the ELF in their respective clandestine ways until opportunities emerged to bring them out into the open. First, in a general air of malaise within and among the military zones, a few Sudan-based Muslim fighters could compare – because of their advantage of distance – the disparity even among the regular fighters in their day-to-day lives. They found it morally and politically unacceptable that fighters from some zones went without want (relatively speaking) while those from the highland-based zones were destitute.[12] Moreover, this same group of twelve "office-based" fighters – not without their own complaints about Zone One's domination by the Beni Amer or conversely about the Beni Amer's grumblings about them – worried about ELF's inconsistency. In the words of one of them, these fighters grew concerned about the wide perception that the ELF lacked "rules and regulations... [and about] the leadership which when in Saudi [Arabia] claimed to be Muslim, when in China to be communist."[13] This early soul-searching exercise grew to become the Islah Movement, which rocked the boat when like-minded and ideologically charged fighters joined it. These early *Islahiyeen* eluded repercussions (and possible elimination) by their political and military superiors

[12] According to Ibrahim Idris Totil (Interview: September 22–27, 2005, Asmara), a few of the Islahiyeen (like Mohammed Osman Ezaz) had served in the Revolutionary Command office in Kassala or were still working there, and all the fighters who came from the field for work or rest passed through that office, for any conscientious person to notice the disparity among the fighters along zonal lines.

[13] Interviews with Mohammed Osman Ezaz (September 3, 2005, Tessenei, Eritrea); and Mohammed Osman Ezaz (January 8, 1988) in RDC, ELF/UO, 0284, Günter Schröder, "Interviews of ELF history" (This is a compilation of interviews conducted by German scholar of the Horn of Africa, Günter Schröder, with veterans of the Eritrean independence war).

because their Syrian training and affiliation with Zone One (only two were from Zone Two) camouflaged their meetings either as friendly reunions or as Zone-related business.[14]

Shocked by the hostility that greeted them in the ELF, a second group of almost exclusively Tigrigna-speaking Christian fighters found the blatant leadership failures unlike the image they had created of the ELF before joining it in the mid-1960s.[15] Determined that it was time the reality matched with their vision, this group of reformers started to circulate their thoughts within a closely guarded circle of confidants. Considering the rising sectarian factionalism and the leaders' repressive acts, Haile "Deru'e" Weldetensae recalled that "clandestine organization within the ELF was the order of the day"[16] for the young, educated nationalists who saw the doomed path of their leaders. Influenced by the then growing international leftist tendencies, they concluded that they needed an ideology or a philosophy in a vanguard "revolutionary party" to turn the Eritrean struggle toward an all-embracing revolutionary movement capable of concurrently achieving independence and social transformation.[17]

Nevertheless, the inherent limitations of clandestine work in an environment highly charged with sectarian suspicion and hostility checked the activities of the above two groups. Both lacked the wherewithal to articulate and canvass the issues and mobilize grassroots support for reform within their respective zones much less without. That is when a convenient third coterie – an obscure Marxist study group of Muslim and Christian fighters – stepped in to fill the gap. From this group, the future secret parties of the Eritrean independence movement (one in the Eritrean Liberation Front another in the Eritrean People's Liberation Front) emerged. According to Tom Killion, this Marxist group was led by the influential ELF ideologue Azein Yassin and included leading figures of the previously mentioned second group.[18]

With these three groups, at least two of which had overlapping membership, the exchange of views and the demand for reform intensified; a

---

[14] Interview with Mohammed Osman Ezaz (September 3, 2005, Tessenei, Eritrea). By the time their existence became public, the Islah Movement was in full swing, and its sympathizers had grown too numerous across all the military zones for the leadership to suppress it.

[15] Most of these were members of secret nationalist organization in Asmara and Addis Ababa during their high school and university days, respectively. Dan Connell, "Inside the EPLF: The Origins of the 'People's Party' and its Role in the Liberation of Eritrea" in *Review of African Political Economy*, 28, no. 89 (2001): 347.

[16] Haile in Connell, *Conversations*, 29.

[17] Haile in Connell, *Conversations*, 42.

[18] Tom Killion, *Historical Dictionary of Eritrea* (Lanham, MD, and London: Scarecrow Press, Inc., 1998), 207–208. The fact that members of this group featured prominently in openly mobilizing for reform between 1968 and 1969, which was the unveiling of the covert reformist mobilization of the previous two years, led Killion to argue that the Marxist group founded the Islah Movement.

consensus on the need to restructure the resistance movement at large started to quickly take shape. Growing numbers of fighters from all zones joined the reformist chorus. In particular, the rank and file and the leaders of Zones Three, Four, and Five almost completely took it over as much out of necessity – in order to overcome their common logistical and other challenges – as out of revolutionary zeal. The summary execution of dozens of fighters of Zone Five in 1967, following the sweeping Ethiopian counterinsurgency operations in highland Eritrea earlier in the year, coupled with the consequent defections and confusion, left that division on the brink of complete disintegration. It also blew the lid off and unleashed the reformist avalanche that culminated in the ELF's eventual implosion.

The Revolutionary Command in Kassala acted swiftly to suspend Hishel from command of Zone Five. In his absence and that of his superior, zonal leadership fell on the next most-senior fighter, platoon commander Abdellah Idris Mohammed. A Beni Amer from the environs of Aqordat in Barka province, Abdellah had completed high school in Egypt and had received military training in Syria between 1966 and 1967, before returning to Eritrea.[19]

Meanwhile, the People's Republic of China had offered to train five political commissars for the ELF at the same time that the Revolutionary Command decided to establish a fifth zone. As a candidate political commissar for the soon-to-be Zone Five, Isaias Afwerki left for Maoist China between late 1966 and early 1967 for an extended training along with four other fighters (including Romedan Mohammed-Nur of Zone Four).[20] Against strict instructions and warnings from their superiors, and repeated threats from the other three co-trainees, Isaias and Romedan spoke of the flaws within the ELF and showed keen interest in the Chinese revolutionary war experience to remedy their own. They were spared persecution or even possible elimination because their return occurred at a critical juncture of Zone Five's near disintegration and the subsequent proliferation of the reform movement.[21] As political commissars of Zones Four and Five, Romedan and Isaias (their Cuban-trained counterparts arrived in 1968) helped provide necessary ideological and organizational cohesion to the amorphous body of reformists. They galvanized the latter with the immediate ripple effect of starting horizontal interaction among the military zones at the highest levels inside the country.

Arriving in Zone Five after Abdellah had assumed command, Isaias, in effect, became second in charge. In June 1968, the two convened the first meeting among all zonal commands – without notifying ELF political

---

[19] Interview with Ibrahim Idris Totil (September 22 and 27, 2005, Asmara, Eritrea).
[20] Interview with Romedan Mohammed-Nur (September 25, 2005); Haile in Connell, *Conversations*, 42–47.
[21] Interview with Romedan Mohammed-Nur (September 25, 2005).

leaders, much less seeking their approval. The participants deliberated on Zone Five's plight[22] and the endemic problems plaguing the entire ELF. Emboldened by their extreme predicament and assisted by demands for systemic reform of the ELF that had been swelling in the grassroots, the meeting discussed and identified mechanisms to overcome the independence movement's ugly reality.[23] These included ending the Algerian model of zonal division, unifying the armed forces under a military command based inside Eritrea, and organizing the Eritrean civilian population and respecting their rights.[24] The following month, at a follow-up meeting held at Aredeyib, zonal commanders and political commissars tentatively adopted the preceding items.[25]

However, two months later at the Anseba Conference, only Zones Three, Four, and Five went ahead with their plan and merged their forces under a provisional leadership made up of twelve elected leaders, the most notable of whom were Mohammed Ahmed Abdu, Romedan Mohammed-Nur, Abdellah Idris Mohammed, and Isaias Afwerki.[26] This merger mitigated the influence and authority of the Sudan-based Revolutionary Command. Nevertheless, during the following heady thirteen months (between July 1968 and August 1969) the ELF nearly split because Zones One and Two refused to join the unified force.[27] Eventually, the two zones relented – perceiving the danger posed by the unified force (pejoratively called "tripartite force" by their opponents) and pressured by their own democratic and nonparochial members – and consented to merge with the rest of the forces.[28]

---

[22] These included the execution of Christian fighters, the planned ELA attacks on Eritrean civilians suspected of being armed by Ethiopia, and the looting of civilian property.

[23] Interview with Romedan Mohammed-Nur (September 25, 2005).

[24] Alamin Mohammed Said, *Al-Defe' wa al-Teredi: Al-Thewra al-Iritriyah. Qisat al-Inshiqaq al-Dakhiliyah Lil-Thewra-al-Iritriyah* (Asmara: Dogoli Printing Press, 1992), 22; and Haile in Connell, *Conversations*, 48–49.

[25] Although the military commanders of first and second zones and the entire Supreme Council declined the invitation to participate, the Aredeyib Meeting was attended by all five zonal political commissars, three military commanders and Omer Damr and Mohammed Omer Abdellah "Abu Tyara," the leaders of the ELF training center and reinforcement contingent, respectively.

[26] Alamin, *Al-Defe' wa al-Teredi*, 23.

[27] Ibid.

[28] Those who broke away from the ELF claim that it was only after the leaders of Zones One and Two found like-minded parochial elements within the tripartite forces that they agreed to merge their forces certain that they would prevail over the younger more radical fighters who had been advocating for change. For their part, reformists who remained with the ELF insist that the leaders of Zones One and Two came under intense internal pressure from their own fighters, and gave in to the broader demand for change. These two explanations are not necessarily mutually exclusive. Both factors – the threat of the tripartite force and pressure from their democratic and nonparochial constituents – must have played a role in persuading the two zonal commanders to eventually consent and join the rest of the forces.

At a landmark meeting held at Adobha in August 1969, the zonal division was abolished at one fell swoop.[29] The five zones were consolidated under a single Eritrea-based leadership called the Provisional General Command (PGC or, in its Arabic acronym, al-qiyadah al-'ama al-muaqetah).[30] Leaving the absentee political leadership intact, the PGC's mandate was to oversee internal matters and lead the army until a permanent body was elected at a national congress within a year.

Jointly headed by Mohammed Ahmed Abdu and Romedan Mohammed-Nur, and including Isaias Afwerki and Abdellah Idris among thirty-four others, the PGC was too big and too diverse to lead the ELF with cohesion and unity of purpose. Moreover, as the unity of the field force denied the rival Supreme Council triumvirate of their traditional clients, Sabbe sought to reposition himself in the new context by flexing his control of the ELF's logistical and materiel pipelines. In November 1969, he in effect dissolved the Supreme Council by launching a new Oman-based General Secretariat (Al-Aman al-'Amah) in isolation of the other members of the ELF's political leadership. To the consternation of emergent power centers, he approached the PGC to discuss the new ways ahead.[31]

Birth of a Secret Party and the Immediate Causes of Breakup

Parallel to the overt project of structurally reforming the ELF's zonal formation, some fighters were quietly searching for permanent mechanisms of resolving the independence movement's strategic leadership shortcomings: ideological, political, and military. In November 1968, leading ELF ideologues like Azein Yassin and Saleh Iyay, among others, secretly set up an Eritrean Democratic Working People's Party (commonly known as Labor Party) as a revolutionary core to steer the movement from within its highest leadership.[32] According to leading Horn of Africa scholar John Markakis, Labor Party founders, in their own words, aimed "'to secure power in the ELF for the revolutionary forces', in order ultimately 'to establish a socialist state in Eritrea.'"[33]

[29] The full detail of what happened between July 1968 and August 1969, when a unified ELF-wide leadership emerged, remains unclear.
[30] This organization was made up of eighteen elected members from the tripartite force, plus ten each from Zones One and Two. It is widely believed that the two zones insisted that they select their representatives, but Mohammed Osman Ezaz (Interview, September 3, 2005, Tessenei, Eritrea) insists that the Commander of Zone One dismissed the appointed representatives and demanded that elected representatives represent his zone.
[31] Interviews with Romedan Mohammed-Nur (September 25, 2005); and Ibrahim Idris Totil (September 22 and 27, 2005, Asmara, Eritrea).
[32] Interviews with Ibrahim Idris Totil (September 22 and 27, 2005, Asmara, Eritrea); and Mohammed Osman Ezaz (September 3, 2005, Tessenei, Eritrea). See also Herui Tedla Bairu's January 1, 2001 interview with awate.com: http://www.awate.com/portal/content/view/352/11/.
[33] Markakis, *National and Class Conflicts*, 128–129.

In the absence of cohesion and unity of purpose within the PGC, the Labor Party's ideologically driven decisiveness accrued sufficient influence. It played an important role during the crucial months between 1969 and 1970. When Sabbe's divorce from the Supreme Council in November 1969 raised the specter of fragmentation, leaving the PGC precariously indecisive, the secret party's unequivocal stand against the splintering of the ELF held sway among powerful PGC elements. They swiftly moved in December to disband what was left of the Supreme Council as a political structure.[34] Nevertheless, its impromptu decisiveness reaped it exactly what it sought to avoid; precisely because of what the new leadership did and what it failed to do, nearly exclusive groups – reflecting the religious and sectarian gulf – congregated out of the mother organization's reach amid a renewed atmosphere of fear and disillusionment.

Whereas a number of fighters were disenchanted by either the removal of their patrons or the PGC's transgression of its agreed-upon mandate, several factors converged to implode the ELF from within. First, the fear among Marxist founders of the Labor Party and among prominent fighters from the Beni Amer of being dominated by Sabbe and his coregionists led to the arrest of some fellow leaders and expulsion of their alleged loyalist fighters.[35] In protest, the former commander of Zone Four Mohammed Ali Omaro filed his formal dissociation from the PGC in a letter addressed to his fellow leaders. Stating the irreversibility of his resignation from leadership, and his readiness to serve as a regular fighter, he wrote, "may God give us consensus" in the interest of the Eritrean people.[36]

---

[34] Interview with Ibrahim Idris Totil (September 22 and 27, 2005, Asmara, Eritrea).

[35] The arrested members of the PGC were former leaders of Zone Four who were close to Osman Saleh Sabbe. According to Mohammed Osman Ezaz, these individuals were arrested because they allegedly refused to merge their forces under the newly formed PGC. That is, however questionable because Zone Four had already united its forces during the pre-PGC tripartite merger and command had moved away from those who had previously assumed the zone's leadership. Ibrahim Idris Totil (Interview, September 22 and 27, 2005, Asmara, Eritrea) offers a more plausible explanation in that the PGC hardliners discovered some of the communications between their arrested counterparts and Sabbe in which the former essentially spoke of themselves as the latter's loyalists (whether out of their regionalist/sectarian allegiance to him or because of the expediency of having a resourceful patron or some combination of both is unknown). Totil also believes that Abdellah Idris and his security assistant Hussein Khalifa and other loyalists of the former Zone One command and its patron Idris Mohammed Adem knew beforehand the reasons and timing of the arrest of these individuals. Interview with Ibrahim Idris Totil (September 22 and 27, 2005, Asmara, Eritrea).

[36] Rough English translation of this letter is included in RDC/ELF/UO, 02847, Günter Schröder, "Interviews on E.L.F. History." A few months later, Omaro articulated the points of divergence with the ELF at a crucial seminar he held for a large crowd of ELF members in the eastern Sudanese city of Ghedarif, splitting the grassroots supporters and cementing the splintering of the ELF.

Sabbe received these disillusioned fighters, and many others, in Khartoum, before flying them to Aden and sailing them back to Eritrea to link up with a similar group that remained in the Denkalia region of Eritrea in mid-1970. At a founding conference in Sodah-Ela, they formed the first of two Popular Liberation Forces (PLF 1) that later merged to become a potent rival to the ELF. Although the ranks of the PLF 1 hailed from the eastern lowlands, fighters from other regions – the late Abu Tyara, Omar Damr, Measho Embaye and Mesfen Hagos – had joined it from the outset.[37]

Second, a new mass arrest, torture, and killing of Christian fighters between late 1969 and early 1970[38] and the simultaneous assassination of two other fighters in Kassala who had played a crucial role in the clandestine reform movement[39] wrenched the largest number of Christian fighters out of the ELF. They congregated around Abraham Tewelde in Ala in early 1970. Like Omaro before him, the former political commissar of Zone Five, Isaias Afwerki, filed his break with the PGC in writing before he went on to play a decisive role in the Christian group. "It is enough," he wrote, that he had kept his misgivings to himself in the interest of maintaining some harmony within the leadership but that he rejected being part of what he called "a flushing whip under a secret leadership," referring to the Labor Party's influence in PGC decisions.[40] Isaias joined the group – shortly after the death of Abraham – and formed Selfi Natsinet Ertra (the Eritrean Freedom Party). In August 1971, they held a conference at a place called Tekhli and announced their transformation into the Popular Liberation Forces, hence PLF 2. A period of tense interaction ensued – filled with suspicion and, at times, open hostility – between the two groups in order to unify their ranks.[41]

Third, the security and military chiefs of the PGC were locked in their own power struggle to mobilize their respective ethnic and/or sectarian groups, the Bilin and Beni Amer, respectively, who had already been unnerved by the removal of their Supreme Council patrons.[42] The Beni Amer elements

[37] Alamin, *Al-Defe' wa al-Teredi*, 82–84; and Gaim Kibreak, *Critical Reflections on the Eritrean War of Independence. Social Capital, Associational Life, Religion, Ethnicity and Sowing Seeds of Dictatorship* (Trenton, NJ, and Asmara: Red Sea Press, 2008), 203–204.
[38] This is what has since come to be called Seriyet Addis for all three hundred fresh volunteers had come from Addis Ababa.
[39] These are Kidane Kiflu and Weldai Ghidey, who were knifed to death by their assailants who were allegedly trying to apprehend them and get them across the border into Eritrea. Markakis, *National and Class Conflicts*, 126–127.
[40] Rough English translations of the two letters are included in ELF/UO, 02847, Günter Schröder, "Interviews on E.L.F. History."
[41] A wave of leftover sectarianism rocked PLF 1 during this time and its members who hailed either from other regions parted ways with it, with the Tigrigna-speaking Christians joining PLF 2. Mesfen Hagos, for example, joined Isaias and others in the leadership of PLF 2. Alamin, *Al-Defe' wa al-Teredi*, 86ff; and Gaim, *Critical Reflection*, 205–206.
[42] Alamin, *Al-Defe' wa al-Teredi*, 85–86; and Markakis, *National and Class Conflict*, 127.

to this rivalry are also believed to have fallen for Idris Mohammed Adem's personal scheme to counter and neutralize Sabbe's unilateral launching of the General Secretariat.[43] Under the guise of being dominated, PGC members Adem Saleh, Ahmed Adem Omar, Osman Ajib, Mohammed Ahmed Idris, and their small force, thus, parted company with the ELF in November 1970 to form what came to be popularly known as the Obel group. Before its liquidation in the hands of what remained of the ELF, this group briefly joined in PLF 1's and PLF 2's efforts to merge.

Confounded by the speed with which things were steering out of control, what remained of the PGC rushed to convene a National Congress. Composition of the large Preparatory Committee caused a further stir among even more fighters. In a clear sign of Labor Party's role, young, left-leaning fighters, among them Ahmed Nasser Mohammed, Abdellah Idris, and the newly arrived Herui Tedla led the Preparatory Committee. Most members of the Preparatory Committee (and certainly the aforementioned three) were either already members of Labor Party or quickly became members before their ascent to the ELF's topmost offices – all subsequent leaders of the ELF had to be members of Labor Party. The revelation of a secret leadership within the fragmented leadership heightened the pre-existing atmosphere of distrust and ruled out the emergence of a "correct leadership" under which Omaro, Isaias, and their colleagues said they were prepared to serve.[44]

Having failed to reform the ELF from within, Eritrean reformists sought to do so from without. Effective reorientation of the existing grand strategy of the Eritrean independence struggle was not accomplished until the splinter groups united to offer a viable alternative in the Eritrean People's Liberation Front (EPLF).[45] EPLF founders set out to turn their vision to reality by structuring and leading the new organization in ways they deemed the ELF failed to do. Meanwhile, the ELF's National Congress had concluded that the Eritrean field could only accommodate one organization and resolved to liquidate the splinter groups.[46] And the splinter groups posed an even

---

[43] Interview with Romedan Mohamed-Nur (September 25, 2005, Asmara Eritrea). But the EPLF's argument is that Idris Mohammed Adem stayed on with the ELF after securing the loyalty of the all powerful Abdellah Idris, the single most decisive person in the ELF since the early 1970s (first as chief of security and then as chief of military staff but never as the highest official of the ELF). The EPLF also claims that it is only after such a deal that Idris Mohammed Adem reigned in commanders of Zones One and Two to merge their forces into a unified, Eritrea-wide liberation army.

[44] Rough English translations of Isaias and Omaro's letters are included in RDC/ELF/UO, 02847, Günter Schröder, "Interviews on E.L.F. History."

[45] Although the EPLF started to take shape in 1973, it was not officially called so until its First Congress of 1977.

[46] Proponents and apologists of this resolution insist that there were special provisions to bring back the Christian group through negotiations. EPLF writings later counter this claim by stating that whatever the congress decided, Abdellah Idris (as chief of ELF military) had authorized his commanders to launch military operations against all splinters, Christian and

greater danger to the Ethiopian government. As a result, both the ELF and Ethiopian government forces geared up to destroy these disparate groups, ironically, expediting their merger and consolidation into a cohesive force that outlasted its rival and defeated the enemy – discussed in following chapters.

Ineffectual Experiment of the East Timorese Resistance

In the confusion of Indonesian airborne units sustaining heavy casualties from retreating FALINTIL and coming under friendly fire from their own advancing marines, FRETILIN leaders ensured the continuation of the resistance by exiting Dili and congregating in the rugged interior toward Aileu. Nevertheless, the brutality that attended the capture of Dili took all East Timorese aback – even those who had anticipated the imminent Indonesian assault. Radio signals in the northern Australian city of Darwin picked up East Timor's Minister of Information, Alarico Fernandes's desperate SOS message: "Indonesian forces have been landed in Dili by sea . . . They are flying over Dili dropping out paratroopers . . . A lot of people have been killed indiscriminately . . . we are going to be killed. SOS, we call for your help, this is an urgent call."[47]

FALINTIL special forces commander Paulino Gama (Mauk Muruk) recounted the circumstances of what he calls FRETILIN's strategic withdrawal: "In the face of these Indonesian atrocities and shocked by the sheer scale of the invasion, the surviving population and the FALINTIL units made a strategic withdrawal to the mountains in order to regroup and reorganize a more effective resistance."[48] Although FRETILIN stood up to the test, efforts to regroup and reorganize were difficult and short-lived. Meanwhile, FALINTIL units continued to delay Indonesian advances, at times engaging in hand-to-hand combat with the invaders. FRETILIN leaders, along with the artillerymen stationed in the hills overlooking Dili, watched in desperation. They could not fire at the invaders in the middle of the confusion in downhill Dili, and Indonesian warships were out of reach of their line of fire. Ducking under cover every time Indonesian ships fired toward them, a junior FRETILIN leader, Xanana Gusmão relates what he saw:

Muslim alike. Be that as it may, the prospect of a negotiated return of the splinters faded as it was not accompanied with sufficient change to assure the splinters. The unification of Eritrean independence fighter has since remained elusive.

[47] Radio message from the Minster of Information of the Democratic Republic of East Timor, Alarico Fernandes quoted in Jill Jolliffe, *East Timor: Nationalism and Colonialism* (Queensland: University of Queensland Press, 1978), 3.

[48] Paulino Gama, "The War in the Hills, 1975–1985: A Fretilin Commander Remembers" in *East Timor at the Crossroads: The Forging of a Nation* ed. Peter Carey and G. Carter Bentley (Honolulu: University of Hawaii Press, 1995), 98.

arriving at Balibar at *Comando da Luta*...we found Nicolau in command. We would look towards Dili whenever the firing of the Miriam gun and naval artillery allowed us to poke our heads over a hill or out from behind a tree. Sebastiao Sarmento tried to aim [the artillery] at the ships anchored in the port. We witnessed days of pillage through [a] huge pair of powerful binoculars. The weapons of war were vomiting fire over Dili's hills while cargo ships emptied the customs house of its contents.[49]

Retaining the initiative, Indonesian advances endangered the safety of Aileu[50] as the headquarters of the Comando da Luta. The latter shuttled between Aileu and Maubisse with only RDTL Prime Minister Lobato exercising some command, but failing to fully control all those under him. Restive FRETILIN leaders in the far west corner of the country, for example, engaged in the extrajudicial killing of East Timorese whom they had imprisoned during the brief internecine conflict of 1975. In Aileu and Same, some FRETILIN leaders eliminated or planned to eliminate dozens of UDT and APODETI prisoners who had been in their custody.[51] Apparently failing to restrain the undisciplined FRETILIN leaders in the field, Lobato returned to Comando da Luta headquarters[52] and reportedly ordered the special forces (and possibly senior FALINTIL commanders) to Same instead.

Paulino Gama and several senior FALINTIL commanders rushed there with hopes of controlling the situation but arrived a little too late for the roomful of Timorese prisoners who had been massacred in retaliation for a few escapees.[53] According to the commander of the special forces, he and his colleagues freed about forty prisoners and marched toward his home district

[49] Sarah Niner (ed.), *To Resist Is to Win! The Autobriography of Zanana Gusmão with Selected Letters and Speeches* (Richmond, Australia: Urora Books, 2000), 38.

[50] The town of Aileu fell to the Indonesians in February 1976 but the district of Aileu continued to be an important hub of the resistance as Indonesian control was limited to the towns and the main roads connecting them.

[51] Xavier do Amaral testified before the CAVR and repeatedly told me in several occasions that FRETILIN's highest leaders (mainly himself and Lobato) arrived in Aileu too late to spare the massacred prisoners the fate that faced them. That assertion, however, assumes that these two leaders and their subordinates exercised control over some of the undisciplined FRETILIN cadres, which becomes questionable in light of subsequent developments.

[52] Gusmão relates how he accompanied Nicolau to restive Same in December 1975/January 1976 around the same time that some prisoners were executed. Niner, *To Resist is to Win!*, 39.

[53] According to CAVR, *Chega!*, Part 7.2: Unlawful Killings and Enforced Disappearances, p. 54, other FALINTIL commanders from the eastern parts of East Timor who disagreed with the killings rushed to Same to rescue the prisoners. These leaders – Guido Soares, Paulino Gama, Ologari Aswain and others – confronted the executioners, narrowly escaping a shootout. The same section of the CAVR report gives an extensive account of these and other similar intra-Timorese killings and violations of human rights.

of Baucau,[54] where he and FRETILIN Central Committee (CCF) member Vicente Sahe joined forces.

Assuming political and military command, Sahe and Gama helped consolidate the resistance in their native locales in the easternmost districts of Baucau, Viqueque, and Lautem (also known by Lospalos, its capital). Later divided into Centro Leste (Center East) and Ponta Leste (Eastern Point) sectors, these operational zones were developed to become safe havens of the resistance. The guerrilla units kept harassing Indonesian forces through ambushes in open areas and surprise attacks.[55] Although that added considerably to their experience in mobile warfare, their political work refined their methods of securing active support (or at least favorable neutrality) of the population residing in their own homes as opposed to the FRETILIN-controlled areas that later on developed into Bases de Apoio. Although this was the earliest uncentralized, postinvasion mobilization of traditional, kinship-based allegiance to the independence movement, FRETILIN leadership quickly agreed to draw on traditional, kinship-based support, parallel to its nonsectarian revolutionary following among the population.

Rampant disillusionment in the immediate aftermath of the invasion demanded that resistance command be decentralized and the fight be carried out from all corners of the country that FALINTIL rank and file had withdrawn (or retired) to. In a tacit approval of those who had remained in their home districts from the beginning, like Sahe in Baucau, Lobato let the CCF members around him "choose their own direction."[56] Nevertheless, with no coordination mechanism in place, and the sense of common purpose not sufficiently ingrained, the scene was set for deadly parochialism, suspicion, and lack of cooperation among the members of CCF who would lead the resistance.

---

[54] Gusmão confirms: "I should say, nevertheless, that the Firakus [warriors from the eastern part of East Timor] freed a lot of the UDT prisoners, taking them along with them to their areas." Niner, *To Resist Is to Win!*, 39. While there is no doubt that Gusmão is referring to Paulino Gama and his forces, it is not clear if his calling them by the traditional warrior name (Firakus) is romanticizing them or denigrating them by not calling them FALINTIL special forces, which they were. I suspect that the latter is the case in light of the dynamics of relations between Xanana and Paulino that resulted in Paulino's surrender to the Indonesians in 1984 and Gusmão's writing of his autobiography after his capture in 1992. Without giving the details of who freed whom or how many, CAVR, *Chega!*, Part 7.2, also claims that the commanders from the east freed many prisoners and took them along.

[55] One famous example of such ambushes was planned and executed by Paulino's brother, Cornelio Gama (also known as L-7) around April 1976. An entire Indonesian battalion was ambushed and many of its weapons captured. Interviews with Cornelio Gama "L-7" (July 1, 2006, Laga, Baucau, East Timor) and Paulino Gama (October 9, 2007, Rijswijk, the Netherlands).

[56] Niner, *To Resist Is to Win!*, p. 40.

Commanding only a platoon of archers, Gusmão, for example, opted to go to his home district of Manatuto with "fewer than a dozen arms." Upon hearing that FALINTIL guerrillas in Baucau had captured weapons, Gusmão visited Sahe and asked him for some. The latter reportedly told him that the news of captured weapons was propaganda fabrication intended to boost the morale of their forces.[57] Nonetheless, Paulino and Cornelio Gama (older and younger brothers, respectively) confirm the successful ambush of an Indonesian battalion and the capture of many weapons.[58] If the Gama brothers were right, Sahe's negative response to Gusmão's request perhaps reflects the lack of coordination and possibly rivalry at the highest levels of the resistance where no centralized leadership yet existed. Nor was this an isolated case. On the western side of the country, for example, a former company commander confirms that units took isolated initiative in their respective localities and that "[s]ome sub-districts had plenty of weapons, while others didn't have any weapons at all."[59]

By and large, therefore, the resistance was in total disarray. FALINTIL's chain of command fell apart, and consequently units seeking to continue the fighting lacked communication, and their scattered resistance remained ineffective at containing the advances of the Indonesian forces, much less in reversing the invasion. Without leadership and guidance, others took a resigned attitude or completely retired from any meaningful engagements. Several mobile units, including FALINTIL special forces that were made up of armed civilians, under individual initiative of their commanders moved around the country in narrowing circuits, nibbling at the edges of Indonesian forces. Meanwhile, in the central area between Aileu and Maubisse, FRETILIN's top leadership was grappling with mechanisms to reorganize the resistance and attend to the needs of the tens of thousands of civilians who fled the Indonesian invasion.

East Timorese nationalists had inflicted sufficient confusion and damage to the invading forces that subsequent Indonesian preparations to invade the hinterland took several months. That afforded FRETILIN breathing space to recuperate from the shock of the initial assault and to try to devise better means of resistance. During the brief lull in fighting, FRETILIN Secretary General Lobato called upon all of FRETILIN's leadership to meet and map out a new strategy for combating the invading forces. Between May 20 and June 2, 1976, the resistance's leadership convened the Soibada Conference in Manatuto district. FRETILIN President Francisco Xavier do Amaral, whose training as a seminarian may have caused him to be suspicious of his colleagues' ideological leanings, disapproved of the ideologically

---

[57] Ibid., 41–42.

[58] Interviews with Cornelio Gama "L-7" (July 1, 2006, Laga, Baucau, East Timor) and Paulino Gama (October 9, 2007, Rijswijk, the Netherlands).

[59] Filomeno Paixão quoted in CAVR, *Chega!*, Part 5: Resistance: Structure and Strategy, 7.

charged proceedings of the conference. He warned against the futility of an ideologized and unrealistic approach to their predicament.

Dominated by Hamis Bassarewan (Hata), Antonio Duarte Carvarino, Sahe, and Lobato,[60] however, the deliberations at Soibada left no room for equivocation. FRETILIN adopted as a principle Amilcar Cabral's dictum of "class suicide," whereby the upper classes would abdicate their privileged status in a bid to create a classless society. To that effect, Lobato and Joaquim Nascimento gave up their private coffee plantations. By contrast, do Amaral's refusal to partake in the ideological communion was perceived as contravening the approved path. Failing to dissuade the attendees, do Amaral fell back on his ceremonial role of opening and closing meetings at Soibada and altogether avoided subsequent meetings.[61] Gusmão later scathingly criticized do Amaral for having enjoyed "his kingdom [in Turiscai] leading a carefree life under the feudalistic care of his brother."[62]

At Soibada, the leadership almost completely overhauled the previous structure and strategy (or lack thereof) and charted out a new course of action along the lines of PAIGC in Guinea Bissau. Accordingly, the country was divided into six sectors (not drastically different from the military zones in Eritrea) that were further subdivided into smaller administrative units: region, zone, village, and sub-village. Maoist teaching that a people's war must serve a matching revolutionary political objective worked on the residues of the *apartidarismo* doctrine to dictate that political commissars held supreme authority within their respective sectors.[63] Finally, FRETILIN proceeded to adapt its "principles of the Maubere Revolution": protracted people's war and self-reliance.[64]

Inception and End of Guerrilla Support Bases

Three times in the twentieth century, East Timor suffered foreign invasion and Portugal's crude counterinsurgency, triggering mass flight to the mountainous hinterlands for safety.[65] Likewise, the looming clouds of war that presaged all-out Indonesian invasion triggered a mass exodus of

---

[60] The first three belong to the group of East Timorese students who returned from Portugal in September 1974 and are allegedly responsible for radicalizing ASDT into FRETILIN. Although a practicing Catholic, Lobato was known for being strict with discipline and a staunch advocate of self-reliance.

[61] As Gusmão put it in his typical criticism of do Amaral, "Xavier, failing to deter the revolutionary avalanche of minds, limited his participation to saying, 'Comrades, the session is open', or 'Because of the late hour the meeting is closed.'" Niner, *To Resist Is to Win*, 43.

[62] Niner, *To Resist Is to Win*, 40.

[63] CAVR, *Chega!*, Part 5: Resistance: Structure and Strategy, 4–8.

[64] CAVR, *Chega!*, Part 5: Resistance: Structure and Strategy, 5.

[65] These were the ruthless suppression, in 1912, of Dom Boaventura's uprising; the 1941 Australian landing in the island of Timor as a forward line of defense against possible Japanese attack on Australia and consequent Japanese invasion of the island, leading to

East Timorese civilians. Supporters and nonsupporters of FRETILIN alike formed "an interminable line of people stream[ing] upwards" out of harm's way and into the rugged interior.[66] FRETILIN spared no effort – cases of abuse notwithstanding – to cater to the needs of these internally displaced persons (IDPs). As its fledgling political establishment was not equipped to handle the scale of social pressure, however, in the early stages its cadres and soldiers only led the fleeing civilians to places where they could find basic shelter and supplies of food and water. The population of the interior helped feed and shelter the exodus of IDPs, along with the FALINTIL among them, until they started to support themselves, raising animals and/or farming patches of land that their hosts offered them.[67]

As incessant Indonesian offensives denied the uprooted civilians any breathing space and at the same time increased their numbers, the independence movement had to come up with systematic mechanisms of addressing the issue in ways that also benefitted the struggle. Soibada conference's drive for a self-reliant people's war had already called for, among other things, the organization and consolidation of the civilian population in the *zonas libertadas*, the FRETILIN-controlled areas, into Bases de Apoio. These support bases were conceived as a core of what might have been an effective apparatus of resistance.

Debates surrounding the Bases de Apoio – their formation and their collapse – epitomize the ill-fated strategic experiments of the East Timorese independence movement. In line with the revolutionary principle that nonconventional war only survives by relying on civilian populations, these Bases de Apoio were expected to serve that purpose: help supply FALINTIL with basic provisions, hide and recuperate the combatants, replenish their ranks, and so on. It was also expected that mobilizing the civilian population into a great revolutionary storm would cleanse society of internal nonprogressive values and practices, and free them from foreign domination. As Gusmão writes, "We had just begun the war and the people were with us [in the interior].... Bases de Apoio were implemented as a mechanism to organize people so they could continue to fight in the war [by providing] logistical and political support, which we could describe as revolution."[68]

Just as FRETILIN exerted a concerted effort to turn the mass exodus of the civilian population into political and military assets for the resistance,

---

massive casualties among the Timorese; and the abortive anti-Portuguese uprising of 1959, which was suppressed in heavy-handed fashion.

[66] Niner, *To Resist Is to Win*, 39.

[67] An example of this is Constâncio Pinto's account of his family's and that of other IDPs' experience in the villages of Bereliurai. Constâncio Pinto and Matthew Jardine, *East Timor's Unfinished Struggle: Inside the Timorese Resistance* (Boston: South End Press, 1997), 44.

[68] Quoted in Ibid., p. 9. It is widely believed that radical elements within FRETILIN envisioned the creation of such a revolutionary society/nation by implementing their ideals in small-scale, manageable groups of people as the Bases de Apoio.

the uprooted civilians benefited from its initiatives between 1975 and 1977. Officials were assigned to oversee various projects, such as education, health and, most importantly, food production. Civilians started to cultivate the fields to sustain themselves and the independence fighters. The movement made a modest effort to produce medicines and offer basic health care services to the population under its control.[69] It also offered them some level of security, while the able-bodied IDPs received military training as Força Auto Defeça (FADE, Self-Defense Forces or militias).[70] Other civilians set up various socioeconomic and military groupings in their respective localities to bolster the resistance. Although lacking uniformity, FRETILIN's earlier programs on literacy and cooperatives resumed in the Bases de Apoio.

Nonetheless, the formation of a progressive society rooted in the Bases de Apoio was not as practical in East Timor as it may have been conceptually sound. Because these bases were not organic, the war-displaced population first had to find a place that ensured their physical and psychological safety; get acclimatized to their new way of life in, or next to, a war zone; and develop their own survival skills. Only then could they support the resistance by becoming the driving force of the envisioned revolutionary society.[71] Most importantly, the flourishing of civilian bases required some safety behind a defensible line, and a cross-border sanctuary out of Indonesian reach. Unlike Eritrea, East Timor did not have any of these necessary preconditions of relative safety.

Geographically, East Timor was too small for any part of the country to be beyond the line of fire of Indonesian forces. Indonesia's heavy-handed counterinsurgency made it impossible for the Bases de Apoio to hold out for long. Direct Indonesian assault or dangerous proximity to the fighting

---

[69] As a former nurse, Lucas da Costa and other health professionals were trying to coordinate the delivery of basic health care services to people in and around FRETILIN-held territories since Indonesian invasion. Interview with Lucas da Costa (April 8 and 12, 2006, Dili, East Timor). Similarly, Constâncio Pinto's father continued giving medical services to the people of their host village. Interview with Constâncio Pinto (April 13, 2006, Dili, East Timor); and Pinto and Jardine, *East Timor's Unfinished Struggle*, 46–47. See also John G. Taylor, *East Timor" The Price of Freedom* (London and New York: Zed Books, 1999), 82.

[70] At the age of twelve years, Constâncio carried a gun and essentially joined the thousands of FRETILIN militias many of whom were his age and older. Interview with Constâncio Pinto (April 13, 2006, Dili, East Timor); and Pinto and Jardine, *East Timor's Unfinished Struggle*, 46–47.

[71] By contrast, and as will be seen in more detail in subsequent chapters, civilian support bases served the Eritrean nationalists very well. But the Eritrean resistance did not develop such civilian bases in the liberated area until the late 1970s when it was using all the forms of protracted people's war (hit-and-run mobile warfare, guerrilla warfare, and conventional warfare). Moreover, at that stage in the Eritrean struggle, there had developed a secure rear base behind a clear, defensible line where almost permanent civilian settlements flourished and the resistance headquarters resided.

deprived the civilian population of breathing space to sustain itself, much less nurture a revolution. Isolated from the rest of the world by complete Indonesian encirclement of their half island country, East Timorese resistance fighters lacked access to a cross-border third-party sanctuary in the event of an Indonesian breakthrough into their safe havens or support bases.

To make matters worse, the deployed Indonesian soldiers heavily outnumbered East Timorese independence fighters. Since Soibada, there existed six sectors in East Timor with an average of 2.5 companies per sector. Each company had an average of three platoons, and each platoon was made up of three squads of a maximum of nine men (and later women) each. That brought regular FALINTIL forces to no more than 1,500 strong, which was infrequently assisted by thousands of militias. At any given time, the Indonesian forces in East Timor numbered a minimum of 15,000 well-armed and supplied soldiers with aerial and naval support, resources that the East Timorese nationalists completely lacked. Taking the entire 15,000-square-kilometer country as the theater of operation, the ratio of this conservative figure of Indonesian soldiers to FALINTIL resistance fighters to the landmass was 15:1:15. Besides its endemic shortage of logistics and materiel, this ratio goes to show that FALINTIL was numerically disadvantaged to ensure the safety of their bases.

John Taylor explains how FALINTIL survived as a liberation army by falling back on an effective and time-honored resistance strategy: rallying vast familial and kinship networks against foreign invasion and occupation. In spite of Portuguese colonial control, Timorese society managed to preserve itself and reproduce its sociocultural and economic systems by retaining its tradition of kinship exchanges.[72] So powerful were kinship-based alliances against foreign intrusion that in 1882, the colonial governor complained that "There has not yet been a single rebellion against the Portuguese flag which is not based in the alliances which result from marital exchange."[73] Taylor argues that such a system survived the brief Japanese interlude and the restored Portuguese colonialism to backstop the nationalist movement against Indonesian secondary colonialism.[74] Sara Niner's biography of second-generation resistance leader Xanana Gusmão best demonstrates this point. Gusmão is shown forging lasting bonds of loyalty and interdependence with individual persons and sacred houses, who, at their own peril, would put their vast kinship and worship networks at his disposal. These were also a beginning and a mainstay of the robust but elusive clandestine front.[75] When localized, kin-based approaches conflicted with the

---

[72] Taylor, *East Timor*, 5–9.
[73] Quoted in Taylor, *East Timor*, 11.
[74] Taylor, *East Timor*, 95, 115.
[75] Sara Niner, *Xanana: Leader of the Struggle for Independent Timor-Leste* (Melbourne: Australian Scholarly Publishing, 2009).

resistance's nationwide strategies, the nationalist movement endeavored to give precedence to the latter. Although it was generally successful in doing this, the few cases in which it failed to rein in traditional identities and loyalties, or harmonize them with its national priorities, shook the movement from within.

The best such example is that of FRETILIN founding President Francisco Xavier do Amaral, who also belongs to the Turiscai-based chiefly families of the Mambai people. These traditional ties had initially won FRETILIN solid support among his people, but when his strategic disagreements with the rest of the revolutionaries set in, he simply retired to his support home base with dire implications to the nationalist movement. Although do Amaral's lack of ideological enthusiasm is well documented, his objection to the decisions at Soibada was a practical one. He argued that the presence of the civilian population was a burden to the fighters who needed to be highly mobile. A prolonged war of resistance that relied on civilian support bases – which would need to be defended by the guerillas – would only deplete FRETILIN's resources. As a result, he suggested freeing FALINTIL from the civilian burden by allowing the latter to return to their previous lives. Not only would they be spared suffering, he argued, but perhaps they also would become an additional source of support to the resistance within the enemy.[76]

This position earned do Amaral the harshest condemnation possible. Lobato called him "an imperialist lackey...trying to undermine...the unity of Fretilin Central Committee, to cause confusion in its ranks, and thus weaken the struggle for the noble cause of liberation of our people."[77] But do Amaral proved to be an ember that almost set the resistance ablaze, and Gusmão could not have been more right when he said that "Xavier [do Amaral] was...like a flame that is not quite extinguished; not shining but refusing to go out."[78] Because of do Amaral's reasoning and perhaps his position in society, his objection to Soibada sent shockwaves that rocked the resistance from within. Consequent internal dissent was brought under control only through the gruesome arrest, torture, and execution of most of the dissenters and their actual or suspected sympathizers.

Former soldiers and the civilians-turned-fighters uniformly challenged the Soibada resolutions once they were communicated to FALINTIL commanders (none of whom had attended the landmark political event). They saw the incongruence of guerrilla warfare with maintaining the Bases de Apoio

---

[76] Interview with Francisco Xavier do Amaral (July 8, 2006, Dili, East Timor).

[77] Speech of Nicolau Lobato on Radio Maubere, September 14, 1977. A full transcription of the speech is available at the Lisbon-based Amilcar Cabral Information and Documentation Center (CIDAC) – CDPM, TL6602-11, "Full text of Speech of Nicolau Lobato, Reading Statement of The Permanent Committee of FRETILIN Central Committee on the High Treason of Xavier do Amaral."

[78] Niner, *To Resist Is to Win*, 33.

and the illogic of subordinating experienced soldiers to inexperienced political commissars on all matters concerning the struggle.

The stiffest criticism came from José da Silva, who had assumed the
second highest rank within the armed forces as the FALINTIL deputy chief
of staff and commander of what became the North Central sector. On his
refusal to implement the restructuring, he was removed from his position as
deputy chief of staff and was replaced by Domingos Ribeiro, who proved
more amenable to the decisions of the politicians. Da Silva was unmoved
by the efforts of the political officers to assert their authority, leading to a
shootout, his capture, and execution.[79]

Sebastião Sarmento (the former artilleryman who went on to spearhead
the formation of FRETILIN's rudimentary military training center) was
removed from his post as the commander of the Northern Frontier sector
and placed under arrest. He had suggested the surrender of the civilian population in light of their worsening conditions under Indonesian violence.[80]
A regional commander in the same sector, Martinho Soares, was executed
for his rejection of Soibada's resolutions. According to a graphic account of
an eyewitness, he was "buried up to his waist in a standing position, without clothes and with his hands tied. Then they burned a car tire, allowing
the melting rubber to burn his body."[81] The commanders of the Southern
Frontier and East Central sectors similarly disagreed with their respective
political commissars on the conduct of the war only to meet their deaths
soon afterward.

After Soibada was adjourned, CCF members Xanana Gusmão and
Ma'Huno[82] stopped by the vicinity of Baucau to pass on the resolutions
of the conference to the FALINTIL units in the area. The challenges they
encountered were similar as in other parts of the country, but this time
put forth by lesser leaders. Paulino Gama claims to have challenged the
two CCF members that FALINTIL's defense of the civilians and the Bases
de Apoio would tie them down, to the detriment of the needed mobility
and agility of waging a guerrilla war.[83] The CCF members reminded him
and everyone present that it was their duty to implement the decisions of
the top leadership before they proceeded to their respective assignments –
Gusmão to East Central sector in Viqueque region and Ma'Huno to Ponta
Leste in Lospalos region. These differences did not get out of hand at that
time possibly because the two sides hailed from the same areas of Baucau
and Manatutu and shared intense loyalty to Lobato and Sahe, but most

---

[79] CAVR, *Chega!*, Part 5: Resistance: Structure and Strategy, 7, 18–19.
[80] Ibid., 22.
[81] Eduardo de Jesus Barreto quoted in CAVR, *Chega!*, Part 5: Resistance: Structure and
Strategy, 13.
[82] Niner, *To Resist Is to Win*, 43–44.
[83] Interview with Paulino Gama "Mauk Muruk" (October 9, 2007, Rijswijk, the Netherlands).

likely also because the challengers were too junior to pose much of a threat.[84]

More-senior military commanders in the eastern side of the country faced the same fate as their westerly brethren. The commander of Ponta Leste sector, Pedro Sanches was accused of being Xavier do Amaral's treasonous accomplice. Military commanders who particularly opposed being controlled by civilians that they held in low esteem, like Aquiles Freitas, Francisco Hornay, and many others, were similarly charged with treason, and many were tortured to death.[85]

The elimination of senior FALINTIL commanders while Indonesian forces retained the military initiative plunged FRETILIN on a downward spiral. Only after Indonesia resumed its offensives in early 1977 with renewed vigor did the correlation between stamping out internal dissension and military setbacks in the hands of the enemy become apparent. FRETILIN began to recognize that greater centralization of leadership was a better way of constructively addressing internal differences and facing the Indonesians.

Between March and May 1977, the leadership convened the Laline conference (in Lacluta, Viqueque district).[86] FRETILIN came out of this conference more convinced than ever that the war was going to be long and arduous, and it geared up, at least ideologically, for protracted struggle.[87]

Meanwhile, Indonesia's aerial and naval blockade of East Timor cordoned off the country from the rest of the world, diminishing the prospect of outside assistance. With their backs to the wall, young, traumatized, and uncompromising FRETILIN leaders latched onto self-reliance as the only way to sustain the long resistance ahead. FRETILIN ideologues mobilized support for the one political ideology they knew best. Openly committing the resistance to a Marxist-Leninist line, they put faith in the path it prescribed toward self-reliance. Political education was offered to FRETILIN cadres and the civilian population on FRETILIN's preferred ideology.

FALINTIL command and operations were restructured at Laline in order to address the previous lack of coordination among FRETILIN companies throughout the regions. Under a new sector-level military command, the operation of FALINTIL units would not be restricted to the specific

---

[84] The interaction of the two CCF members with the military commanders, however, foreshadowed the modus operandi between the two sides and foretold the lines of future dissent when they jointly assumed the leadership of the resistance in the 1980s.

[85] Niner, *To Resist Is to Win*, 50–52; CAVR's *Chega!*, Part 5: Resistance: Structure and Strategy, pp. 18–22. Gusmão claims that he and several of his CCF companions tried to handle the cases with civility and that he freed several such suspects.

[86] In a clear manifestation of his disapproval, FRETILIN President Xavier do Amaral did not attend the meeting.

[87] Interview with Dr. Roque Rodreguez (July 8, 2006, Dili East Timor); and CAVR's *Chega!*, Part 5: Resistance: Structure and Strategy, 16–17.

region each company was assigned to. A certain Shock Brigade[88] was established that was not bound by sector delineations – like the FALINTIL special forces before it. As its name indicates, this was a highly mobile unit intended to deflect the Indonesian forces' forward thrust without lending itself to extended engagements. While sector- and region-based units moved around fixed enemy positions, the Shock Brigade would intervene (hence, also called the Intervention Brigade) by seeking out the weak side of an offensive Indonesian formation. Consolidated as self-defense forces, FADE, the militias in FRETILIN-controlled areas constituted part of the stationary force.[89]

The new chain of command retained elements of the 1976 Soibada resolutions in that regional and zonal commanders reported to the sector command and all were answerable to the sector-level political commissars. This chain of command led up to the restructured FALINTIL General Staff, which was ultimately answerable to Lobato as the commander in chief of FALINTIL. The latter also doubled as the highest political commissar, in a typical adherence to the principle of "politics controls the gun." At the highest level, a narrow circle of leaders, consisting of the FRETILIN president, vice-president, deputy minister of defense, and minister of information and national security, formed a new Concelho Superior da Luta (Supreme Resistance Council).[90] Coming as it did after the brutal containment of the dissenters, the restructuring at Laline ended the almost dogmatic decentralization of the resistance that had proved detrimental to FRETILIN.[91] Very briefly and to a very limited extent, the person of Lobato and his dual role – along

---

[88] It is important to note that the "Brigade" in the name does not mean that this unit was the size of a brigade strong in its common understanding. It was common during the Timorese resistance for various units to be called brigades, which I take to mean units.

[89] Interview with Paulino Gama "Mauk Muruk" (October 9, 2007, Rijswijk, the Netherlands); and CAVR's *Chega!*, Part 5: Resistance: Structure and Strategy, 8–9. The main points of the restructuring are also sketched in an anonymous document of the resistance movement: Arquivo Mário Soares/Resistência Timorense, 05001.009, "Fundamental Thematic of Process. Resume of Central Themes of Armed Struggle," December 1992, p. 7. Written by a later political ideologues-cum-military strategist of the Timorese resistance, possibly Xanana Gusmão himself, the document and the practice of some of the concepts seem to be a Timorese rendition of Maoist doctrine of people's war. Moreover, not only does Gusmão state that *Thoughts of Chairman Mao* was the only belonging he had had that he carried around with him anywhere he went during the resistance, but the poor English of the document seem to indicate that it was a local translation from another language.

[90] These were Francisco Xavier do Amaral, Nicolau Lobato, Hermenegildo Alves, and Alarico Fernandes, respectively, and they represented the full range of perspectives within the leadership.

[91] Although decentralization helps the survival of a guerrilla army or revolutionary movement, centralized command increases its efficiency and accordingly enhances the chances of its success. However, although such centralization is always prone to abuse before the revolutionary war is won, it does not always bode well for the flourishing of participatory institutions afterward.

with the emergence of a more centralized leadership around him – offered the movement some necessary concentration of authority and unity of leadership.

Intensified Indonesian counterinsurgency cut short these positive developments. The replacement of the Indonesian Defense Minister in April 1978 marked the beginning of a new strategy in East Timor with severe consequences for the Timorese resistance and people. With his assumption of the ministerial post, General Mohammed Yusuf brought his experience in counterinsurgency warfare during the South Sulawesi rebellion and energetically pushed the army's doctrine of territorial warfare.[92] Employing a force of at least 20,000 troops, and thousands of unarmed East Timorese civilians, Indonesia intensified its Encirclement and Annihilation Campaign until early 1979.

According to Taylor, and Frederic Durand's cartographic reproduction of his account, the Indonesian forces set out to contain the East Timorese independence fighters into three major encirclements that spanned across the entire country: (1) Indonesian infantry units pushed from West Timor, the navy pounded the northern and southern coasts and an overland cordoning line descended from Liquiça (the environs of Dili) in the north down to Same in the south. This envelopment squeezed inwards with its center at Maliana. (2) While the overland Liquiça-Same cordon stood to the west, another Manatutu-Lakluta-Viqueque line was erected to the east and naval forces from Timor Sea bombed the southern interior. This envelopment sandwiched the resistance fighters around the geographic center of the country. (3) Finally, from the Baucau-Viqueque line in the west, the tip of the island in the east and the navy on both sides of the half island, the Indonesian offensive put the natural fortress of Mount Matebean at the center of the third encirclement of the resistance fighters.[93] With the independence fighters divided into three fully enclosed territories, the Indonesian military mercilessly bombed them before small mobile units combed their interiors.

The Indonesian military followed a scorched-earth policy and targeted food and water sources of the resistance and their civilian Bases de Apoio. The results came swiftly. Unremitting Indonesian assaults pinned most

---

[92] Hamish McDonald, *Suharto's Indonesia* (Blackburn, Victoria, Australia: Fontana Books, 1980), 214. For the purposes here, it suffices to note that territorial warfare doctrine involved the mobilization of the entire population of an area (where the fighting is taking place) to aid the war effort. In the Indonesian context, it was first put to use by the legendary General Abdul Haris Nasution against the Dutch.

[93] Taylor, *Indonesia's Forgotten War*, 85ff.; and Frederic Durand, *East Timor: A Country at the Crossroads of Asia and the Pacific. A Geo-Historical Atlas* (Bangkok: Research Institute on Contemporary Southeast Asia [IRASEC], 2006), 73, also reproduced in the Portuguese scholar José Mattoso's *A Dignidade. Konis Santana e a Resistência Timorense* (Lisboa: Temase e Debates, 2005).

FALINTIL units down to inaccessible caves around the steep mountain ranges and fully encircled the Bases de Apoio. The surviving FRETILIN leaders and FALINTIL units were congregated in three isolated locations – the eastern parts of Ponta Leste, in the steep slopes of Mount Matebean, and Central sector – which made them easier targets for further attacks. From the guerrilla's perspective, Gama recounts how rare it was "for crops to reach maturity because they were systematically destroyed by Indonesian bombardments and sabotage attacks. Springs and wells were poisoned on a number of occasions, which greatly affected the availability of clean water and caused the deaths of many people."[94]

Survivors of these Indonesian sieges give a glimpse of what transpired. Maria José da Costa, who survived an Indonesian siege in Same, described her experience to the Comissão de Acolhimento, Verdade e Reconciliação de Timor-Leste (CAVR, Commission for Reception, Truth and Reconciliation):

In [August] 1978, the enemy began the strategic siege in Dolok [Alas, Manufahi]. The siege was like this: warships fired from the sea, warplanes attacked from the air and burned the dry, tall grass, then the troops attacked on the ground. It was the dry season. The ... fire quickly burned the whole area as if it was soaked with gasoline. ... I witnessed many people being burned to death. ... Many died of starvation. People managed to escape the encirclement when the Indonesian soldiers returned to their camps to rest in the middle of the night.[95]

Although several political leaders had begun to allow the civilian population to surrender, not until December 1978 did the CCF decide for all civilians older than fifty-six and younger than eighteen to surrender. The conflicting viewpoints between those who wanted to keep the people and those who wanted to let the people surrender persisted even after the destruction of the Bases de Apoio. After independence, Taur Matan Ruak put the controversy to rest by arguing that the prevailing circumstances imposed on the resistance leadership the disbanding of the support bases.[96] A long opponent of the idea of Bases de Apoio, Gama explains the circumstances of their destruction:

We simply did not have an administrative organization capable of supporting and protecting the hundreds of thousands of our fellow East Timorese ... This created a huge obstacle for the mobility of our forces, preventing them from responding adequately to the repeated Indonesian land, sea, and air attacks. At the same time, we had to try to organize a logistical structure to remedy the food problem ... of the sizeable civilian population.[97]

[94] Gama, "The War in the Hills," in *East Timor at the Crossroads*, ed. Carey and Bentley, 100.
[95] CAVR, *Chega!*, Part 5: Resistance: Structure and Strategy, 24.
[96] Ibid., 22–25.
[97] Gama, "The War in the Hills," in *East Timor at the Crossroads*, ed. Carey and Bentley, 100.

Critics like Dr. Lucas da Costa believe that the radical elements within FRETILIN used the presence of these civilians under their control as a social laboratory to experiment with their leftist ideologies.[98] Nevertheless, while costly and futile in the intermediate phase of the resistance, the experience of many civilians in FRETILIN-controlled zones in this period facilitated the persistence of the struggle and the ultimate success of the case for independence. Beyond briefly becoming the resistance's support base in the field, these civilians in the long-term constituted the core of anti-Indonesian clandestine networks that latterly sprouted across occupied East Timor. This includes da Costa's own brainchild – the most vibrant and effective Indonesian-based Timorese student movement called the Resistência Nacional dos Estudantes de Timor Leste (RENETIL, East Timorese Student Resistance Movement for Independence).

During the destruction of the Base de Apoio in 1978–1979, FRETILIN asked its supporters, many of whom readily accepted the challenge, to continue the resistance in different form. Even when Indonesian forces herded surrendering civilians into squalid internment camps where many died, survivors in the camps and in towns helped FRETILIN continue the fight. They were a vital source of moral and material support to the guerrillas, and an important conduit for information. According to David Diaz Ximenes, out of filial and kinship loyalty to those who continued the resistance in the jungle, people in towns started to come together secretly and raise money and supplies to send to the field. The same chain through which supplies were sent brought news of their loved ones from the jungle, accompanied by "simple" requests to pass "a message" to someone nearby or for more specific supplies.[99] Traditional ties, thus, took the center stage of resistance to face off the harsh new reality.

In rural East Timor, the trekking guerrilla survivors of the 1978–1979 Indonesian offensives gradually cultivated the people's loyalty during the perilous search for other survivors and resumption of the struggle. The only available extensive account of this period is that of Xanana Gusmão, which is replete with individuals, families, entire hamlets, and sacred houses coming to his aid and, by dint of repeated services to him (and ostensibly to his men too), served the larger movement and effectively became part of the vast underground network. These clandestine activists showed their commitment to the struggle by being loyal to the new, young leader. In some ways, this enabled Gusmão's growing single-handedness as it afforded him the luxury of circumventing the movement's modest structures for expedited actions on his commands.[100]

---

[98] Interview with Lucas da Costa (April 8 and 12, 2006, Dili, East Timor).

[99] Conversations with David Diaz Ximenes (Summer 2006, Dili, East Timor).

[100] That level of centralization inherently carried some grave risks that the movement had to briefly grapple with between his capture in 1992 and his resumption of leadership

Clandestine activism quickly turned into a force to be reckoned with when FRETILIN delivered its first shock strike against Indonesian occupation in June 1980. A radio station and prison and military facilities in and around Dili came under simultaneous attack from within the Indonesian-occupied territories.[101] One coordinator of these attacks was Francisco "Chico" Carvalho, one of FRETILIN president Nicolau Lobato's former bodyguards who had surrendered to the Indonesian military in late 1978.[102] It was in the same spirit of continuing the struggle from within Indonesian control that Lucas da Costa also surrendered to the Indonesians in 1978 and later cofounded the Indonesia-based clandestine RENETIL, of which similarly surrendered young Lucia Lobato and Virgilio Guterres were prominent leaders.[103] Almost a decade after his, along with his family's, surrender, Constâncio Pinto led the Clandestine Front within East Timor from 1990 until his escape to Europe in 1992.[104]

The Fall of Resistance Superstructures and Leadership

FRETILIN errors and Indonesian actions rendered the resistance's repeated restructuring short-lived and ultimately unsuccessful. The inevitable consequences of war, coupled with deliberate Indonesian actions, cost the lives of many civilians in the Bases de Apoio. The physically weakened survivors who surrendered to Indonesian forces were interned in resettlement camps – where many other Timorese from the occupied towns and villages had been resettled. From the Indonesian perspective, internment was necessary to defeat the guerrillas by separating them from the people and purging FRETILIN ideological influences on the latter through indoctrination within controlled quarters.[105]

The consequences were extreme. Without adequate food supplies and medical care, the people were restricted from cultivating sufficient crops and vegetables or collecting fruits from the bush.[106] According to diplomats and experienced relief workers who visited these camps, the consequent diseases, malnutrition, and famines that visited the people were worse than what they had seen in other crisis situations. In October 1979, a staff member of the Indonesian Institute of Social Research and Development in Jakarta

from prison around mid-1994, when field commanders announced that they submitted to his leadership and Ramos-Horta, overseas, openly announced that Gusmão had resumed effective command from prison. See Niner, *To Resist Is to Win*; and Niner, *Xanana*.

[101] Interviews with David Daiz Ximenes (June 30, 2006, Dili, East Timor) and Francisco Carvalho "Chico" (May 13, 2006, Dili).

[102] Interview with Francisco Carvalho "Chico" (May 13, 2006, Dili).

[103] RENETIL is discussed in more detail in Chapter 6.

[104] Interview with Constâncio Pinto (April 13, 2006); Pinto and Jardine, *East Timor's Unfinished Struggle*.

[105] Departemen Pertahanan-Keamanan, "Petunjuk-Pelaksanaan, Nomor: OG/02/V/1979," May 11, 1979 (Defense and Security Department, "Operational Guidance No: OG/02/V/1979" on Operational Activities in East Timor between 1979/1980), 799–809.

[106] CAVR, *Chega!*, Chapter 7.3: Forced Displacement and Famine, 60ff.

confided in Reverend Pat Walsh, an Australian activist for East Timor, about the dire conditions of the people of East Timor: "Some time ago a group of people with many years of experience in the field of emergency aid (Biafra, Sahel, Bangladesh, Indo China refugees) were shocked when they were visiting the area. They had never seen anything like it. In their experience there was nothing which could be compared with it."[107]

Although the human tragedy that had befallen them and their people was devastating, the captures, surrendering and deaths of the leaders and entire FALINTIL units shook the morale of the liberation army and crippled the resistance. By early 1979, the resistance lost its top leaders and the founders of the pioneer pro-independence party, who had led the resistance from within the country.

do Amaral was deposed and arrested by FRETILIN before the Indonesians ambushed and captured him in August 1978. In September 1978, Alarico Fernandes (along with several CCF members) declared his dissociation from the CCF and surrendered to the Indonesians soon afterward on grounds of similar disagreements on the nationalist movement's strategy vis-à-vis Indonesian brute force. He took along with him Radio Maubere, the only direct means of the resistance's communication with the outside world. Delivering the radio to the Indonesians silenced the domestic East Timorese resistance for years and granted Indonesian radio propaganda sole monopoly of the Timorese airwaves for the duration of war – with a brief exception in the mid-1980s.

In the Central sector, Indonesian search for guerrilla leaders turned into massive manhunt for FRETILIN's new president Lobato and his associates, including Hermenegildo Alves. In early December 1978, Indonesian intelligence identified the tracks of someone they believed was important. A pursuit unit of 2,500 soldiers was airlifted from one place to another for three weeks before they located their target.[108] Lobato planned an escape from the encirclement. He sent his forces in one direction and, accompanied by his entourage of aides and bodyguards, he marched in another direction. His only surviving bodyguard, "Chico," remembers how Lobato made an unannounced last-minute change to his escape route only to meet his death. On a fateful Sunday, December 31, 1978, the FRETILIN leader who inspired many lay dead with many bullets piercing his body. An East Timorese was brought to the scene to make a positive identification, after which the embalmed corpse was photographed and the pictures circulated countrywide as part of the ongoing psychological war.

In February 1979, Sahe and Mau Lear were killed in action and in March, Mau Kruma. This brought about the end of the first generation pro-independence leadership inside East Timor – with the ominous (for

---

[107] A confidential letter to Rev. Pat Walsh dated October 5, 1979 available at CDPM's archives at the Centro de Informação e Documentação Amilcar Cabral (CIDAC) in Lisbon, Portugal.

[108] McDonald, *Suharto's Indonesia*, 214.

Indonesia) exception of junior CCF members Gusmão and Ma'Huno. It also marked the neutralization of most FALINTIL forces.

In retrospect, the strategies that the CCF conceived and the policies that its members pursued between 1976 and 1979 were ill suited for the East Timorese predicament. On top of the fact that excessive ideological zeal arrested their capacity to objectively appraise the situation, the resistance leaders' fascination with and their wholesale borrowing from other successful experiences blinded them to how far Indonesia was prepared to go to annihilate them.[109] It took the physical elimination of the first-generation leaders and complete defeat of their ideologically driven strategies for the survivors to pick up from where the earlier leadership left off. A relatively new generation of leaders emerged to resume the struggle. With them, creative and pragmatic thinking prevailed over ideological dogma. Banking on their accumulated experiences, these new leaders brought forth much needed vision and determination to reignite the resistance and eventually win the war.

Conclusion

Eritrean and East Timorese nationalist leaders did not fully comprehend their respective societies and enemies. These shortcomings led them to pursue unrealistic and highly ideologized strategies and to borrow, wholesale, from foreign experiences that were detached from local realities. Although leadership rivalries within the independence movements wreaked havoc, Ethiopia and Indonesia effectively exploited their weaknesses. Yet, within a decade, the two resistance movements managed to regroup, recoup, and refocus. Having experienced firsthand the failed organizational structures and strategies, visionary new leaders rose like phoenixes from the ashes to put both movements on track toward victory. The new leaderships got their movements back in touch with their realities, reenergizing the popular support each had initially enjoyed at the grassroots level. Pragmatism allowed them to selectively borrow from others while learning from their own accumulated experiences. Last but not least, the diligence of the cadres and lower-ranking activists helped devise new ways of combating many previously unforeseen challenges.

---

[109] Every revolutionary war that the Timorese nationalists found inspiration in (from Vietnam in nearby Southeast Asia to the far off former Portuguese colonies of Mozambique, Angola and Guine-Bissau), the independence fighters had either or all of expansive territories that afforded them spatial flexibility, demographic clout that helped replenish their ranks, across-the-border sanctuaries and direct support of global or regional powers. FRETILIN had none of that. Yet, they were enthusiastic about and hoped to replicate one or another of the above mentioned experiences in the same fashion that the Eritreans tried to transplant the Algerian model ten years before them without due consideration to the local realities on the ground.

The strategic initiatives of the Eritrean and East Timorese independence movements had mixed outcomes. Ethiopia and Indonesia intensified their crude counterinsurgencies, and the civilian populations bore the heaviest brunt. The insurgents were left to grapple with seemingly insurmountable odds much of their own making as due to Addis Ababa's and Jakarta's excessive belligerence. The latter's increasingly crude measures only hardened the will and determination to resist.

Determination did not ensure success, however. We have seen how East Timorese defense of their country in conventional warfare was thrown asunder by Indonesia's excessive force. Eritrean hit-and-run tactics during the first decade of their insurgency did not measure up to the massive and indiscriminate Ethiopian retaliations either. Coupled with their own internal weaknesses, Addis Ababa's and Jakarta's massive capacities threw the movements into further confusion.

Ironically, that confusion was the precursor for change, as the nationalists' cognizance of their strategic weaknesses led to the re-evaluation of their means and methods, and the adoption of more appropriate strategies. These processes started with internal restructuring and reorientations of the nationalist movements themselves that were attended by immediate adverse effects. The ELF splintered during the eighth anniversary of the independence war, before a viable alternative consolidated in the Eritrean People's Liberation Front (EPLF). FRETILIN's first generation leaders were gone, and the movement nearly defeated, a mere four years after Indonesian landings in Dili in December 1975 before the Conselho Revolucionario Resistência Nacional (CRRN the Revolutionary Council of National Resistance)[110] emerged to resume and lead the quest for independence.

[110] There is some debate about nature and realness of these organizations. With regard to East Timor, Juan Federe wrote, "Much attention was given to devising pompous sounding titles and the creation of enough of them to co-opt all the vociferous East Timorese pro-independence activists. Little or nothing existed in terms of substantive constitutional documents, definitions of functions, work procedures, information and reporting mechanisms, or work programs and their implementation...." Juan Federer, *The UN in East Timor: Building Timor Leste, a Fragile State* (Darwin: Charles Darwin University Press, 2005), 98.

In the case of Eritrea, such list of resistance structures quickly crystallized into cohesive organizations that eclipsed – in fact and in history – the preceding amorphous or fast changing structures.

I am convinced that many of these organizations were set up in good faith, with as clear command structures and constitutions as their authors could manage. That there is little surviving evidence of this is due to the extremely difficult environment in which these groups were established.

3

Toward Reorganization and Reorientation

Eritrean Fragmentation and East Timorese Near Defeat

> It was revolution and war and I would have to dominate a little if I wanted to accomplish anything. My capacity to direct would depend on my capacity to understand and this would depend on my dedication to study.
>
> Xanana Gusmão[1]

The birth of the EPLF in Eritrea and of the CRRN in East Timor had far-reaching implications for both independence wars. New, reoriented grand strategies emerged, based on a greater understanding of circumstances and aimed at widening the means of resistance. Strategic thinking took precedence, without precluding short-term, tactical preoccupations. Ability to react quickly to fast-changing challenges became a characteristic feature of the new grand strategies. Moreover, previous experiences impressed on the new generation of leaders the need to institutionalize a set of beliefs and practices – military success required secrecy and iron discipline in Eritrea, and the realization that military victory was unlikely compelled East Timorese leaders to diversify the arena of resistance.

Seeing these changes through required sufficiently centralized and unified leaderships as well as cohesive and efficient organization. During this phase of the Eritrean and East Timorese movements, two transformative and enduring figures emerged, and while controversial and condemned in some circles, they personified all, or significant aspects, of their respective organizations. Isaias Afwerki and Kay Rala Xanana Gusmão[2] entered the national stage at critical junctures of the Eritrean and East Timorese nationalist struggles, respectively. They both offered badly needed sense of direction at a time

---

[1] Quoted in Sara Niner, *Xanana: Leader of the Sturggle for Independent Timor-Leste* (Melbourne: Australian Scholarly Publishing, 2009), 69.

[2] One cannot plausibly speak of these two without Romedan Mohammed-Nur (in the case of Isaias) and Ma'Huno (in the case of Xanana) from whom they learned a great deal and on whom they relied for legitimacy and broader support base, at least at the early stages.

of enveloping confusion, and even despair. Neither was initially elected, but both earned the unanimous acclamation of their colleagues because of the strength of their personalities, their determination to turn the vision they shared with others into reality, and their habitual studious preparations. In due course, even their colleagues came to rely on them.[3]

The period after the rise of these two new leaders was marked, in both insurgencies, by a period of consolidation. In each case, previous, haphazard tactics were replaced by methodical and increasingly sophisticated grand strategies. The Eritrean resistance witnessed punctilious political and military work that, among other things, involved increased civilian engagement and stricter internal discipline that sustained the escalation of guerrilla resistance toward conventional warfare in Eritrea. In East Timor, after its severe losses, FRETILIN survived a near-total defeat by drastically shifting from a military-centered conventional strategy into scattered guerrilla warfare, waged by an amorphous and elusive movement that heavily relied on the civilian population. Ultimately, both the Eritrean and East Timorese independence movements, and their strategies, remained dynamic to meet the evolving challenges. That dynamism was the defining feature of the grand strategies of the EPLF and the CRRN.

In order to reconstruct the emergence of the reoriented grand strategies of the two movements, this chapter follows the struggle in Eritrea, after the breakup of the ELF. It also examines the struggle in East Timor after FRETILIN survived its near-total defeat. The chapter offers an integrated analysis of the Ethiopian and Indonesian governments' counterinsurgency measures, on one hand, and the dynamic resistance strategies of the insurgents, on the other. Our understanding is better served first by a brief account of structural factors that determined the convictions and actions of the insurgencies' younger leaders, and then of Ethiopian and Indonesian counterinsurgency dispositions.

Initially, Ethiopian and Indonesian counterinsurgency retained the upper hand over both the Eritrean and East Timorese independence movements. The ELF's implosion in 1969 and the infighting (or even liquidation of dissenters) within FRETILIN between 1977 and 1978 served both forces of occupation. The different trajectories that Eritrean and East Timorese nationalists finally embraced – the first from guerrilla to conventional warfare and the second in the other direction – were as much shaped by the methods and resolve of Ethiopian and Indonesian belligerence as by the geographic and demographic determinants of Eritrea and East Timor themselves. Thus, these key structural factors are examined first.

---

[3] Whereas the East Timorese leader has written, however brief, his own account and his speeches, writing, and leadership have been thoroughly studied albeit by few, there unfortunately is very little along those lines on the Eritrean leader.

Decisive Structural Factors

Geography and demography featured prominently in determining Eritrean and East Timorese nationalist resistance. When rebellion broke out in Eritrea in 1961, the roughly 7,000 soldiers and 5,000 police that Ethiopia had deployed in the 140,000-square-kilometer territory were too thinly stretched to exert effective control over the territory.[4] From a dozen barely armed "bandits" in 1961, Eritrean independence fighters numbered over three hundred in two years and were growing fast with relative ease. By the end of the war, in 1991, Eritrea could marshal more than 100,000 seasoned men and women combatants with surplus weapons of every size and shape. That is because the relatively expansive country (nearly ten times the size of East Timor) granted enough geographical space for maneuvering and, as the independence movement grew in size, the areas of Eritrea that were remote from Ethiopian power center became defensible safe havens for the insurgents.

In its best year since the Indonesian invasion (i.e. during its June 1976 Soibada conference), FALINTIL's regular fighting force numbered no more than 1,500 strong.[5] For their part, Indonesian forces at any given time in East Timor numbered a minimum of 15,000 well-armed and well-supplied soldiers. There were times in the 1980s and 1990s when the resistance forces were reduced to a few dozen widely scattered fighters, while the Indonesian armed presence stabilized at roughly ten battalions, but its police and civilian intelligence operatives increased manyfold. What made this numerical disparity even more crippling, in military terms, was East Timor's geographical size. The 15,000-square-kilometer half island was, in its entirety, within reach of Indonesian forces (aerial, naval, and infantry). It was completely surrounded by Indonesia,[6] and the latter's absolute naval superiority easily and effectively blockaded the territory from the rest of the world. This meant the guerrillas had no secure, defensible safe havens inside their country, or cross border sanctuaries in third-party countries.[7]

---

[4] Moreover, early on Second Division's personnel were stationed in climatically friendly bases and "secured" the territory through infrequent patrols. *Ye 12gna Egregna Brigade-ena Bewestu Yemistedaderut Leyu-Leyu Kefloch Ye-Kefil Tarik* (*The History of the 12th Brigade and Its Special Units*), Ca. 1977/1978, a classified document of the Ethiopian ministry of defense accessed in Eritrea's Research and Documentation Center); and Dawit Wolde Giorgis, *Red Tears. War, Famine and Revolution in Ethiopia* (Trenton, NJ: Red Sea Press, 1989).

[5] CAVR, *Chega!*, Part 5: Resistance: Structure and Strategy, 4–8. According to CAVR, there existed at this time six sectors with an average of 2.5 companies per sector. Each company had an average of three platoons, and each platoon was made up of three squads of a maximum of nine men (and later women) each. That brought regular FALINTIL forces to no more than 1,500 strong.

[6] Australia's de facto and de jure recognition of Indonesian rule in East Timor rendered the latter's maritime borders with Australia redundant.

[7] The Chinese military, for example, reportedly concluded, in the late 1970s, that Indonesian blockade made East Timor inaccessible, leading to Beijing's turning down of FRETILIN's

In contrast, Eritrea borders Sudan and Djibouti by land and shares maritime borders with Sudan, Saudi Arabia, and Yemen. While the sheer length of these borders made it impossible for Ethiopia to cordon Eritrea off from the rest of the world, Addis Ababa's conflict of interest with neighboring countries made Sudan, Somalia, Saudi Arabia, Iraq, Syria, and Yemen willing to grant Eritreans cross-border sanctuaries and access to logistics and materiel. The Eritrean independence movement latterly based itself in parts of Eritrea that, while remote from the Ethiopian power center, were close to the Red Sea (a maritime outlet) and along the Sudanese border. A significant number of them lived beyond the government's reach, including as refugees in neighboring countries, most significantly in Sudan.

Finally, against the 130 million Indonesians offering an abundant reservoir of personnel, East Timorese stood at a paltry 700,000 and was a fast-shrinking population – many of whom were either uprooted because of the war or interned in squalid "strategic hamlets" where they were visited and revisited by diseases and famine.[8] By contrast, more than 2 million Eritreans – while still small in comparison to close to Ethiopia's 40 million – was a sufficient demographic mass to replenish the ranks of the nationalist movement.

These structural factors thus offset Eritrean disadvantages vis-à-vis Ethiopia in the long term, whereas their absence crippled the East Timorese military resistance in the face of overwhelming Indonesian force and numbers. Beyond that, the beginnings and early convictions of the insurgents had a lasting impact on Eritrean and East Timorese grand strategies. After several futile attempts to restore internal autonomy and later wrestle independence from Ethiopia through nonviolent means in the 1950s,[9] Eritreans resorted to armed struggle in 1961, fully convinced that they were capable of defeating the mighty Ethiopian military in battle.[10]

In contrast, in East Timor, the circumstances surrounding their formal emergence and open activities prevented the pro-independence nationalists

---

request for support in military supplies. Interview with Abilio de Araújo (August 5, 2006, Vila Franca de Xida, Portugal).

Moreover, there is an unconfirmed rumor that a Timor-bound shipload of weapons was redirected to Aceh because Indonesia had fully cordoned off East Timor. The glaring irony of an inaccessible East Timor vis-à-vis accessible Aceh notwithstanding, I have been unable to trace the source or general timing of this alleged shipment.

[8] Departemen Pertahanan-Keamanan, "Petunjuk-Pelaksanaan, Nomor: OG/02/V/1979," May 11, 1979 (Defense and Security Department, "Operational Guidance No: OG/02/V/1979" on Operational Activities in East Timor between 1979/1980), pp. 799–809.

[9] Repeated Eritrean appeals to the United Nations and to Emperor Haile Selassie in Addis Ababa went unheeded. In the immediate aftermath of the brutal suppression of a massive labor protest in Asmara in 1958, young nationalists in exile in Port Sudan formed Eritrean Liberation Movement to seek independence through what its founder called "revolutionary coup" or "Al-thewra al-inqilabiyah."

[10] ELF, "Destur Jebhat al-Tahrir al-Iritriyah" (1960). This is a copy of ELF's founding constitution accessed from Dr. Taha Mohamed-Nur's personal Holdings in Asmara, Eritrea.

from clearly identifying and agreeing on what stood between them and their goal. UDT sought continued association with Portugal in order for Lisbon to shoulder the preparation of the country for independence, whereas FRETILIN argued that Portugal would not do in a decade what it failed to do so during centuries of colonialism. FRETILIN came to believe that the immediate independence that it sought had to be fought for, although it was not clear whom the fight was to be against – Portugal had started the decolonization process, and Indonesia had not invaded yet. In fact, FRETILIN continued to jockey for Indonesian backing of East Timorese independence, refusing to give up on Jakarta even after the latter split the pro-independence coalition by co-opting UDT to the integrationist camp.

The East Timorese nationalists found themselves in an even more precarious position when Indonesian incursions turned into an aerial, naval, and land offensive. Facing another conventional army many times its size, FALINTIL units started at a disadvantage and were nearly shattered before resorting to scattered guerrilla resistance. Their Eritrean counterparts, by contrast, started out in small guerrilla formations that gradually evolved to face the full force of the Ethiopian military in mechanized battles.

Both independence movements had to learn quickly from their respective experiences and improvise to better face fast-changing conditions. They relied on their own resourcefulness and drew more heavily from their respective experiences. They pragmatically applied select lessons from other independence struggles, while tapping into any external assistance they could. Through these methods, independence fighters in Eritrea and East Timor eventually succeeded in formulating strategies that suited their circumstances.

While their continued resistance offered ample proof of defiance, their continued survival and success depended on having adaptability and foresight that could not be matched by the crude Ethiopian and Indonesian counterinsurgencies. The movements initially planted themselves amongst the people that they originated from, and eventually appealed more broadly by offering (or promising to offer) badly needed basic services, and adopting appealing ideologies that fit with broader, bottom-up revolutionary struggles of their respective times. By contrast, the unrelenting brutality of Ethiopian and Indonesian methods cost Addis Ababa and Jakarta the hearts and minds of the Eritrean and East Timorese peoples.

Ethiopian and Indonesian Counterinsurgencies

An insurgency wins by turning a people's general sense of malaise, indifference, or even hostility into an effective multifaceted support, among other structural and subjective factors. For a counterinsurgency to succeed it needs – as a minimum requirement – to isolate the insurgents from the civilian population.[11] Breaking the elusive bond between the population and the insurgents does not always require force; in fact, if force is not used with restraint and synchronized with noncoercive options of a coherent strategy, the use of force can be counterproductive.[12] Just as that link is not always physical, breaking it or isolating one from the other does not always require physical separation of the two.

Conventional military doctrines of occupying and holding territory leave states and governments at an inherent disadvantage when faced with guerrilla opponents. Beyond the self-deceptive denial of resistance to their rule, Ethiopian and Indonesian counterinsurgencies were doomed from the beginning for aiming to physically separate the insurgents from the civilian population, mostly by interning civilians in resettlement camps. This study makes it clear that Ethiopia's and Indonesia's highly militaristic methods were imprecise and unrestrained. The two governments, thus, lacked well-thought-out, consistent counterinsurgency strategies because of their own lack of internal cohesion.

A closer look into the power centers in Addis Ababa and Jakarta reveals that Shoan intrigues and the rule through "carefully planned lack of coordination"[13] in Haile Selassie's Ethiopia was matched by what Hamish McDonald calls Javanese "cultural propensity for intricacy and dissimulation, combined with the internal complexities of power"[14] in Suharto's New Order Indonesia. Although the latter was far more formidable in its approach than the former for other reasons, such governance methods were to play an important role in the planning and execution of their respective counterinsurgencies. In the end, just as Ethiopian and Indonesian militaries failed to defeat the insurgents on the battleground, Addis Ababa's and Jakarta's methods failed to win the hearts and minds of the Eritrean and East Timorese people.

"We Need Eritrea for Its Land, Not Its People"

During his first visit to the newly acquired thirteenth province in 1962, Haile Selassie gathered Eritrean elders in his Asmara palace; he was uncharacteristically blunt in telling them: "Eritrea, we need its land not

[11] David Galula, *Counterinsurgency Warfare: Theory and Practice* (Westpoint, CT, and London: Praeger Security International, 2006), 4, 52; and Gebru Tareke, *The Ethiopian Revolution: War in the Horn of Africa* (New Haven, CT, and London: Yale University Press, 2009), 46–53.

[12] Michael Howard, *Studies in War and Peace* (London: Temple Smith, 1970), 195–196.

[13] Haggai Erlich, *The Struggle over Eritrea, 1962–1978. War and Revolution in the Horn of Africa* (Stanford, CA: Hoover Institution Press, 1983), 39.

[14] Hamish McDonald, *Suharto's Indonesia* (Blackburn, Victoria, Australia: Fontana Books, 1980), 189.

its people."[15] The formidable security forces that went after Eritrean insurgents translated this crude declaration into a counterinsurgency that aimed to drain the water in order to kill the fish, in the reverse Maoist jargon. Despite the Twelfth Brigade's show of force in the streets of Eritrean towns since the 1950s, army units remained in climatically acceptable outposts, leaving the police to hunt down the despised "bandits" in the peripheries of the new northernmost province. Stationed in small units across the country, the police happily obliged.

Police and justice officials held regular meetings in western Eritrea, framing Hamid Idris Awate, the founder of the armed struggle, as a bandit. They called on the people not to cooperate with him and assured them of his destruction. The police confiscated his herd and incarcerated his entire family, calling for his surrender in return for their freedom.[16] Meanwhile, Emperor Haile Selassie allegedly sent an emissary to dissuade Idris Mohammed Adem from the insurgency.[17] Undeterred, the Eritrean liberation movement intensified its activities, triggering Ethiopian overreaction and capitalizing on its outcome. Once the angered Ethiopian empire decided to move decisively against the rebellion, it lacked the appropriate know-how to pursue the fast-moving insurgents, well trained and operationally well led as they were by Hamid and the former Sudanese soldiers who joined him early on.

Between March and November 1963 alone, the nascent ELA mounted at least six successful operations against the police and military installations in western Eritrea. Their small numbers, their speed, and their popular support, as well as Ethiopians' lack of preparedness and knowledge of the region enabled the independence fighters to inflict human and material damage on the Ethiopian security forces and capture munitions with minimal causalities to themselves. In October 1963, for example, Adem Mohammed Hamid "Gendifel" and his nascent *fedayin* hit squad of five fighters boarded a public transportation bus on the outskirts of the western Eritrean town of Haikota and raided the police station in broad daylight.

[15] This is a widely circulated quote among Eritrean elders, also quoted in Alemseged Abbay, *Identity Jilted or Re-Imagining Identity? The Divergent Paths of the Eritrean and Tigrayan Nationalist Struggle* (Asmara and Lawrenceville, NJ: Red Sea Press, 1998), 79.

[16] RDC/Biography/03, 006807: "Minutes of Meeting," April 9, 1962, held by the police with traditional administrators and the public in the Eritrean town of Haicota regarding Hamid Idris Awate; and RDC/Biography/3, 006806: Haile Selassie Weldu, "Hatsir Tarikh Hamid Idris Awate kesab 1961," November 30, 1983.

[17] MP Osman Mohammed Hindi to Idris Mohammed Adem (Massawa, 7 October 1961). This is an English translation of a letter in Arabic that a certain group of "Eritrean Liberals" sent to ELF founder Idris to relate to him that Emperor Haile Selassie had recruited the services of a "Nigerian Quack" a certain Haj Abubakar Ibrahim to seek reconciliation with Idris Mohammed Adem and Ibrahim Sultan. The document is available at Eritrea's Research and Documentation Center.

The police were taken by surprise, and their feeble resistance came to naught.[18]

The fedayin continued to stage similar daring operations in small towns, while the guerrillas were actively ransacking isolated government outposts, expanding the ELF's reach of operations, and increasing its popularity among Eritreans, who by the end of 1963 had multiplied its ranks to six platoons mostly armed with captured Ethiopian weapons.[19]

In early 1964, the ELA ambushed a large police convoy, killing seventeen officers (all Eritreans by origin) and capturing about forty machine guns, which prompted the Ethiopian army into one of its retaliatory interventions. The Twelfth Brigade set out to hunt down the independence fighters. Having quickly recovered some of the captured weapons, Ethiopian soldiers continued their chase until, in March 1964, the insurgents offered stiff resistance at Tegorba. That was the first time that the fighters engaged units of the conventional Ethiopian Second Division in open face-to-face combat.[20] As intensified Eritrean guerrilla operations inflicted heavy damage on the police force, the army stepped in and eventually monopolized the antiguerrilla operations.

Held hostage by competing power centers surrounding the emperor, however, Ethiopia's counterinsurgency neither quelled the resistance nor won the hearts and minds of the people. First, a group of Shoan nobility, who were also zealous Christians and Amhara chauvinists, gathered around the emperor's representative in and governor general of Eritrea *Dejazmach* (later *Ras*) Asrate Kassa. The ELF's origins in the Muslim-inhabited parts of Eritrea and the Islamic faith of its leadership played conveniently into the hands of this group in particular, and the Christian Ethiopian state in general. In 1964, Asrate Kassa, who had opted to use a carrot-and-stick strategy toward Eritrea's Christians, but to ruthlessly suppress the country's Muslims, recruited predominantly Christian Eritrean highlanders into a new counterinsurgency force, known as Commandos 101.[21] Trained and

[18] Interview with Adem Mohammed Hamid "Gendifel" (January 7, 1988, Kassala Sudan) in ELF/UO, 02847, Günter Schröder, "Interviews on E.L.F. History."

[19] According to Tesfai Tekle (correspondence, January 1999, Keren, Eritrea), the commanders of these platoons were: Omar Ezaz, Osman Mohammed Idris "Abu Sheneb," Adem Mohammed Hamid "Gendifel," Mahmoud Dinai, Omar Nasser, and Ibrahim Mohammed-Ali.

[20] An ELF song of the 1970s thus glorifies this first combat against Ethiopian soldiers: *Werhi megabit 64 Tegorba abay haben* (March 1964, Tegorba major glory) *Buzuhat nerom antsar wehudat* (There were many against few) *Ghin te'awitom ab-bokhri quinat* (But the [few] won in their first combat).

Nevertheless, with eighteen of its fighters killed, four wounded, and several weapons captured, the ELA also suffered its first major loss to the Ethiopian forces. Correspondence with Tesfai Tekle (Keren, January 1999).

[21] *Andinet*, no. 426, September 5, 1964. According to this newspaper report, the first batch of graduates was 300 strong. According to Erlich, *The Struggle over Eritrea*, p. 38, by

armed by Israel, the commandos (also called Force 101) gained the crudest skills for combating guerrilla fighters. With U.S. and Israeli assistance, Asrate Kassa also inaugurated specialized units – the highly mobile rapid response/expeditionary units (Fetno Derash) – responsible for responding to reports of ELA's movements and launching targeted attacks at the roaming guerrilla units. Such targeted operations, however, were undermined by the counterinsurgency Commandos 101. These commandos earned notoriety for their preemptive ruthlessness against suspect individuals and communities. They targeted Muslim Eritreans, going on wholesale killing sprees and burning their villages.

Asrate Kassa sought to coordinate the activities of the entire security sector with his experimental political and propaganda maneuvers. Coordination was impossible, however, because the military reported to Prime Minister Aklilu Habtewold, who led the the rival camp in Addis Ababa that used the Eritrean counterinsurgency war as means of outdoing each other to be heard by the emperor.[22]

Comprising of other important bureaucrats, the prime minister's group wanted the military to take the primary responsibility in suppressing the rebellion by force. However, even after the Second Division's Twelfth Brigade grew to around seven thousand soldiers after the outbreak of rebellion in Eritrea, the bulk of its force was stationed in the major urban centers. With infrequent patrols by smaller, inadequately informed, underequipped, and undersupplied units, it roamed the rural areas on the tail of Eritrean independence fighters.

During such tours of duty through the countryside, Ethiopian soldiers moved around like a conquering feudal army, avenging their losses on the civilians. In the words of one of its own men, the Twelfth Brigade "did not concentrate on attacking the guerrillas directly; instead it devastated the villages suspected of harboring them."[23] Dawit Wolde Giorgis continues that during its patrolling missions "the army would only carry two or three days rations at a time. After they ran out [of supplies], they were expected to live off the land, to take what they needed from the people. I remember soldiers slaughtering cattle, eating what they wanted, and then leaving the rest to rot. Sometimes soldiers would kill cattle just to get the livers."[24] The Ethiopian army "believed it could command respect and loyalty from the people by sheer show of force" and make an example of the innocent civilians.[25]

---

the end of the 1960s, the commandos constituted a battalion of well-trained and equipped companies.

[22] Erlich, *The Struggle over Eritrea*, 35ff.
[23] Dawit, *Red Tears*, 82.
[24] Ibid.
[25] Ibid.

Ethiopia thus mounted massive, crude counterinsurgency campaigns, the ELF retaliated, and Ethiopia committed more abuses in reprisals. The consequent intensification of resistance and several assassinations of high-ranking Ethiopian army officers nudged Ethiopia's ruling elite out of its complacency. But in another strategic shift that was equally damaging to the overall coherence of Ethiopia's response, the military's increased use of force caused more harm than good in its cavalier and unmethodical pursuit of the insurgents. In 1967, Ethiopian generals devised a similar counterinsurgency strategy to the French Challe Plan in Algeria[26] by channeling most of their strength against one zone at a time. Perhaps also unaware of the parallel brutalities of the Israeli-trained commandos, an Israeli advisor to the Eritrea-based Ethiopian army witnessed in 1967 with apparent surprise:

The 2nd Division is very efficient in killing innocent people. They are alienating the Eritreans and deepening the hatred that already exists. Their commander took his senior aides to a spot near the Sudanese border and ordered them; 'From here to the north – clean the area.' Many innocent people were massacred and nothing of substance was achieved. There is simply no way the Ethiopian army will ever win the struggle over Eritrea by pursuing this line.[27]

Proceeding to Barka in western Eritrea after a brief sweeping operation in the southern Eritrean highlands, Ethiopia set out to "kill the fish by draining the sea": targeting entire villages suspected of harboring the insurgents and interning others in strategic hamlets in a bid to hunt down the guerrillas.[28] In the process, thousands of innocent civilians were deliberately killed and hundreds of western Eritreans villages were razed to the ground. As 1967 came to a close, these atrocities returned to the highlands, starting with Senhit province (around Keren) and continuing to the predominantly Christian highland provinces of Seraye and Akeleguzai. The burning and killing was also attended by looting of property and livestock, leaving the land barren with nothing for the survivors to return to.[29] Its actions, thus, turned the Ethiopian military into what Haggai Erlich called "*shifta* in uniform."[30]

The Eritrean liberation movement intensified its operations only to face the wrath of the humiliated Ethiopian government. In the absence of any meaningful opposition to Addis Ababa in northern Ethiopia, all Second

---

[26] Constantin Melnik, *The French Campaign against the FLN* (Santa Monica, CA: RAND Corporation, 1967); Martin Alexander and J. F. V. Keiger, "France and the Algerian War: Strategy, Operations and Diplomacy" in *Journal of Strategic Studies* 25, no. 2 (2002): –31.

[27] Quoted in Erlich, *The Struggle over Eritrea* 58.

[28] Erlich, *The Struggle over Eritrea*, 40–41.

[29] Mohammed Abul Al-Qasim Hajj Hamad, *Al-Abad Al-Dawliyah Limaereket Al-Iritriyah* (Beirut: Dar Al-Telia', 1974), 126ff.; and Alex de Waal, *Evil Days. 30 Years of War and Famine in Ethiopia: An Africa Watch Report* (New York: Human Rights Watch, 1991), 42ff.

[30] Erlich, *The Struggle over Eritrea*, p. 39.

Division brigades – the Sixth from Tigray and the Eighth from Gonder – were brought into Eritrea, as were additional units of the elite Imperial Bodyguard from Addis Ababa's First Division, along with airborne units from the Air Force. The impact of these reinforcements was directly felt by the Eritrean liberation movement and by civilians. Eritrea was divided into three operational zones, each assigned to the three infantry brigades: the Sixth Brigade in the eastern coastal lowlands, the Eighth Brigade in the vast western lowlands, and the Twelfth Brigade in the entire plateau that lies between. Supported by four expeditionary police battalions, these new arrivals were to hunt down insurgents, without centralized command or an overarching strategic objective.[31] Virtually autonomous, these units had no qualms about doing whatever they deemed necessary to quell the rebellion. Commanders were nonchalant about their deeds in their meticulous reporting. Between September and October 1970, for example, units of the Twelfth Brigade subjected what they claimed were "insurgents, their families and their supporters" to heavy artillery raids and thus reported the outcome:

the bandits, their families and their supporters as well as their property were bombed with 4.2" artillery. On top of their sustaining severe casualties, the heavy bombing of the vicinity and the damage that it caused brought about their failing morale... It is especially believed that the damage and fear caused by the bombings made their supporters think of the further damage they would sustain if the situation continued unchanged and that they will change their beliefs and surrender to the government.[32]

The Twelfth Brigade command believed that expeditionary/patrolling missions would only give the rebels breathing space and ample room to avoid the routes of the soldiers at will. Asking for fresh reinforcements to rebuild its weakened forces, the command recommended that ridding the Akeleguzai province of insurgents required the physical occupation of rebel-infested areas, to stop rebels roaming freely in the territory.[33]

Soon afterward, the ELF sent shockwaves through the Ethiopian military establishment. In late 1970, ELF units ambushed General Teshome Ergetu, the swaggering commander of the Second Division in Eritrea. He was killed and the convoy that accompanied him dispersed. Additional Ethiopian units were called to the scene of the ambush, near the town of Keren, to cleanse the area of insurgents. In the spirit of striking hard at the insurgents' supporters,

---

[31] *Y'huletegna Egregna Kifle-Tor Sostegna Memriya Ye 1964 Amete Mehret Teqlala Y'zemecha ena Y'temhert Riport* ("1964 E.C. General Campaign and Education Report of the Second Infantry Division, Third Directorate"), 1–3. This is one of the still classified Ethiopian documents at the Eritrean Research and Documentation Center.

[32] *Y'12gna Brigade Qedem Memriya Y'tiqimt Wer 63 Amete Mehret Teqlala Riport* (General Report of the 12th Brigade Command for October 1963 E.C.), 4.

[33] *Y'12gna Brigade Qedem Memriya Y'tiqimt Wer 63 Amete Mehret Teqlala Riport* (General Report of the 12th Brigade Command for October 1963 E.C.), 5.

Ethiopian troops descended on the neighboring villages of Ona and Besik-Dira and left more than a thousand innocent men, women, and children dead; their livestock killed; and the entire villages burned to the ground.[34] The Ona–Besik-Dira Massacre and many similar atrocities before and after, undermined the government's ability to win over the people's sympathy.

The counterproductive impact of Ethiopian counterinsurgency is best revealed in a 1971–1972 Second Division report. According to that account, in June 1971 alone, the insurgents tackled Ethiopian troops in ten engagements initiated by the government, while conducting close to two dozen operations across Eritrea on their own initiative.[35] The following months did not bring any reprieve.

Attributing its failure to quell the rebellion to the insurgents' guerrilla war tactics, the Second Division tacitly acknowledged for the first time their inadequate strategy: "Since the combat that takes place is that of bandits, it is clear that other than causing sudden ambush attacks, there are no face-to-face combats that the bandits undertake."[36] The Second Division command went on to recommend a set of solutions that included a few new points, such as "isolating bandits from the people to end the people's informational and organizational assistance to them; just as the bandits propagate their messages, so too the government should send its representatives to counter the bandits' messages and explain to the people the government's goal; controlling the gates to neighboring countries . . . "[37] The report concluded that the size of Eritrea required a bigger and more agile force in order to implement its recommendations. Ethiopian government reinforcements neither revived the troops' waning morale in Eritrea nor reversed the gradual change in the balance of power toward the ELF.

Unlike the French army in Algeria, Ethiopia had neither its neighbors' political goodwill to seal off Eritrea nor the capacity to fully isolate the ELF's military zones from one another. Moreover, before Ethiopian routing of the independence fighters reached all zones and scored a lasting result, the ELF ended its zonal structure and unified its forces. This minimized their exposure while intensifying their resistance. Eritrean insurgents emerged in all corners of the country, and in 1968, ELF's fedayin operations against Ethiopia went international. Ethiopian Airlines came under simultaneous attacks in Rome, Frankfurt, and Karachi. Although the operations in Rome and Frankfurt failed, a four-man ELF squad, led by

[34] Amina Habte, "Ethiopian War Crimes in Eritrea: A Case Study of the Massacres of Besik-Dira and Ona" (BA Thesis, University of Asmara, 2000).

[35] *K'Sene Wer 1963 Amete Mihret Eske Sene 30 Qen 1964 Amete Mehret Dres Yalew Y'Amet Riport* (June 1971-July 7, 1972 Annual Report), 1–10.

[36] *Y'huletegna Egregna Kifle-Tor Sostegna Memriya Ye 1964 Amete Mehret Teqlala Y'zemecha ena Y'temhert Riport* ("1964 E.C. General Campaign and Education Report of the Second Infantry Division, Third Directorate"), 63.

[37] Ibid., 63.

Ali-Said Abdellah, demolished an Ethiopian airliner sitting on the tarmac of the Karachi international airport.[38]

Ethiopia was far more successful in diplomatically isolating Eritreans than defeating them militarily. In the early 1970s, it made brilliant diplomatic moves in the international arena and isolated Eritrean insurgents from their two most important sources of support – China and Sudan. Haile Selassie flew to Beijing and established diplomatic ties with the People's Republic of China, in return for the Chinese withholding support to the Eritreans. Around the same time, he successfully mediated the end of the first Sudanese civil war (the Anya Nya rebellion in the South) and earned Khartoum's alliance.[39]

Overall, the ELF's isolated hit-and-run tactics failed to measure up to sustained government reprisals, and Ethiopia retained the strategic initiative.[40] However, neither the governor's methods nor the prime minister's equally ruthless approach through the Second Division was ultimately effective. Although Ethiopia's security forces failed to end the insurgency, their indiscriminate brutality cost Ethiopia whatever sympathy it may have enjoyed among the Eritrean population. In the long term, this benefited the insurgents. However, the ELF's interim strategy was geared primarily toward short-term objectives: lightning attacks on enemy positions to instill fear in enemy soldiers, selectively assassinating or terrorizing Ethiopian agents, securing supplies to sustain the struggle, and executing tactical operations to uplift the morale of the people.

Throughout the three decades of war in Eritrea, Ethiopia failed to understand Eritrean society, or to address their grievances peaceably. Ethiopia's expansion of meager services prioritized the war effort, and the ultimately

---

[38] "Ertrawyan Komando ab Karachi" in *Hewyet*, No. 8, 1996. June After accomplishing their mission, the four ELF fighters gave themselves up only to be abused by the Pakistani security forces on the spot. Ali-Said remembers how he then pulled out his backup pistol and fired in the air before negotiating their surrender as a political case. During their court hearings, Pakistani student organizations led by the late Benazir Bhutto demanded and secured outright release of the detainees on grounds that they were fighting a legitimate liberation war.

[39] Paul B. Henze, *The Horn of Africa from War to Peace* (New York: St. Martin's Press 1991), 133; and David A. Korn, *Ethiopia, the United States and the Soviet Union* (Carbondale: Southern Illinois University Press, 1986), 3.

[40] On several occasions, ELF fighters would take refuge in isolated villages and hamlets or go there to collect supplies. When Ethiopian security forces approach, instead of protecting the people or helping them flee, the fighters would escape by firing warning shots to cover their exit, leaving the civilian population to bear the brunt of brutal Ethiopian reprisals as was the case in many villages in western lowland province of Barka. During the 1970s' liberation of the towns, however, the ELF had learned from its previous experiences that it exerted significant effort to keep civilians out of combat zones. As the anticipated speedy liberation of Tessenei fizzled out in April 1976, for example, the ELF evacuated civilians who had been caught in the crossfire.

beneficial educational services were seen as an attempt to brainwash the Eritrean population, a point well supported by blatant cultural domination.

As is discussed later in the book, the Ethiopian counterinsurgency after Haile Selassie multiplied with consistency and vigor. But it was sacrificed on the altars of its own militarism because the now battle-hardened independence movement also started to mature politically and galvanize popular support beyond Ethiopian reach.

Indonesian Elite Consensus Falls Short of Victory

Unlike Ethiopia's bureaucratic empire in which a frail monarch presided over subordinate technocrats, professional bureaucrats and military, Indonesia, throughout its occupation of East Timor, remained under a close-knit circle of officers mostly with intelligence backgrounds. Even within this small circle, President Suharto ably managed what David Jenkins calls "creative tension" whereby his subordinates competed with each other around him.[41] He entrusted the East Timor portfolio to BAKIN deputy chief General Ali Murtopo, who oversaw the day-to-day activities of Operasi Komodo and served a diplomatic role as presidential envoy on the question of East Timor while his equally close ally and possible rival General Benny Murdani set in motion an altogether separate enterprise.[42]

Moreover, the multiple, overlapping security forces in Indonesia had considerable experience of working together during *Konfrontasi* with the newly independent Malaysia and the incorporation of West Papua. Not only had Murtopo and Murdani worked together in previous assignments under Suharto, but along with two other generals they also constituted what Jenkins dubbed an "inner core group" within the small circle of officers running the New Order.[43] Finally, the Indonesian elite's self-righteous consensus on the East Timor question, and the virtual absence of an alternative approach, rallied decision makers behind the generals.[44]

---

[41] David Jenkins, *Suharto and His Generals. Indonesian Military Politics, 1975–1983* (Ithaca, NY: Cornell Modern Indonesia Project, 1984), 22.

[42] Foreign Minister Adam Malik and General Yoga Sugama, the Chief of BAKIN (State Intelligence Coordinating Agency) seem to have been only vaguely informed or altogether unaware of the inner workings of the Indonesian scheme to secure East Timor. See the cables of R. A. Ambassador Woolcott in Jakarta to Canberra in Wendy Way (ed.), *Australia and the Indonesian Incorporation of Portuguese Timor* (Melbourne: Melbourne University Press, 2000).

[43] Jenkins, *Suharto and His Generals*, 23.

[44] The only exception to this consensus and seamless collaboration seems to have been President Suharto's concern about the timing and, possibly, the scale of the invasion, which had not received the approval of Indonesia's most important allies – the United States and Australia – and he feared may trigger negative backlash at the anticipated summit of the Non-aligned Countries and other international forums.

In running the show, both subversive and diplomatic, Murtopo was assisted and perhaps rivaled by the powerful military intelligence chief, Murdani. According to Conboy, "Murtopo – and, by extension, his Operation Komodo – was something of a competitor" to Murdani and *Flamboyan*.[45] As an operation based on political control and bankrolling of integrationists, it is possible that Komodo had run its course when developments in East Timor became polarized and explosive. That was at least what Murdani believed, reinforcing Conboy's and Jenkins's point that that competition between the two generals cannot be ruled out, especially given Suharto's skillful balancing of his subordinates. When FRETILIN boycotted the Macao Summit of June 1975 and the hoped-for "consensus" among all the Timorese political parties faltered, Murdani, by his account, resolved that Komodo was not enough to secure East Timor. Instead, he organized a small intelligence-based operation with units of Indonesian special forces disguised as East Timorese integrationists and Indonesian volunteers.[46]

While Murtopo traversed the capitals of countries relevant to Indonesia's grand scheme, Murdani was quietly putting together a far more robust militaristic "Plan B." As Murtopo's efforts seemed to lead to a dead end, Murdani unveiled his contingency plan amid the ongoing Indonesian diplomatic and subversive efforts.[47] In August 1975, Defense Minister Panggabean gave President Suharto a thorough projection of the military operation against East Timor, accompanied by detailed maps that filled the walls of the room. Looking around, the president asked who had prepared those maps and, when told that it was Murdani, exclaimed, "Benny! If you listen to Benny, you'll be in a war every day."[48] Indeed, Indonesia remained at war for the quarter century that followed, failing to emulate the swiftness of India's takeover of Goa in 1961 and pursuing a far-fetched counterinsurgency to pacify the newly acquired province.[49]

The Backlash of Genocidal Invasion and Occupation

An important distinction between the equally grim Eritrean and East Timorese realities was the fact that Indonesian strategy had an unmistakable

[45] Ken Conboy, *KOPASSUS. Inside Indonesia's Special Forces* (Jakarta: Equinox Publishing, 2003), 198ff.

[46] Julius Pour, *Benny Moerdani: Profil Prajurit Negarawan* (Jakarta: Kejuangan Panglima Besar Sudirman, 1993), 392.

[47] McDonald, *Suharto's Indonesia*, pp. 194 ff..

[48] Reported by David Jenkins and quoted in Carmel Budiardjo and Liem Soei Liong, *The War against East Timor* (London: Zed Books, 1984), 22.

[49] Distancing himself from the operation that went awry, General Murdani claims in his official biography that against his advice to wage small-scale, subversive operations, the landings in Dili turned into a full-blown invasion, unnecessarily involving an unwieldy joint command of all sectors of the Indonesian armed forces that took part. Pour, *Benny Moerdani*, 396ff.

genocidal streak. Ultimately proving to be a two-edged sword, with far-reaching significance for the East Timorese struggle, that streak became apparent as early as December 1975, when FRETILIN's modest but resilient resistance perforated unrealistic hopes of "quietly and quickly" taking over the half island. As the Indonesian military offensive lost the element of surprise and what remained of it was chaoticly executed, FALINTIL's early response gave the impression of a major battle, when in fact the fight "in the streets of Dili was little more than a delaying tactic" on the part of FALINTIL, as James Dunn noted.[50] Beyond its far-reaching political implications, therefore, the takeover of Dili itself was a relatively small-scale undertaking hyped in order to cover up the mass killing and pillage that attended the invasion.

Summary and widespread executions left bodies floating on the sea, strewn in the streets, and the only hospital filled with the dead and wounded. An eyewitness to some of the atrocities thus related an incident that quickly became a pattern:

At 2:00 p.m. (on December 7, 1975) 59 men, both Chinese and Timorese, were brought onto the wharf... These men were shot one by one, again with the crowd... being ordered to count. The victims were ordered to stand on the edge of the pier facing the sea, so that when they were shot their bodies fell into the water. Indonesian soldiers stood by and fired at the bodies in the water in the event that there was any further sign of life.[51]

The Indonesian military admitted that its soldiers had gone out of control during the invasion,[52] excesses that Jakarta tried to justify as proportional to the scale of the conflict.

In early February 1976, fewer than three months after the landings, UDT leader Francisco Xavier Lopez da Cruz estimated that between 50,000 and 60,000 East Timorese had perished.[53] He blamed intra-Timorese fighting before and during the Indonesian invasion for the death toll that would otherwise have been unacceptable for such a small-scale operation.[54] Indonesian foreign minister Adam Malik nonchalantly confirmed da Cruz's estimates: "50,000 people or perhaps 80,000 might have been killed" during the takeover, he said, and quickly proceeded to scold journalists: "it was war... what is the big fuss" about?[55] The outrage was about the genocidal

---

[50] James Dunn, *Timor: A People Betrayed* (Auckland: Jacaranda Press, 1983), 258.

[51] "Excerpts of James Dunn's talks with refugees in Portugal, January 1977" in Torben Retbøll (ed.), *East Timor, Indonesia and the Western Democracies. A Collection of Documents* (Copenhagen: IWGIA, 1980), 33–36.

[52] *Melbourne Age*, January 28, 1977.

[53] British Campaign for an Independent East Timor, Press Release, March 15, 1976: "50–60,000 Killed in East Timor since Indonesian Invasion."

[54] Interview with Ambassador Francisco Lopez da Cruz (August 21, 2006, Lisbon).

[55] *Sydney Morning Herald*, April 5, 1977.

occupation of a weak defenseless people, perishing, by most estimates, up to a third of them during the first half of the conflict.

Whereas the binding legal definition of genocide has remained the same since its codification in the Genocide Convention of 1948, social scientists continue to debate what should and should not be added to the defining features of genocide. According to these scholars, the "intent to destroy, in whole or in part, a national, ethnical, racial or religious group"[56] is too narrow to include cases that can legitimately be considered genocide.[57] With regard to East Timor, for example, Geoffrey Robinson points out that there "is *no evidence* that the Indonesian army commanders... *intended* to kill one-third of the population," but goes on to state that efforts to "destroy the resistance... led most decisively to genocide."[58] Moreover, for the same reasons that political killings were excluded in the 1940s, that is the fluidity of political groupings, today ethnicity, and ethnic identity, have become so fluid that they blur the distinction of where one group ends and the next begins.[59]

The existence of the constituent elements of genocide is not contested in the case of East Timor: direct killings; imposition of conditions that make life practically impossible; bodily and psychological harm; depopulation, including forcible transfer of Timorese children; and allegations of preventing births. However, Indonesia rejected any suggestions that its actions in East Timor were remotely genocidal. For its part, the East Timorese Commission for Reception, Truth and Reconciliation (CAVR) resorted to legal obscurantism on the question of genocide after offering an authoritative account of Indonesian gross human rights violations and mass killings:

> The issue of whether the victims of the attacks of the Indonesian security forces constituted a national group seeking to uphold their right to self-determination is one which would require highly technical legal consideration by a court with relevant jurisdiction. The Commission does not consider making such highly technical decisions of international jurisprudence to be within its mandate. It has, therefore, chosen not to reach any findings on whether the actions of the Indonesian security forces did or did not amount to genocide.[60]

---

[56] United Nations General Assembly Resolution 260 A (III), "Convention on the Prevention and Punishment on the Crime of Genocide," 9 December 1948, Article 2.

[57] Robert Cribb, "Genocide in the non-Western World: Implications for Holocaust Studies," Stephen L.B. Jensen (ed.), *Genocide: Cases, Comparisons and Contemporary Debates* (Copenhagen: Danish Center for Holocaust and Genocide Studies, 2003), 123–140.

[58] Geoffrey Robinson, *"If you Leave us Here We Will Die": How Genocide Was Stopped in East Timor* (Princeton, NJ: Princeton University Press, 2010), 49.

[59] Cribb, "Genocide in the non-Western World." This is also the view advanced by, among others, Mahmood Mamdani's account on *Saviors and Survivors: Darfur, Politics and the War on Terror* (New York: Pantheon Books, 2009).

[60] CAVR, *Chega!*, Part 8, Annex 1: "Responsibility and Accountability," 4.

Nonetheless, in line with the argument that outcomes are as good as "intent" to establish that genocide had been perpetrated, the decimation of so many people within such a short time of unbalanced – even low-intensity – fighting by world standards, left many observers and human rights advocates arguing that the Indonesian atrocities constituted genocide.[61]

The East Timorese themselves were convinced that Indonesia had come to exterminate them, as the Catholic Church documented in its damning reports on the condition of the people after the Indonesian take over.[62] Despite being under the strictest surveillance, even ordinary Timorese managed to whisper in the ears of rare foreign journalists and visiting delegations or to pass a note to them with a consistent message: "they are trying to get rid of us."[63] This conviction was important in several respects. First, seeing the worst of barbarities convinced many that it could not get worse, and so they aligned themselves with the independence movement. Indonesian forces could not break that resolve as they could not turn the clock back and undo the harm. Second, with ample evidence smuggled out of the country, and aided by avid advocates around the world, they made a strong case that theirs was a pursuit of justice against ongoing genocide. Timorese activists and foreign solidarity groups endeavored to and, with considerable success, invoked its legal and moral functions to gain widespread sympathy and active support around the world. That support ranged from student activists mobilizing in school grounds to well-connected individuals and groups taking the East Timor question to important corridors of power, especially U.S. and Western European legislatures (discussed in Chapter 5).[64]

Indonesian Approach to Counterinsurgency in East Timor
Almost immediately after occupation, East Timor became the 164th Subregional Military Command (Komando Resort Militer – Korem) Wira

---

[61] Among the earliest are Arnold Kohen and John Taylor, *An act of Genocide: Indonesia's Invasion of East Timor* (London: TAPOL, 1979). See also Antonio Barbedo de Magalhaes, *East Timor: Indonesian Occupation and Genocide* (Porto: Oporto University, 1992); and Mathew Jardine, *East Timor: Genocide in Paradise* (Monroe, ME: Odonian Press, 1999). For an interesting distinction between legal popular conception of genocide and an analysis of where the Indonesian invasion and occupation of East Timor fits, see Roger S. Clark, "Does the Genocide Convention Go Far Enough? Some Thoughts on the Nature of Criminal Genocide in the Context of Indonesia's Invasion of East Timor," 8 Ohio N.U.L. Rev. 321 (1981).

[62] CIDAC-CDPM, TL3174, "Statement of Martinho da Costa Lopes, Apostolic Administrator of East Timor, 1977–1983, to the American Catholic Bishops' Committee for Social Development and World Peace," Washington, DC, June 12, 1984; and CIDAC-CDPM, TL3184, Apostolic Administrator Belo, "Message from the Church of East Timor," January 1, 1985.

[63] Quoted in Taylor, *East Timor*, 106.

[64] For an example of U.S. Congressional sympathy with East Timor since the mid-1980s, see "The United Nations and East Timor," *Indonesia* 42 (October 1986):129–142.

Dharma under the Bali-based Regional Military Command XVI/Udayana (Komando Daerah Militer – Kodam). Korem 164 Wira Dharma was divided into district military commands (Komando Distrik Militer – Kodim), which were further subdivided into subdistrict military commands (Komando Rayon Militer – Koramil). These Koramils detailed their personnel and intelligence agents down to the villages and resettlement camps where many East Timorese had been interned after their surrender. Depending on the security situation of a given locality, these village-level operatives of Indonesian control were either village guidance noncommissioned officers or teams (Bintara/Team Pembina Desa – Babinsa).[65] The continuing insurgency allegedly necessitated the reinforcement of these territorial or organic units, stationed in East Timor for long-term assignments, with nonterritorial units rotated annually to East Timor from other regional military commands.

Moreover, Indonesia managed to quickly and more thoroughly "Timorize"[66] the war and strengthen its intelligence-gathering capacity by aggressively recruiting East Timorese into its security forces.[67] Between 1977 and 1978, for example, two Timorese battalions (Battalion 744 and Battalion 745) were established under Indonesian officer corps.[68] Similarly, Indonesia enlisted many East Timorese as civil defense (Pertahanan Sipil, Hansip/Wanra) and as trained people's units (Ratih). The cruelest exploitation of East Timorese for Indonesia's war effort was the involuntary initiation of the former as Tenaga Bantuan Operasi (or TBO, operational support personnel). Simply put, TBOs were unarmed civilian auxiliaries, including a significant number of underage children (some as young as twelve years old by Indonesian commanders' own accounts) used to help

---

[65] Budiardjo and Liong, *The War against East Timor*, 170.
[66] The initial phase of Indonesia's Timorization of its war to invade and occupy East Timor involved the Timorese partisans from the parties other than FRETILIN that were trained by *Kopassanda* (Indonesian special forces) and took part in the fighting on their side. According to an Australian report from May 1976, Indonesia continued the Timorization of its war effort by recruiting in the first half of 1976 of anti-FRETILIN East Timorese partisans to form the first batches of trained militia force. Way, *Australia*, 758–760. That was further intensified in 1977 with the inauguration of the exclusively Timorese Battalion 744 by Colonel Dading Kalbuadi and later vigorously pursued in accordance with General Yusuf's territorial warfare doctrine, leading up to the 1978 formation of another exclusively Timorese Battalion 745. CAVR, *Chega!*, Part 4: Regime of Occupation, 20; and Robert Lowry, *The Armed Forces of Indonesia* (St. Leonards, New South Wales, Australia: Allen and Unwin, 1996), 153.
[67] As an avid advocate of his people, Father Martinho da Costa was the first to point out the increased Timorization of Indonesian counterinsurgency and unfailingly criticize the practice.
[68] CAVR, *Chega!*, Part 4: Regime of Occupation, 20.

the Indonesian military in whatever their respective commanders deemed necessary.[69]

While these arrangements filled up the lower echelons of military and intelligence structures with East Timorese citizens, ABRI's analogy of itself as a human body best captures its rigid top-down approach to the counterinsurgency war, exacting a heavy price on the Timorese but denying them ownership. "If Korem 164/WD and its components are likened to the human body, with the Korem as the head (or the brain), the Kodims as the trunk and the Koramils as the arms and legs, the Babinsas and the Villages Guidance Teams are the fingers,"[70] wrote intelligence officer, Major Williem da Costa. East Timorese were poorly represented in the military hierarchy. Indonesian military officials circumvented at will whatever hierarchies they put in place. Moreover, the lack of a bottom-up approach for translating intelligence into action deprived the rank and file of ownership of the counterinsurgency strategy, to the long-term detriment of that very strategy. Furthermore, as ABRI's excesses negated its own pronouncements, its agents' forcible extraction of information even from their own conscripts could not prevent a large number of East Timorese from working on both sides.[71] In the short term, however, ABRI's crude execution of this system paid handsome returns in intelligence gathering.

Overall material poverty and physical insecurity of the population clearly offered a fertile ground for Indonesian recruitment of East Timorese as Hansip and Ratih. Some East Timorese saw signing up for service within the Indonesian security system as a way out of the degradation and misery that

---

[69] Interview with Major Alfredo Reinado Alves (June 25, 2006, Maubessi, East Timor). In his early teens, Alfredo was recruited as a TBO before he was involuntarily taken to Indonesia by one of the Indonesian officers under whom he worked as a civilian auxiliary. After independence, Alfredo quickly climbed the military hierarchy of independent East Timor's army, becoming the commander of its military police and navy when, at the height of the country's crisis in 2006, he left his base and remained a renegade soldier until he died on February 11, 2008, in a mysterious scuffle that left President José Ramos-Horta wounded.

On TBOs, also see Peter Carey's "Third-World Colonialism, the *Geração Foun*, and the Birth of a New Nation: Indonesia through East Timorese Eyes, 1975–99," *Indonesia* 76 (October 2003): 23–67.

[70] Korem 164 Wira Dharma Intelligence Section, "Instruction Manual: The Way for Babinsa or Team Pembina Desa to Break up GPK Support Network" in Budiardjo and Liong, *The War against East Timor*, 182.

[71] At the highest levels, Governor Carrascalão's mysterious roles throughout Indonesian occupation and his secret election as CNRT's vice-president in 1997 are examples in the administrative sector. In the police sector Portuguese Ambassador Ana Gomes (interview, August 22, 2006, Cascais, Portugal) related to me how during her first encounter with Paulo Martins in the late 1990s, the highest East Timorese police officer within the Indonesian security forces, she knew he worked with the pro-independence forces.

pervaded their lives. Many others, especially alleged FRETILIN supporters, were forcibly recruited into the Indonesian spy networks.[72] Bishop Belo best characterized these massive inductions of East Timorese into the Indonesian security apparatus, and the latter's consequent penetration down to the village level, as one half of the population spying on the other half.

Even with these structures in place and the war Timorized, however, Indonesia's unfinished project of pacifying the newly acquired twenty-seventh province did not change much over the course of the occupation: closing off the half island from the rest of the world and launching one counterinsurgency campaign after another with impunity. Between 1977 and 1985, Indonesian campaigns involved widespread execution of suspected nationalist sympathizers, indiscriminate bombing of civilian shelters and starving survivors into surrendering through destruction of water and food supplies. It is no exaggeration to state that the whole territory was turned into a prison island with tens of thousands (of surrendered fighters and civilian survivors of the Bases de Apoio) incarcerated in various inaccessible jails, even more interned in undersupplied and squalid "strategic hamlets" as part of counterinsurgency strategy of denying guerrillas the support of their people. Even the least-affected civilians lived in complete isolation from the rest of the world. They lived under constant surveillance, were repeatedly used as human shields, and were forced to work, unpaid, as porters and assistants.

Between June and September 1981, tens of thousands of highly armed regular and specialized Indonesian units launched *Operasi Keamanan* (Operation Security), involving the whole range of East Timorese elements of the Indonesian coercive apparatus. Hoping to weed out the resistance from its strongholds, Indonesia mobilized a minimum of 60,000 East Timorese civilians (145,000 according to another military document) to form a human shield for its troops. Known as "Fence of Legs," the civilians marched through the entire eastern half of the country in front of ABRI units in order to shield them from guerrilla attacks while cordoning off the fighters.[73] The East Timorese Catholic Church wrote in 1981 how during Operasi Keamanan, the people

have been forced to accompany the army to the mountains. A few months ago some villages were ... entirely empty of male inhabitants because all of the male work force was forced to leave their families, houses, field, and work just to accompany the Indonesian army morning and night for months on end ... [74]

---

[72] Conversations with Geoff Robinson (2007–2008, UCLA).
[73] CAVR, *Chega!*, Part 3: The History of the Conflict, pp. 90 ff.
[74] CIDAC-CDPM, TL3230, "Reflections of the East Timorese Religious: A Contribution to the 1981 MASRI Session," July 1981 in *Dossier on East Timor* (March 1982).

The abrupt freeze on these civilians' livelihoods increased their vulnerability to food shortage and famine. Hunger, lack of medical attention, physical exhaustion, and exposure on battlefields also exacted a heavy toll on the lives of marching civilians. An unknown number of civilians in this human shield were killed by Indonesian troops for allowing insurgents to escape. In several instances, hundreds of innocent civilians were killed in purges of areas suspected of harboring guerrillas.[75]

Indonesia Kills Surrendering Insurgents and Commits Many Abuses

Despite repeated promises of amnesty, many members of the resistance movement who surrendered were summarily executed, tortured to death or left to languish in jails across the archipelago. On top of the grave human rights violations and squalid living conditions in the resettlement camps established by the Indonesian military,[76] there were "persistent reports of large numbers of prisons in East Timor to which the International Committee of the Red Cross has no access; of summary execution; of disappearances of people who surrendered under the amnesty proclaimed by President Suharto."[77] Isolated from the rest of the world, an entire population languished in "strategic hamlets" and besieged towns and villages with meager resources.

The physical condition of the Timorese people in the immediate aftermath of the invasion escalated into a human tragedy. So bad was their situation that the chief executive of the Indonesian-appointed provisional government of East Timor, Arnaldo dos Reis Araújo, privately reported to President Suharto in June 1976 how impoverished Timorese would come

---

[75] "Prepared Statement of Michael Williams, Head of Asia Research Department, Amnesty International, Hearing before the Subcommittee on Asian and Pacific Affairs of the Committee on Foreign Affairs House of Representatives, Ninety-Seventh Congress, September 14, 1982" in *Recent Developments in East Timor* (Washington, DC: U.S. Government Printing Office, 1982), 37–39.

[76] Amid calls on Indonesia from humanitarian organizations to allow them to enter East Timor and avert further human catastrophe, in 1979, Benedict Anderson critiqued the U.S. government annual country report on Indonesia's human rights record for its failure to take full note of the appalling conditions in East Timor. The following year, he carried his criticism of U.S. complicity with Indonesian human rights violations in East Timor to the Ninety-Sixth Congress of the United States where he testified before the Congressional Hearing on human rights in noncommunist Asian countries in February 1980. See Benedict Anderson, "Indonesia and East Timor A Critique," in *A Critique of the United States Department of State's Country Reports on Human Rights Practices for 1979* (New York: Lawyers' Committee for International Human Rights, 1980), 271–281. Anderson, "Prepared Testimony on Human Rights in Indonesia and East Timor, Hearing before the Subcommittee on Asian and Pacific Affairs and on International Organizations of the Committee on Foreign Affairs, House of Representatives, 96th Congress, February 4, 6 and 7, 1980" in *Human Rights in Asia: Noncommunist Countries* (Washington, DC: U.S. Government Printing Office), 231–62, 275–77.

[77] Ibid., 233.

to the governor's residence and office asking for food. Having nothing to offer them, he partook in their suffering by shedding his tears with them: "Day and night, at my home [and] office, widows, orphans, children and cripples come begging for milk and clothing. I can do nothing but join my tears to theirs, because the provisional Government owns nothing."[78] Continued looting, wrote Dos Reis Araújo, left everybody "in a state of cruel insecurity." He added that formerly Timorese businesses reopened under new Indonesian owners, and the army occupied private houses while displaced Timorese lived in government buildings like schools, clinics, and offices.[79]

So many crimes were committed on so regular a basis that even the Indonesian-appointed sham Regional People's Representative Assembly, in spite of the inherent political and personal risks involved, protested to Indonesian President Suharto against the unacceptable conditions that their people endured. After receiving regular "verbal as well as written reports or complaints from the people about torture, maltreatment, murders and other unimaginable cases," the Assembly wrote in June 1981 that after five years of integration with Indonesia, the East Timorese people had not been accorded opportunities to enjoy peace, freedom, or the rule of law. The population was subjected to arbitrary military rule under the whims of select ABRI officers and a few strongmen who enjoyed military favor: "some individuals ... have introduced behavior ... of conquerors towards a conquered people [w]ith great brutality." Men and women were tortured, women raped and forced into concubinage, and property looted or destroyed at will. It concluded that seeing "their living conditions as a dangerous threat to their own being," the East Timorese people react, tacitly condoning the people's resistance.[80]

Indonesia's own documents, and the few foreign journalists who had been granted rare access to the blockaded half island, corroborate these conditions in the Indonesian-controlled Timorese towns, villages, and

---

[78] Quoted in Dunn, *Timor*, 265.

[79] Quoted in ibid.. Indonesian appropriation of Timorese houses continued with impunity. In 1982, for example, Amnesty International reported "two large houses in the Colmera area of Dili appropriated from their owners by units of the RPKAD (Resimen Pertempuran Komando Angkatan Darat) which are used for interrogation and detention." "Prepared Statement of Michael Williams, Head of Asia Research Department, Amnesty International, Hearing before the Subcommittee on Asian and Pacific Affairs of the Committee on Foreign Affairs House of Representatives, Ninety-Seventh Congress, September 14, 1982" in *Recent Developments in East Timor* (Washington, DC: US Government Printing Office, 1982), 36.

[80] First Level Regional People's Representative Assembly of the Province of East Timor to President of the Republic of Indonesia, "Report on the Development of Government Affairs in East Timor" June 3, 1981. Available at the Dili-based Archivo e Museo de Resistência.

concentration camps. Indonesian military instruction manuals captured by FALINTIL in 1982 advised that captives or those who surrendered should be physically separated from the rest of the population to avoid their making contacts and passing on information. For interrogation and incarceration purposes, one document instructed that captives should be sent offshore to the islet of Atauro and "other places designated... [to] cut the ties between the support networks in the settlements and the Nureps,"[81] that is the Nucleos de Resistência Popular (Nuclei of People's Resistance). An Australian diplomat filed a confidential report with Canberra that the military's incarceration of suspects in Atauro was "an integral part of the strategy being followed by the Indonesian authorities in an attempt to rid the province of remaining Fretilin... Any family thought to have a relative 'in the mountains' is sent to Atauro. They are sent in family groups."[82] Amnesty International estimated that as early as 1981 or 1982, approximately four thousand prisoners had been incarcerated in Atauro.[83]

Jakarta incessantly denied the existence of prisons in Atauro, but its highest commander in East Timor admitted that they were keeping FALINTIL guerrillas' relatives as hostages in Atauro. Colonel A. P. Kalangi told *Philadelphia Inquirer* journalist Rod Nordland, "You know, east or west, home is best... Maybe some of those who are in the mountains will feel their family is unhappy, so they will come down. It is a positive system." Allowed on a rare but guided and highly restrictive tour of East Timor (including Atauro), Nordland discovered that there were thousands of political prisoners, "most of them simply because they are related, often distantly, to a fighter with the guerrilla group."[84] Yet, Kalangi cynically added that it was for the detainees' own good that they were in Atauro because FRETILIN guerrillas had been harassing them and because "they like to be here."[85]

During the eleven-day tour, Nordland could corroborate large-scale forced resettlement of innocent civilians thus: "Hundreds of thousands have been relocated in a policy to depopulate the countryside and deprive the

---

[81] Korem 164 Wira Dharma Intelligence Section, "Instruction Manual" in Budiardjo and Liong, *The War against East Timor*, 180.

[82] Quoted in Taylor, *East Timor: The Price of Freedom*, 105.

[83] Although the statistics are hard to come by, there is little doubt that many either were killed or died for lack of adequate care. Some were released or transferred to other prisons apparently due to growing pressure from the Red Cross and/or other human rights advocacy groups. Two of my informants had been detained in Atauro before one was transferred to Java while the other was released.

[84] Rod Nordland, "Under Indonesian Control, Timor Remains a Land of Hunger, Oppression and Misery," *The Philadelphia Inquirer*, May 28, 1982.

[85] Ibid.

guerrillas of civilian support." He also observed that there were "virtually no civil liberties [in East Timor]. No one may leave his village or hometown without permission. Telephone calls and telegrams to places outside East Timor are forbidden. No one may leave the province without special – and rarely granted – permission."[86]

People suspected of, or caught collaborating with, the guerrillas were regularly picked up off the streets or from their homes never to be seen again. After Dunn's and Taylor's profiling of a numbing number of cases, the CAVR extensively documented summary disappearances of such civilians as well as surrendered or captured guerrillas.[87] The standard explanation that the authorities gave to the families of the disappeared was that they had "gone hunting," "gone to school," or even "gone to Jakarta."[88] Ainaro won notoriety for being the first district of documented cases of "gone to Jakarta" disappearances as early as 1976. Cliffs around Builico came to be known as "Jakarta II" – where those destined for execution were herded, shot, and dumped down inaccessible escarpments.[89] By all accounts, the detention system, disappearances, and the waves of famine and disease along with the actual fighting caused the decimation of up to 180,000 East Timorese out of a population of less than 700,000.

Surviving and Moving Beyond the Challenges: Eritrean Splinter Groups Coalesce into a Maoist Movement

Breaking free from the ELF in 1969–1970 offered the splinter groups an opportunity, but it also presented them with major challenges. Besides logistical difficulties, they faced a grave danger as the "mother organization" delivered them an ultimatum: rejoin its ranks or face liquidation. In the face of this threat and that of Ethiopia, leaders of the splinter groups needed each other and quickly started discussing ways of overcoming their common challenges. Local and regional hostility speeded up

---

[86] Ibid.

[87] While many pro-Timor advocacy and neutral rights groups had reported on several of these cases with surprising detail given the opaqueness of the regime, the CAVR report added many others that had not come to light before, accompanied by painful recollection of survivors.

[88] CAVR, *Chega!*, Part 7.2: Unlawful Killing and Enforced Disappearances, 67–68.

[89] CAVR, *Chega!*, Part 3: History of the Conflict, 97. While the horrors of Jakarta II is an example, international human rights groups as well as the CAVR have documented that this was a widespread practice within the framework of Indonesian counterinsurgency policy and that it was possibly followed deliberately by the military on the ground with probable encouragement of their superiors in Bali and Jakarta. At the time of writing, the postindependence East Timor-Indonesia Truth and Friendship Commission is expected to release its findings confirming this.

their eventual merger. Moreover, representing the eastern coastal low-lands, the central highlands, and western and northwestern lowlands, respectively, each of PLF 1, PLF 2, and the Obelites offered the other two what they did not have. The all-powerful Sabbe offered access to external assistance and an outlet to the outside world. Nonetheless, as John Markakis, Gaim Kibreab, and many other scholars and direct participants have shown, their individual internal dynamics and their interactions with each other were not free from the sectarian and regional divisions that caused their breaking away in the first place.

The leaders of the splinter groups decided to form a core group to lead the struggle and transform it into a true revolutionary movement. Romedan Mohammed-Nur of PLF 1 and Isaias Afwerki of PLF 2, as well as many of their comrades, had long believed in the concept. As the ELF fractured in the face of the reformist avalanche Islah, they seized the opportunity.[90] During their training in China at the height of the Cultural Revolution of the 1960s, the two had shown a keen interest in the Chinese experience and learned organizing techniques such as the creation of a vanguard party appropriate to the Eritrean context in a bid to reform the defunct ELF.[91]

Suspicion and distrust marred the first post-breakaway meeting between leaders of the first splinter groups in Simoti (in northern Denkalia) in November 1970. Like-minded fighters in the two camps, however, stood behind their Maoist leaders Romedan and Isaias, who, according to a leading cadre Mohamoud "Sherifo", "talked amongst themselves [a]nd...came to an agreement, more or less, that they should form this core group" and unify the splinter groups.[92] On April 4, 1971, about a dozen members from the two PLFs met in Gedem to launch what became the clandestine Eritrean People's Revolutionary Party (commonly called the People's Party)[93] that

---

[90] Haile "Deru" Weldetensae as Isaias's ideological twin and Mahmoud Sherifo as a leading cadre in the Romedan-led PLF-1 acknowledge that their prior exposure to leftist ideas coupled with the reality they found in the ELF prompted them to look toward a core revolutionary group as a way to remedy the problem. But both of them give the credit of leadership in this endeavor to Isaias and Romedan. Connell, *Conversations*, 42, 74–75.

[91] Haile in Connell, *Conversations*, 42–47; and interview with Romedan Mohammed-Nur (September 25, 2005).

[92] Mahmoud Sherifo in Connell, *Conversations*, 74–75.

[93] Ibid., 75. These were Isaias Afwerki, Romedan Mohammed-Nur, Mahmoud Sherifo, Mesfen Hagos, Mohammed Ali Omaro, Abu-Bakr Mohammed Hassan, Ibrahim Afa, Hassan Mohammed Amir, Ali Said Abdellah, Ahmed Tahir Baduri, and Ahmed Al-Qeisi. According to Connell, although Haile "Deru'e" Weld'ensae and Alamin Mohammed Said did not attend this meeting, they belonged to the founding core and went on to play major role as they jointly controlled the political wing of both the clandestine party, also called the People's Party, and the Front, that is, EPLF.

facilitated the merger of the splinter groups into the EPLF and ran the latter from behind the scenes.[94]

With the People's Party in place, the Tekhli Conference of August 1971 consolidated and legitimized the leadership of Isaias in PLF 2, while the October 1971 Embahra Conference brought PLF 1's young, intellectually inclined, and progressive elements to the top, with Romedan Mohammed-Nur at the forefront.[95] Despite this cooperation, early interaction between these two groups remained rocky. PLF-1, for example, denied PLF-2 weapons that the former could spare and that the latter needed badly.[96] In February 1972, PLF-1 and PLF-2 sent separate delegations to Beirut to discuss pressing logistical and materiel challenges with the General Secretariat's Osman Saleh Sabbe.[97] As a resourceful patron of PLF-1, Osman Saleh Sabbe is believed to have urged PLF-1 to talk to PLF-2 and to have also said that he would not release additional supplies to them if they were not willing to share them with PLF-2.[98] It is also possible that the two groups' fear of manipulation by this ambitious and formidable diplomat facilitated the merger of their separate delegations in order to muster the clout to stand up to him. The three sides then agreed, among other things, to form a single front as a step toward full integration of the three groups inside Eritrea, for the General Secretariat to become their foreign delegation, and, in the interim, for the splinter groups (including the Obelites) to share

---

[94] While the inner workings of the Eritrean People's Revolutionary Party (the People's Party) remain a closely guarded secret, Dan Connell is the only scholar who has discussed the party with its founders and leaders and the only one who has published on its early origins. See "Inside the EPLF: the Origins of the 'People's Party' and its Role in the Liberation of Eritrea," *Review of African Political Economy*, September 2001, reprinted in Connell, *Building a New Nation. Collected Articles on the Eritrean Revolution (1983–2002)*, Vol. 2 (Trenton, NJ: Red Sea Press, 2004), 898–924. His account is largely drawn from interviews with Haile and a corroborating interview with Sherifo, both of which have also been published in Connell, *Conversations*.

[95] The elected leaders of PLF-1 were Isaias Afwerki, Mesfen Hagos, Asmerom Gherezghiher, Tewelde Eyob, and Solomon Weldemariam. Elected leaders of PLF-2 are Romedan Mohammed-Nur, Ahmed Hilal, Abubakar Mohammed Hassan, Saleh Tetew, and Abubakar Mohammed-Jimi'e. Alamin Mohammed Said, *Al-Defe' wa al-Teredi: Al-Thewra al-Irtriyah. Qistat al-Inshiqaq al-Dakhilyah Lil-Thewra al-Iritriyah* (Asmara: Dogoli Press, 1992), 99.

[96] RDC/His/Ar/St/9, 06443, "Mewladin Temekron Hizbawi Ghenbar Harenet Ertra" ("The Birth and Experience of the EPLF"), 70.

[97] While Romedan Mohammed-Nur and Ali Said Abdellah represented PLF-1, Isaias Afwerki and Mesfen Hagos represented PLF-2.

[98] Interview with Taha Mohammed-Nur (September 17, 2005, Asmara, Eritrea). Dr. Taha said that he attended those meetings and remembers how PLF-2 delegates reluctantly accepted Sabbe's ultimatum. EPLF literature, on the other hand, is consistent that both PLF-1 and PLF-2 suspected Sabbe's machinations and approached him together in order to avoid being manipulated by him.

procured supplies according to need.[99] Imperatives of survival compelled the two leaderships to overcome their differences and expedite their merger. That became particularly urgent in light of the ELF's and Ethiopia's resolve to eliminate the splinter groups before they consolidated themselves.

Meanwhile, the reluctance of many of its rank and file to fire on fellow fighters impeded the ELF's stealth efforts to liquidate the splinters. Thus, its remaining provisional leaders sought a popular mandate in a hastily organized congress. Held between October and November 1971, the ELF's First National Congress passed an ill-thought-out resolution regarding the splinter groups and adopted a military strategy against Ethiopia that went unimplemented. The ELF acknowledged that its Eritrean Liberation Army had not been structured as it should have been, and announced a new plan of action. Accordingly, the Liberation Army was divided into two: a permanent army stationed in the liberated areas, which would conduct hit-and-run attacks, and small units operating within the occupied territories, which would wage guerrilla warfare. The ELF also decided to establish bases in its liberated areas and to make one of these its central headquarters.[100]

None of these recommendations was implemented because the ELF was preoccupied primarily with carrying out the congress's resolution to eliminate the splinter groups. Its Congress resolved that "the Eritrean experience demonstrates that the Eritrean field can accommodate but one revolution under the leadership of one organization." It accordingly issued an ultimatum for the splinter groups to rejoin ELF ranks. Should they fail to do so, Congress mandated the new leadership to do everything necessary to ensure unity under ELF guardianship.[101] From March 1972, the ELF began to hunt down the splinter groups while Ethiopian efforts to crush all Eritrean rebels continued unabated.

Pressed from all sides, the splinter groups held a joint two-week conference in October 1972 to examine the state of affairs. Their resolutions were of vital importance to the Eritrean independence struggle and are crucial for our understanding of the genesis of an alternative grand strategy of liberation. To facilitate their merger, they set up a fifty-seven-member

[99] RDC/His/Ar/St/9, 06443, "Mewladin Temekron Hizbawi Ghenbar Harenet Ertra," 71–72; and Alamin, *Al-Defe' wa al-Teredi*, 86ff.
[100] RDC/His/ELF/3, "First National Congress of the ELF. Military Work Plan" (Tigrigna), November 12, 1971.
[101] The resolution is available as an index in Alamin, *Al-Defe' wa al-Teredi*, 169–181. Accused by the EPLF for being Abdellah Idris's lieutenant in executing the stealth liquidation operations, Mohammed Osman Ezaz has a nuanced take on this point. According to him, history has proven that ELF's conclusions were accurate. He argues that it was precisely because of that that the EPLF saw the need to push the ELF out of Eritrea and successfully fought against the Ethiopian forces without the distractions of dealing with a rival. Interview with Mohammed Osman Ezaz (September 3, 2005, Tessenei, Eritrea).

proto-legislative body, seven members of which constituted the top leader-ship entrusted with administrative matters. Politically, the groups decided to expose to the Eritrean public that the ELF had started a civil war to liquidate them. This necessitated political work among civilians to galvanize support. The splinter groups would conduct literacy as well as political education and indoctrination of their own soldiers. The differences among the groups were of secondary concern and could be resolved through democratic dia-logue, they determined. Militarily, the three groups decided to make the Sahel in northeastern Eritrea their rear base because of its inaccessible ter-rain, its proximity to the Red Sea and Sudan, and its distance from mainland Ethiopia. They also decided to introduce uniform military standards in the composition of their forces and establish a common military command made up of the top leaders of the three groups.[102]

Splinter Groups Unify around Secular, Inclusive Philosophy

The political and philosophical foundation for unifying the splinter groups was similarly laid during this period. At its Tekhli Conference of November 1971, PLF 2 promulgated a basic document, "Nehnan Elamanan" ("We/Us and Our Goals"),[103] that articulated its ideological orientation and political objectives. Authored by Isaias Afwerki, the document offered a dialectical materialist analysis of Eritrean society before stating that the group was neither Muslim (or Arab) nor preachers of the gospel. Rather, they were res-urrecting the era of the ELM's organized secular advocacy for Eritrean-ness over any other identity. "Nehnan Elamanan" was instrumental in shaping the EPLF's Weltanschauung. During their October 1972 conference, the splinter groups discussed and adopted key principles of the document as their new organization's political cornerstone.[104]

These decisions facilitated administrative efficiency of the splinter groups and unified the political-military organization. Their enthusiasm about involving civilians and their choice of the rear base indicated these leaders' acknowledgment of the looming protracted people's war. Meanwhile, they settled for what they called "temporary/transitional liberation" in which no permanent bases or projects were started and military operations were limited to small-scale guerrilla operations against Ethiopian forces.

The strengthening of Eritrean nationalism and loyalty to Eritrea across ethnic, regional, and religious divides had to be cultivated through vigor-ous work among the people. Liberation from Ethiopian colonialism and domestic social transformation were to go hand in hand. Parallel to its

---

[102] RDC/His/Ar/St/9, 06443, "Mewladin Temekron Hizbawi Ghenbar Harenet Ertra," 72.

[103] RDC/His/Ar/St/8; 02104, "Nehnan Elamanan," November 1971.

[104] After practicing these principles for years, the EPLF convened its First National Congress in 1977 under the slogans "Organize, Conscientize and Arm the Masses" and "Step by Step Liberate the Land and the People."

military operations to liquidate the breakaway groups, the ELF reinvig-
orated its own political work to counter and outdo the EPLF's grassroots
political canvassing. The growing number of educated and left-leaning fighters in its ranks offered a formidable body of cadres to broaden political
education among the fighters and the public. In its strategic sociopolitical
planning, however, the ELF believed, unlike the EPLF, in achieving political
independence first and social transformation second.

Prevailing domestic military conditions and regional diplomatic developments precluded the splinter groups' convening of the congress that had
been anticipated to take place within six months of their October 1972
meeting. First, the signing in 1972 of the Ethiopian-mediated agreement
between Khartoum and the Anya-Nya rebels of South Sudan mended fences
between Haile Selassie and Sudanese president Ja'afer al-Numieri, alienating the latter from the Eritrean cause. The splinter groups' temporary bases
had no more access across the border in eastern Sudan. Second, threatened
by the emergence of this unified force and hoping to take advantage of its
displacement from Sudan, the Ethiopian army launched a massive offensive
against it in March 1973. Finally, between April and May, the ELF resumed
its military campaign against the splinter groups.

The People's Party stepped up its leadership and clandestinely took control of what seemed a dangerously slow merger. The speeded up merger of
the splinter groups, however, prompted the withdrawal of the Obelites from
the process. It also sparked other dissentions, after the remaining two groups
fully merged their forces in September 1973 under a temporary leadership of
nine who became the Field Command.[105] Although the name Eritrean People's Liberation Front was not officially adopted until the 1977 Congress,
that merger signified the birth of the EPLF.

To bring the Obelites back into the fold without undermining concerns
and interests of the two PLF groups, Romedan Mohammed-Nur quietly
planted Abu Tyara among the Obelites to bring the entire group back or,
failing that, to split and weaken them. The ELF attacked the Obelites right
after their withdrawal from the two PLFs, and Abu Tyara succeeded in bringing most survivors back in early 1974, while the rest escaped to Sudan.[106]

This new organization had to recover from the withdrawal of the Obelites
and face another challenge from within. Left-leaning fighters called Menka'e
(literally meaning "bats," so called for their supposed nightly canvassing)

[105] RDC/His/Ar/St/9, 06443, "Mewladin Temekron Hizbawi Ghenbar Harenet Ertra," 73.
These were Romedan Mohammed-Nur, Isaias Afwerki, Mesfen Hagos, Tewelde Eyob,
Asmerom Gherezghiher, Ali Said Abdellah, Saleh "Tetew," and Solomon Weldemariam.
According to Bereket Habte Selassie, by 1975, Saleh Mohammed Idris (Abu Ajaj) and
Mohammed Omar Abdella (Abu Tyara) belonged to this provisional leadership of the
EPLF; *The Crown and the Pen. The Memoirs of a Lawyer Turned Rebel* (Trenton, NJ: Red
Sea Press, 2007), 317.
[106] Interview with Mohammed Omar Abdellah ("Abu Tyara").

challenged the leadership on multiple grounds. The fledgling leadership resorted to harsh methods in containing the threat that Menka'e presented. Having incarcerated those suspected of involvement in alleged subversion, the nascent EPLF leadership held lengthy deliberations, the substance of which is yet to be corroborated by sources other than its own, and determined that Menka'e was a "destructive movement."[107] In June 1974, it accordingly put a "disciplinary conclusion" to it.[108] In August 1975, the EPLF executed the Menka'e ringleaders. This "disciplinary conclusion" set a precedent for future purges and sent the clearest of messages to any individuals or groups who would deviate from the prescribed code and pose a threat to the EPLF.

Soon thereafter, the lead executioner of the Menka'e himself faced the same fate after he sought to challenge the EPLF leadership. This time, internal *dissenters* were dubbed Yemin (Arabic for "right") for their alleged right-wing and regionalist orientations. Much remains to be discovered about the true nature of these dissenters and the process of the EPLF's revolutionary justice. Such methodical efficiency in containing and resolving internal matters and swiftness in clamping down on out-and-out dissent spared the EPLF much outside scrutiny.[109] That is particularly evident in light of the ELF's haphazardness that had prompted such domestic and external commotion.

The ELF's relative openness, its leadership's inability to harmonize differences among themselves and within their ranks, and its repeated failures to efficiently handle internal dissent while the bigger fight against the common enemy was raging sealed its fate. The ELF's leaders insisted that as long as the fighters "adhered to the principle of democratic centralism," the ELF allowed them "to fully exercise publicly their inalienable rights and to participate in forming and holding their opinion."[110] Touring ELF bases in liberated Eritrea in the mid-1970s, Dan Connell confirmed the diversity of views among the ELF ranks, but he also observed their relative inefficiency:

The ELF fighters were an easy going...bunch, far less stiff and somber than the earnest comrades of the EPLF, but also considerably less efficient. Things seemed to happen more by chance than design, discipline was loose, and the guerrillas within the ELF appeared to have more diversity of outlook than those in the EPLF.[111]

---

[107] RDC/Hist/Ar.St/1, 01959, "A'enawi Menqisiqas nay 73" ("Destructive Movement of 1973") to which even Alamin refers his readers.

[108] RDC/His/Ar/St/9, 06443, "Mewladin Temekron Hizbawi Ghenbar Harenet Ertra," p. 75.

[109] Given the EPLF's isolation and its consequent fierce self-reliance, however, the potential of its internal actions drawing external attention and its coming under external scrutiny should not be overemphasized.

[110] Awate.com interview with ELF Chairman, Ahmed Mohammed Nasser, (Jan 29, 2001): http://www.awate.com/portal/content/view/1037/11/

[111] Dan Connell, *Against All Odds: A Chronicle of the Eritrean Revolution* (Trenton, NJ: Red Sea Press, 1993), 75.

ELF bases had what many call "sedi democracy" (that is unregulated democracy), perhaps ideal for the emergence of an open society, but only if it enabled it to survive the cutthroat guerrilla days. Although discipline so strict that it resulted in purges and executions could destroy a guerilla movement, no movement can afford the lack of discipline among its ranks. The ELF could neither resolve simmering rivalry among its leaders nor control what amounted to near anarchy within its rank and file. Necessary ideological, structural, disciplinary and emotional capacity to wage a war and pursue its raison d'être – Eritrean independence – thus withered on the altar of the elusive democratic centralism.

An important distinction in this regard is how, as a supposed revolutionary core, the record of the ELF's Labor Party fades in light of the People's Party in the EPLF. Although prominent ELF leaders in the field belonged to the secret Labor Party, the latter neither maintained secrecy nor cultivated the necessary discipline and ideological uniformity among its highest leaders. It also failed to rein in the actual or aspiring leaders of the front. Labor Party membership was flaunted around in public while others sought membership in order to tactically outmaneuver their rivals within. Once the Labor Party's Marxist orientation became a public secret amid rising mistrust and tension that gripped the party leadership, the non-Marxists and the Islamists in the ELF formed a Ba'athist party and an Islamic grouping, respectively. Similarly, after losing his leadership position in the front, the ELF's former political chief Herui Tedla Bairu formed a new Central Marxist Group which quickly evolved into the Eritrean Democratic Movement (EDM),[112] the bulk of whose forces joined the EPLF in 1977 as the ELF geared up to destroy it.

In contrast to the ELF's unrelenting splintering, the EPLF became highly centralized and ideologically uniform. Connell noticed that it "looked and acted like a highly disciplined political organization" and that there existed within it "an unsettling level of rhetorical uniformity about nearly everything," despite its claim of being "a broad based united front made up of people from many different political persuasions." Connell went on to say that "Whatever its internal debates and differences, there was a tight lid on sharing them."[113] That was at least partially because, unbeknownst to the fighters who were not members, the People's Party detailed its functionaries down to the smallest units of the EPLF and controlled the latter through a clandestine chain of command. Alamin Mohammed Said best captured its purpose when he said, "Everything that the EPLF did was decided by the party beforehand."[114]

---

[112] Awate.com interview with Herui Tedla Bairu (January 1, 2001): http://www.awate.com/portal/content/view/352/11/
[113] Connell, *Against All Odds*, 42.
[114] Interview with Alamin Mohammed Said (September 28, 2005, Asmara, Eritrea).

At its highest level, the EPLF's politburo doubled as the Central Committee of the People's Party and the latter decided the slates of EPLF's central committee, which elected the politburo. Moreover, answerable to its elected chairman Isaias Afwerki, each of these members ran the specialized departments of the EPLF while presiding over the party apparatus within their respective spheres. In such a way, it came under joint leadership of militarily adept politicians and politically conscious military commanders. Moreover, by instituting egalitarianism among its rank and file – empowering its following by pursuing women's rights and the inclusion of ethnic minorities, land reform, and so on – the EPLF/People's Party, in the words of its principal ideologues, articulated an "ideology that could give some light at the end of that dark tunnel. It made people commit themselves. It made each and every individual think of himself [and herself] as part of the whole organization..."[115] Each worked accordingly in every aspect, knowing full well that the fighter next to him or her would do the same or better.[116]

Surviving and Moving Beyond the Challenges: East Timorese Resistance from the Jaws of Defeat

By early 1979, the Indonesian military had wrought havoc on the FRETILIN-led nationalist resistance in East Timor. Only a small group of second-tier leaders and scattered fighters stood between the devastated resistance and a complete Indonesian military victory. With no organized units left standing and almost no communication among survivors, the numerically, materially, and morally diminished FALINTIL was in complete disarray. Contact among the fighters, and between fighters on one hand and civilians in Indonesian-occupied territories on the other was severely limited, what communication did occur was marred by suspicion and distrust.

As Matebean fell to the Indonesians at the height of the Encirclement and Annihilation operations in November 1978, several military and political leaders broke out of the siege. They – FRETILIN Central Committee (CFF) members Xanana Gusmão and Fernando Txay, sector commander Kilik Wae Gae, Mauk Muruk, Ologari Asuwain, and others – escaped toward Ponta Leste,[117] where they linked up with another CCF member, Ma'Huno, and other surviving military commanders. They immediately set out to find their superiors. Before long, they came to realize that the resistance leadership had fallen. Stepping up to the challenge of gathering the shattered

---

[115] Haile in Connell, *Conversations*, 53–54.

[116] Observing this, Connell wrote that the EPLF generated "a palpable excitement... and seemingly boundless enthusiasm that was as infectious as it was seductive." Connell, *Against All Odds*, 42.

[117] Niner, *To Resist Is to Win*, 57ff.; and jnterview with Paulino Gama "Mauk Muruk" (October 9, 2007, Rijswijk, the Netherlands).

pieces and reigniting the resistance, they traversed the country to identify who to reorganize, to assess conditions, reestablish contacts with each other and with the East Timorese civilian population, and evaluate the occupiers' military disposition.[118]

The full story of this search for surviving resistance fighters, who had avoided capture and remained in the jungle to fight, is largely obscure.[119] Xanana Gusmão's and Paulino Gama's (Mauk Muruk) accounts of this stage of the East Timorese independence struggle are complementary, with slight contradictions that can be attributed to their documentation (written and in interviews, respectively) after the two fell out with each other. Gusmão's, as ably detailed by his biographer, shows him traversing the country to locate surviving fighters, reconnecting with the civilian population, and gathering intelligence on the Indonesian forces.[120] "In 1979," he wrote, "I went from house to house, village to village and asked my people if they were still willing to continue to fight."[121] This account also shows Gusmão at the center of similar missions conducted by others under his instructions. While the veracity of Gusmão's centrality is confirmed by his emergence as the highest leader of the reorganized movement, Mauk Muruk's account tells that Gusmão was not alone in conducting the searches and leading the restructuring.

Accordingly, the leaders who now became pioneer reorganizers met in March 1979 at a place called Titilari-Laivai to assess their conditions and devise mechanisms to ensure the continuity of the resistance.[122] It was probably here that they decided to carry out the search in three broad areas: Dili-Same-Suai-Batugade, Dili-Same-Viqueque-Baucau, and Viqueque-Lospalos – assigned to Ologari Asuwain, Xanana Gusmão and Paulino Gama respectively.[123] Their efforts benefited from Indonesian mistreatment of the Timorese population.

Indonesian mistreatment and fear thereof drove many East Timorese into the arms of the resistance movement, even where there had not previously been enthusiastic support for FRETILIN. When itinerant emissaries of the nationalist cause went from one village to another in exploratory treks, people readily offered to help them locate and regroup with their dispersed

---

[118] Niner, *To Resist Is to Win*, 57–59.
[119] The only account written by Gusmão places the author at the center of all that happened from early 1979. The veracity of Gusmão's centrality is not challenged and is, in fact, confirmed by his emergence as the highest leader of the reorganized resistance movement, but he was not alone in this endeavor.
[120] Niner, *Xanana*, 37ff.
[121] Niner, *Xanana*, 66.
[122] Gama, "The War in the Hills" in Carey and Bentley (eds.), *East Timor at the Crossroads*, 101.
[123] Interview with Paulino Gama "Mauk Muruk" (October 9, 2007, Rijswijk, the Netherlands).

comrades hiding from Indonesian forces. After such successful assessments and preliminary reorganization, some of the guerrillas quietly descended into Dili to announce their survival to compatriots and enemies alike. On June 10, 1980, clandestine guerrillas in the capital mounted simultaneous attacks on the Maubara radio and television transmitter as well as on Indonesian military installations at Becora and Lahane in and around Dili.[124] These guerrillas were soon emboldened by the biggest-ever defection of armed East Timorese recruited into the Indonesian security forces as civil guards, Pertahanan Sipil, or Hansips.

In early March 1981, Gusmão and Ma'Hunu convened a meeting of military commanders and middle-ranking political cadres at Maubai (in Lacluta, Viqueque district) to reorganize and resume the struggle. In the first acts of what came to be called the First National Conference for the Reorganization of the Country, the assembled fighters formed the Concelho Revolucionário de Resistência Nacional (CRRN, the Revolutionary Council of National Resistance) and turned themselves into an eleven-man leadership of political cadres and military commanders.[125]

At Maubai, the country was divided into three sectors: the Frontier on the west, the Center, and Ponta Leste on the east. FALINTIL was restructured into light, highly mobile guerrilla units operating within the geographical limits of their assigned sectors. Under Paulino Gama, the former Shock or Intervention Brigade was resurrected as the Red Brigade that was not bound to any territorial delimitation. All these guerrilla forces reported to FALIN-TIL chief of staff Kilik Wae Gae, who was answerable to commander in chief Xanana Gusmão. The latter also doubled as national political commissar.[126]

Although the new leadership grew more realistic, and less ideological, it implemented the ideological orientation adopted during the 1977 Laline Conference and established the Partido Marxista-Leninsta FRETILIN (PMLF). This was done out of loyalty to their fallen leaders and in hope of winning progressive countries' support. Nevertheless, while the Marxist-Leninist party remained obscure until it was altogether abandoned in the mid-1980s, Laline's ideological rendering was not at all followed in the day-to-day operations of the revived movement.

CRRN was the most ingenious and dynamic institution that the new leaders created in March 1981. Although technically guided by the Marxist-Leninist party and drawing its entire leadership from FRETILIN, CRRN

[124] Interviews with David Diaz Ximenes (June 30, 2006, Hera, East Timor) and Francisco Carvalho "Chico" (May 13, 2006, Dili, East Timor); Niner, *To Resist Is to Win*, 64n99; CAVR, *Chega!*, Part 3: History of the Conflict, 90; and Niner, *Xanana*, 61–63.

[125] In addition to Gusmão and Ma'Huno, these are Mau Hodu, Bere Malae Laka, Kilik Wae Gae, Nelo Kadomi, Lemo Rai, Holy Natxa, Lere Anan Timor, Hari Nere, and Paulino Gama (Mauk Muruk).

[126] Interviews with Colonel Lere Anan Timor (July 11, 2006, Hera, East Timor) and Dr. Roque Rodrigues (July 8, 2006, Dili, East Timor).

revolved around the guerrilla insurgency, reflecting the new reality that they were engaged in a protracted war of independence above anything else. Presided over by the elected president, who was also the commander in chief of the FALINTIL and the national political commissar,[127] it was sufficiently centralized for a guerrilla movement. Given Indonesia's extensive spying networks that had penetrated the Timorese society, it seems that CRRN was deliberately amorphous at the grassroots level;[128]; as it loosened down the hierarchy, it remained a confusing tangle of structures.

The Nureps were village-based clandestine units of CRRN. Above them were the subdistrict-level Centros de Resistência Nacional (Cernac, National Resistance Center), which included members of the Nucleos de Resistência as well as full-time FALINTIL fighters. Finally, there were the Comissõs Regionais de Resistência (Committees for Regional Resistance). Although the uneven distribution of these structures across the country and their lack of uniformity in operation obscured their function, structurally, the national political commissar regulated them through a chain of political cadres. The latter, for their part, organized sympathizers in district-level *Caixas or estafeta.*[129]

This period reinforced Gusmão's on-the-job leadership training, which would later enable him to shepherd the resistance to independence. Having observed as early as December 1975, that "the situation of the war demanded a strong grip of command... [that] the majority of us, the members of the CCF, were unpoliticized... [and] were too inexperienced,"[130] Gusmão resolved to become that leader. Developing his political skills, he refused to indulge in what he saw as excessive ideological rhetoric surrounding him. Instead, he leaned toward simplifying issues and speaking to subordinates and civilians in plain language, unencumbered by terminological tangles of leftist ideologies. He reflected that he was in fact practicing the art of becoming "less routinely [*sic*], less dogmatic and less in the revolutionary style" amid their revolutionary resistance. And in that, he found a formidable guide in Mao Tse-tung.

---

[127] Gusmão did not take the title of president, which he most likely convinced his colleagues to bestow on Abilio de Araújo, as the latter claims. But there existed a lack of structural clarity that came to haunt the movement as we shall see later. Niner, *Xanana*, 74–75.

[128] The Indonesian military in East Timor had precise information on the formation and operation of the new resistance structures, and, as early as 1982, the Indonesians sought ways to combat them at the grassroots level. The FALINTIL-captured Indonesian documents that reveal detailed Indonesian knowledge are translated and reproduced in Budiardjo and Liong, *The War against East Timor*, 176ff.

[129] CAVR, *Chega!*, Part 5: Resistance: Structure and Strategy, pp. 28–29. Literally meaning boxes, caixas came to refer to the civilians clandestinely assisting the resistance.

[130] Niner, *To Resist Is to Win*, 39, 43.

As early as 1976, Gusmão had acquired a copy of *Thoughts of Chairman Mao* and "read and reread it, trying to understand Mao's simple way of describing complex things." His other living political mentor, Vicente Sahe, groomed him in what Gusmão called "the dialectic of reality," making sound judgments and projections based on objective reading of the present.[131] These thoughts were the kernel of the reorganized East Timorese independence movement, which the Indonesians failed to grasp or overcome. The 1979–1981 treks across East Timor to locate surviving comrades impressed on Gusmão a new reality: the birth of revolutionary society founded on Bases de Apoio was unattainable, positional warfare against ABRI impossible, and military victory over Indonesia unrealistic. All to the dismay of his second in command Kilik Wae Gae (among others), who, as a former conventional soldier in the Portuguese colonial army, wished for the consolidation of a fortified home base.

Yet, the independence movement had not run its course. Inside the country, it needed to be reconfigured to pursue well-defined and achievable objectives, both tactical and strategic. To that end, resistance leaders endeavored to resolve differences between the soldiers and the politicians, which had hampered their effectiveness before. With most professional soldiers and older, ardent politician rivals killed, the fighting force was actively politicized and the politicians militarized. Distinctions between soldiers and politicians gradually disappeared and the former became an integral part of the fabric of the resistance from its leadership down to its base.[132] Resistance inside the country became a multifaceted, overt, and covert military and political undertaking under a joint, highly centralized command of politically and militarily adept leaders. Thus, did the East Timorese movement enter the phase that Amilcar Cabral used to describe the independence war in his country of Guinea Bissau: "We are not military men. We are armed militants."[133]

But before this practice was institutionalized, the nascent structures solidified, and the resistance picked up momentum, the CRRN sustained severe setbacks at the hands of the Indonesian military. In the thick of Operasi Keamanan in September 1981, four members of CRRN's leadership were killed in action or murdered in captivity. CRRN also lost hundreds of guerrillas, killed or captured along with many of FALINTIL's weapons. This undermined but did not obliterate the resistance. On the contrary, it reinforced the resistance leaders' conclusions that victory had to be sought by other, nonmilitary means, without laying down their arms.

---

[131] Ibid., 41–48.

[132] Previously, subordinate to the politicians, the military did not take part in strategic decision making, but Gusmão took note of their grumblings when their opinions were unsolicited and, when offered, were disregarded by the militarily ill-equipped political leaders.

[133] Amilcar Cabral in Basil Davidson, *The Rise of Nationalism* (documentary film).

Conclusion

Both conflicts had escalated to epic proportions that tested the protagonists' imagination, flexibility, and determination. The Ethiopian and Indonesian armies, and their various security establishments, tried to depopulate regions frequented by insurgents by interning civilians through villagization and resettlement programs. In the process, Ethiopian soldiers in Eritrea burned down hundreds of villages and killed thousands of civilians between 1966 and 1967 alone. The ELF retaliated with violence in the western lowlands, Ethiopia committed more abuses in reprisals, and so went the vicious cycle. Ethiopian brutalities, which mainly (but not exclusively) targeted Muslim Eritreans, seemed to justify some of the ELF leaders' parochial outlook and gave some field commanders an excuse to retaliate against Christian highlanders and their property.[134] These religious cleavages were further pronounced by defections of Christian fighters to Ethiopia (regardless of the causes) and the ELF's tolerance of somewhat haphazard acts of retaliation.[135] It should also be noted, however, that ELF military commanders also resorted to brutal treatment of Eritrean Muslims as well. In 1966, for example, a platoon led by Omar Hammed Ezaz, by his own account, summarily executed thirteen villagers in Senhit province for their alleged collaboration with Ethiopia. They were accused of poisoning his fighters and calling for the commandos.[136]

In East Timor, the nationalist movement developed an intricate web of material and intelligence support, as much from the occupied towns and villages as from the resettlement camps. Indonesia's own impressive

---

[134] There are several allegations that some of ELF Zones encroached into Zone Five territories in the highlands in order to meet their supply needs by looting the local populations. But a well-established classic reaction to Ethiopian marshalling of Christians against Muslims was ELF's localized alignment with the Muslims of Tora'a village in their land dispute against their Christian neighbors in the village of Tsena-Degle. Reignited by Ethiopia's support of the Christian Tsena-Degle's claim and ELF's support of the Muslim Tora'a, the land dispute lasted until after Eritrea's independence. Another case in the western lowlands is ELF's siding with the Nara in their perennial conflicts with the Kunama. Frezghi Teklezghi, "The Toroa Tsenadeghle Reconciliation" (BA Thesis, University of Asmara, 2002).

[135] One of ELF's earliest fighters Saleh Mohammed Idris "Abu-Ajaj" (History Project Interview: June 26, 1996, Eritrea) recalls how a Christian fighter, whom he only mentioned by the first name Mulu, defected to Ethiopia with all the documents regarding the newly introduced zonal division. When the units were dispatched to their respective regions, the Ethiopian government placed its forces in strategic places to block the ELF's implementation of its plan. Abu-Ajaj's statement is confirmed by a letter Mohammed Ali Omaro, the Commander of Zone Four, wrote to his superiors in Kassala on September 26, 1965, in which he explained the delay in reaching their destination. He said that they were first intercepted by about two hundred commandos who forced them to retreat and change course when they were again met with a different force supported by helicopters. Omaro's letter is reprinted in its entirety in Denden, *Ma'erakat Iritriyah*, 80–82.

[136] Denden, *Ma'erakat Iritriyah*, 89.

spy networks identified the most detailed resistance structures that had developed right under the noses of their security forces. In an epic intelligence rivalry, the East Timorese guerrillas knew precisely the extent of ABRI's knowledge.

In the end, the painful experience of losing in battles against more powerful Ethiopian and Indonesian forces taught the nationalist movements to seek other, more expedient, means of resistance. These included reforming their strategies or entirely redirecting their energies. In the long-term, Eritreans also learned from Marxism-Leninism, as well as other leftist revolutions, and evolved to become a formidable fighting force that defeated the Ethiopian military in conventional battles. The East Timorese, without capitulating, shifted their strategy by increasingly relying on clandestine and diplomatic methods, frequently becoming antimilitary for practical purposes. But more difficult reorientations, and evolution toward greater internal cohesion and effectiveness against occupation, still loomed on the horizon for both of the nationalist movements.

4

Victims of Their Own Success

The Revitalized Nationalist Movements and Their Challenges

> In war, tactics are about "the use of armed forces in the engagement; strategy
> [is about] the use of engagements for the object of the war."
> Clausewitz[1]

The Eritrean and East Timorese independence struggles gathered momentum at about the same pace as Ethiopian and Indonesian determination to end them. But the counterinsurgency strategies of both the Ethiopian and Indonesian militaries lacked much-needed discipline and restraint. They failed to take note of Eritrean and East Timorese rejections of imposed Ethiopian-ness and Indonesian-ness, respectively. Their unwise pursuit of the insurgents and retaliation against civilians strengthened the old "us" versus "them" distinctions, to the advantage of the independence movements.

As government counterinsurgencies escalated, the insurgents persevered and developed a better appreciation of the odds against them. Deepening resentment of the crude strategies of the Ethiopian and Indonesian governments benefited the insurgents. They streamlined their operations in ways that enabled them to regularly appraise their means, and adjust strategies accordingly. This flexibility and responsiveness eventually brought them victory.

However, as the insurgents' resilience and sophistication increased, so did friction within the movements. Rival Eritrean nationalist organizations collided head-on. The East Timorese movement faced, at the height of its restructuring and reorientation, the threat of fragmentation.

This chapter follows the David-versus-Goliath struggles between the insurgents and the two governments. It examines the dynamics of change and the rivalries within both insurgent groups, as well as the evolution

---

[1] Carl von Clausewitz, *On War* eds. and trans. Michael Howard and Peter Paret (Princeton, NJ: Princeton University Press, 1976), 146.

of their strategies vis-à-vis changing Ethiopian and Indonesian counterinsurgencies. For Eritrean insurgents, the struggle became far more arduous because of Addis Ababa's ideological shift toward "Ethiopian Socialism," which brought about the Soviet Union's intervention on Ethiopia's side, while the United States persisted in its hostility toward Eritrean nationalists. In East Timor, the balance of physical power remained largely unchanged but the resistance movement outsmarted Jakarta into offering much-needed diplomatic ammunition. It forced Jakarta to sign a ceasefire agreement with a movement whose existence it repeatedly denied in the international arena.

Rivalry and Balance of Power among Eritrean Nationalists

As Ethiopian excesses continued, a growing number of Eritreans were attracted to the nationalist cause and rival organizations competed with each other for their support. The mid-1970s saw Eritreans joining either of the two liberation organizations in large numbers. The fresh flow of support made Eritrean guerrilla groups more-capable adversaries against government forces.

The ELF's Strategic Oblivion and Lethal Internecine Squabbles

The ELF received most of the fresh volunteers (up to seven thousand), but was unable to turn this influx into a strategic asset. This failure signaled its gradual decline and the start of the EPLF's ascendancy. Herui Tedla Bairu, ELF vice-chairman for political affairs at the time, best captured the ELF's failings in this regard:

We did not assess our situation properly...we did not assess what the situation was like in Ethiopia properly; we did not assess our situation internally; how to deal with the new [fighters]: was it a threat? Was it a blessing? Were we sufficiently prepared to assimilate a new element in large doses into our organization? I don't think we assessed the challenge [posed] by the EPLF because the ELF covered the huge middle ground; its support came not only in Eritrea but also from Eritreans in Ethiopia. Also, because the traditions of the ELF in the international arena were highly developed, we did not depend on our own *Hafash* [i.e., masses]. We did not collect money from our Eritrean communities. It was help that came from our friends in our region. The tradition of international relations was quite advanced; we had the language, we had the formulations...[2]

The ELF's training center was frequently ignored or bypassed. Recruits, upon joining the independence fighters, were trained and retained by the units

---

[2] Awate.com interview with Herui Tedla Bairu (January 1, 2001), http://www.awate.com/portal/content/view/352/11/.

with which they first came into contact. In the absence of formal, consistent indoctrination and streamlining of recruits, the influx of volunteers deepened ethnic rifts.[3]

The ELF's political fluidity arrested the evolution of its military doctrine. While its plans for establishing a fixed rear base went unimplemented, its military strategy lacked consistency of vision and execution. After 1977, for example, the ELF reformulated its 1971 military plan of action.[4] In its newly adopted strategy, the ELF set out to liberate the Eritrean countryside first, and then the towns, by tightly defending the Eritrean-Ethiopian border against an influx of fresh Ethiopian reinforcements.[5] Impressive as it looked, however, this was an overly ambitious and unrealistic strategy, considering the ELF's numerical and material deficiencies. Throughout its history, the ELF lacked a realistic strategic program and fixed central base, which cost it dearly.

The ELF's fedayin units proved to be tactically effective. Their selective assassination and terrorization of government officials and their Eritrean collaborators undermined the effectiveness and confidence of the government. At the risk of endangering their own operations, fedayin bravado captivated the imagination of many young Eritreans and inspired nationalist sentiments in both followers and skeptics. Unfortunately, the ELF lost that tactical advantage when an Ethiopian crackdown captured fedayin leader Said Saleh and his prominent protégé Abraham Tekhle narrowly escaped capture a few years later. The network weakened when most of its prominent members were rotated to different branches of the ELF. The remaining ELF fedayin network crumbled in the face of the rival EPLF network, which was better organized and more concealed, had strategic vision, and enjoyed consistent leadership.

The most vibrant branch of the ELF was its cadre school, which housed the organization's most brilliant minds and recruited a capable corps of political cadres. However, in the absence of strict implementation guidelines and a political doctrine or philosophy to glue them together, the ELF failed to reflect the shining qualities of the school and its recruits.[6]

---

[3] This was particularly the case after the vice-chairman for political affairs, Herui Tedla Bairu, with whom many of the fresh Christian fighters identified, was deposed from his post during the ELF's 1975 Second National Congress. Personal conversations with ELF veteran Mana Bahre (spring 2005, Asmara, Eritrea).

[4] RDC/His/ELF/3, "First National Congress of the ELF. Military Work Plan" (Tigrinya), November 12, 1971. This plan stipulated the stationing of a permanent army in the liberated areas, which would conduct hit-and-run attacks, and the formation of small units operating within the occupied territories, which would wage guerrilla warfare.

[5] Correspondence with Tesfai Tekhle (January 1999, Keren, Eritrea).

[6] Today, whether within the government of Eritrea or in opposition to it, former ELF cadres are distinguished by their patience, subtlety, and skill in convincingly pushing their point, whatever it may be.

On the regional Cold War dynamics, for example, the ELF grossly miscalculated the significance of Ethiopia's realignment. Throughout the Ethiopian offensives backed by the Eastern Bloc, the ELF continued to regard the Soviet Union as a strategic ally and its presence in Ethiopia as part of the struggle against imperialism. Ibrahim Idris Totil, ELF political chief since 1975, admits that the ELF lacked the political maturity to correctly appraise Ethiopia's ideological shifts.[7] Zemhret Yohannes, a leading ELF cadre, recalls how the contradiction between the ELF stance and the unfolding regional geopolitical reality caused confusion within the ELF. The lack of consensus regarding common enemies contributed toward its eventual demise.[8]

Finally, the ELF sealed its fate in the long term by depending overmuch on external support. Its Middle Eastern diplomacy benefited initially from the splintering of the Pan-Arabist camp and emergence of competing Pan-Arabists in the region. Just as most Pan-Arabists considered Eritrea as an integral part of the Arab world, Eritrea offered emergent rivals an opportunity to overshadow one another. The increasingly powerful Ba'athists in Syria, for example, championed Eritrea's cause to gain regional influence at the expense of Egypt.[9] As early as 1963, Syria trained and armed a growing number of Eritrean nationalists.[10] Syrian largess enabled the ELF to arm its fighters with the iconic AK 47 assault rifle and lightweight, highly mobile artillery pieces in 1965 – a decade before the USSR did the same for the Ethiopian army. Around the same time, Iraqi Ba'athists seized the helm of power and soon fell out with their Syrian counterparts. Enthusiastic support for Eritreans became one of the many arenas, albeit a minor one, where the two Ba'athist parties sought to outdo each other.[11] The two trained and armed hundreds of Eritrean fighters, hosted some of the most vibrant diplomatic headquarters of the Eritrean nationalist movement, and enrolled growing numbers of Eritrean students in their schools.

Stunted by internal inefficiency and oscillations, the ELF's diplomatic success became its own undoing because it remained beholden to the shifting interests of its rival patrons in Damascus and Baghdad. Rather than conducting international diplomacy from a place of strength and proceeding

---

[7] Interview with Ibrahim Idris Totil (February 4, 1998, Massawa).

[8] Zemhret Yohannes, "Lessons from the ELF's Experience" (fall 2002, Asmara, Eritrea). Giving this lecture to my students at the University of Asmara, Zemhret, among other things, related the lack of unanimity among ELF leaders and ranks as to who the real enemy was to the schism within post-independence Eritrean leadership in the aftermath of the 1998–2000 border conflict with Ethiopia.

[9] John Markakis, *National and Class Conflict in the Horn of Africa* (Cambridge: Cambridge University Press, 1987), 111–112.

[10] Interview with Romedan Mohammed-Nur (September 25, 2005, Asmara).

[11] Osman Saleh Denden, *Ma'erakat Irytriyah. Al-Juzu Al-Awal* (City, Country: NNP, 1996), 373–374.

from a coherent internal political platform, competing ELF potentates vied to ensure their respective patrons' continued support while flirting with their rivals' patrons. For their part, the Syrian and Iraqi Ba'athist parties pitted one group against the other to establish the supremacy of their politics in Eritrea. Nowhere was their interventionism more apparent and damaging than in the ELF's highest leadership circle in the 1970s when a Ba'athist party was formed as a rival to the clandestine Labor Party. The existence of the two internally clashing lines of leadership undermined the stated objective for the latter as a unifying platform for the leadership and nurturer of cohesion among the organization's base. Some leaders assumed their positions in the ELF as members of the Labour Party while simultaneously claiming loyalty to, and active involvement in, the Ba'ath Party. The Ba'athists, in turn, were divided by their competing loyalties to Damascus and Baghdad, leading to the semiofficial Syrian and Iraqi lines within ELF's high-ranking cadres.[12] Fragmented and hamstrung by the whims of its international backers, the ELF was an already collapsing edifice, waiting for an Ethiopian onslaught and a push from its domestic rival, the Eritrean People's Liberation Front.

The Onset of Internal Cohesion and Self-Reliance

In contrast, the nascent EPLF evolved quickly into a highly politicized and disciplined military organization jointly led by militarily adept politicians and politically conscious military commanders. Its military doctrine was grounded in its highly centralized and cohesive political foundation, as well as its leadership's training in, and espousal of, revolutionary war doctrines. The EPLF's top military architect, Ibrahim Afa, who had served in the Ethiopian navy, went to Cuba for military and political training in revolutionary warfare. Other EPLF leaders read thoroughly a wide range of material on revolutionary warfare. Perhaps the most significant experience was the extended training that Romedan Mohammed-Nur and Isaias Afwerki received in China at the height of the Cultural Revolution.

Eritrean police and soldiers, who had started deserting the Ethiopian government, contributed a great deal toward the evolution of the liberation movements' military doctrines. The EPLF particularly campaigned to attract Eritrean commandos from the Ethiopian security forces. One of its October 1974 pamphlets, for example, stressed that commandos cared about their country no less than did independence fighters, but that their mutual enemy drove a wedge between the two, leading to their fighting one another. The pamphlet stressed that the only solution to their infighting lay in their joining

---

[12] Interviews with Ibrahim Idris Totil (September 22 and 27, 2005, Asmara, Eritrea) and Mohammed Osman Ezaz (September 3, 2005, Tessenei, Eritrea).

forces to kick out their mutual enemy. The letter extended an invitation to the commandos to right their implicit previous wrongs, suggesting tacitly that their past record would not be held against them.[13] The response was so positive that former commando commissioner Zerimariam Azazi joined the EPLF and subsequently started to call on others to follow suit.[14]

Advocating that a protracted people's war was the only way to victory, the EPLF set out to "step-by-step liberate the land and the masses."[15] In order to avoid the mistakes of the ELF in this regard, it aimed to raise the consciousness of, organize, politicize, and arm the masses. Although militarily the EPLF implemented the threefold Maoist doctrine of warfare – guerrilla and mobile warfare techniques alongside conventional positional war[16] – the flow of professionally trained soldiers from Ethiopian counterinsurgency units, like the commandos, was an important milestone in institutionalizing military doctrine. Consequently, compared to the ELF, the EPLF showed significantly better understanding and efficient implementation of conventional and nonconventional warfare techniques accompanied by adherence to strict discipline.

Unlike the ELF, the EPLF engaged the civilian population by inculcating a sense of inclusion in something bigger than themselves. It did so, among other things, by first raising funds from among Eritreans inside and outside the country, while increasing their awareness and attachment. Second, it attracted Eritrean youth in such numbers that it had to turn away some at a time when its rival had resorted to forced conscription in some parts of the country. Many young and physically disabled volunteers saw their being turned away as a sign of compassion and care on the part of the nationalists.[17] Third, all new recruits – without exception – were required to travel on foot from wherever they joined the struggle to the EPLF's rear base in Sahel, a trek of more than one hundred miles through the country's

[13] RDC/Call 01/00383, EPLF "Selamtan Metsewa'etan N'ahwatna Comandis Deqi Ertra" ("Greetings and Call to our Commandos Brothers, Children of Eritrea"), 1974.
[14] RDC/Call 01/00386, Maj. Gen. Zeremariam Azazi, "Awajn Seme'etan N'ahwatey Nay Ertra Polis Comandis" ("Declaration and Appeal to my Brotherly Eritrean Police Commandos"), September 1975.
[15] RDC/EPLF/His/Mili:3, *Strategiawi Mizlaq* (*Strategic Withdrawal*), ND. Although this was the slogan of the EPLF's First Organizational Congress in 1977 when it also adapted it as its liberation strategy, it had been practicing it as early as the mid-1970s when it started the liberation of the countryside.
[16] RDC/Hist/Ar/St/09: 06434, EPLF "Seminar Paper # 18: Three Stages of Protracted War," (Undated); RDC/EPLF/His/Mili, 3, *Strategiawi Mizlaq* (*Strategic Withdrawal*), ND, p. 9. The EPLF held its first Congress in 1977 when it officially embraced its improvised strategy.
[17] I have spoken with several individuals, for example, who were turned down for one or another reason, and those who were told they were too young at first were accepted a year or two later. Physically disabled persons were advised to contribute in different ways than joining the liberation army.

most hostile landscape.[18] In the process of surviving hardships of seemingly unending nightly marches, volunteers built endurance, cultivating an early sense of camaraderie with one another and with the fighters who led them to the training center. After months of rigorous military training and political indoctrination, they exited EPLF training center completely transformed into a highly cohesive, disciplined fighting force.[19]

EPLF external relations, during its first few years, carried elements of that of the ELF until leaders inside the country opted to break earlier cycles of external dependence and consequent internal chaotic squabbling. They did this by pursuing fiercely secular, ideologically driven, and autonomous domestic policies. When pioneer Eritrean nationalist diplomat Osman Saleh Sabbe broke away from the ELF in late 1969, the latter's provisional leadership scrambled to save its Middle Eastern lifeline by dispatching its own delegations.[20] The delegations managed to retain some of the political capital and acumen for the ELF that Sabbe had cultivated; however, he continued to maintain his relationships with those same countries for the benefit of the EPLF after the split. Not only was Sabbe an able diplomat, singing to the tune of his hosts to appeal to their generous sides and secure logistical support as well as materiel, he was also savvy and independent. Bereket Habte Selassie, who later became the EPLF's representative to the United Nations, made the following perceptive observation of this enigmatic figure in Eritrean history:

[While] his domain was limited to the Arab world . . . he was perceived to be a one-man show. The guerrilla leaders whom he called "Field Command," thought of him as primadonna, a lone star who "stole the show." They resented his sole control of the financial aid coming from some Arab sources and complained bitterly even as they took the material assistance that he was procuring. Much as I admired Sabbe's service to the Eritrean liberation struggle, I did not share his conservative and highly personalized approach to politics.[21]

More suspicious of Sabbe's ambition than their need for his savvy, EPLF leaders in the field distinguished themselves from their ELF counterparts by directly and more thoroughly involving the Eritrean public and diaspora. Involving the civilian population, both inside Eritrea and internationally, enabled the EPLF to raise international awareness of their cause, as well as extra funds to support it.

---

[18] In his forties, Dr. Bereket was asked to join one such a group and he relates how hard that experience was. Bereket Habte Selassie, *The Crown and the Pen. The Memoirs of a Lawyer Turned Rebel* (Trenton, NJ, and Asmara: Red Sea Press, 2011).

[19] RDC/Hist/Ar/St/EPLF/Mili/01, 03102: "A Short Report from the Training Center to Information Department," 1979.

[20] Interviews with Ibrahim Idris Totil (September 22–27, 2005, Asmara, Eritrea) and Mohammed-Osman-Ezaz (September 3, 2005, Tessenei, Eritrea).

[21] Bereket, *The Crown and the Pen*, 327.

To replace the unpredictable handouts of foreign powers, yet without writing them off as potential future supporters, the EPLF began soliciting financial donations from Eritreans all over the world. They also carried out vigorous political work among nondomiciled Eritreans aimed at cultivating a feeling of inclusion in the nationalist process. It harvested fruits of diasporic activism when Eritreans in Europe and North America launched "Eritreans for Liberation" groups that identified with the field command, generated vast amounts of diaspora cash, and offered new grassroots mechanisms of drawing attention to Eritrea's plight and influencing international public opinion.

So important were these financial contributions and outlets to the outside world that the management and control of this instrument of alternative diplomacy became a bone of contention between the EPLF's Foreign Mission, led by Sabbe, and the Field Command inside Eritrea. Recognizing their significance to the autonomy of field commanders who had started to challenge him on domestic and regional issues pertaining to the independence struggle, Sabbe wanted to bring these resourceful civil society groups under his direct control. Fearing Sabbe's control of these mass organizations, the field commanders, for their part, successfully exhorted Eritreans for Liberation in North America (EFLNA) and its European equivalent (EFLE) to remain autonomous entities, separate from Sabbe's Foreign Mission while retaining direct channels with the Field Command.[22]

Finally, on key regional and global political developments relevant to Eritrea, the EPLF took a clearer, more incisive stand. Cognizant of Ethiopia's realignment with the USSR, it opposed Soviet interference in Ethiopia against Somalia and later called on the Soviet Union and its satellites to refrain from getting involved in the Eritrean struggle.[23] And, finally, having decided at its inception to make Sahel its rear base, the EPLF started in earnest to fortify its headquarters and training center there. For all these reasons, the balance within the Eritrean field began to move gradually in favor of the EPLF against the ELF in the second half of the 1970s. This intensified when a battle-hardened and politically restive group of about one thousand fighters,

[22] Interview with Paulos Tesfaghiorghis (December 29 and 30, 2006, San Jose, California). This was one of the precipitants of Sabbe's 1976 launching of the Eritrean Liberation Front–Popular Liberation Forces (ELF-PLF), signing a unity pact with the ELF, and parting ways with the field command that continued as the EPLF.

[23] RDC/EPLF/His/Ar/St/CR, "Wesanetat Rabe'ay Mudub Akheba Maekelay Shmaghele Hizbawi Ghenbar Harenet Ertra" ("Decisions of the 4th regular meeting of the Central Committee of the EPLF") October 22, 1978, p. 18. It should be noted, however, that the EPLF's refusal to condemn the Soviet Union on the grounds of not engaging in big politics was the reason that the Eritreans for Liberation in North America (EFLNA) ended its association with the EPLF. Previously, the EFLNA played an instrumental role in fundraising, publicity and ideological articulation of the Eritrean cause under the EPLF.

commonly known as *Falul* (literally "anarchist"), joined the EPLF in a bid to escape potential ELF repression.[24]

Eritrean Insurgents Go on the Offensive

Despite the formidable challenge the Ethiopian military continued to present, the disunited Eritrean insurgents started all-out offensives in the mid-1970s. Two crucial factors – besides the previously mentioned – enabled Eritreans to snatch the strategic initiative from Ethiopian government forces. In mid-September 1974, the aging Ethiopian emperor was overthrown by a group of junior army officers called the Derg.[25] Internally fractured, however, this junta had neither the experience nor the resources and stature to restore the government's credibility.[26] During its first three years, the Derg proved even weaker than the emperor as it inherited a thinly stretched and demoralized military of less than 50,000, an arsenal of obsolete U.S.-supplied weapons, a country riddled with a half-dozen armed rebellions, and a formidable civilian leftist urban opposition.[27]

Although such a weakening of the government in Addis Ababa provided Eritrean insurgents with an opportunity to take the initiative, the end of internecine ELF-EPLF fighting made it possible for the two organizations to go on the offensive. Not only did the Eritrean civilian population refuse to be drawn into fratricidal conflict, but they also set up village and regional mediation committees to broker a formal ELF-EPLF ceasefire.[28] Although their sporadic fighting continued, the 1975 ceasefire agreement of Weki-Zagher (environs of Asmara) afforded both to direct their undistracted energies against the Ethiopian government. They aggressively harassed Ethiopian forces through mobile and guerrilla operations, as well as engaging them in open conventional battles. The ELF and the EPLF forces went on strategic offensives so successful that rural areas and towns started to fall to the Eritrean forces one after another.

[24] Interview with Col. Asmelash Ghebremesqel (Asmara, February 9, 1998).
[25] *The Ethiopian Herald*, September 13 and 14, 1974.
[26] To overcome that, the junior officers invited the retired General Aman Andom to act as their leader for his experience and for the respect he had earned both within and without the armed forces.
[27] Archives of the Ethiopian Ministry of National Defense in Addis Ababa/Zemecha-733, "YeAhunu Ghize YeItyopia Hayl Huneta ena Yalebet Segat" ("The Current Conditions of the Ethiopian Force and its Threats"), 20-10-1982 (EC), 1–2.
[28] EPLF, Political Conscientization Programme, *Ta'rikh al-Nidal al-Musallah, al-Marhala al-Mutawassita* (Eritrea: EPLF, 1989); Bereket, *The Crown and the Pen*, 306ff; also see Bereket's May 17, 2001, interview with awate.com: http://www.awate.com/portal/content/view/1038/11/.
Having "turned rebel," Dr. Bereket, the former attorney general of Ethiopia, arrived in the area of mediation around the final stages of the civilian mediation committees, and he, along with Redazghi Gebremedhin, helped give the agreement a modicum of formality.

The new military rulers in Addis Ababa harbored a much stronger belief in the military resolution of the Eritrean question than had emperor Haile Selassie.[29] After taking power in September 1974, the Derg refused to negotiate with Eritrean insurgents and instead dispatched 10,000 soldiers to Asmara to replenish Ethiopian forces there.[30] Failing to reverse or even halt Eritrean advances, in 1976, the Derg gathered tens of thousands of ill-trained and ill-equipped peasant militias in northern Ethiopia. Before these forces could march into Eritrea, however, coordinated Eritrean and Ethiopian rebels dispersed them, turning the undertaking into a total disaster.[31]

With insurgents roaming the Eritrean countryside, Ethiopian troops assumed defensive positions around fortified towns and the main highways that connected them. By 1978, Ethiopian control of Eritrea had shrunk to five completely or partially besieged Eritrean towns – Asmara, Asseb, Adi-Qeyeh, Barentu, and parts of Massawa.[32] The ELF and the EPLF were so confident of taking Asmara that several leaders from the two organizations claimed that only political considerations delayed them from doing so. Ermias Debesai, one of the leading EPLF diplomats, generally mentioned the political calculations that held them back from taking the capital. ELF chairman Ahmed Nasser was clear that ELF-EPLF disagreements stalled the Eritrean imposition of liberation on Addis Ababa's weak military junta.[33] By now, both ELF and EPLF insurgents organized their forces into brigades of about 1,100 to 1,300 men and women, and they could marshal about ten brigades each.[34]

[29] RDC/Mengistu, 3A/78, "Mengistu's Speech on the Fourth Anniversary of the Revolution," 12 (transcription of the speech).

[30] The resolution of the Eritrean question was one of the main bones of contention between the junior officers and General Aman Andom (who incidentally happened to be of Eritrean origin). While the young officers wanted to resolve the problem by crushing the rebels, the general wanted to go about it through peaceful means. This turned out to be a point of departure for the military junta, who sent the reinforcements to Asmara without Aman's approval. Finally, as the general had outlived their need for him, they disposed of him through physical elimination on the same November night when dozens of the imprisoned members of the previous imperial government were executed summarily.

[31] Awet Tewelde, "The Soviet Union and the Eritrean Struggle for Independence" (BA Thesis, Addis Ababa University, 1998 and the University of Asmara, 1999). Also see Bernard Weinraub, "Peasant Forces Move on Eritrea," *The New York Times*, May 23, 1976 and Weinraub, "Sudan is Reported Wary on Eritrea: Khartoum said to have Sent Thousands of Troops to Border With Ethiopia," *The New York Times*, June 07, 1976.

[32] Dan Connell and BBC's Simon Dring spent considerable time with the Eritrean guerrillas during this period. Not only did they report on the guerrillas' battles, but they also reported on the direct intervention of Soviet, Cuban, and South Yemeni personnel, which aided the Ethiopia war effort. See the dossier of news clippings prepared by the Research and Information Center on Eritrea (RICE), *Revolution in Eritrea: Eyewitness Reports* (Rome: RICE), 112–124.

[33] *NewAfrican*, December, 1977, pp. 1183–1185.

[34] Interviews with Col. Yacob Tekhleab (Asmara, August 28, 1997) and Yohannes Tesfase-lassie (Asmara, September 10, 1997, and January 28, 1998).

Ethiopian Realignment that Shifted the Balance of Power

Still convinced that more trained soldiers, with the weapons to arm them, would smash the Eritrean rebellion, the Derg junta went on a worldwide search for arms. As the United States, Ethiopia's traditional arms supplier, grew increasingly reluctant to provide the amount and kind of weapons that the Derg demanded, the latter's adoption of Ethiopian Socialism as the way forward[35] earned Ethiopia an enthusiastic response in Moscow. The USSR readily accepted Ethiopia as a client, and as early as December 1976, a secret military assistance agreement was signed between Ethiopia and the Soviet Union.[36] The first arms package of thirty tanks was delivered in March 1977, and about one hundred more followed in April.[37] Thus, impulsively piling up arms in bulk, the Derg government started to train volunteers and conscripts en masse.

The sudden eruption in 1977 of conflict with the Republic of Somalia over the ethnic Somali-inhabited Ogaden region offered the Ethiopian government a good excuse to more heavily arm itself with sophisticated Soviet weapons. Between September and October 1977 Soviet heavy weapons, including BM-21 Katyusha rocket launchers, BTR60 and 152 armored personnel carriers, T-series tanks, long-range artillery pieces as well as MiG-21 fighter jets and MiG-23 ground attack fighters, were pumped into Ethiopia for "self-defense." Numerous high-ranking Soviet and Cuban advisors were dispatched as were 12,000 Cuban soldiers and Yemeni technicians and experts from Aden. With the Somali threat quickly subdued,[38] the Derg came to be seen as the defender of the "motherland."

The morale of the Ethiopian troops grew as their numbers increased. In 1977–1978 alone, the Ethiopian army increased by 201 percent to 131,334, and in 1978–1979, it further grew by 70 percent to reach 206,117 strong.[39] In addition, Cuban troops were fully engaged in defending Ethiopia, and training Ethiopian troops. According to some sources, some were even

---

[35] *The Ethiopian Herald*, December 21, 1974.

[36] Paul B. Henze, *The Horn of Africa from War to Peace* (New York: St. Martin's Press, 1991), 145; and David A. Korn, *Ethiopia, the United States and the Soviet Union* (Carbondale: Southern Illinois University Press, 1986), 29. On the Soviet Union's policies toward and interventions in the Third World in general, and in Northeast Africa, in particular, see Robert G. Patman, *The Soviet Union in the Horn of Africa. Diplomacy of Intervention and Disengagement* (Cambridge: Cambridge University Press, 1990); and Carol R. Saivetz and Sylvia Woodby, *Soviet – Third World Relations* (London: Westview Press, 1985).

[37] Korn, *Ethiopia*, 27.

[38] The Ethiopian counteroffensive against Somalia lasted from late January to early March 1978, and Somalia was pushed back in defeat. Zemecha-733, "Ke 1967–1982 Megabit dres Yetesera YeHayle Ghembata" 18 October 1982 EC ("Recruitment of Forces Conducted from 1967 until March 1982"), 18-10-82(E.C), 1; and Zemecha-716, *YeItio-Soviet YeGara Komite YeWetaderawi Gudayoch Huneta* (*Conditions of the Ethio-Soviet Committee on Military Affairs*), ND, 3.

[39] Zemecha-733, "Ke 1967–1982 Megabit dres Yetesera YeHayle Ghembata," 5.

dispatched to Eritrea to fight.[40] Soviet weaponry and a large number of trained soldiers were dispatched north to target Eritrean insurgents. The impact could not have been stronger. As these new Ethiopian offensives started in June 1978, the balance of power suddenly tipped in favor of Addis Ababa, and Eritrean fighters found themselves on the defensive and subsequently retreating.

On the eve of these Ethiopian offensives, ELF and EPLF strategic planning differed, despite similarities in their tactical aim to slow down the advance of the Ethiopian army before it crossed into Eritrea. Initially, both the ELF and the EPLF succeeded in slowing the momentum of the Ethiopian advance for over a week. Strategically, however, the ELF decided to engage the advancing Ethiopian forces in positional confrontations and then take measures as the situation unfolded.[41] Out-gunned and outnumbered by superior Ethiopian forces in vast open terrain, lack of ELF-EPLF coordination, repeated tactical miscalculations, and persistent deficiency of internal cohesion combined to knock the ELF out of any meaningful military engagements.

The EPLF avoided the ELF's head-on collision with Ethiopian troops, executing instead an orderly withdrawal while engaging the emboldened Ethiopian military at times and places of its own choosing. Although it is unknown exactly when the EPLF decided to withdraw, it is clear that its clandestine People's Party had predicted the inevitability of a massive setback. Through the courses it offered at its Cadre School and publication and distribution of materials on the Chinese Long March and other similar experiences of withdrawals, the People's Party had prepared most fighters for withdrawal. When push came to shove, the clandestine party structures were in place to ensure that the leadership's strategic decisions were implemented to the letter, despite grassroots resistance.[42] Tenaciously holding to its belief that its cause was righteous, the Eritrean leadership readied itself for any eventuality by reminding its ranks and civilian base that a people's war was not a smooth ride.

[40] Cuban officials insist that no Cuban troops ever set foot in Eritrea (interview with Mr. Miriano Lores Betancourt, Cuban Chargé d'affaires to Ethiopia, October 10, 1997, Addis Ababa). RDC/EPLF/His/Ar/St/CR, "Decisions of the 4th regular meeting of the Central Committee of the EPLF" October 22, 1978, p. 18; the EPLF acknowledged the increased direct intervention of the Soviet Union and Cuba and called on the countries to stop their activities. Higher officers in the Eritrean army are categorical about Cuban presence in Eritrea. Col. Asmelash Ghebremesqel (interview, February 9, 1998, Asmara), for instance, says that 1,600 Cuban soldiers were active in Eritrea. But to former member of the EPLF politburo, Uqbe Abraha (interview, January 31, 1998, Asmara, Eritrea), what the Cubans were doing in Ethiopia was more important than was their presence in Eritrea because it relieved tens of thousands of Ethiopian troops from eastern Ethiopia and made them available for the operations in Eritrea and trained even more.

[41] Interview with Ibrahim Idris Totil (February 4, 1998, Massawa, Eritrea).

[42] EPLF politburo member Uqbe Abraha (interview, January 31, 1998, Asmara, Eritrea) told me that the EPLF knew what would come after Ogaden and that its leadership was morally prepared for the policy of withdrawal.

This conviction was matched by the Ethiopian government's determination to end the Eritrean problem once and for all, and by the Ethiopian popular belief that nothing was more righteous than defending the "unity of the motherland." With the staunch belief that supremacy in armaments would deliver victory, the Ethiopian military boasted that the victory against the Somali Republic in the east would be repeated against the Eritrean insurgents in the north. Its commander in chief, Col. Mengistu, was so confident of a quick military knockout that he denied the existence of a problem in Eritrea. The Ethiopian military command in Eritrea, for its part, declared the annihilation of the rebels at the end of an offensive only to launch another shortly afterward.[43] The Eritrean fronts suffered massive setbacks, and the world began to echo Mengistu's assertion that the outcome was a foregone conclusion.[44]

However, a small group of scholars and journalists traveled to the rear base of the Eritrean combatants, as well as to the frontlines, and documented that the reported defeat of the Eritrean organizations was not true. Analyzing the EPLF and its forces, Richard Sherman concluded that EPLF structures indicated a capacity to defeat Soviet-backed Ethiopia over time: "in the long run, the Eritreans seem capable of militarily defeating the Ethiopian armed forces, even with the massive Soviet hardware build up . . . With their discipline and organization there seems to be little or no chance of them crumbling in the face of a massive counter-offensive."[45]

Similarly, Dan Connell, who witnessed the EPLF withdrawing from cities, argued that in addition to the weapons that the EPLA had captured, its human losses were compensated for by the massive influx of young Eritreans to the organization. Although he recognized the EPLA's inability to face the Ethiopians in conventional, open warfare, he did not doubt its ultimate victory: "Five visits of Eritrea over the past three years, including a month-long tour of the EPLF controlled areas that coincided with the latest round of fighting [Second Round Offensive, November 1978], lead me to conclude that Eritrean predictions of eventual . . . victory are justified."[46]

In the short term, the new Ethiopian arsenal and the influx of troops paid off. The entire Eritrean landscape was recaptured from the nationalist insurgents, with the exception of the northeastern edge. In the long term, though, the outmanned and outgunned EPLF proved that losing territory was quite different from losing the war. It managed to save the lives of

---

[43] RDC/Mengistu 3A/78, "Mengistu's Speech on the Fourth Anniversary of the Revolution," 12 September 1978, Addis Ababa.

[44] Haggai Erlich, *The Struggle over Eritrea 1962–1978: War and Revolution in the Horn of Africa* (Stanford, CA: Hoover Institution Press, 1983), 119.

[45] Richard F. Sherman, "Eritrea in Revolution," (PhD diss., Brandies University, 1980), 163.

[46] Dan Connell, "The Changing Situation in Eritrea," *Behind the War in Eritrea*, ed. Basil Davidson, Lionel Cliffe, and Bereket Habte Selassie (Nottingham: Spokesman, 1980), 55–59.

countless guerrilla fighters and civilians by pulling back in the best-organized manner possible, while exacting a terrible cost on the Ethiopian army.

Throughout the successive offensives, the Ethiopian military employed standard strategies and tactics of a conventional army that relied on technology and numerical superiority. Against these, the EPLA resorted to delaying actions and offensive defenses. They delayed Ethiopian takeover of their liberated towns and outposts until their political branches and civilian dependents were smoothly transported to safer places. With speed and flexibility, the EPLA withdrew to its secure havens where its advantages over the Ethiopian army increased while denying the Ethiopian army the opportunity to apply tactics such as envelopments, double envelopments and turning movements. Moreover, the shrinking theaters of operation curbed the use and effectiveness of Ethiopia's heavy armory. Rather than observing and adapting to the EPLA's methods, Ethiopian strategists remained steadfast and inflexible with their military plan, only making tactical adjustments.[47]

Meanwhile, the series of attempts to reunify the independence fighters by merging their organizations ended with the resumption of rivalry and hostilities between the two in the aftermath of the setbacks that both the ELF and the EPLF endured at the hands of the Ethiopian military between 1978 and 1979.[48] Having retired to areas of no strategic value to the ongoing fighting while the EPLF was engaging the Ethiopian army in major battles, the ELF ceased to meaningfully take on the advancing Ethiopian forces. In the face of Ethiopia's publicly announced preparations for a massive offensive against the Eritrean independence movement, ELF distractions were the last thing the EPLF wanted.[49] Moreover, in the run up to Ethiopia's Sixth Offensive (also called the Red Star Campaign), the EPLF needed geographic flexibility and alternative routes into Sudan unfettered by the ELF.

As Ethiopian forces were putting the final touches on their campaign, the EPLF turned full force against the ELF in 1980 and the civil war erupted

---

[47] For a detailed analysis of this period, see Awet Weldemichael, "The Eritrean Long March: The Strategic Withdrawal of the Eritrean People's Liberation Front (EPLF), 1978–1979," *The Journal of Military History* 73, no. 4 (October 2009):1231–1271.

[48] Amid Ethiopian advances, for example, both the ELF and the EPLF started to implement the "October 20, [1977] Agreement" by gradually merging their forces, allowing two ELA brigades to hold positions along with their EPLA counterparts in defense of EPLF's rear base. And while the relationship between these ELA and EPLA units on the Northeast Sahel front line grew increasingly warm, overall, the ELF-EPLF hostility continued unabated, leading to their forces in Dankalia fighting one another in heated battles over the control of a small Red Sea harbor.

[49] According to Ghirmay "Keshi" (personal conversations, summer 2001, Northern California) who was the political commissar for one of the two ELF brigades, the ELF quietly pulled its two brigades out of the Northeast Sahel frontline in order to pressure the EPLF into pulling its forces from Dankalia. The EPLF discovered and sealed the opening in its defenses before the Ethiopian army could penetrate its rear base.

with a renewed vigor. The long-simmering contradictions within the ELF coupled with its leaders' loss of credibility and trust among their fighters, as well as the latter's general sense of disillusionment, rendered it an easy adversary.[50] It lost ground from the start, and by 1981, it was driven out of Eritrea and into the Sudan.[51]

During long years of stalemate, frontlines on the gates of the town of Nakfa hardly moved. EPLF forces ensured their survival as a guerrilla army by exploiting the barriers – terrain, climate, society – that inhibited the adversary as its forces extended their supply lines into more difficult and unfamiliar terrain in Eritrea.[52] Maintaining these strategic advantages, the EPLA applied conventional principles of war[53] to its defensive guerrilla warfare and held its ground against successive Ethiopian offensives, mainly Addis Ababa's Red Star (that Eritreans remember as the Sixth Offensive) and Stealth Campaigns of 1982 and 1983, respectively.[54] Then, in an underreported 1984 operation, Eritreans demolished the Ethiopian frontline under the Weqaw Command that had blocked Eritrean access to the Red Sea. Eritrean morale in the aftermath of Weqaw's collapse skyrocketed, as did their captured arsenal of high-quality Soviet weapons.[55] Nationalist leaders started to boast of their readiness and capacity to face off any force in any type of warfare. Although subsequent developments were to prove them right, the fight was far from over. The days of guerrilla warfare continued concurrently with conventional battles.

---

[50] Interview with Ahferom Tewelde (August 27, 1999, Asmara, Eritrea).

[51] Subsequently, the latter imploded yet again, but none of the three major opposing factions that emerged posed a serious enough concern to divert EPLF's attention from fighting the Ethiopians.

[52] According to Chairman Mao Tsetung, the survival and eventual success of a guerrilla war hinge on the guerrilla fighters' ability to exploit the weaknesses of their adversaries in these respects. Mao Tsetung, *On Guerrilla Warfare*, trans. Brigadier General Samuel B. Griffith (New York: Frederick A. Praeger, 1961), 42.

[53] David H. Zook, Jr., and Robinson Higham, *A Short History of Warfare* (New York: Twayne Publishers, 1966), 29. Based on Maj. Gen. Fuller, they write that "the objective, which must be realizable, clearly understood, and pursued by the commander; the offensive, which must be undertaken at the proper time and place if victory is to be achieved; security, which must be preserved so that the other principles may be applied unimpeded; concentration or mass, the commitment of means at the decisive time and place; economy of force, the best use of available means; maneuver, the positioning of forces through mobility [flexibility] for maximum advantage; simplicity, especially in planning; unity of command, the concentration of authority and responsibility; surprise, striking the enemy in areas least expected."

    Clausewitz had long noted most of these points throughout *On War* (Book Two, "On the Theory of War"), 153–204.

[54] Gebru, *The Ethiopian Revolution*.

[55] Interview with Isaias Afwerki in James Firebrace and Stuart Holland, *Never Kneel Down: Drought, Development and Liberation in Eritrea* (Trenton, NJ: Red Sea Pres, 1985), 127–137.

Close to four years later, EPLF tactical offensives in western Eritrea lured the government – against the warning of its commanding officer on the spot[56] – into pulling some troops out of Nakfa front lines in order to respond to those attacks. This weakened the Ethiopian positions in Nakfa and enabled the EPLF, in March 1988, to launch an all-out offensive against them. In a historic three-day battle that Basil Davidson famously compared to Dien Bien Phu, Eritreans trounced Ethiopia's ten-year-old Nadew Command.[57] The tide, thus, turned irreversibly against Ethiopian troops, and for the first time, it became indisputably clear that Eritrean military victory was only a matter of time.

Developments in East Timor and Within the Resistance Movement

The guerrillas' tenacity and their bold decision to hold the March 1981 Conference right under the nose of the Indonesian military only strengthened the latter's determination to eradicate the former once and for all. Although Indonesia's Operasi Keamanan failed to hunt down all the remaining FAL-INTIL guerrillas, it dealt them a severe blow. The resistance lost four members of its new leadership in this period, as well as several hundred guerrillas and even more weapons. Several years later, Gusmão described these "as heavy [as] or even heavier than the destruction of the red bases in 1978."[58] The survivors continued putting Humpty Dumpty together again when the Catholic Church reached out to them and they responded positively, becoming increasingly pragmatic and inclusive.

The Catholic Church in East Timor Protests

The Holy See's decision in the late 1970s to directly administer the church in East Timor as a separate diocese, and not part of the Indonesian church, gave the local church unprecedented credibility to speak out against violations on its parishioners and to pursue avenues to protect them. In 1981, the Indonesian Conference of Catholic Bishops (MASRI) invited Dom Martinho da Costa Lopes, the apostolic administrator of the Catholic Church in East Timor, to take part in their yearly session and discuss the Catholic religious

---

[56] Brigadier General Tariku Ayne, *Nadew Ez Memriya: K-hamle 1/1979 eske Tahsas 30/1980 b-Nadew Ez Ghinbar Yetekenawenew Yezemecha Menfeqawi Riport*, Tir 1980 EC. (January 1987); and *Y-Ertra Kifle-Hager Wetaderawi Huneta: Sele-Kifle Hageritu Techebach Huneta Yeqerebe Acheer Riport*, Tir 1980 (January 1988). Classified documents available at the RDC.

[57] Gebru Tareke, *The Ethiopian Revolution: War in the Horn of Africa* (New Haven, CT, and London: Yale University Press, 2009).

[58] "Message from the Supreme Command of the Struggle: 1983-the Year of National Unity" a 1982 end-of-year message of Xanana Gusmão reprint in official FRETILIN organ Nacroma, March/April 1983.

community and its service to its laity. In June and July, in the run-up to that September conference, the East Timorese church gathered a vast pool of data from its clergy on the peoples' conditions. The product, "Reflections of the East Timorese Religious," was devastating. It was the East Timorese church's boldest account on the war.[59]

It embodied a strong consensus on Indonesia's crude policies and argued that the people of East Timor were "suffering ... and being humiliated" under Indonesian occupation. Establishing what had been happening in East Timor since 1975 as "invasion, war, looting, the destruction [and expulsion] of the indigenous population who are replaced by people from other islands," the church decried "attempts for mass mobilization of people ... to make war on each other." Lamenting the Catholic world's silence about their predicament, the East Timorese religious "felt stunned by this silence which seemed to allow us to die deserted."[60] The church reflected that the word of God "takes the form of social justice" that

must be built by the people themselves based on faith and cooperation with God and one's fellow man ... [But since] there is as yet no way out from oppression from above [and since] creating justice together with the present Indonesian government is not possible, we, the religious, must always be alert and thoughtful that the faith of the people is not trodden on. [The church's preaching of faith] without serious endeavors for the building of social justice is the same as making faith merely foreign and mystical. Becoming in accord with faith means always finding new forms of endeavor. [A living church is one that] puts into practice the faith of its people and is also able to express that which they experience, feel, live and suffer.[61]

Putting to rest assumptions of the church's neutrality, the document categorically affirmed that the East Timorese social fabric had been disintegrating, the institution of the family eroding, and the people's physical existence endangered by Indonesian-caused poverty and terror. The consequent "rebellious mood of those who returned to their huts can no longer be denied," according to the East Timorese religious.[62] Indonesia, however, was in complete denial throughout the years of occupation and its military remained religiously consistent in its practices.

Fostering the Church's Sympathy into Active Support
The frustration of the apostolic administrator of the Dili diocese, Father Martinho Lopes, at the silence of the Indonesian Catholics and the Holy See

---

[59] "Reflections of the East Timorese Religious: A Contribution to the 1981 MASRI Session," July 1981 in CIDAC–C DPM/TL3230, *Dossier on East Timor* (March 1982).
[60] CIDAC-CDPM, TL3230, "Reflections of the East Timorese Religious: A Contribution to the 1981 MASRI Session," July 1981 in *Dossier on East Timor* (March 1982).
[61] Ibid.
[62] Ibid.

had reached its peak. Under his leadership, the East Timorese clergy took a stand on the side of their people, even condoning their resistance openly.[63] Taking note of Father Martinho's extended hand, the new resistance leader Xanana Gusmão saw the long-term significance of the church's support and requested to meet with the acting bishop to cement that bond. Initiating contact was made easier for the guerillas as most Timorese resistance leaders, including Gusmão, had received a Catholic education, some of them under Father Martinho himself.

Despite Father Martinho's reluctance, in August 1982, the guerrillas lured his Indonesian military escort (KOPASSUS) into responding to a fake attack while they pulled the church leader into his first secret meeting with Xanana Gusmão at a place called Mehara.[64] It has been difficult to reconstruct the exact details of this meeting, but Father Martinho Lopes is believed to have made it clear to the resistance movement that their only hope of success lay in a united FRETILIN-UDT advocacy for their rights.[65] The church did not hide its aversion to FRETILIN's leftist orientation. It was becoming increasingly clear that FRETILIN's ideological direction had pushed many pro-independence East Timorese away from it, only for them to fall victim to Indonesian traps and deception. The church was ready to assist, but the resistance movement needed to be inclusive of all East Timorese.

Father Martinho empathized with the predicament of the resistance movement and the East Timorese clergy quietly started to support the guerrillas with badly needed supplies and communication with the outside world. This had the ultimate effect of tilting the balance in favor of the insurgents. But only slowly did the resistance leadership respond to Father Martinho's advice. The CAVR claims that the resistance movement introduced CRRN to serve as the "organizational vehicle for everyone who wanted to join the struggle" against Indonesia and that it was an "invitation to all East Timorese to join the resistance."[66] However, Father Martinho's urging to embrace those who had collaborated with the Indonesians appeared an outrageous suggestion to the resistance leader, who is reported to have thought of it as "marrying a frog and a crocodile."[67]

---

[63] For the politics of the Holy See toward Indonesia and East Timor, see Rowena Lennox, *Fighting Spirit of East Timor. The Life of Martinho da Costa Lopes* (London and New York: Zed Books, 2000), 163ff.

[64] Ibid., 188–189; Sara Niner, *Xanana: Leader of the Struggle for Independent Timor-Leste* (Melbourne: Australian Scholarly Publishing, 2009), 82–83; and Xanana Gusmão, *Timor Lives! Speeches of Freedom and Independence* (Alexandria, New South Wales: Longueville Books, 2005), 101.

[65] CAVR, *Chega!*, Part 5: Resistance: Structure and Strategy, 31.

[66] Ibid., 28.

[67] A CRRN political cadre quoted in CAVR, *Chega!*, Part 5: Resistance: Structure and Strategy, 32

As the principal driving force behind the CRRN's slow move toward national unity and ideological moderation, Gusmão made only a lukewarm gesture to that effect by promising to make 1983 "the year of national unity" – without the necessary organizational and ideological changes to validate that invitation. During his New Year declaration given at the end of 1982, for example, he was quick to follow his promise for 1983 with the assertion that the controversial, unilaterally declared Democratic Republic of East Timor (DRET) was "being recognized by several countries of the world. FRETILIN is a movement recognized all over the world as the sole, the truthful and legitimate representative of the Maubere people."[68] These assertions subscribed to a historical perspective that disregarded other non-FRETILIN, non-Marxist pro-independence East Timorese. They also projected an ideologically charged worldview that left no room for an alternative. Transitioning to national unity without transforming the salient features that fomented division in the first place was, therefore, a rhetoric that unnerved FRETILIN without impressing the non-FRETILIN Timorese. CRRN had not made the necessary concessions to achieve unity on a minimum pro-independence platform until the mid-1980s, but Father Martinho had had convincing answers to long-held allegations of external communist support.[69]

Moreover, the new generation impressed Father Martinho as providing a window of opportunity to galvanize the nation. Recognizing the CRRN leadership's reception of his ideas, and confident that it would follow through on his advice for the sake of national unity, Father Martinho started crusading to rectify the distorted image of FRETILIN as a fanatic communist organization.[70] In June 1984, for example, Father Martinho told the American Catholic Bishops' Committee for Social Development and World Peace that the strong resistance of *"the deeply Catholic, nationalist guerrillas of FRETILIN"* (emphasis added) continued to make it necessary for the Indonesian military to "send thousands upon thousands of fresh troops and on top of this enlist the local population... who Indonesian troops try to use as human bait in the fight against their brothers."[71] He was convinced

---

[68] "Message from the Supreme Command of the Struggle: 1983-the Year of National Unity" a 1982 end of year message of Xanana Gusmão reprint in official FRETILIN organ Nacroma, March/April 1983.

[69] During his first secret meeting, Father Martinho was quick to ask Gusmão where they got their guns. The latter replied that all their weapons had been captured from the Indonesians and that reassured the spiritual leader. Lennox, *Fighting Spirit*, 189.

[70] Although Father Martinho had started to speak of thousands of Catholic martyrs as early as 1981, his allusions to FRETILIN became more pointed after his resignation as the Apostolic Administration.

[71] CIDAC-CDPM/TL3174, "Statement of Martinho da Costa Lopes, Apostolic Administrator of East Timor, 1977–1983, to the American Catholic Bishops' Committee for Social Development and World Peace," Washington, DC, June 12, 1984.

that his urgings, along with the prevailing political and military realities, had initiated movement away from hard-line Marxism.

The mending of the estrangement between FRETILIN and the Timorese Catholic Church was a landmark breakthrough for CRRN's drive to restructure and intensify the resistance. The resistance leadership's reluctant reception of the church's urgings for ideological moderation and its increased inclusivity proved to be an invaluable asset in the guerrillas' survival and the advancement of their nationalist cause. In winning the backing of the church, CRRN scored a strategic victory over the Indonesian military. The church helped to sharpen the resistance movement's articulation of its nonmilitary aspects of the struggle, more specifically as pursuit of social justice. After Father Martinho's forced resignation, the church's new leadership adopted a far more nuanced approach, weaving together arguments about human, cultural, religious, and linguistic rights into something that made the East Timorese people deserve self-determination.[72]

Meanwhile, as Indonesian-perpetrated terror and an atmosphere of fear pervaded the lives of the East Timorese, the church became the only place the people could turn to for physical protection and material and moral support, as well as spiritual guidance. As a "source of spiritual solace in a society that suffered trauma," the church, wrote Robert Archer, represented for the Timorese "an important element of continuity in a world overturned by war," and it earned their profound loyalty.[73] The huge increases in the number of Catholics after the Indonesian invasion speak for themselves. According to church sources, out of a population of 688, 769 in 1975, 220,000 (32 percent) were Catholics and the rest were followers of traditional belief systems. Divided into nineteen parishes and served by 155 clergy, the church ran fifty-five schools that catered to 10,263 students. About ten years later in 1984, the population total had decreased, as had the number of clergy, but the number of Catholics had doubled. Out of a population of 578,000, there were now 438,000 (76 percent) Catholics and 30,000 Catechists, all led by eighty-one clergy.[74] Its growing flock gave the church in East Timor the moral ground to speak with confidence on behalf of the people.

[72] The earliest example of the new Apostolic Administrator's defense of the East Timorese people's pursuit of self-determination is his January 1, 1985 "Message from the Church of East Timor," available at CIDAC's CDPM collection: CIDAC-CDPM/TL3184.
[73] Robert Archer, "The Catholic Church in East Timor" in *East Timor at the Crossroads*, ed. Carey and Bentley, 127.
[74] CIDAC – CDPM/TL4788, Apostolic Administrator of Dili, Carlos Filipe Ximenes Belo to Monsenhor Pablo Puente, Apostolic Pro-Nuncio to Indonesia, February 17, 1985. Although it is hard to know precisely, it should be noted that this was also assisted partially by the fact that as "Indonesians" East Timorese had to choose an approved religion under Pancasila, the Indonesian state ideology. Understandably, many East Timorese chose Catholicism, even if nominally.

Under Father Carlos Filipe Ximenes Belo, the new and young apostolic administrator, however, the church had to walk a fine line between the Indonesian military and the FALINTIL guerrillas. On one hand, having secured the replacement of Father Martinho,[75] the Indonesian military sought to co-opt the church in order to win the hearts and minds of the people. The Indonesian government generously supported church projects, and the church was willing to cooperate with the government on many levels, even accepting *Pancasila* as the state ideology.[76] The Indonesian forces particularly sought Monsignor (later Bishop) Belo's active support. Timorese nationalists initially resented Belo's role and suspected his intentions.[77]

On the other hand, the church's inability to take a clear-cut public stand in support of the rebels as it had done before 1983 did not sit well with the independence movement and clergy who sympathized with it.[78] Well-placed priests continued to lend important moral support to the resistance and make as much of the church's resources available to its fighters as security conditions allowed. Timorese priests even joined the ranks of the Caixas and became forerunners of the clandestine struggle by acting as vital conduits of communication with the outside world. Before this, Indonesia had benefited from the lack of credible, uncensored information coming out of East Timor.[79]

Aware of Gusmão's grumbling and of Timorese priests' support for the movement, Bishop Belo did not go out of his way to stop either, in spite of his alleged sympathy toward Indonesian offers of internal autonomy, as Gusmão claimed.[80] Not long after he took office, he championed a far more

---

[75] Although it is not surprising for any of Jakarta's generals in East Timor to seek to replace Father Martinho because of the latter's militancy, it is believed that the Catholic General Murdani's ascendancy to the post of the minister of defense enabled him to better leverage both the Indonesian Catholic Church and the Apostolic Pro-Nuncio to Indonesia (the Holy See's representative) to achieve his goal. Only once has Father Martinho confessed that he was forced to resign. Lennox, *Fighting Spirit*, 215.

[76] CIDAC-CDPM/TL4788, Apostolic Administrator of Dili, Carlos Filipe Ximenes Belo to Monsenhor Pablo Puente, Apostolic Pro-Nuncio to Indonesia, February 17, 1985. Showing how the new Indonesian policy toward the Church was "pendekatan" (bringing closer), Bishop Belo clearly indicates in this report why the Indonesians were doing that and how difficult the Church's position became as a result.

[77] Several priests and an organized group of Catholic Youth were initially suspicion of Belo until the latter's youth-centered programs as well as the guidance and protection that he offered the youth won them over. Conversations with Jacinto Alves (June 10, 2008, Dili, East Timor).

[78] An unnamed guerrilla leader, for example, is on record saying, "The only consistent thing about Bishop Belo is his inconsistency." Quoted in Kohen, *From the Place of the Dead*, 198.

[79] Although the list of these priests and nuns is long and I have only interviewed two of them (Father "Maubere" and Father Francisco Barreto), an Italian priest named Father Locatteli played a very important role as the highest go-between of the resistance leadership with Governor Carrascalão as well as with the outside world.

[80] Niner, *To Resist is to Win*, pp. 87 ff.; Niner, *Xanana*, pp. 109 – 110.

subtle and nuanced advocacy for his parishioners' right to self-determination as a way of guaranteeing their identity, human rights, and culture – without ruling out the possibility of East Timor's merger with Indonesia in a free and fair environment. "The Church believes that the people of East Timor feel that fundamental human rights have been violated. Among these rights is the right of the Timorese people to choose and direct their own future." He rhetorically asked what the reason was for a nine-year war if the people had decided their own future as the Indonesian government claimed. He went on to answer his own question: "[i]f that were so, what would then be the explanation of the arrests, disappearances and the deportation of thousands of civilians" into resettlement camps?[81] "A War that continues for nine years cannot be imputed to the blind obstinacy of a minority."[82]

As he geared the church toward youth-centered programs, he won over the pro-independence youth, as he did the nationalist priests, through his subtle and nuanced endorsement of what their movement had been advocating for. The young Timorese gained confidence in him, and his residence and the church offered them safe haven from Indonesian abuse.[83] The subsequent contributions of Catholic youth organizations and their collective far-reaching grassroots activism in defiance of Indonesia (discussed in Chapter 6) owe their success as much to him and the church as to the activists' courage and creativity.

[81] CIDAC – CDPM/TL3184, "Message from the Church of East Timor," January 1, 1985. The same document is available at the Arquivo Mário Soares, 06473.089, "Statement of the Apostolic Administrator and the Presbyterial Council of Dili Diocese." Both the documents are signed as in January 1985 but Bishop Belo said that they the document was produced in December 1984 following Dom Martinho's precedent and in accordance with the procedures of the Church's information gathering from across East Timor during its preparation of its 1981 "Reflections of the East Timorese Religious." Nevertheless, because of the premature leaking of this document before it even reached the intended recipient, Bishop Belo felt obliged to disown it without forgoing its intentions. Interview with Bishop Carlos Filipe Ximenes Belo (August 25, 2006, Mogofores, Portugal).

[82] CIDAC-CDPM/TL3184, "Message from the Church of East Timor," January 1, 1985. The same document is available at the Arquivo Mário Soares, 06473.089, "Statement of the Apostolic Administrator and the Presbyterial Council of Dili Diocese." Both the documents are signed in January 1985, but Bishop Belo said that they the document was produced in December 1984 following Dom Martinho's precedent and in accordance with the procedures of the church's information gathering from across East Timor during its preparation of its 1981 "Reflections of the East Timorese Religious." Nevertheless, because of the premature leaking of this document before it even reached the intended recipient, Bishop Belo felt obliged to disown it without forgoing its intentions. Interview with Bishop Carlos Filipe Ximenes Belo (August 25, 2006, Mogofores, Portugal).

[83] Conversations with Jacinto Alves (June 10, 2008, Dili, East Timor). The number of incidents involving young Timorese nationalists seeking refuge in the church and the many life-threatening experiences that Bishop Belo survived also speaks to this fact.

The Indonesians Hone Their Intelligence about the Insurgency

Meanwhile, better informed after Operasi Keamanan, Indonesian military architects developed an intricate hierarchy of structures parallel to that of CRRN. Because of the gains of the operation, Korem 164/Wira Dharma had precise knowledge of the structure and strategy of the new East Timorese resistance movement as early as 1982. One of several secret Indonesian documents captured by the East Timorese resistance movement in that year gives a detailed account of the formation and operation of CRRN structures, deployment of forces, composition of the Nureps, and the mechanisms of relaying information and supplies from people under Indonesian control to fighters in the jungle.[84]

Another document described the guerrillas' objectives to persevere and replenish their strength by refusing to engage in major battles, enhancing ties with the population under Indonesian occupation, making their presence felt by launching operations on important dates, and creating a sense of insecurity within the Indonesian military.[85] Indonesian intelligence accurately recognized the resistance movement's guerrilla tactics: determination to inculcate tenacious personal qualities in its fighters, evasiveness, and ability to take initiatives as a group.[86]

To overcome the guerrillas' secrecy, the military adopted an intricate plan of grassroots surveillance and control of the civilian population through a carrot-and-stick approach. In concentration camps and heavily guarded villages, Indonesian strategy aimed to identify relatives of FALINTIL members, as well as capture Nureps and/or fighters redhanded. Once a suspected fighter or Nurep was captured, Indonesian manuals advised interrogating the captive into giving away secrets that would enable the Indonesian security forces to penetrate the clandestine resistance network and find out "who is it who helps them in the settlement, who are the Nureps or GPK [Gerakan Pengacau Keamanan, Security Disrupter Movement] who are in the Cernak."[87] Having advised the physical separation and interrogation of captives, the same Indonesian manuals instructed that repressing the resistance movement should not take place at the expense of efforts to win the hearts and minds of the East Timorese.

[84] Korem 164 Wira Dharma Intelligence Section, "Instruction Manual: The Way for Babinsa or Team Pembina Desa to Break up GPK Support Network" in *The War Against East Timor*, ed. Budiardjo and Liong, 177–181.

[85] Korem 164 Wira Dharma, "Instruction Manual No. Juknis/05/I/1982: System of Security in Towns and Resettlement Area" in *The War against East Timor*, ed. Budiardjo and Liong, 183.

[86] Ibid.

[87] Korem 164 Wira Dharma Intelligence Section, "Instruction Manual: The Way for Babinsa or Team Pembina Desa to Break up GPK Support Network" in *The War against East Timor*, ed. Budiardjo and Liong, 179.

As one manual put it, "exposing the GPK support networks, simultaneously carry out efforts to win the sympathy of the village. Remember that people's sympathy is based first and foremost on the stomach, on their customs and on giving them a picture of a better life."[88] It gave detailed instructions on measures that should be taken to that effect. In reality, however, the hearts and minds work took a backseat to violent counter insurgency.

The secret manuals also advised an increase in local response capabilities through Ratihs, the setting up of village-level security systems, and by conducting regular patrols ostensibly to protect people from insurgents but in actuality to spy on people and to induce them to spy on one another. According to a different manual, the Indonesian security forces would undertake preventive and repressive measures based on *Sishankamrata and Siskan Swakarsa* (i.e., total and self-generated mobilization of the population) from the grassroots in the villages all the way to the towns.[89] Indonesian identification of possible troublemakers indicates their inability to do so due to their failure to win the hearts and minds of the East Timorese. The list of villages identified as likely supporters of the insurgents and hubs of their clandestine cells is telling in its inclusion of the entire country:

Villages that are birth-places of the GPK leaders

Villages whose liurai have sons or daughters who are still in the bush

Villages many of whose inhabitants are still in the bush

Villages where most of the inhabitants have just come down from the bush

Villages most of whose inhabitants consist of ex-GPK and who came down on the basis of plans to destroy ABRI/TNI from within

Villages many of whose inhabitants are disgruntled because of past deeds on the part of ABRI-TNI

Villages that are not yet able to provide sufficient food stuffs for their own inhabitants.[90]

[88] Korem 164 Wira Dharma Intelligence Section, "Instruction Manual: The Way for Babinsa or Team Pembina Desa to Break up GPK Support Network" in *The War against East Timor*, ed. Budiardjo and Liong, 181.

[89] Korem 164 Wira Dharma, "Instruction Manual No. Juknis/05/I/1982: System of Security in Towns and Resettlement Area" in *The War against East Timor*, ed. Budiardjo and Liong, 185.

[90] Korem 164 Wira Dharma Intelligence Section, "Instruction Manual: The Way for Babinsa or Team Pembina Desa to Break up GPK Support Network" in *The War against East Timor*, ed. Budiardjo and Liong, 176–177.

It was one thing, however, to know about insurgents' structure and immediate objectives, and quite another to effectively defeat them.[91] Aware that
the enemy knew it inside out, the resistance movement constantly had to
improvise to frustrate Indonesian counterinsurgency planning. The guerrilla
movement placed a high premium on secrecy surrounding its tactical actions
and strategic objectives. As the Korem command noted, "In developing and
ensuring people's support for the GPK, they organize the people and themselves in ways that make it difficult for ABRI units to bring about their total
destruction."[92]

After ending the blockade and "opening" East Timor to the outside
world in 1989, Indonesia placed East Timor under a reformed Bali-based
Kodam IX. Indonesian armed forces' command in East Timor was renamed
as Kolakops and retained the preexisting trisectoral division of the territory.
Within the new political and structural contexts, the nonterritorial units were
annually rotated from other kodams into East Timor and engaged in combat and noncombat duties. Operating as part of what was called Batalyon
Teritorial, the noncombat units constituted an important component of the
Indonesian intelligence apparatus. They lived among the Timorese civilians across the country, to befriend their neighbors, collect intelligence, and
help Indonesianize Timorese civilians.[93] Nevertheless, continued Indonesian
efforts to pacify East Timor by torturing, raping, imprisoning, and killing
many and by spying on the remaining population doomed its counterinsurgency from the start.

Seeking International Recognition

Nevertheless, neither the Church's contributions, nor the nationalists'
domestic dynamics of resistance, were enough to secure legitimate decolonization because Indonesia was gaining ground in the international arena.
The vote at the UN General Assembly to keep East Timor on the world
body's agenda declined progressively.[94] Sara Niner relates how upon hearing

[91] If Indonesian documents confirm their superior intelligence and accurate knowledge of
CRRN composition, strategy and modus operandi, CRRN's capturing of those very documents was an omen of the Indonesian counterinsurgency's failure.
[92] Military Regional Command XVI Udayana – Korem 164 Wira Dharma, "Established Procedure (PROTAP) on Intelligence No. 01/IV/1982: Instructions for Territorial Intelligence
Activities in East Timor," *The War Against East Timor*, ed. Budiardjo and Liong, 201.
[93] Samuel Moore, "The Indonesian Military's Last Years in East Timor: An Analysis of its
Secret Documents," *Indonesia*, 72 (October 2001):17–23.
[94] The last of these resolutions was adopted in December 1982 during the thirty-seventh session of the UN General Assembly with forty-nine votes in favor and forty-one votes against.
That resolution mandated the Secretary General of the world body to "initiate consultations with all parties directly concerned, with a view to exploring avenues for achieving a
comprehensive settlement of the problem," which was the basis for continued involvement

on the radio that the East Timor question survived being dropped from the UN agenda by a narrow margin in 1982, Gusmão determined to do something inside the country to spare the tattering diplomatic campaign from an irrecoverable collapse.[95] The former FALINTIL deputy chief of staff and Red Brigade commander Paulino Gama (Mauk Muruk) agrees that Gusmão needed the ceasefire for diplomatic purposes.[96]

The CRRN leadership thus prepared to challenge Indonesia's diplomatic successes by supplying proof of East Timor's continued resistance and official Indonesian acknowledgement of it. In 1982 and 1983, the resistance movement intensified its activities, until the Indonesian military sought localized "peace contacts" between its grassroots commanders and their FALINTIL counterparts. Although there is no reason to doubt Taur Matan Ruak's claim that they pursued these "peace contacts" at lower levels out of genuine desire to reach a peaceful resolution to the conflict,[97] CRRN leaders sought to take those talks to the highest levels possible in a bid to undermine Indonesia's upper hand by earning its public recognition of, and drawing international attention to, their continued existence. That, the guerrilla leaders were convinced, would lend credibility to the diplomatic efforts of the movement abroad.

On March 23, 1983, Indonesia's highest military commander Colonel Purwanto, his notorious military intelligence operative Major Iswanto and Governor Mário Carrascalão flew to a designated location in FALINTIL-controlled areas to sign the East Timor–wide ceasefire. CRRN documented the signing ceremony in photographs of Gusmão and Colonel Purwanto shaking hands under parallel flags of FRETILIN and Indonesia. And Gusmão wasted no time in smuggling these documents abroad to show the world proof of their continued struggle, their willingness and ability to negotiate and, perhaps most importantly, Indonesia's acknowledgement of the ongoing war despite its repeated declarations that the war had long been over.

Soon afterward, however, the hawkish General Murdani assumed the defense portfolio in Jakarta, and in May, he served the East Timorese fighters an ultimatum to surrender or face death in the hands of the forces he had amassed for an imminent offensive. In Gusmão's own words, they "received an ultimatum from Benny Moerdani that read: 'Either you surrender

of the successive Secretaries General in the question of East Timor. UN General Assembly Resolution 37/30, "Question of East Timor," November 23, 1982: http://daccessdds.un .org/doc/RESOLUTION/GEN/NR0/425/08/IMG/NR042508.pdf?OpenElement.

[95] Niner, *Xanana*, 87.

[96] Interview with Paulino Gama "Mauk Muruk" (October 9, 2007, Rijswijk, the Netherlands).

[97] Taur Matan Ruak, one of the leaders at the time and Gusmão's assistant, told the CAVR that they agreed to the "peace contacts" out of genuine hope that these would lead to a peaceful resolution of the conflict while the Indonesians' "overriding objective was to use the opportunity to strike at us." Quoted in CAVR, *Chega!*, Part 5: Resistance: Structure and Strategy, 31.

yourselves or we will wipe you out in the bush. We will wipe you out as the serpents and rats that you are.'" In spite of their earlier disagreements and his berating of Governor Carrascalão, Gusmão turned to the latter to plead that the ceasefire held for some time longer: "Immediately, I had to request a meeting with Mario Carrascalão in Larigutu, Venilale. I asked Mario: 'Please, give us your support! Please ensure that this [peace] process is kept alive. Give us time to organise ourselves.' I was asking for time so that we could mobilise the 1983 uprising."[98]

The former UDT leader and Indonesia's newly appointed governor Carrascalão of East Timor left his Thursday afternoons open to the public so that ordinary citizens could have walk-in meetings with him.[99] It was through one such meeting that he received the preceding missive. He met Gusmão, who asked for the governor's help to convince the Indonesian military to abide by the ceasefire for three more months until he reorganized his forces.[100] In the end, the ceasefire held until August.

Internal Friction and Innocuous Divisions among Guerrilla Leaders
Either out of continued loyalty to FRETILIN's old political line and/or its revered fallen leaders or simply using that to legitimize their challenge of Gusmão's increasingly autonomous decision making, some members of the new leadership had initially rejected the ceasefire for it was a reversal of FRETILIN's early policy[101] and later blamed him for violating it.[102] Paulino Gama particularly accuses Gusmão of ulterior motives for wanting to extend

---

[98] In his first address to independent East Timor's National Assembly on October 21, 2002, then president Xanana Gusmão gave an account of the circumstances of his request for help and the former governor's role: "Today, I must say that without his contribution throughout that important period of negotiations, our fate in the jungle could have been tragic." Gusmão, *Timor Lives!*, 102.

   Not knowing this, José Ramos-Horta scathingly dismissed any role his brother-in-law Governor could have played. According to him, Mário Carrascalão "is a good head of family. He loves his wife and kids, but that's all he knows. He doesn't know anything else, and Mário wouldn't have the intelligence to initiate such a political [milestone]. The credit for this political move should go to Murdani. And such a serious political move can come only from Murdani. If Mário mentioned such reversal of political position, he would be shot on the spot." Transcript of Ramos-Horta's interview of early August 1983 in Leiden, available at the Dili-based Arquivo e Museu Resistência Timorense /06443.019.

   For the context of General Murdani's post-ceasefire planning, see Taylor, *East Timor*, 137ff.

[99] His purpose in doing so was in order to remain in touch with the reality on the ground and to protect ordinary people from being tracked down by Indonesian intelligence, the former governor explained to me.

[100] Interview: Mário Carrascalão (July 3 and 7, 2006, Dili); Gusmão, *Timor Lives!*, 102; and Taylor, *East Timor*, 137ff.

[101] Niner, *Xanana*, p. 90.

[102] Interview with Paulino Gama "Mauk Muruk" (October 9, 2007, Rijswijk, the Netherlands).

the ceasefire because, according to him, FALINTIL had already been sufficiently reorganized to resume harassing the Indonesian military across the
country, thanks to the relative freedom that the units and leaders found
to move around and readjust their geographical positions. Although exact
details have never been established, Gama argued that Gusmão ended the
ceasefire in August 1983 after it had served its purpose. Gama holds Gusmão
responsible for the Kraras Massacre that either precipitated, or attended, the
end of the ceasefire. Gusmão did increasingly succumb to making unilateral
decisions, to the chagrin of some of his powerful comrades-in-arms, and did,
by his own account, end the ceasefire.

Having rejected the Indonesian offer of amnesty in return for surrendering, Gusmão scrambled for ways to neutralize or minimize the impact of
the offensive Murdani had promised. Important factors to their emboldened defenses included the defection of a large number of Indonesian-armed
East Timorese to the guerrillas, and their taking the military initiative in
order to surprise the enemy and put them on the defensive – at least tactically. According to Gusmão, they were preparing such uprisings in several
locations:

We had Timorese in the Indonesian Army ready to act and join us, and some in the
Hansips and other military organizations. We had to take the initiative and fixed
the 17 August as the date to mark the end of the ceasefire . . . This action meant that
we broke the ceasefire, but strategically the Indonesian had already broken it by
threatening us. Tactically we broke the ceasefire but strategically they broke it.[103]

Due to bad or miscommunication, the planned simultaneous defections and
uprisings did not take place. Nonetheless, defecting Hansips – possibly also
spurred by localized altercations with Indonesian army personnel in the
area – and FALINTIL units launched a string of attacks against Indonesian forces in Viqueque. In August and September, the Indonesians brought
in reinforcement who massacred innocent civilians in and around the
Indonesian-created settlement of Kraras.[104] The full details of this massacre cannot be fully unraveled as there is no credible Indonesian source.
However, the fact that one or more members of the highest East Timorese
nationalist leadership, who held sensitive positions, believed their leader was
complicit or even responsible for the massacre of their own people bode ill
for the internal cohesion of the guerrilla movement.

This was compounded by Gusmão's continued unilateral decision
making – or within an even narrower circle than the already small leadership – since the onset of the restructuring and reorientation of the East
Timorese resistance. Circumventing CRRN structures almost at will, he

---

[103] Quoted in Niner, *Xanana*, 100.
[104] CAVR, *Chega!*, Part 7.2: Unlawful Killings and Enforced Disappearances, 168ff. For an
outsider's perspective on this, see Taylor, *East Timor*, 102.

cultivated direct contacts with, and loyalty from, party members across the hierarchy and the civilian population. The principal thread that connected the fighters and clandestine members of the resistance was their shared commitment to rid themselves of the Indonesian occupation and, for many, Gusmão personified that quest. Loyalty to the resistance was often reflected through expressed loyalty to him personally. That practice risked limiting the consolidation of the fledgling resistance structures but contributed toward its resilience by giving the leader flexibility to mobilize his followers at a moment's notice without having to go through a chain of subordinates.

In her excellent – and so far the only – biography of the resistance leader, Sarah Niner traces Gusmão's secretive and single-handed leadership style to the debilitating trauma and lack of trust among the fighters who survived Indonesian offensives and started regrouping in 1978 and 1979.[105] Many of their leaders had either perished in combat or been executed in captivity. But a notorious few had surrendered, with their fighters, to the Indonesians. They were quickly turned into propagandists and operatives of Indonesian intelligence. It was only natural that when the nonsurrendered survivors started to slowly locate each other, they would have difficulty telling those who were out in the jungle from those who had been turned around to work for the invading force. Moreover, in the absence of their legitimate senior leaders, and without official authorization for the junior member of the CCF to assume command, many did not readily accept Gusmão's initiatives. To his indignation, some even suspected his intentions. In Gusmão's own account, another CCF member, Fernando Txay, and senior military commander Reinaldo Correia Freitas (also known as Kilik Wae Gae), for example, had in 1979 rejected his proposal to search for survivors and gather intelligence across "the northern plains because they thought I had prepared all this to deliver them to the TNI," the Indonesian military. As hard as those suspicions were for him "to accept in such a difficult situation,"[106] they cultivated a style of leadership that, however expedient at one or another stage of the resistance, became a serious bone of contention among leaders of the resistance movement, and it died hard.[107]

Gusmão learned early on that a commander needed to exercise firm control of his forces. But his attempts to do so after he assumed the top leadership of the Timorese resistance in 1981 were perceived by some of the other leading commanders as self-serving. Gusmão's readiness to do whatever he believed was necessary to ensure national unity, as well as his speedy

---

[105] Niner, *Xanana*, pp. 44–51; 88ff; 111ff.
[106] Niner, *To Resist is to Win*, p. 58.
[107] After independence, Gusmão's style of leadership lay at the heart of several complications that plagued the country, including the 2006 crisis during which Major Alfredo Alves Reinado, the former Commander of the Military Police, deserted – according to him, under Gusmão's instructions. Telephone interview, May 24, 2006, and in person June 25, 2006, Maubisse, East Timor.

and drastic tactics, unnerved several of his powerful comrades-in-arms. In 1982, he began his gradual dissociation from FRETILIN by relinquishing his title as national political commissar – and, later, by dissolving that office altogether on his own initiative. These moves left the defense (genuine or opportunistic) of FRETILIN's legacy, and that of its fallen leaders, a rallying cry of his opponents within the leadership. Finally, in April 1984, the leaders of the resistance movement met and decided to disband the Marxist Leninist Party, formally ending FRETILIN's hard-line ideological orientation and formally embracing its new stand of seeking negotiated resolution to the conflict without laying down arms.[108]

Rival independence leaders had grown increasingly apprehensive of Gusmão's leadership style, especially FALINTIL chief of staff Kilik Wae Gae, his deputy and Commander of the Red Brigade, Paulino Gama, and Red Brigade Deputy Commander Ologari Asuwain. They disagreed on the course the resistance was taking and accused Gusmão of betraying their founding fathers by abandoning their ideology. Gusmão and his supporters dismissed them as lacking any concrete position. Gusmão's group claimed that it had been impossible for the two sides to engage in constructive debate and resolve whatever differences they had. According to Taur Matan Ruak, "nothing [that they did] was ever right" for these dissenters.[109]

No sooner did Gusmão reshuffle his subordinates and demote these three high-ranking dissenting FALINTIL commanders than the latter allegedly refused to take his orders. According to Gusmão, as the dissenters allowed the "continuous loss of guerrillas" in the Central Region, it became necessary for him to "put an end to the demoralizing situation within the Armed Forces and overcome the Companies' complete lack of operational actions, by giving them a higher degree of responsibility to enhance their operational capabilities."[110] For Gusmão "in the military there is no democracy...I gave new instructions on my own initiative...[because] in war the commander gives the orders."[111] Accordingly, he "gave new instructions, gave new direction to the companies, ordering them: 'Now find the enemy and kill them.'" Gusmão alleged that after their demotion the unruly commanders neither had plans against the enemy nor followed instructions.

[After] I carried out a reshuffle...Mauk Muruk [i.e. Paulino Gama] didn't have real plans to lead the company...Ologari, who was the Deputy Commander, just sat

[108] CAVR, *Chega!*, Part 5: Resistance: Structure and Strategy, 32.
[109] CAVR, *Chega!*, Part 5: Resistance: Structure and Strategy, 33.
[110] President Xanana Gusmão's "Message to the Nation" on the occasion of FALINTIL Day, August 20, 2003, Uaimori: http://www.etan.org/et2003/august/17-23/20fal.htm.
[111] CAVR, *Chega!*, Part 5: Resistance: Structure and Strategy, p. 30. Despite his criticism of his predecessors for failing to take note of their subordinates' grumbling, however, Gusmão seems to have neglected that, in war or in peace, not only do good commanders give orders, but they also listen to their subordinates.

around doing nothing. I said: 'if you want to lead a company, then you will.' Because of this [change] they called me a traitor, that I was no longer a Marxist. But the [real] problem was the military reshuffle.[112]

That failed to resolve the differences between the two sides. The dissenters allegedly went on flouting Gusmão's orders. Gusmão insists that the three commanders tried to instigate their forces "to revolt against the Superior Command of the Struggle."[113] Before their alleged revolt even began, however, Kilik was mysteriously killed – reportedly shot from behind – while fighting against Indonesian forces in front.[114] Convinced that if they remained in the field they would die in the hands of their own comrades or the Indonesians, Paulino Gama and Ologari surrendered to the Indonesians in mid-1985.

The death and surrender of the principal dissenters effectively ended further threats to Gusmão's position and friction within the resistance's leadership inside East Timor. Assisted by staunchly loyal staff like Taur Matan Ruak and Nino Konis Santana, Gusmão became FALINTIL chief of- staff in addition to being the CRRN president and FALINTIL commander in chief. Without any further challenges – but unlike a one-man show – and with the undisputed loyalty and support of his subordinates, Gusmão successfully navigated the resistance movement through the turbulent years of struggle until his arrest in November 1992. Even from Indonesian prison, he had the final say on strategic decisions that confronted the resistance movement, while a series of his lieutenants led the resistance on the ground in strict adherence to his instructions.

Conclusion

As tactics shift in war to match fast-changing challenges presented by the adversary, strategy also evolves. Individual engagements are planned based partially on assumptions, but they are adjusted according to realities on the ground.[115] The Eritrean and East Timorese resistance commanders displayed leadership by planning toward strategic goals, without compromising the tactical necessities. Both independence movements established organizational and doctrinal guidelines that struck a balance between controlled tactical fluidity and strategic continuity. They came under the centralized leadership of strong, disciplined political and military commanders, which

---

[112] Quoted in ibid., 33.
[113] President Xanana Gusmão's "Message to the Nation" on the occasion of FALINTIL Day, August 20, 2003, Uaimori: http://www.etan.org/et2003/august/17-23/20fal.htm.
[114] According to Paulino Gama, one eyewitness confirmed that Kilik was not killed by the Indonesians. Rather, a member of FALINTIL shot him from behind while Kilik and his forces were fighting the Indonesians.
[115] Clausewitz, *On War*, 207ff.

afforded on-the-spot tactical adjustments. Strategists' proximity to the actual theatres of operation enabled the concurrent progress of the strategies, without losing sight of the ultimate objective.

In Eritrea, the birth of the EPLF heralded an era of well-articulated and far-sighted strategies against Ethiopian counterinsurgency. Similarly, in East Timor, the CRRN survived massive Indonesian offensives and regained its vitality to harass Indonesian forces militarily. The Eritrean independence movement's effort to place itself within the international context was cut short by Soviet intervention on the side of Ethiopia and by U.S. indifference. Forgotten by Washington and abandoned by Moscow and its allies, Eritrean nationalists were left with no place to turn but inward. By contrast, as is discussed in greater detail in the next chapter, the diplomatic aspect of the East Timorese struggle for independence became increasingly important as it turned progressively outward. On at least one occasion, during the 1983 ceasefire, the resistance movement outsmarted Indonesian commanders into providing the necessary ammunition to challenge Indonesia's international diplomacy.

Crude Ethiopian and Indonesian counterinsurgency strategies increased the appeal of the Eritrean and East Timorese movements for ordinary people of the two territories. Because of the huge price the counterinsurgencies exacted on their lives and in spite of the real risks that things would get worse, Eritreans and East Timorese flocked to the nationalists. Many who did not join their ranks readily assisted them in other ways – raising funds, gathering and passing on information, and so on. Both independence movements offered inclusive infrastructures that enabled more nationalists to become directly involved in their common cause. While increasing the overall effectiveness of the independence movements, the centralized operating mechanism that the two leaderships instituted came with their own downsides with consequential implications for the future. Centralization is inherently prone to abuse, and the more successful it was in Eritrea and East Timor, the less tolerant and more repressive it became of dissenting voices.

5

Eritrean and East Timorese Diplomacy of Liberation

> There now exists no basis on which the United Nations can show any interest in the political situation within the [UN-devised Eritrea-Ethiopia] Federation.
>
> United Nations Assistant Secretary General Andrew Cordier, 1954

> The Security Council, deploring the intervention of the armed forces of Indonesian in East Timor, calls upon all states to respect the territorial integrity of East Timor as well as the inalienable right of its people to self-determination... Calls upon the Government of Indonesia to withdraw without delay all its forces from the Territory... Decides to remain seized of the situation.
>
> United Nations Security Council Resolution 384, December 22, 1975

Often concurrent, war and diplomacy fall at opposite ends of the same spectrum of human interaction. If war is the continuation of that interaction by some means, as Clausewitz famously observed,[1] diplomacy is another. For "the social character of all but the most brutal and simple of relations between groups very quickly brings diplomacy, if not diplomats, into existence."[2] Because an actor's performance in diplomacy has a direct bearing on its position in war, and vice versa,[3] Eritrean and East Timorese military (and political) predicaments reflected their diplomatic dispositions.

East Timor's situation improved because of the international legal regime at the time of its incorporation into Indonesia, and the subsequent sympathy and support it garnered following Indonesian brutalities. That international

---

[1] John Keegan's rendition (in *A History of Warfare* (New York: Vintage Books, 1993)) of what Michael Howard and Peter Paret translated as "continuation of policy by other means," Carl Von Clausewitz, *On War*, ed. and trans. Michael Howard and Peter Paret (Princeton, NJ: Princeton University Press, 1976), 99.

[2] Paul Sharp, *Diplomatic Theory of International Relations* (Cambridge: Cambridge University Press, 2009), 11.

[3] Munroe Smith, "Military Strategy Versus Diplomacy," *Political Science Quarterly* 30, no. 1 (March 1915):37–81.

context – added to the structural challenges to a military solution – encouraged East Timorese nationalists to reinvigorate their diplomacy. Whereas Eritreans, repeatedly beaten by Ethiopian diplomacy, believed they could gain an upper hand over Ethiopia through protracted armed resistance, and they did.[4]

These underlying realities determined the purpose and scope of Eritrean and East Timorese nationalists' relations with the outside world, variously described as "diplomacy of liberation"[5] or "diplomacy of the oppressed."[6] Liberation diplomacy involves at least one weak, nonstate actor, endeavoring to overcome a superior adversary by rallying support from as many sources as possible, without necessarily being in a position to give back in return. Liberation diplomacy, among the emerging alternative mechanisms of "dialogue" or hyphenated diplomacies, is one more testament to the fact that this nonviolent aspect of human interaction is not an exclusive prerogative of sovereign territorial states and their officially accredited representatives.[7]

Liberation diplomacy is not bound by the same deterrent conventions and laws that apply to signatory sovereign states, but liberation diplomacy also operates without the conveniences of immunity and privilege/luxury that are synonymous with its state-centric counterpart. In liberation diplomacy only aspects of instrumentalist (implementing the wishes of the sovereign or conveying the use of other tools) and representational (whereby a cadre of groomed professionals represent their identities and interests overseas and carry the outside world back to the domestic actors) functions become cyclical binaries reinforcing each other.

In search of altruistic aid and to gain a moral upper hand, liberation movements articulate and play up their embedded sense of righteousness and their humanitarian or legal claims in a bid to appeal to potential supporters' ideals, conscience, or legalistic outlook. They often receive ideologically motivated external support in solidarity with their stated political orientation or objectives. Governmental and nongovernmental organizations (NGOs) lend assistance on political or humanitarian grounds, often mixed with geostrategic or economic considerations. Liberation diplomacy – like its conventional counterpart – also seeks alliances with external partners based on religious or ethnic affinities, shared enmities, and actual,

---

[4] ELF Constitution.

[5] Scott Thomas, *The Diplomacy of Liberation: the Foreign Relations of the African National Congress since 1960* (London: Tauris Academic Studies, 1996); and Christopher Landsberg, *The Quiet Diplomacy of Liberation: International Politics and South Africa's Transition* (Johannesburg: Jacana, 2004).

[6] Bereket Habte Selassie, *The Crown and the Pen. The Memoirs of a Lawyer Turned Rebel* (Trenton, NJ: Red Sea Press, 2007).

[7] Richard Langhorne, "Current Developments in Diplomacy: Who Are the Diplomats Now?" *Diplomacy & Statecraft*, 8, no. 2 (1997):1–15.

or potential for, shared long-term interests. Third-party countries frequently support insurgent movements to either fight rivals through proxies or as an investment – albeit a risky one – for future payback.

This chapter deals with the multifaceted diplomatic initiatives that Eritrean and East Timorese nationalists pursued in their quest for liberation. It shows how, as in other liberation wars, less-rigid diplomacy served Eritrean and East Timorese purposes. It allowed them to conduct diplomacy without having to conform to the aura of prestige and officialdom of conventional diplomacy. Often diplomacy was done by frugal, scraggy independence fighters, volunteer-based solidarity groups, and aid organizations, as well as grassroots mobilization and citizen-driven (sometimes) person-to-person initiatives.

As a practice, Eritrean and East Timorese diplomacies of liberation can best be described as instruments insofar as they procured material, moral, and political support to the independence struggles. But their representational purpose differed on the basis of their respective grand strategies – military or otherwise – and the regional and global contexts that shaped them. Whereas the East Timorese, like other nationalists elsewhere, believed "securing diplomatic recognition...preceded achieving political independence and goes a long way to constitute it,"[8] Eritrea's "vigorous campaign for diplomatic recognition...depended much more on its strength on the ground than vice versa."[9]

Liberation Diplomacy in Eritrea and East Timor

The prevailing international legal context, *inter alia*, engendered these contrasting approaches to liberation diplomacy. As previously discussed, in December 1960 (ten years after Eritrea's fate was decided), the United Nations General Assembly adopted two important resolutions that equated the denial of the right to self-determination of non-self-governing territories, that is, colonies, to continued violation of fundamental human rights of the subject peoples. Resolutions 1514 (XV) and 1541 (XV)[10] constituted the legal and moral backbone of East Timor's claim to independence. Indonesia's invasion therefore derailed the formal, UN-recognized decolonization process, enabling Portugal to internationalize the issue. These resolutions

---

[8] Paul Sharp, "For Diplomacy: Representation and the Study of International Relations," *International Studies Review*, 1, no. 1 (Spring 1999):42.

[9] Christopher Clapham, *Africa and the International System. The Politics of State Survival* (Cambridge: Cambridge University Press, 1996), 215.

[10] UN General Assembly Resolution 1514 (XV) "Declaration on the Granting of Independence to Colonial Countries and Peoples" December 14, 1960; UN General Assembly Resolution 1541 (XV): "Principles which Should Guide Members in Determining whether or not an Obligation Exists to Transmit the Information Called for Under Article 73 e of the Charter," 15 December 1960.

were also the basis for the United Nations to continue to treat East Timor as a non–self-governing territory and for the Security Council to call unanimously for the withdrawal of Indonesian forces. This was the basis for multifaceted and robust UN intervention that oversaw the birth of East Timor as an independent country, discussed in more detail in Chapter 7.

But these resolutions came too late to be applicable to Eritrea.[11] In contrast to East Timor, the defeat of Italy and its renunciation of its former colonies deprived the Eritrean nationalist movement of a foreign sponsor with an internationally recognized mandate. Despite the Federal Act's procedural shortcomings, in light of Resolution 1541 (XV), the Eritrean question had been scrapped from the UN agenda in 1950 when the world body decided to federate Eritrea with Ethiopia. In 1954, the American Assistant Secretary-General of the UN Andrew Cordier wrote, "There now exists no basis on which the United Nations can show any interest in the political situation within the Federation."[12] Accordingly, the American legal advisor to Emperor Haile Selassie argued that by making the Federal Act a consensual agreement between his client and the Eritrean Assembly that the parties could amend or terminate, UN legal experts had "divested the United Nations of all further jurisdiction in the federation."[13]

All nonviolent avenues of righting the wrong were thus shut as far as Eritrean nationalists were concerned. They were out to assert their independence by force, and their relationship with the rest of the world was geared toward aiding the realization of that project and legitimizing its success. To that effect, Eritrean diplomats (from the ELF and the EPLF) manipulated ideological, religious, and identity-based (African or Arab) positioning to win the endorsement of individuals, organizations, and states. They also made contact with powers experiencing conflicts of interest with Ethiopia and opponents of the government within Ethiopia itself. Ethiopia's inability to control Eritrean borders with other countries secured cross-border sanctuaries, and sources and avenues of logistical and material support for the Eritrean resistance.

By contrast, as the geographic, demographic, and military conditions made it impossible for the Timorese independence fighters to reverse Indonesian gains by force of arms, their restructured movement reversed its initial military-centered strategy. While, on one hand, its fighters avoided engaging

---

[11] As Bereket Habte Selassie shows, similar provisions of international law that broadly equated the right to self-determination of peoples to their human rights were being implemented while the United Nations was determining the fate of the Eritrean people without proper consultations. Bereket Habte Selassie, *Eritrea and the United Nations and Other Essays* (Trenton, NJ: Red Sea Press), 27ff.

[12] Quoted in Michela Wrong, *I Didn't Do It for You. How the World Betrayed a Small African Nation* (New York: HarperCollins, 2005), 190.

[13] John H. Spencer, *Ethiopia at Bay. A Personal Account of the Haile Selassie Years*, 2nd ed. (Hollywood, CA: Tsehai Publishers, 2006), 236.

the Indonesian forces in major battles, leaning instead toward making East Timorese towns ungovernable and nibbling on the edges of Indonesian control in the countryside, the movement, on the other hand, revived its diplomatic struggle. In the mid-1980s, the nationalists turned decisively toward diplomacy and human rights advocacy. In galvanizing international support for their human rights and right to self-determination, the Timorese nationalists won over international public opinion. This put pressure on powerful countries to lobby Indonesia. What the Eritreans accomplished militarily, therefore, the East Timorese pursued largely by nonviolent means. This approach eventually broke Jakarta's will to continue with its military occupation.

Eritreans' Search for an African India

Regional and global implications of the Cold War limited Eritrea's diplomatic prospects. When the UN General Assembly disposed of Eritrea in 1950, the world body had washed its hands of this former Italian colony, despite its declaration that the Eritrean-Ethiopian Federation was an internationally sanctioned arrangement and that it would continue to monitor the situation. This left Eritreans with little choice other than to struggle to change the military balance of power on the ground. However, they pursued diplomacy of the oppressed in all its forms in order to reinforce their military strategy and legitimize their victory. The advice they received from world leaders was that they either had to be strong or find a strong party to champion their cause, or both.

In 1971, at the height of the India-Pakistan tension over the Indian-supported secession of Bangladesh from Pakistan, members of the nascent EPLF's Foreign Delegation stopped the U.S. Ambassador to the UN, George H. W. Bush, in the corridors of the United Nations in an attempt to win U.S. support for Eritrea's case. Bush told the delegates that they needed an "African India" to capture the attention of the international community.[14] The first Organization African Unity (OAU, the forerunner of the African Union) Secretary General Diallo Teli told the same Eritrean diplomats, "No one will listen to you unless you are powerful."[15] Although acutely aware of the odds against their quest for regional backers, Eritrean nationalists nonetheless pursued liberation diplomacy and, where they did not win material and diplomatic support, they prepared the ground for international legitimization of their military successes in the long run.

Eritrea remained an exception to the rule that Cold War considerations brought the superpowers into opposing camps in localized conflicts,

---

[14] Interview Dr. Taha Mohammed-Nur (September 17, 2005, Asmara Eritrea).
[15] Interview with Dr. Taha Mohammed-Nur (September 17, 2005, Asmara Eritrea). This was affirmation of Jamal Abdel-Nasser's advice to Eritrean students in Cairo decades ago: "Theeru fi tariq al quwah" ("March on the path of power").

because both rivals shunned Eritrean independence fighters and competed for Ethiopia's alliance. During the Reaganite revival of anticommunist rhetoric and support for the United States' anti-Soviet proxies in the mid-1980s, the United States briefly considered backing the Eritrean insurgents. But that recommendation was rejected in powerful U.S. intelligence circles, and the United States persisted in its position of the indivisibility of Greater Ethiopia.[16]

The enormous diplomatic leverage that Ethiopia wielded within the African community of states ruled out the OAU supporting the Eritrean nationalists and deprived them of an African India. The OAU and its member states readily dismissed Eritrea's quest for a legitimate act of self-determination.[17] Penetrating through African legalistic quibbling, obscurantism, and excuses, Ruth Iyob examines the '"Ethiopianism" of early Pan-Africanism to explain Eritrea's inability to counter Ethiopian hegemony in the OAU. Ethiopia's mythical millennial history and its military victory against Italy in 1896 set it on a pedestal as a symbol of African freedom. For many Pan-Africanists, Ethiopia represented the driving spirit behind the ideals that later crystallized as the pillars of the OAU. When Eritreans insisted that they were in essence a colony of Ethiopia – a country that Africans regarded as archenemy of colonialism – the independence activists met with disbelief and angry skepticism. Eritrean solicitation for aid from the Arab world played conveniently into the hands of the Ethiopian empire, which portrayed Eritrean independence as an Arab encroachment at the expense of African unity. Eritrean military gains fortified OAU objections as prospects of Eritrean victory brought closer African fears of surging secessionism.[18]

Eritrean nationalists proved unable to challenge Ethiopia's place in the master-narrative of a proud, free Africa. Nor could any Eritrean rival Emperor Haile Selassie's status as a preeminent African statesman and formidable U.S. client in Africa. Ethiopia's housing of the OAU headquarters and the UN Economic Commission for Africa reflected and reinforced the Ethiopian emperor's public relations successes. Both gave and continued to give Ethiopia enormous diplomatic and moral leverage over other African countries. Numerous promises of support generated enthusiasm and

[16] Paul B. Henze, "Eritrea: The Endless War," a paper prepared for the *Washington Quarterly* (Spring 1986), available in the Thomas L. Kane Collection of the Library of Congress.

[17] A member of the Kenyan delegation to the OAU, for example, is quoted as saying "if they [i.e., the Eritrean independence fighters] want their own state let them go somewhere else but here we are trying to unite a continent." In Abdulrahman Mohamed Babu, "The Eritrean Question in the Context of African Conflicts and Superpower Rivalries" in *The Long Struggle of Eritrea for Independence and Constructive Peace*, ed. Lionel Cliffe and Basil Davidson (Trenton, NJ: Red Sea Press, 1988).

[18] Iyob Ruth, *The Eritrean Struggle for Independence: Domination, Resistance, Nationalism, 1941–1993* (Cambridge: Cambridge University Press, 1995), 50ff.

excitement but fell short of translating into interstate leveraging for Eritrea's right to self-determination. Repeated ELF and EPLF appeals to the OAU failed even to elicit acknowledgement of receipt from the continental organization. Several promises from African statesmen were not kept either. The promises of the government of Equatorial Guinea (and particularly that of Sekou Toure and Diallo Teli), for example, did not go beyond a single televised interview with Eritrean diplomats, and the initial Nigerian sympathy quickly fizzled because of Ethiopia's evocation of Biafra.

Eritrea's African Backers – Ethiopia's Enemy Neighbors

More directly, classic conflicts of interest between Ethiopia and its immediate neighbours, and the allure of proxy fighting, granted Eritreans cross-border sanctuaries and access to supplies. Ethiopia's inability to control its own, and Eritrea's, overland and maritime borders provided insurgents unhampered access to third party countries. Eritrean insurgency, thus, became transnational, whereas international law and sovereignty of third-party states restricted Ethiopian counterinsurgency to its territory.[19]

Because of its strategic conflict of interest with Ethiopia, Somalia constituted the most notable exception to OAU rejection of Eritrean independence. Ethiopia's nineteenth-century expansion into the Ogaden, a vast swath of Somali-inhabited territory, and independent Somalia's desire to unite all the Somali-speaking peoples of the Horn of Africa, put the two countries at loggerheads. It did not take much pleading for Mogadishu to recognize the Eritrean struggle for independence as legitimate. The ELF did not take chances either.

Idris Mohammed Adem made the case for why Somalia should support Eritrean nationalists in a letter to the Somali premier, dated December 20, 1960. He also presented their six-point request for assistance: opening an Eritrean political office in Mogadishu, espousing the Eritrean case in international fora, allowing Eritreans to broadcast from Somali radio, coordinating the simultaneous start of the Eritrean armed struggle with an Ogadeni rebellion, training a division of Eritrean youth "so that they can be ready for the struggle in Eritrea at the proper time," and issuing Eritrean nationalists Somali passports.[20]

Somali response was swift. Led by Idris Mohammed Adem and Osman Saleh Sabbe, a Mogadishu-based Eritreo-Somalia Friendship Association (ESFA) emerged in 1961 to funnel Somalia's multifaceted assistance to the Eritrean struggle. As early as November 1961, on Sabbe's request, the Somali Foreign Ministry issued passports to Eritrean activists in Saudi Arabia after

---

[19] Idean Salehyan, *Rebels Without Borders: Transnational Insurgencies in World Politics* (Ithaca and London: Cornell University Press, 2009), 26ff, 82ff.
[20] Idris Mohammed Adem to the Somali PM.

Ethiopia revoked their passports.[21] From then, and throughout the war, almost all independence fighters trotted the globe on Somali diplomatic or regular passports.[22]

Sudan, like Somalia, constituted a vital exception to OAU indifference. After the removal of the anti-Eritrean Sudanese leader General Ibrahim Abboud in October 1964, the ELF dispatched members of its underground Eritrean cells to various Sudanese towns to organize Eritrean residents there and form friendship associations modelled on the ESFA.[23] Through these grassroots networks and ELF leaders' high-level dealings with Khartoum, the Eritreans procured invaluable assistance. Most importantly, Sudan provided them what any rebellion needs for survival and success: cross-border sanctuaries, secure and reliable supply routes beyond Ethiopian reach, and shelter to waves of Eritrean refugees who, among other things, were to replenish the guerrillas' ranks.

However, official support remained hostage to the instability of successive governments in Khartoum and their fluctuating relations with Ethiopia. As the first Sudanese civil war in the South raged, John Markakis aptly argues, the "Eritrean issue had become a card the Sudan could use to counter Ethiopia's links to the *Anya-nya* [the Southern Sudanese rebels], and was bound to want to keep it in play while southern nationalism remained a problem."[24] That analogy applies equally for the period after 1983, when the second round of Sudanese civil war broke out under John Garang's Sudan People's Liberation Movement (SPLM). Eritrean insurgents were used as a negotiating chip against Ethiopia's support for the SPLM. Eritrean political strategist Alamin Mohammed Said thus characterized Sudanese President Numeiri's policy as *"mesket al 'asa fil-wasat"* ("holding the stick in the middle") to hit either side, depending on the circumstances.[25] Nevertheless, the same corruption and frailty of successive governments in Khartoum, which worked against Eritrean nationalists at numerous junctures,[26] also frequently enabled Eritrean guerrillas to get in and out with supplies, fighters, and weapons even in the face of official Sudanese opposition.

[21] Osman Saleh Sabbe to Minister of Foreign Affairs Abdullah Isa Mahmoud, November 17, 1961. (This is one of several recently acquired and unclassified documents at Eritrea's Research Documentation Center in Asmara.)

[22] One of these was my eldest sister who was based in the Middle East.

[23] Interview with Ibrahim Idris Totil (September 22 and 27, 2005, Asmara, Eritrea).

[24] John Markakis, *National and Class Conflict in the Horn of Africa* (Cambridge: Cambridge University Press, 1987), 112. Haile Selassie's mediation of the first Sudanese civil war earned him Khartoum's official renunciation of its ties with the Eritrean independence movement.

[25] Interview with Alamin Mohammed Said (September 28, 2005, Asmara, Eritrea); and Gaim Kibreab, "Eritrean-Sudanese Relations in Historical Perspective" in *Eritrea's External Relations: Understanding its Regional Role and Foreign Policy*, ed. Richard Reid (London: Chatham House, 2009), 71ff.

[26] Markakis, *National and Class Conflict*, 112.

Sudanese and Somali commitment and crucial support notwithstanding, vacillating and disorganized Khartoum and Mogadishu lacked Addis Ababa's clout within the continent and in the international arena. Ethiopia's widespread networks of influence precluded international diplomatic wheedling on behalf of Eritreans, who, even in the best of times, could not count on Sudan and Somalia as their African India. Moreover, like other countries, Sudanese and Somali positions were not immune to superpower influences. A thumbnail sketch of U.S. and Soviet Eritrean policies must inform our understanding of Eritrea's search for consequential diplomatic support.

In a region that is also home to Islam and cohabited by Arabs, Eritreans benefited from Ethiopia's expansionist policies, its self-image as a millennial Christian empire with Jewish roots, and its contemporaneous network of alliances with the United States and Israel. Moreover, many Eritrean nationalists were drawn to the secular political activism sweeping the Middle East since the 1950s, when leaders and citizens alike were caught up in a heady whirlwind of anti-imperialism, Pan-Arab unity, freedom, and socialism. They framed the Eritrean question within this emergent idea of secular Pan-Arabism[27] and received consequential help from Pan-Arabist and Islamic governments.

Besides the perennial Arab-Israeli conflict, Eritrean nationalists' Middle Eastern diplomacy also benefited from the rise of rival Ba'athist regimes in the region. As Egyptian support for the Eritrean nationalists started to subside, Syria readily stepped in[28] amid its fresh rivalry with its former partner, Egypt. As the Ba'athists took the helm of power in Iraq and quickly fell out with their Syrian counterparts, the ELF benefited from the rivalry as support for the Eritreans became one of the many arenas in which one sought to outdo the other in championing the pan-Arabist agenda of the Ba'athists.[29] As discussed earlier, despite its contributions, this was to have a debilitating effect on the ELF.

---

[27] Interview with Mohammed-Berhan Hassan (September 13, 2005, Asmara, Eritrea).

[28] While three of my informants (Romedan Mohammed-Nur, Mohammed Omer Abdellah "Abu Tyara" and Alamin Mohammed-Said) received months-long military training in Syria in the mid-1960s, since 1965 Syria's largess enabled the ELF to arm its fighters with the light and effective assault rifle, the AK 47, a decade before the Soviet Union did the same for the Ethiopian army. For the broader context of Middle Eastern support or lack thereof for the Eritreans, see also Osman Saleh Denden, *Ma'erakat Iritriyah. Al-Juzu Al-Awal* (No publication information, 1996); and Markakis, *National and Class Conflict.*

[29] It is important to note that being beholden to such conflicting interests contributed to the ultimate disintegration of the ELF as its competing potentates vied for patrons and the Ba'athists in both Syria and Iraq unscrupulously pitted one group against the other to establish the supremacy of their politics. Nonetheless, this level of regional support – including the provision of arms and supplies – stands in stark contrast to East Timor's situation.

Eritrean Alternative Diplomacy

Since the early 1970s, Eritrean grassroots organizations in Europe and North America offered the EPLF's commanders in the field independent sources of information and logistical support from the West while relying on Sabbe's diplomacy in the Middle East. Eritreans for Liberation in North America (EFLNA) and Eritreans for Liberation in Europe (EFLE) alone launched successful information campaigns and raised significant sums of funds to send to the field.[30] Following the 1976 break with Sabbe, the EPLF assigned a member of its politburo (i.e., the central committee of the secret People's Party within the EPLF) to run its foreign mission[31] while the sympathetic mass organizations became answerable to another member in charge of Mass Organizations and Public Administration.[32]

The students and intellectuals in these mass organizations (the ELF and the EPLF as well as in the Middle East and the West) played an important role in Eritrean nationalist diplomacy of the oppressed. As the struggle's intellectuals, many students joined either the ELF or the EPLF and helped to shape their strategies.[33] Their analytical presentation of the Eritrean movement to foreign audiences aligned their respective organizations with the prevailing trend in their host countries.[34] Both the ELF and the EPLF owed their progressive credentials within the Eastern Bloc to the dedication, energy, and enthusiasm of these diasporic constituencies. And when Marxist-Leninist ideology started to lose currency in the second half of the 1980s, Eritrean

---

[30] Interview with Paulos Tesfagiorgis (December 29, 2006, San Jose, CA).

[31] Mohammed Said Bareh, Alamin Mohammed Said, and Ali-Said Abdellah alternated in that capacity and, in due course, what was renamed as Central Bureau of Foreign Relations of the EPLF established its Headquarters in Paris, France.

[32] Until the mid-1980s EPLF Politburo member Sebhat Efrem was in charge of Mass Organizations and Public Administration (the latter generally referred to as Jemaheer) and catered to domestic administrative and civilian intelligence needs as well as overseeing the clandestine mass organizations in Ethiopian-controlled parts of Eritrea and their foreign-based counterparts. Mahmoud Sherifo took over around the mid-1980s and eventually proceeded to become the independent country's minister of local governments with a similar mandate until September 2001. RDC/PublicAdmin/2/04863, "Excerpts of Sebhat Efrem's Presentation," 1983.

[33] Those who joined the liberation fighters in the field included Romedan Mohammed-Nur, Azein Yassin, and many others to the ELF and Alemseged Tesfai, Haile Menkerios, and Yemane Gebreab, among others, to the EPLF. Several of them, and certainly all of the above mentioned, played, and some continue to play, significant roles in the government of independent Eritrea.

[34] Bereket, *The Crown and the Pen*, 336. Although Dr. Bereket did not belong to any of the student organizations, his work fits within the general framework of citizen-driven diplomacy that the student organizations championed. He was behind the groundbreaking People's Tribunal in Milan in 1980, organized numerous international symposia and conferences, and participated in others to promote the Eritrean cause. Those forums featured an impressive array of jurists, scholars, and writers from different countries including other Eritrean scholars and representatives of the Eritrean fighters from the field.

intellectuals continued to play an important role in articulating the root causes of the Eritrean question, devoid of the ideological alignments of the previous decades.[35]

The activism of the Eritrean diaspora attracted a very small but highly talented and dedicated army of advocates around the world. Middle Eastern writers and scholars visited the Eritrean field with the ELF and published favorable firsthand accounts of the reality in Eritrea, informing policy makers and their broad Arab readership.[36] In England, Mary Dines wrote several exposés of Ethiopian atrocities in Eritrean towns and villages, and cofounded an organization called War on Want to push her case.[37] The history of War on Want is not fully documented, nor are the contributions of some prominent U.K.-based scholars and writers who championed the Eritrean cause, such as Basil Davidson, Lionel Cliff, and Abdulrahman Babu. French journalist Christein Sabatier produced short documentary films and articles. In the Untied States, Dan Connell frequently visited the Eritrean field and published extensively in the U.S. and European print media on almost every major episode and item of the Eritrean independence war. In Australia, Thomas Keneally, the well-known author of *Schindler's List*, wrote and lobbied for Eritrea while the renowned Dr. Fred Hallows frequently gave first-class optometric services in the Eritrean war zone free of charge, trained EPLF medical personnel and advocated for, and increased awareness of, the Eritrean struggle not least by publicizing his work and visits in Eritrea.

The preceding, rather short, list of international supporters and the very brief account of their work does injustice to the importance of their contributions. Unlike the international solidarity groups working on East Timor, very little is known about the foreign advocates of the Eritrean right to self-determination beyond the fact that their compositions and methods were diverse and even conflicting at times. Nonetheless, although it is hard to gauge their contributions precisely, it goes without saying that their collective work helped inform ordinary citizens and their conscientious leaders

---

[35] While Dr. Bereket is but a living testimony of this endeavor, his memoir offers a rather humble recollection of their work, too humble in fact for the reader to appreciate the enormity of the challenge and the importance of the accomplishments. Bereket, *The Crown and the Pen*, 334ff. Conversations with José Ramos-Horta, East Timor's pioneer diplomat and statesman who collaborated with Dr. Bereket in the 1980s (Dili, March, 2006, February 2007, and June 2008). Other Eritrean intellectuals who took the Eritrean case to academic fora include Tekie Fesehatsion and Jordan Gebre-Medhin.

[36] Rasheed Al-Asa'ad, *Adwa'e Ala al-Qadiyah al-Irytriyah* (Baghdad, 1969); Asa'ad Jadellah al-Qothani, *Irytriya: Taarikha wa-Thawra* (No publication information) and several works of Dr. Rajab Haraz of the Cairo-based Ma'ehad al-Buhuth wa-al-Dirasat al-Arabiyah (Institute of Arab Research and Studies). I am grateful to Dr. Taha Mohammed-Nur for sharing these and several other documents.

[37] RDC/Atrocities/3, 094797, Mary Dines, "Ethiopian Repression in Eritrea," 1980, submission to the People's Tribunal.

and galvanize individual and collective action around the world on behalf of Eritrea and Eritreans.[38]

The contributions to, and accomplishments of, the Eritrean Relief Association (ERA) is a ready testimony to the EPLF's successful alternative-cum-humanitarian diplomacy in engaging the international community. During the 1975 ceasefire negotiations between the ELF and the EPLF, the two independence organizations agreed to set up joint mechanisms to cater to the growing number of war-affected Eritrean civilians. Although the ELF quickly withdrew its commitment from the venture, its leaders recognized the need for, and promised full cooperation with, such an organization as Bereket Habte Selassie, Redazghi Gebremedhin, and others continued to set up one under the auspices of the EPLF.[39]

Registered in Lebanon as a humanitarian NGO, the ERA initially faced difficulty in procuring food supplies and establishing its credibility. As one of its founders, Bereket relates the challenge thus:

A rebel movement engaged in a struggle to defeat the army of an internationally recognized government must face immense difficulties; and a relief organization associated with such a rebel movement is always suspect and must pass the most rigorous test before securing the assistance of any donor, even for humanitarian purposes.[40]

But after the founders had drafted a basic constitution, Bereket's extensive personal contacts, coupled with international humanitarian support and the enthusiasm of the Eritrean diaspora, helped introduce the ERA into the network of international donors.[41]

Later, Paulos Tesfagiorgis's able leadership, and the dedication of its EPLF personnel, established ERA as a credible and effective organization capable of delivering timely relief to needy civilians affected by famine and war.[42]

---

[38] On learning about Eritrea in the 1980s, a small group of U.S. citizens raised an undisclosed sum of money for the fighters, but the package was returned due to a wrong address. One of these individuals brought the returned package to a meeting in Los Angeles with representatives of the EPLF to hand in their contributions. This is one example of many citizen-actions that the pro-Eritrea activists generated without necessarily having direct knowledge of them. Conversations with Dr. Edmond Keller (2005, Los Angeles, CA).

[39] Bereket, *The Crown and the Pen*, 313.

[40] Ibid., 325.

[41] Ibid., 320–324; and interview with Paulos Tesfagiorgis (December 29, 2006, San Jose, CA).

[42] ERA's impressive work during the mid-1980s famine has received international praise, including from Doctors without Borders that reported of ERA "as the only [one] in the whole region of the Horn which one feels confident to leave alone with their distribution network...it always reaches the affected people wherever they are." Quoted in Roy Pateman, *Eritrea: Even the Stone Are Burning*, rev. 2nd ed. (Lawrenceville, NJ, and Asmara: Red Sea Press, 1998), 207. See also Alex de Waal, *Evil Days: 30 Years of War and Famine in Ethiopia. An Africa Watch Report* (New York: Human Rights Watch, 1991), 178ff.; and Robert D. Kaplan, *Surrender or Starve: Travels in Ethiopia, Sudan, Somalia and Eritrea* (New York: Vintage Books, 2003), 70ff.

The ERA's transparency and accountability overcame the bottlenecks in donor circles, and by organizing donors and transporters into consortiums, it avoided administrative backlogs. Its fiscal conservatism, partially due to its use of unpaid volunteer EPLF fighters, including the director and its staff, generated a significant financial surplus to purchase supplies for the guerrilla fighters, as well as to finance EPLF projects and activities. All of the ERA's governmental and nongovernmental partners knew that, despite its autonomy, ERA was an organic part of the EPLF and that its direct contribution toward the latter conflicted with the stated principles of some donors or their sponsors. But the donor organizations did not stop contributing their share, however small in comparison to what the government in Addis Ababa received and how many hungry the EPLF had to feed. Paulos particularly remembers the generous donations ERA received from the United States Agency for International Development despite the United States' consistent hostility toward the Eritrean independence struggle.[43]

East Timor's Three-Pronged Resistance

Six days after its unilateral declaration of independence on November 28, 1975, FRETILN dispatched a high-level delegation abroad to canvass international recognition for the Democratic Republic of East Timor (DRET). Four days later, José Ramos-Horta, Mari Alkatiri, and Rogerio Lobato arrived at Lisbon Airport, where Abilio de Araújo received them with the news that completely changed their mandate: that same morning, Indonesian forces had overrun Dili. Suddenly transformed into a permanent mission, the nascent Delegação da Fretilin em Serviço no Exterior (DFSE, FRETILIN's Delegation for External Services) focused its energies on gaining material and diplomatic support for the resistance. Under de Araújo's leadership, the larger part of the delegation (which swelled with the addition of several students whose scholarships had been suspended by the Portuguese government) moved to Mozambique due to Portuguese hostility toward them.[44] While de Araújo's Portuguese citizenship allowed him to work from Lisbon, and Mari Alkatiri joined middle-ranking FRETILIN leaders in Mozambique and Angola, Ramos-Horta took on representation to the United Nations.

When Portugal introduced the invasion to the floor of the United Nations, both the General Assembly and the Security Council deplored the Indonesian action. They called for the respect of the East Timorese people's inalienable right to self-determination, called on Indonesia to desist from further violation of the territorial integrity of East Timor, and to immediately withdraw its forces. They also called on Portugal to resume the decolonization

[43] Interview with Paulos Tesfagiorgis (December 29, 2006, San Jose, CA).
[44] Interview with Abilio de Araújo (August 5, 2006, Vila Franca de Xida, Portugal).

process.[45] The DFSE capitalized on these fresh UN rejections of the Indonesian invasion to further the international attention on and goodwill towards their cause. In July 1976, Mari Alkatiri wrote to the Non-Aligned Movement requesting that East Timor be placed on the agenda of the then upcoming Sri Lanka summit and that FRETILIN be granted observer status.[46] The FRETILIN delegation was granted attendance at both the Sri Lankan and Cuban summits of the Non-Aligned countries in which the member states called for compliance with the UN resolutions and the respect of the Timorese people's right to self-determination.[47]

Despite repeated Soviet refusals to meet members of the DFSE, Cuba and Vietnam were as hospitable to them as they were morally and diplomatically supportive of their cause. On a third trip to Beijing in mid-1976, FRETILIN secured important financial support from the People's Republic of China without any strings attached. The Chinese government gave an undisclosed number of US$200,000 (equivalent at that time) installments that sustained FRETILIN's diplomatic work for years.[48] FRETILIN's request for Chinese support in military supplies was not met because the Chinese military concluded that the Indonesian blockade made arms delivery impossible.[49] Such international attention, combined with the stream of generally optimistic news of resistance that flowed out of East Timor, boosted the morale, and increased the efficiency of the DFSE's diplomatic work.

Soon afterward, however, developments in East Timor exacted a heavy toll on the otherwise resourceful DFSE. As Indonesian military gains started to dampen prospects for the East Timorese nationalists, Jakarta's diplomatic upper hand in Canberra severely curtailed the flow of information out of East Timor. After the Indonesian blockade of East Timor, FRETILIN's only outlet to the outside world was through a Darwin-based two-way Outpost

---

[45] General Assembly Resolution 3485 (XXX), "Question of East Timor," December 12, 1975; Security Council Resolution 384, "East Timor," December 22, 1975, and all subsequent UN resolutions until 1982 when the Secretary General was mandated to find avenues of resolving the problem, leading up to the Secretary General–mediated tripartite meetings with Indonesia and Portugal. These and other important UN documents (until 1996) are reproduced in Geoffrey C. Gunn, *East Timor and the United Nations: The Case for Intervention* (Lawrenceville, NJ, and Asmara: Red Sea Press, 1997), 107ff.

[46] Arquivo Mário Soares/Resistência Timorense, 05000.003, Mari Alkatiri to the Non-Aligned Countries Coordinating Committee, July 1, 1976.

[47] *Tapol*, no. 7, October 15, 1976.

[48] Interview with Abilio de Araújo (August 5, 2006, Vila Franca de Xida, Portugal). Dr. de Araújo was not willing to disclose the number of installments or how long the cash flow continued.

[49] There is an unconfirmed rumor that a Timor-bound shipload of weapons was redirected to Aceh because Indonesia fully blockaded East Timor. The glaring irony of an inaccessible East Timor but accessible Aceh notwithstanding, I have been unable to trace the source or general timing of this alleged shipment. Moreover, Dr. de Araújo who made the request to the Chinese insists that no attempt was made on their part because of the Chinese military's conclusions that it was not possible to do so.

Radio, which received and disseminated dispatches from the East Timorese jungles. In September 1976, however, the Australian government captured the radio, ending its transmissions.[50] Although the Darwin end of the service resumed shortly afterward, radio communication with East Timor was completely severed in September 1978 when the DRET's minister of information and security, Alarico Fernandes, surrendered to the Indonesians. Moreover, as noted earlier, by the first half of 1979, East Timorese nationalist leaders who had not surrendered had either been killed in combat or died in Indonesian captivity. Having eliminated the home-based leadership of the Timorese resistance and silenced Radio Maubere, Indonesia effectively cut off the remaining FALINTIL guerrillas from the diplomats of the DFSE for three long years. During this period, Indonesia exploited its monopoly of the airwaves to launch vigorous propaganda and psychological war.

Shuttling between Portuguese Neglect and a Constitutional Mandate

Indonesia's resort to a military takeover of East Timor embarrassed the Portuguese political elite who had already been blamed by the repatriated citizens from their former African colonies for mismanaging the process of decolonization. Under growing domestic pressure to act, Portuguese leaders were divided on how to proceed: one side wanted to recognize the DRET, as well as FRETILIN, as the legitimate representative of the Timorese people in retaliation for Indonesia's supposed betrayal, while another group advised a more cautious and long-term approach, involving international instruments that could guarantee the rectification of the blunder by genuinely ascertaining the East Timorese people's choice.[51] In the meantime, Portugal took actions that had great strategic significance to the Timorese resistance.

In the immediate aftermath of Indonesia's invasion, for example, Portugal broke off diplomatic ties with Indonesia and took the case to the United Nations, calling for an international response to Indonesia's invasion. Within a few weeks of the invasion, both the General Assembly and the Security Council reaffirmed Portugal's position as the administering power and called on Indonesia to respect the rights of the people of East Timor and withdraw

---

[50] Interview with Abilio de Araújo (August 5, 2006, Vila Franca de Xida, Portugal). In early 1976, the Australian solidarity group, Campaign for an Independent East Timor (CIET), needed an East Timorese to assist in manning the radio. The head of FRETILIN's External Delegation, Abilio Araújo, assigned his trusted secretary, Estanislau da Silva, who dutifully accepted the challenge, interrupted his plans to resume his studies in Mozambique and, instead, instantly left Portugal for Australia. As the Australian government wanted to shut down the radio, da Silva went underground with the radio in the jungles of the Northern Territories of Australia from which he continued communication with East Timor for about six months. In September 1976, however, Australian authorities managed to capture him and briefly cut off the direct contact with East Timor. Upon his expulsion from Australia, da Silva joined FRETILIN's External Delegation in Mozambique and Angola. Interview with Estanislau da Silva (June 6, 2008, Dili, East Timor).

[51] Interview with Dr. Carlos Gaspar (August 31, 2006, Lisbon, Portugal).

its forces.[52] While these resolutions remained at the core of all diplomatic campaigns for East Timor, Portugal elevated the political future of its former colony to a constitutional mandate. According to the Constitution of April 1976, Portugal bound itself to "promote and safeguard the right to independence of Timor Leste" and entrusted the Portuguese Republic to do everything possible within the limits of international law to achieve that goal.[53]

Although no Portuguese party dared to remove this constitutional mandate, for several years, none of the successive governments in Lisbon pursued it actively. In fact, Lisbon became increasingly hostile to FRETILIN representatives as well as East Timorese scholarship students. Until the early 1980s, as Ramos-Horta relates, Portuguese political circles "acted as if they had accepted the *fait accompli*. Portuguese politicians, diplomats and officials simply shrugged when they were approached on the subject of East Timor."[54] Portugal's inconsistent championing of the East Timor question did not help the resistance movement internationally. Its actions and statements consistently sent mixed signals.

In 1979, Lisbon briefly took up the question only to relapse to its acquiescent silence in the international arena. It dispatched several special envoys to its allies and other important countries to rally support. But when the CDPM activists visited the Portuguese foreign minister in late 1983 with the documents of the March 1983 ceasefire agreement between the Indonesian military and FALINTIL as proof of the continuing Timorese resistance and Indonesia's acknowledgment of their relative strength, the foreign ministry dismissed their argument and refused to use the evidence in Portugal's transient diplomatic fervor regarding East Timor.[55] Although Portugal's official statement of July 1984 asserted its status as the administering power and its desire to seek a peaceful resolution of the conflict, it went on to invoke UN resolutions and claim that the Timorese people's right to self-determination was the responsibility of the international community.[56]

---

[52] UN General Assembly Resolution 3485 (XXX), "Question of Timor," December 12, 1975; UN Security Council Resolution 384 (1975), December 22, 1975.

[53] Article 307, "Independence of Timor" of the Constitution of Portugal, 1976, p. 136; also reproduced in *East Timor and the International Community. Basic Documents*, ed. Heiki Krieger (Cambridge: Cambridge University Press, 1997), 36.

[54] José Ramos-Horta, *Funu. The Unfinished Saga of East Timor* (Lawrenceville, NJ, and Asmara: Red Sea Press, 1987), 125–126.

[55] Interviews with Luisa Pereira (January 11, 2006, Lisbon, Portugal) and António Barbedo de Magalhães (August 29, 2006, Porto, Portugal). Professor Barbedo was furious with the foreign minister who, according to the professor, the day after their meeting told a Portuguese newspaper that the East Timorese resistance had been defeated.

[56] Portuguese government statement of July 19, 1984, originally published in *Timor Newsletter*, 2, no. 4 (August 1984), and reproduced in Torben Retbøll (ed.), *East Timor: The Struggle Continues* (Copenhagen: International Working Group on Indigenous Affairs, 1984), 116–117.

The East Timorese Diplomatic Front

Portugal's distancing of itself from the East Timor question dealt the latter's diplomacy a serious blow. Disowned by Lisbon and generally neglected by the international community, the DFSE started to crack, and the energy and resourcefulness of its individual members seemed like lone and futile voices of a lost cause. Although the campaign of FRETILIN's diplomats was founded on historical and legal grounds, the news of the deteriorating resistance back home eroded their earlier optimism and hampered their struggle. Shaken by the news of the surrender or death of their top leaders and their tottering resistance, and disillusioned by the extreme pressure of isolation, difference of opinion among these diplomats turned, in the late 1970s, into serious personal quarrels.

According to Engineer Estanislau da Silva, the main difference was between Abilio de Araújo and Rogerio Lobato, on one hand, and the rest of the external delegation, on the other. While the former held that they would not negotiate with Indonesia, the latter advocated in favor of pursuing any and every means available to them in order to end the suffering of the people, including negotiating with the Indonesians. The disagreement deteriorated to an extent that at one point in the late 1970s Rogerio Lobato held the rest of the FRETILIN delegation hostage until the then Mozambican Foreign Minister Joaquim Chissano intervened and ensured a safe end to the deadlock.[57]

Between 1978 and 1982, FALINTIL guerrillas inside East Timor and their diplomatic brethren were effectively separated. The former commander of the FALINTIL Red Brigade, Paulino Gama, confirms that "there was total silence" on the part of the FRETILIN delegation abroad and that the resistance inside East Timor "only received its communiqués from 1982 onwards."[58] Nor did the external delegation receive any communication from the FALINTIL command until 1982, when de Araújo says he received reports of the 1981 reorganization conference. According to Ramos-Horta, during these seven years of Indonesian invasion, "FRETILIN was virtually alone in the lobbying efforts at the United Nations."[59] The indomitable pioneer of East Timorese diplomacy who went on to win the Nobel Peace Prize in 1996 confessed that he often "felt crushed" by the lone and uphill diplomatic fight against the regional and global powers. Only images and

---

[57] Interview with Estanislau da Silva (June 6, 2008, Dili, East Timor). Although it is not clear how it played itself out in the period preceding the hostage-taking, President Ramos-Horta (interview, June 5, 2008) claims that the intra-DFSE dynamics had always been characterized by rivalry between Alkatiri and de Araújo.

[58] Paulino Gama, "The War in the Hills," in *East Timor at the Crossroads: The Forging of a Nation*, ed. Peter Carey and G. Carter Bentley (Honolulu: University of Hawaii Press, 1995), 102.

[59] Ramos-Horta, *Funu*, 128.

thoughts of the plight of the Timorese people "have given me the determination to stand up to these powerful forces," he reminisced.[60]
There is no doubt that the other members of the DFSE shared Ramos-
Horta's determination to fight against the horrors that had befallen their
people. Nevertheless, as their physical distance from their country diminished their influence on the developments inside the resistance, the differences
among them increased to the detriment of their cause. For example, in the
mid-1980s, at the height of U.S. hostility toward Libya, Rogerio Lobato
appeared in Libya for uncertain reasons, which put the rest of the DFSE on
the defensive.[61] The Australians, who had been running out of public relations material to justify their continued support of Indonesia, eagerly seized
upon this piece of information. In 1987 Australian Prime Minister Hawke
expressed concern that Libya was having an influence in his region, charging
that FRETILIN received help from the pariah North African oil giant. On
June 16, other FRETILIN leaders, namely, de Araújo and Ramos-Horta,
declared that they had not received any help from Libya and demanded that
Hawke withdraw his accusation.[62]
As relationships between East Timorese diplomats were going through
rough times, the resumed communication between them and the new leaders
inside the country got off to a poor start. With the death of all first generation
leaders of FRETILIN inside the country confirmed, the surviving fighters
inside the country named the senior-most ideologue, de Araújo, to head
FRETILIN (as secretary general) and the DRET (as president), which they
still recognized.[63] Later, however, Gusmão disputed de Araújo's claim to
the presidency. In reply to Sara Niner's questions in 1999, he wrote,

An important point to emphasise about the structure of CRRN at this time concerned the Office of the Presidency. Those of us inside thought the Office was the
responsibility of Commander-in-Chief... We thought this because in the 'Constitution of RDTL', the President of the Republic was also the Commander-in-Chief
and, as I have said, we generally 'continued' to follow that previous structure. If the
President of the Republic 'was out of the country' (during this particular period),

---

[60] Ibid., p. 132.
[61] Interview withPaulino Gama "Mauk Muruk" (October 9, 2007, Rijswijk, the Netherlands).
It may be important to note that while almost all FRETILIN leaders have visited the United
States for one reason or another, there is no record of Rogerio Lobato ever visiting, possibly
because of his suspicious visit to Libya. It was also reported that later in 1993, he would
accompany General Galvao de Melo, one of the Portuguese officers who overthrew the
Caetano government in 1974, who became an avid advocate of the Indonesian position on
the East Timor question. Geoffrey C. Gunn, *East Timor and the United Nations: The Case
for Intervention* (Lawrenceville, NJ, and Asmara: Red Sea Press, 1997), 46.
[62] CIDAC/Peace is Possible, PP0808, "FRETILIN Press Release," June 16, 1987.
[63] Sarah Niner, *Xanana: Leader of the Struggle for Independent Timor-Leste* (Melbourne:
Australian Scholarly Publishing, 2009), 74–75.

it logically meant that he would have been unable to command the Forces directly, so the designation of the Commander-in-Chief remained unchanged. As we had not clearly explained this structural anomaly of CRRN to the DFSE, Companheiro Abilio Araújo used the designation of president in his first radio message [of 1985] to us to the surprise and distress of all of us.[64]

The controversy aside, de Araújo's designation, on the one hand, does not seem to have endeared the new commander in chief of FALINTIL and National Political Commissar Gusmão to the rest of the FRETILIN old guard in exile. In spite of their initial attempt to challenge Gusmão, however, most members of DFSE continued to work within the new framework, except Dr. Ramos-Horta who declined to become a member of the newly inaugurated Patrido Marxista-Leninista FRETILIN (PMLF).[65]

On the other hand, as increasing arrivals of East Timorese refugees in Portugal in the 1980s enabled the external delegation to piece together the tragedy that had befallen the people both under FRETILIN and the Indonesians, de Araújo sought to assert the authority of his office, touching off a quarrel with Gusmão. de Araújo claims how he was particularly troubled by stories that FRETILIN had perpetrated summary executions and by rumors that in the mid-1980s, some of the highest-ranking guerrilla leaders had been either physically eliminated by their comrades or forced to surrender to the Indonesians. de Araújo claims that he raised questions with Gusmão regarding accountability for what had happened and called for extensive deliberations on how to avoid them in the future.[66] In the ensuing squabbles between the two leaders, de Araújo completely blocked the flow of information from the FRETILIN leaders outside the country to the guerrilla movement inside.[67] So severe was the blockade that, according to

---

[64] Niner, *Xanana*, 75.

[65] Interviews with President José Ramos-Horta (June 5, 2008, Dili, East Timor) and Dr. Roque Rodriguez (July 8, 2006, Dili, East Timor). Ramos-Horta, nonetheless, continued diplomatic work as a regular member of FRETILIN, and his dissociation from its PMLF core is also likely to have helped his standing among the staunch anti-Marxists whose corridors of power he frequented.

[66] Interview with Abilio de Araújo (August 5, 2006, Vila Franca de Xida, Portugal).

[67] Interview with President José Ramos-Horta (June 5, 2008, Dili, East Timor). According to Ramos-Horta, he disagreed with fellow FRETILIN leaders outside East Timor, Mari Alkatiri and Abilio de Araújo, when the two tried to challenge Gusmão's leadership while competing with each other. As he put it, Ramos-Horta even withdrew from FRETILIN in 1989 because he got "fed up with Alkatiri and de Araújo quarreling for power and also challenging Gusmão's authority in the country. My view was always 'we in the diaspora cannot have more legitimacy than those on the ground.' So I could not agree with anyone trying to challenge Xanana Gusmão from outside; absolute stupidity! But they did that again and again." Ramos-Horta is more dismissive of de Araújo for hardly doing anything outside of Lisbon and accuses him of seeking to challenge Gusmão's authority because of his egotistic ambition for personal power.

Luisa Pereira, for some time, Gusmão relied almost exclusively on foreign solidarity groups like CDPM and Tapol, which used church channels for their communication.[68]

De Araújo, however, was the first to negatively react when Gusmão, in his own terms and analytical perspective, brought up the very issues that the former claims to have demanded. In December 1987, on the twelfth anniversary of the Indonesian invasion, Gusmão made a landmark speech that was taped and disseminated around the world. In it the resistance leader announced a "significant change of position" that he conceded was "an expression of our very weakness" but, according to him, also "affirm[ed] that we are becoming, finally, more realistic!"[69] Critically analyzing FRETILIN's experiment with Marxist ideology as an adventurous "political infantilism that tried to defy the world, obsessed with our non-existent 'capacities,'" Gusmão renounced "doctrines that promote suppression of democratic freedoms in East Timor." What he called "senseless radicalism [that] paid no attention to our concrete conditions and limitations" left no room for disagreement and led to treatment of internal dissent on the same footing as the Indonesian enemies, to the great detriment of the nationalist cause. Gusmão concluded that the new reality – decreasing Indonesian capacity to crush the resistance, Timorese resilience and international recognition of the Timorese right to self-determination – called for the resistance to take a new direction. Accordingly, he withdrew from FRETILIN to become a nonpartisan leader of all pro-independence East Timorese and made FALINTIL a neutral apparatus of the resistance movement in pursuit of the Maubere people's desire for national liberation and individual liberties.[70]

With that speech, Gusmão laid the cornerstone of the CRRN's transformation to the more robust and inclusive National Council of Maubere Resistance (CNRM). Although its launch was attended by internal and diasporic commotion, CNRM was conceived as a multifaceted umbrella organization that grew to attract and retain increasingly diverse pro-independence East Timorese. As the new worldview and strategic realism of the leaders inside the country dictated the drifting away from seeking to overcome Indonesia militarily, CNRM sought to systematically intensify and coordinate the diplomatic work abroad, and underground nationalist activities in East Timor and Indonesia, with the armed struggle. These specialized

---

[68] It is important to note that not only did Father Martinho da Costa Lopes carry important 1983 Cease Fire documents with him as he left the country that same year, but he had firmly put the church's services at the disposal of the resistance movement. Hence, from then onward, church channels were frequently used to expedite communications with the outside world.

[69] "Ideological Turnaround," December 7, 1987, in Sarah Niner (ed.), *To Resist Is to Win! The Autobiography of Xanana Gusmão with Selected Letters and Speeches* (Richmond Australia: Urora Books, 2000), 129–136.

[70] Ibid.

fronts crystallized to become the armed, diplomatic, and clandestine pillars of resistance that eventually carried the independence struggle to victory.

Nevertheless, Dr. de Araújo was astounded by what he perceived as Gusmão's explicit charge that FRETILIN's actions had triggered the tragedy that had befallen their people. He thought that Gusmão seemed to want to destroy the party that had, from the outset, fought for independence at an enormous cost to itself. Moreover, as FRETILIN's president and, perhaps more importantly, as the author of its political ideology that was the subject of Gusmão's scorn, de Araújo felt obliged to challenge Gusmão's attacks. In a 1989 letter to Ma'Huno and Mau Hudo, de Araújo reasoned that only a FRETILIN congress had the legitimate authority to alter party structures (including FALINTIL) and exhorted the two CCF members to convene an extraordinary FRETILIN congress to deliberate on the matter. De Araújo recognized Gusmão's prerogative to withdraw his membership from FRETILIN. But the fact that Gusmão did actually withdraw from FRETILIN made it all the more necessary to stop him from meddling in internal party structures and orientation, according to de Araújo, who also believed that FALINTIL constituted an inextricable part of FRETILIN structures.[71]

In 1989, shortly after de Araújo sought to challenge Gusmão, the resistance leadership inside East Timor concretized Gusmão's designation of FRETILIN as *a* party within (and not *the* party of) the resistance, led by the newly formed National Council of Maubere Resistance (CNRM). CNRM had a ten-member executive committee with three from FALINTIL command, five from the Clandestine Front, and two from FRETILIN.[72] The latter set up the Comissão Diretiva da FRETILIN (CDF), with a president and vice-president along with FRETILIN's external delegation constituting the highest leadership of the CDF. Ma'Huno (as secretary) and Mau Hodu (as vice-secretary) oversaw its day-to-day activities.[73] CNRM also imposed the restructuring of the DFSE into Resistance Delegation for Overseas Service (Delegação da Resistência em Serviço Exterior, DRSE).[74]

The other members of the DFSE were, by and large, amenable to working within the constantly changing structures of the resistance movement inside East Timor except José Ramos-Horta. Having declined to join the Marxist-Leninist leadership of the resistance after the inauguration of the PMLF as

---

[71] Interview with Abilio de Araújo (August 5, 2006, Vila Franca de Xida, Portugal); Niner, *Xanana*, 119.

[72] Niner, *Xanana*, 118.

[73] Arquivo Mário Soares/Resistência Timorense, 07153.102, "Organograma da LEP" (no publication information). It is not clear who the president and vice-president were throughout the existence of the CDF; but for all practical purposes, the secretary and vice-secretary remained its highest officials, subordinating even the DFSE.

[74] Niner, *Xanana*, 118.

the official ideological guide of the resistance in the early 1980s,[75] Ramos-Horta was automatically excluded from the newly formed CDF structures. Moreover, he completely withdrew his membership from FRETILIN in 1989 and went on to establish the Secretariado Internacional da Resistência (SIR, International Secretariat of Resistance) around the same time.[76]

Meanwhile, de Araújo's relationship with Gusmão and the rest of the leaders hit rock bottom and he started to drift gradually away from the main course of the nationalist movement for self-determination.[77] In May 1990, FRETILIN leaders inside the country expelled de Araújo and replaced him with Jose Luis Guterres. They also affirmed their confidence in and solidarity with Ramos-Horta's leadership of external delegation as an autonomous component of the resistance movement.[78] Despite his disappointment that his actions did not deserve Ramos-Horta's "complete trust," Gusmão, who

---

[75] Interviews with President José Ramos-Horta (June 5, 2008, Dili, East Timor) and Dr. Roque Rodriguez (July 8, 2006, Dili, East Timor).

[76] Interview with Dr. Roque Rodriguez (July 8, 2006, Dili, East Timor). The structure, membership, and mission of SIR is not clear partly because Ramos-Horta was quickly brought into the fold of the resistance movement within the CNRM umbrella.

[77] In the aftermath of de Araújo's effective sidelining and amidst his accusations that Gusmão was seeking to surrender to the Indonesians, the de Araújo-Gusmão tussle escalated and took an irreversible personal turn. De Araújo's sister, Aliança de Araújo, was married to Gusmão relative Augusto Pereira, who was an Indonesian police officer but also an underground operative of the resistance movement. The de Araújo house where this couple lived was one of Gusmão's safe houses, renovated with an underground bunker specifically for the resistance leader. On November 20, 1992, Indonesian security forces captured Gusmão in that safe house, leading to the arrest of the latter's entire family (including the seventy-four-year-old Mrs. de Araújo) and the subsequent torture of Aliança. Interview with Aliança Conceicao de Araújo (May 16, 2006, Dili East Timor); and Niner, *Xanana*, 137, 150.

This further inflamed the disagreement between the two leaders. Furious, Abilio de Araújo concluded that Gusmão was not a "good man." By his own account, de Araújo was the first to declare that Gusmão was no longer the leader of the East Timorese resistance movement after his capture. Severing ties with a captured leader from an ongoing struggle to some degree insulates the latter from the potentially coerced confessions of the former, and de Araújo's insistence that his declaration aimed to protect the broader interest of the Timorese resistance deserves the benefit of the doubt. Nonetheless, the preceding personal hostility and subsequent stands of de Araújo suggest otherwise. Interview with Abilio de Araújo (August 5, 2006, Vila Franca de Xida, Portugal). Starting in 1993, Dr. de Araújo and Ambassador Francisco Xavier Lopes da Cruz set in motion the All Inclusive Intra-Timorese Dialogue (AIETD) in London under Indonesian urging. FRETILIN and UDT seem to have joined later for reasons of political expediency. Meanwhile, in 1995, Gusmão wrote a letter to de Araújo: "brother, I know that you are in Jakarta. If you would like to meet, I am ready. Our country needs us to have a meeting." De Araújo refused to meet the resistance leader in prison, and his lobbying with the highest Indonesian officials to meet Gusmão out of jail did not bear fruit. From 1994, de Araújo started to be loosely identified with the Indonesian camp, and in July 1999, he launched a political party – the Timorese Nationalist Party (PNT) – that openly espoused autonomy within Indonesia during the referendum.

[78] Arquivo Mário Soares/Resistência Timorense, 06430.010, CNRM-FRETILIN, "Declaração de Voto," May 30, 1990.

had recently narrowly escaped capture, or death, in the hands of Indonesian troops and was hiding in a Dili safe house, expressed his personal confidence in the latter's leadership of the diplomatic front: "We are certain that, relaunched [*sic*] into the fray, you will pursue the struggle with us – a struggle which you began before me."[79] As he became the special representative of CNRM and personal envoy of FALINTIL Commander Gusmão, Ramos-Horta presided over the entire diplomatic machinery of the resistance with significantly greater legitimacy, answerable only to Gusmão.[80]

The rest of FRETILIN's external delegation accepted Ramos-Horta's new role and backed wholeheartedly Gusmão's leadership. In September 1992, FRETILIN leaders in Maputo wrote a letter to the resistance leadership inside the country expressing their confidence in Gusmão. Six weeks before his capture, Gusmão wrote back his reflections on the divergences of the 1980s: "Were dishonesty, pride, and ambition the cause of the rupture between us? Well, if the (theoretical/strategic) thought of CNRM was not convincing, the practice of the struggle imposed its laws and demonstrated its validity, and above all proved its capacity for action." Gusmão went on to placate and assure his compatriots in Maputo that he meant neither to undermine FRETILIN nor to block their political future. "I never had the intention of minimizing FRETILIN; it was the homeland that required me to draw away from the Party that taught me to fight for her [and that] no one should consider me an adversary to their political objectives."[81]

Reiterating his bestowal upon Ramos-Horta of all the powers to represent CNRM abroad, restructure the external delegation as well as strategize and lead its diplomatic offensive, while only answering to CNRM and FALINTIL commanders inside the country, Gusmão explained the logic behind the centralized, simple structures:

the regulation of institutional functioning should be the most basic, not losing oneself in the confusion of capitals, articles and paragraphs with no end, that only reflect a "necessity" to satisfy all of the components of structure, as if it were the primary objective . . . It is in this sentiment that we advocate a simple, but functional 'structure of war,' in which the sentiment of duty will prevail more than a description of rules of a "democratic" game.[82]

---

[79] "Letter to José Ramos-Horta about the Leadership of the Resistance," November 1990, in Niner, *To Resist Is to Win*, 144–147. Gusmão's disappointment seems to have stemmed from Ramos-Horta's founding of the little-known Secretariado Internacional da Resistência (SIR, International Secretariat of the Resistance) in 1989 that Gusmão understood as a counterbalance or even challenge to his CNRM (after Structural Readjustment of the Resistance) within which the External Delegation was assigned specific tasks.

[80] Interview with President José Ramos-Horta (June 5, 2008, Dili, East Timor).

[81] Arquivo Mário Soares/Resistência Timorense, 05001.009, Xanana Gusmão to leaders in Maputo, October 10, 1992.

[82] Ibid.

Despite the aforementioned division and hostilities among some of the Timorese leaders in the diaspora, the arrival of Father Martinho do Costa Lopes in Portugal in 1983 had boosted the resistance movement's drive for national unity between FRETILIN and UDT on a minimum pro-independence platform. The exact details can only be inferred: Dom Martinho had significant influence among the devoutly Catholic, non-FRETILIN East Timorese who supported independence, and it is possible that he impressed upon them the new face of the resistance movement inside their country that sought to embrace all Timorese. The grim reality of facing off against the Indonesian armed forces inside East Timor and challenging its aggressive diplomacy overseas also increased the appeal of working together. UDT leader João Carrascalão insists that all East Timorese regardless of party affiliation had carried out the armed resistance inside the country. Outside the country, however, complete political harmony between the two major proponents of independence was slow in coming.[83]

In December 1985, FRETILIN and UDT representatives in Portugal started discussing mechanisms for collaboration, and in March 1986 they jointly announced what they said was a nationalist convergence. Accordingly, the two political parties declared their whole-hearted support of the CRRN-led guerrilla resistance inside East Timor and agreed to work together in the diplomatic field without compromising their respective historical and doctrinal/philosophical identities.[84] In the words of João Carrascalão, however, the nationalist convergence was a mere "smoke screen" to give the impression of unity outside the country, something the resistance inside the country had long achieved because of the ordinary people's rejection of Indonesian rule.[85] The following year, UDT representatives separately went to the UN Decolonization Committee where they condemned Indonesian occupation and declared that they had always been committed to the independence of their homeland.[86]

In 1994, UDT and FRETILIN further hammered out their differences and launched the Coordinating Council of the Diplomatic Front of the Timorese Resistance (CCFDRT) in order to strengthen their diplomatic work.[87] According to Carrascalão, in the run-up to the CCFDRT agreement,

---

[83] Interview wtih João Carrascalão (June 28, 2006, Dili, East Timor).
[84] CIDAC/Peace is Possible, PP864, FRETILIN and UDT, "Joint Communiqué," March 18, 1986, Lisbon.
[85] Interview with João Carrascalão (June 28, 2006, Dili, East Timor). For him, it was not until the birth of CNRT in 1998 that unity was achieved and Gusmão recognized not just as a symbol but a leader of the resistance.
[86] CIDAC/Peace is Possible, PP888, "Statement by the Delegation of the Timorese Democratic Union to the Special Committee on Decolonization," August 13, 1987, New York.
[87] Interviews with Dr. Roque Rodriguez (July 8, 2006, Dili, East Timor) and João Carrascalão (June 28, 2006, Dili, East Timor).

FRETILIN formally withdrew its unilateral declaration of independence and started calling for self-determination. With its Coordinator Carrascalão based in Canberra, the CCFDRT appointed its proficient leaders and their dedicated diplomatic corps in countries and regions of significance to their resistance: Alkatiri, who was based in Maputo and supported by a cadre of diplomats in Angola and Mozambique, covered the Third World; José Luis Guterres was appointed to North America and was based in New York; and, finally, out of Brussels, Zacarias da Costa coordinated the diplomatic work in Europe.[88] As an autonomous branch of CNRM (and later CNRT), this joint FRETILIN-UDT diplomatic work came under the general purview of Ramos-Horta who, as the special representative of CNRM and personal envoy of the FALINTIL commander in chief, maintained regular contact with the imprisoned commander and rather loosely coordinated the diplomatic front with the clandestine and guerrilla fronts.

The United Nations Takes On and Portugal Resumes the East Timor Mandate

Meanwhile, amidst the shrinking number of votes to keep the East Timor question on the UN General Assembly agenda, FRETILIN's diplomats scored a strategic victory in 1982. Mobilizing East Timor's key supporters at the United Nations and their allies, Ramos-Horta drafted and Brazil cosponsored a resolution that the thirty-seventh session of the General Assembly adopted as Resolution 37/30 with a narrow margin of four votes.[89] The resolution mandated the UN Secretary General to "initiate consultations with all parties directly concerned, with a view to exploring avenues for achieving a comprehensive settlement of the problem. . . . "[90] With the basis for continued involvement of the UN Secretary General on the question of East Timor securely in place, East Timorese diplomats and their UN-member allies desisted from tabling the East Timor question for voting in subsequent General Assembly sessions. Resolution 37/30 made it incumbent upon the successive UN secretaries general to use their good offices to facilitate Indonesian-Portuguese negotiations, which, in the long run, provided for the UN-supervised referendum in the 1999.[91]

---

[88] Conversations with Zacarias da Costa (summer of 2006, Dili, East Timor).

[89] Ramos-Horta gives a fascinating account of the lobbying and arm-twisting that went into Resolution 37/30 both at the UN and world capitals. Ramos-Horta, *Funu*, Chapter 14: "The Game Nations Play," 125 ff.

[90] UN General Assembly Resolution 37/30, "Question of East Timor," November 23, 1982, http://daccessdds.un.org/doc/RESOLUTION/GEN/NR0/425/08/IMG/NR042508.pdf? OpenElement.

[91] The most authoritative account from the Indonesian perspective on the negotiations between Indonesia and Portugal leading up to the referendum is Indonesian Foreign Minister Ali

Lisbon's interim distancing of itself from the question of East Timor until Portugal joined the European Economic Community (EEC) was an astute tactical move as EEC members wanted to build stronger economic ties with Indonesia.[92] The UN Secretary General's papers show that tripartite UN-Indonesian-Portuguese negotiations between 1984 and 1986 neared a "comprehensive and internationally-acceptable settlement" on East Timor. Among other items, Portuguese civil servants and cultural artifacts were to be repatriated to Portugal,[93] East Timorese in Portugal who wished to return to their country were to be allowed to do so, and Indonesia was to guarantee the East Timorese people's religious, cultural, and political rights.[94] The last round of these "substantive talks" was held as late as May 1986 when drafts of Indonesian assurances were filed.[95] The situation suddenly changed two months later when Portugal secured veto-wielding membership in the European Community.

Having ensured Portugal's full membership in the European Community during his premiership, in 1986, the newly inaugurated President Mário Soares asked his advisors, and the government, to take up the East Timor question.[96] In July, he took the floor of the European Parliament, urging his fellow Europeans to give the East Timorese right to self-determination its long-overdue consideration. "We are obliged to recall, with indignation and disgust, the dramatic situation which exists in East Timor, an offence to the most elementary rules of coexistence between nations as well as to the fundamental rights of man," he declared. Promising "Portugal is not

Alatas's *The Pebble in the Shoe: The Diplomatic Struggle for East Timor* (Jakarta: Askara Karunia, 2006). It is important to note that these negotiations were tripartite, involving the UN Secretary General or his personal representative, Portugal and Indonesia.

[92] Domestically, Portugal's principal preoccupation between the late 1970s and mid-1980s was overshadowed by its bid to consolidate its own fledgling democracy.

[93] So confident was Indonesia that it contracted the Lisbon-based Fundação Oriente to collect all traces of Portuguese cultural heritage from East Timor in an attempt to fully Indonesianize East Timor by obliterating the distinctive markers of its Portuguese colonial history. On Prime Minister Mário Soares' private advice, the Director of Fundação Oriente withdrew his foundation from the project at the last minute. The Director of Fundação Oriente told Professor António Barbedo de Magalhães (interview, August 29, 2006, Porto, Portugal) that his friend, Soares, warned him against believing all that is said in public on the question of East Timor and advised him to stay away from that Indonesian project.

[94] UN Archives, Secretary General's Personal Papers, S-1024–0027-08, Rafeeuddin Ahmed to Secretary General, Draft "Memorandum of Understanding," 10 March 1986. Then Indonesian Permanent Representative to the United Nations and future Foreign Minister, Ali Alatas, also offers the procedural details of how Indonesia and Portugal planned to permanently remove "the East Timor Question" for UN agenda items through the agreement that never reached its climax. Alatas, *The Pebble in the Shoe*, 33ff.

[95] UN Archives, Secretary General's Personal Papers, S-1024–0027-08, "Preliminary Draft: Assurances," 2 May 1986.

[96] Interview with Dr. Carlos Gaspar (August 31, 2006, Lisbon, Portugal).

disposed to abandon East Timor to its fate," he exhorted the European Parliament to "demonstrate the attention and interest that a problem of this gravity requires,"[97] all to Indonesia's understandable "displeasure on the content and tone" of Soares's statement.[98]

The fortunes of East Timorese diplomacy of liberation in general and FRETILIN's External Delegation in particular changed dramatically with Portugal's EEC membership. During that same July 1986 session, the European Parliament adopted a resolution calling for the respect of East Timorese right to self-determination.[99]

The Clandestine Front

Domestically, in 1990 CNRM moved to systematize and coordinate the Clandestine Front, an important third pillar of the struggle against the Indonesian occupation. As discussed in Chapter 4, the clandestine front started spontaneously out of familial loyalty of those who were in Indonesian controlled parts of East Timor to their brethren fighting the Indonesian military in the jungles. Although this element of spontaneity continued unhindered throughout the period of Indonesian occupation, the resistance movement made a concerted effort to secure the support of the youth.[100] In 1985, for example, a group of Catholic youth formed a clandestine cell called 007 that linked with David Alex, one of the FALINTIL commanders, providing his guerrillas with logistical supplies and information. In a very short time, according to Constâncio Pinto, 007-affiliated underground cells of seven members sprang up through East Timorese towns and countryside. As its cells grew in number, 007's links to the resistance leadership expanded, connecting also with Xanana Gusmão and Mau Hodu. In a bid

[97] Excerpts of July 9, 1986 Speech of President Mário Soares at the European Parliament, quoted in Alatas, *The Pebble in the Shoe*, 39.

[98] UN Archives, Secretary General's Personal Papers, S-1024–0040-02, Indonesian Foreign Minister Mochtar Kusumaatmadja to UN Secretary General Javier Perez de Cuellar, 15 July 1986.

[99] Resolution of the European Parliament on "The Situation in East Timor," July 17, 1986. In the following years, President Soares hardened his position and went all out in condemning Indonesia after the Santa Cruz Massacre. His message to Queen Elizabeth of April 27, 1993 is only an example (1993, Organizacoes Internacionais, Portugal, 06465.090): "I cannot refrain from mentioning the present drama of the people of East-Timor, whose decolonization process was interrupted by the violent and illegal occupation by Indonesia, who insists in disregarding United Nations resolutions and the most elementary human rights of the Maubere people. This is a flagrant violation of International Law by a bloodthirsty dictatorship which should be condemned by the international community."

[100] Prominent among these youth groups was the Catholic Youth in East Timor and Students in Indonesia who initiated correspondence with Gusmão in September 1985 to which he responded on May 20, 1986. "A History that Beats in the Maubere Soul. Message to Catholic Youth in East Timor and Students in Indonesia" in Niner, *To Resist Is to Win*, 85ff.

to coordinate the activities of its fast expanding cells, 007 formed in 1987 a new leadership organ called Orgão Oito (Organ Eight).[101]

Moreover, the movement cemented the loyalty of the people by winning over the Umas Lulik (Sacred Houses) throughout East Timor. While the Uma Lulik constituted an important component of the clandestine network of the resistance movement, [102] several leaders fostered amorphous groups camouflaged as sacred associations but with a clear secular and nationalist objective. Prominent among them was Cornelio "L-7" Gama's Sagrada Familia that mostly operated in the parts of the country east of the capital, Dili.[103] In the western districts of East Timor, Colimau 2000 was formed by a group of young martial artists who were religiously zealous and dedicated to independence.[104] Several other martial arts groups that clandestinely worked for the nationalist resistance also mushroomed in and around Dili.

Although CNRM sought to implement loose coordination among these and other groups for better efficiency, it was not until June 1990 that it managed to introduce an effective coordinating body, in anticipation of the Portuguese Parliamentary Delegation's visit. CNRM launched the Comité Executivo da CNRM na Frente Clandestina (Executive Committee of the Clandestine Front, also called the Executive Committee) as a coordinating body of all clandestine activities of the nationalist movement. Led by Constâncio Pinto, the Executive Committee of the Clandestine Front drew most of its leaders from Orgão Oito. In a sweeping centralization of its power, the Executive Committee received its orders directly from CNRM President and FALINTIL Commander in Chief Gusmão and answered directly to him as well, without ending the preexisting ties of individual cells to individual leaders, but always with Gusmão's knowledge and approval.[105]

Solidarity Groups as Alternative-Diplomacy Vehicles of Resistance
One of the hallmarks of the new resistance leaderships inside East Timor was its newfound appreciation for, and direct collaboration with, international solidarity organizations as effective means of galvanizing public opinion in their respective countries. A host of such groups and individuals had long played a crucial role in drawing international attention to the plight of the East Timorese people and constituted an important component

---

[101] Constânio Pinto and Matthew Jardine, *East Timor's Unfinished Struggle: Inside the Timorese Resistance* (Boston: South End Press, 1997), 97–98.

[102] Even after the conversion of the majority of the Timorese to Catholicism, the Uma Lulik continue to muster the allegiance of almost the entire population. So powerful are they that as recently as 2006 and 2007, the then president Gusmão is believed to have consulted them before he launched his new political party – the Timorese Council of National Reconstruction – to compete in the 2007 parliamentary elections.

[103] Interview with Cornelio Gama "L-7" (July 1, 2006, Laga, East Timor).

[104] Interview with Gabriel Fernandes (June 26, 2006, Dili, East Timor).

[105] Pinto and Jardine, *East Timor's Unfinished Struggle*, 121 ff.

of the East Timorese nationalists' struggle in the international arena. Some of them had a direct link with the resistance movement inside East Timor, but they became vital alternative conduits of information to the guerrillas and influenced their strategic decisions after the reorganization of the mid-1980s. They helped amplify, and in some cases render more credible, the information coming to them from the resistance movement inside East Timor.

One of these solidarity organizations was the Lisbon-based Centro de Informação e Documentação Amílcar Cabral (CIDAC, Amílcar Cabral Information and Documentation Center). The new Portuguese leaders' inability to make controlled progress toward democratization during the first eighteen months of the Carnation Revolution of April 1974, together with their unwillingness to resort to coercive means of control, opened Portugal's political space, allowing the formerly clandestine Progressive Catholics to emerge as CIDAC.[106] Introduced to East Timor in September 1974 as a case of precarious decolonization, CIDAC started cooperating with FRETILIN by putting the latter in touch with the liberation movements in the African Portuguese colonies.[107] First, in collaboration with Timorese students in Portugal, and single-handedly after the latter returned to East Timor, CIDAC became the only organization in Portugal capable of campaigning for East Timor.[108]

Under the pretext that the suffering of the East Timorese people had become disproportionately high, different forces exerted pressure on the CIDAC not to inflame the conflict and instead to help end it. They advocated advising the Timorese to accept the status quo, or at least to keep quiet about it. Refusing to cave in, CIDAC activists persistently invoked Article 307 of the Portuguese Constitution to remind successive Portuguese governments of their mandate. While CIDAC's composition helped it to withstand the pressure to silence its members, Luisa Pereira admits that their blissful ignorance of Indonesia's size and capabilities helped them remain steadfast in their belief that the invasion was illegal and had to be reversed.[109] Moreover, the two-way radio communication between the Timorese independence fighters and the outside world brought them news of continued

---

[106] http://www.cidac.pt/; and interview with Luisa Pereira (January 11, 2006, Lisbon, Portugal).

[107] These are the Frente de Libertação de Moçambique (FRELIMO), Movimento Popular da Libertação de Angola (MPLA), and Partido Africano da Independência da Guiné e Cabo-Verde (PAIGC).

[108] http://homepage.esoterica.pt/~cdpm/quemsomos.htm; and interview with Luisa Pereira (January 11, 2006, Lisbon, Portugal).

[109] One-half of CIDAC's members were young progressives, like Pereira, who were staunch in their political principles, and the other half was made up of people like Professor António Barbedo de Magalhães, who had worked in East Timor and knew that the Timorese people wanted to become independent.

Timorese resistance, which gave them the material proof and moral inspiration to fight on.[110]

This vital communication was facilitated by the Australian-based Campaign for an Independent East Timor (CIET).[111] Based in Sydney, CIET opened branches in major cities across Australia and New Zealand, lobbying governments, parliaments, and civil society organizations on behalf of East Timor.[112] By far, the most remarkable role CIET played immediately after the Indonesian invasion was to run the Darwin-based two-way Outpost Radio, communicating with FRETILIN's leadership inside East Timor and disseminating their messages across the world. What CIET could not do, activists of various Australian aid organizations within the umbrella Australian Council for Overseas Assistance (ACFOA) did. From the very beginning, the ACFOA had believed that the humanitarian crisis in East Timor was a man-made problem and that addressing it required the resolution of underlying political problem, that is, the respect of the people's right to self-determination.[113]

In the United States, disparate individual sympathizers and groups assisted the East Timorese cause either because of academic interests or because of personal convictions. Since its inception in 1976, the East Timorese diplomatic struggle benefited from scholars and activists – Benedict Anderson, Noam Chomsky, Elizabeth Traub, Richard Tanter, and others – bringing their expertise and reputations to bear. A vital element of continuity between the activism of the 1970s and the 1990s is the consummate activist Arnold Kohen, who not only galvanized the previously mentioned sympathizers but also meticulously laid the foundation for Congressional hearings on East Timor as well as extensive media coverage – the "Arnold Kohen Effect" as Clinton Fernandes aptly called it.[114]

---

[110] Interview with Luisa Pereira (January 11, 2006, Lisbon, Portugal).

[111] Founded just before the Indonesian invasion by Australian activists for East Timor – Denis Freney, Andy Alcock, and Bob Hanney – CIET became the Australia-East Timor Friendship Association after East Timor's independence in 2002. http://www.communitywebs.org/AustEastTimorFriendship/aboutus.html. Also see Ben Kiernan, "Cover-Up and Denial of Genocide. Australia, the USA, East Timor, and the Aborigines," *Critical Asian Studies*, 34, no. 2 (2002):163–192.

[112] Stephen Hoadley, "Diplomacy, Peacekeeping, and Nation-Building: New Zealand and East Timor" in *Southeast Asia and New Zealand: A History of Regional and Bilateral Relations*, ed. Anthony L. Smith (Singapore: Institute of Southeast Asian Studies, 2005), 124–143. According to Hoadley, CIET also spread its activities in cities across New Zealand.

[113] Interview: Patrick "Pat" Walsh (June 7, 2008, Dili, East Timor).

[114] Clinton Fernandes, *The Independence of East Timor. Multi-Dimensional Perspectives: Occupation, Resistance, and International Political Activism* (Brighton: Sussex Academic Press, 2011), 49–60, 67. In telling the account of East Timor through the biography of Bishop Belo – *From the Place of the Dead* (New York: St. Martin's Press, 1999) – Kohen himself is silent about his personal role.

Such high caliber engagement may not have succeeded in reversing Western governments' policies on East Timor and Indonesia, but in the immediate aftermath of the invasion and during the war-induced famine of the late 1970s, they helped draw international attention to the plight of the East Timorese people.[115] They also crucially assisted in articulating the resistance movement's effective challenge to sophisticated Indonesian state diplomacy. Beyond Anderson's Congressional testimonies, Chomsky's writing and public lectures, and Kohen's facilitation of them, as well as mainstream media coverage, Jose Ramos-Horta relates how Roger Clark's meticulous legal rebuttal of Indonesian claims[116] constituted an important document in the dossier he distributed to potential sympathizers. As academic research and media coverage on East Timor increased, so did the dossier of papers and media clippings that international activists circulated for greater attention. This initial activism laid an important foundation for the post-1991 solidarity movement.

After the November 1991 Santa Cruz Massacre (discussed in the next chapter), U.S.-based sympathizers coalesced into the East Timor Action Network (ETAN) in New York City with affiliated cells across the United States. With active financial and intellectual support of the preceding activists, Charles Scheiner and John M. Miller mobilized a grassroots avalanche of direct appeals and lobbying of U.S. Congress.[117] So astounding was their success that ETAN received widespread recognition, including from the celebrated American author Howard Zinn, who wrote that not only did ETAN "prove that independence for East Timor was possible but helped make it happen. ETAN harnessed the power of ordinary people in the United States...to redirect the policy of the most powerful government in the world. I can't think of a better recent example of grassroots action changing U.S. foreign policy."[118]

While the United States Conference of Catholic Bishops regularly denounced Indonesian violations of East Timorese rights, a few of them are known for having lobbied with their congregations to push the East Timor question into the highest circles of U.S. policy making. Professor Barbedo

---

[115] Geoffrey Robinson, *"If You Leave Us Here, We Will Die": How Genocide was Stopped In East Timor* (Princeton, NJ: Princeton University Press, 2010), 53–54.

[116] Roger S. Clark, "The 'Decolonization' of East Timor and the United Nations Norms on Self-Determination and Aggression" in *International Law and the Question of East Timor* (1995):67–68.

[117] Charles Scheiner, "Grassroots in the Field: Observing the East Timor Consultation," in *Bitter Flowers, Sweet Flowers: East Timor, Indonesia and the World Community*, ed. Richard Tanter, Mark Sheldon and Stephen R. Shalom (Oxford: Rowman and Littlefield Publishers, INC., 2001), 110; Fernandes, *The Independence of East Timor*, 91–93; John M. Miller, "Reflecting on ETAN at 20," http://etan.org/etan/20anniv/miller.htm.

[118] Quoted in ETAN website: http://etan.org/etan/default.htm.

de Magalhães particularly recalls the role of the bishops of Boston and New York in securing Washington's favorable view toward East Timor.[119]

One organization that fervently advocated for the human rights of the East Timorese people and never ceased its campaigning was the London-based Tapol (standing for Tahanan Politik, which is Indonesian for "political prisoner"). Cofounded in 1973 by a former Tapol, Carmel Budiardjo, to advocate for the rights of Indonesian political prisoners held by Suhato's New Order in connection with the events of September 1965, Tapol picked up the question of East Timor in October 1975. While its members testified before the United Nations and several Western parliaments, Tapol organized rallies and workshops, published regular bulletins and pamphlets and piggybacked the activities of other solidarity groups like Lord Eric Avebury's Parlaimentarians for East Timor.[120] Its mouthpiece, a magazine named *Tapol*, uniquely carried interviews, news updates, and analyses on East Timor and was instrumental in influencing international public opinion in Europe and the United States.[121] Tapol took over from British Campaign for an Independent East Timor (BCIET), about which little is known beyond the fact that future preeminent scholar of East Timor, John Taylor, was a founding member in December 1975.[122]

In 1979, CIDAC, FRETILIN and another obscure and short-lived organization called East Timor-Portugal Friendship Association (ETPFA) co-organized an international conference on East Timor that attracted wide attention. The tripartite organizing committee was called the Comissão para os Direitos do Povo Maubere (CDPM, Commission for the Rights of the Maubere People). At the conference, CDPM learned about the People's Tribunal and was granted a session in 1981. CDPM then took its case to the tribunal, and the latter gave a favorable legal opinion, which constituted an important component of the diplomatic dossier on East Timor. Soon afterward, the CIDAC-based activists took over CDPM (without FRETILIN and the ETPFA) to advocate for East Timor. As CIDAC was a hub for diverse groups or individual activists who wanted to advocate for specific cases – Palestine, Western Sahara and even Eritrea – CDPM became necessary in order to give due weight to the East Timor question and to better execute its goals. Led from the beginning to end by a founding member of CIDAC, Luisa Pereira, CDPM worked independently, as well as in concert with FRETILIN and other solidarity groups, to increase international public

[119] Interview with Professor António Barbedo de Magalhães (August 29, 2006, Porto, Portugal).

[120] http://tapol.gn.apc.org/history.htm; CIDAC-CDPM, TL6506, "Memo: Parliamentarians for East Timor," July 14, 1988.

[121] The success of its advocacy work can also be measured by the wrath it generated in Indonesian power circles and the condemnations it earned. My research benefited from the long series of *Tapol* issues, which are duly acknowledged.

[122] Fernandes, *The Independence of East Timor*, 78–79.

awareness about East Timor's national question, to expose the human rights violations perpetrated by Indonesia, and to lobby foreign governments to act.[123]

When the friction between the leaders of the guerrilla resistance inside East Timor and their diplomat brethren grew more pronounced in the 1980s, the former intensified the direct contacts with the solidarity groups. According to CDPM Director Pereira, after de Araújo imposed an information blackout on Gusmão, the latter came to rely on CDPM for information, advice, and political analysis of developments inside Portugal and around the world. The communication took place at two levels. On the public level, there were contacts between CDPM as an organization and CNRM, whereby the former sent press clippings and materials from the public domain. As CNRM's leader, Gusmão cemented the organizational ties between the resistance, on one hand, and the solidarity groups, on the other, by sending personal letters, thanking the groups for their work.[124] On a more discreet level, Gusmão initiated a private communication with Pereira in which more sensitive policy issues were discussed over lengthy letters going both ways and, after Gusmão's arrest, through long telephone conversations as the latter had a secret cellular phone in prison.[125]

Unlike its Eritrean counterpart, the East Timorese diplomacy of the oppressed benefited from the fact that the international community accepted the legal and moral dimensions of its case, as demonstrated amply by high-level UN involvement. Based on the aforementioned General Assembly and Security Council Resolutions, the Decolonization Committee held regular hearings on the up-to-date developments of the derailed decolonization process. United Nations agencies and other international human rights organizations, like Human Rights Watch and Amnesty International, deplored the lot of the East Timorese people and regularly demanded that their human rights be respected. As discussed in more detail in Chapter 7, in the process of the successive secretaries general holding continuous tripartite talks with Indonesia and Portugal, the UN Secretariat developed a favorable view toward East Timor. Particularly after Kofi Annan succeeded Butros Butros-Ghali, the UN Secretariat assumed a more proactive stance which was perhaps the most significant contribution that the United Nations made toward allowing the East Timorese to exercise their right to self-determination.

East Timorese and Eritrean diplomats faced rather similar challenges – most importantly the hurtful neutrality and/or outright hostility of the world's most powerful countries. While the guerrilla war raged inside East Timor, Timorese diplomats abroad tenaciously waged their own diplomatic

---

[123] Interview with Luisa Pereira (January 11, 2006, Lisbon, Portugal).

[124] CIDAC-CDPM, TL3676, Xanana Gusmão to CDPM, October 15, 1987; CIDAC-CDPM, TL3675, Xanana Gusmão to Peace is Possible in East Timor, October 15, 1987.

[125] Interview with Luisa Pereira (January 11, 2006, Lisbon, Portugal).

war. The resistance leadership, however, realized the futility of their domestic and external strategies without an additional angle: changing Jakarta. To that effect, they sought Indonesian sympathizers and allies to challenge Suharto's New Order from within.

Conclusion

However successful it was, diplomacy of the oppressed, or liberation diplomacy, had its limits. Nowhere were those limits more apparent than in the case of Eritrea. The Eritrean and East Timorese nationalist movements realized that only their continued resistance on the ground would earn them the international attention required to find a lasting solution. The farthest-reaching strategic vision of the nationalists was their recognition that victory in Eritrea and East Timor alone would be incomplete or altogether infeasible. Success at home had to go hand in hand with the military defeat of the government in Addis Ababa and the reform of that in Jakarta. The two movements went about achieving these goals in ways that best fit their respective circumstances.

Denied any international legal recourse and dejected by both superpowers' incessant desire to befriend Ethiopia, Eritrean nationalists became convinced of the need to change the balance of power on the ground, so that they could speak from a position of strength.[126] While this made defeating Ethiopia necessary, that necessity became feasible only because of Eritrea's geographic and demographic characteristics. Material assistance (especially military support in training and weapons) that the Eritrean nationalists received from foreign countries also proved crucial to their success. As they became stronger, Eritrean nationalists were determined to defeat the Ethiopian government inside Ethiopia proper. They eventually did this by fostering Ethiopian rebel groups and by forging alliances with preexisting ones.

By contrast, with the international legal system favoring their cause, many countries and solidarity groups advocating on their behalf and the United Nations actively engaged in pursuit of a solution, the East Timorese fared far better in the diplomatic sphere than their Eritrean counterparts. The East Timorese nationalists did well to build alliances with UN member states, and in a system that relied heavily on reciprocal voting practices, they stacked up General Assembly votes without offering anything in return. East Timorese nationalists understood they would not defeat Indonesia militarily, but they believed that far-reaching political reform in Indonesia was essential to

---

[126] As previously discussed in this chapter, that was also precisely what several powerful political figures and diplomats advised the Eritrean nationalists. Jamal Abdel Nasser: "[M]arch on the path of power"; George H. W. Bush: "[F]ind an African India"; and Diallo Teli: "[N]o one will listen to you unless you are powerful"; and so on.

the success of their struggle for self-determination. Cooperating with sympathetic Indonesians to accomplish that goal, Timorese nationalists diversified their strategy, incrementally drifting away from their initial military approach and peacefully demanding respect of their basic human rights. That shift doubled their effectiveness. It also consolidated their struggle's moral upper hand and further increased the appeal of their cause to local (both East Timorese and Indonesian) and international audiences. In the process, they exposed Jakarta's appalling human rights record and irreversibly Indonesianized and internationalized their cause.

6

To Asmara Through Addis Ababa and Dili Via Jakarta

> It is impossible to see how the Eritreans could ever inflict a definitive defeat on the Ethiopian army without a parallel anti-monarchical revolution inside Ethiopia itself. In that sense the victory of the opposition inside Ethiopia appears to be a strategic precondition for the liberation of Eritrea.
>
> Fred Halliday[1]

International isolation made it increasingly difficult for the Eritreans to single-handedly combat the mighty Ethiopian empire. So, too, was the isolated East Timorese resistance ineffective. For Eritrea, military victory against the Ethiopian armed forces was not enough. To gain international recognition, the liberation movement needed Addis Ababa to relinquish its political hold on Eritrea. For Ethiopia to acquiescence to Eritrea's right to self-determination, the government in Addis Ababa had to be replaced with a "democratic alternative." Summing up these factors, the EPLF's military architect, Sebhat Efrem, famously said, "the road to Asmara lies through Addis Ababa." By the same analogy, East Timor's Dili had to be reached through Jakarta as the latter's change of attitude toward East Timor needed to precede any change of policies and actions regarding its future.

Parallel to their efforts in international diplomacy and their continued resistance on the ground, Eritrean and East Timorese nationalists realized that they also had to prevail in Addis Ababa and Jakarta. Both independence movements proved their adaptability by exploiting historic oppression and human rights abuses in the Ethiopian and Indonesian heartlands in order to win allies within Ethiopia and Indonesia. They thus embarked on the road to Asmara through Addis Ababa and to Dili through Jakarta, by forging alliances with Ethiopian and Indonesian forces.

The preeminent scholar of nationalism Benedict Anderson observed that the "explosive combination of development, education, and repression"

---

[1] Fred Halliday, "The Fighting in Eritrea" *New Left Review* no. 67 (May–June 1971):65. Reproduced with permission of New Left Review.

under aggressive colonial policies contributed to the development of territorial nationalism in the former European colonies.[2] If Italian and Portuguese colonialism did not see the full-fledged manifestation of Eritrean and East Timorese nationalisms, Ethiopian and Indonesian secondary colonialisms did. Ethiopia and Indonesia sealed their fate in their newly acquired provinces when, parallel to their repression, they granted the East Timorese and Eritreans far better educational opportunities than they had experienced under their former European colonizers.

When educational opportunities reached East Timorese students, and the brightest of them won scholarships to institutions of higher learning in Java and Bali, they helped sensitize the Indonesian public to the war in East Timor and broke the government's information monopoly. These students also offered a crucial link between the guerrilla front inside East Timor and solidarity groups and human rights advocates outside.

Similarly, after education expanded in Ethiopian-controlled Eritrea, and high school- and university-educated men and women joined the independence movement en masse, they had a transformative impact. As a result, the independence movement better articulated its ideology, policies, and goals. It devised a more cohesive program, galvanizing grassroots support and waging resistance in different forms beyond the battlefield. The education of their leaders, among a plethora of important factors, enabled the independence wars in Eritrea and East Timor to go on for decades, while Ethiopia and Indonesian contemptuously went on describing the nationalists as ungrateful sellouts and many other nomenclatures.

This chapter shows how local, regional, and global approaches to liberating Eritrea and East Timor were geared to "conquer" the conquerors through military action in Addis Ababa and by securing legitimacy in Jakarta. Eritrean and East Timorese successes rested on changes in Addis Ababa and Jakarta. Nationalists in both territories matured to see that the road to their Promised Land lay through the lion's den in Addis Ababa and garuda's nest in Jakarta. Addis Ababa's structural violence offered Eritreans an opportunity to court antigovernment forces in the Ethiopian heartland, in the same way Jakarta's internal repression offered East Timor an ally in the increasingly audacious reform movement in mainland Indonesia. Ultimately, Eritrean nationalists prevailed by joining forces with Ethiopian insurgents against the Derg regime in Addis Ababa and the East Timorese movement succeeded by coalescing with Indonesian reformists, human rights advocates and solidarity groups to stand up to the Orde Baru in Jakarta.

The nature of these alliances differed, however. They were determined by the different circumstances that the two liberation movements faced and the grand strategies that they devised to overcome them. Without compromising

---

[2] Benedict Anderson, "Gravel in Jakarta's Shoes," in *The Spectre of Comparisons: Nationalism, Southeast Asia and the World* (London and New York: Verso, 1998), 131ff.

their ultimate goals and preferred methods of ending their subjugation, the Eritrean and East Timorese nationalists advocated that Addis Ababa's and Jakarta's democratic resolution of the Eritrean and East Timorese questions were a litmus test for their domestic transformation. Ethiopian and Indonesian opposition forces and reformist solidarity groups that sought to end their own oppression recognized that point; that is, the resolution of the Eritrean and East Timorese questions could be crucial starting points for the democratic transformations of their own countries.

Convinced that they could only reverse international inattention by changing the balance of power on the ground, Eritrean nationalists determined to win their case by military means. They incrementally perfected their battlefield tactics and overall military strategy (to include simultaneously mobile, guerrilla, and even conventional-position warfare tactics) in order to defeat the Ethiopian military in Eritrea and depose the government in Addis Ababa, in collaboration with Ethiopian allies. Through military-political backing, they secured what they called a "democratic alternative" to replace the repressive Ethiopian government and let Eritreans decide their own political future.

Similarly cognizant of the fact that they would not be able to exercise their right to self-determination without a change of attitude in Jakarta, East Timorese nationalists successfully introduced East Timor into the struggle for political change for which many Indonesians had long been struggling. Intensifying their clandestine and diplomatic fronts, in coordination with the scattered but methodical guerrilla war inside East Timor, they worked hand in glove with Indonesian reformists. Ultimately, they marched in the streets of Jakarta and other major cities to openly demand Timorese right to self-determination as well as human rights and democracy in Indonesia.

The Democratic Alternative in Addis Ababa

Eritreans had a much longer association with Ethiopia, especially in comparison to that of East Timorese with Indonesia. During their schooling in Ethiopian controlled Eritrea and in mainland Ethiopia, Eritrean students were active promoters of progressive demands. They featured prominently in the leadership of the Ethiopian Student Movement in the 1960s and early 1970s, and some were active members of the progressive political parties that proceeded from that movement – the Ethiopian People's Revolutionary Party (EPRP) and the All-Ethiopian Socialist Movement (Me'ison). Nevertheless, the Eritrean Liberation Front had not identified the gains of rebellion in mainland Ethiopia with its own strategic dividends when, as Fred Halliday identified early on, "the victory of the opposition inside Ethiopia appears to be a strategic *precondition* for the liberation of Eritrea."[3] Although it is

---

[3] Halliday, "The Fighting in Eritrea," 65.

plausible that the ELF was too preoccupied with internal challenges to make any overtures or lend support to the anti–Addis Ababa rebellions in Bale and Gojjam during the second half of the 1960s, Fred Halliday intimates that the ELF actively avoided engagement with Ethiopian opposition forces because doing so purportedly conflicted with its Arab/Islamic claims and support base.[4]

The lack of strategic partnership between Eritrean nationalists' and Ethiopian grassroots revolutionaries who brought about the downfall of the monarchical regime is partially to blame for the subsequent escalation of the war for Eritrea. But the Eritrean independence war was an important contributing factor to the overthrow of Emperor Haile Selassie in 1974. The Eritrean nationalist movement underwent important transformations after its splintering into ELF and EPLF that the most defining difference between the presplintering and postsplintering nationalist organizations is the latter's initiative to win over Ethiopian allies and alacrity to collaborate with any number of them. They were handsomely assisted by the long history of oppression in the Ethiopian heartland.

The Empire's Domestic Abuses and Its Dissenters

Violently founded and held together by force, the Ethiopian state lived on as an imperial entity, whose track record of internal oppression predates and overshadows its image as a symbol of freedom among peoples far afield. Increasing decay of the state and rampant social injustice, as well as abusive and often condescending authority of an Amhara elite who saw themselves as born to rule, fed a growing ideological militancy and popular unrest ever since the 1960 abortive coup by the Imperial Bodyguard. Between the 1960s and 1970s, the Ethiopian Student Movement provided a progressive ideological and political groundwork against the imperial regime's domestic policies (or lack thereof) and global alignment that culminated in the overthrow of Emperor Haile Selassie.[5]

Christopher Clapham's characterization of rebellions in Ethiopia as flare-ups of "age-old tensions between center and periphery" when the center became or appeared weak[6] could not have been truer than in the 1970s. Addis Ababa's weakening apparatus of coercion that attended Haile Selassie's overthrow continued to plague the equally tyrannical military regime of the Derg, giving oppressed Ethiopian people the opportunity to

---

[4] Ibid.

[5] Bahru Zewde, *A History of Modern Ethiopia, 1855–1974* (Addis Ababa: Addis Ababa University Press, 1992), 220–226. Also see Richard Greenfield, *Ethiopia: A New Political History* (London: Pall Mall Press, 1965); Gebru Tareke, *Ethiopia: Power and Protest. Peasant Revolts in the Twentieth Century* (Lawrenceville, NJ: Red Sea Press, 1996).

[6] Christopher Clapham, *Transformation and Continuity in Revolutionary Ethiopia* (Cambridge: Cambridge University Press, 1988), 207.

rise up in arms and assert their rights. The northernmost Ethiopian province of Tigray (which shares the longest border with Eritrea) alone saw the mushrooming of four armed organizations. The activism of the Ethiopian Student Movement in the run-up to the end of the emperor's rule furnished the progressive ideological and political groundwork to coalesce around in opposition of the budding military rule under the Derg.[7]

Just when Eritreans sought to exploit structural weaknesses that made armed insurgency in mainland Ethiopia inevitable, the nascent insurgents looked to the thirteen-year-old Eritrean armed struggle for inspiration and assistance. They needed – and for the most part received – crucial support in military training, weapons, experience in guerrilla warfare, and access to the outside world. A combination of ideological affinity and strategic self-interest compelled Eritreans to court these antigovernment forces. While both Eritrean organizations laid down conditions that Ethiopian insurgents had to meet in order to receive Eritrean support, they also showed varying levels of pragmatism to cultivate the oppositions' alliance against the powerful government forces. At the end of the fighting, collaborating with Ethiopian insurgents granted the Eritrean cause an alternative government in Addis Ababa that recognized Eritrea's colonial past and respected its people's right to self-determination and independence.

As early as 1972 and 1973, members of the antimonarchical EPRP started receiving military training in the EPLF bases inside Eritrea. According to Günter Schröder, the EPRP, under the influence of one of its powerful leaders Tesfaye Gebreselasie, had recognized the Eritrean question as a colonial one, which earned it EPLF backing.[8] Meanwhile, in 1974, EPLF clandestine cells in Addis Ababa and Asmara got in contact with progressive Tigrayans,[9] whose leaders and earliest recruits headed northward to Eritrea for military training with the EPLF, upon deciding to launch armed rebellion as the Tigray People's Liberation Front (TPLF).[10] These two allies of the EPLF had

[7] For a succinct analysis of student activism during this period, see Gebru, *Ethiopia*, 24–34; and Bahru Zewde (ed.), *Documenting the Ethiopian Student Movement: An Exercise in Oral History* (Addis Ababa: Forum for Social Studies, 2010).
[8] Personal conversations with Günter Schröder (February 3 and July 14, 2011, Cologne and Frankfurt, Germany).
[9] Seyum Mesfin in *Asser* 3, no. 9 (December 1997–February 1998):25; Aregawi Berhe, "The Origins of the Tigray People's Liberation Front," *African Affairs* 103, no. 413 (2004):585.
[10] Tesfaye Gebreab, "Ye Mussie Ghedl," in *Teraroch Yanqeteqete Tiwlid, Vol. II* (Addis Ababa: Mega Publishing Enterprise, 1997), 34ff; and John Markakis, *National and Class Conflict in the Horn of Africa* (Cambridge: Cambridge University Press), 253. After the Tigrayans completed their training, the EPLF armed them and dispatched two of its own veteran Eritrean fighters (of Tigrayan descent) – Mehari Tekhle "Mussie" and Yemane Kidane "Jamaica" – to offer the pioneer Tigrayan fighters military and political assistance during the early stages of their struggle. As Mehari Tekhle led the founding TPLF fighters back into Tigray, the latter fondly nicknamed him as "Mussie" after the Biblical Moses who led the Jews out of Egypt into the Promised Land.

fundamental programmatic differences: the EPRP espoused a pan-Ethiopian, multi-ethnic project, whereas the TPLF was ethnically and regionally oriented.

EPLF leaders found a progressive political program for an unbalkanized Ethiopian mainland in the EPRP. Although many EPRP leaders (other than Tesfaye and his close associates) gave lukewarm support to Eritrea's unique status, the EPLF secured in the TPLF an unconditional recognition of Eritrea as a colonial case different from the nationalities question in the rest of the Ethiopian empire. Harmonized, the two could offer an ideal combination for Eritrean interests – a united Ethiopia under a popular, inclusive government that would let Eritrea go its own way. Hence, EPLF hopes that the EPRP and the TPLF would unite – or would at least work together on minimum common grounds – when it received them both at its rear base around the same time and started to train their earliest fighters, including their founding leaders.[11]

The EPLF arm-twisted both EPRP and TPLF leaders in Sahel to participate in political discussions that it convened in order to smooth out their differences and to identify and unite them on their commonalities. Like the ELF, so too did the EPLF fail to resolve programmatic differences of its allies as those semi-formal meeting broke out in tirades. The TPLF remained firm that the mistrust and hatred prevalent among Ethiopian nationalities was too deep for a project with multiple nationalities. Instead, the TPLF called for the struggle of all Ethiopian nationalities, in their respective ways, against the "oppressing Amhara nation."[12]

Furious, EPRP leader Berhanemesqel Reda shouted back, "Thinking to wage a nationalist struggle for the people of Tigray [alone] is an expression of immature mentality."[13] He fatefully decided that "from now on, there is nothing that relates us [the EPRP and the TPLF]. I do not have any common stand that relates me to you." He dashed out insisting that his organization would start fighting from Tigray and push southward to the rest of Ethiopia to the dislike of the TPLF.[14] Whereas any hopes of EPRP-TPLF cooperation dissipated thus, the TPLF issued its political program in 1976 that made matters even worse for the Eritreans who brought immense pressure on TPLF (because of its territorial pretensions) and worsened its relations with EPRP.

---

[11] Tesfaye, "Ye Mussie Ghedl," 34ff.; Markakis, *National and Class Conflict*, 253; and EPLF, "Documents of the Congress: Approved during the Second and Unity Congress of EPLF and ELF-CL," (Tigrigna), (1978), 78–80.

[12] RDC/TPLF/2226, TPLF, "Program and Principle of the TPLF," (Tigrigna), November 1976, 9.

[13] Tesfaye, "Ye Mussie Ghedl," 43

[14] After completing training with the EPLF, the EPRP established itself at Mount Asimba in northeastern Tigray. Tesfaye, "Ye Mussie Ghedl," 43.

The TPLF argued that the Tigray question was a "national" (as opposed to colonial) one, and claimed to be pursuing the establishment of a separate Tigrayan republic. Quoting Lenin, its program stated that "national oppression is solved by 'self-determination of the oppressed nations, i.e. establishing one's own independent government through political separation from the oppressing nation'."[15] The EPLF was particularly prickly about this because the potential separation of Tigray from the rest of Ethiopia threatened to deprive Eritrea of an amenable alternative in Addis Ababa. The TPLF's championing of secession also weakened the Eritrean nationalist claims to separate statehood based on Africa's colonial legacy. According to Schröder, the EPLF suspended its relationship with the TPLF for nearly three years on this ground.[16]

Territorially, having stated that it was set to rectify the violation of Tigray's rights and land, the 1976 TPLF program included a vast swathe of Eritrea into Tigray that was hub of ELF operations. Tigray accordingly stretched from Alawaha stream in the south to River Mereb in the north and, to the west, Welqayt and Tselemt.[17] Mereb constitutes a natural boundary between Eritrea and Ethiopia up to the point where the Mai Ambessa stream joins River Mereb. From that point to the west, the latter flows into Sudan deep through Eritrean territory pivotal for the ELF. Whereas the omission of Eritrea as bordering Tigray and unqualified declaration of River Mereb as constituting Tigrayan boundary were not acceptable to both Eritrean organizations, ELF was enraged about it. Moreover, ELF had been organizing and mobilizing Eritrean peasants in rural Tigray long before the emergence of the TPLF. The latter's advent into northwestern Tigray and early land redistribution practices discombobulated Eritrean civilians and undermined the ELF's activities in that region.[18]

Meanwhile, the ELF had established relations with an earlier Tigrayan rebel organization, the Tigray Liberation Front (TLF), that rejected Eritreans claim to independence on grounds of colonial past yet seeking independence for the northernmost Ethiopian province of Tigray. During its drive to make Tigray its exclusive zone, the TPLF liquidated the TLF. The latter's Eritrean

---

[15] RDC/TPLF/2226, TPLF, "Program and Principle of the TPLF," (Tigrigna), November 1976, p. 8; TPLF: People's Democratic Program, May 1983 in Kahsay, 16; Abraham Yayeh in *Yeweyanew Talaq Sera be Qedmow Abalatu Sigalet* (Addis Ababa: No publisher, 1990 Tir 1982 EC), 10–11.

[16] Personal conversations (January 2011, Cologne, Germany).

[17] RDC/TPLF/2226, TPLF, "Program and Principle of the TPLF," (Tigrigna), November 1976.

[18] Personal conversations with Tesfay "Degiga" Weldemichael (winter 2001, Northern California). These were the issues of contention between the ELF and the TPLF and not "ELF's interpretation of Eritrea [that] went beyond the Italian defined colonial boundaries to include parts of north-western Tigray," as John Young claims in "The Tigray and Eritrean People's Liberation Fronts: A History of Tensions and Pragmatism," *The Journal of Modern African Studies* 34, no. 1 (March 1996):106.

ally sent a delegation to the former demanding an investigation and threatening action only to abandon all that upon knowing that EPLF-TPLF relations had deteriorated, giving the ELF an opportunity to forge alliance with the increasingly powerful TPLF.[19]

The EPLF's fortunes suddenly turned in 1977 when the key proponent of EPRP's pro-Eritrean program Tesfaye Gebreselassie was killed in an intra-EPRP shootout. The pan-Ethiopian armed party subsequently withdrew its recognition of Eritrea as colonial case and ended its endorsement of Eritrean right to self-determination in isolation from Ethiopian nationalities question.[20] The EPRP did not automatically fall out of EPLF's favor. For a few months, the latter quietly tried but failed to persuade EPRP leaders to retract their new position, whereupon it terminated its support, leaving them exposed to the TPLF's pent-up violent wrath. The combination of TPLF hostility and EPLF's dejection sealed the EPRP's fate as a political force; the TPLF chased it out of Tigray in 1978, and the EPLF denied it shelter; only after the ELF granted safe conduct did its remaining force retire into Sudan.[21]

The TPLF was convinced that – unawares of the full extent of ELF-EPRP relations – the EPLF was the only organization that TPLF can rely on for support. It made itself indispensable to the EPLF by cementing its grip of Tigray – strategic buffer between Eritrea and mainland Ethiopia – through elimination of its rivals.[22] As the EPLF persisted in its rejection of the TPLF's secessionism, a reformed TPLF program of 1979 made a modest concession that the EPLF had little choice but to live with. The new, reformed TPLF program stated that "Self-determination of an oppressed nation could be implemented through . . . either voluntary unity based on equality or secession and formation of an independent government. . . . [T]he TPLF struggles for both ends to let the people of Tigray decide their future."[23]

Only on the failure of its struggle for the equality and freedom of the oppressed nationalities within the framework of a united Ethiopia would

[19] Personal conversations with Günter Schröder (January 2011, Cologne, Germany).

[20] EPLF, "Documents of the Congress: Approved during the Second and Unity Congress of EPLF and ELF-CL" (1978), 79.

[21] Günter Schröder interview with Tesfay Weldemichael "Degiga" (January 12, 1988, Kassala, Sudan). The promising rise and tragic demise of the EPRP is best documented in Kiflu Tadesse's *The Generation, Part II. Ethiopia, Transformation and Conflict: The History of the Ethiopian People's Revolutionary Party* (Lanham, MD: University Press of America, 1998).

[22] Tesfaye, "Ye Mussie Ghedl"; Markakis, *National and Class Conflict*, 254–256; Bereket, *Conflict and Intervention in the Horn of Africa* (New York and London: Monthly Review Press, 1980), 89–96.

[23] RDC/TPLF/4/2233, TPLF, "Program and Principle of the TPLF," (Tigrinya), 22 Yekatit 1971 EC; and Kahsay Berhe, "The National Movement in Tigray," 14 (an unpublished paper available at Eritrea's Research and Documentation Center in Asmara).

the TPLF opt for separation.[24] The EPLF seamlessly resumed courting the TPLF while continuing to pressure it to adjust its political objective because the latter's dualistic approach did not sit well with EPLF's leaders who still regarded the potential separation of Tigray as unraveling their own case. The EPLF, thus, continued to reject the TPLF's secessionist program and refused to recognize the grounds for Tigray's separation from Ethiopia. Instead, the EPLF continued calling for the formation of a coalition or front among all of the democratic Ethiopian movements opposed to the Derg dictatorship.[25] Not until after they jointly pushed the ELF out of Eritrea into Sudan and survived a punishing government offensive in the early 1980s did their differences come out into the open.

In the aftermath of the Soviet-backed five rounds of government offensives between 1978 and 1979, the ELF had retired from the actual fighting against Ethiopian troops. Meanwhile, the ELF-EPLF rivalry and hostilities started to gather momentum at the same pace as government forces' preparations for a momentous Sixth Offensive (also known as the Red Star Campaign). A senior TPLF fighter thus explains the consequent crucible of danger awaiting them both: "The ELF was attacking the EPLF, the Dergue [government] was very strong and it was preparing its major offensive," which necessitated "cooperation militarily, not out of sheer desire to support the EPLF, but out of self-interest . . . The collapse of the Eritrean revolution was not going to have a pleasant effect on our [i.e., Tigrayan] self-interests."[26]

In coordinated, sweeping operations, the TPLF and EPLF forces herded the poorly led, division-ridden ELF out of Eritrea between 1980 and 1981. Shortly afterward, government forces launched the much talked of offensive in early 1982 while many TPLF fresh recruits – in the thousands by some estimates – were receiving military training at the EPLF rear base, the rugged northeast Eritrean mountains facing the Red Sea.[27] Both the EPLF and the TPLF agreed for these fresh recruits to remain in the EPLF bases to help defend Eritrean lines.

As the TPLF grew increasingly battle-hardened, it became more and more assertive in its relationship with its Eritrean counterpart, the EPLF. After

[24] Markakis, *National and Class Conflict*, 245.

[25] Isaias Afwerki in James Firebrace and Stuart Holland, *Never Kneel Down: Drought, Development and Liberation in Eritrea* (Trenton, NJ: Red Sea Press, 1985), 137. As early as the mid-1970s, "Mussie" sought to impress on the EPLF-supported Ethiopian rebels that they had a common enemy and shared enough political views to enable them to fight their common enemy together. See Tesfaye, "Ye Mussie Ghedl," 43.

[26] TPLF Central Committee member Tewelde Hagos quoted in Alemseged Abbay, *Identity Jilted or Re-imagining Identity. The Divergent Paths of the Eritrean and Tigrayan Nationalist Struggles* (Lawrenceville, NJ: Red Sea Press, 1998), 14.

[27] Gebru Tareke, "From Lash to Red Star: the Pitfalls of Counter-insurgency in Ethiopia, 1980–82," *Journal of Modern African Studies* (2002):465–498; and Young, "The Tigray and Eritrean People's Liberation Fronts," 107.

1982, the TPLF started "challenging the EPLF on a range of military [doctrine] and political [ideology] issues."[28] Just as Young attributed part of this to "an historical sense of inferiority on the part of many Tigrayans in their relations with Eritreans,"[29] however, so too did EPLF leaders dismiss them as "manifestations of self-confidence crisis" among TPLF leaders.[30] In 1985, however, the EPLF publicly articulated its long-held rejection of the TPLF's secessionist program as well as its own motives for supporting the TPLF and its intentions to continue to do so as long as its interests were granted due respect:

> As long as a repressive and expansionist government that does not recognize Eritrea's especial identity and its people's right to independence is in Addis Ababa, there would be no guarantee for the peace, stability and independence of Eritrea even after Eritrean forces defeat the Ethiopian in the battle field. Therefore . . . the government in Addis Ababa has to be replaced by a popular and democratic one. For this reason the EPLF had been collaborating with Ethiopians capable of establishing a democratic alternative to the government in Addis Ababa.[31]

To the TPLF's chagrin, the EPLF stressed that the exercise of the right to self-determination required the replacement of the oppressive Addis Ababa regime with a democratic one. In the process of installing a democratic government, the suspicions and contradictions among Ethiopian nationalities would give way to a system based on equal rights and opportunities that would make secession unjustifiable.

An acrimonious exchange ensued[32] that the EPLF unsuccessfully tried avoid been drawn into.[33] It eventually decided to openly sever its ties with the TPLF in June 1985,[34] while persistently calling on all anti-Derg forces in Ethiopia to discuss the formation of a united front from the grassroots up,[35] a call that eventually culminated in the formation of the Ethiopian Peoples'

---

[28] Young, "The Tigray and Eritrean People's Liberation Fronts," 108.

[29] Young, "The Tigray and Eritrean People's Liberation Fronts," 118.

[30] EPLF/PFDJ political strategist Yemane Gebreab quoted in Alemseged Abbay, *Identity Jilted or Re-imagining Identity*, 128.

[31] Voice of the Broad Masses, "The EPLF and its Relationship with the Democratic Movements in Ethiopia," January 31–February 2, 1985.

[32] RDC/TPLF/6/2399, TPLF, "People's Voice on our Differences with the EPLF," March 1985, pp. 4, 6.

[33] Voice of the Broad Masses, "The EPLF is silent because it preferred to remain silent," October 6, 1985.

[34] Voice of the Broad Masses, "The EPLF is silent because it preferred to remain silent," (Tigrigna) October 6, 1985. EPLF's decision has to also be seen in light of the Derg government's preparations that had been going on at the time for one more round of large-scale military offensive. Having just survived the punishing, the stealthily organized Seventh Campaign, EPLF was weary of what more the government might throw against it during the forthcoming offensive.

[35] Voice of the Broad Masses, "The EPLF calls upon all the democratic movements in Ethiopia for the establishment of Neighborliness Democratic Front," October 7, 1985.

Revolutionary Democratic Front (EPRDF) as a pan-Ethiopian coalition in early 1989.

Nonetheless, as long as the Derg was in power and their resistance against it continued, the EPLF needed the TPLF and vice versa, notwithstanding their ideological and political differences, which had estranged their relationship. Recognizing the strategic importance of each to the other, the two insurgent groups carefully avoided permanently burning bridges. Despite their disagreements, the EPLF did not stop supporting the TPLF or contemplating a different democratic alternative to the Derg government. Nor did the TPLF repudiate its stance that the Eritrean question was a colonial one that needed to be resolved through the respect of the Eritreans' right to self-determination.

The EPLF capitalized on its military gains to revitalize its regional network of alliances with the Ethiopian rebel movements and to project a moderate image of the nation-state that it was poised to declare independent. But the TPLF beat the EPLF to it as its military gains against government forces increased its chances of taking the helm of power in Addis Ababa.[36] The resumption of relations were preceded and made possible by two other developments. The ferment within the TPLF's leadership settled when a pragmatic group led by Meles Zenawi replaced the extremists.[37] Almost immediately, Meles quietly reached out to the EPLF leadership through ordinary Eritreans (at least one of whom was his close relative) who had found the past vitriol distasteful. Just as quietly, the mediators convinced the Eritrean leadership of the conducive developments within the TPLF to mend fences. Beyond that point, no one knows what issues the two leaderships discussed and for how long. The accessible records show the TPLF making a goodwill gesture first and the EPLF reciprocating in kind.

Celebrating the EPLF's victory, the TPLF made a very pragmatic overture for rapprochement and displayed a dramatic policy reversal by embracing the EPLF's analysis that peace and democracy in Addis Ababa was a necessary requirement for any act of self-determination to take place.

---

[36] But this should not be taken to mean only their gains brought the all-jubilant insurgents back together again. There were as many potentially negative dynamics that had to be proactively mitigated. According to John Young, these included Eritrean and Tigrayan fears of adverse effects of tens of thousands of government troop freed up from the Ogaden in the wake of a new Ethio-Somali Memorandum of Understand, and ongoing peace talks between the EPLF and the government threatened to leave Tigray in isolated opposition to the government. Young, "The Tigray and Eritrean People's Liberation Fronts," 117.

[37] Meles Zenawi's saavy pragmatism and strategic thinking about the major issues confronting TPLF, Tigray and Ethiopia comes out at its best during his meeting with Paul Henze, when it seems the former won over the latter for the rest of his life (Henze died in May 2011). See "Memorandum for the Record from Paul B. Henze. Conversation with Meles Zenawi," April 3 and 5, 1990, available at the Thomas Kane Collection of the Library of Congress.

Without any reference to the ideological polemics of the mid-1980s, the TPLF's statement stressed that the EPLF and the TPLF had a common enemy and that a regime change in Ethiopia was necessary for peace in the Horn of Africa.[38]

In April 1988, EPLF and TPLF leaders met and decided to resume full cooperation.[39] Around the same time the stunning military gains of the TPLF suddenly stalemated, and the government forces seemed poised to reverse their losses as the one-year long battle for the town of Shire demonstrated between March 1988 and February 1989. Averting TPLF setbacks and depriving the government of breathing space required EPLF's expertise in offensive action through coordinated mechanized and infantry units inside Ethiopia. As a result, the EPLF deployed one of its mechanized brigades in Tigray and northern Ethiopia alongside the TPLF forces that in early 1989 forged the EPRDF coalition with other ethnic rebels.[40] With the EPLF assistance, the TPLF seized the strategic town of Shire, took control of the entire northerly province of Tigray, and moved on to the neighboring provinces in the direction of Addis Ababa.[41] To further distract the Ethiopian army, these allies helped revive the Oromo Liberation Front (OLF) that reentered the fold of regional insurgent alliances within the framework of self-determination rights of Ethiopian nationalities. The EPLF sent an entire division to revitalize OLF forces and opened a new front in Wollega (in western and southern Ethiopia).[42] The military noose was tightening on Addis Ababa.

---

[38] RDC/TPLF/6/2499, TPLF, "Organizational Statement on the Occasion of the Victory on the Naqfa-Afabet Front" (Tigrigna), ND, 2.

[39] RDC/TPLF/5/2284, TPLF, "EPLF-TPLF Joint Statement," (Amharic) April 1988.

[40] Tekeste Melake, "The Battle of Shire (February 1989): A Turning Point in the Protracted War in Ethiopia," *New Trends in Ethiopian Studies*, Vol. 1, ed. Harold G. Marcus (Lawrenceville, NJ: Red Sea Press, 1994), 963–980. Tekeste also confirmed to me in several private conversations that he saw confidential intelligence reports of the Ethiopian troops in the frontline that conclusively established the deployment of the EPLF mechanized and other elite units.

[41] But before it continued its operations outside of Tigray in the direction of Addis Ababa, up to 30,000 of the TPLF's peasant army retired to their home districts, claiming that they had fulfilled their mission and instead called on other Ethiopian groups to liberate their respective provinces. That required increased Eritrean participation in fighting inside mainland Ethiopia; and at the end of the hostilities in May 1991, there were, according to some estimates, 20,000 of the EPLF's seasoned fighters.

[42] Abiyu Geleta, "OLF and TPLF: Major Issues and Outcomes of a Decade of Negotiations since 1991," Oromo Studies Association Conference, 2002 Washington, DC. Available at http://www.oromia.org/Articles/Issues_and_outcomes_of_a_decade_of_OLF-TPLF_Negotiations_p.htm. Whereas Eritreans were unprepared to see concurrent referenda in Ethiopia alongside that in Eritrea and the TPLF was not to preside over the balkanization of Ethiopia once it took the helm of power, OLF was left frustrated and bitter that a referendum was not held to ascertain the wishes of the Oromo people which was its reading of the agreements among the insurgent groups.

Indonesianizing the East Timor Conflict

Unlike Eritrea, East Timor was suddenly added to the Indonesian body politic in 1975 and did not enter the intra-Indonesian political discourse until the second half of the 1980s. It hardly penetrated the political psyche of ordinary Indonesian citizens, and according to Benedict Anderson, Indonesians failed to imagine East Timor as part of "us" for a number of reasons. Two key reasons were Indonesia's policy of keeping East Timor closed (even from Indonesians) and the almost complete silence of the Indonesian media on East Timor before 1975 and its inadequacy afterward.[43] During much of the occupation, Indonesian media coverage of East Timor was limited in scope, and tightly controlled by the Indonesian intelligence agency, BAKIN. The media blackout was so pervasive that the prominent Indonesian human rights advocate Adnan Buyung Nasution admitted in December 1977 that Indonesians "hear little or nothing at all about the situation in East Timor. It's a kind of [a] secret war."[44] Nevertheless, as news of the Indonesian-perpetrated atrocities started to trickle into Indonesia along with reports of Indonesian casualties, Nasution's conviction and that of many other Indonesians that "Timor should never have been Indonesia's national claim" furnished a favorable environment for the East Timorese cause.[45]

When the newly acquired territory was sufficiently pacified to offer opportunities of higher education, a whole generation of young men and women had grown up with trauma of the war. Young East Timorese students arriving in Indonesia to attend university, even those who were young enough to forget the horrors and had started to accept their Indonesian-ness, could not help but be struck by the contrast between their war-ravaged country and the relative peace, stability, and opportunities in Indonesia proper. Discontented, these students found inspiration in the pioneer Indonesian nationalists of the early twentieth century who used educational opportunity under Dutch rule to break free from colonial oppression. They connected with the rest of the world to tell the plight of their people under firm Indonesian military blockade, completing the cycle of resistance and taking the fight to an international arena.

The growth in the Indonesian public's awareness of the tragedy of East Timor emerged after East Timorese students started to stream into Indonesian universities in the second half of the 1980s. The presence of Indonesian-educated East Timorese who rejected Indonesia and challenged its regime accentuated the uneasiness felt by a growing number of Indonesians concerning the overall lack of civil liberties and respect of human rights

---

[43] Benedict Anderson, "Imagining East Timor," *Arena Magazine*, no. 4 (April–May 1993).
[44] Interview with Adnan Buyung Nasution in *Tapol*, no. 27, April 1978.
[45] Ibid.

in their country. Indonesians who sought to reform their own political order thus started to see the resolution of the East Timor question as a critical component of their country's democratization.[46] Likewise, prodemocracy and pro–human rights activists of diverse religious and political persuasions started to openly stand in solidarity with the East Timor nationalist cause. This rise in Indonesian public awareness about and solidarity with East Timor emboldened the East Timorese students' peaceful challenge and generally helped the guerrilla resistance inside East Timor by enhancing its links with the outside world and galvanizing international support.

In the mid-1980s, the Indonesian-appointed governor of East Timor, Mário Carrascalão, pleaded with Jakarta to admit East Timorese high school graduates into Indonesian institutions of higher education.[47] Happy to cultivate an Indonesianized corps of educated East Timorese, Indonesian officials readily accepted the request. Starting in 1986, East Timorese students were offered government scholarships to study at universities in Java and Bali. At the end of the centuries-old Portuguese rule of East Timor, Lisbon had left its colony with fewer than a dozen university-educated nationals. By contrast, in the first year alone, Indonesia sent dozens of East Timorese to its best universities, and the figure grew exponentially each year.[48] In making this decision, Indonesia sowed the seeds of destruction of its rule of East Timor in the same way that the Dutch had done in the Netherlands Indies in the early twentieth century.

The Netherlands' capitalist economy prospered in the beginning of the twentieth century to the benefit of the Dutch colonial order in what became Indonesia. That prosperity enabled the colonizers to invest more in infrastructural development of the colony, educate a growing number of its natives, and strengthen their security apparatus there. According to Anderson, the convergence of these processes led to an "explosive combination of development, education, and repression" out of which Indonesian nationalism emerged.[49] While some pioneer Indonesian nationalists who

---

[46] It should be noted, however, that not all reformist Indonesians shared the same views about the importance of the East Timor question for Indonesia's democratic change.

[47] Interview with Mário Carrascalão (July 3 and 7, 2006, Dili, East Timor).

[48] As governor, Mário Carrascalão visited East Timorese students in Indonesia, and on returning to East Timor, they visited him as well. In one of his gatherings with them in Bali, he told them that while studying in Lisbon, he had been involved in the underground movement, particularly with the African students from the former colonies. The more engaged those students were, the lower their performance was in school. But after their countries gained independence, they became ministers and high-level officials in their new governments because they were good at what they did. So, whatever it is the Timorese students wanted to do, he urged them to do it well and work toward their objective with diligence. Interview with Fernando "Lasama" de Araújo (July 5 and 7, 2006, Dili, East Timor).

[49] Benedict Anderson, "Gravel in Jakarta's Shoes," in *The Spectre of Compairson*, 134. Also see Anderson, "East Timor and Indonesia: Some Implications," in *East Timor at the Cross*

had ventured to the Netherlands were struck by the disparity between the colony and the metropole, others did not need to leave their homeland to perceive the difference. On the centennial of the Netherlands' independence from France, Soewardi Soerjaningrat put down his imaginings in one of the first articles to be written by an Indonesian in the Dutch language: "If I were a Dutchman," Soewardi wrote, "then I would hold no independence celebrations in a land where we deny the people their independence."[50] Thus started the conceptual undoing of the Netherlands' colonial project at the hands of the Dutch-educated Indonesian nationalists who benefited from the educational and physical infrastructure in spreading their cause against the repressive colonial order.

Decades later, East Timorese students in Indonesian universities were similarly shocked by the overall disparity between their homeland and the towns and cities where they studied, and found lessons and inspiration in Indonesia's own path to independence. The contemporaneous security and basic development comparisons were too glaring to ignore for many of the young students who went back and forth between East Timor and their schools in Indonesia. For example, Virgilio Guterres, one of the early recipients of a government scholarship, had accepted his Indonesian-ness[51] until the relative tranquility and abundance he witnessed in Indonesia compelled him to revisit the hardship he had endured when Indonesia took over his homeland.[52] The relatively older and politically more conscious students, like Fernando de Araújo "Lasama" and Lucas da Costa, came to Indonesia determined to continue the fight for independence by different means. One of them, Carlos da Silva "Saky," best recounted how they went about starting their new mission:

We read and studied a lot. We learned that our struggle for independence existed from the start of colonialism. But every attempt was defeated because there was no unity among the Timorese, hence our priority to find unity of purpose amongst us. We particularly found inspiration in the history of Indonesian struggle for independence from the Dutch. Young Indonesians who studied in Indonesia and in Holland started challenging Dutch colonialism and so we put our heads together to see what we can benefit from our studying in Indonesia so that we can advance our cause for independence and we found a lot.[53]

Roads: The Forging of a Nation, ed. Peter Carey and G. Carter Bentley (Honolulu: University of Hawaii Press, 1995), 145.

[50] Quoted in R. E. Elson, "Constructing the Nation: Ethnicity, Race, Modernity and Citizenship in Early Indonesian Thought" *Asian Ethnicity* 6, no. 3 (2005):145–160.

[51] This is a measure of the success of Indonesia's early school curriculum in East Timor that was mainly geared toward Indonesianizing the East Timorese youth. For an analysis of this, see John G. Taylor, *East Timor: The Price of Freedom* (London and New York: Zed Books, 1999), 127–129.

[52] Interview with Virgilio Guterres (April 13 and May 9, 2006, Dili, East Timor).

[53] Conversations with Carlos da Silva "Saky" (June 27, 2006, Dili, East Timor).

In June 1988, ten of these students in Bali spontaneously came together and secretly formed what was to become the Resistência Nacional dos Estudantes de Timor Leste (RENETIL, National Resistance of East Timorese Students). Its three key objectives were to (1) insulate the East Timorese students in Indonesia from being absorbed into the integrationist scheme, (2) expose – to the Indonesians and the international community – the crimes that were being perpetrated by the Indonesian military, and (3) prepare a corps of educated East Timorese for peacetime national reconstruction.[54] In all three of these goals, they had a record of success.

RENETIL immediately pledged allegiance to Xanana Gusmão as the highest leader of the resistance. In his first letter of December 1988, Gusmão advised the founders of RENETIL to remain autonomously affiliated with CNRM under his direct command and to accept all East Timorese students who supported independence regardless of their backgrounds.[55] Gusmão and RENETIL's founding members regularly communicated through letters in which RENETIL Secretary General Fernando de Araújo "Lasama" sought clarification on the overall orientation of the resistance, while Gusmão offered guidelines on its strategic objectives while leaving matters of execution entirely to RENETIL.[56] Parallel to his request that Ramos-Horta work strictly under his instructions, Gusmão also enforced RENETIL's strict compliance with his directives by fiercely lashing out at its leaders for any deviations.[57]

[54] Interviews with Dr. Lucas da Costa (April 12 and 18, 2006, Dili, East Timor) and Fernando de Araújo "Lasama" (July 5 and 7, 2006, Dili, East Timor).

[55] Conversations with Carlos da Silva "Saky" (June 27, 2006, Dili, East Timor). When the Executive Committee was formed to coordinate all the clandestine activities of the resistance movement in 1991, CNRM similarly advised its structural affiliation with CNRM and not FRETILIN to avoid any ill feelings of non-FRETILIN East Timorese working for independence. Also see Constâncio Pinto and Matthew Jardine, *East Timor's Unfinished Struggle: Inside the Timorese Resistance* (Boston: South End Press, 1997), 123, regarding such efforts of the resistance movement to embrace all pro-independence East Timorese.

[56] Interview with Fernando de Araújo "Lasama" (July 5 and 7, 2006, Dili, East Timor). In 1991, Lasama traveled to Dili and for the first time (and possibly the last time before the two met again in jail) met Gusmão in Dili for face-to-face policy discussions.

[57] During a visit to East Timor from the Australian ambassador to Indonesia in the early 1990s, Gusmão found out about the RENETIL plan to organize a demonstration before their letter informing him about it reached him. According to Carlos da Silva, one of the RENETIL leaders in Indonesia, Gusmão furiously told them, "If the resistance's chain of command cannot be strictly respected in its current state, then the command may as well be transferred to RENETIL HQ." Similarly in 1999 during the Dare meeting in Jakarta as part of the Confidence Building Measures between the pro- and anti-independence blocs, RENETIL leaders made transportation and accommodation arrangements for José Ramos-Horta without consulting with Gusmão, who had his own plans for the roving Timorese diplomat. On learning under house arrest that Ramos-Horta had been whisked from the airport and kept in an undisclosed location until he walked into the corridors of the meeting venue, Gusmão excluded Lasama and Lucas da Costa from further participation in the meetings as a penalty for their deviating from his wish. Although they say they did not

RENETIL also received regular communications – verbal and written – from the other leaders of the resistance. In March 1989, for example, Ma'Hodu and another resistance leader sent to RENETIL a lengthy analysis of how RENETIL's role fit within the broader struggle, inculcating in the students the prevailing mind-set of the resistance leaders – national unity.[58] Speaking about the socialist students such as Avelino Coelho, Nino Konis Santana similarly pressed the point of embracing all pro-independence East Timorese regardless of difference by verbally urging RENETIL leaders to "embrace the smaller enemy in order to defeat the bigger enemy."[59] RENETIL dutifully embraced all East Timorese students who supported independence. Nonetheless, only under strict induction standards did each of RENETIL's founders recruit ten students under oath, and each new recruit inducted another ten, and the cycle continued until almost all pro-independence East Timorese students joined its ranks.

In his first communication with RENETIL, Gusmão also urged the students in Indonesia to work together with the preexisting Organization of East Timorese Catholic Youth (OJECTIL) inside East Timor. The two groups met soon afterward, agreed to drop OJECTIL, to adopt RENETIL as an all-embracing organization, and to turn OJECTIL's structures into RENETIL's branches in East Timor.[60] On this basis, RENETIL quickly set up mechanisms to work with the amorphous clandestine networks and their leaders inside East Timor. As its new tentacles gave it instant access to all corners of East Timor, detailed information about Indonesian-perpetrated human rights abuses were immediately fed to its headquarters in Indonesia. At the same time, RENETIL leaders started to experiment with techniques of internationalizing their struggle.

Having fled Bali after the initial Indonesian crackdown on East Timorese student activism, several of RENETIL's leaders tried to internationalize their case by, among other things, seeking political asylum in embassies of countries that had close ties with Indonesia. In 1989, they identified three embassies – Austria, the Vatican, and Japan – although only four students ended up in the Vatican compound and two in the Japanese. Unfortunately, they failed to draw international attention. Indonesia succeeded in securing their ejection from the embassies by promising the two embassies that it would not prosecute the students,[61] a promise that the

---

hold grudges against Gusmão, Lasama and Lucas da Costa insist that they did what they did for Ramos-Horta's safety because the place Gusmão had reserved was neither safe nor appropriate for the Nobel Peace laureate.

[58] Arquivo Mário Soares/Resistência Timorense, 07191.054, Bukar and Hodu Ran Kadalak, "Carta a RENETIL," March 1989.

[59] Interview with Joaquim Fonseca "Ruso" (May 6, 2006, Dili, East Timor).

[60] Conversations with Carlos da Silva "Saky" (June 27, 2006, Dili, East Timor).

[61] Ibid.; and interview with Fernando de Araújo "Lasama" (July 5 and 7, 2006, Dili, East Timor).

Indonesian authorities kept for two years. Nevertheless, they succeeded in helping internationalize their struggle by gradually developing personal connections and institutional links with Indonesian and international human rights advocates, journalists and foreign embassies as the CNRM-FALINTIL command continued to urge.[62] RENETIL passed on to the latter accurate reports of crimes and violations committed anywhere in the half island.[63]

From "Opening" to Santa Cruz Massacre

During the second term of his governorship of East Timor, Mário Carrascalão proposed to President Suharto and his generals the "opening" of his province to the rest of the world. In early 1989, the Indonesian government obliged within the framework of its propaganda that, having been pacified, its twenty-seventh province had been benefiting from integration. Accordingly, the Indonesian government started to extend invitations to visitors only to take those who accepted the offer on strictly guided tours of preselected sites. During these trips, the Indonesians stage-managed the display of the people's contentment with integration and set up security measures to silence those opposed to it. The two most important visits, however, exposed the limits of Indonesian control as the Clandestine Front of the Timorese resistance exploited the presence of prominent foreigners to demonstrate their dissatisfaction with Indonesian rule.

In October 1989, Pope John Paul IV visited East Timor after over a decade of directly administering the Catholics there against the requests of the Indonesian church to integrate the two. While the Timorese church's direct relationship with the Holy See gave it significant autonomy and proved to be of strategic value to the nationalist movement, as discussed earlier, the visit of the pope offered the resistance an important tactical opportunity to protest against the status quo. The pope celebrated an outdoor mass

---

[62] Arquivo Mário Soares/Resistência Timorense, 07153.081, "Orientacoes do CNRM-FALINTIL A RENETIL," May 10, 1991. This handwritten note seems to come from a RENETIL leader receiving verbal instructions about the need for complete secrecy regarding the plans for the visit of the Portuguese Parliamentary Delegation (DPP), followed by how RENETIL should mobilize its members and its network of friends to give as much coverage to the planned insurrection. It is possible that the document was produced during one of the several brainstorming sessions that Gusmão and other CNRM-FALINTIL leaders had in the run up to the cancelled trip of the DPP.

[63] As a former Amnesty International official responsible for Indonesia, Geoffrey Robinson cultivated strong personal relationships with East Timorese student leaders who supplied him with reliable information, and Amnesty International staff acted on it as fast as they could. Reports of human rights violations were conveyed almost immediately after they happened because of RENETIL's networks on the ground and its connections with the international community. Conversations with Dr. Geoffrey Robinson (winter 2008, Los Angeles, CA).

with close to 100,000 East Timorese worshipers.[64] Although the Vatican insisted that the visit was purely pastoral and not political, His Holiness knelt and kissed a cross lain on the ground during the outdoor mass, and during his sermon, he empathized with their persecution and called for the respect of human rights to the cheering of the crowd. Several anti-integration youth unfurled their political banners, leading to a significant scuffle between Indonesian security forces in plainclothes and the youth. Despite Indonesian authorities' efforts to present the fight as their attempt to control the crowd and ensure the pope's safety, the latter saw that even the youth who were trying to climb up onto the podium with their banners were chanting, "Viva Il Papa."[65]

Every time an opportunity offered itself, the clandestine front staged peaceful demonstrations aimed at an international audience – like the visit of the Jakarta-based U.S. Ambassador Monjo. The Indonesian military was consistent in its heavy-handed reaction to such peaceful challenges.[66] Although as tragic as many other that came before and after it, none of Indonesia's heavy-handed responses to peaceful demands was as consequential as the incident of November 12, 1991.

In the run-up to the planned visit of the Portuguese Parliamentary Delegation (DPP), the Indonesian security forces tragically failed to avoid humiliation at the hands of the pro-independence elements. Six years after it was first discussed during the Indonesian-Portuguese negotiations under the auspices of the UN Secretary General, the visit of the DPP seemed ready to come to fruition in 1991 as a date was set for its arrival in November.[67] In anticipation of the delegation, the Indonesian forces launched an elaborate operation named Halo Kapaz (to make better), spanning the three months preceding the planned arrival of the delegation in November. In a

---

[64] To signify the importance of the visit of Pope John Paul II, the government of independent East Timor erected a landmark monument in his honor at the very place he gave the outdoor mass at Taci Tolu on the outskirts of Dili. That monument was inaugurated on June 15, 2008.

[65] Clyde Haberman, "Melee Erupts as Pope Speaks in East Timor," *The New York Times*, October 13, 1989.

[66] Geoffrey Robinson, *"If You Leave Us Here, We Will Die": How Genocide Was Stopped in East Timor* (Princeton, NJ: Princeton University Press, 2010), 81ff. For an insider account of East Timorese youth's peaceful anti-Indonesian demonstrations and their treatment at the hand of the Indonesian military, see Donancio Gomes, "The East Timor Intifada: Testimony of a Student Activist," in *East Timor at the Crossroads* ed. Carey and Bentley, 106.

[67] UN Archives, Secretary General's Personal Papers, S-1024–0027-10, a confidential "Non-Paper" detailing the preliminary terms for the visit of the Portuguese Parliamentary Delegation dated June 27, 1991. Those terms clearly stipulated – what later became a deal breaker – that twelve international journalists would accompany the delegation (with each country selecting six and only informing the other of its selection three weeks prior to the visit). In the same collection of documents, a letter from the Portuguese permanent mission to the United Nations dated July 19, 1991, confirms Lisbon's agreement to those terms.

150-page document, the army prepared detailed security measures around the routes of the delegation's visit and in the towns and the financing of development projects during the visit, the display of support for integration and ensured that the anti-integrationists did not come out. To do that, according to Moore, the Indonesians brought in additional "Strike Force" units that numbered over 1,600 strong and placed 10,000 of the preexisting troops along the routes of the planned tour.[68]

The East Timorese nationalists geared up to receive the delegation with an equally meticulous but far more daring plan. Led by Constâncio Pinto, the Executive Committee of the Clandestine Front received its planning orders directly from CNRM President and FALINTIL Commander in Chief Gusmão,[69] who had almost permanently moved to Dili. Gusmão closely supervised the planning of the highest leaders of the Clandestine Front – Constâncio Pinto, José Manuel Fernandes, Gregorio Saldanha, Jacinto Alves, Francisco Miranda Branco, and others. The Timorese resistance invited to Dili a large number of civilians from across the country and prepared enough transportation – vehicles and horses – as well as walkie-talkie communication with one another. They planned to place a human blockade around and storm the airport and to take control of the Portuguese parliamentarians. They knew that the Indonesians would have to kill many civilians to control the situation and hoped that they would not do so in the presence of the delegation, which was expected to be accompanied by UN personnel. And if the Indonesians did open fire, then that would show to the international community the true face of Indonesian occupation. After taking control of the Portuguese parliamentarians, it was planned to force part of the delegation to tour the war-ravaged countryside that they would otherwise not see under Indonesian guides and to bring the rest of the delegation into the Government Palace and impose on them a meeting with Gusmão himself. The planners knew that openly bringing in Gusmão to meet the Portuguese would mean his eventual arrest, but they believed that the Indonesians would not shoot him beforehand. To rule out the possibility of the latter from happening, they planned to bring Gusmão on a horseback surrounded by human shield of thousands of civilians.[70]

---

[68] Samuel Moore, "The Indonesian Military's Last Years: An Analysis of its Secret Documents," *Indonesia* 72 (October 2001):23–24.

[69] The clandestine network was very vast for any single individual to control and even after the consolidation of the Executive Committee as a coordinating body, the latter maintained regular consultations with, took orders from, and passed information to the various leaders of the guerrilla movement but, according to Constâncio, "always with the knowledge of Xanana." Pinto and Jardine, *East Timor's Unfinished Struggle*, 125.

[70] Interviews with Constâncio Pinto (April 13, 2006, Dili), Gregorio Saldanha (July 11, 2006, Dili), and Fernando de Araújo "Lasama" (July 5–7, 2006, Dili); and personal conversations with Jacinto Alves (June 10, 2008 Dili, East Timor).

Gusmão sent a secret letter to CDPM's Luisa Pereira and Tapol's Carmel Budiardjo regarding what he called an "insurrectionary demonstration" that the resistance movement was planning in anticipation of the DPP. Through Pereira, Gusmão disclosed the details of this operation to the Portuguese parliamentarians who were unnerved by the grave danger that it engendered. In the words of Pereira, Gusmão assured the delegation: "We have been spilling our blood for the past fifteen years and it is our blood that will be spilled."[71] That only aggravated the concerns of the Portuguese parliamentarians. For their part, although there are no indications that they were aware of the Clandestine Front's exact plans, the Indonesians seem to have sensed the intense underground activities that had been going on. The fears of the Portuguese parliamentarians, thus, converged with the Indonesians' lack of preparedness to face any eventualities in the presence of the DPP and their uncertainty of their capacity to rule out another embarrassment. As the two sides sought to abort the planned trip, the Indonesians and the Portuguese offered each other a convenient excuse to do so: the Portuguese parliamentarians planned to bring along with them Lisbon-based Australian journalist Jill Jolliffe. Having been long offended by the content and tone of her coverage of East Timor since 1975, the Indonesians denied Jolliffe an entry visa. The Portuguese refused to proceed with the trip without her.[72]

Faced with the potential collapse in morale of its members, the Executive Committee urgently sought and found an opportunity to vent the frustration of its members who had reported en masse to Dili to participate in the DPP reception demonstration. The UN Special Rapporteur on Torture Pieter Koojimans happened to be in Dili on November 12, 1991, which coincided with the fifteenth day memorial of a murdered pro-independence

---

[71] Interview with Luisa Pereira (January 11, 2006, Lisbon, Portugal). Abilio de Araújo is likely to have heard this plan through his Portuguese links before declaring that Gusmão was planning to surrender to the Indonesians in public. Luisa Pereira felt compelled to disclose parts of her secret communication with Gusmão in order to protect the resistance leader and calm the commotion that de Araújo's accusations triggered. I am not privy of the contents of the newspaper publication, but Gusmão was fully aware of what was being said in Portugal, and on November 15, 1991, he lamented with Ramos-Horta: "You know how I insisted on the Portuguese parliamentary delegation visit even before Portugal had accepted the Indonesian invitation. Now they are claiming that I am responsible for the cancellation of the visit." Excerpts of Gusmão's 15 and 17 November 1991 letters to Ramos-Horta available in the Arquivo e Museu Resistência Timorense, Timor-Leste/1991/Resistência Armada, 06487.001. Also published in *O Publico* of November 29, 1991.

[72] Jolliffe is known for being friendly to the Timorese nationalist cause and had been one of the harshest and most effective critics of Indonesia since 1974. It was not surprising for the Indonesians to refuse her entry, but it was unfortunate for the Portuguese to refuse to move beyond that denial, especially given that other journalists were accompanying the Portuguese parliamentarians. Jolliffe correctly believes, as do many others, that the Indonesians used her as an excuse to provoke the Portuguese into cancelling their planned visit. Conversations with Jill Jolliffe (May 2006, Dili, East Timor). The CAVR adds that Portuguese journalist Rui Araújo was also denied entry visa.

activist – Sebastião Gomes. With Gusmão's approval, the Executive Committee decided to turn that memorial service into a pro-independence rally and stage a demonstration in front of Hotel Tourismo, where the special rapporteur was staying. After a prayer service at Motael Church, the mourners went on a procession of unprecedented political vibrancy toward the grave of their fallen brethren at the Santa Cruz Cemetery. On the way, the activists exposed their slogan-filled undershirts and took out the banners and flags that they had been preparing for the arrival of the Portuguese delegation. With the Indonesian security marching alongside the chanting and frenzied crowd, the procession entered the Santa Cruz Cemetery, and the Indonesian troops came from three directions and encircled them inside. The soldiers started to fire at the crowd, killing about two dozen demonstrators on the spot and disappearing many more in the subsequent crackdown. Most of the injured also died in hospitals when "their doctors" administered poison injections to their helpless patients.[73]

Indonesian generals shrugged off what had transpired at the Santa Cruz Cemetery as something the victims had brought on themselves. For General Rudolf Samuel Warouw, the highest operational commander inside East Timor, for example, which angle the killings were seen from was more important than the fact that they had taken place: "But which glasses should we be looking at it through? They [the deceased] were Fretilin. If for example you were marching under a flag apart from the Indonesian one, what would you expect?"[74] On his part, General Mantiri, the kodam commander in Bali, defended the actions of the Indonesian military by arguing that what had transpired was an attempt to control troublemakers:

We don't regret anything. What happened was quite proper.... They were opposing us, demonstrating, even yelling things against the government. To me that is identical with rebellion, so that is why we took firm action.... [T]heir theme was opposing the government. Long Live Fretilin. Long Live Xanana, waving Fretilin flags. If they try that now, I will not tolerate it. I will order strong action.... I don't think there's anything strange in that.[75]

---

[73] CAVR, *Chega!*, Part 7.2: Unlawful Killings and Enforced Disappearances, 201ff.; and interview with Max Stahl (June 9, 2008, Dili, East Timor). Traveling on a British passport, journalist Stahl captured the massacre on video and hid the videotapes until he was allowed to leave the country after twelve hours of interrogation. Stahl relates that he returned to East Timor in 1993 on a different passport in order to investigate claims that some of the survivors of the massacre had been poisoned in the hospital. He claims to have confirmed, with the help of a laboratory, which examined the sample he acquired from the hospital lab technician, that the survivors had indeed been murdered. According to CAVR, several individuals who claimed to have witnessed such killings came forward in 1994 and testified before the UN Human Rights Commission.
[74] "'Tanggung Jawab Saya': Wawancara dengan Warouw," *Tempo* 21, no. 42 (1991), quoted in McRae, "A Discourse on Separatists," *Indonesia* 74 (October 2002):42.
[75] See H. B. L. Mantiri's interview: "Mantiri: Jenderal Success" in *Cerita Dari Dili*, a magazine-type publication (in Bahasa Indonesia) regarding the Santa Cruz Massacre available at the

Fortunately for the East Timorese people and their resistance movement, experienced documentary film maker Max Stahl, who was in Dili to cover the visit of the DPP, had filmed the tragedy that had befallen the unarmed civilians. Stahl had to destroy the most gruesome footage of the Santa Cruz Massacre that was in his video camera in order to avoid it falling into the hands of the Indonesians and jeopardizing his safety. He, nonetheless, managed to hide in a grave the earlier phase of the massacre, which he said was significantly less gruesome than what he had destroyed just before his capture. Smuggled out of East Timor with the help of a priest and a Dutch visitor, that footage was turned into a documentary – *In Cold Blood* – to shake its viewers' conscience into doing something about it. Aired on several TV channels around the world, *In Cold Blood* irreversibly turned the previous tide of international apathy toward the suffering of the East Timorese people by the world powers. The strongest impact of the broadcast was showing the world a faraway people praying over graves and the Indonesians killing them.[76]

The tragedy of Santa Cruz brought East Timor into the spotlight that did not fade until the root cause of the problem was resolved. As a result, several doors opened for the Timorese nationalist movement and its diplomats who had been waging an uphill struggle in countries and among influential leaders who were averse to confronting Indonesia over a minor inconvenience that East Timor was to them. Although Gusmão did not know or did not appreciate the gesture,[77] Portugal took immediate diplomatic action. It summoned eighty of its ambassadors and dispatched more diplomatic representatives abroad with instructions to more vigorously pursue the East Timor question and to expose Indonesian violations.[78] Portugal also used President Mário Soares's socialist credentials and historic ties with powerful European socialists to introduce the East Timor question to the agenda of the European socialist pressure groups – among them then French President Francois Mitterrand and his family.[79] Current Timorese President José

Arquivo Mário Soares/Resistência Timorense, 06432.018. Also quoted in Robinson, *"If You Leave Us Here, We Will Die"*, 67.

[76] Interviews with Lurdes Bessa (April 13, 2006, Dili, East Timor) and Max Stahl (June 9, 2008, Dili, East Timor).

[77] In the immediate aftermath of the Santa Cruz Massacre, Gusmão was exasperated with Portuguese inaction prior to 1991, its failure to set up a Timor lobby in powerful capitals afterwards and the Timorese's own lack of resources to set one up. Excerpts of Gusmão's November 15 and 17, 1991, letters to Ramos-Horta available in the Arquivo e Museu Resistência Timorense, Timor-Leste/1991/Resistência Armada, 06487.001.

[78] Interview with Ambassador Leonardo Mathias (January 11, 2006, Lisbon). Ambassador Mathias's information is also confirmed by Ramos-Horta in Excerpts of Gusmão's November 15 and 17, 1991, letters to Ramos-Horta available in the Arquivo e Museu Resistência Timorense, Timor-Leste/1991/Resistência Armada, 06487.001.

[79] Interview with Dr. Carlos Gaspar (August 31, 2006, Lisbon, Portugal); according to this longtime Portuguese presidential advisor, the European socialists were very instrumental in

Ramos-Horta best summed up the turn of the tide thus: "Timor gained visibility through that tragedy that was filmed . . . the Santa Cruz Massacre made my work a bit easier because those who were skeptical before . . . started to say 'yes you are right after all.'"[80]

By contrast, the massacre constituted a turning point for Indonesian diplomacy. In the words of Indonesia's own chief diplomat Ali Alatas, "12 November 1991 constituted a watershed in Indonesian diplomacy on East Timor and since that date, international support for Indonesia's position inexorably declined while that for the independence movement in East Timor markedly increased."[81] Santa Cruz was "a severe setback" from which his country never recovered; once-soaring international support for Indonesia started to wane and ultimately plummeted.

Keeping East Timor in the Spotlight

In a bid to keep the East Timor question in the spotlight, the incarcerated resistance commanders and RENETIL leaders planned another asylum seeking events in the Swedish and Finnish embassies during the United Nations Conference on Human Rights in Vienna in June 1993. According to Robinson, who was the Amnesty International Researcher covering island Southeast Asia, the asylum seekers and their letter (well timed and worded as it was in the language of human rights) drew wide and sustained attention in Europe. Jakarta-based friends of East Timor coordinated with human rights advocates, and a network of solidarity groups in order to give the asylum seekers maximum attention, with Amnesty International issuing a press release within twenty-four hours and Indonesian foreign minister firing back the next day.[82]

RENETIL even smuggled foreign journalists, researchers, and activists into the East Timorese jungles to meet with the resistance leadership.[83] Those same channels also delivered to the resistance movement important information and supplies that RENETIL procured or that it simply passed on from the members of the diplomatic front.

---

the campaign to free Nelson Mandela in Europe and after Mandela was freed in 1990, East Timor was the next major issue that they took up.

[80] Interview with President Jose Ramos-Horta (June 5, 2008, Dili, East Timor).

[81] Ali Alatas, *The Pebble in the Shoe: The Diplomatic Struggle for East Timor* (Jakarta: Aksara Karunia, 2006), 64.

[82] Robinson, *"If You Leave Us Here, We Will Die,"* 8off.

[83] In September 1990, the Australian lawyer and journalist Robert Domm became the first foreigner to sneak beyond Indonesian lines and interview Xanana Gusmão. See Pinto and Jardine, *East Timor's Unfinished Struggle*, 126ff., for firsthand account of Domm's risky trip to the meeting. After that, many activists and researchers were taken to the East Timorese jungles where the guerrilla movement roamed. Dr. Joseph Nevins (formerly at UCLA) and Mindo Rajagukguk (formerly of SOLIDAMOR) are two of many examples.

These East Timorese students combined imagination with lessons learned from the history of the Indonesian independence struggle to turn every obstacle that the authorities posed against them into an asset. The Indonesian intelligence, for example, fostered a certain Ikatan Mahasiswa dan Pelajar Timor Timur (IMPETTU, East Timor Students' Association) and required every Timorese student in Indonesia to become a member as a way of controlling his or her activities. Far from controlling them, however, IMPETTU offered the pro-independence students a convenient camouflage for the activities of RENETIL. It subverted the legally recognized IMPETTU by making sure that RENETIL members were elected as IMPETTU's leaders and executed RENETIL's programs that naturally went against the stated interests of the Indonesian government.[84]

Indonesian security forces started to crack down on IMPETTU for its flagrant defiance, only to give its captured leaders a legal and open forum to powerfully present their case, that is, RENETIL's case. The first such case took place when Lasama was arrested in November 1991 and charged with subversion in May 1992. In his defense plea, Lasama rejected the charge on the grounds that, as an East Timorese, he was not subject to Indonesian laws. In a lengthy analysis of the history of East Timor, Lasama characterized Indonesia as a colonial power for seeking to trade off the basic rights of the Timorese people "for luxurious houses and asphalted roads." Moreover, Lasama asserted that, in charging him with subversion because he advocated for his people's human rights, the Indonesian state was in fact enforcing the same laws that the Dutch used against Indonesian nationalists.[85] For close to five years before his arrest, Lasama had studied Indonesian Literature in Bali. Eloquently delivered in Bahasa Indonesia, Lasama's defense plea was perhaps as jarring a condemnation of Indonesia's occupation of East Timor as Soewardi Soerjaningrat's 1913 article was of the Netherlands' colonial subjugation of Indonesia, or perhaps was comparable to Sukarno's defense plea in 1930.

While shielding its members from being Indonesianized, RENETIL aimed to Indonesianize the fight for the human rights of the Timorese people and their right to self-determination. This was particularly the case after the infamous November 1991 Santa Cruz Massacre when a funeral procession turned into a bloody spectacle upon the Indonesian military's shooting at the unarmed civilians. As Domingos Sarmento Alves put it, after this massacre, "we came to the understanding that the East Timorese and Indonesians

---

[84] Interviews with Dr. Lucas da Costa (April 12 and 18, 2006, Dili, East Timor) and Mariano Sabino (May 3, 2006, Dili, East Timor); and conversations with Laurentina "Mica" Barreto Soares (spring 2006, Dili, East Timor).

[85] CIDAC-Peace is Possible, PP 0548, "Why and for What I am Struggling? The Defense Plea of Fernando de Araújo Presented to the Public Prosecutors Team in the Central Jakarta State Court" May 11, 1992.

had the same enemy, which was the Indonesian military . . . and the Suharto dictatorship. We needed to bring Indonesians into our struggle because it was their struggle too."[86] RENETIL encouraged its members to join Indonesian student organizations and political groups with a clear purpose of bringing the East Timor question to their attention and accessing broader Indonesian audiences through them.

In 1992, three RENETIL members played an active role in founding one of the pioneer pro-democracy student organizations in Yogyakarta, Solidaritas Mahasiswa Indonesia untuk Demokrasi (SMID, Solidarity of Indonesian Students for Democracy). Joaquim Fonseca "Ruso," a forestry student at Gadjah Mada University, relates how the formation of SMID offered them access to the Indonesian student body as well as to the faculty, who were generally sympathetic to change. Placing the East Timor question within the framework of change, the RENETIL students found institutional forums to

engage the Indonesian academics and students in discussions about East Timor . . . not as an exclusive case pertaining to the Timorese; it is something that belonged to them as well; that was an issue to them as well . . . a reflection that democracy does not exist in Indonesia because of the profile of the East Timor case. We invited them to assess the opportunity where they can actually have a bigger impact in their struggle if they decided to join hands with the Timorese.[87]

After working together on several preliminary projects, the two sides gained confidence in one another and started whole-hearted cooperation in openly defying the New Order regime and exposing its record of oppression and human rights violations. Indonesian activists "start[ed] to write about East Timor and start[ed] to go to jail for East Timor."[88] They also followed Lasama's lead in using the courts to push their point through their lengthy, analytical, and sometimes impassioned pleas. From that point, the East Timor question entered Indonesian public discourse as a human rights issue.[89]

Meanwhile, the resourceful and avid advocate for East Timor Professor António Barbedo de Magalhães of Porto University had been working to Indonesianize the East Timor question in his own way. Banished to Portuguese Timor in the early 1970s because of his activities against the

---

[86] Quoted in Maria J. Stephan, "Fighting for Statehood: The Role of Civilian-Based Resistance in the East Timorese, Palestinian, and Kosovo Albanian Self-Determination Movements" in *Heinonline – Fletcher F. World Affairs* 30.2 (Summer 2006), available at http://scholar.google.com/scholar?hl=en&lr=&q=info:oLHxXRNNm4kJ:scholar.google .com/&output=viewport .

[87] Interview with Joaquim Fonseca "Ruso" (May 6, 2006, Dili, East Timor).

[88] Interview with Joaquim Fonseca "Ruso" (May 6, 2006, Dili, East Timor).

[89] James Goodman, "Indonesians for East Timor: A small but growing Indonesian movement supports self-determination in East Timor, for the sake of Indonesian democracy," *Inside Indonesia* no. 59 (July–September 1999), http://www.insideindonesia.org/edit59/goodm. htm.

Salazar dictatorship, Professor de Magalhães had learned that the democ-ratization of Portugal had to go hand in hand with the liberation in the colonies and vice versa, and he brought that lesson to his advocacy for East Timor. Recognizing that the Timorese fight could not succeed with-out democratization in Indonesia, he sought to develop a strong relation-ship with what he considered Indonesian democratic elements sympathetic toward East Timor. In 1990, he started to convene a workshop to bring together like-minded Indonesians and East Timorese and help establish an Indonesian solidarity group with East Timor that equated democratization in Indonesia with the liberation of East Timor.[90] Indonesian prodemoc-racy activist Dr. George Aditjondro attended the first of these workshops in Portugal, and on returning to Indonesia, he cofounded Solidarias untuk Penylesaian Damai Timor-Leste (SOLIDAMOR, Solidarity for East Timor's Peaceful Solution). Principally founded to advocate for the Timorese peo-ple's right to self-determination, SOLIDAMOR's strategy included raising the Indonesian public's awareness about all aspects of the East Timor ques-tion, spreading information about developments in East Timor, and working with other human rights advocates and proponents of democracy to assist the Timorese people in deciding their own future. Like the other solidarity and human rights advocacy groups, SOLIDAMOR benefited from the East Timorese activists who joined its ranks as volunteers and staff.[91]

Caught by the animated activism for human rights that shaped the 1990s, the greatly developed middle class in Indonesia mobilized its clout to demand the opening up of the country's political system. The continued brutality with which Jakarta handled the East Timor question increased the uneasiness of many Indonesians about the lack of respect for basic rights and liberties. After East Timorese students staged a major demonstration in Jakarta in the aftermath of the Santa Cruz Massacre in November 1991, Indonesian secu-rity forces rounded up East Timorese students in large numbers, prompting several groups of lawyers in Jakarta to come together under a certain Joint Committee in Defense of East Timor.[92] The clash between Orde Baru and the increasingly assertive middle-class groups came to a head when several of them took the regime to task on the treatment of political prisoners, in general, and the East Timorese, in particular.

As more Indonesians got involved in solidarity with East Timor and/or opposition to the New Order regime, various types of organizations that

---

[90] Interview with Professor António Barbedo de Magalhães (August 29, 2006, Porto, Portu-gal). Preeminent scholar of East Timor John Taylor similarly concluded in his 1991 book, *Indonesia's Forgotten War. The Hidden History of East Timor* (London: Zed Books, 1991), that East Timorese victory rested on the degree of their success in Indonesia proper.

[91] Conversations with Mindo Rajagukguk and Mica Barreto Soares (spring 2006, Dili, East Timor).

[92] Goodman, "Indonesians for East Timor."

helped bring the fight for East Timor to Jakarta's doorstep, thus, mush-roomed. In 1993, Lembaga Studi dan Advokasi Masyarakat (ELSAM, Institute for Policy Research and Advocacy) was launched, and East Timor constituted one of its important agenda items. In the late 1990s, close to a dozen nongovernmental, secular, and religious organizations formed a solidarity consortium with the people of East Timor. Under the slogan "No Democracy in Indonesia without Freedom in East Timor," the Forum Solidaritas Untuk Rakyat Timor Lorosae (FORTILOS, Solidarity Forum for the People of East Timor) was launched in 1998 and played an important role in informing Indonesian and international public opinion about and taking Indonesian authorities to task on the violations perpetrated in the run-up to the August 1999 referendum.[93]

Excessive Indonesian attempts to control the situation only helped RENETIL draw further international attention and to spread its message beyond Indonesia. The third anniversary of the Santa Cruz Massacre coincided with the 1994 annual summit of the Asia-Pacific Economic Conference (APEC) that was held in Indonesia. RENETIL leaders were split between writing petitions and holding demonstrations until Gusmão weighed in from his prison cell in favor of the latter. As Indonesian authorities apprehended the East Timorese students who streamed to Jakarta for the demonstration, those who eluded the authorities unfurled their banners in front of the U.S. embassy, and twenty-nine of them jumped over the fence to avoid capture by the Indonesian police.[94] In contrast to 1989, they spontaneously stole media attention from the APEC meeting, and President Bill Clinton felt compelled to make his first public appeal for Jakarta's respect of Timorese rights.[95]

As the international attention they drew secured them a safe exit from Indonesia, these students were granted Portuguese citizenship and flown out to Portugal where they set up the hub of RENETIL activities in Europe. The growing interest of Portuguese people in East Timor and their government's intensified advocacy after the Santa Cruz Massacre were served well when, RENETIL co-founders Carlos da Silva "Saky" and Domingos Sarmento Alves founded the Delegação Externa da Resistência Nacional dos

---

[93] Interview with Nugroho Kacasungkana (July 3, 2006, Dili, East Timor). According to FORTILOS's statement in relation to the Liquiça Massacre of April 1999, these organizations are "ELSAM (Institute for Policy Studies and Advocacy), LBH Jakarta (Jakarta Legal Aid Foundation), PBHI (Association of Indonesian Legal Aid and Human Rights), ISJ (Jakarta Social Institute), Bindik PGI (Counseling and Education division of the Indonesian Council of Churches), JK-LPK (Network of Christian Service), POKASTIM (Working Group for the Welfare and Education of the East Timorese), Justice and Peace Secretariat of Indonesian Catholic Churches Commission, LPPS (Institute for Social Research and Development), JKB (Collective Cultural Network)." http://www.etan.org/et99/april/11-17/12press.htm.

[94] Conversations with Carlos da Silva "Saky" (June 27, 2006, Dili, East Timor) and Stephan, "Fighting for Statehood."

[95] Andrew Pollak, "Anti-Indonesian Protest at US Embassy," *The New York Times*, November 13, 1994; "Indonesia's Embarrassment," *The New York Times*, November 15, 1994.

Estudantes de Timor Leste (DIGAREX, External Delegation of the National Resistance of East Timorese Students) in Lisbon, Porto, and Coimbra. One of the cofounders and forerunners of DIGAREX, Lurdes Bessa, recalls how they drew so much attention without having to do much work and how they were sought after for consulting and speaking tours throughout Portugal and Europe. With two of RENETIL's founders in Portugal and with direct telephone access to the rest of RENETIL in Indonesia, and through them to East Timor, DIGAREX became an important center of fresh and reliable information on East Timor and Indonesia. Working with CDPM and CDPM-affiliate Peace is Possible in East Timor, DIGAREX leaders were frequent consultants to the Portuguese Ministry of Foreign Affairs. The Ministry for its part offered DIGAREX generous financial support for their speaking tours as well as other projects in Portugal and elsewhere.[96]

While RENETIL operated covertly in Indonesia and East Timor, DIGAREX worked openly as a branch of RENETIL overseas. Because that exposed IMPETTU as RENETIL's cover, the Indonesian government sought to withdraw IMPETTU's legality to which East Timorese and Indonesian activists reacted by protesting against the outlawing. Whatever the outcome of that tussle, a network of Indonesian and international civil society organizations, human rights activists, and solidarity groups had taken up the advocacy of the East Timor question so that no disbanding of an organization or arresting of activists would muffle their voices. The right to self-determination of the people of East Timor had, therefore, become thoroughly Indonesianized and internationalized so that any government in Jakarta could not stifle the question of East Timor without an acceptable act of self-determination. It was only a matter of time until Jakarta relented.

Doomed Counterinsurgencies

The success of either an insurgency or a counterinsurgency rests on the support of the people in the contested areas and a successful guerrilla or antiguerrilla strategy must necessarily isolate the civilian population from the opponent.[97] But "if a guerrilla movement, in spite of repeated defeats and heavy losses, can still rely on a sympathetic population among whom its survivors can recuperate and hide, then all the numerical and technical superiority of its opponents may ultimately count for nothing." Because of that, Michael Howard warns, force must be "exercised with precision and control... [and] integrated in a policy based on a thorough comprehension of the societies" in question; otherwise, it is counterproductive.[98] Throughout their occupations of Eritrea and East Timor, Ethiopian and Indonesian

---

[96] Interview with Lurdes Bessa (April 13, 2006, Dili, East Timor).
[97] Galula, *Counterinsurgency Warfare*, 4, 52.
[98] Michael Howard, *Studies in War and Peace* (London: Temple Smith), 195–196.

counterinsurgency strategies lacked an element of restraint. More particularly, the Ethiopian and Indonesian generals' belief in military solutions
were too deeply entrenched to allow them to apply force with restraint,
much less to strike a balance between their military and nonmilitary strategies. Moreover, Addis Ababa's and Jakarta's projects in Eritrea and East
Timor were fated to end in defeat because of their fundamental flaws that
went unrectified.

Ethiopianizing Eritreans and Indonesianizing East Timorese

As the actions of the Ethiopian and Indonesian governments constantly
contradicted their rhetoric, efforts to win the hearts and minds of the two
peoples were understood as bolstering the Ethiopianizing and Indonesianizing projects of domination. Based on a true story that only a few knew
at the time of its writing in the Eritrean field, Alemseged Tesfai's famous
play *Eti Kale-ay Kwinat (The Other War)* best captures Addis Ababa's
project of "Amharizing" Eritrea by fighting the war in the wombs of Eritrean
women and harvesting Eritrean children to Amhara fathers, hence loyalty
to Ethiopia. In a later work,[99] Alemseged elaborated the background to *The
Other War*. He also argued that the Imperial Ethiopian government sought
to experiment that practice in the Somali-speaking region of Ethiopia. He
relates his experience in the early 1970s when, as a young legal aide to
Ethiopia's finance minister, he accompanied several of Shoa's nobility who
made up the core of Haile Selassie's government on a tour to the Ogaden.
During the trip that lasted several days, one of the nobles bragged about the
beauty of being born Amhara and how they could only overcome the Somali
sentiments in that part of Ethiopia by bastardizing the Ethiopian-Somalis
with Amhara children.

As far as East Timor is concerned, although I have not come across hard
evidence that shows a systematic Indonesian policy to bastardize East Timorese as another way of winning the war against the independence fighters,
a glance at the Timorese society after independence leaves little doubt that
Jakarta's policy of transmigration into an already inhabited half island had
a similar effect of Indonesianizing many East Timorese children. Moreover,
as Samuel Moore's analysis of Indonesian secret military documents shows,
the Indonesian soldiers in East Timor were divided into organic and nonorganic units. The latter were rotated on a regular basis in apparent response
to the then ongoing insurgency whereas the organic (also the territorial)
units were stationary. Often, young soldiers from the nonorganic troops
would be assigned to what was called a territorial battalion and were made

---

[99] Alemseged, "The Other War: An After word," in Alemseged Tesfai, *Two Weeks in the
Trenches: Reminiscences of Childhood and War in Eritrea* (Trenton, NJ: Red Sea Press),
211ff. The play *Eti Kale-ay Kwinat* is also reproduced on pp. 167ff., in its English translation.

to live outside their barracks among the East Timorese people. Although this deliberate intermixing had immediate security objectives, its long-term Indonesianizing influences were as important as the transmigrants were.[100]

Ethiopia and Indonesia Consume Their Own Propaganda

Moreover, Ethiopian and Indonesian forces were more intimidating than effective, strategically speaking. Ethiopian and Indonesian military reports from Eritrea and East Timor tacitly admitted their forces' ineffectiveness in guerrilla warfare while the nationalists' operations in the occupied towns speak to the governments' failures there as well. Yet, in their disdainful attitude toward the insurgents, Ethiopian and Indonesian military commands declared the crushing of the nationalist insurgents at the end of each offensive only to launch another shortly afterward with the promise of annihilating them once and for all. Writing about Ethiopian counterinsurgency, even Ethiopia's leading apologist Paul Henze compared this phenomenon to "a drama that gets stuck in the third act and repeats itself over and over again...."[101] Similarly, David McRae exposes the Indonesian propaganda gimmick of persistently identifying the insurgents as remnants of one or another pariah organization while launching increasingly massive military operations against them.[102]

In their refusal to acknowledge the true nature of the insurgencies, the Ethiopian and Indonesian forces seem to have been the prime consumers of their own propaganda regarding the Eritrean and East Timorese resistance movements. The successive Ethiopian governments' views of the Eritrean insurgency did not deviate from Haile Selassie's 1962 declaration that Eritreans had gallantly defended their supposed Ethiopian-ness but that the cowardice of a few permitted their selling out to foreign powers bent on dividing Ethiopia.[103] Indonesian documents captured by FRETILIN in the early 1980s as well as others from the 1990s show the Indonesian military's adequate awareness of the popular support that sustained the Timorese resistance movement. Like its Ethiopian counterpart, however, ABRI seemed to believe its own propaganda. Its reports and internal communications were

---

[100] Moore, "The Indonesian Military's Last Years in East Timor," 20–23. Perhaps relevant to the concept of making societies active battlegrounds of one or another of the warring sides is serious allegations of Indonesia's forced sterilization of East Timorese women as part of Suharto's demographic control policies through family planning.

[101] Paul B. Henze, "Eritrea: The Endless War." article prepared for *The Washington Quarterly* (Spring 1986), 9, available from the Thomas Kane Collection of the Library of Congress.

[102] McRae, "A Discourse on Separatists," 40.

[103] The Ethiopian Government, *Selected Speeches of His Imperial Majesty Haile Selassie First, 1918 to 1967* (Addis Ababa: The Imperial Ethiopian Ministry of Information, 1967), 462; and RDC/Mengistu. 2/77, "Mengistu Haile Mariam, Interview," September 12, 1978, Addis Ababa.

replete with analysis and conclusions based on the misinformation that it spread about the insurgents. There accordingly persisted a gaping hole in ABRI's argumentation and analysis that prompted Samuel Moore to write, in an equally representative analysis of Indonesian and Ethiopian counterinsurgencies, that the Indonesian military "never came to the obvious conclusion that many people ... were strongly determined to feed, shelter, and provide information to Falintil and continually replenish its ranks."[104]

Adamant that Eritreans and East Timorese were Ethiopians and Indonesians, respectively, the two governments sought to explain what they chose to believe was limited popular support for the resistance movements by dismissing their civilian supporters as inferior, confused, and/or deceived. Broadly speaking, General Ali Murtopo advocated the depoliticization of the broad Indonesian population (including the East Timorese) because their being a mindless "floating mass" made them prone to manipulation from different corners.[105] More particularly, the Indonesian military intelligence found the East Timorese youth lacking an understanding of "integration and the meaning of independence, whether as a result of being left out of the integration process or a lack of proper explanation ... they are easily influenced by issues and propaganda so that consciously or unconsciously, they want to stage anti-integration demonstrations."[106]

Retention of Colonial Borders Reinforces Insurgents' Identity

European colonialism furnished the infrastructure that gave Eritrea and East Timor distinct, territorialized identities. Ethiopia and Indonesia maintained those territorial referents to the detriment of their counterinsurgencies. Ethiopia administered all of Eritrea as a single province during the formative years of the Eritrean national resistance for over two decades after the abolition of the Eritrean-Ethiopian federation. It was only in the second half of the 1980s that the Derg government tried to dismantle the territoriality of Eritrea by splitting the coastal region of Dankalia and proposing to grant the rest of Eritrea internal autonomy. That plan, however, came about too late when Eritrean national consciousness had consolidated over time and sustained the then ongoing protracted armed resistance. Moreover, the Eritrean cosponsors of the division-with-autonomy plan were elements of the ELF's leadership who had lost to the EPLF during the 1981 civil war and were more committed to settling old scores than to the arrangement itself. Finally, the project lost momentum and whatever credibility it may have had when Mussie Bekhit, one of the plan's Eritrean forerunners, abandoned the

---

[104] Moore, "The Indonesian Military's Last Years in East Timor," 17.

[105] Ibid., 11.

[106] Ibid., 12–13. The Indonesian military newspaper, *Angkatan Bersenjata*, similarly characterized East Timorese as "A primitive and backward community" of "[f]eeble mentality." Quoted in Taylor, *East Timor: The Price of Freedom*, 109, 129.

Derg government and went over to the nationalist side.[107] Similarly, East Timor remained the twenty-seventh province of Indonesia throughout the period of its occupation with a Timorese civilian administrator, subordinate to the military commanders who oversaw an iron-fisted grip over the territory. Despite ethnolinguistic resemblance to the other half of Timor Island, East Timor was highly militarized and suffered excessively, thus reinforcing its distinctiveness.

Meanwhile, the maintenance of security in Eritrean and East Timorese towns and countryside meant tight control over the population and forced conscription of their adult members into the Ethiopian and Indonesian security institutions, often to the detriment of their providing for their respective families. Expanded hospitals catered to wounded Ethiopian soldiers in Eritrea. In East Timor, the war economy and direct subsidies from Jakarta enabled the expanding of infrastructure and services. At least from the mid-1980s onward, Indonesian administrations invested in socioeconomic and infrastructural projects, mostly in collaboration with the East Timorese church. Through a policy of pendekatan Gereja (bringing the church closer) and through the church, the people, the Indonesian government started to finance reconstruction programs and schools. But according to Bishop Belo (then apostolic administrator), that posed a major problem:

The schools represent the gravest problem for the Diocese... The teaching is... not commensurate with the freedom of establishing a school where it gives independent teaching, or where the teaching is in Portuguese, or Tetun. All is Indonesian. Because the teachers are paid by the government, the state makes changes or calls when they want, without advising the Ecclesiastic Authorities.[108]

Bishop Belo dismissively characterized that policy as "*omnia tibi dabo, si cadens adoraveris me...*" ("I give you all, if you adore me"). Moreover, although hard to measure accurately, the expanding services were stretched thin by the migrant Indonesians in East Timor[109] along with the heavy troop presence and never-ending counterinsurgency and security operations. They also fed into the sense of indignation and relative deprivation among many

---

[107] RDC/Security/1, 05285, EPLF, "Kab Mussie Bekhit Zeterekhbe Habereta" (intelligence gathered from governor of Eritrea's Senhit province, Mussie Bekhit, after he defected from Ethiopia).

[108] CIDAC-CDPM/TL4788, Apostolic Administrator of Dili, Carlos Filipe Ximenes Belo to Monsenhor Pablo Puente, Apostolic Pro-Nuncio to Indonesia, February 17, 1985.

[109] Former governor Mário Carrascalão and Bishop Belo repeatedly appealed for the halting of settling Indonesians from the other islands in East Timor as part of Jakarta's long practice of easing over-population in some islands through the trans-migration of some of the inhabitants off to underpopulated islands. According to Carrascalão, these migrants inevitably settled in lands that belonged to native East Timorese and ran businesses that either once belonged to East Timorese or were in fierce competition with them.

native East Timorese who remained in the peripheries of the expanding services and closer to the resistance movement.[110]

Far from diluting the sense of distinctive Eritrean and East Timorese identities, therefore, the Ethiopian and Indonesian states reinforced them by leaving them intact and subjecting their peoples to crude counterinsurgencies. Moreover, lacking restraint and precision in their use of force, and a parallel noncoercive approach to either contain the insurgencies or meet their demands, Addis Ababa and Jakarta failed to win over the Eritrean and East Timorese peoples, nor did their troops defeat the Eritrean and East Timorese insurgents on the battleground. Eritrean and East Timorese independence movements, thus, owe their successes to a cyclical combination of their strategic brilliance and blunders of the Ethiopian and Indonesian governments.

[110] Taylor (*Indonesia's Forgotten War*, 98), for example, quotes a group of East Timorese as having written: "The Indonesian armed forces impede the medical and food aid which is needed by the people. Food stuffs...are sold by the local military command...in the shops at high prices."

7

Winning Insurgencies and Counterinsurgencies in a Changing Global Order

No small nation, and few great ones, can stand the [war induced economic] deprivation indefinitely. Yet the painful fact is that guerrillas, for their part, can carry on indefinitely.

Robert Taber[1]

Guerrilla warfare goes through various stages up to the point of its success or its effective suppression, and successful guerrilla wars may come to a triumphant end with or without a final showdown. Realizing their inability to pursue a successful counterinsurgency, or unconvinced of its continued expediency, governments may give in to guerrilla demands, as Indonesia did with East Timor. Alternatively, as with Ethiopia, governments may be unaware of their waning military capacity, or unwilling to admit it, and so may continue to fight until they are defeated. Because the final blow to such oblivious regimes is delivered in an all-out confrontation through engagement by conventional armies, successful guerrilla forces must evolve into conventional militaries before the final showdown. Whereas Ethiopia was a conventional army in its organization, composition, training, and armament, the Eritreans had to develop into a full-fledged conventional force in order to defeat them.[2]

---

[1] Robert Taber, *War of the Flea. The Classic Study of Guerrilla Warfare* (Washington, DC: Potomac Books, 2002), 39. Reproduced with permission of Potomac Books, Inc.

[2] André Beaufre, "Battlefields of the 1980's," in *Unless Peace Comes; a Scientific Forecast of New Weapons,* ed. Nigel Calder (New York: Viking Press), 11–15. Conventional wars involve counter-insurgency war, the "war to establish a fait accompli" whereby one of the adversaries would strike with the goal of scoring a quick victory to dictate its terms on the other side, and the "conventional 'great war'" fought between two fairly matched conventional armies – from Blitzkrieg (lightning war) to a prolonged war, which comes to an end with the exhaustion of the "weaker or less determined party, or ending with nuclear escalation or some kind of revolutionary war."

The military doctrines and political philosophies that eventually triumphed in Eritrea and East Timor are Maoist in nature – albeit they used divergent practical methods – in that, because they were facing superior adversaries, they had to juggle space, time and will. The challenge of Eritrean and East Timorese guerrilla leaders was not unlike that of Mao, which, in Katzenbach's words, "was how to organize *space* so that it could be made to yield *time*. His political problem was how to organize *time* so that it could be made to yield *will*, that quality which makes willingness to sacrifice the order of the day, and the ability to bear suffering cheerfully the highest virtue."[3] In other words, the nationalist resistance in the two territories had to make territorial concessions to the powerful conventional forces of the opponent (withdraw or even disperse) in order to gain time that they could use to mobilize the population. Mao had also added that the time would enable any inherent weaknesses of the powerful to grow increasingly apparent, and slip out of hand under the pressures of a drawn-out conflict.

The momentum of Ethiopian and Indonesian counterinsurgency withered further, and the morale of the governments' troops waned every day the EPLA held off Ethiopia's advances and FALINTIL survived Indonesian campaigns. Inversely, the morale of the Eritrean and East Timorese independence fighters steadily developed, as did the loyalty and support of their respective peoples. In the end, Eritreans marked the fait accompli liberation of Eritrea when they took Asmara on May 24, 1991, disintegrating the Ethiopian military in Eritrea and herding its remnants into Sudan. Their East Timorese counterparts picked up momentum, taking their resistance to a new level of domestic intractability and diplomatic offensive until Indonesia exhausted its resolve to carry on the fight. Although Addis Ababa and Jakarta devised equally dogmatic and heavy-handed counterinsurgencies, they responded differently to internal and external pressures to enable the independence movements to achieve their respective goals.

The local environments within which the Eritrean and East Timorese peoples exercised their rights to self-determination were conspicuously different from one another. This chapter analyzes the decaying Ethiopian and Indonesian inter- and intrastate dynamics and the evolving strategies of the Eritrean and East Timorese insurgents, all against the backdrop of fast-changing global geopolitics. It segues into the conclusion of this project by examining Eritrea's peaceful ascent to sovereignty, in spite of the indifference of the international community, and East Timor's tortuous birth to independent statehood, despite unprecedented international engagement. Just as the Cold War interests of, and rivalry among, the superpowers made Ethiopia's and Indonesia's secondary colonialism over Eritrea and East Timor possible, so too did the onset of a new world order contribute to their demise. Eritrea and East Timor emerged to independence at a crucial transformation of the

---

[3] E. L. Katzenbach quoted in Taber, *War of the Flea*, 43.

normative comfort zone that allowed great powers to fight their wars through local proxies. The age of human rights discourse and advocacy had started to slowly displace militant nationalism when Eritrean forces marched into Asmara. The evolution of this human rights discourse into an international regime of humanitarian interventionism made the independence referendum in East Timor possible.

The Debilitation of Ethiopia's Capacities

The beginning of the end of the Cold War had a direct impact on Ethiopia's standing with regard to Eritrea. The ascent of Mikhail Gorbachev to the leadership of the Soviet Union in the mid-1980s introduced a new political thinking in Moscow and accordingly changed the dynamics of Soviet-Third World relations. The post–World War II decline of the linkage between local wars and an international one had heightened the Soviet Union's interest and direct intervention in the Third World. Having failed to appeal to a large number of countries, however, the Khrushchev era's rigid formulations gave way to Brezhnev's détente rhetoric toward the United States while actively supporting Third-World forces deemed to be progressive. In the early 1970s, the Soviet Academy of Sciences introduced a rather simplistic formulation – the State of Socialist Orientation – under which the Soviets essentially financed expensive wars of corrupt and dictatorial Third-World regimes under the guise of cultivating their socialisms.[4] The advent of Gorbachev to the Kremlin began the end of Moscow's consistent disregard of these regimes' failures to live up to their promises.

In his attempt to extricate the USSR from its unwinnable wars and those of its clients, Gorbachev initiated a deliberate course of cutting supplies to failing African governments, particularly Ethiopia and Angola. He is believed to have bluntly told Ethiopian dictator Mengistu Hailemariam to cut his losses and change course on Eritrea. The Soviets sent an early warning to the Ethiopian government in January 1989 that they might not renew the Ethio-Soviet military assistance agreement beyond its anticipated expiration in 1991.[5] Although, until its defeat, the Ethiopian government received military hardware from the Soviet defense establishment, the policy articulations of the new political thinking in Moscow and consequent denunciations of

---

[4] Carol R. Saivetz and Sylvia Woodby, *Soviet – Third World Relations* (London: Westview Press, 1985), 9–14; also see Okbazghi Yohannes, *Eritrea, a Pawn in World Politics* (Gainesville: University of Florida Press, 1991), 240–253, for an analysis of Soviet behavior in the developing countries and the Horn of Africa in particular.

[5] Herman J. Cohen, *Intervening in Africa. Superpower Peacemaking in a Troubled Continent* (New York: St. Martin's Press, 2000), 4–5, 24. According to Cohen (p. 230n9), this message was conveyed to Mengistu through Viktor Chebrikov, member of the Soviet Politburo and former KGB chief.

Addis Ababa's failed socialist orientation were clear signs that the peak of Ethio-Soviet arms deals had long passed.[6]

The Derg government's scrambling search for an alternative weapons supplier to the USSR converged with the U.S.-Israeli need for some kind of understanding with Addis Ababa to address the delivery of relief aid and the crossover to Israel of the Bete Israel–Ethiopian Jews. Herman Cohen, the former U.S. assistant secretary of state for African Affairs, and Robert Houdek, U.S. chargé d'affaires in Ethiopia, concluded that Soviet pressure left Mengistu no choice but "to swallow his pride and act like a pussycat" when in August 1989 Cohen presented to him U.S. demands for normalization of relations.[7] While Washington pressed the embattled Mengistu that the timely delivery of relief aid required peaceful resolution of the spiraling insurgencies, his government was happy to trade the stranded Bete Israel for generous weapons shipments from Tel Aviv. Dismissing U.S. preconditions as unrealistic and impatient to wait until Mengistu was replaced, Israel started to provide Ethiopia some weapons and military training.[8] The commodification of the Bete Israel, however, was an inherently short-lived affair because so few remaining members of that community wished to migrate to Israel's expanding border settlements. Moreover, Israel lacked the enthusiasm and the reservoir of weapons that the USSR had to sustain the Derg for long. As EPLF leader Isaias Afwerki accurately observed, Israeli-Ethiopian cooperation had only been tactical and temporary, and although Israel delivered to Ethiopia prohibited weapons like cluster and napalm bombs, the potential for their strategic partnership had not been realized.[9]

Moreover, the Derg had long been suffering from internal weaknesses that, compounded by the external pressures, neutralized the impact of any new infusion of weapons, regardless of size. Ethiopian strategy that relied on brute force failed to sustain its troops' superiority in numbers, armaments and morale in Eritrea. Having quickly reversed the Somali invasion of 1977, Ethiopian rulers chanted, "The victory in the East will be repeated in

---

[6] G. A. Krylova, "National-Democratic Revolution in the Light of the New Political Thinking (The Example of Ethiopia)," *Narody Azii I Afriki (Peoples of Asia and Africa)*, no. 1 (1989):42–53; translated, analyzed, and reproduced by Paul Henze, *Glasnost About Building Socialism in Ethiopia: Analysis of a Critical Soviet Article* (Santa Monica, CA: RAND, 1990).

[7] Cohen, *Intervening in Africa*, 25.

[8] Colin Legum, "Ethiopia: Divergent Policies of United States and Israel," in *Third World Reports*, London, August 1, 1990.

[9] "Answer of the Secretary General to Questions from the People and the Fighters" in *Sagem*, 2 no. 10 (October 1990):56. Cohen (*Intervening in Africa*, 35) claims that "What really worried us was the possible secret [Israeli] delivery [to Ethiopia] of highly destructive weapons such as cluster bombs. Since we found none, we had no reason to protest." Nonetheless, the use of Israeli-supplied cluster and napalm bombs is well documented in the final years of the independence war.

the North" and dispatched their well-armed troops northwards to militarily resolve the Eritrean question in three months. As previously noted, the Ethiopian military consistently promised to crush the Eritrean independence fighters and declared victory after every offensive only to repeat the same cycle over and over again. Meanwhile, the Eritrean independence movement gnawed at the Ethiopian military superiority and accelerated the decline of the morale of its troops.[10] In the process, most of the able Ethiopian army commanders were either assassinated by their adversaries, sentenced to death by their own government, fell in action, or were captured by the Eritreans.

Several of the surviving senior Ethiopian officers scrutinized the Derg government's conduct of the war in Eritrea and recommended alternatives, which reflected the dwindling internal cohesion, further eroding the government's capacity when it acted drastically against them. Prominent among these officers was the Russian-trained General Tariku Ayne, who first entered Eritrea in 1978 and had climbed the ranks of the military command while fighting against the EPLF only to realize ten years later that their strategy had not left room for nonmilitary methods of ending the war in Eritrea. Within the limited scope of his authority in the Nadew Command (on the gate of Nakfa, the EPLF's headquarters), his peaceful gesturing toward and his generosity during his interaction with the population of the strategic town of Afabet alarmed Ali Ibrahim, the EPLF commander across the line.[11] As discussed in more detail later in this chapter, General Tariku also questioned the wisdom of his superiors' orders for how his forces should respond to the EPLF's tactical maneuverings in other parts of Eritrea. The general was immediately demoted and executed shortly afterward along with several of his leading officers.

An April 1988 investigation by Addis Ababa into the collapse of the strategic *Nadew* Command did not bode well for the stability of the Derg regime. It reinforced the timeliness of the officers' scrutiny of their government by confirming the accuracy of Tariku's conclusions and the

---

[10] For detailed analysis of this aspect of the Eritrean independence war, Awet T. Weldemichael, "The Eritrean Long March: The Strategic Withdrawal of the Eritrean People's Liberation Front, 1978–1979," *The Journal of Military* 73, no. 4 (October 2009):1231–1271.

[11] According to one of Ali Ibrahim's former aides, the EPLF commander had considerable respect for General Tariku's skills (which seemed to be mutual) and appreciated the danger his military and newly introduced nonmilitary strategies engendered for the EPLF. The two closely followed one another's movements, and Ali set up several traps and ambushes to eliminate Tariku from which the latter narrowly escaped, at least once as the sole survivor. In January 1988, Ethiopian dictator Mengistu relieved Tariku from his command and had him physically eliminated shortly afterwards while in March the revered Ali Ibrahim was killed in an Ethiopian aerial raid right after he advanced beyond Tariku's headquarters in Afabet when the EPLF crushed the Nadew Command.

government's blatant disregard of his warnings.[12] A year later, in May 1989, the remaining senior officers staged an ill-thought-out coup d'état when Mengistu was in East Germany. The coup was brutally put down, and none of the coup-makers survived; some of the officers were killed in shootouts with Mengistu's loyalists, and the rest were tortured to death before their mutilated bodies were tied to cars and dragged through the streets. As that incident further besieged Mengistu, the dictator issued in June, and the rubberstamp parliament instantly approved, an urgent call to the Eritrean independence fighters and Ethiopian rebels for peace talks, for the first time, without preconditions. As the Derg was cornered by its tactical errors and strategic blunders, the Eritrean independence fighters and the Ethiopian rebels did well to exploit this window of opportunity and bring the Derg to its knees. As the next section shows with regard to the Indonesian government, the Ethiopian government was also victim of factors beyond its own control, particularly the end of the Cold War and Soviet reluctance to continue supporting it.

Faltering Indonesian Resolve

Throughout the quarter century of Indonesia's occupation of East Timor, President Suharto remained in control and was on the same page as his generals. So confident was Suharto (and his broader constituency) that Foreign Minister Alatas's 1994 proposal of granting East Timor extensive internal autonomy in lieu of a referendum did not even fly. Nevertheless, the end of the Cold War had already removed a key ideological justification for Indonesia's continued occupation of East Timor, in the same way that it speeded the debilitation of Ethiopia's capacity to carry on the fight against the Eritrean independence fighters. Then the president's efforts to diversify his constituency started to dent Indonesian consensus on East Timor as the newcomers had little to no vested interest in what they saw was an ungrateful burden of a Catholic half island. This was particularly the case with his bringing in powerful elements in Indonesian society like the Ikatan Cendekiawan Muslim Se-Indonesia (ICMI, Indonesian Association of Muslim Intellectuals).[13] Furthermore, the Asian economic crisis of the late 1990s gripped the Indonesian economy, which cast East Timor to the backburner of Jakarta's priorities and forced it to give in to the persistent demands of the East Timorese nationalist resistance.

---

[12] "Be-Nadew Ez Ghinbar Seletekesetew Huneta Tetarto Yeqerebe Riport," Miaziya 1980 EC ("Investigative Report about the Conditions that Transpired on the Frontline of the Nadew Command," April 1988).

[13] Salim Said, "Suharto's Armed Forces: Building a Power Base in New Order Indonesia, 1966–1998," *Asian Survey*, 38, no. 6 (June 1998):535–552.

Meanwhile, although East Timor featured more frequently in Indonesian publications from the late 1980s, the coverage of the resistance movement and its goals were consistently and deliberately misrepresented. Despite the transformations within the resistance movement, Indonesia persisted in calling the evolving resistance movement FRETILIN and in branding it as security disrupter group, GPK. According to Akihisa Matsuno, such a depiction of the resistance of the East Timorese people "freezes the whole history of the [unfolding] drama at the pre-invasion period of 1975 where the alleged root of the trouble [the FRETILIN-UDT civil war] lies."[14] The persistent reference to FRETILIN as communist and comparisons with failed Indonesian rebellions were intended to perpetuate communism's status as a permanent threat that required the people's vigilance. Furthermore, the term GPK aimed to depoliticize the resistance movement, dehumanize it, and legitimize the state's crude actions against it.[15]

Such bias can also be partially attributed to the media's reliance on officialdom for information even in better-established democracies let alone in authoritarian New Order Indonesia. These problems compounded the blatant cover up in the mainstream media outlets around the world, which, according to Edward Sherman, "have policies and agendas that make truthfulness inconvenient."[16]

The regional and global developments of the 1990s, however, undercut Jakarta's monopoly of the media with regard to East Timor and removed the threat of communism as a convenient justification for its actions. The end of the Cold War removed the raison d'être for Jakarta's "National Resilience" strategy of being on the ideological frontline against the spread of communism. Furthermore, the Internet grew steadily through the 1980s, and the East Timorese nationalists and their growing network of international supporters exploited it to break the media bias and altogether circumvent the already porous government control over information flow.[17] The Internet

---

[14] Matsuno, "Reading the Unwritten: An Anatomy of Indonesian Discourse on East Timor," in *The East Timor Problem and the Role of Europe* ed. Pedro Pinto Leite, (Dublin: International Platform of Jurists for East Timor-IPJET, 1996), 199.

[15] David McRae, "A Discourse on Separatists," *Indonesia* 74 (October 2002):41ff.

[16] Edward S. Sherman, "Manifestations of Media Bias: The Case of the *New York Times* Reporting on Indonesia and East Timor," in *Censored 2001: 25 Years of Censored News and the Top Censored Stories of the Year*, ed. Peter Phillips and Project Censored (New York: Seven Stories Press, 2001), 266. In this astute analysis of the *New York Times'* embracing and propagation of the lies and propaganda of an ally country, Sherman shows, for example, how the crimes that were been perpetrated against the East Timorese people were presented in the passive voice without hinting human agency much less the agents. Accordingly, the Timorese died, while Cambodians and Kosovars were slaughtered and massacred by murderous tyrants and genocidists.

[17] In "East Timor and the Internet: Global Political Leverage in/on Indonesia" (*Indonesia* 73 [April 2002]:25–51), David T. Hill shows how the East Timorese resistance gained virtual independence and cyberspace information freedom to carry out internet activism called

and other technologies provided cost-efficient and fast means of communication between the resistance movement and its supporters, who further disseminated the information to their own networks and media contacts. Through reliable intermediaries, the Internet, and other high-tech communications systems offered the incarcerated Gusmão, the supreme commander of the resistance movement, secure lines of communicating sensitive information to Ramos-Horta, his principal diplomatic representative abroad. Since the mid-1990s, therefore, the internet offered some cyberspace freedom of information for the East Timorese nationalists. It also allowed their international supporters, particularly those in Ireland, to claim virtual independence for an independent East Timor in the waiting.[18]

Meanwhile, in 1997, the Asian economic crisis hit the Indonesian economy with serious consequences across the social strata of Indonesian society. Alatas put it succinctly thus:

That crisis cut down Indonesia's GDP growth...to minus 13.5 percent in 1998. Indonesia also suffered hyper-inflation, which reached 77.6 percent in 1998, food shortages in several parts of the country, the loss of millions of jobs, the collapse of the banking sector, the sharp depreciation of the Rupiah, a ballooning debt burden and hemorrhagic capital flight.[19]

President Suharto resigned in May 1998 as the popular outburst against the growing economic and political woes spilled over to the streets of major Indonesian cities. His appointee, Vice-President B.J. Habibie, stepped up and took over the reins of power. Preoccupied by the economic and political crisis, "President [Habibie] and his Cabinet Ministers... did not give much thought to the East Timor Question," which offered Foreign Minister Alatas a "window of opportunity" to revive his earlier proposal of special autonomy for East Timor.[20] About a month after Suharto's resignation, Alatas's proposal for "special status to East Timor with wide ranging autonomy" was approved and officially announced by President Habibie in June 1998. According to that proposal, a Special Autonomous Region of East Timor (SARET) was to be set up with, if implemented to its word, wide-ranging internal autonomy though without addressing the crux of the matter, self-determination.[21]

Suharto's sudden resignation in May 1998 left the doors wide open for the East Timorese nationalists and their international solidarity network

---

"hactivism," both spreading information and hacking into the Indonesian government's internet resources in an effort to incapacitate them.

[18] Hill, "East Timor and the Internet," 33–37.

[19] Ali Alatas, *The Pebble in the Shoe: The Diplomatic Struggle for East Timor* (Jakarta: Aksara Karunia, 2006), 133.

[20] Ibid., 135ff.

[21] Ibid., 135. Also see appendix 11: "A Constitutional Framework for a Special Autonomy for East Timor," 227–291, for the details of rules that were to govern the proposed SARET.

to walk right through and exert maximum pressure on his successor, B. J. Habibie. An example of this was the Australian Labor Party's rein-statement of its long-suspended call for the respect of the East Timorese people's right to self-determination. That fractured the consensus among the Australian political elite, which spoke against Indonesian violations of human rights in East Timor while in opposition but failed to lift a finger against them once they were in office. It also gave ammunition to the sol-idarity groups in that country and the sympathetic public to pressure the conservative government of John Howard into leveraging Indonesia.[22]

Finally, the East Timorese proponents of independence, collectively and individually, exploited Indonesia's moments of weakness by intensifying their multifaceted activities for independence. Side by side, the riots and civil disobedience in the rest of Indonesia, for example, pro-independence demonstrations and strikes in East Timor brought the local government to a screeching halt. In October 1998, Governor Abilio Soares's threats against his civil servants who he said faced forced retirement if they did not choose autonomy only angered the people who demanded his resigna-tion and the return of his predecessor, Mário Carrascalão. The intensified, nerve-wracking hit-and-run operations of FALINTIL wrought havoc and compounded the momentary confusion that befell the Indonesian military in East Timor subsequent to the death of its highest commanders in a heli-copter accident in mid-1998.[23]

The domestic and international factors that had enabled Indonesia to invade East Timor in the mid-1970s and get away with it changed fun-damentally in the late 1990s, leading to the undoing of the invasion. The increasing domestic pressure for change, the regional economic crisis, and the new global order left Jakarta cornered. As the East Timorese nation-alists and their international solidarity networks had long been poised to snatch such an opportunity, in the words of Pat Walsh, the pressures on

---

[22] I am grateful to leading Australian human rights activist and advocate for East Timor Patrick "Pat" Walsh (interview, June 7, 2008, Dili, East Timor) for firsthand and insightful infor-mation on the advocacy of the Australian humanitarian groups under ACFOA's umbrella. Also see Clinton Fernandes, *Reluctant Saviour: Australia, Indonesia, and the Independence of East Timor* (Victoria, Australia: Scribe Publications, 2004), 26–47.

   It is probably in reference to this unprecedented Australian involvement that former Indonesian Foreign Minister Alatas (*The Pebble in the Shoe*, 147, 173) accused unnamed for-eign governments of collusion to exploit Indonesia's weaknesses in the immediate aftermath of Suharto's resignation. An analysis of Australia's public pronouncements and leveraging of Indonesia behind closed doors seems to substantiate Alatas and many of Indonesians' resentment of Australia. For example, while Alatas, (p. 173) shows how, as early as April 1999, Prime Minister Howard requested the deployment of an international force before the vote; however, Fernandes aptly analyzed Canberra's persistent statements and declarations that clearly favored Indonesia up until Australian military deployment in the aftermath of the postballot rampage.

[23] Fernandes, *Reluctant Saviour*, 33–34.

Jakarta opened a door that "they walked right through." The East Timorese nationalists succeeded in doing so by intensifying their resistance domestically and reframing their cause within broader norms on human rights and international law.

Dynamic Insurgencies and Their Victories: The Eritrean Endgame

A number of factors worked on one another to paralyze whatever remained standing of the Ethiopian army and render it incapable of sustaining any major attack. These included the decline of the Soviet Union and the consequent cutting of its supplies to Ethiopia, the latter's steady loss of its more capable generals at the hands of the government and its enemies and, most importantly, its successful thrashing by the Eritrean liberation forces as well as Ethiopian opposition movements. This phenomenon was not a linear process; but an analysis of the EPLF's internal dynamics and its execution of its strategy will better our understanding of the extreme desperation of the Ethiopian predicament.

In 1986, the EPLF's secret People's Party held its second congress in anticipation of the front's congress the following year. During the deliberations that lasted several weeks, the party heard detailed reports from all sectors of the resistance movement and concluded that the Ethiopian military was decaying and Eritrean victory was inevitable. The People's Party, thus, decided that the EPLF should seize the strategic initiative and intensify its offensive military action. To better coordinate the military operations with the political and propaganda aspects of the war, the executive pyramid of leadership of the independence movement was further centralized. The People's Party reelected Isaias Afwerki as its Secretary General and in accordance with its determination of the slates, he was also elected in 1987 as the EPLF's Secretary General, replacing the co-founding and longest-serving predecessor Romedan Mohammed-Nur. Additionally, the intelligence and military staffs as well as the media and political guidance branches of the EPLF came under his direct control – a drive for further centralization in light of the anticipated fast changes on the ground and the supposed need to make equally fast decisions.

EPLF boosted its credentials as an all-embracing nationalist force by merging with one of the factions of the former ELF – the ELF Central Command (ELF-CC, also called Sagem). With its realization that national independence remained to be achieved and the only force actively pursuing that objective was the EPLF, Sagem crossed over into Eritrea determined to come to an accommodation with the EPLF; whatever their differences, their strategic objective was the same.[24] While a powerful minority within

---

[24] Interview with Ahferom Tewelde (August 27, 1999, Asmara, Eritrea); and personal conversations with Zemhret Yohannes.

Sagem entertained the idea of becoming an autonomous alternative power-base within the EPLF, for the majority of its members, postmerger organizational and personal positions mattered less than did their contribution to the fight against the common enemy.[25] The EPLF was not prepared to entertain anything short of complete merger, and it pursued the merger through a drawn-out negotiation process when EPLF leaders, prominently Isaias Afwerki, engaged the young but capable ELF cadres who came to lead Sagem in numerous and sometime overnight political debates and negotiations about longer-term political programs and strategies. Meanwhile, more-senior ELF leaders – former political chief Ibrahim Idris Totil and senior cadre Dr. Giorgish Habte – joined Sagem, although they remained above the intra-Sagem differences regarding the conditions of joining the EPLF. Some political sticking points needed to be hammered out, but the EPLF continued to ensure the safety of the Sagem camp in northwestern Eritrean against the raging Ethiopian offensives and Sagem dispatched its own force to fight alongside their EPLF counterparts as part of the confidence building measures.

Totil's former position within the ELF and the loyalty he commanded among several hundred well-armed militias from his own Nara ethnic group in the Gash region of western Eritrea seem to have added to the intrinsic value of Sagem's merger into the EPLF. Totil met Isaias separately to help resolve some of the concerns that the young Sagem leaders had. Isaias went straight to the point: the EPLF had enough Christian fighters to show for if it so wished, but it was interested in genuine national unity, and it needed Totil's representation of his minority ethnic group in their nationalist movement.[26] For all practical purposes, the merger between Sagem and the EPLF was essentially completed in 1986. It was formalized a year later in what became the Second and Unity Congress of the EPLF and the ELF-CC.[27] On top of its political value, this merger enhanced the security of EPLF forces' mobility and increased their ability to strike at the Ethiopian army in the former ELF-controlled parts of Eritrea where the Ethiopians retained an overall upper hand.

Militarily, the EPLF banked upon its previous offensive experiences to prepare an elaborate plan of attacking Ethiopian frontlines and strongholds

---

[25] Personal conversations with Manna Bahre (spring 2005, Asmara, Eritrea). According to Manna, some Sagem members even declined leadership positions to which they were nominated in the EPLF after the merger, insisting that they decided to merge with the EPLF not for leadership positions.

[26] Interview with Ibrahim Idris Totil (Asmara, Eritrea).

[27] Personal conversations with Zemhret Yohannes and Tesfai "Degiga" Weldemichael reveal that the EPLF followed the same approach and nearly succeeded to bring about the merger of ELF-Revolutionary Council (ELF-RC). But the process stalled when the EPLF attacked ELF-RC forces based on misinformation provided by Tesfamehret Temesghen, a renegade former ELF platoon commander who had broken away from the ELF and roamed western Eritrea until, on his refusal to surrender, he was killed and his forces dispersed by the EPLF.

one at a time with impressive speed and strategic foresight. Since the 1984 knockdown of Ethiopian front line that resumed Eritrean fighters' access to the Red Sea, EPLF was capturing military supplies in such huge quantities that its forces did not have enough personnel to collect them. Although EPLF leaders do not seem to have harbored false hopes for quick and easy victory, they started boasting of their capability to outgun the Ethiopian military at any time and any terrain. When the recruitment of regional militias continued in earnest in the 1980s, the EPLF had enough weapons and ammunition to turn them into an effective fighting force.[28]

In March 1988, the EPLF trounced Ethiopia's ten-year-old Nadew Command on the Nakfa Front in a historic three-day battle that Basil Davidson famously compared to the Vietnamese defeat of the French at Dien Bien Phu. After the Eritrean nationalists executed the Strategic Withdrawal of 1978–1979, the rugged terrain of Sahel in northern Eritrea became the EPLF's last line of defense. The front lines at the gates of the town of Nakfa signified the EPLF's mere survival and an Ethiopian upper hand, which the latter kept reinforcing for close to ten years. In due course, as EPLF rotated some of its forces and started to flank Ethiopian lines, the government pulled some of its forces out of the Nakfa Front to respond to EPLF attacks in western Eritrea. As late as January 1988, the revered commander of the Nadew Command, General Tariku Ayne, warned headquarters that the Nadew Command was weakening as a result and that the EPLF had been launching tactical offensives to gauge its own capacity and that of his forces before what he implied was an imminent full-blown offensive. His overall evaluation of his forces' capacity to withstand it was not optimistic.[29] The general was immediately demoted and executed, as were his immediate subordinates who shared some of his thinking and briefly replaced him after his demotion.[30] Nevertheless, the government's investigation into the collapse of this strategic front line later concluded that his predictions were on target. Prepared by seven

---

[28] Interview with Isaias Afwerki in *Never Kneel Down: Drought, Development and Liberation in Eritrea*, ed. James Firebrace and Stuart Holland (Trenton, NJ: Red Sea Press, 1985), 127–137.

[29] Brigadier General Tariku Ayne, *Nadew Ez Memriya: K-hamle 1/1979 eske Tahsas 30/1980 b-Nadew Ez Ghinbar Yetekenawenew Yezemecha Menfeqawi Riport*, Tir 1980 EC. (*Nadew Command: Semi-Annual Campaign Report of Nadew Command Frontline from July 8, 1987 to January 7, 1988,*" January 1988), a classified document at the Eritrean RDC accessed under special permit.

[30] *Y-Ertra Kifle-Hager Wetaderawi Huneta: Sele-Kifle Hageritu Techebach Huneta Yeqerebe Acheer Riport*, Tir 1980 (*The Military Condition of the Eritrean Province: A Short Report about the Prevailing Conditions in the Province*, January 1988), a classified document signed by Kassaye Aregaw and available at the RDC. The immediate causes for the demotions and executions are the disapproval of the officers in the front line of their superiors' management of the war effort (a charge that laid ultimate responsibility on the dictator, Col. Mengistu Haile Mariam) and these officers' realization that peaceful resolution of the conflict had not been given due weight.

officers, the fifty-page report particularly highlighted the points that General Tariku had warned about as the leading causes for the collapse of the front line: personnel shortages, control of commanding positions or lack thereof, and rotation of forces to the lowlands when they were most needed on the Nakfa Front.[31] Perhaps without the knowledge of this strategic blunder on the part of the Ethiopian government, the EPLF snatched victory that irreversibly turned the tide in its favor.

Parallel to revitalizing its regional network of alliances with the Ethiopian rebel movements, the EPLF capitalized on its military gains to take center stage and project a moderate image of the nation-state that it was poised to declare independent. Armed with the EPLF's revised program of 1987, EPLF Secretary General Isaias Afwerki toured the West ostensibly to assure the world that the nationalist movement had moderated its radical leftist orientation.

The international charm campaign aimed to challenge the master-narrative of Ethiopia as a guarantor of regional stability and to debunk anti-Eritrean propaganda about the independence struggle as an Islamist movement or anti-Israel regional spoiler. Transformative measures of its 1987 Congress backstopped EPLF's diplomatic initiative. First, it toned down its ideologized foreign relations rhetoric in favor of "pursuing peaceful and nonaligned foreign policy." More specifically, it stipulated that independent Eritrea would seek cordial neighbourly relations with countries of the region and establish diplomatic ties with all countries "regardless of their economic and political systems." Second, the EPLF Congress had resolved to launch a multiparty political system after independence.[32] With that, the EPLF reiterated its readiness to reach a negotiated solution that does not compromise Eritrean right to self-determination, and renewed its call for a referendum as a means of ascertaining the people's wishes.[33]

Military gains that made its victory inevitable along with its receptiveness to negotiations earned the EPLF the attention of both the United States and Soviet Union, who had just achieved a nebulous "peace without losers" to the Namibian independence war in late 1988 and sought a similar end to the Eritrean war. Former U.S. President Jimmy Carter offered to mediate, and in April, the EPLF formally accepted his offer to directly meet with the Derg without preconditions. In order to preclude Carter's monopoly of the mediator role, however, the EPLF sought to pursue an internationalized and

---

[31] *Be-Nadew Ez Ghinbar Seletekesetew Huneta Tetarto Yeqerebe Riport*, Miaziya 1980 EC (*Investigation Report about the Conditions that Transpired on the Frontline of the Nadew Command*, April 1988).

[32] EPLF, *National Democratic Program*, 1987.

[33] Alamin Mohammed Said, *Hidget Zeyefiqid Mesel* (Asmara: Hidri Publishers, 2002). As its title – *The Right that Does not Allow for Compromises* – suggests and written as it is by one of EPLF's top leaders and negotiators, this book is the only account from the Eritrean side on the EPLF's long negotiations to find a peaceful resolution to the Eritrean question.

transparent process that involved the UN, the OAU, and the Arab League. Moreover, to reverse the persistent Ethio-Soviet rejection of the Eritreans' right to self-determination, the EPLF also decided to intensify its military operations and change the balance of power on the ground.[34]

As the Carter-mediated negotiations continued to stumble over technical sticking points, successful military operations by the Eritrean and Ethiopian insurgents further tightened the noose around Mengistu's neck. With EPLF assistance, the TPLF seized the strategic town of Shire, took control of the entire northerly province of Tigray, and moved on to the neighboring provinces. On the south and southwest, OLF forces operating alongside EPLF's commandos and other specialized units drove government forces from one stronghold to another. In February 1990, the EPLF took the port city of Massawa and effectively cut off the Ethiopian forces in the Eritrean highlands from direct access to the Red Sea and to mainland Ethiopia. Soon afterward, most of southern Eritrea fell to the independence fighters. Holding their ground in a defensible chain of natural fortresses between the highlands on one hand and the eastern and western lowlands on the other, the EPLF effectively blockaded the Ethiopian forces in Eritrea and made fast military inroads in the shrinking enclosure in the central highlands, surrounding the capital Asmara.

In the aftermath of the Iraqi invasion of Kuwait, the United States started to take a lead in seeking the peaceful resolution of regional conflicts, and the Eritrean independence war was one of them. The U.S. initiative, led by Assistant Secretary of State Herman Cohen in late 1990 failed because the Ethiopian government promised to offer only internal autonomy to parts of Eritrea while the EPLF insisted on a UN-supervised referendum to establish the wishes of the entire Eritrean people. The EPLF conceded to the postponement of a referendum, but demanded the withdrawal of Ethiopian troops and their replacement by UN peacekeepers in the interim. Another round of U.S.-mediated talks in February 1991,[35] however, recommended the postponement of the final resolution of the Eritrean question for a future date[36] when the Eritrean independence fighters were poised to deliver a military solution to the Eritrean question faster than the negotiations.

Failure to take note of EPLF's military upper hand and what seemed a deliberate ploy to give the beleaguered Ethiopian government new breathing space was alarming to EPLF negotiators, who decided that an irreversible military victory had to be achieved to avoid compromising its successes in

---

[34] Alamin, *Hidget Zeyefiqid Mesel*, 155ff.

[35] Alamin, *Hidget Zeyefiqid Mesel*, 209; and Herman J. Cohen, *Intervening in Africa. Superpower Peacmaking in a Troubled Continent* (New York: St. Martin's Press, 2000), 40–41.

[36] Eritrean Foreign Minster Haile "Deru" Weldetensae's talk to Eritreans residing in the greater Los Angeles area, March 2000; H. J. Cohen, *Intervening in Africa*, 43; and "Chronology of Conflict Resolution Initiatives in Eritrea," Institute for Conflict Analysis and Resolution, George Mason University, 1991, 145ff.

the next round of talks planned for May 1991. To that end, EPLF leaders returned to Eritrea and fell off the American negotiators' radar screen until the planning of the final military showdown was charted.[37] They did not avail themselves of the negotiations until they were certain the endgame was within their grip.

In coordination with allied Ethiopian rebels, EPLF exerted maximum pressure on government forces. Shrinking theaters of operations inside Eritrea along with increasing volunteer enlistment into the liberation army enabled the EPLF to deploy an increasing number of its forces in direct action alongside Ethiopian opposition forces in northern and western Ethiopia. As about 30,000 of TPLF's peasant army retired to their home districts claiming that they had fulfilled their mission – liberation of their province – and called on other Ethiopian groups to liberate their respective provinces, EPLF's personnel was needed inside Ethiopia as much as its expertise in mechanized offensive action and logistical capacity. By the end of the hostilities in May 1991, approximately 20,000 of the EPLF's seasoned fighters were operating alongside the TPLF-dominated Ethiopian People's Revolutionary Democratic Front (EPRDF) coalition.

Moreover, having already revitalized Oromo insurgent operations in western Ethiopia in 1989, the EPLF dispatched two separate expeditionary commando units in 1990 to rescue OLF units sandwiched by the Derg and their allied southern Sudanese rebels, the SPLM.[38] More particularly, between February and April, Eritrean mechanized and commando units in tandem with Ethiopian allies drove government forces from one stronghold to another. Already caught between a rock and a hard place, with insurgents making inroads into the capital Addis Ababa from all directions, the Ethiopian army saw its position deteriorate even further when military dictator Menghistu Haile Mariam fled to Zimbabwe on May 21 and the EPLF captured Asmara on May 24.

The fait accompli liberation of Eritrea was, thus, accomplished while preparations for the second round of negotiations were underway in London. Such a clear-cut military victory was unique in the African context. It also made the international community and the United States hard-pressed to continue evading the respect of a people's right to self-determination. Despite earlier plans to postpone the resolution of the Eritrean question, Assistant Secretary of State Cohen, "decided to endorse the referendum because Eritrea was historically a 'special case'... A self-determination

---

[37] Eritrean Foreign Minster Haile Weldetensae's talk to Eritreans residing in the greater Los Angeles area, March 2000; and personal conversations with Zemhret Yohannes.

[38] Interview with Alamin Mohammed Said (September 28, 2005, Asmara, Eritrea). These were units of Division 70 pulled out from Massawa. Twice, the EPLF expeditionary forces passed through the eastern Sudanese town of Kassala, where I lived as a teenager with my parents.

referendum [for Eritrea] was clearly a key element of . . . the transitional package being put together [for Ethiopia] in London,"[39] he declared.

Cohen also lifted the U.S. ban on the EPRDF from marching into Addis Ababa in order to restore order in the agitated capital. Accordingly, on May 27, 1991, EPLF units spearheaded EPRDF's triumphant march into Addis Ababa with the collapse of the Derg government. The EPLF turned itself into the Provisional Government of Eritrea (PGE) and started to administer the country while preparing for the internationally monitored referendum in 1993. All Eritreans were to vote yes or no for the country to be independent and sovereign.

Dynamic Insurgencies and Their Victories: East Timorese Irriversible Gains amid Adversity

The 1982 U.N. General Assembly resolution along with Lisbon's 1986 policy reversal emboldened the Portuguese diplomats on the question of East Timor. Convinced that time was on their side, President Mário Soares put Portugal on a gradualist pursuit of the right to self-determination of East Timorese people.[40] Although successive diplomats carried out their latent constitutional mandate[41] with steady doggedness, it was not until after the November 1991 Santa Cruz Massacre that they started to put up a fierce fight against Indonesia.[42] While Prime Minister Antonio Guterres, for example, proposed to Suharto in 1996 the release of Gusmão and other political prisoners in return for mutual opening of interest sections in friendly embassies in Jakarta and Lisbon, his foreign minister, Jaime Gama, consistently chal-

---

[39] Cohen, *Intervening in Africa*, 50.

[40] Interviews with President Mário Soares (August 22, 2006, Lisbon, Portugal) and Dr. Carlos Gaspar (August 31, 2006, Lisbon, Portugal).

[41] Portuguese Presidents Mário Soares and Jorge Sampaio as well as senior Portuguese officials I spoke with were consistent in saying that they were pursuing the right to self-determination of the East Timorese people as a principle enshrined in international law and their own constitution.

[42] On one hand, senior Portuguese diplomats believed that, as a matter of principle, it was their responsibility to see to it that the Timorese people exercise their right to self-determination. Interviews with Dr. Carlos Gaspar (August 31, 2006, Lisbon, Portugal) and Ambassador Leonardo Mathias (January 11, 2006, Lisbon, Portugal). On the other hand, a younger generation of Portuguese diplomats felt an added sense of guilt because they knew some of the martyred Timorese nationalist leaders for their activism within the anticolonial leftist movement in Portugal. Interview with Ambassador Ana Gomes (August 22, 2006, Cascais, Portugal). The most prominent of the latter group is José Manuel Durão Barroso, who, before the Carnation Revolution, was a leading activist within the underground Maoist movement to which most of the Timorese students in Portugal belonged. Professor Barbedo praises Barroso's personal commitment to the East Timorese cause, and Barroso's dogged diplomatic fights earned him the respect of his Indonesian counterpart, Foreign Minister Ali Alatas.

lenged his Indonesian counterpart Ali Alatas that Portugal would only accept the final resolution of the question based on the outcome of a genuine act of self-determination.[43]

Although Portugal's new diplomatic initiatives started to garner tangible results for the Timorese diplomats, the East Timorese nationalist movement determined to expedite Indonesia's exhaustion or its leaders' realization that such a possibility was inevitable. In the 1990s, East Timorese nationalists geared up to increase the costs of occupation for individual Indonesian soldiers and the Indonesian state. In the international arena, Ramos-Horta intensified the diplomatic war. The current Timorese president related how their success in blocking the delivery of several F-16s to Indonesia was a major victory not because those jet fighters were used in East Timor but because it was a major diplomatic blow to Indonesia.[44]

Waves of Arrests and Succession of New Leaders

Indonesia intensified its operations to neutralize the underground cells of the Timorese nationalist resistance and nearly broke the back of the Clandestine Front. A massive crackdown during the immediate aftermath of the Santa Cruz Massacre landed the entire leadership of the underground movement in Indonesian jails. A week later, members of RENETIL staged the first demonstration of its kind in Jakarta, denouncing the massacre and calling for a negotiated resolution of the conflict. That also resulted in further arrests and to the incarceration of the first-generation RENETIL leaders.

Indonesian arrest of these Timorese nationalist leaders, however, proved to be a double-edged sword. On one hand, these waves of arrests paralyzed the activities of the Clandestine Front. CNRM had to assign two new leaders – David Alex and Sabalae – to reactivate its clandestine structures and activities. On the other hand, in captivity, the Indonesian authorities furnished the Timorese clandestine leadership with a new, physically safer, and effective forum to advocate their case. While Fernando Lasama drew, in court, parallels between their struggle and that of the pioneer Indonesian nationalists struggling against Dutch colonialism (as previously discussed), all of the Timorese political prisoners wrote regular appeals to the Indonesian president and consistently turned down routine Indonesian offers of amnesty in return for the renunciation of their cause.[45] Moreover, the increased activism on their behalf in Indonesia and beyond kept the East Timor question on a high profile.

Undeterred, Indonesian security forces continued their crackdown and a year after the Santa Cruz Massacre they captured Xanana Gusmão in Dili

---

[43] Alatas, *A Pebble in the Shoe*, 81–83.
[44] Interview with President Jose Ramos-Horta (June 5, 2008, Dili, East Timor).
[45] Personal conversations with Jacinto Alves (June 10, 2008, Dili, East Timor).

in November 1992. The capture of Gusmão shook the morale of many East Timorese and their supporters throughout the world.[46] Nonetheless, the resistance movement emerged stronger out of its difficult predicament, in what has become a typically Timorese tradition of resilience. Although the diplomatic representatives abroad declared the dissociation of the resistance movement from Gusmão in the interest of protecting it from his forced public denunciations, FALINTIL remained loyal to him and later religiously followed his leadership.

In the immediate aftermath of the capture, however, Ma'Huno conferred with the Ainaro parish priest, Father Francisco Barreto, and another seminarian about his succession.[47] With the help of the two priests, the only surviving member of the CCF of 1975 issued the "November 20" Declaration in which he upheld Gusmão's role as the "symbol" of resistance but declared that his leadership role had been frozen, invalidating any claims and declarations that he may be forced to make. Ma'Huno declared that CNRM would continue in its established trajectory toward national unity and that FRETILIN and UDT were the legitimate representatives of the Timorese people. He also upheld the nonpartisanship of FALINTIL. Confirming Ramos-Horta's leadership outside the country as the highest representative of CNRM, Ma'Huno restructured the internal leadership to fill the consequent vacuum, with himself as the highest field commander, Francisco Guterres "Lu-Olo" and Konis Santana as his vice-secretaries, and Taur Matan Ruak as FALINTIL's operational commander.[48]

As Ma'Huno was captured by the Indonesian military soon afterward in March 1993, Father Barreto claims that the same Timorese priests who facilitated Ma'Huno's succession installed a replacement in an effort to spare the movement treading forward without a central leading figure and in order to avoid the building of an image that it does not have a leader.[49] As FALINTIL operational commander Ruak, the most senior of the remaining leaders, could not be reached, the priests called on Nino Konis Santana to replace Ma'Huno, which also meant his becoming the Secretary of the CDF. Konis signed a declaration that they prepared, saying that he had stepped up to take the leadership[50] to the disappointment of the two

[46] In Cipinang penitentiary in Jakarta, for example, Fernando Lasama prayed to God to blind the Indonesians to where Gusmão was. But when he was captured, Lasama and his colleagues in the same prison were demoralized until Gusmão joined them in Cipinang and they started to comfort one another.

[47] Interview with Father Francisco Barreto (May 11, 2006, Dili, East Timor).

[48] Arquivo Mário Soares/Resistência Timorense, 5000.225, CNRM-CDF, "Declaracão '20 de Novembro,'" November 28, 1992.

[49] Interview with Father Francisco Barreto (May 11, 2006, Dili, East Timor).

[50] Arquivo Mário Soares/Resistência Timorense, 5000.228, CNRM-Frente Armada, "Declaração Sobre a Captura do Novo Lider do Resistecia: O Companheiro Ma'Huno . . . " April 1, 1993.

most-senior FALINTIL commanders, Ruak and Lere Anan Timor.[51] Although there is no record of a schism or an open defiance of orders of the new FALINTIL commander, Konis is believed to have moved his headquarters from the eastern parts of East Timor to the center in Ermera in order to avoid Ruak and Lere's hostility. When Konis died of a debilitating illness in 1998, however, Ruak was the undisputed successor to lead FALINTIL until independence.

The succession of new leaders kept the resistance moving forward despite the wave of their captures. Under their leadership, FALINTIL did its share of increasing the costs of occupation for Indonesia. As Margherita Tracanelli, former media advisor and liaison officer of FALINTIL Vice-Commander Taur Matan Ruak, put it, the Timorese guerrillas wrought panic upon the Indonesian troops and rendered them ineffective before launching their attack:

They'd sneak up to the barracks firing a single shot, immediately disappearing into the blackness. The sound of the shot cracking the still night sent the TNI leaping from their bunks, preparing for battle, only to find their enemy had dissolved into the night. They found the guerilla tactics unnerving. After many of these well-timed and unsettling irritations, the enemy were exhausted and their guard was down. It was then Falintil would launch a successful attack.[52]

The successive commanders on the ground in East Timor and the conditions of Gusmão's imprisonment made the latter a far better leader in effectively coordinating all the fronts of the resistance movement. Throughout the rounds of captures and successions, Gusmão's authority remained intact as his successors only assumed operational command of FALINTIL with the title of vice-commander. Gusmão had cultivated staunch loyalty and trust among his subordinates so that he retained undisputed strategic decision-making powers of the resistance movement throughout the chain of successors. Captivity also brought Gusmão closer to RENETIL leaders who had been incarcerated in Cipinang penitentiary since November 1991. These young, well-educated nationalists proved to be dedicated and capable advisors for the supreme resistance leader to consult and brainstorm with on as many issues as he brought forth to them.[53] Finally, thanks to the network that the Clandestine Front had laid down, and the sympathy and attention that the Santa Cruz Massacre attracted, Gusmão remained connected to the resistance movement in the East Timorese jungles, the clandestine front under Indonesian occupation and the diplomatic front. In

[51] Interview with Father Francisco Barreto (May 11, 2006, Dili, East Timor).
[52] Margherita Tracanelli, "The Pain of the Sinner Betrayed," http://www.margheritatracanelli. com.au/thepainofthesinnerbetrayed.pdf.
[53] Interviews with Fernando "Lasama" de Araújo (July 5–7, 2006, Dili, East Timor) and Virgilio Guterres (April 13 and May 9, 2006, Dili, East Timor).

the final years of his confinement, Gusmão even had a secret satellite phone in his prison cell, which he used to remain connected with the rest of the world.[54] University-educated, highly intelligent, and dedicated lieutenants and advisors surrounded Gusmão in prison, and all corners of the resistance movement and global network of solidarity groups fed him with valuable information. As a result, in the words of one of his and Horta's former aides, "Xanana [Gusmão] became like a sponge, absorbing everything and making well-informed decisions" without being held back by the day-to-day management of FALINTIL affairs on the ground.

After laying a solid foundation for international uproar upon his arrest, it is possible that the resistance leader staged his own capture by the Indonesians in 1992. Having come two years after the release of South Africa's Nelson Mandela, Gusmão perhaps succeeded the former as the world's most famous political prisoner with world leaders lobbying Jakarta on his behalf and keeping East Timor in the international limelight. While world leaders continued to press Jakarta for his release, newly elected President Mandela paid him a secret visit, allegedly in one of Suharto's government palaces.[55] Because of that and other efforts, international public opinion in conjuncture with regional and global political and economic factors nudged Jakarta from its stubborn position.

East Timorese nationalists persisted in making East Timor ungovernable and Indonesian forces there insecure, in Indonesianizing the East Timor question and in seeking international support in order to force Indonesia to respect the East Timorese right to self-determination. The East Timorese position on a negotiated solution to their conflict was consistent with the peace proposal that CRRN put forth during the 1983 cease-fire agreement with Indonesia. The most important components of that proposal were the withdrawal of Indonesian troops, their replacement by UN peacekeepers, and the holding of a referendum to ascertain the East Timorese people's wish.

1997: The Turning Point
An important turning point in the history of the East Timorese independence war is 1997 when the nationalists started to reap the harvest of their two decades of struggle. In December 1996, José Ramos-Horta and Bishop Belo

---

[54] Interview with Luisa Pereira (January 11, 2006, Lisbon, Portugal). Pereira, for example, remembers how, after Gusmão's capture, their communication continued through long letters crossing paths until the latter got the satellite phone in his cell and they shifted to lengthy nighttime phone conversation, some of which went on for hours.

[55] According to Ambassador Francisco Xavier Lopes da Cruz (interview, August 21, 2006, Lisbon, Portugal), not only did Mandela plead with Suharto for the release of Gusmão, but on his first trip to Indonesia, the first president of multiracial and democratic South Africa secretly met Gusmão in Suharto's residential palace in the suburbs of Jakarta.

were awarded the Nobel Peace Prize for their work on behalf of the East Timorese people, the impact of which was intensified diplomatic work from CNRM's and Ramos-Horta's Nobel offices as well as Bishop Belo's international standing. Although he was the first Roman Catholic bishop to win the Nobel Prize, the subtly adamant advocate of his people's human rights does not seem to have changed the content or intensity of his advocacy after receiving the award. But it opened the doors to the highest circles of powerful countries. President Clinton, for example, "dropped by" while Bishop Belo was meeting Sandy Berger, the president's national security assistant, and promised to "try to be more helpful" to the Timorese pursuit of respect for their human rights.[56]

While intrinsically raising the profile of the East Timorese question in the international arena, the award multiplied the pressure on Ramos-Horta who, in the words of one of his former aides, had already been a "relentless campaigner for his people's right to self-determination." Initially working from Ramos-Horta's Nobel office, the aide recalls the amplified political activities in and out of the office and wherever Ramos-Horta went. Although tireless even in the darkest years of the resistance movement, the renewed and multifaceted political engagements and campaigns made it incumbent on Ramos-Horta getting all the help he could get from his fellow East Timorese. Although the intensified political and diplomatic work and Ramos-Horta's need for assistance accentuated the importance of a more unified Timorese front for independence, the Nobel Prize added to his international standing and strengthened the legitimacy of his leadership among the Timorese.

The growing appreciation among the East Timorese nationalists of the need to form a single cohesive pro-independence bloc in order to harness the emerging opportunities and face the challenges ahead culminated in their launching of the Conselho Nacional Resistência Timorense (CNRT, National Council of Timorese Resistance) in April 1997. Despite CNRM's existence since 1987, the various pro-independence Timorese had not been brought under one umbrella, and their work only continued on individual basis without effective overarching organizational structures. For the non-FRETILIN East Timorese, the word *Maubere* in CNRM, for instance, denoted the radical, leftist orientation of the pre-invasion days. Meeting in Peniche, Portugal, however, they collectively decided to replace CNRM with CNRT, which proved to be a truly inclusive umbrella organization. Gusmão's leadership was confirmed by his election as president, Ramos-Horta and Mário Carrascalão (secretly) as vice-presidents.

---

[56] Arnold S. Kohen, *From the Place of the Dead. The Epic Struggle of Bishop Belo of East Timor* (New York: St. Martin's Press, 1999), 23–24.

Also in 1997, Kofi Annan succeeded Butros Butros Ghali[57] as UN Secretary General and took a much keener personal interest on the East Timor issue.[58] According to former Indonesian Foreign Minister Alatas, seven rounds of Indonesian-Portuguese negotiation under the auspices of the UN secretaries general resulted in nothing until the eighth round in June 1996, when the tripartite meetings came out with a confidential nonpaper agreement on "Establishing the parameters within which the two parties are prepared to negotiate."[59] Kofi Annan appointed Pakistani Ambassador Jamsheed Marker as his personal representative who remained in that capacity throughout the negotiations until independence, offering an element of continuity in high-profile representation. Perhaps ironically, the Eritrean Tamrat Samuel also offered an important element of continuity for throughout the 1990s he remained the point person for East Timor and Indonesia at the UN's Department of Political Affairs in New York.[60]

Ambassador Marker[61] was supported by a dedicated team of UN officials, Tamrat Samuel among them, and regularly consulted with the Timorese nationalists. Marker himself made bold moves and statements that sometimes offended Indonesia. One of the venues at which he made a bold statement representative of the Secretary General's commitment to the East Timorese right to self-determination was the Indonesian-initiated confidence-building All-inclusive Intra-East Timorese Dialogue (AIETD), where nothing political was supposed to be discussed. During the final AIETD meeting in late October 1998, Ambassador Marker told his Timorese

---

[57] While his work as UN Secretary General with regard to East Timor could have been constrained by several factors of the time, as Egypt's former senior foreign ministry official, Butros Butros-Ghali is on record opposing Eritrea's separation from Ethiopia when EPLF forces defeated the Ethiopian military and liberated Eritrea in 1991.

[58] Tamrat Samuel, "East Timor: The Path to Self-Determination" in *From Promise to Practice: Strengthening UN Capacities for the Prevention of Violent Conflict*, ed. Chandra Lekha Sriram and Karin Wermester, (Boulder, CO: Lynne Rienner Publishers, 2003), 206.

[59] Alatas, *The Pebble in the Shoe*, 80.

[60] Tamrat, "East Timor: The Path to Self-Determination," in *From Promise to Practice*, 206.

[61] Although several diplomats and politicians I spoke with have little to attribute to Ambassador Marker, perhaps the most articulate critic of Ambassador Marker is Geoff Robinson. After long scholarly research on Indonesia and half a decade of work with Amnesty International focusing on Indonesia and East Timor, Robinson had known too well the workings of the Indonesian state and its armed forces beyond diplomatic promises of the higher political circles. Working with Ambassador Marker as UNAMET Political Affairs Officer, Robinson closely observed that the former's old school diplomacy along with his friendship with the Indonesian Foreign Minister, Alatas, was an unhelpful mix amidst the intensifying crisis on the ground: "A diplomat of the old school, Ambassador Marker was a firm believer in the value of cordial face-to-face discussion. In keeping with that philosophy and because of his friendship with Indonesian Foreign Minister Alatas, he was more inclined than many others in the United Nations to accept assurances of good faith offered by Indonesian officials." Robinson, *"If You Leave Us Here, We Will Die,"* 129.

and Indonesian audience that "the time is fast approaching when East Timor will deservedly run its own affairs, whatever the framework and legal issues may be ... prepare for the imminent prospect of self-determination...."[62]

Real Prospects of the Special Autonomous Region of East Timor (SARET)

Finally, the impact of all these developments converged with the toll the Asian financial crisis started to exact on the Indonesian economy to leverage Jakarta into reversing its twenty-four-year-old policy toward East Timor as a way of appealing to the donors and global financial institutions. That paved the way for Alatas's special autonomy proposal to get the new Indonesian government's seal of approval. When Indonesia presented its Special Autonomy proposal in June 1998, both the East Timorese independence movement and the Portuguese had to consider it seriously. But they could not accept it as anything more than an interim solution as it failed to address or resolve the key bone of contention of the past twenty-four years. During his meeting with Ambassador Jamsheed Marker in Cipinang in July 1998, for example, Gusmão expressed his enthusiasm in the interim solution the proposal was expected to bring until conducive conditions were created for the people to exercise their right to self-determination. From Gusmão's perspective, during that interim period, the two sides would cease hostilities, Indonesians were to reduce troop presence in East Timor, and the United Nations would have physical presence in the form of a peacekeeping force.[63] Similarly, the Portuguese political establishment viewed the proposal as an interim one and, during the negotiations, Foreign Minister Gama remained firm in that only through a referendum could a lasting and acceptable solution be achieved.[64]

Consequently, the August 1998 Alatas-Gama meeting in New York deadlocked until Kofi Annan's creative intervention prevented the breakdown of negotiations by proposing that the two sides agree on the substantive aspects of the proposal without compromising their basic positions.[65] Nonetheless, the progress was limited because Indonesians regarded the proposal as a final solution whereas Portuguese negotiators saw it only as an interim solution.

Meanwhile, the postponement of subsequent Indonesian Portuguese meetings because of tragic developments inside East Timor gave the Portuguese side a chance to further deliberate on the proposal. President Sampaio invited Foreign Minister Gama to attend his meeting with the Portuguese Council of State (the president's advisory body) in order to hear the range of Portuguese (as well as East Timorese) opinions and analyses

---

[62] Quoted in Alatas, *The Pebble in the Shoe*, 96.
[63] Ibid., 140.
[64] Ibid., 142.
[65] Ibid.

on the question of special autonomy and self-determination. The overall assessment was that while the Indonesian proposal left the basis of Portugal's constitutional mandate hanging, that is, ascertaining the wishes of the East Timorese people, it was an irresistible opportunity that should not be squandered at any cost.[66] After consulting with the East Timorese nationalist leaders and with the approval of their superiors, therefore, the Portuguese team left for New York in late November to discuss the implementation modalities of SARET project and to sign an agreement. But an impromptu decision by President Habibie took the two negotiating teams by surprise and introduced a second option before the Special Autonomy project was finalized.[67]

On December 19, 1998, Australian Prime Minister Howard sent a letter to Indonesian President B. J. Habibie, which proved to be the proverbial straw that broke the camel's back. In the letter, Howard advised Habibie to follow the French example in New Caledonia, whereby an interim compromise solution was reached without the final resolution of the latter's status.[68] Its merits aside, the comparison of Indonesia, whose politicians prided on its being an anticolonialist bulwark, with an erstwhile colonial power angered Habibie. On January 21, Habibie forwarded Howard's letter to six of his cabinet ministers, asking them to "please analyse." "If the question of East Timor has become a burden to the struggle and image of the Indonesian Nation and if after 22 years ... the people of East Timor cannot become united with us," the President jotted down his ideas on the margins of the forwarded letter, "then it would be appropriate and wise ... that East Timor be allowed to separate honourably."[69] The longtime Minister of Technology and Research, who rose to the highest power by dint of friendship with Suharto, had no vested interest in East Timor, nor did his political constituency, ICMI.

Although Habibie and many of his ministers' main concern was the financial crisis, several key ministers with military backgrounds seem to have convinced the President that the East Timorese people would prefer autonomy within Indonesia to independence. These ministers persisted in their conviction that the East Timorese would accept autonomy because the

---

[66] Interview with President Jorge Sampaio (August 25, 2006, Lisbon, Portugal).

[67] Interview with Ambassador Ana Gomes (August 22, 2006, Cascais, Portugal). The negotiations progressed well to a point that the two teams agreed to open interest sections in friendly embassies in one another's capitals, and Ambassador Gomes, who was in New York as part of the Portuguese team, was dispatched from New York directly to Jakarta to be on the ground as Portugal's representative to Indonesia. On January 30, 1999, unexpected media paparazzi welcomed Gomes at the Seokarno-Hatta International Airport in Jakarta. The local and international media in Jakarta wanted to know if Portugal had anything to do with the government's sudden change in course.

[68] Fernandes, *Reluctant Saviour*, 26–47.

[69] Quoted in Fernandes, *Reluctant Saviour*, 151; also see, pp. 41–42.

pro-independence side had been vanquished. That view was so widespread
in Jakarta that in mid-1999 General Garnadi of the Home Affairs Ministry
warned that the government's optimistic attitude about the people's likely
choice might have been misplaced and that there needed to be a contingency
plan in the event Timorese people rejected the autonomy option.[70] Although
how much the President (and his closest civilian advisors) shared the belief
that East Timorese would choose to remain part of Indonesia was unclear,[71]
he was determined not to let East Timor be a lingering problem for Indonesia's future governments and wanted to offer the full range of options in
order to reach a permanent solution.

Subsequently, on January 27, 1999, Habibie's cabinet of ministers reap-
proved Alatas's ongoing Special Autonomy proposal along with the President's new decision to give the East Timorese people a "second option" of
choosing to be independent.[72] Even then, further negotiations between the
Indonesians and the Portuguese stumbled due to the fact that the Special
Autonomy was still on the plate "with the Indonesian delegation view-
ing... [it] as being accorded to a province of Indonesia and Portuguese side
regarding it as being conferred to East Timor as a non-self governing territory...."[73] Although not to the point of imperiling what was already on
the table, the Portuguese understandably wanted to make the best out of
the "second option" and succeeded to make preambular reference to Resolutions 1514 and 1541 on decolonization in the final agreement.

Fortunately for Portugal, President Habibie, several of his ministers, and
ICMI advisors were, for their own reasons, not enthusiastic about East
Timor's autonomy-based association with Indonesia. Whereas they feared
that the wide-ranging autonomy for East Timor would set a bad precedent

[70] Garnadi's memo ("Gambaran umum apabila Opsi I gagal" ("General Assessment if Option
I Fails") no M.53/Tim P4-OKTT/7/1999 of July 3, 1999) is differently interpreted by different scholars. Moore in "The Indonesian Military's Last Years in East Timor: An Analysis
of its Secret Documents," *Indonesia* 72 (October 2001): 33–34, and Fernandes in *Reluctant
Saviour*, 42–44, for example, claim that Garnadi believed that the people would choose
autonomy over independence. Robinson's most recent analysis, however, reveals that at the
time of writing, Garnadi's memo was more of a call for caution regarding the government's
optimism and warning for lack of contingency plan in the event of independence. Robinson,
"If You Leave Us Here, We Will Die," 133. All these scholars, however, agree that retired
General Sintong Panjaitan and General Feisal Tanjung were some of the key proponents of
the idea that the East Timorese people would choose autonomy. According to Fernandes,
that conclusion was based on the fact that more than two thirds of East Timorese participated in the sham Indonesian elections of June 1999 and that the majority of them voted
for ruling GOLKAR party.
[71] Given his ICMI background, it is likely that Habibie viewed East Timor as nuisance that
not only Indonesian could afford to let go but also would benefit from doing so, in the
same way that his fellow Muslim intellectual constituency saw East Timorese as ungrateful
bunch.
[72] Alatas, *The Pebble in the Shoe*, 152–153.
[73] Ibid., 156.

for the other Indonesian provinces, they believed that the East Timorese people would not opt to separate from Indonesia.[74] Yet, President Habibie's initial reaction was "Why should we continue to carry the political and financial burden of governing and developing East Timor... and then, after five or ten years, only to be told by the East Timorese: 'Thank you, but we now want to be independent'?"[75] Whatever the calculations, Habibie's dislike of the idea of special autonomy paved the way for the popular consultation in East Timor stipulated in the May 5 Accords between Indonesia, Portugal, and the United Nations.[76]

Referendum at Long Last

The different paths of the Eritrean and East Timorese independence movements merged in the immediate pre-independence days only to diverge again immediately afterward. Although both the Eritrean and East Timorese nationalists fought an arduous struggle for independence because of international collusion with Ethiopia and Indonesia, both movements sought the support of the international community without which they could neither hold referendum nor legalize the outcome. Nevertheless, the structural disparity between the international legal standing of the Eritrean and East Timorese independence movements played out in the kind and degree of international response the two received. Corresponding divergences were marked by the different international responses toward each, the local environments within which the referenda took place, and the political systems that emerged afterward in the two countries.

Legalizing a Foregone Conclusion in Eritrea

EPLF's May 1991 blitzkrieg securely placed Eritrea's landmass and coastline under EPLF control. Its extensive clandestine and grassroots networks in formerly Ethiopian-controlled towns fed into its field-based security apparatus to consolidate its grip on the entire country as the Provisional Government of Eritrea (PGE). These two combined with fresh excitement of freedom among Eritreans to facilitate the creation of an enabling stability for the PGE to carry out its functions from Asmara. With its entire military personnel ordered into barracks immediately after liberation and no weapons allowed into any of the towns, the PGE's control inside Eritrea remained subtle.[77] In Ethiopia, coordinated EPLF, EPRDF, and OLF onslaughts

---

[74] Ibid., 164.
[75] President B. J. Habibie quoted in Alatas, *The Pebble in the Shoe*, 149.
[76] United Nations, Question of East Timor. Report of the Secretary-General, A/53/951-S/1999/513, May 5, 1999.
[77] It was not uncommon, however, for people to be stopped or pulled over by security agents in civilian outfits to confirm their identities without even the people accompanying them noticing it. Having gone to Eritrea for the first time in September 1991, I witnessed many

shattered the Derg government and its defense apparatus, replacing it with the viable Eritrea-friendly coalition, that is, the EPRDF, in Addis Ababa. Overall, therefore, a stable environment prevailed that, to the satisfaction and praise of all international observers, enabled the Eritrean people to decide their future at long last and to live in peace with their choice afterward.

Determined to internationally legalize and legitimize their military gains, Eritrean leaders had long planned to hold referendum. Lacking the means and the necessary international support to hold the vote on its own, in 1992 the PGE filed request with the World Bank for a loan in the amount of US$ 25 million in order to run the popular vote. Because Eritrea was not a member, "the Bank determined it could participate if the loan were technically made to Ethiopia and passed on to the autonomous region of Eritrea, with Eritrea's agreement to assume full responsibility for the liability upon independence."[78] Neither military victory nor readiness to finance the referendum moved the United Nations and the OAU, however. Neither would witness the process and approve its outcome without Ethiopia's green light. Eritrean leaders appealed to the new Ethiopian government[79] over which they had far more significant leverage than the Eritrean commando and elite security units that were helping consolidate its hold on power in Addis Ababa and other Ethiopian towns.

In late 1991, Eritrean leaders brokered an agreement between the EPRDF coalition and the OLF, the second-strongest rebel force in post-Derg Ethiopia.[80] By interning OLF forces at remote camps, the agreement allowed the EPRDF's guerrilla army to turn itself into the national Ethiopian army and spared the country from having two victorious guerrilla armies competing for legitimacy. The EPLF strengthened the EPRDF's position within Ethiopia even further, it is alleged, by quietly withdrawing its guardianship of the agreement and abandoning the OLF to the EPRDF's surprise attack. The OLF was effectively disarmed and almost immediate paralyzed. The OLF was the final price the EPLF had to pay for Eritrea to earn the EPRDF's

---

such nonincident scenarios but did not realize what they were until the persons being asked told me what had happened. So professional was the EPLF security personnel that, looking back, those encounters were always respectful and quick. Nevertheless, where deemed necessary, brute security measures were easily brought to bear throughout Eritrea.

[78] The World Bank – Operations Evaluation Department, "Eritrea: Country Assistance Evaluation" (Report No. 28778, April 2004), p. 29.

[79] Former Eritrean Foreign Minister Haile Weldetensae, talk to Eritreans residing in the greater Los Angeles area, March 2000.

[80] Leencho Lata, *The Ethiopian State at the Crossroads: Decolonization and Democratization or Disintegration* (Lawrenceville, NJ, and Asmara: Red Sea Press, 1999). This former OLF leader offers the first, and so far the only of its kind, detailed firsthand account of the complex dynamics of OLF-EPRDF relationship in the early post-Derg Ethiopia.

blessing of the referendum, for its invitation of the OAU, and for the United Nations to verify the process and recognize its outcome.[81]

In a December 1991 letter addressed to UN Secretary General Boutros Boutros-Ghali, then President Meles Zenawi granted Ethiopia's approval of the Eritrean plebiscites, affirming "the people of Eritrea have the right to determine their own future by themselves . . . in a referendum."[82] This paved the way for an uncomplicated consummation of Eritrea's ascent to formal independence with UN and OAU verification of the process and approval of the outcome. The technical work for an internationally sanctioned initiation into sovereign nationhood still loomed on the horizon.

In April 1992, Eritrea's provisional government set up an independent commission to administer the referendum. Close to 2 million eligible voters (aged eighteen years and older) registered, and a record number of over 90 percent of them turned out to cast their votes between April 23 and 25, 1993. Local and international observers were consistent in their praise of the process's orderliness and transparency, and the popular anticipation before voting and the euphoria afterward. After observing voting in different locations, the Director of the Massachusetts-based Grassroots International Tim Wise wrote,

Everywhere, the story was the same. Despite having three days to vote, virtually every able-bodied voter in the country's . . . electorate braved long lines and a searing desert sun to vote on the first day of balloting. Overall turnout was estimated to be about 98%, including over 90% on the first day. One U.S. observer from the U.N. told me afterward, he never would have believed such a result if he hadn't witnessed the process himself. Another U.N. observer told me she had never seen such a meticulous process. . . . It may have been the most elaborate process in history every carried out to achieve a foregone conclusion.[83]

Indeed, with the Eritrean people's euphoria and national consciousness at unprecedented levels, the EPLF as the only power in Eritrea whose ideals and drive for independence impacted Eritreans everywhere and from all walks of life, and with a friendly government in Ethiopia, the outcome of a referendum was a foregone conclusion. What was also remarkable was that over 60,000 of the voters were Eritreans living in Ethiopia and among the most prominent international observers was the large, high-profile Ethiopian delegation led by then Prime Minister Tamrat Layne. On April 27, the

---

[81] In the longer term, however, EPLF's exclusive relationship with the TPLF/EPRDF deprived Eritrea of an alternative political force in Ethiopia when the two countries went to war in 1998.

[82] UN Doc. A/C.3/47/5 (1992), Ethiopian President Meles Zenawi to UN Secretary-General Boutros Boutros-Ghali, Dec. 13, 1991.

[83] Tim Wise, "Eritrea's Referendum on Independence. The Meaning of a Free Vote," http://archive.fairvote.org/reports/1993/wise.html.

referendum commission announced that 98 percent of the registered voters cast their ballot and 99.8 percent voted for independence. A month later, Eritrea joined the United Nations; three weeks earlier, Ethiopia had become among the first countries to recognize independent Eritrea.

"Liberation Came to East Timor like a Whirlwind"

Without renouncing armed struggle or laying down its weapons, the East Timorese independence movement had mobilized its domestic, regional, and international resources in order to relate to the outside world the appalling conditions of the East Timorese people. Whereas the totality of these efforts spurred the international community into action and involved Indonesians in exerting pressure – from within and without – on Jakarta, the latter did not relent until a combination of domestic and regional political as well as economic factors culminated in the end of the New Order with Suharto's resignation. Under pressure from all corners, his successor, B. J. Habibie, broke the self-righteous consensus of the Indonesian political elite regarding East Timor when he allowed the people there to decide their own future through Popular Consultation, as the Indonesians insisted the referendum should be called.

Article 2 of the May 5 Agreements requested the United Nations Secretary General "to establish, immediately after the signing of this Agreement, an appropriate United Nations mission in East Timor to enable him to effectively carry out the popular consultation." Accordingly, on June 11, 1999, the United Nations Security Council by its Resolution 1246 set up the United Nations Mission in East Timor (UNAMET) to administer the referendum. With the Modalities Agreement setting August 8 as the voting date, the world body's notoriously sluggish bureaucracy had to put together an unprecedented mission, under less-than-optimum security conditions. Having already appointed Ian Martin as the Special Representative of the Secretary General for East Timorese Popular Consultation, that is, the Dili-based UNAMET's chief, and Tamrat Samuel in charge of UNAMET in Jakarta before the end of May, Kofi Annan had set the mission on motion at a breakneck speed.[84]

Indonesian approach on the ground was so confusing that SRSG Ian Martin lamented afterward "[i]t was hard to know which was the real policy of the Indonesian government."[85] But a twofold approach is apparent,

---

[84] Many scholars and participants documented this phase of UN involvement on the East Timor question. The best, authoritative accounts remain Ian Martin's *Self-Determination in East Timor. The United Nations, the Ballot, and International Intervention* (Boulder, CO: Lynn Rienner Publishers, 2001) and Tamrat's "East Timor: The Path to Self-Determination" in *From Promise to Practice*, 197–230.

[85] Martin, *Self-Determination in East Timor*, 48.

one peaceful and another violent.[86] First, pro-autonomy parties emerged to canvass for votes in favor of staying within Indonesia. These are the Forum Persatuan, Demokrsi dan Keadilan (FPDK, Forum for Unity, Democracy and Justice) led by Domingos Soares and Barisan Rakyat Timor Timur (BRTT, East Timor People's Front) of Francisco Lopes da Cruz.[87] While active and retired generals in Jakarta were assuring President Habibie that the people of East Timor would choose to remain part of Indonesia, their colleagues in East Timor set another plan of thuggish action in motion. The latter track involved coercing people to swear oaths, threatening civil servants with suspension or dismissal should they reject autonomy, and finally using naked violence to eliminate pro-independence activists and terrorize the population into rejecting independence.[88] For that purpose, preexisting and new pro-Indonesian militias were trained, armed, and financed by the Indonesian military in East Timor.[89]

So widespread and blatant was the terror campaign that in April 1999 Gusmão called on FALINTIL to defend the people: "the situation has reached an intolerable limit... [and] I am compelled to authorize Falintil guerrillas to undertake all necessary action in defense of the population. . . . " He also called on his followers to begin a "general popular insurrection against the armed militia groups who have been killing the population with impunity under the indifferent eyes of the international community."[90] But, although it is said that FALINTIL Vice-Commander Taur Matan Ruak refused to follow through on those orders,[91] on the advice of his close associates as well as international actors, the CNRT President retracted that call.[92] Not only did that policy reversal rescue the fragile process from hitting a snag or altogether collapsing, but it also showed the one-sided violence that was being perpetrated by the Indonesian side.

The terror campaign continued unabated after the May 5 Accords in spite of Indonesia's commitment to ensure that the referendum was "carried out in a fair and peaceful way in an atmosphere free of intimidation, violence

---

[86] Tamrat, "East Timor: The Path to Self-Determination," in *From Promise to Practice*, 197–230.

[87] Although with limited support, Abilio Araújo also joined this effort by officially launching the pro-autonomy Timorese Nationalist Party (PNT) in July 1999.

[88] Martin, *Self-Determination in East Timor*, 43–45.

[89] See Geoffrey Robinson, "People's War: Militias in East Timor and Indonesia," *South East Asia Research* 9, no. 3 (2001):271–318, for a general historical and contemporaneous pattern of the use and abuse of militias by the Indonesian security forces across the archipelago (including in East Timor).

[90] "Falintil Resumes Their Mission in Defense of the People of East Timor," Jakarta, April 5, 1999, also quoted in Robinson, *"If You Leave Us Here, We Will Die,"* 107; and Alatas, *The Pebble in the Shoe*, 168.

[91] Interview with Dr. Carlos Gaspar (August 31, 2006, Lisbon, Portugal).

[92] Martin, *Self-Determination in East Timor*, 30; and Robinson, *"If You Leave Us Here, We Will Die,"* 107.

or interference inference" and because Jakarta remained "responsible for maintaining peace and security in East Timor" during the consultations. Indonesian security command let off leash their East Timorese militia allies to intimidate and terrorize the population and possibly even derail the process. The Indonesian military is, by most accounts, also believed to have actively taken part in the ravaging of East Timor both before and after the referendum.[93]

The violence rose at an alarming rate in the weeks preceding the planned vote to an extent that UNAMET advised UN Headquarters in July against proceeding with the registration process because the conditions on the ground failed to meet the security benchmarks that the Secretary General had laid out.[94] Nonetheless, all the involved parties were averse to delaying the vote for their respective reasons. President Habibie wanted to hold the referendum before the end of August, when the country's People's Consultative Assembly (MPR) was due to meet to elect a new president. Indonesia's western allies wished a speedy end to the process in order to not harm their relationships. Senior UN officials feared that Indonesia might back out of its commitments if the date were delayed. And, finally, aware of the unrealized Western Saharan referendum after POLISARIO conceded to Moroccan technical excuses in 1992 and agreed for a postponement, East Timorese nationalists were eager to go ahead with the registration and the referendum. In their view, because there was no mechanism for making the Indonesian military help end the militia violence (especially given that administration and security was left under Indonesian control), delaying the referendum would only have prolonged the suffering of the people and benefited those who did not wish to see the people exercise their right to self-determination.[95]

---

[93] Geoffrey Robinson's UN report, *East Timor 1999: Crimes against Humanity*, presented a compelling story of how the Indonesian military planned, financed, and supervised the terror campaign that mired the referendum in East Timor. So compelling was this work that the East Timorese CAVR appended it to its voluminous and groundbreaking report, *Chega!*, Part 12: Annex 1. The Joint Indonesian-East Timorese Truth and Friendship Commission (TFC) recently concluded its own report essentially agreeing with the findings of the CAVR and with Robinson. Although the release of the TFC report was awaiting President Susilo Bangbang Yudhoyono's approval, people close to the commission conveyed to me in mid-2008 that TFC commissioners and their consultants had confirmed Robinson's findings and in fact relied heavily on his report but refrained from indicating that to spare TFC's report the intense dislike that many powerful Indonesians have for Robinson. The latter's human rights advocacy and several years' tenure as the Amnesty International official responsible for Indonesia and East Timor had earned him the enmity of many of Orde Baru's operatives, with the result that he was barred from entering Indonesia for several years.

[94] Martin, *Self-Determination in East Timor*, 45ff.

[95] I am grateful to Geoffrey Robinson, Ana Gomes and Tamrat Samuel for much of the insider information during those difficult days. Also see Martin, *Self-Determination in East Timor*, 45–50; and Tamrat, "East Timor: The Path to Self-Determination" in *From Promise to Practice*, 197–230.

UNAMET faced a dilemma. "The stakes were high," wrote SRSG Martin.

To proceed with the consultation in the midst of violence could not only put the East Timorese and the UN's own staff at risk but also set the scene for the UN to sanction an outcome that was the result of intimidation. Yet to suspend the process risked handling victory to those who were bent on preventing the vote from taking place and losing what many East Timorese, including Gusmão, believed might prove the unique window of opportunity for them to determine their own future.[96]

UNAMET persisted in taking Indonesian leaders to task on their stated commitments, and a string of militia violence triggered broader international condemnation. Indonesian officials responded to pressure; they started to cooperate and violence declined briefly to allow the delayed registration to start just in time for the polling to take place before the end of August.

During the three-week registration period, more than 450,000 eligible East Timorese voters (aged seventeen and above) registered amid spiraling violence that UNAMET unfailingly documented, took up with Indonesian authorities, and reported to headquarters in New York. With more than 50 percent of the voters at the polling stations before they opened at 6:30 AM on August 30, Ian Martin relates how most of the stations finished processing their respective voters two hours before the official closing at 4:00 PM the same day.[97] The closing of the polling did not bring any reprieve to the atmosphere. In fact, a worse tension descended, and many pro-independence Timorese fled their homes, further swelling the internally displaced.

The D-day came on September 4 with the announcement of the outcome of the referendum. Of the 446,953 who cast their vote, 78.5 percent rejected autonomy within Indonesia and chose to be independent. The tension that had been rising in the preceding days imploded as pro-Indonesia militias went on a frenzy of killing and an uncontrolled rampage across the country. International observers and most foreign journalists had already left. A significant part of UNAMET's personnel had also been evacuated in anticipation of the escalated violence after the announcement of the results. The cantoned FALINTIL units grew increasingly restive and Vice-Commander Ruak requested Gusmão's approval to deploy in defense of the people. In a dramatic reversal of roles from mid-1999, Ruak pleaded for a green light while Gusmão insisted on FALINTIL staying in their assigned cantons. One of Gusmão's aides recalls how, during his house arrest in Jakarta, one of these heated conversation between the two resistance leaders ended with

---

[96] Martin, *Self-Determination in East Timor*, 50.
[97] Ibid., 90.

Gusmão threatening to resign should Ruak allow FALINTIL out. Agitated, Gusmão hung up the phone on the vice-commander.[98]

Nonetheless, sustained media attention on the spiraling violence with live coverage from the ground, the refusal of a few of UNAMET's international staff to evacuate, and UN and individual countries' high-level diplomacy, as well as that of Portugal and the Vatican, fixed outraged international attention on East Timor. Increased pressure, including from the World Bank and the International Monetary Fund that had been planning on an economic rescue package for Indonesia, compelled Jakarta to rein in its military's traditional intransigence and allow an interim International Force for East Timor (INTERFET) moved in to fill the gaping security void caused by Indonesian goading of and complicity in the militia violence.[99]

Albeit neither peaceful nor orderly as stipulated in Article 6 of the May 5 Agreements, Indonesia had to transfer authority in East Timor to the United Nations for the consummation of the process. This meant a new UN mission to shepherd the country to independence. But up to 1,500 people had reportedly been killed in the wake of the announcement of the referendum results. An entire population had become displaced, with tens of thousands herded across the border into Indonesia by fleeing pro-autonomy militias. Up to 90 percent of the country's rudimentary infrastructure had been destroyed. Civil service and all services ceased to exist. East Timor's struggle for independence had endured a final torturous trial, for which its people continue to demand justice and struggle for durable peace.

Conclusion

The Eritrean and East Timorese independence movements outdid Addis Ababa and Jakarta in winning the hearts and minds of the Eritrean and East Timorese peoples. The 1993 referendum in Eritrea and 1999 consultation in East Timor magnificently displayed that. Almost all Eritreans and more than two-thirds of East Timorese voted for independence. Nevertheless, the processes through which the two movements accomplished their goals

---

[98] Gusmão's orders notwithstanding, Cornelio Gama "L-7," one of the longest-serving and revered FALINTIL commanders, took a small force out of the cantons in pursuit of the pro-autonomy militias who had been ravaging the countrymen and townspeople alike. Although L-7 was quickly brought back into the barracks, his brief absconding and the almost mystical image he had cultivated among many superstitious and nonsuperstitious Timorese probably explain the government's rush to push him out of the independent country's force and into retirement along with many former members of FALINTIL.

[99] For the international diplomatic crescendo and coordinated pressure on Indonesia during the postreferendum violence in East Timor and the logic of international intervention, see Martin, *Self-Determination in East Timor*, 103–112; and Robinson, *"If You Leave Us Here, We Will Die,"* chapter 9, 184ff.

explain the environment within which the acts of self-determination took place and the immediate backlash (or absence thereof) that followed.

The shift in the thinking and practice of the Eritrean and East Timorese nationalist leaderships from isolated resistance to regionalized and internationalized approaches carried with them a potential strategic liability to the political psyche of the two peoples in question and their independent political systems. Coupled with the cutthroat domestic and regional rivalry that the Eritrean movement had to endure, the traditional neglect from Washington (and its allies), and eventual rejection by Moscow and its allies' jilting left their permanent marks on Eritrean political thinking. Every future interaction with the outside world came to be filtered through the sense of betrayal that these experiences had engendered.[100] Moreover, as the Eritrean nationalists were left with little choice but to look into their own capacities in order to carry on the fight, the fierce inward turn that they took incubated a philosophical epiphany – self-reliance and militarism. Unbeholden to any external interests, the Eritrean nationalists took by force what they could not achieve through international mechanisms and instruments. Moreover, while the growth of the EPLF meant the fruition of the worldview that gave birth to it, its success was a measure of the consolidation of its leadership atop a highly secretive and disciplined military organization bent on asserting its worldview against real and/or perceived odds, external and domestic. Eritrea's current monistic political landscape is a direct outcome of the nationalist movement's centralization of power, and its indoctrination and thorough disciplining of its followers.

In East Timor, by contrast, the leadership's centralizing thrust was inherently limited by its physical separation from its other branches, and CRRN, and later CNRT, had to make do with those limitations. Arguably, the structural inability of the leaders inside the country to keep a tight rein on all of its resistance apparatus, to instill its worldview and to enforce discipline gave birth to the fractured political landscape in present-day East Timor. Because of widespread distrust among the rival political parties and personalities, the East Timorese repeatedly called on the international community to investigate and arbitrate in domestic conflicts. That is also because high-profile UN involvement along with extensive international advocacy of solidarity groups on behalf of the East Timorese enabled the independence

---

[100] During his first address of the OAU and the United Nations as President of the independent State of Eritrea, Isaias Afwerki lambasted both organizations and lamented the community of states' silence when fundamental norms of the international order were being violated and neglecting the consequent suffering of the Eritrean people. He, nonetheless, pledged that Eritrea would play a constructive role to help ensure international peace, which it had been denied by the international community but it took on its own. Although factually accurate, the President's oratorical forays coupled with the Eritreans' historically contingent suspicion of the international order did not augur well for independent Eritrea's diplomacy.

movement there and the new republic to become more trusting of international benevolence toward them.

The disparity between the international legal standing of the East Timorese and Eritrean cases played out in the international support the two cases received. Having consistently classified East Timor as a non-self governing territory, it fell on the United Nations to hold the referendum when Indonesia allowed it to and oversee the birthing of an independent country when the majority of East Timorese rejected the Indonesian offer of constitutional internal autonomy. What the East Timorese accomplished with less reliance on violence owing to decisive international backing, Eritreans had set out to achieve, and achieved, by sheer force for lack of any meaningful international backing.

Although the world powers could not persist in rejecting the legitimacy of the Eritreans' quest for self-determination, the UN and the OAU (the African Union's predecessor) were neither moved by the swift Eritrean victory nor by the Provisional Eritrean Government's readiness to finance and administer the vote. Only after Addis Ababa's green light did the United Nations dispatched an Observer Mission to Verify the Eritrean Referendum (UNOVER) as did the OAU, fortifying Eritrean conviction that they went it all on their own. Needless to add, these disparate roles of the United Nations and, generally, the international community, on the decolonization of Eritrea and East Timor contributed to the divergent dynamics of interaction that the two sets of former independence fighters and their respective fledgling states were to have with the international community.

8

The Promise and Quandary of "Infusing Fresh Blood" and "Inaugurating New Politics"

> This leadership has been tested through fire and it is not going to relinquish power to a bunch of opportunists.
>
> Isaias Afwerki at one of the final meetings of EPLF's secret party, 1993

A successful grand strategy is like an edifice under permanent construction. It retains an element of fluidity, even after assuming a coherent form, in order to meet evolving challenges. Although the Eritrean and East Timorese grand strategies of liberation remained dynamic, at their height they were polar opposites – the Eritrean approach essentially military and the East Timorese strategy mainly diplomatic.

Unable to diplomatically reverse international inattention toward their situation, Eritreans took up arms. Eritrea's demographic, geographic, and geostrategic realities enabled the nationalists to sustain a protracted insurgency. That the United Nations had long absolved itself of further responsibility to its own plan and that both of the rival Cold War superpowers alternated in their active support of Ethiopia spurred the Eritreans to take the Ethiopian empire by force. Embracing self-reliance during their armed struggle, the Eritrean nationalists forged tactical and strategic alliances with Ethiopian rebel movements to defeat the Ethiopian government and replace it with an alternative that accepted Eritrea's ascent to independence. The end of the Cold War, and Ethiopia's consequent economic and military decline, compounded the state's moral and political decay, allowing the insurgents to triumph.

By contrast, East Timor's small demographic and geographic size and the collusion with Indonesia by its other neighbor, Australia, enabled Indonesia to physically isolate the half island from the rest of the world and nearly annihilate the resistance movement. Surviving nationalist leaders realized they would not overcome the Indonesian military through armed struggle and turned instead to defeating Indonesia through nonmilitary means. The East Timorese eventually forged alliances with Indonesian reformists and nurtured the attention of the citizens of many powerful countries in order to advocate for their basic human rights, and the respect of UN resolutions and international law. The East Timorese simultaneously increased the cost of occupation for Indonesia by making their towns ungovernable and the countryside unsafe for ABRI units. Jakarta dismissed this as a "pebble in the shoe" or "pimple on the face," but the resistance in East Timor and the international attention it attracted became a huge resource drain and diplomatic liability for Indonesia. These domestic and international environments, combined with the financial crisis that hit the Indonesian economy in the late 1990s and the political turmoil that attended it, broke Jakarta's resolve, and so it bowed to East Timorese demands.

However successful in their respective circumstances, the grand strategic choices made by the Eritrean and East Timorese independence movements had far-reaching consequences. The political landscapes of the newly independent countries, the nation-building challenges that they encountered, and continue to encounter, as well as their mechanisms of handling them, are as divergent as the grand strategies themselves.

Their domestic political systems also started out on different footings and grew farther removed from one another, in spite of their similar ambitions to infuse new blood into their politics or to inaugurate completely new politics. It is one thing to make euphoric promises after victory; it is quite another to stay the course of implementing them when faced with the challenges of realpolitik – postconflict day-to-day governance and fast-changing regional and global dynamics.

EPLF's Ominous Monopoly of Organized Politics in Eritrea

We have seen how trouncing Africa's largest and strongest military against regional and global odds required the Eritrean nationalists to develop the necessary political and military savvy to outmaneuver their foe. In the process of cultivating such an effective war machine, secrecy, centralization, and military discipline became deeply ingrained in the Eritrean political landscape. As a consequence, the newly independent Eritrean government became no less militaristic than the movement that gave birth to it. International isolation and betrayals (domestic and external as well as real and/or perceived) had turned the Eritrean independence movement austerely inward, and fierce self-reliance became the foundational principle of the State of Eritrea. As if to reinforce the self-imagining of the scarred psyche of the Eritrean body politic, world powers with vested interests in the Horn of Africa consistently afforded the new country no better than secondary place in their regional calculations. The cumulative outcome was that the international community lost any leverage regarding the direction that the independent country took.

Domestic Eritrean politics was doomed to stagger as organized politics remained an exclusive enterprise of the EPLF, without a balancing alternative voice. Vowing to avoid the fragmented politics of the past, the EPLF asked members of the various political organizations (mostly fragments of the defunct ELF who continued organized political existence outside Eritrea) to return to Eritrea as individuals and to participate in nation building and national reconstruction. Almost the entire first generation of fighters, including the surviving former members of the Sudanese army, embraced the call, returned to Eritrea, and threw their lot behind the EPLF government. Organizationally, Omar Buruj, the late Osman Saleh Sabbe's successor, for example, dissolved the ELF-PLF and asked his members to return to Eritrea if they so wished. Leading members of the ELF-PLF, like Taha Mohammed-Nur and ELM cofounder Mohammed-Seid Nawud, moved back to Eritrea as private citizens. Several members of ELF-Revolutionary Committee, like the other ELM cofounder Saleh Iyay and Eritrea's former ambassador to China Mohammed-Nur Ahmed, also returned, as did Herui Tedla Bairu. On the other hand, the ELF-Revolutionary Council (ELF-RC) that had almost merged with the EPLF in the second half of the 1980s refused to disband and return as individuals. The initial negotiations to arrange for their entry into Eritrea stalled when, en route to Asmara, the ELF-RC negotiators informed the EPLF that they had notified the U.S. and European governments of their planned arrival. Once suspended, those negotiations never resumed.

Once back in Asmara, however, several Eritreans, prominently two lawyers of different political persuasions and generations, called on the Eritrean leadership to open the political space to accommodate all nationalists, regardless of their previous political-organizational loyalties. Almost immediately after his voluntary return to Eritrea, ELF cofounder Taha Mohammed-Nur wrote to Eritrean leader Isaias Afwerki recommending that the government invite all Eritreans to a conference of national unity and give people the room for political activity, within the parameters of the rules that would be agreed upon at the conference. Around the same time, Paulos Tesfagiorgis, the former chief of the Eritrean Relief Association (ERA), personally appealed to Isaias to make Eritrea a nation where the rule of law prevailed and human rights were respected, so that it might become a model polity in the region. According to Taha, Isaias responded verbally by saying that many shared Taha's views and assured him that the government was seriously looking into the matter.[1] Although none of Taha's recommendations seem to have been allowed to get off the ground, Paulos's idea was more favorably received. The latter managed to launch an Eritrean Human Rights Institute in 1992, which got off to a promising start, training local observers for the Eritrean referendum.[2]

Despite those positive signs, however, the EPLF remained largely unencumbered by urgings from the peripheries of power for legal political pluralism. It inaugurated the single-party state of Eritrea where military discipline

[1] Interview with Taha Mohammed-Nur (September 17, 2005, Asmara, Eritrea).
[2] Interview with Paulos Tesfagiorgis (December 29, 2006, San Jose, CA).

reigned supreme, with a leadership base that entered a controversial phase of speedy transformation in 1993. The dust has not sufficiently settled for a definitive account, but it is presented in the following in its broad contours.

In May 1993, days before Eritrea's formal declaration of independence, liberation fighters rejected a plan, put forward by their leaders without any consultation or warning, to keep them in service without pay for an additional two years of postindependence transition. In their urgent request for the reversal of that policy, commando and other units in and around the capital Asmara shut down the airport, seized government offices and installations, and demanded that the leadership address them immediately. The drama ended within twelve hours in a climactic gathering with the President in Asmara Stadium. This meeting revealed Isaias's charisma, fearless determination, and perhaps even his single-handedness. A stream of fighters took the stage, filing their complaints about wasteful personal behaviors of the leaders – including drunkenness and prostitution – that explicitly and tacitly put them in sharp contrast to the ordinary fighters' impoverished lot, as well as that of their still-waiting families. In rejecting the leaders' new policy, one fighter even went so far as to deride them as resembling the other African leaders. He questioned who had chosen these leaders and allowed them to make such decisions regarding the fighters' long-term future. To a cheering crowd, the speaker asked, "*Men mera'at mes beleken tekwahala?*" which is Tigrinya proverb that translates to something like "Who said you were the bride for you to beautify yourself?"

In a pointed response to this challenge, Isaias announced that he was not interested in rolling forward and back at the helm of power: "*Ab seltan sheshey mebal.*" The response was a popular uproar: "We are not talking about you!" With the vote of confidence from this crucial constituency thus secured through consensus by acclamation, Isaias proceeded to reprimand their methods as "illegal" and "infantile" while at the same time placating them for the correctness of their cause. The proposed contentious policy was reversed on the spot; funds that had been allocated for national reconstruction programs were to be redirected for their salaries and arrears. The fighters jubilantly returned to their barracks the same night, calming fears (and anticipation among some Ethiopians) that the official proclamation of independence may be derailed. Quietly, the government picked up and arrested – for several years – the alleged ringleaders without any public pronouncements of what was happening. They were released upon receiving a presidential pardon attached to "punishment of conscience," the legal expression of which is as unknown as its practical limits have being untested.[3]

---

[3] Legendary revolutionary vocalist and musician Tekleab Kiflemariam (also known as Wedi-Tukhul) dismissed the whole incident as an intrafamily misunderstanding in which some members step out of line and the rest bring them back.

Toxic Infighting Within the 1960s Generation

Also in 1993, signs of an impending change in the Eritrean leadership base emerged in the run up to the Third Congress of the EPLF, when the former independence movement transformed itself into the People's Front for Democracy and Justice (PFDJ). Perhaps nudged out of several years of dormancy by the fighters' challenge, the secret People's Party, which had run the EPLF from behind the scenes, held nightly marathon meetings to prepare the ground for the Third Congress (held in early 1994). It is believed that the People's Party was suspended since 1987, although the exact details have never been confirmed. The accepted explanation for its suspension is that it had grown redundant by the second half of the 1980s when its membership – previously limited to a small "revolutionary core" – expanded, parallel to the EPLF's growth. Its work was done. It had successfully inculcated the desired political traditions – discipline and unquestioning sacrifices – across the Front's hierarchy; contained internal threats and slowly but surely eliminated external rivals and minimized international hostility.

The preceding claims leave at least two unresolved oddities and confirm something else. First and equally factual was that the secret party was suspended not long after a heightened centralizing drive had left the secretary general in direct command of key instruments of the state-in-waiting – armed forces, intelligence, information/media, and external relations. Second, it is curious that for nearly six years (the last two of which were after the victorious end of the independence war), none of the other leaders seems to have raised the fate of the institution that was so vital to their success. And finally, the President so reasserted his decisiveness and determination to get his way that not until he reconvened select leaders of the People's Party did the question of its suspension come up.

During the first of several meetings of the high-ranking cadres of the People's Party, jointly presided over by Isaias Afwerki and Haile "Deru'e" Weldetensae, former Defense Minister Mesfen Hagos demanded an explanation for who suspended the secret party in the late 1980s and why. The People's Party's Secretary General and Eritrea's President Isaias took responsibility for suspending the operations of the secret party, announcing, "Anyone who has questions about that will have to take it up with me." When no one took Mesfen's initiative any further, the President explained that the leadership had become "rotten" and needed an infusion of "fresh blood." Mahmoud Sherifo interjected, saying that if the leadership had actually turned rotten, then time had come for its replacement in its entirety. With little more said but much implied in the ensuing tension, the question was left hanging until the follow-up meeting.

At the start of the subsequent gathering, a question came from the floor as to what the resolution was for the problem of "rotten leadership." Tacitly retracting his statement, the People's Party Secretary General praised the tested leadership of the EPLF: "This leadership has been tested through fire and it is not going to relinquish power to a bunch of opportunists." Nonetheless, the spirit of infusing fresh blood into the EPLF leadership overtook the congress when the old guard was ejected from the newly inaugurated PFDJ's topmost positions, the Executive Committee. Most of the EPLF's old guard retained their ministerial posts in the government, but the President had an exclusive prerogative to appoint and dismiss any of them at will. That was exactly what happened when he fell out with most of his fellow old guard.[4]

The leaders presented a united face in galvanizing grassroots participation in the constitution-making process that dominated Eritrea's politics for nearly three years until 1997, when the Constitution was unanimously ratified. An important component to that democratic exercise was the open and highly competitive regional elections that, without much notice of the international community and as little local fanfare, preceded the May 1997 session of the Constituent Assembly. In a live interview on Eritrean television, Minister of Local Governments Mahmoud Ahmed Sherifo who administered and oversaw the elections acknowledged what little shortcomings they identified in the process that involved about 80 percent of eligible citizens, more than 90 percent of whom cast their ballot. He declared with smug confidence that the elections proved homegrown technical and logistical capacity to hold elections in one day across the country without outside help.

In spite of active and responsible popular participation in the early democratic experiments and the annual presidential discourses in response to questions sent directly from the public, however, there were hardly any institutionally sustainable discussions on day-to-day politics and long- and short-term policies of the state that involved the vast majority of the people. It could be in reference to this that the former military commander and chief of intelligence Petros Solomon reportedly scoffed, "What have we accomplished after independence? We only became people of more words and less deeds." To make matters worse, in 1998, a border conflict broke out with Ethiopia, leading to the postponement of the implementation of the constitution and large-scale mobilizing of the entire population and the Eritrean diaspora toward the war effort.

The dust has not fully settled to objectively decipher the causes and dynamics of a supposed border conflict that quickly endangered the very existence of Eritrea. In May 2000, Ethiopian forces broke through Eritrean

[4] Petros Solomon, one of the former EPLF leaders who fell out with the President, predicted what awaited them in a way that best resonates with how the daily practices of struggle during the liberation movement left their marks on Eritrean politics after independence: The President, he said, "will try to freeze us as members of the Central Committee [of the PFDJ] . . . and then court-marshal [*sic*] us according to the traditions and ways of doing things of the party [i.e., People's Party]." Petros Solomon in Dan Connell, *Conversations with Eritrean Political Prisoners* (Trenton, NJ: Red Sea Press, 2005), 132.

defenses and penetrated deep into Eritrean territory. The Ethiopians swept through a third of the country, in an area considered Eritrea's traditional breadbasket. With the bulk of Eritrean forces withdrawn to defensible lines without enduring heavy casualties, Ethiopian gains were untenable and they were wise to pull out shortly afterward. Since then the chances of Ethiopia permanently reconquering Eritrea – in whole or in part – have remained small. But the border incident resurrected the latent tension within Eritrean leadership, particularly among the EPLF old guard. Before it burst into the public domain through the fledgling private newspapers, a few concerned Eritreans in the diaspora got wind of the escalating acrimonious internal friction.

Former Minister of Information and Culture and renowned educator and historian Alemseged Tesfai came to the United States from Eritrea in the summer of 2000 as a keynote speaker at the annual Eritrean festivals across the country. In Washington, he linked up with Paulos Tesfagiorgis, who had also come from Eritrea. The two spoke to close colleagues, who themselves had either belonged to the EPLF top brass or were forerunners of solidarity and mass organizations, among them Dr. Assefaw Tekeste and Dr. Bereket Habte Selassie, of what was going on behind closed doors in Asmara. The group decided to offer to help negotiate a truce within the leadership. They invited a select group of Eritrean professionals from around the world and met in Berlin with the assistance of a foundation associated with the German Green Party. The outcome of their deliberations was a well-articulated, highly deferential but also critical letter addressed to President Isaias. The authors – popularly known as G 13 – reflected on what they believed was going on in Eritrea and its image around the world, while offering to help break the internal impasse and halt the slide into an unfavorable international position.[5]

Meanwhile, in May 2001, fifteen former leaders of the EPLF took their case to the entire membership of the successor political organization, the PFDJ,[6] and shortly afterward to everyone else, through Eritrea's private newspapers. The public record shows them questioning the strategic considerations behind the government's conduct of the 1998–2000 war with Ethiopia, and taking the President to task on the implementation of the 1997 Constitution and holding of elections. The public record also shows

---

[5] The letter is reproduced in its entirety in Bereket Habte Selassie, *The Wounded Nation. How a Once Promising Eritrea was Betrayed and its Future Compromised* (Trenton, NJ, and Asmara: Red Sea Press, 2011), 289–296. The letter was leaked reportedly before it arrived at the President's Office in Asmara and went viral in cyberspace. During its authors' meeting with the President, upon the latter's invitation, the leaking of the document is reported to have dominated the discussion that some said was not substantive.

[6] "An Open Letter to All Members of PFDJ," May 5, 2001. English translation of this letter signed by fifteen of the EPLF old guard and the attached correspondences between them and the President is reproduced in Connell, *Conversations*, 171ff.

that the President dismissed them from government positions, biding his time for a robust action without saying anything more than privately warning them that they were "mistaken".[7] FPDJ Secretary Alamin Mohammed Said, himself an EPLF old guard, led the government's first open rebuttal against the signatories of the letter to members of the PFDJ. In an interview with government newspaper *Hadas Erta*, Alamin accused the G-15 – as they came to be called – of treasonous defeatism and conspiracy.[8]

While the President was quietly ensuring that the entire chain of command of the security sector remained on his side, his new rivals' canvassing for support among civilian personalities had mixed outcomes. Whereas some politely declined to join the G-15, including questioning their democratic credentials, perhaps most tellingly the late Saleh Iyay ridiculed the G-15 for asking him to stand with them against the President, when they had not secured the support of even the Finance Police (Guardia di Finanaza, an institutional leftover from Italian colonialism that deals with financial crimes, and with the least military muscle).

In his rare interview with the private papers on the matter, the President went public only to say that his opponents were "empty vessels" making more noise. Shortly afterward, on September 18, 2001, he had them all arrested in one fell swoop on charges of treason and ordered the suspension of the private newspapers and arrest of nearly everyone who had worked for them. The arrest of the former resistance leaders, who, after independence, had held top government offices, permanently transformed and shrank the leadership pool and the near-simultaneous closure of the nascent free press nipped what many believed was a promising participatory political system in the bud. Although a court of law is yet (as of 2012) to see the merit of the charges against the arrested, who remain in prison, the charges against them include conspiring with the Ethiopian regime to overthrow the government.[9]

If the border dispute was at the heart of the renewed war with Ethiopia, Eritrea may have been vindicated by the final and binding ruling of the Eritrea Ethiopian Boundary Commission that awarded the flashpoint of the conflict – the village of Badme – to Eritrea in 2002. But tens of thousands

---

[7] This was said in a two-liner response the President penned down to Sherifo, who had by then become the undeclared spokesperson of the group corresponding with the head of state on behalf of the dissidents.

[8] *Hadas Erta* (the government newspaper run by the Ministry of Information), August 8, 2001.

[9] The Eritrean government accuses its former ministers that they used as intermediary former American National Security Advisor Anthony Lake, who, as President Clinton's envoy, had conducted shuttle diplomacy between Asmara and Addis Ababa to mediate. Lake and his team of National Security and State Department officials rejected that accusation and praised the jailed former Minister of Foreign Affairs Haile Weldetensae's leadership. But the "Lake Papers" in the Manuscript Division of the Library of Congress dubiously carries not a single correspondence between, or report of meeting with, the Eritrean Foreign Minister and Clinton's foreign policy team that was working on the Eritrea-Ethiopia conflict.

of deaths, hundreds of thousands of displacements, and four years later, the conflict took a different form with Ethiopia first rejecting the ruling outright, then accepting it "in principle," and finally accepting it "unconditionally" but demanding negotiations on what it considers are sticking points. Eritrea has refused to budge. It insists that the final and binding ruling is not up for negotiation and has accused Ethiopia of deliberately stalling in an attempt to cripple Eritrea's economy that had been badly hit by the conflict. Eritrea's response to Ethiopian prevarication was to turn inward yet again. It redirected its uniformed men and women, older than eighteen years of age, toward building and rebuilding expanded physical infrastructure.[10] The gains of doing so have been considerable but it came at a hefty price that can, in the long-term, prove more of a threat than Ethiopia's menacing military.

Since 1994, when the eighteen-month-long national service was instituted as a national duty of every adult citizen, only the first four batches had fulfilled their duties and discharged from service when the Eritrea-Ethiopia border war started in 1998. At that point, even these first four groups were recalled back into the army, and since then no national service batch has been discharged. During the two-year active conflict – in three rounds of large-scale, highly mechanized, and trench warfare across each of the three widely dispersed frontlines – Eritrean national service reservists proved their mettle with selfless courage, endurance, and initiative. As the standoff with Ethiopia dragged on and Eritreans from all walks of life started to feel squeezed by consequent deterioration of the economy, however, the morale of Eritrea's young warriors started to wane. Years of putting their lives and those of their families on hold exacted a toll on their discipline and patience, and many of them took to illegally crossing into Sudan and, ironically, Ethiopia, as stepping-stones to better lives elsewhere.

The statistics on Eritrean youth flight from the country are inherently patchy and sketchy; hence, there is no consensus about them. A 2007 source, for example, estimated that every week 120 young Eritreans arrived in one Sudanese refugee processing camp alone.[11] More recently, an official of the United Nations High Commission for Refugees (UNHCR) put the count of Eritreans fleeing into Ethiopia anywhere between 800 and 1,000 per month. His counterpart in the Ethiopian government claimed that the figure was actually between 1,200 and 1,500 Eritrean arrivals per month.[12] The Eritrean government has repeatedly dismissed the claims, plausibly stating that Eritrea would soon be depopulated – if it had not been already – if these figures were accurate.

---

[10] See Hagos "Kisha" Gebrehiwet's extensive interview on the Eritrean economy in *Hidri*, January-February 2005.

[11] http://www.unhcr.org/46cc4a974.html.

[12] http://allafrica.com/stories/201108051072.html.

But the youth who are fleeing Eritrea are leaving behind an impressive record of accomplishments that is at the heart of the country's successful combating of the 2011 droughts. USAID's Famine Early Warning System Networks (FEWS NET) warned that repeated rain failures have exposed vast part of Africa. More specifically, the Horn of Africa faced the worst drought in sixty years, reportedly affecting 10 million people across the region. With thousands of lives lost and livelihoods destroyed due to crop failures and/or decimation of livestock, the United Nations declared famine in some pockets. Since the end of the conflict with Ethiopia in 2000, Eritrea has been building dams, expanding irrigable farming, introducing heavy machinery in bulk, all to boost its agriculture and ensure food self-sufficiency, with promising returns.[13] With little to no relief aid from the outside world, Eritrea seems to have overcome the scourge of the draught on its own. Reconstruction and expansion of physical infrastructure have also continued and, coupled with Eritrea's domestic stability, the country has attracted considerable foreign investment into a promising mining sector. Proven large deposits of various precious minerals are expected to generate hundreds of billions of dollars in the coming decades, and the country is at the cusp of a mineral rush and an unprecedented economic boom. Nonetheless, as the long overdue demobilization is pushed back indefinitely, domestic political process/transition remains stalled, and immigration reform postponed, until the stalemated relations with Ethiopia is not resolved, not only will youth flight continue at Eritrea's own peril but the lagging political process is likely to forestall the much-anticipated economic progress, with dire long-term consequences to the country's stability.

The Onset of Fractured Democracy in East Timor

The church and other international groups supported the East Timorese nationalists on the premise that the resistance was all embracing and that its ideals were democratic in nature. To convince the East Timorese and the world (including Indonesians) that this was the case, the reoriented East Timorese movement allowed politically diverse proponents of independence to participate. This meant that independent East Timor would be more strongly inclined – perhaps even obliged – to accept a participatory liberal democratic form of government than it otherwise might have been. Moreover, high-level outside support for independence, and a predominantly donor-based economy in the formative years of independence, seemed too great for the country to stray far from the democratic ideals under which it

---

[13] In 2005 alone, more than one thousand tractors and agricultural machinery were introduced to expand agriculture across the country. On requesting official data on these developments in mid-2012, I was informed that the government was in the process of finishing the compilation of the data and would make it available for the public.

gained its independence. Nonetheless, the absence of political cohesion and discipline, and the lack of unified control of the state's coercive apparatus, inaugurated a fractured political system in East Timor.

Its unique predicament had compelled the East Timorese resistance movement to develop specialized fronts – guerrilla inside East Timor, clandestine in East Timor and Indonesia, and diplomatic in the rest of the world. The leadership inside the country was aware of the inherent limitations to instill discipline across the loose structures and amorphous constituencies with diverse and, sometime, nonconformist members. The guerrilla leaders were, thus, content before independence to coordinate the activities of people of varying backgrounds, capacities and outlooks, who operated the two other fronts. The vast leverage of the international community went untapped after independence when a group of leaders instituted an ill-advised political structure under which a single party dominated day-to-day politics, and the widely revered independence war leader ended up constitutionally bound to stay out of the affairs of government. With their common goal of independence achieved, this political structure contributed to the erosion of pre-independence intra-Timorese cooperation. This gave way to fierce, and sometimes violent, political contestation that frequently paralyzed the state.

Resurrecting the Politics of 1975 under UNTAET

Article 6 of the May 5 Agreements mandated the United Nations to assume authority in East Timor and implement the outcome of the referendum. Accordingly, on September 15, Security Council Resolution 1264 invited "the Secretary-General to plan and prepare for a United Nations transitional administration in East Timor." Pursuant to the Secretary General's October 4 request, the Security Council authorized the formation of the United Nations Transitional Administration in East Timor (UNTAET) to "provide security and maintain law and order;" "establish an effective administration;" "assist in the development of civil and social services;" "ensure the coordination of delivery of humanitarian assistance, rehabilitation and development assistance;" "support capacity-building for self-government;" and "assist in the establishment of conditions for sustainable development."[14] UNTAET, thus, became an unprecedented UN government of a territory, until East Timor was ready to look after itself.

Meanwhile, East Timorese leaders started to grapple with the prospects of their independent country post-UNTAET. During the first pan-Timorese gathering of October 1999 in Darwin, Gusmão, Ramos-Horta, Mário Carrascalão, João Carrascalão, and Mari Alkatiri held a closed-door meeting. Gusmão proposed, and Ramos-Horta and Mário Carrascalão seconded,

---

[14] United Nations Security Council Resolution 1272, October 25, 1999, http://daccess-dds-ny .un.org/doc/UNDOC/GEN/N99/312/77/PDF/N9931277.pdf?OpenElement.

the dissolution of FRETILIN and UDT in order to put to rest the division-fraught and blood-spattered past of the 1975 generation and to inaugurate an era of new politics. João Carrascalão and Mari Alkatiri, representing UDT and FRETILIN, respectively, rejected the idea.[15] This is not surprising given the fact that the first three leaders seemed to have been prepared to retire. But even if they were to stay in politics, as they eventually did, they had accumulated sufficient political capital to compete under different political party constellations: Gusmão as the most popular liberation war hero, Ramos-Horta as diplomat par excellence of the independence movement and Nobel Prize laureate, and Mário Carrascalão as a popular Indonesian-time governor who had secretly and crucially supported the independence movement. By contrast, João Carrascalão and Mari Alkatiri were neither prepared to retire from politics nor did they have much to show the increasingly young electorate without the historic parties that they helped found and lead.

FRETILIN leader Alkatiri was particularly unnerved by what a source said was Gusmão's excessive assertiveness – slamming the table to get his point across and telling the other leaders what they were going to do.[16] Such personality conflicts and different worldviews – themselves carrying marks of their 1975 ideological orientations and divergences during twenty-four years of resistance – set the scene for the independent country's rocky start, compounded by challenges of state and nation building among war-torn communities. Alkatiri and his right hand person Ana Pesoa allegedly saw danger ahead should Gusmão assume executive powers. Despite Gusmão's long political experience and strategic vision, Alkatiri's political finesse consequentially ensured that the former liberation leader became little more than a figurehead during the government's first term.

The internal dynamics of the resistance inside the country had relegated some of FRETILIN's founding leaders, who had been in Africa and Australia, to a less significant second tier in the nationalist movement, accentuated by their physical and temporal distance. But these leaders did not lose their political edge. Since the mid-1990s, they had been preparing for a post-independence political contest. They cemented their leadership of FRETILIN inside the resistance movement by inviting Mau Hodu from East Timor to Australia in 1998 to attend their last meeting before independence. At that moment, Mari Alkatiri was elected along with Mau Hodu, Ma'Hunu, and Francisco Guterres "Lu-Olo" to form FRETILIN's reorganized

---

[15] Interview with João Carrascalão (June 28, 2006, Dili, East Timor).

[16] Four months prior to Darwin summit, Sara Niner, *Xanana: Leader of the Struggle for Independent Timor-Leste* (Melbourne: Australian Scholarly Publishing, 2009), 195, has the following to say about the first gathering of CNRT leaders in June in Jakarta, at Gusmão's Salemba prison house: "CNRT leaders from Mozambique, Portugal, Australia and Timor all jammed into the tiny Salemba lounge room and held a 'consolidating meeting'. They sat in the stifling heat, receiving order from their Commander face-to-face for the first time. For some his military-style leadership and the discipline he expected was a shock."

leadership.[17] On Mau Hodu's disappearance and Ma'Hunu's stroke, which left him incapacitated, Lu-Olo remained the only legitimate successor to FRETILIN's top leadership inside the country with Mari Alkatiri outside.

Immediately after the October 1999 Darwin meeting of East Timor's top leaders, FRETILIN leaders from the diaspora joined their counterparts inside East Timor and started rebuilding FRETILIN structures in earnest. Prominently, Ana Pesoa, who had lived in Mozambique since 1976, was instrumental in recruiting almost all of the members and leaders of the Dili-based clandestine front as forerunners of FRETILIN's grassroots revitalization.[18] In June 2000, FRETILIN held a major conference for its political cadres to help socialize the former diaspora-based leaders with those inside, and to cement their bond. While thus consolidating its separate party infrastructure, not only did FRETILIN remain within CNRT but it also played active part in the National Consultative Council (later the National Council) that was formed to represent East Timorese parties and interests in interacting with UNTAET.

Secretary-General Kofi Annan had appointed his longtime friend and veteran of many UN peacekeeping missions, the Brazilian Sergio Vieria de Mello, to be his special representative responsible for UNTAET. During UNTAET's tenure between November 1999 and May 2002, de Mello was empowered as "Transitional Administrator...to enact new laws and regulations and to amend, suspend or repeal existing ones."[19] In spite of UNTAET's slow start (compared to UNAMET and INTERFET), its overly broad mandate, the dire conditions on the ground and several other personnel and infrastructural challenges, the special representative and his administration did well to bring East Timorese into the governance structures before handing authority over to them.

In discharging his duties by "consult[ing] and cooperat[ing] closely with the East Timorese people," de Mello took several consequential steps. In July 2000, UNTAET formed the East Timor Transitional Administration (ETTA) composed of nine ministries, five of which were led by East Timorese. Although some are critical of the special representative,[20] that move started the gradual transfer of power to the East Timorese, giving them hands-on experience in governance, before their complete assumption of power. UNTAET then started preparing for Constituent Assembly elections of August 30, 2001. In the run up to the elections, FRETILIN withdrew from CNRT in order to compete independently for political office.

---

[17] Interview with Estanislau da Silva (June 6, 2008, Dili, East Timor).
[18] Interview with Gregorio Saldanha (July 11, 2006, Dili, East Timor).
[19] Security Council Resolution 1272
[20] João Carrascalão (interview, June 28, 2006, Dili, East Timor), who held the first Infrastructure portfolio accused de Mello of favoring FRETILIN and traces his affinity to his early appointment in Mozambique when he befriended FRETILIN leaders like Mari Alkatiri who lived there during the entire period of Indonesian occupation.

Besides diligent grassroots work, FRETILIN arrogated the entire legacy of the anticolonial struggle and accompanying nationalist symbols for itself. As already discussed, in midcourse, the nationalist movement embraced all pro-independence East Timorese and came under non-FRETILIN leadership. To the chagrin of Gusmão and other leaders, the postoccupation FRETILIN read history differently and succeeded in convincing the electorate. Having long withdrawn their membership – in the interest of the nationalist cause – Gusmão and Ramos-Horta now found themselves with little to no say on what FRETILIN could and could not do to win elections.

Recognizing this, Ramos-Horta says that he advised Gusmão to turn CNRT into a political party and create FRETILIN-CNRT equilibrium. But Gusmão dissolved the umbrella organization to the dismay of those who found themselves in a weak opposition to FRETILIN along lines not too different from 1975 with few exceptions. Almost eight years later, newly elected President Ramos-Horta sounded angry talking about what he called was "a mistake by Xanana [Gusmão]. He did it unilaterally... which was typical of Xanana at that time."[21] The remaining politicians launched their respective political parties: João Carrascalão had already started reviving UDT bases; Francisco Xavier do Amaral relaunched ASDT (FRETILIN's predecessor); Mario Carrascalão attracted a younger generation of former UDT families and former student activists, to launch the new Social Democratic Party (PSD); almost all of the former Indonesia-based clandestine activists of RENETIL formed the Democratic Party (PD) under Fernando Lasama and so on. Gusmão gravitated toward PD, and the latter did hope that he would join them, but neither did he join them nor did his sympathy for them make much of an impact at the ballot box – despite their energy and appeal to many of those who came of age under Indonesian occupation. Lacking FRETILIN's history, mobilizing experience, and early and painstaking political canvassing, no other party stood a chance.

Taking sixty-five of the eighty-eight seats, FRETILIN won the elections by a landslide. In the short-term, such a victory enabled FRETILIN Secretary General Mari Alkatiri to become the Chief Minister of the first all-Timorese Transitional Government, responsible for the East Timorese Public Administration that replaced ETTA. In the long-term, the overwhelming majority in the Constituent Assembly afforded FRETILIN free rein – under UNTAET's watch – to lay out the constitutional framework of political pluralism that best served its interests. Repeatedly outvoting Gusmão during the constitution-making process, FRETILIN statecraft vested all the executive powers on the prime minister, who derived from the parliamentary majority, with a figurehead president who would be directly elected by voters. Without a party base, the most popular liberation war hero Gusmão stood no chance

---

[21] Interview with President Jose Ramos-Horta (June 5, 2006, Dili, East Timor).

of assuming executive powers as prime minister. In a country where the majority of people had only known Indonesia's strong presidency, Gusmão was safely relegated to the largely ceremonial position of president in East Timor because most of the people would vote for him.[22] But those who underestimate former guerrillas do so at their own peril.

For a number of additional reasons unavoidable under the circumstances, independent East Timorese politics got off on a rocky start. To begin with, FRETILIN turned the Constituent Assembly into East Timor's first National Parliament,[23] which angered the opposition who also wrongly accuse FRETILIN of contravening its promises of the pact of national unity.[24] At the end of UNTAET's mandate in May 2002, a FRETILIN-dominated legislature and government took over and started running the country in a way that left everyone else (and even some within FRETILIN) feeling as though they had no room in the country's politics.[25] FRETILIN's exclusive grip on political power (which was not illegal but politically imprudent in a divided and fragile postconflict society) and its nonchalance toward – and even blatant scorn for – the opposition only helped make it a target of popular anger about postindependence challenges, some of which were not of its making: the language question, demobilization of veterans, continuing poverty and soaring unemployment, and justice for pre-independence crimes, among many others.

The majority of East Timorese came of age under Indonesian occupation, speaking Melayu (Bahasa Indonesia).[26] But in early 2000, the Lusophone-dominated CNRT leadership decided to adopt Portuguese (spoken by

[22] That actually turned out to be the case, because Gusmão won the first presidential election with a landslide against Francisco Xavier do Amaral, who claims to have entered the race to give the elections an element of competition.

[23] FRETILIN used its majority to push through a constitutional clause that provided for the transformation. Section 167, No. 1 of the Constitution states that "The Constitutional Assembly shall be transformed into a National Parliament with the entering into force of the Constitution of the Republic."

[24] As a political affairs officer for the new UN peacekeeping mission in the aftermath of the 2006 conflict (UNMIT), I was assigned to discuss with the political parties a pact of nonviolence among them during the 2007 national elections. All of the opposition parties bitterly recalled what they continued to believe was FRETILIN's betrayal of the promises of the 2001 pact. But nowhere in that pact was a suggestion that the winner would form a government of national unity.

[25] While all members of the opposition parties are unanimous on this question, at the height of the 2006 crisis, many FRETILIN middle- and high-ranking cadres conceded privately that their party could and should have done more to accommodate the other parties' complaints – at least as a political move to combat the growing perception that FRETILIN was authoritarian.

[26] The widespread use of the Indonesian language is reflected in the Indonesian version of the final report of CAVR is authoritative in the event of controversy with either the English or the Portuguese versions.

less than 1 percent of East Timorese) as the official language.[27] The East Timorese Constitution makes a transitional stipulation that English and Indonesian were "working languages within the civil service side by side with official languages [Portuguese and Tetum] as long as deemed necessary."[28] Nonetheless, in early 2004, the East Timorese court system introduced what came to be called as the Language Directive that made it incumbent on all litigants to use the official languages – so long as Tetum remained insufficiently developed, this meant the Portuguese language.[29] Whereas this move could restrict access of poor ordinary citizens to the country's justice system, the use of Portuguese in Parliament is believed to significantly reduce the level of debate among the non-Lusophone parliamentarians during legislative deliberations – an advantage to the concentrated Portuguese-speaking FRETILIN leaders.

Popular expectations that justice would be meted out to those who had committed crimes under the Indonesian occupation were frustrated by the United Nations' failure to prosecute "the big fish," and East Timorese and Indonesian leaders' giving precedence to harmonious relationships. Both Indonesian and international inquiry commissions into the pre- and post-ballot violence in East Timor separately reached similar conclusions: that crimes against humanity had been committed, particularly by Indonesian-funded rogue militias who attacked and murdered pro-independence East Timorese, and destroyed their property before and after the August 1999 vote.[30] Accordingly, Jakarta formed an Ad Hoc Human Rights Tribunal with the aim of bringing those responsible to justice, while UNTAET established the Special Panels for Serious Crimes within Dili District Court.

Both are widely considered to be failures.[31] Of those whom KPP-HAM found responsible, only a few were actually investigated and indicted; and

---

[27] Interview with Joaquim Fonseca "Ruso" (May 6, 2006, Dili, East Timor); Damien Kingsbury, "Political Development," in *East Timor: Beyond Independence*, ed. Damien Kingsbury and Michael Leach (Clayton, ST: Monash University Press, 2007), 23; Sara Niner, "Martyrs, Heroes and Warriors: the Leadership of East Timor," *East Timor*, ed. Kingsbury and Leach, 114. Ruso and all former clandestine activists understand the political implications for the older generation to adopt Melayu as the official language. They nonetheless think it a mistake to impose Portuguese on 99 percent of the population and believe that it is destined to change in due course.

[28] Constitution of the Democratic Republic of Timor Leste, Sections 13 and 159.

[29] Kerry Taylor-Leech, "Sustaining Language Policy and Language Rights: Where to from Here?" in *East Timor*, ed. Kingsbury and Leach, 246.

[30] These are the Indonesian Commission of Inquiry into Human Rights Violations in East Timor (KPP-HAM) that the National Commission for Human Rights launched in September 1999, and the International Commission of Inquiry on East Timor set up by the United Nations Human Rights Commission in October 1999.

[31] The best critique of both courts is by UC Berkeley's David Cohen, *Intended to Fail. The Trials before the Ad Hoc Human Rights Court in Jakarta* (International Center for Transitional Justice, ICTJ, 2003): http://ictj.org/sites/default/files/ICTJ-Indonesia-Rights-Court-2003-English.pdf; and "'Justice on the Cheap' Revisited: The Failure of the Serious

even then they were acquitted on first trial or on appeal. The only jail sentence that seemed to stand, against East Timorese militia leader Eurico Gueterres, was later repealed, and he was set free before serving his sentence. The hybrid tribunal in Dili performed better in indicting close to four hundred suspects, including General Wiranto. Nevertheless, with Jakara refusing to recognize the court and cooperate in implementing the arrest warrants, more than three hundred of the indicted were out of the court's reach in Indonesia. The remaining East Timorese were, in the grand scheme of things, lower-level functionaries, and foot soldiers of bigger forces.

UNTAET Regulation No. 2001/10 established the Comissão de Acolhimento, Verdade e Reconciliação de Timor-Leste (CAVR) to, among other things, establish past human rights violations, promote reconciliation and "support the reception and reintegration of individuals who had caused harm to their communities. . . . " Where it deemed appropriate, CAVR was also mandated to recommend for prosecution suspects of more serious crimes. Whatever its weaknesses – substantive or methodological – CAVR helped communities confront their troubled past and accept the wrong doers back, upon the latter's expression of remorse. It also reliably profiled the violations and their circumstances, producing a historic and sobering document that might help prevent future crimes. The evidence that CAVR presented was enough to seek the indictment of Indonesian perpetrators of serious crimes. As one commissioner put it to me confidentially, however, realpolitik relegated CAVR's findings to no more than a tool that only NGOs and the international community can use to bring the perpetrators to book. Dili and Jakarta had given precedence to political reconciliation and friendship instead.

As CAVR prepared to launch its monumental report titled *Chega!* (*Enough*), Indonesia and East Timor launched a dubious joint Commission for Truth and Friendship (CTF) to establish the conclusive truth (*kebenaran akhir*) about the violations, assign "institutional responsibility," and make recommendations on how best to build lasting friendship between East Timor and Indonesia.[32] Although CTF was intended to deflect international pressure for justice, the commission's final report surprised many by confirming that crimes against humanity had been committed, finding TNI and the civilian Indonesian government structures institutionally responsible, refusing to grant amnesty to any individual, and – perhaps most importantly – leaving open the possibility of future trials of those who bore individual and command responsibility. Nonetheless, whereas Dili's emphatic rejection seemed to dampen prospects of an international tribunal, East Timorese

Crimes Trials in East Timor," *AsiaPacific Issues* No. 80, East-West Center, Honolulu, HI (May 2006).

[32] *Per Memoriam Ad Spem. Final Report of the Commission of Truth and Friendship (CTF) Indonesia – Timor-Leste* (2008).

leaders continue to add insult to their aggrieved people's injury by commuting sentences and granting amnesty to those who had been convicted and were serving time.[33] They continue to bend backward in order to accommodate Indonesia, even short-circuiting the young country's nascent judicial process.[34]

The future of FALINTIL and independent East Timor's armed forces became a sensational issue under UNTAET and nearly nose-dived the country into civil war four years after UNTAET closed shop. At the outset, the East Timorese were not unanimous on the need for, and mandate of, a national army with even CNRT's leaders (including Gusmão and Ramos-Horta) erring on the side of having a demilitarized state.[35] International actors were also divided between those (mainly INTERFET) who looked on FALINTIL as a party to the conflict that should be disarmed like all armed civilian groups,[36] and others who feared the political repercussions of interfering in such a sensitive question. Some observers of the independent country, however, continue to argue that the new army was nothing more than a job creation project for some of the former guerrilla fighters.[37]

Only when INTERFET tried several times to forcibly disarm FALINTIL – confrontations that undermined its command structures and threatened to humiliate the liberation army – did Gusmão seem to change his opinion about a national army. After an INTERFET – FALINTIL confrontation and a subsequent attempt by the former to disarm the latter in early October, Gusmão lashed out at the peacekeepers' indiscretion: "I am the Commander of Falintil, InterFET will have to negotiate with me." He went on to reject INTERFET commander General Casgrove's demand to disarm and

---

[33] For an excellent up-to-date overview thus far of all the local and international efforts to bring the question of impunity for crimes against humanity to a just conclusion, see Robinson, *"If You Leave Us Here, We Will Die,"* 205ff.

[34] A prominent example that outraged many is the release of Laksaur militia leader Maternus Bere who had been indicted for the September 6, 1999 Church massacre in Suai (Covalima district). On the basis of a 2003 warrant for his arrest, East Timorese police took him into custody on August 8, 2009, when he quietly returned from Indonesia. Upon Indonesian pressure, the President and Prime Minister handed him back to the Indonesian Embassy in Dili three weeks later. "East Timor defends Indonesian's pardon," September 2, 2009: http://www.aljazeera.com/news/asia-pacific/2009/09/20099251144407187.html; "Maternus Bere Indicted for Crimes Against Humanity in Suai Church Massacre and other Laksaur Militia activities: Arrested by PNTL, then Released to Indonesia by Timor-Leste Political Leaders," November 13, 2009, http://www.laohamutuk.org/Justice/99/bere/09MaternusBere.htm.

[35] Niner, *Xanana*, 196. This should not be taken to imply that these leaders had differences on FALINTIL's legacy. In fact, both challenged INTERFET in defense of FALINTIL's legitimacy as a liberation army.

[36] "An Overview of FALINTIL's Transformation to F-FDTL and its Implications," *La'o Hamutuk Bulletin* 6, no. 2 (April 2005): http://www.laohamutuk.org/Bulletin/2005/Apr/bulletinv6n1.html.

[37] Kingsbury, "Political Development," 25.

demanded instead to be treated as an "army of liberation and not as a band of bandits . . . We were never involved in acts of terrorism." Likewise, several senior commanders of the liberation army felt their legacy threatened and authority undermined.[38] This marked a turning point, when Gusmão came to foresee a post-independence role for FALINTIL, considering it an indispensable symbol of national pride.

Meanwhile, UNTAET had altogether considered the matter beyond its mandate. Not until the physical living conditions in their consolidated cantonment in Aileu[39] turned FALINTIL nearly rebellious did the international community move to contain the potentially troublesome question. The earliest drive to disarm, demobilize, and reintegrate (DDR) former fighters, thus, started as a "political process with a political aim – to prevent FALINTIL from becoming problematic"[40] instead of a genuine process of transitioning victorious combatants to a dignified civilian life with alternative means of supporting themselves and their families.

DDR projects succeeded in their immediate objectives but did not resolve – nor has the government – the long-term veterans question that took on important moral and political significance to the country's long-term stability.[41] DDR programs mostly excluded the tens of thousands who fought for independence on the other fronts (mainly the clandestine front). Nor did it satisfy those who were targeted, not least because some of them wanted to stay in the force that was being formed. By then, Gusmão and his top military lieutenants had set their minds on preserving FALINTIL's legacy by establishing a successor national army.

UNTAET and CNRT determined to establish a 1,300-strong army, made up of 650 former FALINTIL fighters and an equal number of fresh recruits from across the country. Aptly called FALINTIL-FDTL (Forças Armadas de Defesa de Timor-Leste or Timor-Leste Armed Forces), the composition of the initial 650 was internally determined by FALINTIL and CNRT, leaving

---

[38] Niner, *Xanana*, 208.

[39] In the run-up to the referendum, the close to two thousand FALINTIL guerrillas were cantoned in several locations across the country, which were later consolidated into one at Aileu after TNI withdrew and INTERFET took over.

[40] An unnamed official involved in the 2000–2001 FALINTIL Reinsertion Assistance Program (FRAP), quoted in Gordon Peake, "What the Veterans Say: Unpacking Disarmament, Demobilization and Reintegration (DDR) Programs in Timor-Leste" (University of Bradford's Center for International Cooperation and Security, July 2008), 11. Edward Rees, "UNDER PRESSURE: FALINTIL – Forças de Defesa de Timor Leste, Three Decades of Defence Force Development in Timor Leste 1975–2004," Center for Democratic Control of Armed Forces, Geneva, 2004.

[41] Edward Rees, "The UN's failure to integrate Falintil veterans may cause East Timor to fail," *On Line Opinion*, September 2, 2003: http://onlineopinion.com.au/print.asp?article=666.

See also "Observations Regarding the RESPECT Program in Timor Leste," *La'o Hamutuk Bulletin* 5, no. 5–6 (December 2004): http://www.laohamutuk.org/Bulletin/2004/Dec/bulletinv5n5.html.

some of the discharged fighters discontented by the decision.[42] Controversially, famous former FALINTIL commander and leader of Sagrada Familia Cornelio Gama L-7 led an association of ex-combatants to protest their treatment. They found an ally in CPD-RDTL that claimed loyalty to the unilaterally declared independent republic of 1975 and its leadership, in which Rogerio Lobato had held the defense portfolio.[43] Increasingly marginalized from the resistance before independence, Lobato sought to make himself relevant in state and government structures by piggybacking on the ex-combatants challenging the fledgling army's composition and on the CPD-RDTL's of the legitimacy of the state.

To avoid making him an enemy of the state, the new government brought Lobato onboard as Minister of Interior, responsible for the police. At Gusmão's insistence, the police had recruited hundreds of former Indonesian police officers.[44] Lobato earnestly began building an armed powerbase of layered units within PNTL, which was also hoped to counterbalance F-FDTL that was reportedly loyal to Gusmão.

This fluidity came to a head in early 2006 when 591 of the newly recruited F-FDTL soldiers from the ten western districts went on strike against and petitioned (hence the Petitioners) for an end to their unfavorable living conditions and promotions, that they blamed to the regionalism of the commanders.[45] Upon the Petitioners' refusal to heed orders to return to their barracks, then F-FDTL commander General Taur Matan Ruak – with the approval of Prime Minister Alkatiri – dismissed the entire group in one fell swoop in mid-March. Gusmão called the decision a mistake that they all had to live with, but went on to identify with the Petitioners and called on the government to find a sustainable solution to the root causes of the problem. Abetted by intellectuals and businesspeople from the western districts, the Petitioners continued to protest and were joined by thousands of unemployed youth in Dili when their peaceful five-day demonstration, in front of the government palace, turned violent. The Prime Minister called

---

[42] As early as 2003, Edward Rees warned of the consequences of the nepotism-tainted selection of a third of FALINTIL that formed the core of F-FDTL. "The UN's failure to integrate Falintil veterans may cause East Timor to fail," *On Line Opinion*, September 2, 2003, http://onlineopinion.com.au/print.asp?article=666.
    Also see Rees, "UNDER PRESSURE: FALINTIL."

[43] Interview with Antonio Thomas Amaral da Costa, also known as Aitahan Matak (May 15, 2006, Dili, East Timor).

[44] The public moral dilemma of recruiting those who had been in active service of the erstwhile oppressive occupier aside, one should not discount the possibility that former members of the Indonesian Police (PolRI) clandestinely supported the independence movement in one form or another of which only the topmost leaders of the Clandestine Front can give fuller account.

[45] This along with the President's speech of March 23, 2006 harked back to historical dichotomy between the Kaladi in the west and Firaku in the east that had also briefly emerged during the resistance days.

on F-FDTL to restore order and a few days later the commander of the navy and military police Major Alfredo Reinado deserted from the army in protest of government mishandling of the Petitioners. Reinado claimed that he received his orders from the President and continued to act under his orders.[46]

Security broke down even further with several armed groups operating simultaneously. On one hand, F-FDTL and PNTL sought to rein in the lawlessness, separately and in coordination with each other. On the other hand, Interior Minister Lobato illegally armed a group (led by a certain Vicente da Conceicao, also known as Railos) under the guise of helping restore order. Major Reinado's ambush of F-FDTL and PNTL units, Railos's attack on government soldiers and F-FDTL's arming of loyal civilians followed each other at dizzying speed, which ultimately ended in a bloody confrontation between the army and the police. On May 25, F-FDTL and their civilian allies gunned down unarmed PNTL officers who were been escorted by UN officials out of the confrontation, effectively dismantling the police force.[47]

East Timor's constitution was undermined, its political system and state institutions were shaken to their base and fractured, and the poverty-stricken population was pillaged by yet another cycle of physical insecurity. Unable to maintain a peaceful consummation of its birth into liberal democracy, the nearly collapsing East Timorese state called on international forces and UN Police to maintain law and order.[48] Nevertheless, and despite the divisions among them, East Timorese political leaders have shown, yet again, remarkable resilience and adaptability in keeping the country from teetering on the verge of anarchy. President Gusmão demanded and secured the resignation of the defense and interior ministers and took on both positions personally, which he retained entering the 2012 elections more than five years later. Three weeks later, he demanded the Prime Minister's resignation and had him replaced with then Foreign Minister Ramos-Horta.

What was apparent throughout this chaotic phase was the conflict between the powerful, methodical, and taciturn Prime Minister and constitutionally weak but impatient-for-change, passionately involved, populist

---

[46] Interviews (telephone, May 24, 2006; and in-person on June 25, 2006, Maubessi, East Timor). He demanded the resignation of the Prime Minister only to continue as a renegade in command of most of the Petitioners after Alkatiri's resignation and the mid-2007 elections that brought Gusmão as Prime Minister and Ramos-Horta as President.

[47] For a reliable account of what transpired between April and May 2006, see "Report of the United Nations Independent Special Commission of Inquiry for Timor-Leste" (Geneva, October 2, 2006) that the United Nations High Commissioner for Human Rights conducted upon the request of then Foreign Minister Ramos-Horta.

[48] With Australian forces arriving as early as May 26, Malaysian, New Zealander, and Portuguese peacekeepers followed soon afterwards as the United Nation launched a revamped mission with a renewed peacekeeping mandate, the United Nations Integrated Mission in Timor-Leste (UNMIT).

President. The two leaders' fundamental differences on how to run the country and the domestic economy are best captured in their messages on the 2006 UNDP Human Development Report. Without denying the challenges, Alkatiri wrote how during the "three short years since independence, Timor-Leste has a solid National Development Plan which helps to guide the country's vision and future." As if to rebut the Prime Minister, President Gusmão's message concluded by stating "Timor-Leste has the resources to reduce poverty or even eliminate it. But setting a goal is one thing and achieving it is quite another," suggesting government failure in translating it's NDP into action to alleviate poverty.[49]

This also reflects the different experiences of the two leaders during the period of Indonesian occupation. Alkatiri was informed by the failures of the former Portuguese colonies in Africa – Mozambique and Angola, in particular – where imposed impractical programs and widespread corruption had long held back development. It is little wonder that, given nascent East Timor's lack of structures to retain financial injections into the economy, his government erred on the side of frugality in terms of cash transfers, preferring to gradually invest in public assets instead. In light of the people's impatience for the dividends of independence and betterment of their lot – an impatience not only shared but also personified by the President – Alkatiri was blamed for letting East Timor's petroleum income sit in U.S. Treasury bonds. By the time of his forced resignation, these had exceeded US$5 billion and at the time of this writing that sum has nearly doubled. However, Alkatiri deserves credit for putting in place a mostly clean, stringent, and efficient administration that, according to the UNDP Human Development Report, made significant strides within the framework of an aggressively propoor development agenda that successor government took on.[50]

President Gusmão for his part seemed to consider Lusophone African experiences less relevant to an economy that for nearly three decades had been directly tied to, and wholly dependent on, the larger economy of a next-door occupier. Indonesian military expenditures in East Timor and subsidies aimed at benefitting Indonesian immigrants there had rendered most East Timorese marginal beneficiaries or passive onlookers. Consultations with East Timorese intellectuals, and professionals close to Gusmão, reveal that they believed a less stringent and less frugal economic approach – than Alkatiri's – was required, at least as a transitional step from the fake economy that had wholly depended on Indonesian subsidies. The only way Gusmão could then turn a propoor National Development Plan that was on paper

[49] UNDP, *The Path out of Poverty. Integrated Rural Development: Timor-Leste Human Development Report 2006*, i–ii.
[50] UNDP, *Managing Natural Resources for Human Development. Developing the Non-Oil Economy to Achieve the MDGs: Timor-Leste Human Development Report 2011*.

into an East Timor-relevant actionable project was for him to take on the executive powers of the Prime Minister.

Beyond his ill-advised incendiary speeches, there is no conclusive evidence that Gusmão instigated the chaos that culminated in Alkatiri's resignation in June 2006, but his bid for the premiership benefited greatly from it. Long before FRETILIN's popularity suffered a dent during the 2006 crisis, Gusmão had quietly started to explore the possibilities of establishing a political party capable of eclipsing the ruling party – as early as 2005 according to some sources.[51] Parallel to government-sponsored traditional reconciliation efforts (Simu Malu), the President launched a separate National Dialogue Commission, including Halot Meik No Kroat[52] that he is believed to have used to take his idea of forming a political party to his old and reliable rural support base through the Sacred Houses (Uma Lulik).

As election 2007 approached, the very same former CNRT officials, who as officials in President Gusmão's office had spearheaded the Halot Meik No Kroat, unveiled plans to launch a new party called National Congress of Timorese Reconstruction, carrying the same acronym as the pro-independence umbrella "CNRT".[53] In preparing the ground for a new political party, they targeted former CNRT activists and structures, capitalizing on the weight of the Uma Lulik who had long supported Gusmão – since his reorganization of the resistance in the early 1980s. "CNRT" did well to win 23 percent of the vote and reduce FRETILIN's gains at the polls (27 percent). With all the capable opposition parties refusing to join a FRETILIN-led coalition, newly elected President Ramos-Horta called on the second highest voted "CNRT" to form a minority government. PD, PSD and ASDT readily agreed to join "CNRT" and form the "Parliamentary Majority Alliance" (AMP) government under Gusmão's premiership.

The nascent free press and political pluralism survived the upheavals of 2006, although the liberal democratic system that is being experimented with played more to the satisfaction of, and support from, the international community than that among the Timorese. Today, East Timor continues to confront the structural violence inherited from colonial neglect and secondary colonial brutality, as well as the consequences of its independence movement's grand strategies of liberation. Nonetheless, despite the socioeconomic and political setbacks of 2006, the country has continued to make

---

[51] But as late as October 2006, smaller parties like PD, PSD and ASDT rejected the idea of merging with a party that the then president would soon launch.

[52] Meaning "Putting the Weapons Back in their Places," this project was meant to facilitate the end of violence by putting to rest the ancestors who had been invoked during the independence war.

[53] These include but are not limited to Eduardo Baretto "Du Sae" in Ermera, Virgilio Smith in Same, Manufahi, Duarte Nunes in Los Palos, Marito Reis in Baucau, Candido "Maubere" in Manatutu, Aquilino Etioko in Viqueque, Julio Meta Malik in Ainaro, and Francisco Martins "Teki Liras" in Aileu.

remarkable strides toward pulling itself out of poverty across many human development indicators. In spite of widespread allegations and some credible indicators of rising corruption, partly fueled by increased withdrawals from the Petroleum fund and by increased levels of direct transfers to target groups, the UNDP's 2011 Timor-Leste National Human Development Report shows East Timor's human development indicators ranking higher than many of its neighbors in Southeast Asia and most sub-Saharan African countries.[54] More encouraging is East Timor's leading position in the g7+ group – of the world's poorest, war-torn, and most fragile seventeen countries – that are demanding alternative benchmarks to the Millennium Development Goals because of the mismatch between the latter and their unique situations. Whereas the accomplishments are great, what remains to be done is greater and the institutional odds, challenges in human capacity, and volatility of the fractured political landscape persist, leaving the specter of relapse hovering.

Conclusion

There is concrete and circumstantial evidence that both Eritrean and East Timorese guerrilla leaderships were genuinely committed to establishing democratic systems, handing over power, and retiring from active politics in their respective independent countries. The Eritrean leader Isaias Afwerki and his East Timorese counterpart Xanana Gusmão, in particular, are said to have had a keen interest in agriculture and the arts that they reportedly wished to pursue after retiring from politics. But power politics of independent countries coupled with considerations of domestic political constituencies and realpolitik came to play on their individual and collective characteristics and traditions to keep them wanting to stay in power.

Most importantly, when the two top guerrilla leaders felt not only personally challenged but also their accomplishments imperiled by former colleagues or rivals (in collusion with familiar old enemies, at least in the case of Eritrea), then the tested methods of the successful resistance strategies reasserted themselves. In spite of their genuine commitment to infusing fresh blood into their politics, the two independent countries remain under the firm grip of the 1960s generation in Eritrea and the 1975 generation in East Timor. In spite of some legitimate and many unhealthy vitriolic attacks these two leaderships have been subjected to, not only do they remain powerful but also the longer-term stability of the two countries demands their presence in real and historical terms – until their dignified exit from politics.

Beyond their polarizing actions or inactions, their image – in the present and in history – as unifiers requires responsible transitioning of the two

54 UNDP, *Managing Natural Resources for Human Development*.

countries to second-generation leaders through a transparent, participatory process that also involve genuine forgiveness and reconciliation. That is inevitable, ultimately. But it is important that the two leaders enable it while they are still healthy and alive. That can go a long way to help ensure social harmony and full coming to grips with the two people's long, bloody, and fratricidal quest for freedom and liberation.

Conclusion

Ethiopian and Indonesian secondary colonialism and the anticolonial strategies of the Eritrean and East Timorese liberation movements have left indelible marks on the politics of the independent countries that emerged upon their victory. A detailed analysis of these dynamics is indispensable to understanding Eritrea and East Timor today. In the process of doing so, this book challenged several common perceptions about the Third World. It demonstrated that colonialism is not confined to the West, but was practiced by both Ethiopia and Indonesia when they absorbed their smaller neighbors. It examined how Eritrean and East Timorese liberation movements developed their own grand strategies, previously also thought to be a preserve of the West. Despite the differences in geographic, demographic, and political circumstances, both liberation movements devised strategies that were increasing sophisticated and ultimately victorious. Through a detailed analysis of events and of methods, the study also showed that not all insurgents in the Third World are terrorists. In fact, when the Eritrean and East Timorese liberation movements avoided terrorism, the Ethiopian and Indonesian states used terrorist methods with impunity.

The book concludes with a look at how the political and physical circumstances that shaped these grand strategies also influenced the new states that emerged from the liberation struggles. It also examines how international attitudes towards colonialism and the Third World changed during these classic struggles against secondary colonial oppressors. Classic colonial refusal to heed the voices of the colonized compelled the Eritrean and East Timorese people to violence. Increasing revulsion with colonialism and its barbarities gradually won both anticolonial insurgencies the moral and – belatedly – the legal high ground. But there existed intrinsic contradictions between the ideal of liberation on one hand and the means of realizing it on the other. Whereas no expectations of independence have ever been met fast enough – nor will they be – that contradiction between methods and ends blighted the process of liberation in Eritrea and East Timor and will continue to plague these independent countries.

In the process of executing their liberation grand strategies against far superior adversaries, the two independence movements institutionalized governing practices and introduced political philosophies that continue to influence the trajectories of the Eritrean and East Timorese states. Generally, the greater centralization in Eritrea and amorphous, disparate structures in East Timor ensured the success of the two liberation movements. However, these two factors also had an adverse impact on the political environment in each country after independence. In the Eritrean case, a lot can get done, but the system is, as it has always been, prone to abuse. The Timorese system is less prone to be abused by the powerful, but little, if anything, gets done. But the political systems in both states have generated intense frustration, scorn, condemnation, and even hostility from different corners within the two countries and without.

Consequently, the politics of the State of Eritrea and that of the Democratic Republic of Timor-Leste leave much to hope for. In pursuit of its still potent revolutionary ideals of transforming the Eritrean society, Asmara insists on giving precedence to social justice over all other considerations and in near complete neglect of external ideas and concerns. Politically and economically beholden to external forces and morally obligated to its pre-independence advocacy for individual rights and political pluralism, Dili remains fixated on electoral politics to the high office. Nonetheless, long-term impediments to these endeavors and threats to the accomplishments thereof remain to be Eritrea's relegation of individual liberties to a distant secondary consideration at best and East Timor's of the abject poverty of the vast majority of its people.

Important assets – at least the semblance of collective leadership, popular democracy, accountable governance, and reconciliation in Eritrea and cohesive leadership and all-inclusive politics in East Timor – cultivated during the years of struggle are also corroding in the face of beliefs and practices inherited from the same pre-independence era. With the generation of the 1960s still in charge in Asmara, and the politics of 1975 in full swing in Dili, the promised infusion of fresh blood or the inaugurating of new politics have yet to be realized. As of this writing, under a politically monistic order Asmara has yet to fully redeem many of the promises of the liberation movement while, for its part, a politically divided Dili struggles to alleviate poverty and heal the wounds of the past. In the final analysis, the two have produced an inauspiciously sufficient mass of disaffected citizens in both countries about the delayed dividends of independence.

Meanwhile, the discourse on recently independent countries is caught in a binary of optimism versus pessimism, a standoff that, according to one historian, is "reinforced by journalists in search of pathos and humanitarians in need of funds."[1] The novelty of human rights and the grave abuses in many parts of the global South cannot be denied, nor is turning a blind eye to the shortcomings of the two governments an option. Just as Eritrea should learn from the unfortunately rich history around it that national liberation loses its significance without fundamental individual liberties, so too should East Timor beware that independence fades when its dividends are late incoming. A dream deferred does explode.

Whatever Eritrea's and East Timor's shortcomings, however, it is neither fair nor – in the grand scheme of historical perspective – viable to judge either country, for a decade or two is an insufficient timeframe. State formation out of the myriad experiences of wrenching liberation from colonialism and secondary colonialism takes generations. As a result, contemporary history, like grand strategy, becomes an incomplete, constantly developing project. I am hopeful that this book has made a modest contribution toward that project in the Horn of Africa and island Southeast Asia, in general, and in Eritrea and East Timor, in particular.

---

[1] Stephen Ellis, "Writing Histories of Contemporary Africa," *Journal of African History*, 43 (2002):1–26.

Bibliography

Primary Materials: Eritrea – Ethiopia

Be-Nadew Ez Ghinbar Seletekesetew Huneta Tetarto Yeqerebe Riport, April 1980 EC (*Investigation Report about the Conditions that Transpired on the Frontline of the Nadew Command*, April 1988), a classified document at the Eritrean RDC accessed under special permit.

Brigadier General Tariku Ayne, *Nadew Ez Memriya: K-hamle 1/1979 eske Tahsas 30/1980 b-Nadew Ez Ghinbar Yetekenawenew Yezemecha Menfeqawi Riport*, January 1980 EC. (*Nadew Command: Semi-Annual Campaign Report of Nadew Command Frontline from July 8, 1987 to January 7, 1988*, January 1987), a classified document at the Eritrean RDC accessed under special permit.

K'Sene Wer 1963 Amete Mihret Eske Sene 30 Qen 1964 Amete Mehret Dres Yalew Y'Amet Riport (June 1971–July 7, 1972 Annual Report), a classified document at the Eritrean RDC accessed under special permit.

RDC/Atrocities/3, 094797, Mary Dines, "Ethiopian Repression in Eritrea," 1980, submission to the People's Tribunal.

RDC/Biography/03, 006807 "Minutes of Meeting [between the security authorities and the residents of Haicota]," April 9, 1962.

RDC/Biography/3, 006806, Haile Selassie Weldu, "Hatsir Tarikh Hamid Idris Awate kesab 1961" ("Short History of Hamid Idris Awate") November 30, 1983.

RDC/Call 01, 00383, EPLF "Selamtan Metsewa'etan N'ahwatna Comandis Deqi Ertra" ("Greetings and Call to our Commandos Brothers, Children of Eritrea"), 1974.

RDC/Call 01/00386, Maj. Gen. Zeremariam Azazi, "Awajn Seme'etan N'ahwatey Nay Ertra Polis Comandis" ("Declaration and Appeal to my Brotherly Eritrean Police Commandos"), September 1975.

RDC/ELF/UO, 02847, Gunter Shröder, "Interviews on E.L.F. History."

RDC/EPLF/His/Ar/St/CR, "Decisions of the 4th regular meeting of the Central Committee of the EPLF" October 22, 1978.

RDC/EPLF/His/Ar/St/CR, "Wesanetat Rabe'ay Mudub Akheba Maekelay Shmaghele Hizbawi Ghenbar Harenet Ertra" ("Decisions of the 4th regular meeting of the Central Committee of the EPLF") October 22, 1978.

RDC/EPLF/His/Mili, 3, *Strategiawi Mizlaq* (*Strategic Withdrawal*), ND.

RDC/Hist/Ar/St/1, 01959, "A'enawi Menqisiqas nay 73" ("Destructive Movement of 1973") *Sagem*, vol. 2 no. October 10, 1990.

RDC/His/Ar/St/8, 02104, "Nehnan Elamanan," November 1971.

RDC/Hist/Ar/St/09: 06434, EPLF "Seminar Paper # 18: Three Stages of Protracted War," (Undated).

RDC/His/Ar/St/9, 06443, "Mewladin Temekron Hizbawi Ghenbar Harenet Ertra" ("The Birth and Experience of the EPLF").

RDC/Hist/Ar/St/EPLF/Mili/01, 03102: "A Short Report from the Training Center to Information Department," 1979.

RDC/His/ELF/3, "First National Congress of the ELF. Military Work Plan" (Tigrigna), November 12, 1971.

RDC/Mengistu 3A/78, "Mengistu's Speech on the Fourth Anniversary of the Revolution," (transcript), September 12, 1978, Addis Ababa.

RDC/Mengistu, 2/77, "Mengistu Haile Mariam, Interview," September 12, 1977, Addis Ababa.

RDC/PublicAdmin/2/04863, "Excerpts of Sebhat Efrem's Presentation," 1983.

RDC/Security/1, 05285, EPLF, "Kab Mussie Bekhit Zeterekhbe Habereta" (no date).

RDC/TPLF, 2226, TPLF, "Program and Principle of the TPLF," November 1976.

RDC/TPLF/4, 2233, TPLF, "Program and Principle of the TPLF," February 22, 1971 EC.

RDC/TPLF/5, 2284, TPLF, "EPLF-TPLF Joint Statement," April 1988.

RDC/TPLF/6, 2399, TPLF, "People's Voice on our Differences with the EPLF," March 1985.

RDC/TPLF/6, 2499, TPLF, "Organizational Statement on the Occasion of the Victory on the Naqfa – Afabet Front," ND.

Research and Information Center on Eritrea (RICE), *Revolution in Eritrea: Eyewitness Reports*.

Voice of the Broad Masses. "The EPLF and its Relationship with the Democratic Movements in Ethiopia," Janury 31–February 2, 1985, transcription available at the Eritrean RDC.

Voice of the Broad Masses. "The EPLF calls upon all the democratic movements in Ethiopia for the establishment of Neighborliness Democratic Front," October 7, 1985, transcription available at the Eritrean RDC.

Voice of the Broad Masses. "The EPLF is silent because it preferred to remain silent," (Tigrigna) October 6, 1985, transcription available at the Eritrean RDC.

Y'12gna Brigade Qedem Memriya Y'tiqimt Wer 63 Amete Mehret Teqlala Riport (*General Report of the 12th Brigade Command for October 1963 E.C.*), a classified document at the Eritrean RDC accessed under special permit.

Y'huletegna Egregna Kifle-Tor Sostegna Memriya Ye 1964 Amete Mehret Teqlala Y'zemecha ena Y'temhert Riport (*1964 E.C. General Campaign and Education Report of the Second Infantry Division, Third Directorate*), a classified document at the Eritrean RDC accessed under special permit.

Y-Ertra Kifle-Hager Wetaderawi Huneta: Sele-Kifle Hageritu Techebach Huneta Yeqerebe Acheer Riport," Tir 1980 (*The Military Condition of the Eritrean Province: A Short Report about the Prevailing Conditions in the Province*, January 1988), a classified document at the Eritrean RDC accessed under special permit.

Zemecha-716, "YeItio-Soviet YeGara Komite YeWetaderawi Gudayoch Huneta" ("Conditions of the Ethio-Soviet Committee on Military Affairs"), ND, p. 3, document accessed at the Ethiopian Minister of National Defense.

Zemecha-733, "Ke 1967–1982 Megabit dres Yetesera YeHayle Ghembata" 18 October 1982 EC ("Recruitment of Forces Conducted from 1967 until March 1982"), 18–10-82(E.C), document accessed at the Ethiopian Minister of National Defense.

Zemecha-733, "YeAhunu Ghize YeItyopia Hayl Huneta ena Yalebet Segat" ("The Current Conditions of the Ethiopian Force and its Threats"), 20–10-1982 (EC), document accessed at the Ethiopian Minister of National Defense.

Primary Materials: East Timor – Indonesia

"Message from the Supreme Command of the Struggle: 1983-the Year of National Unity" a 1982 end of year message of Xanana Gusmão reprint in official FRETILIN organ *Nacroma*, March/April 1983.

Arquivo e Museo Resistencia, 06443.019, Interview transcript of José Ramos-Horta August 1983 in Leiden.

Arquivo e Museo Resistencia, 05000.003, Mari Alkatiri to the Non-Aligned Countries Coordinating Committee, July 1, 1976.

Arquivo e Museo Resistencia, 05000.056, President of the Democratic Republic of Vietnam Ton Duc Thang to President Francisco Xavier do Amaral, Ha Noi, January 27, 1976.

Arquivo e Museo Resistencia, 05000.274, José Ramos-Horta to the Ambassador of the People's Republic, Canberra, September 28, 1974.

Arquivo e Museo Resistencia, 06487.001, Xanana Gusmão to Ramos-Horta, November 15 and 17, 1991.

Arquivo Mário Soares/Organizacoes Internacionais/Portugal, 06465.090, 1993.

Arquivo Mário Soares/Resistência Timorense, 5000.228, CNRM-Frente Armada, "Declaração Sobre a Captura do Novo Lider do Resistecia: O Companheiro Ma'Huno..." April 1, 1993.

Arquivo Mário Soares/Resistência Timorense, 05001.009, "Fundamental Thematic of Process. Resume of Central Themes of Armed Struggle," December 1992.

Arquivo Mário Soares/Resistência Timorense, 06430.010, CNRM-FRETILIN, "Declaração de Voto," May 30, 1990.

Arquivo Mário Soares/Resistência Timorense, 06432.018, "Mantiri: Jenderal Success," *Cerita Dari Dili* (No Date).

Arquivo Mário Soares/Resistência Timorense, 07153.081, "Orientacoes do CNRM-FALINTIL A RENETIL," May 10, 1991.

Arquivo Mário Soares/Resistência Timorense, 07153.102, "Organograma da LEP" (no publication information).

Arquivo Mário Soares/Resistencia Timorencia, 07191.054, Bukar and Hodu Ran Kadalak, "Carta a RENETIL," March 1989.

BPKI Chairman Radjiman Wedijodiningrat during the BPKI meeting of May 31, 1945, quoted in TAPOL, *The Territory of the Indonesian State; Discussions in the Meeting of Badan Penjelidek Usaha Persiapkan Kemerdekaan Indonesia. Background to Indonesia's Policy Toward Malaysia* (no date).

Chega! The Report of the Commission for Reception, Truth, and Reconciliation (CAVR). East Timor, 2006.

CIDAC-CPDM, TL6720, Secret Correspondence of Australian Ambassador in Jakarta to Canberra, August 23, 1975.

CIDAC-CDPM, TL3174, "Statement of Martinho da Costa Lopes, Apostolic Administrator of East Timor, 1977–1983, to the American Catholic Bishops' Committee for Social Development and World Peace," Washington, DC, June 12, 1984.

CIDAC-CDPM, TL3184, Apostolic Administrator Belo, "Message from the Church of East Timor," January 1, 1985.

CIDAC-CDPM, TL3230, "Reflections of the East Timorese Religious: A Contribution to the 1981 MASRI Session," July 1981 in *Dossier on East Timor* (March 1982).

CIDAC-CDPM, TL3675, Xanana Gusmão to Peace is Possible in East Timor, October 15, 1987.

CIDAC-CDPM, TL3676, Xanana Gusmão to CDPM, October 15, 1987.

CIDAC-CDPM, TL4788, Apostolic Administrator of Dili, Carlos Filipe Ximenes Belo to *Monsenhor* Pablo Puente, Apostolic Pro-Nuncio to Indonesia, February 17, 1985.

CIDAC-CDPM, TL6506, "Memo: Parliamentarians for East Timor," July 14, 1988.

CIDAC-CDPM, TL6531, "Statement [of Admiral Gene R. La Rocque] delivered to the Fourth Committee of the United Nations General Assembly," October 20, 1980.

CIDAC-CDPM, TL6602–11, "Full text of Speech of Nicolau Lobato, Reading Statement of The Permanent Committee of FRETILIN Central Committee on the High Treason of Xavier do Amaral."

CIDAC-Peace is Possible, PP0548, "Why and for What I am Struggling? The Defense Plea of Fernando de Araujo Presented to the Public Prosecutors Team in the Central Jakarta State Court" May 11, 1992.

CIDAC-Peace is Possible, PP0808, "FRETILIN Press Release," June 16, 1987.

CIDAC-Peace is Possible, PP864, FRETILIN and UDT, "Joint Communiqué," March 18, 1986, Lisbon.

CIDAC-Peace is Possible, PP888, "Statement by the Delegation of the Timorese Democratic Union to the Special Committee on Decolonization," August 13, 1987, New York.

Departmen Pertahanan Keamanan, "Keputusan Menteri Pertahanan-Keamanan/ Panglima Angkatan Bersenjata nomor Kep/23/X/1978 tentang Normalisasi Penyelenggaraan Pertahanan-Keamanan di Daerah Timor-Timur dan Pembubaran KODHANKAM Tim-Tim," October 1978.

Departemen Pertahanan-Keamanan, "Petunjuk-Pelaksanaan, Nomor: OG/02/V/ 1979," May 11, 1979.

Department of Information, *Government Statements on the East Timor Question* (No publication information; a compilation of five statements issued in succession by the Indonesian government between December 4 and December 22–23, 1975).

First Level Regional People's Representative Assembly of the Province of East Timor to President of the Republic of Indonesia, "Report on the Development of Government Affairs in East Timor" June 3, 1981. Available at the Dili-based Archivo e Museo de Resistência.

National Security Archives, "East Timor Revisited" (declassified proceedings of the meeting with Suharto): http://www.gwu.edu/~nsarchiv/NSAEBB/NSAEBB62/doc4.pdf.

President Xanana Gusmão's "Message to the Nation" on the occasion of FALINTIL Day, August 20, 2003, Uaimori: http://www.etan.org/et2003/august/17-23/20fal.htm.

Recent Developments in East Timor. Hearing before the Subcommittee on Asian and Pacific Affairs of the Committee on Foreign Affairs House of Representatives, Ninety-Seventh Congress (Second Session), September 14, 1982 (Washington, DC: US Government Printing Office, 1982).

TAPOL, *The Territory of the Indonesian State; Discussions in the Meeting of Badan Penjelidek Usaha Persiapkan Kemerdekaan Indonesia. Background to Indonesia's Policy Toward Malaysia* (no date).

U.S. National Archives, "For Newsom from Habib: Ford/Suharto Discussions, July 5," 1975.

U.S. National Archives, "General Brown Meeting with General Panggabean," April 7, 1975.

Interviews

Abilio de Araujo (August 5, 2006, Vila Franka de Xida, Portugal).

Ahferom Tewelde (August 27, 1999, Asmara, Eritrea).

Ahmed Mohammed Nasser with awate.com (January 29, 2001). Available from http://www.awate.com/portal/content/view/1037/11/.

Alamin Mohammed Said (September 28, 2005, Asmara, Eritrea).

Aliança Conçeicão de Araujo (May 16, 2006, Dili, East Timor)

Ambassador Ana Gomes (August 26, 2006, Cascais, Portugal).

Ambassador Francisco Lopez da Cruz (August 21, 2006, Lisbon, Portugal).

Ambassador Leonardo Mathias (January 11, 2006, Lisbon, Portugal).

Antonio Thomas Amaral da Costa, also known as Aitahan Matak (May 15, 2006, Dili, East Timor).

Avelino Coelho da Silva (May 5, 2006, Dili, East Timor).

Bereket Habte Selassie with awate.com (February 28, 2001). Available from: http://www.awate.com/portal/content/view/1038/11/.

Bishop Carlos Filipe Ximenes Belo (August 25, 2006, Mogofores, Portugal).

Carlos da Silva "Saky" (June 27, 2006, Dili, East Timor).

Colonel Asmelash Ghebremesqel (February 9, 1998, Asmara, Eritrea).

Colonel Yacob Tekhleab (August 28, 1997, Asmara, Eritrea).

Colonel Lere Anan Timor (July 11, 2006, Hera, East Timor).

Constâncio Pinto (April 13, 2006, Dili, East Timor).

Cornelio Gama "L-7" (July 1, 2006, Laga, East Timor).

David Daiz Ximenes (June 30, 2006, Dili, East Timor).

Dr. Carlos Gaspar (August 31, 2006, Lisbon, Portugal).

Dr. Lucas da Costa (April 12 and 18, 2006, Dili, East Timor).

Dr. Roque Rodrigues (July 8, 2006, Dili, East Timor).

Dr. Taha Mohammed-Nur (September 17, 2005, Asmara, Eritrea).

Estanislau da Silva (June 6, 2008, Dili, East Timor).

Father Domingos "Maubere" Soares (May 22, 2006, Dili, East Timor).
Father Francisco Barreto (May 11, 2006, Dili, East Timor).
Fernando de Araujo "Lasama" (July 5 and 7, 2006, Dili, East Timor).
Francisco Carvalho "Chico" (May 13, 2006, Dili, East Timor).
Francisco Xavier do Amaral (July 8, 2006, Dili, East Timor).
Gabriel Fernandes (June 26, 2006, Dili, East Timor).
Gregorio Saldanha (July 11, 2006, Dili, East Timor).
Günter Schröder (Conversations: February 3, 2011, Cologne, Germany, and July 14, 2011, Frankfurt, Germany).
Herui Tedla Bairu with awate.com (January 1, 2001). Available from http://www.awate.com/portal/content/view/352/11/.
Ibrahim Idris Totil (February 4, 1998, Massawa; September 22 and 27, 2005, Asmara, Eritrea).
João Carrascalão (June 28, 2006, Dili, East Timor).
Joaquim Fonseca "Russo" (May 6, 2006, Dili, East Timor).
Luisa Pereira (January 11, 2006, Lisbon, Portugal).
Lurdes Bessa (April 13, 2006, Dili, East Timor).
Major Alfredo Reinado Alves (June 25, 2006, Maubessi, East Timor).
Mariano Sabino (May 3, 2006, Dili, East Timor).
Mário Carrascalão (July 3 and 7, 2006, Dili, East Timor).
Marito Reis (June 30, 2006, Dili, East Timor).
Max Stahl (June 9, 2008, Dili, East Timor).
Miriano Lores Betancourt (October 10, 1997, Addis Ababa, Ethiopia).
Mohammed Omar Abdellah "Abu Tyara" (September 2, 2005, Tessenei, Eritrea).
Mohammed Osman Ezaz (September 3, 2005, Tessenei, Eritrea).
Mohammed Said Nawud (April 23–25, 2005, Asmara, Eritrea; conducted by Nerayo Bahre for RDC's History Project).
Mohammed-Berhan Hassan (September 13, 2005, Asmara, Eritrea).
Mahmoud Dinai (June 26, 1995); History Project Interview.
Nugroho Kacasungkana (July 3, 2006, Dili, East Timor).
Patrick "Pat" Walsh (June 7, 2008, Dili, East Timor).
Paulino Gama aka Mauk Muruk (October 9, 2007, Rijswijk, the Netherlands).
Paulos Tesfaghiorghis (December 29 and 30, 2006, San Jose, California).
President Jorge Sampaio (August 25, 2006, Lisbon, Portugal).
President José Ramos-Horta (June 5, 2008, Dili, East Timor).
President Mário Soares (August 2006, Lisbon, Portugal).
Professor António Barbedo de Magalhães (August 29, 2006, Porto, Portugal).
Romedan Mohammed-Nur (September 25, 2005, Asmara, Eritrea).
Saleh Mohammed Idris "Abu-Ajaj" (History Project Interviews, June 26, 1996, Eritrea).
Seyoum Ogbamichael with awate.com (June 21, 2002). Available at http://www.awate.com/portal/content/view/196/11/.
Uqbe Abraha (January 31, 1998, Asmara, Eritrea).
Virgilio Guterres (April 13 and May 9, 2006, Dili, East Timor).
Yohannes Tesfaselassie (September 10, 1997, and January 28, 1998, Asmara, Eritrea).
Zemhret Yohannes (February 2, 1998, Asmara, Eritrea).

UN Documents

"Report of the United Nations Independent Special Commission of Inquiry for Timor-Leste" (Geneva, 2 October 2006).

UN General Assembly passed Resolution 1514 (XV) "Declaration on the Granting of Independence to Colonial Countries and Peoples" December 14, 1960.

UN General Assembly Resolution 1541 (XV): "Principles which Should Guide Members in Determining whether or not an Obligation Exists to Transmit the Information Called for Under Article 73 e of the Charter," 15 December 1960.

UN General Assembly Resolution 3485 (XXX), "Question of Timor," December 12, 1975.

UN General Assembly Resolution 37/30, "Question of East Timor," November 23, 1982.

UN General Assembly Resolution 37/30, "Question of East Timor," November 23, 1982.

UN General Assembly – Fifth Session, Resolution 390 (V). "Eritrea: Report of the United Nations Commission for Eritrea; Report of the Interim Committee of the General Assembly on the Report of the United Nations Commission to Eritrea," December 2, 1950.

UNDP. *The Path Out of Poverty. Integrated Rural Development: Timor-Leste Human Development Report* 2006.

UNDP. *Managing Natural Resources for Human Development. Developing the Non-Oil Economy to Achieve the MDGs: Timor-Leste Human Development Report 2011.*

United Nations Security Council Resolution 384 (1975), December 22, 1975.

United Nations Commission for Eritrea, "Communiqué by the Commission to the Inhabitants of Eritrea Inviting Written Statement by Individuals or Groups," 15 February 1950 (available at UCLA Research Library Special Collections, Ralph Bunche Papers, Box 92, "Eritrea Mission Cables").

United Nations Commission for Eritrea, "Fifth Confidential Report," 23 March 1950, pp. 3–6 (available at UCLA Research Library Special Collections, Ralph Bunche Papers, Box 92, "Eritrea Mission Cables").

Hearing Testimonies, Scholarly Articles, and Theses

"Chronology of Conflict Resolution Initiatives in Eritrea," Institute for Conflict Analysis and Resolution, George Mason University, 1991.

"Prepared Statement of Michael Williams, Head of Asia Research Department, Amnesty International, Hearing before the Subcommittee on Asian and Pacific Affairs of the Committee on Foreign Affairs House of Representatives, Ninety-Seventh Congress, September 14, 1982" in *Recent Developments in East Timor*. Washington, DC: U.S. Government Printing Office, 1982.

Per Memoriam Ad Spem. Final Report of the Commission of Truth and Friendship (CTF) Indonesia – Timor-Leste (2008).

Abiyu Geleta, "OLF and TPLF: Major Issues and Outcomes of a Decade of Negotiations since 1991," Oromo Studies Association Conference, 2002 Washington, DC. Available at http://www.oromia.org/Articles/Issues_and_outcomes_of_a_decade_of_OLF-TPLF_Negotiations_p.htm.

Alemseged Tesfai. "Diversity, Identity and Unity in Eritrea. A View from Inside."
    Unpublished paper presented at the "Identity and Conflict in Africa" conference,
    African Studies Unit, University of Leeds, September 1997.
Alexander, Martin, and J. F. V. Keiger. "France and the Algerian War: Strategy,
    Operations and Diplomacy." *Journal of Strategic Studies* 25, no. 2(2002):1–31.
Aregawi Berhe. "The Origins of the Tigray People's Liberation Front" in *African
    Affairs* (2004), 103/413:569–592.
Amina Habte. "Ethiopian War Crimes in Eritrea: A Case Study of the Massacres of
    Besik-Dira and Ona." BA thesis, University of Asmara, 2000.
Anderson, Benedict. "Statement delivered to the Fourth Committee of the United
    Nations General Assembly on East Timor, October 20, 1980." In *East Timor,
    Five Years after the Indonesian Invasion: Testimony Presented at the Decolo-
    nization Committee of the United Nations General Assembly, October 1980*, ed.
    Jason Clay, 29–34 . Cambridge, MA: Cultural Survival, Occasional Paper No. 2,
    1981.
Anderson, Benedict. "Indonesia and East Timor A Critique," in *A Critique of the
    United States Department of State's Country Reports on Human Rights Practices
    for 1979* (by Lawyers' Committee for International Human Rights, New York).
Anderson, Benedict. "Prepared Testimony on Human Rights in Indonesia and East
    Timor," Hearing before the Subcommittee on Asian and Pacific Affairs and on
    International Organizations of the Committee on Foreign Affairs, House of Rep-
    resentatives, 96th Congress, February 4, 6 and 7, 1980," in *Human Rights in Asia:
    Noncommunist Countries*. Washington, DC: U.S. Government Printing Office,
    1980.
Anderson, Benedict. "Imagining East Timor."*Arena Magazine* no. 4 (April–May
    1993).
"An Overview of FALINTIL's Transformation to F-FDTL and its Implications,"
    La'o Hamutuk Bulletin, Vol. 6, No. 2: April 2005: http://www.laohamutuk.org/
    Bulletin/2005/Apr/bulletinv6n1.html.
Arendt, Hannah. "Ideology and Terror: A Novel Form of Government," *The Review
    of Politics*. 15, no. 3 (July 1953):303–327.
Bhabha, Homi K. *The Location of Culture*. London and New York: Routledge,
    1998.
Carey, Peter. "Third-World Colonialism, the *Geração Foun*, and the Birth of a New
    Nation: Indonesia through East Timorese Eyes, 1975–99," *Indonesia* 76 (October
    2003):23–67.
Chomsky, Naom et al. "Ideology and Terror: A Novel Form of Government."
    Anthropology Today 18, no. 2 (April 2002):22–23.
Clark, Roger S. "Does the Genocide Convention Go Far Enough? Some Thoughts
    on the Nature of Criminal Genocide in the Context of Indonesia's Invasion of East
    Timor," 8 *Ohio N.U.L. Rev.* 321 (1981).
Clark, Roger S. "The 'Decolonization' of East Timor and the United Nations Norms
    on Self-Determination and Aggression," *International Law and the Question of
    East Timor* (1995):67–68.
Cohen, David. "'Justice on the Cheap' Revisited: The Failure of the Serious Crimes
    Trials in East Timor." *AsiaPacific Issues*, No. 80, East-West center, Honolulu, HI,
    May 2006.

Connell, Dan. "Inside the EPLF: The Origins of the 'People's Party' and its Role in the Liberation of Eritrea." *Review of African Political Economy* 28, no. 89 (2001):345–364.

The East Timor Situation. Report on Talks with Timorese Refugees in Portugal. Canberra: Legislative Research Services, Australian Parliament, 1997.

Ellingson, Lloyd Schettle. "Eritrea: Separatism and Irredentism, 1941–1985." PhD diss., Michigan State University, 1986.

Ellis, Stephen. "Writing Histories of Contemporary Africa," *Journal of African History*, 43 (2002):1–26.

Elson, R. E. "Constructing the Nation: Ethnicity, Race, Modernity and Citizenship in Early Indonesian Thought." *Asian Ethnicity* 6, no. 3 (2005):145–160.

Falk, Richard "The East Timor Ordeal: International Law and its Limits," in *Bulletin of Concerned Asian Scholars. East Timor, Indonesia and the World Community: Resistance, Repression, and Responsibility*, 32, no. 1 and 2 (January–June 2000).

Frezghi Teklezghi. "The Toroa Tsenadeghle Reconciliation." BA thesis, University of Asmara, 2002.

Gebru Tareke. "From Lash to Red Star: The Pitfalls of Counter-insurgency in Ethiopia, 1980–82." *Journal of Modern Africa Studies* 40, 3 (2002):465–498.

Halliday, Fred. "The Fighting in Eritrea." *New Left Review* no. 67 (May–June 1971), pp. 57–67.

Henze, Paul B. "Eritrea: The Endless War" (1986). An Article Prepared for *The Washington Quarterly* (Spring 1986); available at the Thomas Kane Collection of the Library of Congress.

Henze, Paul B. *Glasnost about Building Socialism in Ethiopia: Analysis of a Critical Soviet Article.* Santa Monica, CA: RAND, 1990.

Hill, David T. "East Timor and the Internet: Global Political Leverage in/on Indonesia" in *Indonesia* 73 (April 2002):25–51.

Hobsbawm, Eric. "Barbarism: A User's Guide." *New Left Review*, 206 (July–August, 1994):44–54.

Jolliffe, Jill. *Report from East Timor. AUS Representative on Australian Delegation to East Timor, March 12–20 1975.* Canberra: Australian National University Students' Association, 1975.

Kieman, Ben. "Cover-Up and Denial of Genocide. Australia, the USA, East Timor, and the Aborigines." *Critical Asian Studies* 34, no. 2 (2002):163–192.

Krylova, G. A. "National-Democratic Revolution in the Light of the New Political Thinking (The Example of Ethiopia)." *Narody Azii I Afriki (Peoples of Asia and Africa)* no. 1 (1989).

Langhorne, Richard. "Current Developments in Diplomacy: Who Are the Diplomats Now?" *Diplomacy & Statecraft* 8, no. 2 (1997):1–15.

Legum, Colin. *Colin Legum's Third World Reports. London*, 1990.

Legum, Colin. "Ethiopia: Divergent Policies of United States and Israel." In *Colin Legum's Third World Reports.* London, 1990.

McRae, David. "A Discourse on Separatists," *Indonesia* 74 (October 2002):37–58.

Moore, Samuel. "The Indonesian Military's Last Years in East Timor: An Analysis of its Secret Documents," *Indonesia* 72 (October 2001):9–44.

Nairn, Tom. "The Modern Janus." *New Left Review* no. 94 (November–December 1975):2–27.

Nordland, Rod. "Under Indonesian Control, Timor Remains a Land of Hunger, Oppression and Misery," *The Philadelphia Inquirer*, May 28, 1982.

"Observations Regarding the RESPECT Program in Timor Leste," *La'o Hamutuk Bulletin* 5, no. 5–6 (December 2004): http://www.laohamutuk.org/Bulletin/2004/Dec/bulletinv5n5.html.

Peake, Gordon. "What the Veterans Say: Unpacking Disarmament, Demobilization and Reintegration (DDR) Programs in Timor-Leste." Paper at the University of Bradford's Center for International Cooperation and Security, July 2008.

Rees, Edward. "UNDER PRESSURE: FALINTIL – Forças de Defesa de Timor Leste, Three Decades of Defence Force Development in Timor Leste 1975–2004." Paper at the Center for Democratic Control of Armed Forces, Geneva, 2004.

Rees, Edward. "The UN's failure to integrate Falintil veterans may cause East Timor to fail," On Line Opinion, September 2, 2003: http://onlineopinion.com.au/print.asp?article=666.

Robinson, Geoffrey. "East Timor 1999: Crimes against Humanity." CAVR, *Chega!* 2006, Annex 12–1.

Robinson, Geoffrey. "People's War: Militias in East Timor and Indonesia." *South East Asia Research* 9, no. 3 (2001):271–318.

Said, Salim. "Suharto's Armed Forces: Building a Power Base in New order Indonesia, 1966–1998." *Asian Survey*, 38, no. 6 (June 1998):535–552.

Sharp, Paul. "For Diplomacy: Representation and the Study of International Relations." *International Studies Review* 1, no. 1 (Spring 1999):33–57.

Sherman, Edward S. "Manifestations of Media Bias: The Case of the *New York Times* Reporting on Indonesia and East Timor." In *Censored 2001: 25 Years of Censored News and the Top Censored Stories of the Year*, edited by Peter Philips and Project Censored, 265–275. New York: Seven Stories Press, 2001.

Sherman, Richard F. "Eritrea in Revolution." PhD diss., Brandies University, 1980.

Stephan, Maria J. "Fighting for Statehood: The Role of Civilian-Based Resistance in the East Timorese, Palestinian, and Kosovo Albanian Self-Determination Movements." *Heinonline – Fletcher F. World Affairs* 30:2 (Summer 2006):57–79.

Salih, Tayeb. *Season of Migration to the North.* trans. trans. Denys Johnson-Davies. Oxford: Heinemann, 1969.

Smith, Munroe. "Military Strategy versus Diplomacy." *Political Science Quarterly* 30, no. 1 (March 1915):37–81.

Tekeste Melake. "The Battle of Shire (February 1989): A Turning Point in the Protracted War in Ethiopia." *New Trends in Ethiopian Studies*, Vol. 1, ed. Harold G. Marcus. (Lawrenceville, NJ:Red Sea Press, 1994):963–980.

Tesfaye Gebreab. "Ye Mussie Ghedl." *Teraroch Yanqeteqete Tiwlid, Vol. II.* Addis Ababa: Mega Publishing Enterprise, 1997.

"The United Nations and East Timor," *Indonesia* 42 (October 1986):129–142.

Weatherbee, Donald E. "Portuguese Timor: An Indonesian Dilemma." *Asian Survey* 6, no. 12 (December 1966):683–686.

Weldemichael, Awet Tewelde. "The Eritrean Long March: The Withdrawal of the Eritrean People's Liberation Front, 1978–1979," *The Journal of Military* 73, no. 4 (October 2009):1231–1271.

Wolfe, Patrick. "History and Imperialism: A Century of Theory, from Marx to Postcolonialism." *American Historical Review* 102, no. 2 (April 1997):388–420.

Young, Crawford. "Nationalism, Ethnicity and Class in Africa: A Retrospective." *Cahiers d'Etudes africaines* 103 no. 26-3 (1989):421–495.

Young, John. "The Tigray and Eritrean People's Liberation Fronts: a History of Tensions and Pragmatism." *Journal of Modern African Studies* 34, no. 1 (1996):105–120.

Books and Book Chapters

Abir, Mordechai. *Ethiopia: The Era of the Princes. The Challenge of Islam and the Re-unification of the Christian Empire, 1796–1855.* New York: Frederick A. Praeger, 1968.

Alamin Mohammed Said. *Al-Defe' wa al-Teredi: Al-Thewra al-Iritriyah. Qisat al-Inshiqaq al-Dakhiliyah Lil-Thewra al-Iritriyah.* Asmara: Dogoli Printing Press, 1992.

Alamin Mohammed Said. *Hidget Zeyefiqid Mesel.* Asmara: Hidri Publishers, 2002.

Alatas, Ali. *The Pebble in the Shoe: The Diplomatic Struggle for East Timor.* Jakarta: Aksara Karunia, 2006.

Alemseged, Abbay. *Identity Jilted or Re-Imagining Identity? The Divergent Paths of the Eritrean and Tigrayan Nationalist Struggles.* Lawrenceville, NJ: Red Sea Press, 1998.

Alemseged Tesfai. *Aynefelale. Eritrea, 1941–1950.* Asmara: Hidri Publishers, 2001.

Alemseged Tesfai. *Federation Ertra ms Ityopiya: Kab Matienzo kesab Tedla, 1951–1955.* Asmara: Hidri Publishers, 2005.

Alemseged Tesfai. *Two Weeks in the Trenches: Reminiscences of Childhood and War in Eritrea.* Trenton, NJ: Red Sea Press, 2002.

Anderson, Benedict. *The Spectre of Comparisons: Nationalism, Southeast Asia and the World.* London and New York: Verso, 1998.

Anderson, Benedict. "Gravel in Jakarta's Shoes." In *The Spectre of Comparisons: Nationalism, Southeast Asia and the World,* 131–138. London and New York: Verso, 1998.

Anderson, Benedict R. O'G. *Imagined Communities. Reflections on the Origin and Spread of Nationalism.* Rev. ed. London: Verso, 1991.

Babu, Abdulrahman Mohamed. "The Eritrean Question in the Context of African Conflicts and Superpower Rivalries." In *The Long Struggle of Eritrea for Independence and Constructive Peace,* ed. Lionel Cliffe and Basil Davidson, 47–63. Trenton, NJ: Red Sea Press, 1998.

Bahru Zewde. *A History of Modern Ethiopia, 1855–1974.* Addis Ababa: Addis Ababa University Press, 1992.

Bahru Zewde (ed.). *Documenting the Ethiopian Student Movement: An Exercise in Oral History.* Addis Ababa: Forum for Social Studies, 2010.

Bairu Tafla. *Ethiopian Records of the Menilek Era: Selected Amharic Documents from the Nachlass of Alfred Ilg, 1884–1900.* Weisbaden: Harrassowtiz Verlag, 2000.

Barbedo de Magalhaes, Antonio. *East Timor: Indonesian Occupation and Genocide.* Porto: Oport University, 1992.

Bereket Habte Selassie. *Conflict and Intervention in the Horn of Africa.* New York and London: Monthly Review press, 1980.

Bereket Habte Selassie. *Eritrea and the United Nations and Other Essays.* Trenton, NJ: Red Sea Press, Inc, 1989.

Bereket Habte Selassie. *The Crown and the Pen. The Memoirs of a Lawyer Turned Rebel*. Trenton, NJ: Red Sea Press, 2007.

Bereket Habte Selassie. *The Wounded Nation. How a Once Promising Eritrea Was Betrayed and its Future Compromised*. Trenton, NJ, and Asmara: Red Sea Press, 2011.

Blakeley, Ruth. *State Terrorism and Neoliberalism: The North in the South*. New York: Routledge, 2009.

Budiardjo, Carmel, and Liem Soei Liong. *The War against East Timor*. London: Zed Books, 1984.

Bulletin of Concerned Asian Scholars. East Timor, Indonesia and the World Community: Resistance, Repression, and Responsibility 32, no. 1 and 2 (January–June 2000).

Calder, Nigel (ed.). *Unless Peace Comes; a Scientific Forecast of New Weapons*. New York: Viking Press, 1968.

Carey, Peter, and G. Carter Bentley (eds.). *East Timor at the Cross Roads: The Forging of a Nation*. Honolulu: University of Hawaii Press, 1995.

Césaire, Aimé. *Discourse on Colonialism*. trans. Joan Pinkham. Marlborough, England: Adam Matthew Digital, 2007.

Clapham, Christopher (ed.). *Africa and the International System. The Politics of State Survival*. Cambridge: Cambridge University Press, 1996.

Clapham, Christopher. *African Guerrillas*. Oxford: James Currey, 1998.

Clapham, Christopher. *Transformation and Continuity in Revolutionary Ethiopia*. Cambridge: Cambridge University Press, 1988.

Clarence-Smith, Gervase. *The Third Portuguese Empire, 1825–1975. A Study in Economic Imperialism*. Manchester: Manchester University Press, 1985.

Clausewitz, Carl Von, *On War*. Michael Howard and Peter Paret (eds. and trans.) Princeton, NJ: Princeton University Press, 1976.

Clay, Jason (ed.). *East Timor, Five Years After the Indonesian Invasion: Testimony Presented at the Decolonization Committee of the United Nations' General Assembly, October 1980*. Cambridge, MA: Cultural Survival, 1983.

Cliffe, Lionel, and Basil Davidson (eds.). *The Long Struggle of Eritrea for Independence and Constructive Peace*. Trenton, NJ.: the Red Sea Press, 1988.

Cohen, David. *Intended to Fail. The Trials before the Ad Hoc Human Rights Court in Jakarta*. ICTJ, 2003.

Cohen, Herman J. *Intervening in Africa. Superpower Peacemaking in a Troubled Continent*. New York: St. Martin's Press, 2000.

Conboy, Ken. *KOPASSUS. Inside Indonesia's Special Forces*. Jakarta: Equinox Publishing, 2003.

Connell, Dan. *Against All Odds: A Chronicle of the Eritrean Revolution*. Trenton, NJ: Red Sea Press, 1993.

Connell, Dan. *Building a New Nation. Collected Articles on the Eritrean Revolution (1983–2002), Vol. 2*. Trenton, NJ: Red Sea Press.

Connell, Dan. "The Changing Situation in Eritrea." In *Behind the War in Eritrea* edited by Basil Davidson, Lionel Cliffe, and Bereket Habte Selassie, 55–59. Nottingham: Spokesman, 1980.

Connell, Dan. *Conversations with Eritrean Political Prisoners*. Trenton, NJ: Red Sea Press, 2005.

Crenshaw, Martha (ed.). *Terrorism in Context*. University Park: The Pennsylvania State University Press, 2007.

Cribb, Robert. "Genocide in the non-Western World: Implications for Holocause Studies." In Stephen L. B. Jensen (ed.), *Genocide: Cases, Comparisons and Contemporary Debates*, 123–140. Copenhagen: Danish Center for Holocaust and Genocide Studies, 2003.

Crenshaw, Martha. "The Logic of Terrorism: Terrorist Behavior as a Product of Strategic Choice." In *Origins of Terrorism: Psychologies, Ideologies, Theologies, States of Minds*, edited by Walter Reich, 7–24. Washington, DC: The Woodrow Wilson Center Press, 1998.

Crenshaw, Martha. "Thoughts on Relating Terrorism to Historical Contexts." In *Terrorism in Context*, edited by Martha Crenshaw, 3–24. University Park: The Pennsylvania State University Press, 2007.

Dahm, Bernhard, *History of Indonesia in the Twentieth Century*, translated by P. S. Falla. London: Praeger Publishers, ND.

Davidson, Basil. *The People's Cause. A History of Guerrillas in Africa*. London: Longman, 1981.

Davidson, Basil, Lionel Cliffe, and Bereket Habte Selassie (eds.). *Behind the War in Eritrea*. Nottingham: Spokesman, 1980.

Dawit Wolde Giorgis. *Red Tears. War, Famine and Revolution in Ethiopia*. Trenton, NJ: Red Sea Press, 1989.

de Waal, Alex. *Evil Days: 30 Years of War and Famine in Ethiopia. An Africa Watch Report*. New York: Human Rights Watch, 1991.

Dedijer, Vladimir. "The Poor Man's Power." In *Unless Peace Comes; a Scientific Forecast of New Weapons*, edited by Nigel Calder, 18–26. New York: Viking Press, 1968.

Denden, Osman Saleh. *Ma'erakat Iritriyah. Al-Juzu Al-Awal*. (NNP, 1996).

Doyle, Michael. *Empires*. Ithaca, NY: Cornell University Press, 1986.

Dunn, James. *Timor: A People Betrayed*. Auckland: the Jacaranda Press, 1983.

Durand, Frederic. *East Timor: A Country at the Crossroads of Asia and the Pacific. A Geo-Historical Atlas*. Bangkok: Research Institute on Contemporary Southeast Asia (IRASEC), 2006.

Earle, Edward Mead (ed.). *Makers of Modern Strategy. Military Thought from Machiavelli to Hitler*. Princeton, NJ: Princeton University Press, 1943.

East Timor, Indonesia and the World Community. Lanham, MD: Rowman and Littlefield Publishers, 2001.

ELF, *Erytriyah: Burkan Al-Qern Al-Afriqi*. 1986.

EPLF, Political Concientization Programme, *Ta'rikh al-Nidal al-Musallah, al-Marhala al-Mutawassita* (Eritrea: EPLF, 1989).

Erlich, Haggai. *Ethiopia and the Challenge of Independence*. Boulder: Lynne Rienner Publishers, 1986.

Erlich, Haggai. *The Struggle Over Eritrea, 1962–1978. War and Revolution in the Horn of Africa*. Stanford, CA: Hoover Institution Press, 1983.

Ethiopian Government. *Selected Speeches of His Imperial Majesty Haile Selassie First, 1918 to 1967*. Addis Ababa: The Imperial Ethiopian Ministry of Information, 1967.

Ethiopian Ministry of Information. *Speeches Delivered by His Imperial Majesty Haile Selassie 1st, Emperor of Ethiopia, on Various Occasions, May 1957– December 1959*. Addis Ababa: Berhan ena Selam.

Fanon, Frantz. *The Wretched of the Earth*. Trans. Constance Farrington. New York: Grove Press, 1968.

Federer, Juan. *The UN in East Timor: Building Timor Leste, a Fragile State.* Darwin: Charles Darwin University Press, 2005.

Feith, Herbert and Lance Castles (eds.). *Indonesian Political Thinking. 1945–1965.* Ithaca and London: Cornell University Press, 1970.

Fernandes, Clinton. *Reluctant Saviour: Australia, Indonesia, and the Independence of East Timor.* Victoria, Australia: Scribe Publications, 2004.

Fernandes, Clinton. *The Independence of East Timor. Multi-Dimensional Perspectives: Occupation, Resistance, and International Political Activism.* Brighton: Sussex Academic Press, 2011.

Firebrace, James, and Stuart Holland, *Never Kneel Down: Drought, Development and Liberation in Eritrea.* Trenton, NJ: The Red Sea Press, 1985.

Freire, Paulo. *Pedagogy of the Oppressed,* trans. Mytra Bergman Ramos. New York: Herder and Herder, 1970.

Michael Gabir. *The History of the Bilen.* Baghdad: no publisher information, 1992.

Gaim Kibreak. *Critical Reflections on the Eritrean War of Independence. Social Capital, Associational Life, Religion, Ethnicity and Sowing Seeds of Dictatorship.* Trenton, NJ, and Asmara: Red Sea Press, 2008.

Galula, David. *Counterinsurgency Warfare: Theory and Practice.* Westpoint, CT, and London: Praeger Security International, 2006.

Gebru Tareke. *Ethiopia: Power and Protest. Peasant Revolts in the Twentieth Century.* Lawrenceville, NJ: The Red Sea Press, 1996.

Gebru Tareke. *The Ethiopian Revolution: War in the Horn of Africa.* New Haven, CT, and London: Yale University Press, 2009.

Geertz, Clifford. *Islam Observed: Religious Development in Morocco and Indonesia.* Chicago: University of Chicago Press, 1971.

Gellner, Ernest. *Nations and Nationalism.* Ithaca, NY: Cornell University Press, 1983.

Grant, Bruce. *Indonesia.* Melbourne: Melbourne University Press, 1964.

Gomes, Donancio. "The East Timor Intifada: Testimony of a Student Activist." In *East Timor at the Cross Roads: The Forging of a Nation,* 106–108, edited by Peter Carey and G. Carter Bentley. Honolulu: University of Hawaii Press, 1995.

Greenfield, Richard. *Ethiopia: A New Political History.* London: Pall Mall Press, 1965.

Guevara, Ernesto "Che." *Guerrilla Warfare.* Lincoln: University of Nebraska Press, 1961.

Gunn, Geoffrey C. *East Timor and the United Nations: The Case for Intervention.* Lawrenceville, NJ, and Asmara: Red Sea Press, 1997.

Gurr, Ted Robert. *Why Men Rebel?* Princeton, NJ: Princeton University Press, 1970.

Gusmão, Xanana. *Timor Lives! Speeches of Freedom and Independence.* Alexandria, New South Wales: Longueville Books, 2005.

Hainsworth, Paul and Stephen McCloskey (eds.). *The East Timor Question: The Struggle for Independence from Indonesia.* London and New York: I.B. Tauris Publishers, 2000.

Harbeson, John W. *The Ethiopian Transformation: the Quest for the Post-Imperial State.* Boulder: Westview Press, 1988.

Hart, B. H. Liddell. *Strategy,* rev. 2nd ed. London: Meridian, 1991.

Henze, Paul B. *The Horn of Africa from War to Peace.* New York: St. Martin's Press 1991.

Hill, Charles. *Grand Strategies: Literature, Statecraft, and World Order*. New Haven, CT, and London: Yale University Press, 2010.

Hill, Helen. *The Timor Story*. Melbourne: Timor Information Service, 1975.

Hoadley, Stephen. "Diplomacy, Peacekeeping, and Nation-Building: New Zealand and East Timor." In *Southeast Asia and New Zealand: A History of Regional and Bilateral Relations* edited by Anthonly L. Smith, 124–144. Singapore: Institute of Southeast Asian Studies, 2005.

Hobsbawm, Eric. *Nations and Nationalism since 1780: Program, Myth, Reality*. Cambridge: Cambridge University Press, 1992.

Howard, Michael. *Studies in War and Peace*. London: Temple Smith, 1970.

Huntington, Samuel P.. *Political Order in Changing Societies*. New Haven, CT: Yale University Press, 1968.

Ikenberry, G. John (ed.). *American Foreign Policy. Theoretical Essays*. New York: Longman, 1999.

International Law and the Question of East Timor. Catholic Institute for International Relations (CIIR) and International Platform of Jurists for East Timor (IPJET), 1995.

Jacquim-Berdal, Dominique. *Nationalism and Ethnicity in the Horn of Africa. A Critique of the Ethnic Interpretation*. Lewiston, NY: Edwin Mellen Press, 2002.

Jardine, Matthew. *East Timor: Genocide in Paradise*. 2nd ed. Monroe, ME: Odonian Press, 1999.

Jeffrey, Robin (ed.). *Asia – the Winning of Independence. The Philippines, India, Indonesia, Vietnam, Malaya*. London: Macmillan, 1981.

Jenkins, David. *Suharto and His Generals. Indonesian Military Politics 1975–1983*. Ithaca, NY: Cornell Modern Indonesia Project, 1984.

Jensen, Stephen L.B. (ed.). *Genocide: Cases, Comparisons and Contemporary Debates*. Copenhagen: Danish Center for Holocaust and Genocide Studies, 2003.

Johnson, Chalmers. *The Sorrows of Empire: Militarism, Secrecy, and the End of the Republic*. New York: Metropolitan Books, 2004.

Jolliffe, Jill. *East Timor: Nationalism and Colonialism*. Queensland: University of Queensland Press, 1978.

Jolliffee, Jill. *Cover-Up: The Inside Story of the Balibo Five*. Melbourne: Scribe Publications, 2001.

Jordan Gebre-Medhin. *Peasants and Nationalism in Eritrea. A Critique of Ethiopian Studies*. Trenton, NJ: Red Sea Press, 1989.

Kahin, Audrey R., and George McT. Kahin. *Subversion as Foreign Policy: The Secret Eisenhower and Dulles Debacle in Indonesia*. New York: New Press, 1995.

Kahin, George McTurnan. *Nationalism and Revolution in Indonesian*. Ithaca, NY: Cornell University Press, 1952.

Kaplan, Robert D. *Surrender or Starve: Travels in Ethiopia, Sudan, Somalia and Eritrea*. New York: Vintage Books, 2003.

Keller, Edmond J. *Revolutionary Ethiopia from Empire to Revolutionary Republic*. Bloomington: Indiana University Press, 1988.

Kemp, Tom. "The Marxist Theory of Imperialism." In *Studies in the Theory of Imperialism*, edited by Roger Owen and Rob Sutcliffe, 15–33. London: Longman, 1972.

Kennedy, Paul (ed.). *Grand Strategies in War and Peace*. New Haven, CT, and London: Yale University Press, 1991.

Killion, Tom. *Histroical Dictionary of Eritrea*. (Lanham, MD, and Londong: Scarecrow Press, 1998).

Kingsbury, Damien and Michael Leach (eds.). *East Timor: Beyond Independence*. Clayton, Victoria: Monash University Press, 2007.

Kingsbury, Damien. "Political Development." In *East Timor: Beyond Independence*, edited by Damien Kingsbury and Michael Leach, 19–28. Clayton, Victoria: Monash University Press, 2007.

Kohen, Arnold S.. *From the Place of the Dead. The Epic Struggle of Bishop Belo of East Timor*. New York: St. Martin's Press, 1999.

Kohen, Arnold, and John Taylor. *An act of Genocide: Indonesia's Invasion of East Timor*. London: TAPOL, 1979.

Korn, David A. *Ethiopia, the United States and the Soviet Union*. Carbondale: Southern Illinois University Press, 1986.

Krieger, Heike (ed.). *East Timor and the International Community. Basic Documents*. Cambridge International Documents Series, Vol. 10. Cambridge: Cambridge University Press, 1997.

Landesberg, Christopher. *The Quiet Diplomacy of Liberation: International Politics and South Africa's Transition*. Johannesburg: Jacana, 2004.

Laqueur, Walter. *The Age of Terrorism*. Boston: Little, Brown, 1987.

Leencho Lata. *The Ethiopian State at the Crossroads: Decolonization and Democratization or Disintegration*. Lawrenceville, NJ, and Asmara: Red Sea Press, 1999.

Legge, J. D. *Sukarno: A Political Biography*. Sydney: Allen and Unwin Australia Pty Ltd, 1984.

Leiden, Carl, and Karl M. Schmitt (eds.). *The Politics of Violence. Revolution in the Modern World*. Englewood Cliffs, NJ: Prentice-Hall, Inc, 1968.

Leite, Pedro Pinto (ed.). *The East Timor Problem and the Role of Europe*. Dublin: International Platform of Jurists for East Timor-IPJET, 1996.

Lenin, N., and Leon Trotsky. *The Proletarian Revolution in Russia*, edited by Louis C. Fraina. New York: The Communist Press, 1918.

Lennox, Rowena. *Fighting Spirit of East Timor. The Life of Martinho da Costa Lopes*. London and New York: Zed Books, 2000.

Levine, Donald N. *Greater Ethiopia: The Evolution of a Multiethnic Society*. Chicago: University of Chicago Press, 1974.

Lowry, Robert. *The Armed Forces of Indonesia*. St. Leonards, NSW: Allen and Unwin, 1996.

Magalhães, António Barbedo de. *East Timor: Indonesian Occupation and Genocide*. Porto: Oporto University, 1992.

Mamdani, Mahmood. *Saviors and Survivors: Darfur, Politics and the War on Terror*. New York: Pantheon, Books, 2009.

Mamdani, Mahmood. *Citizen and Subject. Contemporary Africa and the Legacy of Late Colonialism*. Princeton, NJ: Princeton University Press, 1996.

Marcus, Harold G.. *The Politics of Empire: Ethiopia, Great Britain, and the United States, 1941–1974*. Berkeley: University of California Press, 1983.

Markakis, John. *Ethiopia: Anatomy of a Traditional Polity*. Oxford: Clarendon Press, 1974.

Markakis, John. *National and Class Conflict in the Horn of Africa*. Cambridge: Cambridge University Press, 1987.

Martin, Ian. *Self-Determination in East Timor. The United Nations, the Ballot, and International Intervention.* Boulder, CO: Lynn Rienner Publishers, 2001.

Matsuno, Akihisa. "Reading the Unwritten: An Anatomy of Indonesian Discourse on East Timor." In *The East Timor Problem and the Role of Europe*, edited by Pedro Pinto Leite, 195–210. Dublin, International Platform of Jurists for East Timor-IPJET, 1996.

Matsuno, Akihisa. "The Balibo Declaration: Between Text and Fact." In *The East Timor Problem and the Role of Europe*, edited by Pedro Pinto Leite, 159–194. Dublin: International Platform of Jurists for East Timor-IPJET, 1996.

Mattoso, José. *A Dignidade. Konis Santana e a Resistencia Timorense.* Lisboa: TemasTemase e Debates, 2005.

McDonald, Hamish. *Suharto's Indonesia.* Blackburn, Vic.: Fontana Books, 1980.

Melnik, Constantin. *The French Campaign against the FLN.* Santa Monica, CA: RAND Corporation, 1967.

Memmi, Albert. *The Colonizer and the Colonized.* Boston: Beacon Press, 1965.

Mohammed Abul Al-Qasim Hajj Hamad, *Al-Abad Al-Dawliyah Limaereket Al-Iritriyah.* Beirut: Dar Al-Telia', 1974.

Mohammed Said Nawud, *Harakat al-Tahrir Al-Irytriyah.* Khartoum: NP, 1995.

Mohammed-Berhan Hassan. *Menqisiqas Harenet Ertra (Haraka): Me'arfo kab Me'arfotat Gu'ezo Hagherawi Qalsna. Welqawi Mezekir.* Asmara: Publisher, 2001.

Nairn, Tom. *The Break-up of Britain. Crisis and Neo-Nationalism.* London and New York: Verso, 1981.

Negussay Ayele. *In Search of the DNA of the Ethiopia-Eritrea Problem: Recent Articles on the Nature and Evolution of the Conflict in Northeast Africa.* San Diego, CA: Media Ethiopia, 2003.

Neumann, Peter R. *Old and New Terrorism: Late Modernity, Globalization and the Transformation of Political Violence.* Cambridge: Polity Press, 2009.

Newitt, Malyn (ed.). *The First Portuguese Colonial Empire.* Exeter: University of Exeter, 1986.

Niner, Sarah (ed.). *To Resist is to Win! The Autobiography of Xanana Gusmão with Selected Letters and Speeches.* Richmond, Australia: Urora Books, 2000.

Niner, Sara. *Xanana: Leader of the Struggle for Independent Timor-Leste.* Melbourne: Australian Scholarly Publishing, 2009.

Niner, Sara. "Martyrs, Heroes and Warriors: The Leadership of East Timor." In *East Timor: Beyond Independence* edited by Damien Kingsbury and Michael Leach, 113–128. Clayton, Victoria: Monash University Press, 2007.

Nzongola-Ntalaja, Georges (ed.). *Conflict in the Horn of Africa.* Atlanta, GA: African Studies Association Press, 1991.

Okbazghi Yohannes. *Eritrea, a Pawn in World Politics.* Gainesville: University of Florida Press, 1991.

Owen, Roger and Rob Sutcliffe (eds.). *Studies in the Theory of Imperialism.* London: Longman, 1972.

Pagden, Anthony. *Lords of All the World. Ideologies of Empire in Spain, Britain and France c. 1500-c. 1800.* New Haven, CT: Yale University Press, 1995.

Paget, Roger K. (ed. and trans.). *Indonesian Accuses: Soekarno's Defence Oration in the Political Trial of 1930.* Kuala Lumpur: Oxford University Press, 1975.

Pantja Sila: the Basis of the State of Republic Indonesia. Jakarta: National Committee for the Commemoration of the Birth of Pantja Sila, 1964.

Parker, Richard. *John Kenneth Gailbraith: His Life, His Politics, His Economics*. New York: Farrar, Straus and Giroux, 2005.

Pateman, Roy. *Eritrea: Even the Stones are Burning*. Trenton, NJ: Red Sea Press, 1990.

Patman, Robert G. *The Soviet Union in the Horn of Africa. Diplomacy of Intervention and Disengagement*. City: Cambridge University Press, 1990.

Paynton, Clifford T., and Robert Blackey (eds.). *Why Revolution? Theories and Analysis*. Morristown, NJ: Schenkman, 1971.

Perham, Margery. *The Colonial Reckoning: The End of Imperial Rule in Africa in the Light of British Experience*. London: Collins, 1961.

Phillips, Peter, and Project Censored (ed.). *Censored 2001: 25 Years of Censored News and the Top Censored Stories of the Year*. New York: Seven Stories Press, 2001.

Pinto, Constâncio, and Matthew Jardine. *East Timor's Unfinished Struggle: Inside the Timorese Resistance*. Boston: South End Press, 1997.

Portal, Gerald H. *My Mission to Abyssinia*. London: Edward Arnold, 1892; reprinted New York: Negro Universities Press, 1969.

Pour, Julius. *Benny Moerdani: Profil Prajurit Negarawan*. Jakarta: Kejuangan Panglima Besar Sudirman, 1993.

Preston, A.Richard et al. *Men in Arms. A History of Warfare and its Interrelationships with the Western Society*, 5th ed. (Fort Worth, TX: Harcourt Brace Jovanovich College Publishers, 1991).

Primoratz, Igor (ed.). *Terrorism. The Philosophical Issues*. New York: Palgrave Macmillan, 2004.

Ramage, E. Douglas. *Politics in Indonesia: Democracy, Islam, and the Ideology of Tolerance*. London and New York: Routledge, 1995.

Ramos-Horta, José. *Funu. The Unfinished Saga of East Timor*. Lawrenceville, NJ, and Asmara: Red Sea Press, 1987.

Reich, Walter (ed.). *Origins of Terrorism: Psychologies, Ideologies, Theologies, States of Mind*. Washington, DC: The Woodrow Wilson Center Press, 1998.

Reid, Anthony. *The Indonesian National Revolution, 1945–1950*. Westport, CT: Greenwood Press Publishers, 1974.

Reid, Anthony. "Indonesia: Revolution without Socialism." In *Asia – the Winning of Independence. The Philippines, India, Indonesia, Vietnam, Malaya*, edited by Robin Jeffrey, 107–157. London: Macmillan, 1981.

Reid, Richard (ed.). *Eritrea's External Relations: Understanding its Regional Role and Foreign Policy* (London: Chatham House, 2009.

Renan, Ernest. "What Is a Nation?" In *Modern Political Doctrines*, edited by A. Zimmern, 186–205. Oxford: Oxford University Press, 1939.

Republic of Indonesia. *East Timor: Building for the Future. Issues and Perspectives*. Jakarta: Ministry of Foreign Affairs, July 1992.

Republic of Indonesia. *The Province of East Timor: Development in Progress*. Jakarta: Department of Information, ND.

Retbøll, Torben (ed.). *East Timor, Indonesia and the Western Democracies. A Collection of Documents*. Copenhagen: IWGIA, 1980.

Retbøll, Torben (ed.). *East Timor: The Struggle Continues.* Copenhagen: International Working Group on Indigenous Affairs, 1984.

Robinson, Geoffrey. *"If You Leave Us Here, We Will Die": How Genocide Was Stopped in East Timor.* Princeton, NJ: Princeton University Press, 2010.

Ruth Iyob. *The Eritrean Struggle for Independence: Domination, Resistance, Nationalism, 1941–1993.* Cambridge: Cambridge University Press, 1995.

Sabbe, Othman Saleh. *Tarikh al-Irytriyya.* Lebanon: Dar al-Mesira, 1974.

Said, Edward W. *Culture and Imperialism.* London: Vintage Books, 1994.

Saivetz, Carol R., and Sylvia Woodby. *Soviet – Third World Relations.* London: Westview Press, 1985.

Saldanha, João Mariano de Sousa. *The Political Economy of East Timor Development.* Jakarta: Pustakan Sinar Harapan, 1994.

Salehyan, Idean. *Rebels without Borders: Transnational Insurgencies in World Politics.* Ithaca, NY, and London: Cornell University Press, 2009.

Samuel, Tamrat. "East Timor: The Path to Self-Determination." In *From Promise to Practice: Strengthening UN Capacities for the Prevention of Violent Conflict,* edited by Chandra Lekha Sriram and Karin Wermester, 197–230. Boulder, CO: Lynne Rienner Publishers, 2003.

SarDesai, D.R. *Southeast Asia, Past and Present.* 4th ed. Boulder, CO: Westview Press, 1997.

Scheiner, Charles. "Grassroots in the Field: Observing the East Timor Consultation." In *Bitter Flowers, Sweet Flowers: East Timor, Indonesia and the World Community,* edited by Richard Tanter, Mark Sheldon, and Stephen R. Shalom, 109–126. Oxford: Rowman and Littlefield, 2001.

Sharp, Paul. *Diplomatic Theory of International Relations.* Cambridge: Cambridge University Press, 2009.

Shumet Sishagne. *Unionists and Separatists: The Vagaries of the Ethio-Eritrean Relation, 1941–1991.* Hollywood, CA: Tsehai Publishers and Distributors, 2007.

Smith, Anthony D. *The Ethnic Origins of Nations.* Oxford and New York: B. Blackwell, 1986.

Smith, Anthony D. (ed). *Nationalist Movements.* London: Macmillan, 1976.

Smith, Anthony L. (ed.). *Southeast Asia and New Zealand: A History of Regional and Bilateral Relations.* Singapore: Institute of Southeast Asian Studies, 2005.

Smith, Gervase Clarence. *The Third Portuguese Empire, 1825–1975. A Study in Economic Imperialism.* Manchester: Manchester University Press, 1985.

Smith, Michael G. *Peacekeeping in East Timor: The Path to Independence.* Boulder, CO: Lynne Rienner, 2003.

Soeharto. *Pikiran, Ucapan dan Tindakan* Saya. Jakarta: PT Citra Lamtoro Gung Persada, 1988.

Solomon Berhe. *Wefri Segre-Dob (Campaign Beyond the Border).* No publication information.

Spencer, John H.. *Ethiopia at Bay. A Personal Account of the Haile Selassie Years.* 2nd ed. Hollywood, CA: Tsehai Publishers 2006.

Sukarno, "Lahirnja Pantja Sila." In *Pantja Sila: the Basis of the State of Republic Indonesia.* Jakarta: National Committee for the Commemoration of the Birth of Pantja Sila, 1964.

Sukarno. *Pantja Sila: the Basis of the State of Republic Indonesia.* Jakarta: National Committee for the Commemoration of the Birth of Pantja Sila, 1964.

Taber, Robert. *War of the Flea. The Classic Study of Guerrilla Warfare.* Washington, DC: Potomac Books, 2002.

Tadesse, Kiflu. *The Generation, Part II. Ethiopia, Transformation and Conflict: The History of the Ethiopian People's Revolutionary Party.* Lanham, MD: University Press of America, 1998.

Tahir Ibrahim Feddab, *Harakat al-Tahrir Al-Irytriyah wa Masiretaha al-Tarikhiyah fi al-Fetrah ma bayna 1958 ila 1967. Kitab Watha'iqi.* Cairo: Metabi' al-Shurq, 1994.

Tanter, Richard et al (eds.). *Masters of Terror: Indonesia's Military and Violence in East Timor.* Lanham, MD: Rowman and Littlefield, 2006.

Tanter, Richard, Mark Sheldon, and Stephen R. Shalom. *Bitter Flowers, Sweet Flowers: East Timor, Indonesia and the World Community.* Oxford: Rowman and Littlefield, 2001.

Tarling, Nicholas (ed.). *The Cambridge History of Southeast Asia. Volume Three. From c. 1800 to the 1930s.* Cambridge: Cambridge University Press, 1999.

Tarling, Nicholas. "The Establishment of the Colonial Regime." In *The Cambridge History of Southeast Asia. Volume Three. From c. 1800 to the 1930s,* 1–71. Cambridge: Cambridge University Press, 1999.

Taylor, John G. *East Timor: The Price of Freedom.* London and New York: Zed Books, 1999.

Taylor, John G. *Indonesia's Forgotten War. The Hidden History of East Timor.* London: Zed Books, 1991.

Taylor-Leech, Kerry. "Sustaining Language Policy and Language Rights: Where to from Here?" In *East Timor: Beyond Independence* edited by Damien Kingsbury and Michael Leach, 239–249. Clayton, ST: Monash University Press, 2007.

Tekeste Negash. *Italian Colonialism in Eritrea, 1882–1941: Policies, Praxis and Impact.* Uppsala: Universitatis Upsaliensis, 1987.

The Eritrean Case. Rome: The Research and Information Center on Eritrea, 1982.

Thomas, Scott. *The Diplomacy of Liberation: The Foreign Relations of the African National Congress since 1960.* London: Tauris Academic Studies, 1996.

Tilly, Charles. *From Mobilization to Revolution.* New York: McGraw-Hill, 1978.

Trevaskis, G. K. N. *Eritrea. A Colony in Transition: 1941–1952.* Westport, CT: Greenwood Press, 1975.

Trotsky, Leon. "The Farce of Dual Power." In *The Proletarian Revolution in Russia,* by N. Lenin and Leon Trotsky, ed. Louis C. Fraina, 185–192. New York: The Communist Press, 1918.

Tse-tung, Mao. *On Guerrilla Warfare,* translated by Brigadier General Samuel B. Griffith. New York: Frederick A. Praeger, 1961.

Way, Wendy (ed.). *Australia and the Indonesian Incorporation of Portuguese Timor, 1974–1976.* Melbourne: Melbourne University Press, 2000.

Wolters, O. W. *History, Culture, and Region in Southeast Asian perspectives.* Ithaca, NY: Cornell University Southeast Asia Program Publications, 1999.

Wrong, Michela. *I Didn't Do it for You. How the World Betrayed a Small African Nation.* New York: HarperCollins, 2005.

Young, John. *Peasant Revolution in Ethiopia: The Tigray People's Liberation Front, 1975–1991.* Cambridge: Cambridge University Press, 1996.

Zook, David H. Jr., and Robinson Higham. *A Short History of Warfare.* New York: Twayne Publishers, 1966.

Index